COMPUTER CRIMES
AND DIGITAL INVESTIGATIONS

SECOND EDITION

COMPUTER CRIMES AND DIGITAL INVESTIGATIONS

SECOND EDITION

Ian Walden

OXFORD

UNIVERSITY PRESS

OXFORD

UNIVERSITY PRESS

Great Clarendon Street, Oxford, OX2 6DP,
United Kingdom

Oxford University Press is a department of the University of Oxford.
It furthers the University's objective of excellence in research, scholarship,
and education by publishing worldwide. Oxford is a registered trade mark of
Oxford University Press in the UK and in certain other countries

© Ian Walden 2016

The moral rights of the author have been asserted

First Edition published in 2007
Second Edition published in 2016

Impression: 1

Crown copyright material is reproduced under Class Licence
Number C01P0000148 with the permission of OPSI
and the Queen's Printer for Scotland

Published in the United States of America by Oxford University Press
198 Madison Avenue, New York, NY 10016, United States of America

British Library Cataloguing in Publication Data
Data available

Library of Congress Control Number: 2016931117

ISBN 978–0–19–870559–8

Printed and bound by
CPI Group (UK) Ltd, Croydon, CR0 4YY

PREFACE TO THE SECOND EDITION

Writing the first edition of this book took me the best part of a year, during a sabbatical from teaching and administration. The second edition has taken a considerably longer time span to complete, due in large part to the lack of any similar opportunity to dedicate exclusive time to the project. Another excuse for the delay is the amount of change that had taken place between the first edition and this, a period of some nine years. This is a result of continuing rapid developments in, and ever-greater integration of, information and communication technologies into our daily lives; as well as events, such as the revelations by Edward Snowden, which have generated vast amounts of new material to examine and incorporate. Computer crime, or now more commonly cybercrime, continues to be regularly in the news and in the minds of policy makers, legislators, industry, and the general public.

As with the first edition, I remain indebted to all those whose work I came across during the course of writing, both the good and the bad inspires me, either as a standard to work towards or a consolation that what I was doing has at least some merit. For the past three years, I have co-taught an LLM course entitled 'International Cybercrimes and Investigations', as well as various other related training courses, which have provided abundant reasons for considering developments in the field. I therefore owe a debt to the students who have asked the awkward questions that made me think on my feet, or failed to react at all, but inspired me to re-cast how to communicate the issues. I would also like to reiterate my thanks to my colleagues at the Centre for Commercial Law Studies, and those at other academic institutions, for their valuable input to my understanding of these fascinating and complex areas of law.

Colleagues at Baker & McKenzie, and the clients with whom I have had dealings, have also exposed me to issues and generated insights that are not normally available to academics. In addition, my involvement as Board Member and Trustee of the Internet Watch Foundation (2004–09); on the Executive Board of the UK Council for Child Internet Safety (2010–12); the Press Complaints Commission (2009–14), at the height of the phone-hacking scandal; and as a member of the RUSI Independent Surveillance Review (2014–15) have each contributed considerably to my knowledge and understanding of the issues addressed in the book.

I had hoped to have this opportunity for a second edition to correct all the mistakes present in the first edition, which I discovered or were brought to my attention over the years. I hope that most have been corrected, but whether I have inserted new mistakes at a faster rate than I was able to correct will become apparent in due course. If you come across anything, please let me know!

Finally, I dedicate this book to my family, Claire, Ben, and Rhys, who are always the best of everything. With love.

Ian Walden
27 November 2015
i.n.walden@qmul.ac.uk

ACKNOWLEDGEMENTS

The text of the *Council of Europe Cybercrime Convention (2001) and its Additional Protocol (2003)* in Appendix 2 is reproduced with the kind permission of the Council of Europe: http://www.coe.int/en/web/portal/home (Home page) and http://conventions. coe.int/ (Treaty Office).

The text of the *Directive 2013/40/EU of the European Parliament and of the Council of 12 August 2013 on attacks against information systems and replacing Council Framework Decision 2005/222/JHA* in Appendix 3 is reproduced from the EU website <http://eur-lex. europa.eu,> with the kind permission of the European Union. Disclaimer: only European Union documents published in the Official Journal of the European Union are deemed authentic.

The text of the *ACPO Good Practice Guide for Digital Evidence* (March 2012) in Appendix 4 is reproduced with the kind permission of the National Police Chiefs' Council.

CONTENTS

TABLE OF CASES

AUSTRALIA

BELGIUM

CANADA

COURT OF JUSTICE OF THE EUROPEAN UNION

UNITED STATES

TABLE OF LEGISLATION

TABLE OF INTERNATIONAL
TREATIES AND CONVENTIONS

1

INTRODUCTION

A. An Ever-changing Environment

Books can take considerable time to gestate, or at least this one did. As such, in the inter-   **1.01**
vening period, significant changes may occur both in the author's life as well as the world
at large. For this book, the terrorist attacks in London on 7 July 2005 occurred on the first
(disturbed) day of my sabbatical, and caused a sea change that has impacted directly on
the book. In terms of substantive offences, the impact has primarily been in the areas of
content crimes relating to hate speech[1] and conduct threatening the integrity of computer
systems and networks.[2] The latter is also a consequence of the terrorism threat evolving
into concerns about cyber-attacks from hostile states and organized crime.[3] Much of this
book concerns criminal procedure, the investigative process in a digital environment. In
this area, the cumulative effects of 9/11 and July 2005 have resulted in a rate of change that
has challenged all writers and commentators in the area. Some of these developments were
things that the law enforcement community had already been calling for, often for several
years, and the terrorism threat simply moved them from the 'could do' into the 'will do'
column of policy makers. Other measures were genuinely new and reactive to the changed
environment. More recently, as the second edition was being prepared, pressure for reform
in criminal procedure has come from a different direction as a result of the Snowden revelations that began in June 2013. This has led to calls for greater controls and transparency over
the conduct of law enforcement agencies, particularly the intelligence services.

The world, particularly the developed world, seems a more vulnerable place than it did prior   **1.02**
to these attacks. Addressing such insecurities, both real and perceived, is the job of governments. Governments have therefore adopted numerous measures to support law enforcement agencies in their efforts to combat terrorism. Such measures impact on computer
and network crime directly, to the extent that terrorists use such tools to support either

---

[1] eg Terrorism Act 2006, s 1 (Encouragement of terrorism) and Racial and Religious Hatred Act 2006.
[2] eg Amendments to the Computer Misuse Act 1990 made in 2006 and 2015. See further Chapter 3.
[3] See HM Government, *A Strong Britain in an Age of Uncertainty: The National Security Strategy*, Cm
7953, October 2010.

real-world or virtual terrorist activities. Indirectly, non-terrorist criminals therefore face a more effective law enforcement environment, even if resource has been diverted towards the 'war on terror'. The hackers and virus writers of the 1990s continue to be a major concern, although motivation and target become the touchstone triggering law enforcement attention, rather than the activities themselves.

B. What It Is and Is Not

1.03 The classic problem for a law student embarking on a piece of research is one of boundaries: what falls legitimately within the topic for consideration and what falls outside? This seemingly simple proposition regularly causes significant problems as both the nature of the subject matter and the student's enthusiasm conspire to embrace ever more material. Several sessions may be spent discussing with students why they have words by the thousands discussing one topic when the title and thesis indicate another direction. The answer generally lies in something they have read which captured their imagination and which proceeds to haunt the dissertation until excised, often painfully and sometimes with force, by the tutor. However, since we must practise what we teach, it is my task to confront the boundaries of this book. We can proceed from an exclusionary perspective, what is not being addressed, or by outlining what is viewed as within the balloon. What follows is intended to do both, inclusion first.

1.04 The project started out as a book on computer crime, plain and simple. But, then again, perhaps not so plain and simple! At one level, the title kept changing as the work progressed, expanding to take into account its broadening scope; it was perceived to encompass computers, networks, and information crimes. For a start, the Internet is the obvious environment that currently dominates any discussion of computers and their usage—hence the use of the prefix 'cyber' in much of the literature, including this book. The Internet is primarily about communications and the networks that enable connectivity between computers on one side of the world with those on the other. So computers per se are not the sole object of concern: rather, computers connected to other computers, the networked computer.

1.05 The liberalization of the global telecommunications market over the past twenty years has led to an unprecedented array and availability of communications mechanisms, from mobile phones to the Internet. Networks are now therefore fundamental to any study of computer crime, not simply as a given infrastructure, similar in kind to the need for electricity to power computers, but as a technological phenomenon of equal import to that of computers.

1.06 The concept of 'information crimes' is a more problematic term for inclusion. Without entering into a philosophical examination of the expression, the term 'information' is being used in the book to denote that which is being processed by computers and communicated via networks, ie it is the substance on which computers and networks operate. It is also used synonymously with 'data', a term more familiarly connected with the world of computing and networks.

1.07 Information is now a key resource of the global economy. The legal treatment and protection of information is an increasingly important topic, for policy makers, legal practitioners and law students. It is also a topic for another book, written at another time (hopefully by the author!). As we shall see, however, the manner in which the book categorizes the criminal activities under examination revolves around computers and networks as the principal tools used for the processing and communication of information in modern societies. As tools, they may be utilized by criminals to manipulate information in the course of committing crime or to facilitate the creation, use, and transmission of information that is itself illegal. The criminal conduct may also target the tools that process the information, impairing or compromising their functionality, through hacking and viruses. It is this final category, however, which is the popular conception of what constitutes computer crime. In each of these scenarios, information is intimately bound up with the tools in question and hence forms a pillar on which this book is built.

The book may also be viewed simply as a criminal law text, with the focus on conduct **1.08** related to computers, networks, and information operating as a filter through which we can examine the whys and wherefores of criminal law and policy. It is a case study illustrating many of the problems faced by our modern criminal justice system, from law making, to catching, prosecuting, and sanctioning those that commit criminal acts against us, as individuals and society as a whole. Whether seen as a computer crime book or a book on crime, with a cyberspace filter, will likely depend on the motivations of the reader when picking up the book. However, I expect to meet more satisfactorily the demands of the former than the latter!

Another way of categorizing this book would be as an Internet or cyberspace law book, **1.09** focusing on crime rather than the multiplicity of other aspects of law that are impacted by the environment; from electronic contracting, through trade marks and domain names to private international law. As such, many if not all the core themes that are debated by academics of cyberspace are present in this book, specifically issues of identity, location, and enforcement. The problem of regulating technology is another theme that informs the analysis. Principle-based, technology-neutral laws are often seen as the most appropriate response to a rapidly evolving technical environment, although computer misuse laws cannot claim to be technology-neutral at one level!

Having established what we consider to be the main focus of this book, what is 'in', we must **1.10** now consider what this book is not intended to be about. First, the study of crime can be divided into four dimensions: the criminal, the criminal conduct, the victim, and enforcement. This book is primarily concerned with the criminal conduct and enforcement, rather than the criminal and victim. As such, it can be distinguished from the majority of existing literature in the field, which has tended to be criminological in focus.

'Cyber-terrorism', 'cyber-warfare', and 'cyber-security' are terms often used in the literature **1.11** in conjunction with computer crime, generally rightly so, but are not points of departure for the analysis in this book. It would not really be appropriate to describe these topics as 'out' of the book, since they each inform the discussion and analysis at various times. Rather, none of these topics is central to our attention, and should not result in the book being filed under one of these headings (unless of course it improves sales!).

Cyber-terrorism concerns the motivation of a perpetrator, which is one means of charac- **1.12** terizing criminal activities, since motivation is related to intent, a common criterion for establishing criminal liability. However, this is a criminal law, not a criminology text, so motivation, while very much of interest in terms of drivers of the activities investigated in this book, is not a core topic. Likewise with serious organized crime, an increasing proportion of criminal acts under consideration, the organizational structures that underpin a perpetrator are of interest to us, and must inform our analysis, but are not central to the objects of this book.

1.13 Warfare, on the other hand, is a classic state-based activity that may engage the criminal law, through such developments as the International Criminal Court, but is primarily an issue of public international law and international relations. While neither cyber-terrorism nor cyber-warfare is the focus of this book, both, and particularly the former, have been critical in driving the response of policy makers and legislators to the criminal activities examined in this book.

1.14 Prevention being better than cure, cyber- or data security is a third topic closely related to the issues at the heart of this book. Security is primarily concerned with victims or potential victims of crime, a perspective which goes beyond our objectives in many circumstances, since security policies and measures should be concerned as much with the dangers posed from accidental loss and damage to an organization's information, computer, and network resources. Cyber-security does, however, raise critical policy issues for discussion in the course of the book. Issues concerning the responsibilities of users to implement adequate security; the relationship between the existence of security measures and the criminality of certain activities; obligations to report security breaches; and achieving an appropriate balance between privacy and security needs, all go towards informing our considerations of law enforcement powers.

1.15 As a book concerned with technologies, specifically computers and networks, there is an essential need to understand the manner in which such technologies operate and are utilized, whether by victims, perpetrators, or law enforcement agencies. Legal analysis without such an understanding is likely to be fundamentally flawed and limited. At the same time, we must accept a certain degree of ignorance and innocence about where the technology is developing, within five years let alone fifty, which can frustrate the lawyer within us, brought up on a diet of relative stability and certainty. Allied with technological developments are the economics of the market within which such technologies operate. The liberalization of the telecommunications sector has not only brought forth a burgeoning array of network services, but has also fundamentally altered the economics of communications, a factor which is having a profound impact on the nature of the criminality under examination. The fraudulent obtaining of communication services, for example, now has more to do with the avoidance of detection than high call charges. However, the book is first and foremost a law text and, as such, the depth of technical and market detail will be restricted both by the room available as well as the author's own (mis)understandings. Wherever possible, the reader will be guided to alternative sources, where a more comprehensive technical treatment of the issues can be found.

1.16 As noted above, the purpose of the book extends beyond the legal framework criminalizing certain activities, to the procedural framework governing the investigation and prosecution of such crimes. In respect of the former, the author has the freedom, subject to traditional standards of academic rigour, to draw a bright line between which activities are to be examined and those that fall outside the scope. When considering procedural issues, from the commencement of a forensic investigation through to any eventual court proceedings, the applicable rules are generally distinct from the nature of the offences themselves.

So, for example, computer-derived evidence may be used in a shoplifting prosecution, or an interception may be carried out of a call between members of a terrorist cell. As a consequence, the boundaries are indistinct and our analysis will need to embrace a broader perspective and range of considerations than that necessarily required for the substantive framework.

C. For Whom?

Having discussed what the book is about, the inevitable corollary question is: for whom has **1.17** the book been written? What kind of audience has the author been directing his thoughts towards? The answer, however, as with the book's subject matter, is not straightforward. The author's career to date has encompassed both the academic world, since 1987, and legal practice, since 1990, running in parallel. As such, my work is primarily concerned with four categories of person: students, fellow academics, fellow practitioners, and clients. This book has been written with all four types of reader in mind.

In legal practice, we generally speak of a division between criminal and commercial lawyers. **1.18** I consider myself within the latter camp, being regularly asked to advise companies, particularly in the telecommunications/eCommerce sector, about computer- and cybercrime-related matters, either assisting a company to implement appropriate security measures, to comply with statutory obligations, or to deal with the consequences of an attack or threat. This work is not unique to me or the firm with whom I work; therefore I am aware that commercial law practitioners in many law firms are being asked to give advice on such matters. However, the volume of such work those firms are asked to advise upon will vary considerably in terms of quality and quantity, often inhibiting practitioners from developing a depth of experience. This book is therefore designed to assist commercial law practitioners and their clients to address these new and complex criminal law issues, offering an in-depth consideration of the governing legal framework and the consequences of such law in terms of compliance and protection.

This book is also obviously intended for the criminal law fraternity, those engaged in the **1.19** day-to-day handling of criminal cases. Indeed, some of the inspiration behind the writing of this book arose from my involvement in training solicitors from the Crown Prosecution Service in 'hi-tech' crime issues, as part of its initiative to train specialized prosecutors across the UK. As with commercial lawyers, some will have far greater experience than the author of the legal and forensic issues arising when prosecuting or defending particular crimes addressed in this book. However, the majority will not have had the volume or variety of work in this area to enable an overview of the field offered in this book.

Computer and cybercrime are not topics generally taught to undergraduate law students; **1.20** it tends to be a specialized area which is provided at a postgraduate level, and even then rarely in the detail attempted by the book. However, the author teaches an LLM course on 'International Cybercrimes and Investigations, as well as a distance-learning module on computer crime at Queen Mary.[4] As such, the book is aimed at these students, as well as the

---

[4] See <http://www.law.qmul.ac.uk/postgraduate/llm/modules/102780.html> and <http://www.law. qmul.ac.uk/postgraduate/distancelearning/DL_modules/index.html#CCDM009ComputerCrimesandD igitalInvestigations>.

vast postgraduate legal market made up of future and current practitioners, either studying part time or having a year out.

1.21 There is a substantial academic community actively researching into all the aspects addressed in this book, from privacy to electronic commerce and issues of public international law. This book modestly attempts to add to the work being produced by this community.

1.22 In addition to the four categories discussed above, during the course of my career I have dealt with two other categories of person that deserve mention. First, I have been fortunate to have been involved in law reform initiatives at an individual state and intergovernmental level, which has introduced me to politicians and policy makers. As this book is as concerned with what the law should be as it is with what the law currently is, it is hoped that some of the discussions will be of value to policy makers. The second group is the non-legal computing and communication professional, such as computer security and cyber-forensic experts. Our work often overlaps and we have much to learn from each other. This book should therefore also be seen as a contribution to achieving greater understanding between our different but interrelated disciplines.

1.23 Professor David Wall has noted that one of the areas of debate within cybercrime is between what he terms 'regulators' and 'cyberlibertarians'.[5] The former he describes as being primarily reactive in nature, viewing criminality in cyberspace as a symptom of a lack of regulation, requiring law reform and strengthened powers for law enforcement. He portrays the latter as being more concerned with the causes of criminality, promoting the need for greater information and education about issues, challenging the adoption of regulatory measures that impose collateral restrictions on legitimate cyberspace users without significantly impacting on the underlying cause. This book attempts to embrace both perspectives. It comprehensively examines and tries to understand the existing legal and regulatory framework governing certain types of cybercrimes; to evaluate the suitability of this framework to appropriately address the activities; and to assess ways and means of recasting the rules to more effectively meet the policy objectives that underpin such rules. As such, the book is both explanation and argument. As explanation, it shows how the law is or is likely to be, where uncertainty exists. As argument, it questions why certain things are as they are and why misconceptions about how the technology functions, as well as used and abused, may give rise to bad arguments in policy and law. Sometimes it teaches, sometimes it debates.

1.24 In conclusion, the book is intended to sit between an academic and practitioner work since, in my experience, this is what is missing in the market for legal books, and in reality the academic/practitioner distinction is not as relevant in this field as it may be in others. Trying to appeal to such a broad readership may be overambitious, and may not be achieved to the satisfaction of all, but the nature of the subject matter would seem to attract a potentially wide audience.

---

[5] Wall, DS, 'Policing the Internet: Maintaining order and law on the cyberbeat', in Walker, C and Wall, D (eds), *The Internet, Law and Society*, Longman, 2000, Chapter 7, at 162–3.

D. Laws and Laws and …

In terms of scope, this book is primarily concerned with the UK, although in any criminal **1.25**
law book it is important to remember that Scotland and Northern Ireland are separate
criminal jurisdictions from England and Wales. In Scotland, substantive criminal law, such
as fraud, is based primarily on common law, ie past decisions from the courts, rather than
statute, while criminal procedure is codified. However, many statutory offences in Scotland
and Northern Ireland are shared with England and Wales through UK-wide legislation
such as the Computer Misuse Act 1990. For the purposes of this book, references to the UK
and England are used synonymously, but Scottish readers beware!

This area of law, reflecting its environment, is undergoing constant change, with new legis- **1.26**
lative proposals and amendments and case law. For an author, such developments engender
both excitement and frustration: the former when difficult points of law are subject to judicial consideration and (hopefully) clarification; the latter when trying to achieve some sense
of stability and finality before completing a manuscript. During the course of writing both
editions, significant legal developments have inevitably arisen, at both a legislative level and
in case law, creating problems for the author in terms of incorporation. However, apart from
some last-minute tweaks at proof stage, the law is as stated on 1 September 2015.

As a Member State of the European Union (for now!), as well as other intergovernmental **1.27**
organizations such as the Council of Europe, the Organisation for Economic Co-operation
and Development (OECD), the Commonwealth, and the G8, UK policy and law sometimes drive, or are driven by, initiatives within these bodies, rather than acting in isolation.
As such, our analysis and attention must encompass the work of these entities. Such international developments have become more prevalent and relevant in our global economy,
where there is an ever-greater recognition by governments of de facto national interdepend-
ence, even if they remain wary of surrendering de jure sovereign control.

In the same manner, the frequently transnational nature of the criminal activities being **1.28**
examined means that we need to consider the manner in which national laws differ and
interact in a situation of either conflict or cooperation. It is beyond the scope of this book
to carry out a comprehensive comparative study of national computer crime laws, but reference will be made to other jurisdictions, when known and where pertinent to the analysis. Such comparisons provide a fertile basis for critically assessing the approach taken
in English law, as well as sometimes providing defence counsel with ideas to pursue in the
defence of their clients!

E. 'Lies, Damned Lies, and Statistics'

Empirical data is generally not a central feature of a law text,[6] except perhaps in the area of **1.29**
criminology. Law books are generally concerned with understanding the rules, applying
them to particular scenarios, and, perhaps, suggesting amendments or wholesale revision.
This book follows this normal pattern of behaviour. However, issues concerning statistics

---

[6] The title quote is widely associated with Mark Twain, although he in fact attributed it to Disraeli: see
Dictionary of Quotations, Bartleby.com, available at <http://www.bartleby.com/73/1769.html>.

impact on the book in a number of contexts. First, amending and extending the criminal law should, in a rational world, be predicated on information about the nature and scale of the problem being addressed. Yet statistics about computer and cybercrime are scarce and unreliable. Second, the available facts and figures about the environment in which criminal activity is being examined, ie cyberspace, must be considered to be a transient snapshot, even if reliable, not least because the rate of change taking place is such that any data will likely have little value to a reader six months after the book was published.[7] Third, much of the law enforcement activity being carried out against perpetrators, whether by public or private bodies, inevitably takes place in secret and is only relatively rarely subject to the full gamut of the criminal justice system and the glare of publicity.

1.30 As such, the book makes scant reference to statistics concerning the purported volume and value of computer crime, and is somewhat limited in the stories it can authoritatively relate. A presumption is made that this is a substantial and growing area of criminal activity, however, worthy of the attention of policy makers and legislators, practitioners and academics. Instead, attention is focused on qualitative themes that the author has discerned or been informed about during his research about where the problems lie in the investigation and prosecution of computer and cybercrimes.

F. Method and Madness

1.31 The book is divided into five core chapters, representing (to the author at least) the major areas of concern in computer crime. Chapter 2 examines the nature of the subject matter and reviews some of the legal and criminological elements of this area of activity. It is intended to provide a series of building blocks to complement the main analysis, especially for those without a legal or criminal law background. The first block concerns the nature of the subject matter, computer crime, considering various schemes for classifying such activities, including through the history of computing. Since laws articulate policy concerns, whether political or judicial, it is important to give consideration to the evolving framework of policy concerns that have driven or underpin governmental responses to computer crime. The third block reviews the nature of criminal law, from the commission of substantive offences to the rules governing their investigation and the outcomes of the criminal justice system as sanctions and remedies. Those that engage in computer crime are also examined, touching on the 'whom' and 'why' of such criminality, as well as the legal treatment of the persons involved depending on their role. Finally, we consider the policing issues in a cyberspace environment, which requires the involvement and cooperation of public and private law enforcement players.

1.32 The third chapter reviews the range of substantive offences that may be committed by those engaged in computer crime, in parallel or series. It divides such treatment into three broad categories, computer-related, content-related, and computer-integrity offences. It examines the fault and conduct elements that comprise each offence and the problems that have been experienced when legislating and prosecuting such criminality.

---

[7] Approximately twelve months after the text was submitted to the publishers.

Chapter 4 shifts focus to the legal rules governing the investigative process in a digital environment. Consideration is given to the various problems that data generates for investigators, from identifying a real perpetrator to capturing and handling the volumes of potentially valuable forensic material. Forensic rules and procedures are examined in respect of three major sources of material: covert surveillance, communication service providers (CSPs), and coercive search and seizure. The use of monitoring and filtering techniques as a crime control mechanism is also examined, as a form of surveillance, whether instigated by the state, CSPs or network users. CSPs play an increasingly important role in supplying evidence in cybercrime investigations, and the nature and impact of such obligations on CSPs is scrutinized in detail. Finally, the process of seizing data is considered, under criminal and civil procedure, as well as the increasing problem of accessing material that is subject to some form of protection mechanism. **1.33**

The fifth chapter moves us from a national focus to transnational and international issues. The transnational nature of computer crime means that national laws overlap with each other, raising questions about whether certain rules are applicable and when they are applied in a particular case. Complex jurisdictional scenarios arise from the criminal activities themselves, but are also present in the exercise of investigative powers, resulting in possible sovereignty disputes. Harmonization of both substantive offences and procedural rules are designed to mitigate or remove such disputes and consequent obstacles to cross-border law enforcement. The two primary institutions engaged in harmonization initiatives impacting on computer crime, directly or indirectly, are the Council of Europe and the European Union; however, the nature of the latter enables far greater progress than that achievable through other forums. **1.34**

The use and abuse of computer-derived evidence in criminal proceedings is the topic of Chapter 6. Consideration is given to all stages of the trial process, from pre-trial disclosure to the presentation of evidence in court. Computer-derived evidence was initially treated with suspicion, based on perceptions of it being inherently unreliable, inhibiting its use. Such concerns have largely dissipated or are now addressed before a judge and jury. On the other hand, network-derived evidence, intercept product, continues to be subject to complex rules regarding its use, which benefits defendants but which are designed to protect the investigative process. **1.35**

The final chapter reviews some of the themes and developments addressed in the preceding chapters, identifying some of the key fault lines in computer crime and digital investigations that are likely to continue to challenge policy makers and the criminal law over the coming years. **1.36**

2

FROM COMPUTER ABUSE
TO CYBERCRIME

A. Introduction

The proliferation and integration of computer and communication technologies into every **2.01** aspect of our society have inevitably led to criminal activities involving their use. Such activities, labelled with the shorthand 'computer crime' or 'cybercrime', are the subject matter for this book. The media regularly feature stories on computer crime, covering topics from hackers to viruses, 'web-jackers' to Internet paedophiles; sometimes accurately portraying events, sometimes misconceiving the role of technology in such activities. The Internet, in particular, is seen as the source of any number of ills and illegalities from which we need the protection of criminal law. This book aims to comprehensively examine the legal treatment of such criminality, from the offending behaviour to investigating the perpetrators and their eventual prosecution.

In this chapter, consideration will be given to some basic building blocks that are thought **2.02** fundamental to an understanding of the subsequent analysis. It is not designed for the criminal law practitioner, who will be familiar with at least the legal aspects; rather, it is more for the commercial law practitioner, for whom criminal law has long since become somewhat vague, as well as the academic and non-legal audience wanting to place the rules within a broader legal, historical, policy, and criminological context.

First, we must understand our subject matter, computer crime: as an evolving phenomenon; **2.03** as terms and terminology; and as embracing a variety of types of criminal conduct from computer abuse to cybercrime. Second, we examine some of the public policy concerns driving law reform in the area, to help us to understand the complexities of the interaction between policy, law, and regulation in the field. Third, the nature of criminal law and the criminal process is reviewed, with one eye on the needs of the lawyer who has forgotten his criminal law and the non-lawyer trying to fathom the mysteries! Fourth, consideration is given to the participants in computer crimes, from the perpetrator with his hands on the device, to the intermediaries that provide the technological infrastructure and services over which the criminality is carried out. Finally, the nature of law enforcement is examined, from investigation through to prosecution.

2.04 Through the process of examining successive topics, directly or indirectly related to computer crime, this chapter also introduces a number of themes which the book will return to again and again throughout the remaining chapters. The first theme concerns the nature of the subject matter. When first conceived, the title and the shorthand description of my research was 'computer crime'. This seemed to satisfy people who asked, nodding sagely with a muttered 'interesting' before moving swiftly on to other topics. However, 'computer crime' was clearly not a sufficient descriptor in and of itself. For a start, the dominant computing environment is the Internet, which is a network of computers. A computer communicating with other computers, and ultimately with ourselves, is obviously central to our concern, so the critical role of networks in criminal activity using computers has to be acknowledged up front. The distinctive characteristics of such 'cybercrime' are, first, that the computers are interconnected through networks; and, second, that we are not concerned with the criminal physical taking of a computer or its component parts. The other element is of course the data or information being processed by the computers and transmitted over the networks. In our increasingly 'Information Society', data is the raw material on which computers and networks operate, creating and enhancing the value of data through their capability to manipulate and distribute it at the speed of light.

2.05 The chosen title, *Computer Crimes and Digital Investigations*, should therefore be read with an implicit sub-title in mind, 'computers, networks, and information crimes'; using a Boolean 'and' connector places some limit on the scope of the subject matter, particularly in respect of information. Within that space, however, two further distinctions can be made, creating other areas of interest to us, which reappear throughout the book. The first concerns the target of the criminal activity, either the information being handled by the technology, or the technology itself, the computers and networks processing the information. Second, where the target is the information, that information may be 'at rest' within a computer, or be 'in transmission' over a network.

2.06 If information, computers, and networks form the boundaries of criminal activity with which we are concerned, then another theme is how the law has changed and evolved to address the growth of such activity. Existing rules and regulations may be sufficiently flexible to adequately cope with such crime. However, as is made clear throughout, governments and legislators have, for a range of reasons, had to amend and adopt new laws to establish a more appropriate legal framework. In some cases, the reform agenda had been specifically focused on computers and networks; but more often, the problem being tackled has a more indirect bearing on the underlying technologies, the most obvious examples being organized crime and terrorism. In either case, one aspect of our inquiry is whether the policy objectives require or justify law reform and whether the reform does, can, or will succeed in achieving the stated objectives. Clearly, these questions may be addressed from different perspectives. In human rights terms, for example, such questions require considerations of proportionality, balancing any potential infringement of the rights of individuals with the needs of society. From a technology perspective, if the technology is exploited or develops in an unanticipated fashion, then legal controls may miss their target or prove ineffective.

While criminal law reform will have specific policy objectives that have driven the reform **2.07** process, the use of criminal law as opposed to civil or administrative legal mechanisms, involves more generic considerations such as deterrence, incapacitation, and retribution— goals which differ in kind and nature from other branches of law. This book is concerned with activities that are considered criminally illegal under UK law, although not necessarily in other jurisdictions, and is not directly concerned with the broader topic of controlling harmful but legal activities. However, to the extent that civil proceedings may be used as a complementary or supplementary enforcement mechanism, brief consideration will be given to where such procedures overlap with the criminal law.

Law enforcement in terms of identifying, apprehending, and sanctioning those that com- **2.08** mit criminal acts is central to an effective legal framework. The Internet as an environment has brought law enforcement issues to the fore as a topic for study, as well as impinging on wider public consciousness. This book is therefore concerned as much with criminal pro-cedure, the suitability of the powers given to those tasked with law enforcement responsibil-ities, as it is with issues of substantive criminal law. The manner in which law enforcement is achieved in a computer and networking environment will differ in many respects from our traditional physical environment, a theme that will be examined throughout the book.

B. Subject Matter

This section examines the nature of the subject matter this book deals with. First, consid- **2.09** eration is given to the three key elements of concern to us: information, computers, and networks. All are seemingly familiar, yet all raise interesting and difficult issues in terms of boundaries, bright lines, and, consequentially, legal certainty, a principle of particular import in the criminal field. Second, various attempts are made to define and classify the phenomenon of computer and cybercrime, the field of study for this book. The final part is a brief history of the study of computer and cybercrime to illustrate the changing nature of people's concerns in the field, which reflects in large part the evolving environment at both a technical and legal level.

Matters of technology and terminology

With regard to technology and its terminology, computers, and networks, or the common **2.10** shorthand 'ICTs' (information and communications technologies), are notorious for the level of ignorance and confusion that is present or may arise. In some instances, such ignor-ance has direct legal implications, which are to be examined further: from poorly drafted legislation to unexpected judicial interpretations, and acquittals of defendants on good and bad grounds. Ignorance inevitably also extends sometimes into the legal framework that governs such technology. However, it is not possible, within the scope of this book, to provide an extensive list of all the concepts and terminology that will be touched upon in the course of our analysis. As a starting point for readers, however, a useful glossary can be found in the ACPO Guide reproduced in the appendices.[1]

---

[1] Association of Chief Police Officers (ACPO), *Good Practice Guide for Computer Based Electronic Evidence*, Appendix IV, available at <http://www.cps.gov.uk/legal/assets/uploads/files/ACPO_guidelines_computer_

2.11 To an extent, an author has a certain right to define terms as he chooses to use them. This freedom need only be curtailed when analysing the applicability of terms written into the criminal code in a particular situation or jurisdiction, as we shall see in Chapter 3. Under English law, legislators are notoriously wary about defining certain terms, often preferring to rely on the tribunal of fact to be able to recognize what they are dealing with. One area of exception to this is where law is supplemented by a regulatory regime, such as exists for the communications sector, which demands a greater degree of certainty due to the nature of the obligations imposed and the scope for regulatory intervention. Other jurisdictions consider that ignorance among the general public and judiciary requires that certain terms be expressly defined, to mitigate against inappropriate decision-making. There are advantages and disadvantages of each approach, flexibility versus certainty, which will be an issue that we will return to throughout the book. For the purposes of our analysis, it is necessary to clarify how 'information', 'computers', 'networks', and related terms are to be used in general within the course of the book, as well as constrained by law.

2.12 There is general agreement within the academic literature that 'data' is a broader concept than 'information', as Wacks notes:

> 'Data' become 'information' only when they are communicated, received and understood. 'Data' are therefore potential 'information'. Thus when the data assume the form of the printed word, they are immediately transformed into information by the reader. Where, however, data consists in acts or signs which require any meaning, they remain in this state of pre-information until they are actually understood by another.[2]

This is one reason why European data protection law uses the term 'personal data', rather than 'personal information', because threats to privacy arise from the accumulation of raw data before it is transformed into information that can be used in relation to an individual; therefore the law intervenes at this earlier stage. However, while accepting this distinction, the book uses data and information interchangeably, sometimes preferring one over the other, depending on the context. Their use as synonyms also reflects how the terms are currently treated under English law.

2.13 Computers and communication technologies process data or information; it is the substance on which the technologies operate. However, data should not simply be viewed as something distinct from the technology, since there is often a duality present in our use of the term. One issue of relevance to our later discussion, for example, is the legal treatment of computer 'software' or 'programs' as a form of data, as distinct from software as a tool or device that acts on or processes data.[3] This blurred boundary is similar to the debate that has raged over the years about the treatment of computer software as both a literary work protected by copyright and as a patentable invention.[4]

---

evidence[1].pdf>. See also Peter Sommer, *Information Assurance Advisory Council Digital Evidence, Digital Investigations and E-Disclosure*, 4th edn, November 2013, at 150, Appendix 12 'Glossary of terms used in digital evidence', available at <http://www.iaac.org.uk/media/1347/iaac-forensic-4th-edition.pdf> ('IAAC Guide').

  [2] Wacks, R, *Personal Information, Privacy and the Law*, Clarendon Press, 1989, at 25.
  [3] See further discussion at paras 3.224–3.234.
  [4] See eg Press, T, 'Patent protection for computer-related inventions', in Reed, C (ed), *Computer Law*, 7th edn, Oxford University Press, 2011, Chapter 6.

In terms of forensics, investigators are generally more concerned with data generated by the **2.14** technology itself, such as machine logs, than the content of the data that has been supplied to, and processed by, the technology. This so-called 'metadata' 'describes and gives information about other data',[5] and will be generated by different elements within each of the computers and networks that process the content. Such forensic data is a critically important component of our analysis.[6]

The term 'computer' is used expansively to cover the hardware, software, and 'firmware'[7] **2.15** contained in a computer. An alternative term used in some laws is 'information system',[8] which, bearing in mind the scope of this book, perhaps may seem more suitable, but is not commonly used in public discourse. As noted above, some jurisdictions have chosen to explicitly define various ICTs in a criminal context, such as the term 'computer':

> . . . an electronic, magnetic, optical, electrochemical, or other high speed data processing device performing logical, arithmetic, or storage functions, and includes any data storage facility or communications facility directly related to or operating in conjunction with such device, but such term does not include an automated typewriter or typesetter, a portable hand held calculator, or other similar device.[9]

A key element of these statutory definitions is the requirement that a computer 'processes' **2.16** data, which itself requires to be understood. As a verb, the term 'processing' is used to describe any action, or series of actions or operations, that computer and communication technologies carry out in relation to the data supplied to them. Indeed, such an expansive approach is adopted under the Data Protection Act 1998 (DPA):

> 'processing', in relation to information or data, means obtaining, recording or holding the information or data or carrying out any operation or set of operations on the information or data, including—
> (a) organisation, adaptation or alteration of the information or data,
> (b) retrieval, consultation or use of the information or data,
> (c) disclosure of the information or data by transmission, dissemination or otherwise making available, or
> (d) alignment, combination, blocking, erasure or destruction of the information or data.[10]

Under this broad conception, acts such as storage and communication are seen as modes of processing, as well as distinct operations in their own right. This simple approach will not, however, be sufficient for the purpose of our analysis, since in certain contexts, processing is construed as being some form of manipulation of data, altering it from one state to another, beyond that of simple storage or holding data. This potentially excludes devices such as USB memory sticks and some Smart Cards, which are only capable of storing data and are not usually perceived to be a 'computer'. However, if such devices were considered to be

---

[5] 'metadata', in Oxford English Dictionary online, available at <http://www.oed.com/view/Entry/117150>.
[6] See in particular Chapter 4.
[7] Generally defined as a program or software that is embedded in a hardware device, such as a read-only memory (ROM) integrated circuit.
[8] eg Directive 2013/40/EU on attacks against information systems, OJ L 218/8, 14 August 2013.
[9] 18 USC s 1030(e)(1). See also Singapore's Computer Misuse and Cybersecurity Act (1993), as amended, s 2(1).
[10] Data Protection Act 1998 (DPA), s 1(1).

'processing' data simply by storing and making it available, it raises the issue of the proper scope of computer crime laws, specifically in relation to those *sui generis* laws concerned with the integrity, confidentiality and availability of ICTs.

2.17 An obvious potential disadvantage of a statutory definition is that technological developments may render historically accepted and politically negotiated statutory concepts unsuitable. Conversely, the absence of a definition relies on the judiciary being able to recognize a computer when they see one. The development of handheld wireless devices, for example, such as 'Blackberrys' and smart phones, may not fit most people's conception of what comprises a computer, while the integration of semi-conductor chips into an ever greater number of household items, from televisions to washing machines and the general trend towards the 'Internet of Things',[11] could result in over-criminalization, as unauthorized uses of such items could be determined to be a form of computer crime. The future heralds the possibility of household devices containing embedded systems with Internet connectivity,[12] enabling enhanced functionality such as remote control, but also inevitably giving rise to whole new forms of criminal activity.

2.18 While processing includes the act of communication, the means through which such communications take place are 'networks'. Broadly conceived, the term extends to all forms of systems that permit the transmission of data between different points, encompassing wireless (eg '3G', 'WiFi', and 'Bluetooth') and wireline systems (eg 'twisted pairs' and optical fibres), and fixed and mobile access technologies. While the term 'computers' has not generally required definition under English law, reflecting the unregulated environment in which the sector has developed, by contrast, networks fall within the historically heavily regulated field of telecommunications or communications law.

2.19 The current regulatory term is 'electronic communications networks', which is defined under the Communications Act 2003 in the following terms, although the term originates in European Union law:[13]

(a) a transmission system for the conveyance, by the use of electrical, magnetic or electro-magnetic energy, of signals of any description; and
(b) such of the following as are used, by the person providing the system and in association with it, for the conveyance of the signals—
  (i) apparatus comprised in the system;
  (ii) apparatus used for the switching or routing of the signals; and
  (iii) software and stored data.[14]

---

[11] See Martin, G, 'The case of the hacked refrigerator—Could "The Internet of Things" connect everything?', *California Magazine*, 5 February 2014, available at <http://alumni.berkeley.edu/california-magazine/just-in/2014-03-05/case-hacked-refrigerator-could-internet-things-connect>.

[12] Made possible, in part, through the introduction of Internet Protocol version 6 (IPv6), with huge additional IP address space potentially enabling every device in the world to be assigned a unique address.

[13] Directive 2002/21/EC on a common regulatory framework for electronic communications networks and services, OJ L 108/33, 24 April 2002, Art 2(a). See generally Walden, I, 'European Union Communications Law', in Walden, I, *Telecommunications Law and Regulation*, Oxford University Press, 2012.

[14] Communications Act 2003 (CA), s 32(1). The term 'signal' includes 'anything comprising speech, music, sounds, visual images or communications or data of any description' (ibid, s 32(10)(a)).

From this definition, it is important to recognize that the network comprises 'apparatus', which would include computers, as well as data, such as software, which is used to process data. In this context, 'signals' would include the content being transmitted by the communicating parties, as well as 'metadata' generated by the transmission process itself.[15] Therefore, once again, a clear line cannot necessarily be drawn between use of the terms computer, data, or a network.

From a regulatory perspective, and for the purposes of our subsequent discussion, it is neces- **2.20** sary to further qualify the concept of a network in a number of ways. Since the network will be a tool or medium through which criminal acts are carried out, the law may place responsibility upon the person providing the network, in respect of the prevention, detection, and/ or investigation of such criminality.[16] It is necessary, therefore, to identify the person on whom such obligations rest. The Communications Act 2003 places responsibility for the provision of a network upon the person who 'directs' or 'controls' it.[17] Legal ownership may be a relevant criterion for determining control, but it is by no means a decisive criterion, since a network may wholly comprise components (eg routers and circuits) that have been leased from others. The concept of a network has become substantially more complex in the past twenty years with the liberalization of the telecommunications sector at a national and global level. Where we used to have a single national telecommunications provider, such as BT, and one or two providers of broadcasting networks, we now have a proliferation of literally thousands of converged networks of all shapes and sizes. Such diversity is driven both by technological developments and the economics of network design and supply, and even, in certain cases, by regulatory dictate.

While 'control' represents one regulatory criterion, focusing on the relationship between **2.21** the network and the person that creates or operates the network, a boundary must also be drawn between the network and those that use it to communicate, operating at the edges of the network. From a regulatory perspective, the computers and other apparatus that 'end-users'[18] connect to a network, from handsets to computers, are referred to as 'terminal equipment',[19] which connect via an 'interface', either in the form of a physical 'network termination point' or a radio path between radio equipment.[20] This then could enable us to distinguish between criminal activities that take place 'on' the network and those which occur 'off' the network, which can have a range of policy and legal implications in terms of cybercrime. The ability and means of controlling the distribution of illegal content, for example, is very different where the content resides 'on' the network, in the form of a website, than when it is made available 'off' the network via peer-to-peer (P2P) file exchange systems. Police surveillance of a suspect's communications is subject to very different

---

[15] ibid, s 32(10).
[16] See further paras 2.233–2.253.
[17] CA, s 32(4)(b).
[18] ibid, s 151(1). Strictly speaking, the term is only applicable to those connecting to 'public electronic communication services', although we are using it to refer to all categories of network user. Another important regulatory distinction exists in telecommunications law between 'users' and 'subscribers', those that actually contract with the service provider.
[19] Directive 1999/5/EC on radio equipment and telecommunications terminal equipment and the mutual recognition of their conformity, OJ L 91/10, 7 April 1999. Implemented into UK law by the Radio Equipment and Telecommunications Terminal Equipment Regulations 2000 (SI No 730), as amended.
[20] SI No 730, reg 2(1).

procedural controls depending on whether it is carried out 'on' the network, through interception, or 'off' the network, through various bugging techniques.[21]

2.22 A third important criterion for distinguishing different types of networks is the division
between 'public' and 'private' networks, which focuses on the availability of the network
for use by others, end-users. As we shall see, this distinction may also be relevant to
the commission of an offence in certain circumstances[22] or the imposition of liability;[23]
although such a distinction will generally be of greater relevance in terms of criminal
procedure.

2.23 The Internet as the 'network of networks' must be distinguished from the multitude of ser-
vices that operate across it, such as email, newsgroups, and file transfer applications. In the
US, child protection legislation has been adopted that is specifically targeted at one type of
Internet communication service, ie the World Wide Web. The Child Online Protection Act
(COPA) establishes an offence of 'knowingly' communicating by means of the World Wide
Web, for commercial purposes, material that is 'harmful to minors',[24] where the 'World
Wide Web' is defined in the following terms:

> placement of material in a computer server-based file archive so that it is publicly accessible
> over the Internet, using hypertext transfer protocol or any successor protocol.[25]

While much of the discussion in this book will be about the applicability of traditional
statutory terminology to situations involving ICTs, the approach above can be criticized for
being too specific to current technology, when developments are occurring so rapidly that
attempts to address a specific technological environment may render legislation obsolete
within a few years.

2.24 'Cyberspace', a term first coined by William Gibson in *Neuromancer*,[26] is being used here as
a collective noun for the diverse range of environments that have arisen using the Internet
and its various services. While much of our subsequent analysis will focus on the use and
abuse of different Internet services, the underlying communications platform, the networks
that comprise the 'network of networks', are also the subject matter of our consideration and
should not be overlooked or misunderstood.

2.25 In terms of law enforcement against computer crime, questions of technology and terminology may arise at various points, from classifying behaviours as criminal to their subsequent forensic investigation and prosecution. In nearly each and every case, some level of
determination will need to be made as to the nature of the ICTs involved in a particular
criminal activity. Achieving legal certainty when treating such interconnected and rapidly
evolving subject matter as computers, networks, and data is itself a matter for concern when
criminalizing conduct in relation to them.

---

[21] See further paras 3.318–3.325.
[22] eg Regulation of Investigatory Powers Act 2000, s 1.
[23] eg 'common carrier' status may exempt a communications service provider (CSP) from liability for
illegal content: see para 2.227.
[24] 47 USC s 231(a)(1).
[25] 47 USC s 231(e)(1).
[26] HarperCollins, 1984.

Matters of taxonomy

Defining our subject matter is not only classic legal technique, but also assists us in teasing **2.26** out a taxonomy or scheme of classification, which is a 'basic intellectual tool'[27] for carrying out critical legal analysis. While this book is concerned primarily with the phenomenon of computer and cybercrime, we must acknowledge that cybercrime is a subset of computer crime and therefore our attention must encompass the broader field. Identifying a scheme of classification for computer and cybercrime can also assist policy-making, identifying common strands and themes that can offer predicative capabilities, as well as help isolate and discount popular misperceptions and misrepresentations of the issues involved. It has also been argued, however, that conceptualizing crime on the Internet as a unique category may itself create the perception of a problem that brings forth a state response.[28]

There is no agreed definition of what constitutes computer or cybercrime, and indeed there **2.27** has been some debate about whether such labels can even be said to have meaning. Wall, for example, used the phrase 'new wine, no bottles' to describe not only cyberspace, but also the new types of criminal behaviour he saw emerging; while Grabosky suggested that it was more a case of 'old wine in new bottles', since the crimes are fundamentally familiar.[29] However, there is broad acceptance within the literature that computer and cybercrime involves traditional crimes committed in a new environment as well as new crimes made possible in the new environment. Flanagan expresses this distinction in terms of 'issues of degree' and 'issues of kind', the former covering traditional crimes that are enhanced or facilitated by ICTs, the latter where the offence is fundamentally new.[30] The UK government distinguishes two categories of cybercrime: 'cyber-enabled' and 'cyber-dependent'.[31]

Statutory terminology may not always be appropriate guidance on the scope of the subject **2.28** matter. In the UK, for example, the leading statutory measure in the field is the Computer Misuse Act 1990. However, the common use of the word 'misuse' would seem to encompass an employee using his legitimate access to a computer or the Internet to engage in non-work-related activities, such as booking a holiday or organizing his weekend football team. Obviously, such activities may, in themselves, involve the commission of crimes, such as the downloading of pornography that could give rise to criminal liability being imposed upon the employer under principles of vicarious liability. In most cases, however, misuse by employees is not viewed as criminal in nature, but is an issue of employment law.[32]

'Computer abuse' is another term sometimes used in the literature,[33] although it has certain **2.29** anthropomorphic connotations that seem inappropriate for an enabling tool that, however

---

[27] Horder, J, 'The classification of crimes and the special part of the criminal law', in Duff, R and Green, S (eds), *Defining Crimes*, Oxford University Press, 2005, at 21.

[28] Palfrey, T, 'Surveillance as a response to crime in cyberspace', 9(3) *Information and Communications Technology Law* 173 (2000).

[29] Wall, DS, 'Cybercrimes: New wine, no bottles?', in Davies, P, Francis, P, and Jupp, V (eds), *Invisible Crimes: Their Victims and their Regulation*, Macmillan, 1999 and Grabosky, P, 'Virtual criminality: Old wine in new bottles?', 10 *Social & Legal Studies* 243 (2001) . The phrase can be traced back to the Bible, at Matthew 9:17: 'Neither do men pour new wine into old wineskins.'

[30] Flanagan, A, 'The law and computer crime: Reading the script of reform', 13(1) *International Journal of Law and Information Technology* 98 (2005) .

[31] HM Government, *Serious and Organised Crime Strategy*, Cm 8715, October 2013, para 2.54, available at <https://www.gov.uk/government/publications/serious-organised-crime-strategy>.

[32] eg *Denco v Joinson* [1991] 1 WLR 330.

[33] eg Parker, D, *Crime by Computer*, Charles Scribner's Sons, 1976.

much we may love and hate it at times, may be used for engaging in real abusive behaviour, such as child pornography. Acts of computer misuse and abuse are therefore not generally considered to fall within the scope of this book.

2.30 Various classification schemes are possible, based around differing, but overlapping, perspectives. The following briefly outlines five possible schemes:

- technology-based,
- motivation-based,
- outcome-based,
- communication-based, and
- information-based.

2.31 Technology-based schemes focus on the role of the ICTs. The US Department of Justice, for example, adopts a tripartite categorization based on the computer.[34] A distinction is made between acts where the computer is the 'object' of the crime, a relatively narrow category primarily addressing the theft of hardware and software components; where the computer is the 'subject' of the crime, for the purpose of breaching its confidentiality, integrity, and availability or the data it processes; and crimes where the computer is the 'instrument' of the crime, encompassing both fraud and computer pornography offences.[35] This typology is based on the work of Donn Parker, who also proposed a fourth 'symbolic' role of computers, based on the fact that people implicitly accept computer-generated output as accurate and true.[36]

2.32 Motivation can be used as an alternative basis for classifying different forms of computer crime, taking the perpetrator as the focus, rather than the nature of the criminal act. Thomas and Loader, for example, propose three categories of cybercriminal: hackers and phreaks; information merchants and mercenaries; and terrorists, extremists, and deviants.[37] The primary motivation for the first category is that of curiosity, essentially seen as benign rather than malicious. The second group are interested in financial reward, a desire to make money, a core criminal motivation. The final group are engaged in illegal political or social activity. However, motivation is more the concern of criminologists than the legal practitioner. Motivation also fails to correlate with the legal rules that comprise the primary focus of our analysis. While it may drive policy in the area or influence the sanction applied against a perpetrator, motivation does not generally dictate the legality of an act, being distinguishable from intent as the *mens rea* for a crime,[38] or the procedure governing its investigation. An important exception to this rule, relevant in the current environment, is in respect of terrorism, where, controversially,[39] motivation comprises an element of an 'act of terrorism'.[40]

---

[34] US Department of Justice, *Computer Crime: Criminal Justice Resource Manual* (1989), at 2.

[35] A variant of this scheme adopts the basic division between target/subject and instrument, but replaces the third category with crimes where the computer is simply an incidental aspect of the crime. See Brenner, SW, 'Defining Cybercrime: A review of state and federal law', in Clifford, R (ed), *Cybercrime: The Investigation, Prosecution and Defence of a Computer-related Crime*, 3rd edn, Carolina Academic Press, 2011, at 15–103.

[36] Parker, above, n 33, at 21.

[37] Thomas, D and Loader, B, 'Cybercrime in the information age', in Thomas, D and Loader, B (eds), *Cybercrime: Law Enforcement, Security and Surveillance in the Information Age*, Routledge, 2000, at 6–7.

[38] See para 2.111.

[39] eg Stella Rimington, ex-Director General of MI5, has stated that we should 'treat terrorism as a crime, and deal with it under the law—not as something extra, that you have to invent new rules to deal with': see 'Free Agent—Decca Aitkenhead', *The Guardian*, 17 October 2008, available at <http://www.theguardian.com/commentisfree/2008/oct/18/iraq-britainand911>.

[40] See para 3.306.

Motivation can often be inferred from the outcome of the criminal activity;[41] therefore **2.33** another point of departure for a classification scheme is to identify the types of potential misuse or harms with which we are concerned: an outcome-based approach.[42] Standard criminal law texts traditionally distinguish between offences against the person, whether individuals, legal persons, or the nation state; against property, mainly through forms of misappropriation or damage; and against various states of being, such as public order and the proper administration of justice.[43]

At the most basic level, of course, computer hardware and related peripherals may be used **2.34** (eg thrown) to directly injure a person, although such acts are not of concern to us! In terms of crimes against the person that are within our remit, a computer may be used to injure an individual in various ways, physically and psychologically, directly and indirectly. As a tool of direct harm, a medical facility's computer systems may be hacked to alter drug information that results in a person being misprescribed and dying as a result. As a tool facilitating harm, laws against child pornographic images are primarily concerned with the child abuse that occurred in the creation of the image, more than the effect of the image itself. Cyberterrorism is an online manifestation of a threat against the state, whether in the form of distributing bomb-making information or attacking the systems that form part of a nation's critical infrastructure, such as air traffic control systems.

In terms of crimes against property, computers, and networks may be misappropriated as **2.35** objects of a crime, as a valuable asset in themselves,[44] or through containing valuable components. With the introduction of Intel's 'Pentium' chip, for example, problems with the supply caused spikes in the market price and created a lucrative black market supplied by the criminal fraternity.[45] As high-value but small items, semiconductor chips, and mobile phones are currently a favourite of those engaged in 'carousel fraud', which exploits the VAT system governing the trade in goods within the EU.[46] In some countries, the value of the copper in a telecommunications network may make it the target of theft. Such crimes of corporeal seizure are of minor concern to us and are generally beyond the scope of this book. However, crimes of corporeal possession are of concern to us, especially in respect of devices that enable the commission of computer-integrity offences.[47]

To the extent that information has value, crimes aimed at obtaining information may be **2.36** classified as 'crimes of acquisition'.[48] With information, an inevitable first question concerns the proprietal nature of information. Under English law, information is not considered a form of property per se capable of theft, or the object of criminal misappropriation; although certain types of public, commercial, and personal information are granted the

---

[41] BloomBecker, JJB, 'Computer crime and abuse', 2 *The EDP Auditor Journal* 34 (1990), at 39.

[42] ibid.

[43] See eg Ormerod, D and Perry, D (eds), *Blackstone's Criminal Practice 2016*, Oxford University Press, 2015, and Ormerod, D and Laird, K (eds), *Smith & Hogan Criminal Law*, 14th edn, Oxford University Press, 2015.

[44] eg *Byrne* (1994) 15 Cr App R (S) 34.

[45] See Mead, DF, 'High-tech intruders', 10(6) *Washington Technology*, 22 June 1995.

[46] See Serious Organised Crime Agency (SOCA), *The United Kingdom Threat Assessment of Serious Organised Crime: 2006/7*, 31 July 2006, para 7.3.

[47] See paras 3.336–3.349.

[48] Grabosky, P, Smith, RG, and Dempsey, G, *Electronic Theft: Unlawful Acquisition in Cyberspace*, Cambridge University Press, 2001, at 1.

protection of criminal law.[49] Information is primarily used as an instrument of criminal misappropriation, from fraud to forgery, causing funds to be transferred and credentials to be accepted. We will be concerned with both types of activity.

2.37 An alternative form of misappropriation is where the computer or network is appropriated as a resource or facility for an unauthorized use. This may range from an internal person, such as an employee, using the resources to run another business or produce illegal copies, to external persons, storing material or laundering communication activities through a third-party resource, such as a PBX.[50] In these situations, the appropriation of the property is generally partial rather than total, and may not cause the rightful owner to experience any interference with, or degradation to the ICT resource.[51]

2.38 While appropriation is concerned with the assumption or usurpation of property or a right or interest in property,[52] the major other form of crime against property is the causing of damage or modification to the property, whether or not related to any intended gain to the perpetrator involved. At this stage, damage is being conceived broadly to include both tangible and intangible property, absent any statutory limitation. Malware and denial-of-service attacks are designed to interfere with the integrity and availability of computer, network, and information resources, which may result in crimes against persons, such as the medical example given above.

2.39 Wall adopts a similar outcomes-based approach, distinguishing four groups of activities: 'cyber-violence', 'cyber-obscenity', 'cyber-theft', and 'cyber-trespass'.[53] The first covers different forms of crime against the person; as does the second group, although the person being harmed varies depending on the subject matter. For child pornography, the concern is the abuse suffered by the subject, while for other obscene material it is the impact on the viewer that is the focus of concern justifying the imposition of criminal sanctions. 'Cyber-theft' matches crimes against property. However, the last category raises interesting issues, since the law of trespass is primarily concerned with defining the boundaries of property, distinguishing public from private space, and is both criminal and civil in nature. While cyberspace challenges existing conceptions of space, as we shall see further in Chapter 3, the analogy made between trespass and unauthorized access to a computer system raises not only boundary issues, but also questions over the appropriate use of criminal law.

2.40 A fourth possible means of categorizing our subject matter could be derived from the communications element in the commission of the crime; the network rather than the computer. Criminal activities with a communication element are sometimes subject to specific legislative measure. In the US, for example, 'wire fraud'[54] is a specific form of computer-related crime where the means of communications is a central feature of the offence. In a networked environment, crimes relating to acts of supply become assimilated with acts of communications when the item being supplied comprises digital information. In the case of child pornography, for example, supply (*read* 'communications') is the more serious offence

---

[49] See paras 3.08–3.51.
[50] ie a 'private branch exchange' that connects an office network to the public communications network.
[51] However, following *Gomez* [1993] AC 442, an offence of theft can be made out where an assumption has been of any of the rights of the owner.
[52] Theft Act 1968, s 3.
[53] Wall, above, n 29, at 113 et seq.
[54] 18 USC s 1343. See para 3.66.

than that of possession, while the use of a communication service to send certain types of illegal content is a separate offence.[55] In terms of computer-integrity offences, the interception of communications is criminalized.[56]

We could therefore conceivably categorize according to different types of criminal communications. So, for example, illegal communications, where the message from A to B infringes the rights of a third party C or is abusive, such as an illegal music file and child pornographic image; unsolicited communications, where the message from A to B is in the course of a criminal act, such as spam (in certain jurisdictions) or harassment; and unauthorized communications, where the message from A to B is of an unauthorized nature, such as hacking and denial-of-service attacks. Also, as discussed below, the inchoate acts of incitement and conspiracy are inherently communicative in nature, whether the message from A to B is to encourage B to commit a criminal act or is in respect of a non-cyberspace criminal activity, such as a terrorist act. **2.41**

For the purpose of this book, the categorization used to distinguish between different types of computer and cybercrime is based on that adopted in the primary international legal instrument in the area, the Council of Europe Convention on Cybercrime (2001).[57] In the Convention, substantive offences are distinguished into four categories, which are here reduced to three: computer-related crime, content-related crime, and computer-integrity offences. **2.42**

The first category is traditional types of criminal offence that may be committed using computers as the instrument of the crime, such as fraud. The second category, content-based cybercrimes, such as criminal copyright infringement and child pornography, concern reliance on the use of computer and communications technologies to facilitate the distribution of unlawful content or illegal data. The distinction being made between computer-related and content-related crime is primarily one of focus. In both, computers are a tool or instrument for the commission of a crime, rather than the target itself. However, in computer-related crime, the data or information being processed is also a tool or instrument for committing a criminal act; while in content-related crime, the data or information *is the crime*, not just a tool or instrument. The third category includes offences that have been established to specifically address activities that attack the integrity of computer and communications systems, such as distributing computer viruses. **2.43**

While the Convention on Cybercrime could be viewed as utilizing a technology-based scheme of categorization, similar in kind to the object, subject and instrument scheme described above, it would also seem that the categories could perhaps be more accurately described as 'information crimes', since the object of the crime is the information processed by ICTs, whether accounting data or pornographic images, rather than the computer itself.[58] Even for the computer-integrity offences, the public policy rationale underpinning **2.44**

---

[55] Communications Act 2003, s 127. See paras 3.201–3.213.

[56] Regulation of Investigatory Powers Act 2000, s 1.

[57] For alternative categorizations, see Sieber, U, *The International Handbook on Computer Crime*, Wiley, 1986, and Kerr, O, 'Cybercrime's scope: Interpreting "access" and "authorization" in computer misuse statutes', 78(5) *New York University Law Review*, 1596, 1602 fn 19 (2003) .

[58] The G8 categorizes computer-related and content-related together as 'computer-assisted threats', as distinct from 'threats to computer infrastructures'.

the category is the protection of the information being processed rather than computers and systems for their own sake.

2.45 Information may be the perpetrator's prime, convertible, or transitional target.[59] Theft of trade secrets and cracking copyright protection mechanisms are examples where information is the prime target; credit card data from hacked websites is information used for conversion into products and services; while password-sniffing programs are used to obtain information required to gain access to the password owner's system. However, no legal system protects information per se; instead, laws and regulations protect particular types of information driven by different public policy objectives and constraining particular types of behaviour in relation to that information.[60] Governments in many jurisdictions have, however, adopted *sui generis* measures to protect particular technologies that are used for processing information, ie computers and networks.

2.46 As the various schemes outlined above indicate, computer and cybercrime do not exhibit clear boundaries, neatly demarcating some topics from others. In addition, a criminal act will often comprise offences under one or more of any of the categories; concurrently or in series, in the course of events. The purpose of a taxonomy or classification scheme is not an attempt to describe the world as it is, but, rather, as noted at the beginning of this section, to provide a framework on which we can effectively analyse the different types of criminal activity present in cyberspace.

2.47 The subject matter of this book could have been defined narrowly to address only those crimes that are applicable to computer-integrity offences, such as 'hacking' and distributing viruses. Indeed, a substantial proportion of our attention and the examples considered will be concerned with such crimes. However, the impact of computers on criminal law has been much more substantial than this narrow field of activities would suggest, challenging traditional criminal concepts, such as deception, and facilitating particular types of crime, such as child pornography. As such, it seems only appropriate that we take into account the wider influence of computer and communication technologies on criminal conduct.

2.48 The study of criminal law is also not just about whether a particular act should be considered criminal or not. It is also about law enforcement, investigating those that commit criminal acts and prosecuting them, a process often considerably more difficult in a computer or digital environment. This book therefore takes a broad perspective on the topic, considering computer-specific and computer-based crimes and procedural issues as well as substantive offences.

Matters of history

2.49 As with any good law text, this book intends to describe the law as it is to date, ie the point at which control of the manuscript is handed over to the publishers. Achieving this objective does not preclude the equally worthy pursuit of other objectives, including a consideration of how and why we got to the current position; criticism of the current status quo coupled with suggestions for where we should (perhaps) be; as well as plenty of speculation on where we may be going. These objectives will also generally be carried out in parallel, when

---

[59] Newman, G and Clarke, R, *Superhighway Robbery: Preventing e-Commerce Crime*, Willan Publishing, 2003.
[60] See paras 3.08–3.51.

examining discrete topics of concern. However, it is also interesting to note that the topic as a subject matter for study has a strong pedigree. As the bibliography illustrates, books, articles, and reports on computer and cybercrime are both voluminous and date back over three decades to the 1970s, the oldest UK-published book of which the author is aware being 1973.[61] While this is not surprising, reflecting as it does the history of ICTs, the nature of such interest has obviously varied and developed over time, reflecting the environment in which such work has taken place.

Hollinger, for example, identifies four distinct periods of research and writing in the area **2.50** up until 1997.[62] In the 'discovery' period, from 1946 until 1976, the abuse of computers and communications technologies, such as phone phreaking, was first being recognized, recorded, and written about. The 'criminalization' period, from 1977 until 1988, was when problems with existing criminal law were the focus of attention, reflecting the commencement of legislative activity in many jurisdictions. The US state of Florida apparently wins the prize for the first 'stand-alone' computer crime statute.[63] The third period, entitled the 'demonization of the hacker', from 1988 until 1993, is considered to be a period when law enforcement agencies strived, often unsuccessfully, to pursue those considered to be threatening the ICT revolution, primarily the 'hackers' and 'phreakers'. Finally, Hollinger described the time he was writing as the 'censorship' period, with concern moving from computer-integrity crimes to concerns about the potentially illegal content made available over the Internet, such as child pornography and related material.

Without needing to wholeheartedly accept Hollinger's portrayal, one could at least recog- **2.51** nize, as noted in the Introduction, that current concerns in computer and cybercrime are dominated by the twin threats of terrorism and organized crime; although illegal content remains high on the political agenda. As such, this period could be given the epithet the 'critical infrastructure' period, since societal rather than user level issues are driving policy, substantive, and procedural law reform in the area.

Alternative ways of depicting the history of computer crime have obviously been proposed. **2.52** Ulrich Sieber, for example, has identified six 'main waves' of national laws addressing computer crime, reflecting legislative responses to the need to tackle emerging issues.[64] The first 'wave' during the 1970s and 1980s were laws addressing data protection and privacy issues, which arose in response to concerns about the capabilities of computers to process data about us.[65] In the early 1980s, criminal laws were amended and updated to address computer-related economic crimes, which were inadequately addressed by existing rules. During the course of the 1980s and early 1990s, enhancements were made to national intellectual property regimes, to reflect the new forms of property generated by ICTs, such as computer software, and the new means of handling traditional protected works.[66] The arrival of the Internet, during the mid-1990s, focused attention on the need to update laws

---

[61] McKnight, G, *Computer Crime*, Michael Joseph, 1973.
[62] Hollinger, RC, *Crime, Deviance and the Computer*, Dartmouth, 1997, at xviii.
[63] Florida Computer Crimes Act, Fla Stat ch 815, came into force 1 August 1979.
[64] Report for the European Commission, written by Sieber, U, 'Legal Aspects of Computer-Related Crime in the Information Society: COMCRIME Study', 1 January 1998, Pt I.B.2, available at <http://www.echo.lu/legal/en/comcrime/sieber.html>.
[65] See paras 3.27–3.38.
[66] See paras 3.105–3.128.

protecting against illegal and harmful content. Reforms to criminal procedural law began in the 1980s, as ICTs challenged traditional practices and procedures. The final 'wave' identified by Sieber were regulations on security measures such as cryptography and digital signatures, during the latter half of the 1990s.

2.53 Another parallel history could be constructed around the shifting motivations of those that engage in criminal conduct, such as hackers and virus writers. The early hackers, during Hollinger's so-called 'discovery' period, were primarily driven by curiosity and experimentation, rather than misappropriation. As the technology spread, economically motivated, industrial-scale computer crimes have become the norm. Most recently, concerns about terrorism have come to the fore since the attacks on New York in 2001, ICTs being seen as both a tool and weapon for cyber-terrorists.

2.54 Finally, a fundamental historic distinction that must be acknowledged when discussing computer crime is that between activities that occurred pre-Internet and those that have emerged in the cyberspace era. While we are concerned with both, as Hollinger notes, the first phase of legislative activity in the field, against conduct targeting the technology, occurred pre-Internet, or during its early years, in a very different environment. Our examination must, therefore, acknowledge the seismic shift that has been brought about as a result of the Internet.

C. Public Policy

2.55 Law and regulation are about facilitating and restraining certain types of behaviour. The imposition of criminal sanctions upon an activity, particularly where the sanction involves the deprivation of liberty through imprisonment, clearly falls at one end of the spectrum in terms of the enforcement of public law. As such, criminal sanctions should not generally be imposed without clear policy objectives being identified and articulated by the executive and legislative branches of government, and sometimes explicitly referenced in statute or articulated by the judiciary. In terms of criminal policy, such objectives are generally conceived in terms of preventing certain behaviours or harms from being suffered. In turn, those behaviours and harms are normally considered deserving of criminal sanction due to the scale of such activity and/or the scale of harm suffered. This section first examines various policy objectives that underpin the use of criminal law against cybercrimes, particularly in relation to data insecurity; while in the second part, the scale of incidence and cost of such crimes are considered.

2.56 Statutory rules and regulations are a manifestation of policy-making, political agendas, and expedience, whether originating within national or international fora.[67] To better understand the laws that comprise the subject matter of this book, it is necessary to consider some of the policy objectives that have driven the legislative response to computer and cybercrime since the late 1970s, in the same manner that examining the motivations of perpetrators should feed into the policy-making process. We may object to certain policies, and the law and regulations that flow from them, on grounds of principle, practicality, and

---

[67] See generally Hosein, I, 'The sources of laws: Policy dynamics in a digital and terrorized world', 20(3) *The Information Society* 187 (2004).

performance, but we must understand the 'why' in order to be able to critically analyse the 'what' of law.

It is also important to note, however, that the different categories of criminal behaviour   **2.57**
identified above 'render inadequate attempts to aggregate cybercrimes for the purpose of policy formation'.[68] Each category will raise different policy concerns and may require a different response, in terms of law and other forms of control. In terms of computer-related offences, the public policy objectives behind the criminalization of such activities are generally unaltered by the use of computer technology, since these activities are merely a tool. However, ICTs have been seen as facilitating certain criminal activities, which has led to calls for further criminalization. The growth of 'identity theft', for example, is widely associated in the public's mind with the Internet. While the response of policy-makers to identity theft covers a range of different initiatives, specific law reform has been mooted as one element of the strategy, even though existing laws may be considered sufficient, seemingly to meet public expectations that something be seen to be done.[69]

In terms of content-related crimes, specifically copyright infringement and the distribu-   **2.58**
tion of child pornography, the ease with which computer and communication technologies handle digital information has had a substantial impact in terms of facilitating activities concerning illegal content. This has resulted in legislative amendment to try and restrain such growth. Indeed, content-related crimes, from child pornography to religious hatred and the glorification of terrorism, have increasingly dominated the political agenda and consequentially policy initiatives,[70] despite the problems with crystallizing such conduct in workable legal rules.

The policy objectives that have driven the criminalization of activities specifically targeted   **2.59**
at computers and networks, particularly hacking and the distribution of viruses, have been concerned with the cost to users of such activities. The direct origins of the Computer Misuse Act 1990 can be found in a Law Commission report on 'Computer misuse' published in October 1989.[71] In justifying its proposal for legislation, the Law Commission made it clear that protecting information processed by computers was not the sole consideration:

> The most compelling argument for the criminalization of hacking are those stemming from, first, the actual losses and costs incurred by computer system owners whose security systems are (or might have been) breached; secondly, that unauthorized entry may be the preliminary to general criminal offences; and thirdly, that general willingness to invest in computer systems may be reduced, and effective use of such systems substantially impeded, by repeated attacks and the resulting feeling of insecurity on the part of computer operators.[72]

The types of harm that a person may suffer, particularly in a commercial context, include   **2.60**
the loss of information assets, such as intellectual property or personal information, which extends to a loss of control over how such information is used even if the information itself is not lost; the loss or disruption of an activity, such as 'denial-of-service' attacks against a

---

[68] Wall, DS (ed), *Cyberspace Crime*, Dartmouth, 2003, at 158.
[69] See paras 3.73–3.76.
[70] Interview with Tim Wright, Home Office, 1 February 2006.
[71] Report No 186, Cm 819, HMSO, 1989. See also previous reports: Law Commission 'Computer misuse', Working Paper No 110, 1988, and Scottish Law Commission 'Report on computer crime', Cm 174, HMSO, 1987.
[72] Report No 186, above, n 71, para 2.14.

website or the receipt of large number of unsolicited communications; and the damage to a person's reputation and privacy, from either a security breach or from being used as a location from which cybercrimes are committed, such as the person's machine being operated as a 'botnet'.[73]

2.61　As noted by the Law Commission, harm, or fear of harm, can be seen as acting as a brake on the take-up and exploitation of ICTs and related activities, such as electronic commerce, which can have an impact on economic development. If people do not feel a certain level of trust and security in cyberspace, so the argument goes, then they may either be deterred from using it, or will be circumspect about the range of activities they will engage in. Such reticence, if too widespread, may inhibit the growth and development of the Internet and the services made available over it.

Data insecurity

2.62　Prevention being better than cure, policy-makers have recognized that criminalizing specific activities is not a complete or sufficient response to the threat of hackers, virus writers, and cyber-terrorists. The targets or potential victims of such attacks are usually best placed to implement the appropriate physical, logical, and organizational security measures that will prevent, deter, or limit the consequences of such attacks, often referred to as 'target hardening',[74] thereby contributing to general crime control.

2.63　While the virtuous link between data security and cybercrime should clearly be in the interests of users,[75] there is much evidence that data security measures are not given adequate attention or are not properly understood within many organizations or among the general public.[76] However, since an interconnected and interdependent environment means significant negative externalities and collateral vulnerabilities from a failure by users to take measures to protect themselves, policy-makers have recognized the need to facilitate data security through a variety of mechanisms, including the imposition of legal obligations and encouraging compliance with internationally recognized security standards, such as the ISO 27100 family of standards for keeping information assets secure.[77]

2.64　In terms of obligations to implement data security measures, different sources of legal treatment can be identified. In terms of express provision, there are currently few examples. At a general level, European data protection law is the most familiar, requiring the implementation of 'appropriate security measures' by those processing personal data, 'in particular where the processing involves the transmission of data over a network'.[78] As implemented

---

[73] Where a computer is inadvertently controlled, as a robot, by a third party. See further para 3.295.

[74] See Morris, S, *The Future of Netcrime now: Part 2—Responses*, Home Office Online Report 63/04, December 2004, at 23.

[75] As noted in the United Nations' *Manual on the Prevention and Control of Computer-related Crime*, 1994, as well as by the European Commission in its Communication 'Creating a safer information society by improving the security information infrastructures and combating computer-related crime', COM(2000) 890 final, 12 September 2009.

[76] Schneier, B, *Secrets and Lies: Digital Security in a Networked World*, Wiley, 2000.

[77] International Organization for Standardization (ISO), 'ISO/IEC 27001—Information security management', available at <http://www.iso.org/iso/home/standards/management-standards/iso27001.htm>.

[78] Directive 95/46/EC on the protection of individuals with regard to the processing of personal data and on the free movement of such data, OJ L 281/31, 23 November 1995, Art 17.

in the DPA, however, failure to comply can give rise to regulatory sanction or grounds for a civil claim, but will not generally be subject to criminal sanction.[79]

At a sectoral level, providers of particular types of services may be subject to security obliga-   **2.65**
tions that reflect specific perceptions of risk and public interest concern. Suppliers of 'public electronic communication services', for example, such as Internet service providers (ISPs), have an obligation to notify subscribers of any security breach, as well as any residual risks that may exist, despite the security put in place by the ISP, and measures that the subscriber may take to mitigate such risks.[80] So, for example, broadband subscribers should be informed about the increased risks of viruses and related malware that may compromise their systems from being 'always on' the Internet. Compliance regimes in other regulated sectors also require the implementation of security and control measures to counter the risk of crime, such as the financial services sector.[81]

The threat of terrorism has extended risk sensitivities from sectoral activities to location-   **2.66**
based concerns. In 2005, following the terrorist attacks in London, the police called for new measures placing private and public sector entities under a duty 'to install and maintain to approved standards protective security in designated locations', which would encompass computer systems.[82] While this proposal received little support within Government, nor did large-scale data retention schemes until the events of 11 September.[83]

In terms of criminal sanction, the Official Secrets Act 1989 creates three offences in respect   **2.67**
of a 'failure to safeguard' certain types of information,[84] although this is an exemption rather than the rule under English law. However, it has been proposed by Brenner that the failure by 'users' and 'architects' of the Internet to adequately utilize or build products and services with data security features should be subject to criminal liability in order to provide the necessary incentives to protect themselves and others who may be harmed by their failure.[85] Criminalizing negligence is uncommon in English criminal law,[86] but less so in other legal systems. Arguments that may be marshalled in favour of criminalizing negligence in the protection of systems and networks are that the harm is great, the risk is (or should be) obvious and the defendant has the capacity to address such risk through precautions.[87] In the US, the implementation of inadequate security by a manufacturer of mobile devices

---

[79] See paras 3.27–3.38 for a discussion of data protection law.

[80] Directive 02/58/EC concerning the processing of personal data and the protection of privacy in the electronic communications sector, OJ L 201/37, 31 July 2002, Art 4, as amended by Directive 09/136/EC, OJ L 337/11, 18 December 2009. Transposed into UK law by the Privacy and Electronic Communications (EC Directive) Regulations 2003 (SI No 2426), reg 5 (as amended).

[81] eg *Financial Conduct Authority Handbook*, SYSC 3.2.6R: 'Systems and controls in relation to compliance, financial crime and money laundering', available at <https://www.handbook.fca.org.uk/handbook/SYSC/3/2.html>.

[82] See ACPO, 'Chief Police Officers recommend changes to counter the terrorist threat', Press Release 55/05, 21 July 2005.

[83] See paras 4.228–4.230.

[84] Official Secrets Act 1989, ss 8(1), (4), and (5).

[85] See Brenner, S, 'Distributed security: Moving away from reactive law enforcement', 9(1) *International Journal of Communications Law and Policy* 11 (2005).

[86] However, personal criminal liability is often imposed on persons acting in a corporate capacity, as a 'director, manager, secretary or similar officer of the body corporate' who through neglect are responsible for the corporate body committing an offence. See eg DPA, s 61 and the Fraud Act 2006, s 12.

[87] See Ashworth, A and Horder, J, *Principles of Criminal Law*, 7th edn, Oxford University Press, 2009, at 181 et seq.

has been held to constitute an unfair or deceptive trade practice in breach of US consumer law.[88] As such, the law can be one element in a strategy to change the economics of data security and thereby raise levels of deployment.[89]

2.68 As well as express obligation, laws may provide indirect incentives to system operators to implement security measures. Illegal access to computer systems is criminalized in some jurisdictions, for example, only where it involves the infringement of security measures.[90] The onus is therefore placed upon a victim to have such measures in place in order to be able seek a criminal law remedy.

2.69 However, for the foreseeable future, legal obligations and incentives are likely to remain a minor element in any public policy strategy to address data security, when compared with the opportunities presented by the technology itself, in terms of 'engineering out' opportunities for crime by industry itself,[91] as well as the availability of techniques, such as encryption and digital signatures, anti-virus, and spyware applications.

2.70 Market forces are also critical, influencing technological developments and their adoption by users. On the demand side, increasing user awareness and concern is encouraging the ICT industry to take data security more seriously. On the supply side, one potential source of market pressure would be insurance companies, since they are in a position to effectively force organizations to address the risks they face from cyberspace and act to adequately protect their assets, through the withdrawal of coverage[92] or raising of premiums, although current take-up of cyber-related insurance products among business remains low.[93] The stream of revelations about the surveillance activities of the National Security Agency (NSA) and others, from the materials disclosed by Edward Snowden since June 2013, have had a clear impact on the attitudes and practices of both industry and users towards the deployment of security technologies.

Critical infrastructure

2.71 Increasing dependence on cyberspace, especially for a nation's 'critical national infrastructure', such as power, financial, communication, and transport networks, escalates the potential loss suffered by an individual user up to society as a whole. Post 11 September 2001, cybercrime has inevitably become one element of the developed nations' fear and fascination with terrorism. Attention has focused on the possibilities for 'cyber-terrorism', cybercrime with a premeditated political motivation, as well as for 'cyber-war', state-based activity, with the image of a future 'electronic Pearl Harbor' haunting policy-makers.[94]

---

[88] *In the matter of HTC America Inc*, FTC File No 1223049 (2013), the Federal Trade Commission (FTC) reached a settlement with HTC, at <http://www.ftc.gov/enforcement/cases-proceedings/122-3049/htc-america-inc-matter>.

[89] See generally Grady, MF and Parisi, F, *The Law and Economics of Cybersecurity*, Cambridge, 2006. See also Anderson, R, 'Economics and Security Resource Page', available at <http://www.cl.cam.ac.uk/~rja14/econsec.html>

[90] See paras 3.242–3.243.

[91] Schneier, above, n 76.

[92] See eg *Tektrol Ltd v International Insurance Company Ltd* [2005] EWCA Civ 843, where the insurer tried, unsuccessfully, to argue that damage caused by a virus was excluded because it could not be shown that it was directed at the computer system in question.

[93] See Computer Emergency Response Team (CERT), *Cybersecurity Watch Survey*, available at <http://www.cert.org/insider-threat/research/cybersecurity-watch-survey.cfm?>, since 2004.

[94] Smith, G, 'An electronic Pearl Harbor? Not likely', 15(1) *Issues on Science and Technology* 68 (1998), available at <http://www.issues.org/15.1/smith.htm>.

Over recent years, for example, the US has been subjected to a series of sustained attacks against governmental information resources which seem to originate from a particular province in China and are thought to be being carried out with the support, express or tacit, of the Chinese government.[95] The objective is presumed to be access to sensitive commercial and military information to assist China's economic development, as well as improving the defensive and offensive capabilities of the People's Liberation Army.[96]

As concern about cybercrime as cyber-terrorism has increased, governments have expressly **2.72** addressed the vulnerabilities created by cyberspace for so-called 'critical infrastructures', those 'facilities, networks, services and assets which, if disrupted or destroyed, would have a serious impact on the health, safety, security or economic well-being of citizens or the effective functioning of governments'.[97] While the specific scope of what constitutes 'critical infrastructure' may vary between countries, computer and communications networks including the Internet are usually explicitly identified.[98]

At a G8 level, Member States have adopted a set of principles specifically addressed at the **2.73** protection of 'critical information infrastructures'.[99] In South Africa and the US, statutory recognition is given to the need to protection 'critical data', as well as the infrastructure systems that process such data. In South Africa, requirements exist for the identification and management of 'critical data', defined as that which the Minister of Communications considers 'of importance to the protection of the national security of the Republic or the economic and social well-being of its citizens'.[100] Obligations are placed upon 'critical database administrators' to implement measures to protect such databases and a failure to comply may itself result in the commission of an offence.[101]

In the US, the Clinton Administration first established a National Infrastructure Protection **2.74** Center in 1998, to address and coordinate policy and strategy in the area,[102] which has since been integrated into the Information Analysis and Infrastructure Protection Directorate of the Department of Homeland Security.[103] The Critical Infrastructure Information Act 2002 places criminal sanctions on the disclosure of 'information not customarily in the public domain and related to the security of critical infrastructure or protected systems';[104] while US sentencing guidelines provide for enhanced sentences where it involves a computer system used to maintain or operate a critical infrastructure.[105]

---

[95] Warren, P, 'Smash and grab, the hi-tech way', *The Guardian*, 19 January 2006, available at <http://www.theguardian.com/politics/2006/jan/19/technology.security>.

[96] See US Department of Defense, *The Military Power of the People's Republic of China*, Annual Report to Congress, 20 July 2005, at 36 'Computer Network Operations'.

[97] Commission Communication to the Council and the European Parliament on Critical Infrastructure Protection in the fight against terrorism, COM(2004) 702 final, 20 October 2004.

[98] eg Commission Green Paper 'on a European Programme for Critical Infrastructure Protection', COM(2005) 576 final, 17 November 2005, Annex 2 'Indicative list of critical infrastructure sectors', at No 7.

[99] G8 Principles for Protecting Critical Information Infrastructure, adopted May 2003, available at <http://www.justice.gov/sites/default/files/ag/legacy/2004/06/03/G8_CIIP_Principles.pdf>.

[100] Electronic Communications and Transactions Act 2002, Art 52(1)(a).

[101] ibid, Art 58(2).

[102] 'Critical Infrastructure Protection', Presidential Decision Directive, PDD63, 22 May 1998, available at <http://fas.org/irp/offdocs/pdd/pdd-63.htm>.

[103] See <http://www.dhs.gov/national-protection-and-programs-directorate>.

[104] 6 USC ss 131 et seq. The maximum penalty is one year's imprisonment (s 133(f)).

[105] US States Sentencing Commission, *Guidelines Manual* (effective 1 November 2014), ss 2B1.1(b) (18)(A)(i) and (iii); 2B2.3(b)(1)(A); and 2B3.2(b)(3)(B)(V), available at <http://www.ussc.gov/guidelines-manual/guidelines-manual>.

2.75 The US Government has also published a 'National Strategy to Secure Cyberspace', which is a component of its broader national strategy for homeland security. The phraseology used in the document makes clear the potential or perceived scale of vulnerability, by stating that cyberspace is 'the control system of our country' and that 'the healthy functioning of cyberspace is essential to our economy and our national security'.[106] Recognition of the strategic importance of the Internet was one of the reasons for the US Government's intransigence over suggestions, within the context of the United Nations World Summit on the Information Society (WSIS), that control over the domain name system, a critical Internet resource, should be transferred from the US Government to some international governing body.[107]

2.76 In the UK, there has been no legislative measure directly addressing critical infrastructure, although the Civil Contingencies Act 2004 places obligations upon communications providers to assist preparations against a future 'emergency', such as the 'disruption of a system of communication'.[108] At an institutional level, the National Infrastructure Security Coordination Centre (NISCC) was established in 1999 as an inter-departmental initiative, with the remit to oversee protection of all critical infrastructure systems, and issues regular reports and briefings on threats emanating from cyberspace. In 2007, NISCC was merged with the National Security Advice Centre to form the Centre for the Protection of National Infrastructure (CPNI).[109]

2.77 We can therefore see a duality in the nature of the vulnerability created by cyberspace: as a source of vulnerability, the conduit for those that wish to attack critical infrastructure, such as ports and power stations, as well as being a vulnerable entity itself, as an essential infrastructure. Our vulnerability to the loss of the Internet as a critical information infrastructure is particularly ironic given the origins of the Internet as a US Defense Department initiative designed to provide a robust communications network against attack.[110]

2.78 While governments are keen to promote security and trust in cyberspace as a mechanism for facilitating its development, security technologies themselves present a source of risk and vulnerability. Certain cryptographic products, in particular, as the dominant technological solution to the need for authentication, integrity, and confidentiality in cyberspace, are categorized under EU law as 'dual-use', having military as well as civil applications. As a consequence, cryptographic technologies are subject to export control regimes designed to limit the proliferation and use of products and services that can threaten us,[111] while their

---

[106] US Government, *The National Strategy to Secure Cyberspace*, February 2003, available at <http://georgewbush-whitehouse.archives.gov/pcipb/>.

[107] However, in March 2014, the US announced its intention 'to transition key internet domain name functions to the global multistakeholder community', see National Telecommunications and Information Administration (NTIA), 'NTIA announces intent to transition key internet domain name functions', Press Release, 14 March 2014, available at <http://www.ntia.doc.gov/press-release/2014/ntia-announces-intent-transition-key-internet-domain-name-functions>.

[108] Civil Contingencies Act 2004, s 1(2)(f). Under the Act, there are three 'privileged access' schemes relating to telecommunications, covering mobile and fixed systems. See further Cabinet Office, 'Resilient Communications', Public safety and emergencies—guidance, 20 February 2013, available at <http://www.cabinetoffice.gov.uk/content/privileged-access-schemes-mtpas-ftpas-and-airwave>.

[109] See <http://www.cpni.gov.uk>.

[110] Grewlich, K, *Governance in Cyberspace*, Kluwer Law International, 1999, at 34.

[111] See Council Regulation (EC) No 428/2009 setting up a Community regime for the control of exports, transfer, brokering and transit of dual-use items, OJ L 134/1, 29 May 2009. See also Koops, B-J, *Crypto Law Survey*, edn February 2013, available at <http://www.cryptolaw.org/>.

widespread use by the criminal fraternity to protect data being stored and communicated has increasingly become a dominant feature in digital investigations.[112] Governments therefore have to achieve a difficult balancing act, encouraging the implementation of security technologies of sufficient strength to provide 'appropriate' protection for cyberspace users, while preventing such security becoming a weapon in the hands of cybercriminals, cyberterrorists, and for cyber-warfare.[113]

Incidence

In terms of criminal policy-making, the first stage in a perfect world would be to identify **2.79** the scale of any perceived threat or problem (presuming of course that problems continue to arise in the perfect world!). The next stage would be to identify those things that we ought to know in order to develop an appropriate response, in current terminology 'evidence-based' policy-making. However, of those things we ought to know, we must then distinguish 'between those we can know and what is infeasible to know',[114] since much resource can be wasted trying to obtain the latter. Where evidence is not available, policy-making may be based on the precautionary principle, where a risk is apparent, but the evidence is uncertain.[115]

As noted above, this chapter is concerned with examining the evolving legal framework **2.80** to address the phenomenon of computer and cybercrime. Consideration will be given to the adequacy of existing laws and proposals for law reform to better tackle the problem. However, a preliminary issue that must be addressed concerns the actual scale of the problem. Public policy agendas generally respond to a need articulated through one or more channels, such as the media or business. Such needs generally emerge from experience, victims suffering from such activities often coupled with a real or perceived sense of inadequate protection from the law and the agencies responsible for its enforcement. Therefore a first question to be asked is: What is the scale of computer crime?

Reliable statistics about the scale of computer crime are notoriously difficult to come by. **2.81** A lack of consensus about what constitutes computer and cybercrime is clearly one obstacle to the collection of data, as discussed above. Also, measurement may be taken at different points, from surveys of victims to the number of successful prosecutions. Cornwall suggests that statistics provide two things of value: figures about the total incidence of a particular type of crime, and data about the proportion of different methods, perpetrators and victims.[116] While the former may be somewhat doubtful, the latter is certainly important for influencing public policy. In attempting to obtain estimates of the prevalence of cybercrime, Moitra distinguishes between a micro-level approach and a macro-level approach,[117] the former focusing on the generation of cybercrime, utilizing data about numbers of active

---

[112] See paras 4.291–4.297 for a discussion about protected data.

[113] Organisation for Economic Co-operation and Development (OECD), *Guidelines on Cryptography Policy*, 19 December 1997, available at <http://www.oecd.org/sti/ieconomy/guidelinesforcryptographypolicy.htm>.

[114] Moitra, SD, 'Developing policies for cybercrime: Some empirical issues', 13(3) *European Journal of Crime, Criminal Law and Criminal Justice* 435 (2005), at 437.

[115] See eg the Treaty on the Functioning of the European Union (TFEU), OJ C 83/47, 30 March 2010, Art 191(2).

[116] Cornwall, H, *Data Theft*, Mandarin, 1990, at 63.

[117] Moitra, above, n 114, at 438–9.

persons and groups, such as that obtained through self-reporting,[118] while the latter relies on data found in reports and surveys of victims.

2.82 The relative paucity of empirical data concerning computer crime is generally seen as being due to a range of factors. A lack of experience and resources among law enforcement and prosecuting authorities, for example, has often meant that investigations and prosecutions are not considered a priority area, particularly when competing for attention with other public concerns, such as violent crime.[119] This will often be exacerbated through inadequate training of personnel, which has sometimes meant that the suspect has had to educate the investigator about the nature of his crime. As John Perry Barlow, co-founder of the Electronic Frontier Foundation, noted after being interviewed by the FBI in the course of a hacking investigation: 'You know things have rather jumped the groove when potential suspects must explain to law enforcers the nature of their alleged perpetrations'![120] This second factor obviously contributes to the under-reporting of cybercrimes since, where victims perceive that they will receive a poor response from law enforcement agencies, they will be less likely to make the effort to report.

2.83 The transnational nature of computer crimes and digital investigations, with the associated jurisdictional problems, contributes to the complexity and therefore cost of investigating and prosecuting offenders.[121] In addition, the nature of computers, particularly when networked, creates significant forensic challenges to law enforcement agencies when obtaining evidence and subsequently presenting it before the courts.[122] All law enforcement agencies are under pressure to perform, either expressly or implicitly, and are short of resources. Tackling international computer and cybercrimes and the related forensic and evidential challenges is resource-intensive, requiring the obtaining of evidence from abroad, yet has low clear-up rates, ie successful prosecutions, all of which operates as a significant disincentive for law enforcement activity.

Statistics and survey data

2.84 In the UK, official crime statistics are based on a number of different sources. A primary source is crimes that are reported by victims to the police. Of these, those that are classified as 'notifiable' offences become 'recorded crime', which means the data is passed on to the Home Office to form 'recorded crime statistics'.[123] Within the Home Office 'counting rules', the range of computer crimes considered in this book are not surprisingly classified separately. Computer-integrity offences fall within the general category of 'Fraud'.[124] The

---

[118] eg Hollinger, RC, 'Crime by computer: Correlates of software piracy and unauthorized account access', 4 *Security Journal* 2 (1993). Such approach would seem more problematic where the criminal activity is of an organized nature.

[119] See Goodman, MD, 'Why the police don't care about computer crime', 10 *Harvard Journal of Law and Technology* 465 (1997).

[120] Barlow, JP, 'Crime and puzzlement: In advance of the law on the electronic frontier', *Whole Earth Review*, 22 September 1990. While this occurred well over a decade ago, the author knows of a similar situation in an investigation in the UK in 2005.

[121] See further Chapter 5.

[122] See further Chapters 4 and 6.

[123] See further Office for National Statistics (ONS), 'Police recorded crime', available at <http://www.ons.gov.uk/ons/guide-method/method-quality/specific/crime-statistics-methodology/guide-to-finding-crime-statistics/police-recorded-crime/index.html>.

[124] Home Office Counting Rules for Recorded Crime (with effect from April 2014), available at <https://www.gov.uk/government/publications/counting-rules-for-recorded-crime>.

rules specify a general rule for the counting of different types of crime. So, for example, with computer viruses and malware, one crime should be recorded for each intended victim; whereas for hacking into personal computers, one crime should be recorded for each computer affected.[125]

While the situation in the UK has improved over recent years, the failure of law enforcement **2.85** agencies to specifically collate data in relation to computer crime remains widespread.[126] This may be due to a lack of resources, but is more likely due to the complexities of recording such events. Of the three categories outlined above, computer-related and content-related are traditional crimes using computers as the instrument of commission. As such, it may not always be obvious to record it as a computer crime or, if recorded, it may artificially inflate the crime statistics through double counting. In the UK, with respect of computer misuse offences, Action Fraud recorded nearly 18,000 cases in the year to June 2014.[127] According to official figures, between 1990 and 2013, there have been 339 proceedings where the Computer Misuse Act 1990 has been the principal offence, resulting in 262 convictions.[128] As with any type of crime, prosecution numbers represent a small proportion of the number of offences actually occurring; however, it is difficult to know how to extrapolate an estimated total from these relatively small numbers.

A second source of official crime statistics is the Crime Survey, which uses survey data to **2.86** measure people's experience of crime, including unreported crimes.[129] In addition to these official figures, there are numerous surveys carried out by a range of organizations on the scale and cost of computer crime in the UK and around the world.[130]

Such survey data is generally based on organizational victims, generally business users, vol- **2.87** untarily responding to a request for information about the incidence and impact of criminal activities perpetrated against them. Although it is generally designed to provide quantitative data about the scale of cybercrime, the sample size often means that the results do not have statistical significance and are more appropriately categorized as qualitative indicators of the range of the acts being experienced and the consequences suffered. In addition, survey figures are often produced by commercial entities operating in the data security sector, which clearly have an incentive to overstate the problem, and extrapolate the economic costs of computer crime on the basis of scant real data.[131]

---

[125] ibid, see 'Counting rules for fraud', at NFIB50–NFIB52E.
[126] See United Nations Office on Drugs and Crime (UNODC), *Comprehensive Study on Cybercrime*, February 2013, at 259, Annex 2 'Measuring Cybercrime', available at <http://www.unodc.org/documents/organized-crime/UNODC_CCPCJ_EG.4_2013/CYBERCRIME_STUDY_210213.pdf>.
[127] See ONS, 'Crime Statistics, year ending September 2014', available at <http://www.ons.gov.uk/ons/publications/re-reference-tables.html?edition=tcm%3A77-372973>.
[128] See Ministry of Justice, Justice Statistics Analytical Services, quoted in a written answer from Justice Minister, Mike Penning, to a Parliamentary question (PQ 222192) on 4 February 2015, available at <http://www.parliament.uk/business/publications/written-questions-answers-statements/written-question/Commons/2015-01-27/222192/>.
[129] ONS, *Crime Survey for England & Wales*, available at <http://www.crimesurvey.co.uk>.
[130] eg Home Office, *Cyber crime: A review of the evidence*, Research Report 75, October 2013, available at <https://www.gov.uk/government/publications/cyber-crime-a-review-of-the-evidence>.
[131] See Anderson, R et al, 'Measuring the Cost of Cybercrime', in Moore, T, Pym, D, and Ioannidis, C (eds), *The Economics of Information Security and Privacy*, Springer, 2013, at 265–300. See also Kabay, M, 'Understanding Studies and Surveys of Computer Crime', January 2013, available at <http://www.mekabay.com/methodology/crime_stats_methods.pdf>.

2.88 The process of obtaining the empirical data by the state to support policy-making may raise its own legal issues. An example of government trying to address the need for data to support policy-making is the dispute in early 2006 between the US Government and Google over access to data concerning search terms and web addresses. In January 2006, the US Department of Justice (DoJ) issued a subpoena requesting data from various firms offering Internet search facilities, such as Yahoo!, Microsoft, and Google. The stated purpose for the request was to assist the DoJ to address the problem of child pornography over the Internet. A previous attempt to legislate on the issue in 1998, under the COPA, is currently blocked by the Supreme Court on constitutional grounds.[132] However, the case was remanded for a retrial to 'allow the parties to update and supplement the factual record to reflect current technological realities'.[133]

2.89 In the course of the preparing a report for the retrial, the DoJ wanted to provide evidence to the court that pornography continues to be easily accessible over the Internet posing a continuing threat to children, despite attempts to control through industry self-regulation and the use of filtering software. Such statistical evidence would be based on a random sample of data provided by the search companies about (a) addresses accessible through their search engines and (b) search queries submitted by users over the course of an average week. While the other providers supplied the requested data, Google challenged the legality of the request before the courts. The challenge was rejected by a federal court, although the scope of the request was modified by the judge to cover a more restricted data set.[134]

2.90 The case highlights that the process of data collection itself may raise issues of collateral interference with the rights of others, effectively shifting some types of incidence data from that 'which we can know' to that which is 'infeasible to know'!

Crime reporting

2.91 Victim crime reporting is likely to be a highly problematic source of information for public and private statistical and survey data for a range of different reasons. It is widely recognized that there is general under-reporting of computer and cybercrime incidents by victims, especially commercial organizations eager to avoid adverse publicity that may affect their reputation and share price. As Wall notes, 'the model of justice which public law enforcement organizations offer to corporate victims is not generally conducive to their business interests'.[135]

2.92 A second problem area is to whom and how a person reports an incidence of computer or cybercrime? A domestic broadband Internet user, for example, is likely to feel unsure whether his local police station can or should be notified of a fraudulent scam website he has fallen foul of, based seemingly in another jurisdiction, while the local station officer may be equally unsure about how to record such an incident were the user to try and report! Operating reporting mechanisms is an expensive business, and something which resource-tight law enforcement agencies will be concerned to control. In the UK, in the areas of concern to this book, a number of public–private sector initiatives exist, such as Action

---

[132] *Ashcroft v ACLU*, 535 US 656 (2004), 122 S Ct 1700.
[133] ibid, 535 US, at 672.
[134] Decision of US District Judge James Ware (17 March 2006) in *Gonzales v Google Inc*, 234 FRD 674; 79 USPQ 2D (BNA) 1832.
[135] Wall, above, n 68, at 161.

Fraud,[136] establishing reporting mechanisms distinct from the investigative agency itself. While this makes sense from the perspective of the agencies, it may also exacerbate a perception of distance, and therefore lack of concern, in the minds of victims of crime.

Survey evidence suggests that victims are much more likely to report a virus or hacking **2.93** incidence to their Internet service provider or website and system administrator, than to the police.[137] However, the extent to which such reports are then passed on to the police is unclear; although the police are likely to welcome any such private-sector filtering as reducing their burden. There are also various public and private entities, such as US Computer Emergency Response Team (CERT)[138] or the Internet Watch Foundation (IWF), who have an explicit intermediary role providing opportunities for self-reporting, although how widespread they are recognized among the general public is unclear.

As well as deliberate non-reporting, it will also be the case that many victims are unaware **2.94** that they have suffered, or are suffering, an incident of computer or cybercrime. The phenomenon of 'zombie' computers, where the victim is unaware that a perpetrator has taken control of some of the available processing resource, is testament to our general level of ignorance.[139]

Finally, there are also factors that may conversely lead to over-reporting of computer and **2.95** cybercrime. There is a recognized tendency, for example, among inexperienced computer and Internet users to place the blame for a problem with their computer on criminal interference, rather than inherent problems with the system or their lack of knowledge. This phenomenon has been labelled 'cyber-hypochondria' by Moitra.[140] In addition, automated detection systems, such as firewalls and filters, will usually generate high levels of false positives, recording benign traffic as potentially harmful, which sometimes ends up being reported.[141]

One approach to address the problem of non-reporting has been to impose a legal obliga- **2.96** tion on organizations to report incidents of security breach. Since 2003, for example, the Civil Code[142] of the state of California has obliged private businesses and public agencies to report if they have suffered 'a breach of the security'[143] of a system that contains personal

---

[136] Action Fraud, 'Report Fraud and Cyber Crime', available at <http://www.actionfraud.police.uk/report_fraud>.

[137] Wilson, D et al, *Fraud and technology crimes: Findings for the 2003/04 British Crime Survey, the 2004 Offending, Crime and Justice Survey and administrative sources*, Home Office Online Report 09/06, at 7.

[138] See <http://www.us-cert.gov>.

[139] eg, the 'ZeroAccess' botnet was estimated to involve some 2 million infected computers when Microsoft, Europol, and others disrupted it in December 2013. See further EUROPOL, 'Notorious botnet infecting 2 million computers disrupted', Press Release, available at <https://www.europol.europa.eu/content/notorious-botnet-infecting-2-million-computers-disrupted>.

[140] Moitra, S, 'Modelling and simulation for cybercrime policy analysis', Research Brief No 28, December 2005, available at <https://www.mpicc.de/shared/data/pdf/fa-moitra.pdf>.

[141] eg, see 'BT sounds child web porn warning', BBC, 7 February 2006, available at <http://news.bbc.co.uk/2/hi/uk/4687904.stm>. For criticism of these figures, see McCarthy, K, 'Twisting the facts to fit the story', 7 February 2006, available at <http://kierenmccarthy.co.uk/2006/02/07/twisting-the-facts-to-fit-the-story-child-porn-nonsense/>.

[142] California Civil Code, ss 1798.29 and 1798.80 et seq. The majority of US states have since enacted similar legislation; see National Conference of State Legislatures (NCSL), 'Security breach notification laws', available at <http://www.ncsl.org/research/telecommunications-and-information-technology/security-breach-notification-laws.aspx>.

[143] California Civil Code, s 1798.82(d): 'means unauthorized acquisition of computerized data that compromises the security, confidentiality, or integrity of personal information'.

information, including financial data.[144] While the stated purpose of the statute was to tackle the growing problem of 'identity theft',[145] the initiative also represents a recognition that the data processed by an organization often engages the private interests of individuals, as subjects of the processed data, as well as public interests, which may not coincide with the private interests of the victim organization. The EU adopted similar security breach notification obligations for providers of 'public telecommunication services' in 2009;[146] and there are currently two proposals to extend such notification requirements to all data controllers processing personal data,[147] as well as public administrations and 'market operators'.[148] Such laws can vary considerably between jurisdictions, with respect to whom notification should be made (eg regulator, data subjects, general public); the threshold scale of breach (eg level of seriousness); the subject matter of the breach (eg financial and health data); on which the obligation should be placed; and remedies for non-compliance.

2.97   As well as the imposition of reporting requirements upon the victim, another approach is to impose reporting obligations upon certain intermediaries that may play a role in the criminal activity. Such 'intermediary reporting' requirements can be divided into those rules which impose a proactive monitoring obligation upon the intermediary and those that are reactive in nature, arising only when the intermediary has become, or been made, aware of the illegality. Whether the obligation is proactive or reactive will generally depend on the perceived extent of involvement that the intermediary plays in the criminal conduct. To tackle crimes of appropriation, for example, many states have adopted money-laundering laws, which impose requirements upon financial institutions and professional advisers, backed by criminal sanction, to report suspicious transactions to the appropriate authorities.[149] In the area of content-related cybercrimes, some states require that Internet service providers report child abuse images to the authorities as soon as they 'obtain knowledge'[150] or become 'aware'[151] of their existence, again backed by criminal sanction for a failure to report. In the UK, the Terrorism Act 2000 imposes an obligation on persons to disclose, 'as soon as reasonably practicable', information that 'he knows or believes might be of material assistance' in the prevention of an act of terrorism or the apprehension, prosecution, or conviction of a person involving terrorism.[152]

Trends and characteristics

2.98   The absence of strong empirical data to support the frequent public claims made about the growth and impact of computer and cybercrime creates problems for public policy-makers.

---

[144] The obligation to notify may be delayed if a law enforcement agency determines that it would impede a criminal investigation (ibid, s 1798.82(c)).

[145] See paras 3.73–3.76 for a discussion about 'identity theft'.

[146] Directive 2009/136/EC, OJ L 337/11, 18 December 2009, which amended Art 4 of Directive of Directive 02/58/EC, above, n 80.

[147] Proposed Regulation on the protection of individuals with regard to the processing of personal data and the free movement of such data, COM(2012)011 final, January 2012, Arts 31 and 32.

[148] Proposal for a Directive concerning measures to ensure a high common level of network and information security across the Union, COM(2013)048 final, February 2013, Art 14.

[149] eg Proceeds of Crime Act 2002, s 330.

[150] See US federal law at 42 USC s 13032 ('Reporting of child pornography by electronic communications service providers').

[151] Australian Criminal Code Act 1995, s 474.25 ('Obligations of Internet service providers and Internet content hosts').

[152] Terrorism Act 2000, s 38B.

On the one hand, adopting legislative measures against a phenomenon that is little known may easily result in an inappropriate set of rules, either failing to adequately address the mischief or overextending criminal law to activities that should not be criminalized. On the other hand, the basis for taking any measures at all is weak, and therefore potentially flawed, undermining the rationale for public policy-makers to act and again leading to an unsuitable criminal code.

Although the true figures concerning computer and cybercrime may be suspect from a **2.99** quantitative perspective, certain common or qualitative characteristics do emerge from the data available, which can provide important insights to help guide policy-makers. As already discussed, the unwillingness of victims to report a computer crime, particularly business users, means that the scale of incidence is likely to be significantly greater than that recorded in any of the statistical sources.

A significant proportion, sometimes the majority, of computer-related and computer- **2.100** integrity offences are committed by, or with the assistance of, persons within, or associated with, the victim organization, such as an employee or independent contractor.[153] This should not be surprising, however, since both categories of crime generally involve interaction with the victim or, more relevantly, the victim's ICT systems and resources, whether misappropriating assets or interfering with the systems and resources themselves. By contrast, content-related crimes, while by no means victimless, do not usually require any such interaction, whether distributing infringing copyright works or child abuse images or engaging in hate speech.[154] Instead, the ICT systems and resources involved are simply those controlled, or used, by the perpetrator. With the former, interaction with the victim's ICT will often involve some degree of authorization. As such, obtaining authorization through the circumvention of protection mechanisms or establishing false credentials requires a much higher level of knowledge, skill, and motivation than exceeding the scope of an existing authorization, hence the prevalence of insider crimes.

The 'insider' characteristic may have policy implications for computer crime in that govern- **2.101** ments may see primary responsibility for tackling such behaviour as resting with the victim organizations themselves, through improved security and insurance, rather than that of governments. In addition, civil proceedings under employment law can be seen as an alternative legal redress against the perpetrators, which also results in the under-reporting of such crimes.[155]

When measuring the incidence of computer and cybercrime, the concern is not only with **2.102** the volume of such activities but also their value, in terms of the damage, harm, and loss such acts cause both to the victims themselves as well as collateral damage incurred by others, including society and the nation state. While cybercrime is most popularly associated with acts of hacking and viruses, the most prevalent form of cybercrime *by value* would seem to be computer-related crimes, where computers are simply a tool for the commission

---

[153] eg PricewaterhouseCoopers (PwC), *US cybercrime: Rising risks, reduced readiness. Key findings from the 2014 US State of Cybercrime Survey*, June 2014, available at <http://www.pwc.com/en_US/us/increasing-it-effectiveness/publications/assets/2014-us-state-of-cybercrime.pdf>.

[154] The exceptions are malicious, improper, and harassing communications (see paras 3.201–3.219), which lie somewhere between computer and content-related crimes.

[155] See eg *Denco v Joinson* [1991] 1 WLR 330; *British Telecommunications plc v Rodrigues* [1998] Masons CLR Rep 93; *Bolton School v Evans* [2006] IRLR 500.

of economic and financial crimes,[156] while prevalence *by volume* is likely to be content-related, software piracy and child pornography, as ICTs are the pre-eminent tool for the reproduction and distribution of digital information.

2.103 Clearly, the scale of the loss or damage caused will vary greatly according to which form of cybercrime is involved. In terms of computer-related offences, the nature of the loss and damage will obviously be dictated by the underlying criminal activity for which the computer, as a tool, was being used. Most modern large-scale economic and financial crime, for example, will utilize computers at some point, whether in terms of the inputting, processing, or outputting of fraudulent data. In 1994, for example, Citibank suffered a significant breach of security in a cash management system for financial institutions. Once the system was hacked, the perpetrator was able to transfer funds out of the accounts of certain Indonesian banks. As such, computer-related crime is capable of representing a threat to sustainable development for developing countries, in the short term, such as diverting resources from aid programmes, and in long-term investor confidence in the market.[157]

2.104 For perpetrators of computer-integrity crimes, cyberspace offers individuals and criminal networks possibilities unparalleled in other environments, in terms of anonymity, mobility, geographical reach, and the scope of loss and damage that can be inflicted. The range and scale of potential loss that may flow from attacks against computers and data is substantial and well reported, however unreliably: from individual inconvenience when a virus infects and corrupts a system to billions of dollars in lost revenue resulting from business interruption, or the loss of life when medical systems malfunction. Where such attacks target, or inadvertently impact on, a nation's critical national infrastructure, such as power systems or transportation networks, the consequences of such attacks are obviously of great significance and concern. In 2003, for example, the Port of Houston in the US was brought to a standstill after a denial-of-service attack crippled the computer system on which the port's operations were dependent.[158]

2.105 It should also be recognized that the adoption and dispersion of ICTs are not uniform, particularly between developed and developing nations. Wireless communication technologies, for example, have rapidly eclipsed wireline systems in many developing countries, where the legacy of fixed infrastructure was greatly underdeveloped. As such, it must be recognized that differential levels of economic development and technological usage may mean different patterns of threats and vulnerabilities in terms of computer and cybercrime.[159] In 2004, for example, the first virus designed specifically to attack mobile phones was reported, the 'Cabir' virus. The attacks were against a certain brand of Nokia phones found largely in developing countries, such as the Philippines, Vietnam, and India.[160]

---

[156] See Discussion Guide presented at the Eleventh United Nations Congress on Crime Prevention and Criminal Justice, Bangkok, April 2005, para 103.

[157] ibid, paras 104 et seq.

[158] See 'Questions cloud cyber crime cases', BBC News, 17 October 2003, available from <http://news.bbc.co.uk/1/hi/technology/3202116.stm>.

[159] United Nations, 'Workshop 6: Measures to Combat Computer-related Crime', Background Paper, Presented at the Eleventh UN Congress on Crime Prevention and Criminal Justice, Bangkok, 18–25 April 2005, A/CONF.203/14, 14 March 2005, paras 14 et seq.

[160] Macan-Markar, M, 'Developing countries not immune from cyber crime–UN', Inter Press Service, 25 April 2005, available at <http://www.ipsnews.net/2005/04/technology-developing-countries-not-immune-from-cyber-crime-un/>.

Mapping the scant empirical data from developed countries to developing countries is obvi- **2.106**
ously fraught with difficulties and potentially meaningless. On the one hand, the economic
activity of developing countries may be viewed as being less dependent on computer and
communications networks, since ICT resources are also less integrated into every aspect of
people's daily lives. On the other hand, the cost and resources required to secure systems
from attack and exploitation, in terms of the deployment and maintenance of organizational, physical, or logical measures, may often be beyond the means of those using systems
in developing countries, thereby resulting in greater vulnerability than developed nations.

D. Criminal Law

To address the threat of computer and cybercrime and to enhance the security of cyber- **2.107**
space, governments have set about establishing legal frameworks to deter and punish those
who engage in such activities and assist those investigating such crimes, the core subject
of this book. However, the use of the criminal law against certain types of act is in itself
sometimes controversial. Free speech advocates, for example, express concern when certain types of content are made illegal, while 'hacktivism' is viewed as a legitimate form of
political protest when used against targets such as the World Trade Organization through
denial-of-service attacks.[161] Accessing systems without authorization is also seen by some as
analogous to the act of trespass, which generally gives rise to civil remedies.[162] It is generally
accepted in liberal democracies that the onus, or burden of proof, should always lie with
the state when justifying any extension of criminal law. Indeed, such a principle underpins
human rights law and jurisprudence, where the right of a state to infringe a person's freedoms is made subject to considerations of necessity and proportionality.[163]

A regime addressing computer and cybercrime must not only appropriately identify the **2.108**
different types of criminal activity, a question of substantive law, it should also facilitate the
investigation and prosecution of such activities, a question of criminal procedure. A failure
to adequately address the latter may undermine the rationale for the former. Unenforceable
criminal laws are somewhat of a stain on any legal regime, but need not result from an inad-
equacy of procedural law.

While this book is targeted primarily at legal practitioners, academics, and students, it **2.109**
is also hoped that the subject matter will attract the attention of a non-legal audience,
especially information and communication technologists, such as forensic and IT security
professionals. As such, it seems appropriate to review the nature of the criminal law and
process to address common misunderstandings and misconceptions about how the criminal framework operates, as well as raise matters of general relevance when thinking about
criminal law and policy in the area of computer and cybercrime. It is not intended to be
comprehensive; rather, it is a selection of issues considered necessary or valuable for a better
understanding of the subject matter of the book. Also, as stated in the Introduction to this
chapter, it must always be borne in mind that the English criminal legal system differs in

---

[161] See Jordan, T and Taylor, PA, *Hacktivism and Cyberwars: Rebels with a Cause*, Routledge, 2004.
[162] See para 3.244.
[163] eg European Convention on Human Rights, 4 November 1950, entered into force 3 November
1953, 213 UNTS 222, Arts 8 (right to privacy) and 10 (freedom of expression). See generally Ashworth, A,
Macdonald, A, and Emmerson, B, *Human Rights and Criminal Justice*, 3rd edn, Sweet & Maxwell, 2012.

many respects from its common law relations and its European neighbours; therefore differences will be, and should be, noted where pertinent and known!

Criminal code

2.110 Under English law, the concept of a 'criminal code' is currently still somewhat inappropriate as a term of description, since there is no single instrument of codification, in contrast to our continental partners with their Penal Codes, and other common law jurisdictions.[164] In addition, common law offences, such as conspiracy to defraud and public nuisance, continue to play an important role in English criminal law, including against those activities of concern to this book.[165] However, the term 'criminal code' has been adopted in this book as a label to indicate the field of substantive criminal law.[166]

2.111 As traditionally conceived, the commission of an offence is differentiated into two elements, the prohibited act or conduct (referred to as the *actus reus*) and the mental or fault element (referred to as the *mens rea*), such that the defendant or principal has a culpable state of mind. Such states are primarily described in terms of intention, knowledge, or recklessness on the part of the defendant.[167] As noted previously, negligence is usually not considered an appropriate basis for imposing criminal liability, due in part to the difficulty of characterizing the mental state of the perpetrator.[168] Any particular offence may require the presence of more than one form of conduct and/or fault to attract criminal liability.[169]

2.112 It is worth briefly considering the nature of the different conduct and fault elements under English criminal law, both in terms of better understanding the offences themselves and the process of prosecuting them, as well as in terms of considerations of policy-making in the field.

2.113 As well as the conduct and fault elements applicable to a particular offence, such as unauthorized access or 'hacking', differing elements may need to be present depending on the point in time at which the person was apprehended or the role the person played in the commission of the offence. First, the principal may only succeed in attempting to commit the offence, which is a separate inchoate offence,[170] where both the conduct and fault elements differ from the substantive offence. So, for example, the use of password-cracking software against a system may constitute an attempt to hack into that system. An attempt is conduct that is 'more than merely preparatory',[171] which itself will be a question of fact for

---

[164] eg Australia, Criminal Code Act 1995, No 12 (Cth).

[165] However, the English courts have clearly rejected the idea that they have 'some general or residual power either to create new offences or so to widen existing offences....'; see *Knuller (Publishing, Printing and Promotions) Ltd v DPP* [1973] AC 435, at 457–8 per Lord Reid.

[166] We would note that the Law Commission has shifted the focus of its work in the criminal law field from 'codification' (see *A Criminal Code for England and Wales*, Law Com No 177, 17 April 1989, available at <https://www.gov.uk/government/uploads/system/uploads/attachment_data/file/235826/0299.pdf>) to 'simplifying' (see *Tenth Programme of Law Reform*, Law Com No 311, 10 June 2008, para 1.6, available at <https://www.gov.uk/government/uploads/system/uploads/attachment_data/file/250282/0605.pdf>).

[167] As indicated by the previous references, the meaning of these terms has evolved through case law, not statutory definition, although definitions have been proposed by the Law Commission.

[168] See Ashworth and Horder, above, n 87, at 181 et seq, and *Smith & Hogan Criminal Law*, above, n 43, at 6.4.

[169] eg Computer Misuse Act 1990 (CMA), s 1.

[170] Criminal Attempts Act 1981, s 1(1).

[171] ibid.

the judge and/or jury to decide. The existence of password-cracking software on a person's system, for example, is unlikely to be sufficient evidence of an attempt to hack, without further corroborative evidence.

English law also distinguishes between the 'principal' who commits an offence and accessories, those that 'aid, abet, counsel or procure' a principal, where the fault element for such 'secondary liability' differs.[172] The supply of password-cracking software in our example may fall into this category of conduct. The offences of conspiracy and incitement also involve distinct conduct and fault elements. The former would involve an agreement to hack into the target system, while the latter could be applicable where access codes for a specified system are posted on a bulletin board. In each of these examples, there are unique conduct and fault requirements that require consideration and would need to be evidenced.

2.114

A mental element is not required where the offence is one of strict liability, where conduct alone is sufficient. While strict liability comprises the position for the majority of offences under English criminal law,[173] which may come as a surprise to many, strict liability is not applicable to the offences that form the core area for examination in this book. However, even for strict liability offences, fault may comprise an element of the act itself, such as in possession offences; proceedings may only be brought where fault is present,[174] or fault may be a relevant consideration at the point of sentencing. It is also a judicial presumption to import *mens rea* into the interpretation of a statutory offence,[175] unless Parliament has made it clear that it is one of strict liability, or sometimes based on considerations of efficacy or the nature of the penalty.[176]

2.115

In terms of the *actus reus*, a division may be made into 'conduct' crimes, where the attention is focused on the actions of the perpetrator, such as offences in respect of child abuse images[177] and computer misuse,[178] and 'result' crimes, where the harm caused or the condition of the victim comprises the focus, such as obscene material[179] and the old deception offences in relation to fraud.[180] In the latter category, the necessary *actus reus* may be completed by the victim, rather than the perpetrator, such as in a fraud, where the deceived account holder initiates a transfer of funds for the benefit of the perpetrator, or a person downloads an obscene image. Some crimes combine elements of both conduct and result. An obscene publication, for example, requires an act of publication and must have a tendency 'to deprave and corrupt' the recipient, ie the victim.[181]

2.116

---

[172] See paras 2.203–2.208 for a discussion of accessory liability.

[173] See Ashworth, A and Blake, M, 'The presumption of innocence in English criminal law', *Criminal Law Review* 306 [1996] .

[174] As many strict liability crimes are regulatory in nature, the enforcement authority, such as the Office of the Information Commissioner, will often pursue a compliance strategy rather than one of deterrence: Ashworth and Horder, above, n 87, at 160 et seq.

[175] *Sweet v Parsley* [1970] AC 132, at 148H. See also *B v DPP* [2000] 2 AC 428 and *K* [2002] 1 Cr App R 121.

[176] *Blackstone's Criminal Practice 2016*, above, n 43, para A2.23.

[177] eg Protection of Children Act 1978 (POCA), s 1. See further paras 3.154–3.187.

[178] eg CMA.

[179] eg Obscene Publications Act 1959.

[180] eg Theft Act 1968, s 15. See paras 3.53–3.55.

[181] See further paras 3.130–3.139.

2.117   Determining the various elements that comprise the relevant *actus reus* will be a question of fact for which evidence will be tendered by the prosecutor or an objective question for the tribunal of fact to decide upon, such as whether an article is 'indecent'[182] or a network is public or private.[183]

2.118   As stated above, while a crime may commonly not require *mens rea*, liability for a failure to act or omission (so-called 'omission liability') is rare, except where the law specifically imposes a duty to act, whether it is through statute, official duty, or breach of contractual obligation, such as a failure to report the knowledge or suspicion of money laundering.[184] It should be noted, however, that the distinction between omission liability and liability for complicity, as an accessory, is sometimes blurred.[185]

2.119   In respect of the forms of crime examined in this book, possession is an important area of criminality, from the possession of articles for use in fraud,[186] to the possession of articles or devices designed to circumvent technological protection measures and the possession of child abuse images.[187] However, possession offences can appear as a somewhat odd category of offence, since one may conceivably possess an item without engaging in an act, although knowledge would be required.[188] Such offences are generally enacted to prevent the commission of a particular wrong or harm, by extending liability to a moment in time prior to that covered by the law of attempts. As such, the *mens rea* effectively transforms from being one of intention as to consequences to that of knowledge of circumstances by the perpetrator. Thus, possession offences can be criticized for criminalizing activities too remote from the eventual harm.[189]

2.120   The nature of ICTs can raise particular challenges in respect of evidencing the knowledge of a perpetrator, due, in part, to the level of ignorance that exists about how the technologies operate among the general public, including the criminal fraternity! The existence of knowledge is to be determined by the tribunal of fact, on the evidence presented to it. However, there is case law in the computer crime field where acquittals have occurred because the prosecution were unable to present evidence that the defendant was aware of the manner in which information was viewed over the Internet or deleted from digital media.[190] However, as Lord Bridge has noted:

> it is always open to the tribunal of fact, when knowledge on the part of the defendant is required to be proved, to base a finding of knowledge on evidence that the defendant had deliberately shut his eyes to the obvious or refrained from inquiry because he suspected the truth but did not want to have his suspicion confirmed.[191]

The following tabulates the main categories of offence under English law that fall into the three categories of crime being examined in this book in terms of the applicable *mens rea*:

---

[182]   eg *Smethurst* [2002] 1 Cr App R 6.
[183]   See paras 3.320–3.322.
[184]   Proceeds of Crime Act 2002, ss 330–2.
[185]   See Ashworth and Horder, above, n 87, para 10.8.
[186]   See para 3.63.
[187]   Copyright, Designs and Patents Act 1988, s 296ZB and Criminal Justice Act 1988, s 160 respectively.
[188]   See *Warner v Metropolitan Police Commissioner* [1969] 2 AC 256.
[189]   See Ashworth and Horder, above, n 87, at 98.
[190]   See paras 3.171–3.174.
[191]   Lord Bridge in *Westminster City Council v Croyalgrange Ltd* (1986) 83 Cr App R 155, at 164.

Mens rea	Offences
Intention	Computer Misuse Act 1990, s 1; Fraud Act 1996; Communications Act 2003; Forgery and Counterfeiting Act 1981
Knowledge	Protection from Harassment Act 1997; Protection of Children Act 1978; Criminal Justice Act 1988
Recklessness	Criminal Damage Act 1971; Computer Misuse Act 1990, s 3

Comparative jurisdictions may adopt different *mens rea* standards applicable to similar *actus reus*. Under US federal law, for example, unauthorized access causing damage is criminalized where the perpetrator has intent, is reckless, or even just negligent,[192] while under New Zealand law, recklessness is sufficient in respect of unauthorized access.[193] Such differences can obviously undermine efforts made to harmonize criminal conduct in respect of computer and cybercrime.

2.121 These categorizations of *actus reus* and *mens rea* may have implications for the nature of the charge, or alternative charges, brought against a defendant, since the nature of the evidence required will differ accordingly. Results crimes, for example, will require evidence of a causal link between the act and the result, in terms of both factual and legal causation,[194] which has implications for what is required to be obtained or generated through digital forensic techniques.[195]

2.122 The task of the prosecution in criminal proceedings is substantial. First, the prosecutor will generally have the burden of proving that the required *actus reus* and *mens rea* are present. Second, the standard of proof required is that of 'beyond reasonable doubt',[196] in contrast to the standard of 'balance of probabilities' which the defendant may be required to meet on a particular issue.[197] Both may be formidable tasks, but proving *mens rea* will generally constitute the greater hurdle, hence the modern trend toward strict liability offences. In that respect, however, it is important to distinguish strict liability offences from offences where there is a reverse burden of proof in respect of the *mens rea* element, which may encroach on the presumption of innocence enshrined in Article 6(2) of the European Convention on Human Rights.[198]

2.123 Under English criminal law, there can be no presumption of intention based on an *objective* assessment of what was likely to result from a particular action, rather it is for the prosecution to present evidence to show that the perpetrator had *subjective* intention or foresight. This principle has been given statutory expression:

---

[192] 18 USC s 1030(a)(5)(A)(i), (ii), and (iii) respectively.

[193] Crimes Act 1961, s 252(1).

[194] Legal causation requires that the act was an 'operating and substantial' cause (*Smith* [1959] 2 QB 35).

[195] See generally Chapter 4.

[196] *Woolmington v DPP* [1935] AC 462. The standard as generally explained to a jury is that of being 'sure' that the defendant is guilty of the offence. Also referred to as an 'error preference', since meeting the standard will generally result in more errors in terms of acquitting the guilty than convicting the innocent: Ashworth, A and Redmayne, M, *The Criminal Process*, 4th edn, Oxford University Press, 2010, at 25.

[197] This is the evidential standard required to prevail in civil proceedings, although in reality the difference between the criminal and civil standard is often not that great, since in civil proceedings the evidential standard sought by the court will generally reflect the seriousness of the issues being argued and the remedies being sought.

[198] See para 4.328 in respect of key disclosure.

A court or jury, in determining whether a person has committed an offence,—

(a) shall not be bound in law to infer that he intended or foresaw a result of his actions by reason only of its being a natural and probable cause consequence of those actions; but

(b) shall decide whether he did intend or foresee that result by reference to all the evidence, drawing such inferences from the evidence as appear proper in the circumstances.[199]

This has been supplemented through judicial pronouncement:

In a contested case based on intention, the defendant rarely admits intending the injurious result in question, but the tribunal of fact will readily infer such an intention . . . from all the circumstances and probabilities and evidence of what the defendant did and said at the time.[200]

This may be contrasted with the position for other categories of fault, where it is for the tribunal of fact to make an objective assessment. In respect of recklessness, for example, where an objective consideration of 'reasonableness' to take the risk of which the perpetrator is aware lies with the tribunal of fact,[201] dishonesty, which involves evaluating the defendant's behaviour according to the 'standards of ordinary decent people',[202] and in criminal negligence, where the objective standard is that of what care, skill, or foresight a 'reasonable man' would have exercised.[203]

2.124 Distinctions between subjective and objective criteria are another means of categorizing the various forms of *mens rea*, although the dividing line may not always be clear.[204] Subjective factors focus on the perpetrator and their state of mind, while objective factors are based on the conception that the perpetrator owes a duty of care towards others and the need to protect social welfare. In terms of criminal policy, reliance on subjective factors tends to favour the individual perpetrator, while objective factors gives scope to the court and jury 'to make social judgements about the limits of the criminal sanction'.[205] Where the criminal standard should be fixed in respect of any particular crime examined in this book, on a continuum from strict liability to intention, represents a moral and political choice as much as a question of law.

2.125 While the prosecution has to evidence the presence of any *mens rea* element detailed in the offence, defence counsel may put forward a range of responses designed to avoid or mitigate criminal liability. Indeed, as noted by Lanham:

As a matter of analysis we can think of a crime as being made up of three ingredients, *actus reus*, *mens rea* and (a negative element) absence of a valid defence.[206]

2.126 First, it may be argued that the necessary culpable state of mind is not made out due, for example, to a mistake, accident, or mental illness, such as addiction. The latter has been

---

[199] Criminal Justice Act 1967, s 8.

[200] *G* [2004] 1 AC 1034, para 39 per Lord Bingham.

[201] ibid.

[202] *Ghosh* [1982] QB 1053.

[203] Law Commission, *The Mental Element in Crime*, Working Paper No 31 (1970) at 31.

[204] See eg Duff, RA, 'Subjectivism, objectivism and criminal attempts', in Simester, AP, and Smith, ATH (eds), *Harm and Culpability*, Clarendon Press, 1996, at 19–44.

[205] Ashworth and Horder, above, n 87, at 186.

[206] Lanham, D, 'Larsonneur revisited', *Criminal Law Review* 276 [1976] .

successfully deployed in a computer-integrity case.[207] Second, a range of excuses may be proffered, such as duress, coercion, and provocation. Third, defence counsel may argue that the action was justifiable, ie the act is not wrong, such as self-defence, which negates the criminal nature of the conduct:

> A person may use such force as is reasonable in the circumstances in the prevention of crime, or in effecting or assisting in the lawful arrest of offenders or suspected offenders or of persons unlawfully at large.[208]

A person could, for example, be prosecuted for causing an unauthorized act against a person's system by operating an Intrusion Detection System (IDS) on his network configured to 'attack' the source IP address of any purported hacker. If this act was considered justifiable on the grounds of self-defence, then the person could not be convicted of criminal damage to the property of a third party, or be subject to civil liability.[209]

The concept of 'force' has traditionally been conceived in terms of physical acts against persons or property. It is therefore questionable whether the courts would be prepared to extend the concept to the carrying out of intangible acts against a computer system. However, were the courts to consider such acts as 'force', the second issue to be decided is whether such force is considered 'reasonable in the circumstances'. This will be for the court or the jury to decide, on an objective basis, although it is not generally seen as reasonable to cause harm unless it was necessary to do so to prevent the crime, or the nature of the crime was such that the reasonable person would think the harm justifiable on the basis of preventing the crime.[210] **2.127**

A fourth category of argument that may be put forward by defence counsel is to invoke **2.128** certain public policy or legal process grounds against the proceedings themselves, such as entrapment as an abuse of process or claims of infringement of the person's right to a 'fair trial'.[211] Each of these arguments has different rationales and degrees of intellectual coherence, which has been the subject of much academic comment and criticism.[212] For our purposes, we simply need to be aware that in our adversarial system, defence counsel will not simply refute prosecution claims and evidence, but may also raise various defences.

Criminal procedure

Whereas the idea of what constitutes the field of computer and cybercrime revolves around **2.129** the issue of substantive offences, the activities being criminalized, we are also concerned here with the process of investigating and prosecuting such offences, questions of criminal procedure. Computer and cybercrime raise significant issues in respect of the powers of law enforcement agencies to gather computer-derived evidence.[213]

Law enforcement agencies have been lobbying governments for a number of years to **2.130** grant them the necessary powers to enable them to operate effectively in a computer and

---

[207] *Bedworth*, Southwark Crown Court, 17 March 1993. See further para 3.293.
[208] Criminal Law Act 1967, s 3(1).
[209] eg *Sears v Broome* [1986] Crim LR 461.
[210] See *Blackstone's Criminal Practice 2016*, above, n 43, at paras A3.54 et seq.
[211] See generally Chapter 6.
[212] See eg Wilson, W, 'The structure of criminal defences', *Criminal Law Review* 108 [2005] ; and Simester, AP et al (eds), *Simester and Sullivan's Criminal Law: Theory and Doctrine*, 5th edn, Hart, 2013, Chapter 17.
[213] See generally Chapter 3.

communications environment. Calls for reform have received substantial political backing as a result of the growth in the threat of terrorism, especially following major events such as the attacks of 11 September 2001 (New York), 7 July 2005 (London), and 13 November 2015 (Paris). In many jurisdictions, including the UK, the process of law reform has been considerably more vigorous, contentious, and comprehensive in respect of criminal procedure than in the area of substantive offences. Such activism in the field of procedural law must, however, be broadly subdivided into those that can be labelled 'pipeline' changes and more innovative initiatives designed specifically to address the new perceived threats. The former pre-date the 'war on terrorism', but have been enacted on the back of legislative instruments implementing the latter.

2.131 Criminal procedure rules contain a series of offences that may be committed either by the investigator,[214] a person assisting an investigation,[215] or the person under investigation.[216] However, such offences comprise a category generally distinct from those detailed in the criminal code. As with English substantive law, there are on-going efforts to codify criminal procedure rules,[217] although for the purposes of this book we will reserve use of the term 'code' to the substantive law.

2.132 In terms of criminal procedure, ie investigation and enforcement, we need to bear in mind not only the statutory rules that govern the regime, but also the inevitable exercise of discretion involved at many points in the whole process, from investigation and prosecution, to the tribunal of fact and courts on appeal. Such discretion will take many forms: the discretion to make new rules, to interpret a rule, and apply it or depart from it.[218] There are certain decisions that will be made which have been termed 'dispositive', as they dispose of the case without the need for the full rigours of English criminal procedure to be pursued.[219] The decision to prosecute,[220] determining the mode of trial,[221] and whether to accept a guilty plea[222] on a lesser charge are all key decisions where discretion is inevitably exercised. The final determination of a sentence by a court involves a similar exercise of discretion.

2.133 The exercise of discretion may require discussions between different entities, such as the police and prosecution service, as well as taking place at an international level, where multiple jurisdictions are involved and jurisdiction has to be negotiated.[223]

2.134 Although the exercise of discretion interferes with the need for legal certainty, we should avoid viewing discretion as a weakness in the criminal justice system, or indeed in other

---

[214] eg the common law offence of misconduct in public office.

[215] eg an unauthorized disclosure of information about an interception warrant (Regulation of Investigatory Powers Act 2000, s 19(4)).

[216] eg a failure to deliver up cryptographic keys. See paras 4.320–4.321.

[217] See Spencer, JR, 'Codifying criminal procedure', *Criminal Law Review* 279 [2006] .

[218] Baldwin, R and Hawkins, K, 'Discretionary justice: Davis reconsidered', *Public Law* 570 [1984], at 572.

[219] See Ashworth and Redmayne, above, n 196, s 2.6.

[220] Either initially by the police, eg to give a caution, or at a later review stage by the CPS, eg on the grounds of public interest.

[221] ie between Magistrates' Court and Crown Court.

[222] Note that in other legal systems, such as France and Germany, a guilty plea does not dispose of the case, since it is considered only as an item of evidence. See Spencer, J, 'Evidence', in Delmas-Marty, M and Spencer, JR (eds), *European Criminal Procedures*, Cambridge University Press, 2002, at 595.

[223] See paras 5.33–5.43 for a discussion about resolving jurisdictional conflicts.

areas of law where it is an essential feature.[224] In the author's experience, there is a general tendency to mistrust discretion, often pronounced in ICT professionals who generally have a more 'rationalist' notion of decision-making, which can result in a miscomprehension of the complex context in which decisions are made in the field of criminal law. Indeed, somewhat ironically, a common response to the problems of regulating technology in a constantly evolving environment has been to avoid detailed rule-making in favour of the application of principle-based criteria.[225] However, such an approach clearly introduces a higher level of discretion into the regulatory system, which is then vulnerable to mistrust and accusations of a lack of certainty and clarity.

When thinking about the criminal process, another complex interrelationship exists **2.135** between the view of the investigative process as one of gathering reliable evidence to enable the tribunal of fact to accurately determine whether a defendant is guilty or innocent; and the need for the process to operate with legitimacy, so that persons involved are treated fairly and are seen to be so treated.[226] Clearly conflicts may arise between the two, where, for example, evidence has been obtained using unlawful techniques, such as torture[227] or entrapment, or following improper procedures. The legal system may treat such evidence as a distinct class subject to a strict exclusionary rule, as was the historic approach to hearsay and applies to intercept product; or the treatment of such evidence may be left to the discretion of the courts, as a general factor for consideration or as an abuse of process. Whether the flexibility of the latter approach is seen favourably will depend, as with any exercise of discretion, on the trust one has in the decision maker, ie the judiciary.

Related to the need for the exercise of discretion in the criminal process, the tribunal of fact **2.136** will also obviously be required to consider all the facts and circumstances of the specific case. Taken together, discretion and specific circumstance may be viewed as lying at the edge of the criminal code, where an inevitable level of uncertainty exists, in much the same way that control mechanisms, such as traceability, dissipate at the edge of a network.

Another feature of criminal procedure that will arise throughout the book arises from its **2.137** intrusive nature. Whether we are concerned with the suspect, victim, or a third party, the process of investigation and enforcement can interfere with a person's property interests, liberties, and privacy. Issues relating to whether a person's rights, under either European Convention on Human Rights or the EU Charter,[228] have been interfered with in a necessary and proportionate manner are increasingly raised in case law involving criminal procedure, particularly the exercise of law enforcement powers.

Criminal procedure therefore engages human rights issues to a far greater extent than sub- **2.138** stantive criminal code, although such issues obviously arise there as well. However, the extent to which the rights of a defendant are respected will sometimes vary over time, according to the prevailing political culture and circumstance, between what has been described as the 'due process model' and the 'crime control model'.[229] The former emphasizes procedural protections, while the latter gives priority to the suppression of crime. Current Government

---

[224] See Endicott, T, *Vagueness in Law*, Oxford University Press, 2000.
[225] eg data protection rules.
[226] Ashworth and Redmayne, above, n 196, at 23 et seq.
[227] See *A (FC) and Others (FC) v Secretary of State for the Home Department* [2005] UKHL 71.
[228] Charter of Fundamental Rights of the European Union, OJ C 303/1, 14 December 2007.
[229] Packer, H, *The Limits of the Criminal Sanction*, Stanford University Press, 1969.

policy in respect of both the 'war on terrorism' and anti-social behaviour exhibits a clear shift toward the 'crime control model', which has had an indirect impact on computer and cybercrime investigations, as will be examined primarily in Chapter 4.

2.139 Extending law enforcement powers as a response to rising criminality is often controversial. Oft-quoted fears of civil libertarians when proposals to extend law enforcement powers are muted often revolve around the so-called 'slippery slope' argument. This comprises two closely related elements, first a concern about 'scope creep' and, second, that permission granted in one context will be too readily extended, explicitly or implicitly, to other areas, operating as a global licence for the agency.[230] Scope creep may be driven by a range of factors, including institutional, the classic empire building exhibited by many organizations; resource-based, with governments looking for economies of scale from expanding the functionality of an agency, and due to the nature of the subject matter and the overlap with other issues. In terms of calls for enhanced powers, using the language of anti-terrorism and child protection may often seem like a convenient wagon on which to place the law enforcement band.

Sanction and remedy

2.140 Issues of criminal sanction are often seen as the end product of the criminal process, although it is an inappropriate characterization for two reasons. First, the nature of the criminal process often means that the trial process is avoided wherever possible. Second, the maximum level of sanction, and hence the degree of seriousness with which a particular form of criminal conduct is viewed, is determined by legislators and specified in the criminal code, even though the judiciary retain substantial discretion about the actual sanction imposed.

2.141 In terms of sanctions, the focus is on the perpetrator and the use of different measures to deter and punish his criminal conduct. We are primarily concerned with the use of four forms of sanction in a computer and cybercrime context: the imposition of jail terms; restraints placed on a perpetrator's future conduct; and forfeiture and recovery by the state of the ill-gotten gains from the perpetrator's conduct. Remedies are more normally seen as forming part of the civil law, compensating the victim for the losses he has suffered. While sanctions are generally state-initiated, remedies have historically been for the victim to pursue.

Sentencing

2.142 Fines and jail terms are designed both to deter the commission of crime and punish those that may commit crimes. A distinction should be made between criminal penalties and administrative fines imposed by regulatory authorities, such as the Financial Conduct Authority, which are more administrative than criminal in nature and are generally beyond the scope of this book. The ultimate state sanction is the death penalty, which is not generally relevant to the subject matter of this book, although it has been reported that China has taken this extreme position in respect of a hacking incidence.[231]

---

[230] See eg the comments of the Earl of Erroll concerning proposals for new police powers, reported in 'Police decryption powers "flawed"', BBC News, 15 August 2006, available from <http://news.bbc.co.uk/2/hi/technology/4794383.stm>.

[231] In 1998, Hao Jing-long and Hao Jing-wen were convicted of hacking into a bank's computer network and transferring funds into accounts they controlled; the former was sentenced to life imprisonment, while the latter was sentenced to death. See Lixian, C., 'Chinese e-commerce (2) and legal environment', in Kariyawasam, R, *Chinese Intellectual Property and Technology Laws*, Edward Elgar, 2011, at 279.

One common concern is that computer crime, like much 'white-collar crime' with which **2.143**
it is rightly or wrongly associated, is not viewed with the same seriousness as other crimes,
and consequently receives lighter sentences.[232] As with other forms of crime, some areas
have been subject to tariff inflation over the years, sometimes to a substantial degree,[233]
reflecting evolving public concern and policy priorities. However, debate continues to exist
over whether harsher penalties have a concurrent deterrent effect. None of the offences
under consideration are subject to the imposition of a mandatory minimum tariff under
English law, such as that imposed for offences such as burglary[234] and firearms offences.[235]
However, in other common law jurisdictions, minimum sentences, either operating stand-
alone or as part of a wider sentencing policy (eg 'three strikes'[236]) may exist; while in civil law
jurisdictions, minimum and maximum tariffs are more common. In developing countries,
minimum sentences may not only reflect a cultural belief that harsh penalties act as a deterrent, but also a mistrust of the judiciary being capable of exercising appropriate discretion
in such cases.

The scale of a tariff may also be constrained by the nature of the legal instrument being **2.144**
used to criminalize a particular behaviour. Under the European Communities Act 1972,
secondary legislation adopted to transpose EU law may only create criminal offences with
a maximum tariff of two years imprisonment.[237] This provision was disapplied in respect of
the eCommerce Directive, which imposes liability on Information Society Service providers established in the UK.[238]

Under English criminal procedure, the mode of trial has an impact on the sentence available **2.145**
to the court. A trial on indictment takes place in the Crown Court before a judge and jury,
although a jury is only required where the defendant has pleaded 'not guilty'. Summary trials
take place in a Magistrates' Court. Where an offence is triable both ways, on indictment or summary trial, the former attracts a greater maximum tariff that can be handed down than the latter.

As noted above in respect of criminal procedure, the statutory tariff attached to a particular **2.146**
offence generally only sets the maximum possible applicable penalty, while the sentencing practice of the courts in respect of a particular offence may diverge substantially from
that figure. In addition, prison and probation practices, coupled with limitations on the
size of the prison population, will mean that a given sentence in reality falls far short of
that imposed by the judge. In developed legal systems, guidance is often provided to assist
judges in making sentencing decisions. Such guidance may be statutory, laying down a
standard for assessing the seriousness of any offence:

> In considering the seriousness of any offence, the court must consider the offender's culpabil-
> ity in committing the offence and any harm which the offence caused, was intended to cause
> or might forseeably have caused.[239]

---

[232] See Smith, R, Grabosky, P, and Urbas, G, *Cyber Criminals on Trial*, Cambridge University Press, 2004.
[233] eg child pornography, IP crimes, and computer-integrity offences.
[234] Powers of Criminal Courts (Sentencing) Act 2000, s 11(2), which requires the imposition of a minimum three-year sentence for a third conviction, unless the court feels that in the circumstances such a tariff
would be unjust.
[235] Firearms Act 1968, s 51A, inserted by the Criminal Justice Act 2003, s 287.
[236] eg many US states.
[237] European Communities Act 1972, Sch 2, para 1(1)(d). See further para 2.224 below.
[238] Coroners and Justice Act 2009, s 143(1)(a).
[239] Criminal Justice Act 2003, s 143(1).

So, for example, in *Harvey and Bradley*,[240] members of an international hacking group, known as the 'THr34t Krew', who wrote and distributed a worm malware that infected some 19,000 computers, were given reduced custodial sentences because the judge accepted that they had acted for reasons of 'power and ego' rather than malicious or nefarious purposes.[241]

2.147   Other statutory guidance may address the impact of the presence of 'aggravating circumstances', such as an activity being part of a criminal organization;[242] or the consequences of recidivism, where the defendant is a repeat offender.[243] In the US, recidivism is a factor in sentencing under the Computer Fraud and Abuse Act, where the previous offence was under the same section,[244] while in Belgium, the Computer Crime Act 2000 provides for a doubling of the applicable penalty when an offence is committed within five years of a previous conviction.[245]

2.148   Alternatively, non-statutory guidelines may be promulgated in relation to specific categories of crime, such as those issued by the Sentencing Council, which lay down factors or criteria that should guide the sentencing judge.[246] To date, guidelines have been issued in respect of fraud and child pornographic images, but not in relation to offences under the Computer Misuse Act 1990. In the US, the ability to program a computer has been determined to be a 'special skill' enabling the imposition of an enhanced sentence,[247] although the level of skill required to do certain tasks inevitably falls as they become more widely used, such that building a website has not been considered a 'special skill'.[248] The nature of such guidance, or 'soft law', obviously provides flexibility to address developments in technology.

2.149   As the workings of the criminal justice system have become increasingly politicized, we have also seen legislative intervention in the sentencing process to further restrict or guide judicial discretion. In the US, for example, the Cyber Security Enhancement Act of 2002[249] directed that the US Sentencing Commission review and amend its guidance relating to computer crimes to 'reflect the serious nature of the offenses … the growing incidence of such offenses, and the need for an effective deterrent and appropriate punishment to prevent such offenses'.[250] Under the revised guidelines, hackers face a 25 per cent uplift in their tariff if they hijack email accounts or steal personal data, while virus writers may face a 50 per cent tariff increase.[251] Calls for such intervention arise when public opinion, an influential sectional interest, and/or the perceptions of politicians shift substantially ahead of existing court practice, inevitably nearly always in the direction of more rather than less.

---

[240] Newcastle Crown Court, 7 October 2005, unreported.

[241] Quoted in 'Computer hackers jailed', *The Guardian*, 7 October 2005, available at <http://www.the-guardian.com/technology/2005/oct/07/hacking.internetcrime>.

[242] eg Council Framework Decision 2005/222/JHA on attacks against information systems, OJ L 69/67, 16 March 2005, Art 9(4).

[243] Criminal Justice Act 2003, s 143(2).

[244] 18 USC s 1030(c).

[245] Computer Crime Act 2000, Art 550 *bis*, s 8.

[246] See <http://www.sentencingcouncil.org.uk>.

[247] *United States v Petersen*, 98 F 3d 502 (9th Cir 1996), at 506–7.

[248] *United States v Lee*, 296 F 3d 792 (9th Cir 2002), at 796–9.

[249] 6 USC s 145.

[250] Ibid, s 145(b)(1).

[251] See United States Sentencing Commission, *Guidelines Manual* (2014), Chapter 2, Pt B, 1, available at <http://www.ussc.gov/guidelines-manual/2014/2014-ussc-guidelines-manual>.

Prohibitions and forfeiture

As a supplement or alternative to fines and the imposition of a jail term, a court may issue **2.150**
orders imposing controls on the activities that a defendant can engage in after being convicted.[252] Controls may be placed on the activities a person engages in, the places he goes,
or the things he owns. In a traditional environment such orders may, for example, prohibit
the perpetrator from leaving or entering a designated geographical area in order to restrict
the person's movements and/or protect potential victims. In a cybercrime environment,
an obvious subject for control is the person's use of the technologies used in the course of
his criminal activities. This may comprise the confiscation of existing equipment or voluntary forfeiture,[253] as well as prohibitions on future conduct in respect of the use of certain
ICTs.[254]

When Kevin Mitnick, the US hacker, was tried, the prosecution requested that he be **2.151**
prohibited from using or possessing any computers, software, or networking equipment.
This was contested, and the court eventually imposed conditions providing that he was
only permitted computer access with the consent of his probation officer.[255] Indeed, during the trial itself, Mitnick was restricted as to the telephone numbers he could call.[256]
Similarly, the hacker Kevin Poulsen was given the following 'special conditions' when on
probation:

> ... you shall not obtain or possess any computer or computer related equipment or programs
> without the permission and approval of the probation officer; and you shall not seek or main-
> tain employment that allows you access to computer equipment without prior approval of
> the probation officer.[257]

In the UK, in *Collard*,[258] the defendant was found guilty of offences of making and pos- **2.152**
sessing indecent images of children. As well as imposing jail terms, the court also made
a restraining order under the then Sex Offenders Act 1997, s 5A,[259] the terms of which
stated:

> that you be prohibited from owning, using, possessing or having any access to any per-
> sonal computer, laptop computer or any other equipment capable of downloading any
> material from the Internet. That prohibition does not apply to any such equipment which
> you have and use for the purpose of any lawful employment at and only at a place of such
> employment.

---

[252] Such conditions may also comprise bail conditions, ie pre-conviction, where there are specific concerns that a suspect may engage in inappropriate behaviour. Gary McKinnon, eg, the hacker extradited to
the US in 2006 for hacking into defence systems, was banned from using the Internet.

[253] eg as a condition for receiving a formal caution.

[254] eg a 'prohibited activity' requirement issued as a requirement of a 'community sentence', under the
Criminal Justice Act 2003, s 203.

[255] See Bowker, A and Thompson, G, 'Computer crime in the 21st century and its effect on the probation
officer', 65(2) *Federal Probation* 18 (2001) .

[256] Hafner, K and Markoff, J, *Cyberpunk: Outlaws and Hackers on the Computer Frontier*, Simon and
Schuster, 1991, at 342.

[257] Letter from Marc J Stein, US Probation Officer to Kevin Poulsen, 22 May 1996, quoted in Thomas,
D, 'Criminality on the electronic frontier', in Thomas and Loader, above, n 37, at 30.

[258] [2004] EWCA Crim 1664.

[259] The provision has been repealed and such an order would now be a 'sexual offences prevention order',
made under the Sexual Offences Act 2003, ss 104–13.

An appeal was taken against the scope of this order. The court accepted the appeal, noting that such a wide prohibition would effectively deprive his wife and children from access, ie collateral damage, and therefore amended the order in the following terms:

> that you be prohibited from downloading any material from the Internet, that prohibition not applying to downloading for the purpose of any lawful employment or lawful study.

The indefinite period, however, was not considered to be excessive. In *Halloren*,[260] a similarly broadly drafted order was quashed on the grounds that the sentencing judge had not adequately considered the statutory criteria or whether the order was necessary rather than desirable.[261]

2.153 Forfeiture is a process whereby the courts are able to order that property belonging to an offender that has been, or is intended to be, used for committing or facilitating the commission of an offence be surrendered to the state, such that the person loses any rights in that property. While such forfeiture does not extend to real property, such as a house, it would include computer and networking equipment used in the commission of an offence, as well as the subject matter that comprises the crime, such as child abuse images; together often referred to as the 'instrumentalities of crime'.[262]

2.154 Under English law, a general power is granted to the courts under s 143 of the Powers of Criminal Courts (Sentencing) Act 2000,[263] known as a 'deprivation order', as well as forfeiture provisions in other statutes relating to specific offences. Under the Protection of Children Act 1978, forfeiture of child abuse images was, originally, possible only when it was seized under a warrant issued under the Act or a person was convicted for an offence in relation to those images.[264] However, this was amended in 2006, such that images and the devices holding them can now be forfeited irrespective of the power they were seized under, such that indecent material inadvertently found during the course of a forensic investigation in any other circumstances may be retained by the police, as occurred in *O Ltd v Z*,[265] where illegal images were found on a hard disk in the course of a civil search for confidential information.

2.155 Forfeiture orders made by foreign courts may also now be enforced in the UK, as part of the Government's ratification of the United Nations Convention Against Organized Crime.[266] The Criminal Justice (International Co-operation) Act 1990 provides that such orders will be enforced where the offence 'corresponds to or is similar to' an offence under English law,[267] which would clearly include computer crime offences given the harmonization initiatives in the field.

---

[260] [2004] EWCA Crim 233; [2004] 2 Cr App R (S) 57.

[261] See further Walden, I and Wasik, M, 'The Internet: Access Denied Controlled!', 5 *Criminal Law Review* 377 [2011] , and Gillespie, A, 'Restricting access to the internet by sex offenders', 19(3) *Int'l J Law Info Tech* 165 (2011) .

[262] eg United Nations Convention Against Transnational Crime (UNTOC), signed 12 December 2000, entered into force 29 September 2003, 40 ILM 335 (2001), Art 12(1)(b), available at <http://www.unodc.org/documents/treaties/UNTOC/Publications/TOC%20Convention/TOCebook-e.pdf>.

[263] See eg *Lewys Stephen Martin* [2013] EWCA Crim 1420.

[264] POCA, s 4(3).

[265] [2005] EWHC 238 (Ch). See para 4.288.

[266] See para 2.201.

[267] Criminal Justice (International Co-operation) Act 1990 (CJIC), s 9(6). See also the CJIC (Enforcement of Overseas Forfeiture Orders) Order 2005, SI No 3180.

As an element of the Government's 'war on terrorism', control orders as a means of control- **2.156**
ling the activities of suspects who have not been tried before a court have been fraught with
legal difficulties.[268] Post-conviction, the imposition of similar controls is an accepted and
important tool of law enforcement. In our increasingly 'Information Society', however, a
complete prohibition on the use of computers and access to the Internet would likely be an
unacceptable and disproportionate restriction on a person's ability to participate and operate in society, except in the most extreme of circumstances.

Recovery

As discussed above, computer and cybercrimes fall into different categories, defined in vari- **2.157**
ous ways. However, with the increasing involvement of criminal organizations in all forms
of cybercrime, a dominant element of such crimes is misappropriation, ie making money.
As a consequence, attention is being paid to state-based methods of recovering the proceeds
of such misappropriation, as part of the sentencing process.[269]

In the UK, the Assets Recovery Agency was established by the Proceeds of Crime Act 2002 **2.158**
to recover the assets obtained by criminals from 'unlawful conduct',[270] although it subsequently became part of the Serious and Organised Crime Agency and now the National
Crime Agency. Recovery may be pursued through criminal procedures, such as confiscation orders,[271] or through civil proceedings under a 'recovery order'.[272]

In *McKinnon*,[273] for example, a confiscation order was made in respect of proceeds received **2.159**
by the defendant from a commercial website located in the US containing obscene images,
which had been taken in the UK and then sent to the US. On appeal, the defendant argued
that not all the proceeds generated by the website should be regarded as proceeds of crime,
since many of the customers accessing the site were from foreign jurisdictions where such
material was not illegal. This argument was rejected, partly on the grounds that none of the
proceeds would have been generated but for the original commission of an offence within
the UK.

Compensation

One reason for the low level of reporting by organizations that are victims of computer **2.160**
crime is the perceived costs involved. Direct costs are associated with supporting a prosecution, in terms of management time and resources related to the provision of evidence,
as well as any losses flowing from the offence itself, such as restoring systems and data. In
addition, there are considerable fears about the indirect or consequential losses, in terms of
the reputational damage to the organization. Although a proportion of direct costs may be
recoverable under insurance, full recovery will not be possible and the opportunity costs
and reputational tarnish are unrecoverable. To try and address these realities, some jurisdictions have made express statutory provision for compensatory remedies to be made available to the victims. Compensation may either be granted to the victim by the court, at the

---

[268] See *Secretary of State for the Home Department v JJ & five others* [2006] EWCA Civ 1141; and *Secretary of State for the Home Department v MB* [2006] EWCA Civ 1140.
[269] See *Benjafield* [2003] 1 AC 1099.
[270] POCA, s 241.
[271] ibid, Pt 2.
[272] ibid, Pt 5.
[273] [2004] 2 Cr App R (S) 46.

culmination of criminal proceedings, or the victim is given the right to pursue a remedy on his own behalf.

2.161 As an example of the former, court-granted compensation exists in Singapore, where the Computer Misuse and Cybersecurity Act expressly grants a court the power to make a restitution order against a person convicted of an offence to pay compensation to any party that has suffered damage from the offending activity.[274] In the UK, no civil remedy provisions are contained in the Computer Misuse Act, although the courts have the power within their general jurisdiction to make compensation orders 'for any personal injury, loss or damage resulting from that offence'.[275] Alternatively, where goods have been stolen and subsequently sold, over eBay, for example, a court could issue a restitution order entitling the victim to the proceeds of any such sale.[276]

2.162 By contrast, under US law, a victim of a computer-integrity offence has the right to seek compensation, divorced from any criminal proceedings. Under the Computer Fraud and Abuse Act (CFAA), it is provided that:

> Any person who suffers damage or loss by reason of a violation of this section may maintain a civil action against the violator to obtain compensatory damages and injunctive relief or other equitable relief. . . . No action may be brought under this subsection unless such action is begun within 2 years of the date of the act complained of or the date of the discovery of the damage.[277]

As a consequence, in a litigious environment such as the US, there are as many civil cases examining the terms of the CFAA as there are criminal. Indeed, the provision enables a civil action to proceed where the entire basis for the action is a breach of criminal law.[278] It has been held that the use of misappropriated confidential commercial information by a competitor does not fall within the definition of what constitutes a recoverable 'loss' under the CFAA,[279] which is an important limitation on the level of compensation that may be sought by victims.[280]

2.163 Such civil actions can greatly facilitate judicial consideration of a statute, potentially enhancing legal certainty and strengthening the deterrent impact of such legislation. Conversely, granting victims an explicit right to bring an action may result in it being used in situations not originally envisaged by legislators, thereby over-extending the reach of criminal law; as has been noted by a court:

> Because the CFAA has largely been addressed in the civil context, courts may be adopting a more expansive view of 'authorization' than they would have taken in the criminal context.[281]

---

[274] Singapore Computer Misuse and Cybersecurity Act, s 13 (originally enacted in 1993, it was amended in 1996, 1998, and 2007).

[275] Powers of Criminal Courts (Sentencing) Act 2000, s 130.

[276] ibid, s 128.

[277] 18 USC s 1030(g).

[278] *Shurgard Storage Ctrs, Inc v Safeguard Self Storage, Inc*, 199 F Supp 2d 1121 (WD Wash 2000).

[279] ie 'any reasonable cost to any victim, including the cost of responding to an offense, conducting a damage assessment, and restoring the data, program, system, or information to its condition prior to the offense, and any revenue lost, cost incurred, or other consequential damages incurred because of interruption of service' (18 USC s 1030(e)(11)).

[280] *Nexans Wires SA v Sark-USA Inc*, 13 February 2006, 166 Fed Appx 559 (2d Cir 2006).

[281] *Lockheed Martin Corporation v Speed*, 2006 US Dist, LEXIS 53108, 1 August 2006, at fn 11. See also Kerr, above, n 57, at 1641–2.

As a consequence, the CFAA provision was amended in 2001, by the USA Patriot Act, to add the following qualification: 'No action may be brought under this subsection for the negligent design or manufacture of computer hardware, computer software, or firmware.'[282] This was designed to halt the increasing number of lawsuits being brought in the US against IT companies for damage caused when installing new hardware devices and programs.[283]

As well as criminal compensation provisions, a person will obviously often have the possibility of pursuing civil proceedings, generally based in tort law, to obtain protective and/or compensatory remedies, such as an injunction or damages. Such an approach has been examined in respect of viruses[284] and denial-of-service attacks.[285] A key advantage of civil proceedings is the lower standard of proof that needs to be met by the plaintiff/victim, ie on a balance of probabilities, in order to prevail before a court. **2.164**

Law reform: Problems and principles

In general, law reform addressing computer and cybercrime will involve considerations of adaptation designed to ensure that the criminal code and criminal procedure are capable of being applied against acts involving the use of computers and networks, rather than wholesale revision of existing rules. English criminal law has developed over hundreds of years; as such, much of English law was drafted using concepts and terminology that reflect the physical world rather than the virtual world. **2.165**

The following lists some of the areas where English law, and indeed other jurisdictions, have faced legal difficulties when applying traditional criminal law in a computer and cybercrime environment. However, these difficulties are by no means unique to criminal law; indeed, some will arise more frequently in a commercial context: **2.166**

- *Information acquisition*: As information has become a more valuable commercial asset, such as intellectual property and personal data, the misappropriation of such information may deserve to be made subject to the protection of criminal sanctions (eg identity theft) or to enhanced penalties (eg counterfeiting). In terms of criminal procedure, the exercise of a power of seizure against information may not simply equate with rules designed for the taking of physical items.
- *Dealing with machines*: Some criminal acts may be cast in terms of doing something to someone, such as deception (fraud). In a cybercrime environment, acts will often involve no human interface, being completely automated. The criminal code may need to ensure that human-to-machine and machine-to-machine conduct are subject to the law.
- *Intangible damage*: The nature of computer and communication technologies means that damage may be committed against a system which is not tangible or directly perceivable by persons, such as altering the magnetic state of a disk to erase data. Such intangible damage, modification, or impairment of an ICT resource needs to be acknowledged in the criminal code.

---

[282] 18 USC s 1030(g).

[283] eg *Shaw v Toshiba A Info Sys, Inc,* 91 F Supp 2d 942 (ED Tex 2000).

[284] eg Samuelson, P, 'Legally speaking: Can hackers be sued for damages caused by computer viruses?', 32(6) *Communications of the ACM* 666 (1989).

[285] eg Chandler, JA, 'Security in cyberspace: Combating distributed denial of service attacks', 1 *University of Ottawa Law and Technology Journal* 231 (2003–4).

- *Digital manipulation*: Digital information is capable of manipulation to an unprecedented extent. As such, statutory provisions based on fixed, real-world conceptions of capturing and presenting information (eg an indecent photograph) may need to be amended to reflect such flexibility.
- *Digital time*: It is well recognized that events can happen in cyberspace in a different timescale to traditional conceptions. The criminal code may need to reconsider the use of terminology, such as 'recorded' or 'stored', which may imply a requirement for something more permanent than the sometimes transitory nature of events in cyberspace.
- *Determining location*: As with time, traditional criminal concepts of location are challenged in cyberspace. At one level, things occur on or in real-world physical objects, such as servers and networks, although identifying the location may prove problematic. At another level, however, conceptions of public and private space may vary in an Internet context, which can raise complex procedural law issues. The criminal law needs to adequately reflect the potential transnational scope of cybercrime activities.[286]

2.167 Policy-makers and legislators have therefore been required to review existing criminal law to address such issues and to reflect the nature of criminal activities in a computer and cyberspace environment. However, law reform is a generally slow process, requiring parliamentary time, political enthusiasm, and external lobbying. Sometimes, the length and nature of the process is to the detriment of the end product, a compromise of interests and issues, while the world has often moved on.

2.168 Translating policy objectives into workable laws and regulations can obviously be a complicated task in any area of human endeavour; technology, however, presents particular challenges to law-makers, primarily due to the pace of change that occurs in the subject matter itself, for example software, computers, and networks, as well as the manner in which such technology is utilized. The limits of our imagination are as manifest in our ignorance of where the technology is developing as it is about how it will be taken up by users. Much has been written about the nature of regulation in an environment of ubiquitous information, computers, and networks. Reidenberg's concept of *lex informatica*[287] and Lessig's phrase 'code as code',[288] for example, highlight the role of technology itself in regulating users' behaviour.

2.169 In response to the challenges, policy-makers have attempted to discern principles that can guide regulatory initiatives in the field. The leading, oft-quoted, regulatory principle in an ICT context is that of 'technology neutrality'. Much reference and deference is made by policy-makers to the concept of 'technology-neutral' regulation, based on an acceptance that the environment is moving too rapidly to try and tie legal rules to a particular technology or market model:

> The moment you try and do definitions which rely on some kind of implicit technology model, then you know that those definitions are doomed, certainly within ten years and probably within five.[289]

---

[286] See generally Chapter 5.
[287] Reidenberg, JR, 'Lex informatica: The formulation of information policy rules through technology', 76 *Texas Law Review* 553 (1998).
[288] See Lessig, L, *Code and other laws of cyberspace*, Basic Books, 2000.
[289] European Informatics Market (EURIM) submission to the All Party Internet Group (APIG) Report on Communications Data, January 2003.

The principle, and variants of it, has been used in two key senses in policy statements made in relation to ICT regulation: that which is regulated offline should be regulated online; as well as the need to treat different technologies similarly to the extent that they have the same effect.[290]

The principle has been applied in the context of both substantive and procedural law reform **2.170** initiatives, although disputes exist about the relevance and manner in which the principle should be applied. Computer integrity offences, for example, are responses to technology-specific activities that have either no equivalent in an offline environment, or the analogies are considered an inadequate response to the perceived mischief. In terms of criminal procedure, extending historic distinctions between content and communications data have been criticized for failing to recognize the unique features of modern IP networks, as noted by Hosein and Pascual:

> Attempts to be technology-neutral should be interrogated, lest in our blindness we reduce democratic protections and oversight under the deterministic veil of progress.[291]

The principle also fails to provide help to policy-makers when making the choice between the adoption of different regulatory models. The Internet, for example, is the perfect example of the convergence phenomenon, with different forms of content being transmitted across interconnected networks using a common protocol. But whether the IT industry, telecoms, or broadcasting models of regulation should apply to the services being made available and content being transmitted, continues to test policy-makers and regulators.[292]

Other reform principles relate to the manner in which regulation is implemented. Self- **2.171** regulation by industry or professional groups, or at least co-regulation, based on some form of public–private partnership, is seen as a key 'soft law' mechanism for reducing the need for governmental intervention and providing a flexible and responsive regulatory regime, particularly appropriate in a cyberspace environment.[293] However, self-regulation can also be criticized for failing to credibly reflect the interests of individuals and the wider general public, as well as often lacking sufficient accountability.[294]

Effective self-regulation requires the operation of a policing function to identify, inves- **2.172** tigate, and enforce against those operating within the self-regulated sector. As examined below, private sector law enforcement is a key element in the fight against computer and cybercrime. However, while effective sanctions are available and used against the illegal or harmful activities of third-party users, such as 'notice and take down', the limit of the sanction available against a recalcitrant industry participant will often be expulsion from the scheme and attendant bad publicity, or the organization may simply not be a scheme member in the first place.

Layered on top of principles for law reform in the ICT sector, there are generic principles **2.173** against which laws are traditionally assessed and evaluated, especially in respect of criminal

---

[290] See Koops, B-J, 'Should ICT regulation be technology-neutral?', in Koops, B-J et al (eds), *Starting Points for ICT Regulation*, TMC Asser Press, 2006, at 77–108.

[291] Hosein, I and Pascual, A, 'Understanding traffic data and deconstructing technology-neutral regulations', 7 March 2002, available at <http://www.it46.se/docs/papers/unece-latest-escuderoa-hoseini.pdf>.

[292] See generally Reed, C, *Making Laws for Cyberspace*, Oxford University Press, 2012.

[293] See Marsden, C, *Internet Co-regulation*, Cambridge University Press, 2011.

[294] See generally Price, M and Verhulst, S, *Self-regulation and the Internet*, Kluwer Law International, 2005.

matters.[295] The principle of legal transparency or 'fair warning', for example, demands that those made subject to the law are aware, or have the possibility of becoming aware, of the rules applicable to a particular activity. Under European human rights law, transparency is one element of the requirement that restrictions on a person's rights be 'in accordance with the law'. Legal certainty requires that the law be sufficiently clear to enable a person to know whether his conduct is unlawful or not. Certainty may have wider economic benefits to the extent that it facilitates good behaviours, such as encouraging people to trade online.

2.174 Closely related to certainty is the demand that laws be sustainable. Sustainability can be seen as having two key aspects. First, the length of time that a set of legal rules remains workable in terms of meeting the policy objectives in the environment in which it operates. Second, that the rules are enforceable against the prohibited conduct. While 100 per cent enforceability in any area of law is never attained, particularly in a cyberspace environment of multiple and conflicting jurisdictions, a large-scale inability to enforce undermines the value of any set of legal rules.

2.175 Law reform is an essential feature of any legal system, in all areas of activity. Calls for reform may emerge from expressions of public concern, industry lobbying, or other scrutiny mechanisms, from the Law Commission to parliamentary committees. Identifying the problems and choosing the most appropriate and effective solution is a constant challenge, more so perhaps in the criminal law field, where the consequences of mistakes may be more significant. That challenge is substantially greater in a field, such as computer and cybercrime, characterized by a rapidly evolving technological and market environment and an inherently international nature.

E. Criminal Types and Actors

2.176 Crimes are committed by persons, natural or legal, even where the components of a crime may be carried out by a computer system or the victim themselves. As such, any examination of computer crime must be concerned with those who commit, assist, or are otherwise tied up in the commission of criminal conduct, although this is a topic for more thorough investigation by criminologists.[296] This section therefore briefly considers four different categories of person involved in computer and cybercrimes: the perpetrators themselves; criminal organizations; persons directly associated with the perpetrator; and Internet service providers.

2.177 The perpetrator is the traditional focus of criminal law enforcement. Building a profile of the type of person likely to commit a certain form of crime can impact on criminal policy, the legal framework, and the effective response of law enforcement.[297] For computer crime, multiple profiles would be necessary for each category, if not specific type, of activity of concern to us, reflecting different motivations, opportunities, and levels of skill at using ICTs, from the white-collar fraudster, by way of the paedophile, to the teenage hacker.

---

[295] See Ashworth and Horder, above, n 87, s 3.5.
[296] See eg Mann, D and Sutton, M, 'NETCRIME: More change in the organization of thieving', 38 *British Journal of Criminology* 201 (1998).
[297] Goodman, above, n 119, at 469.

As noted earlier, criminal policy has increasingly shifted in focus from the individual to that **2.178** of the criminal organization. Such a change has a significant impact at the level of the criminal code, framing offences that reflect the organizational underpinnings of the activity, as well as criminal procedure, the investigation and prosecution of the organization and its participants. We therefore need to briefly consider the concept of the criminal organization and its treatment in law, although the organized crime phenomenon informs many other aspects of the book.

As well as the 'principal offender', the perpetrator of the criminal act, we also need to **2.179** address the role and liability of others, those who may commit an offence through association, direct or indirect, with the criminal conduct. In an environment of global and organized criminality, such persons have become a more significant target for law enforcement attention. For our purposes, such persons are distinguished into three distinct but overlapping roles.

The first is the criminal liability of an accessory. The second and third are the inchoate acts of conspiracy and incitement. A subsection of incitement, often treated as a category in its own right, is that of the provider or supplier of 'devices' that are, or can be, used in the commission of the primary offence. In a cybercrime environment a 'device' may be broadly or narrowly conceived, but both the supply and possession have been subject to specific legislative treatment and are discussed further in Chapter 3.

The final category is the Internet service provider, which provides the end-user with access **2.180** to the Internet, transmission, and storage capacity, as well as related services that are necessary to commit all the categories of cybercrime under consideration. While the use and abuse of communication networks pre-dates cyberspace, in an Internet context we have seen the emergence of service providers that offer substantially enhanced services and facilities than those present in a traditional voice telephony environment. This, together with the liberalization of provision in the market, has created some unique issues in terms of the attribution of criminal liability.

Perpetrators

Those who commit computer and cybercrimes are variously described as perpetrators and **2.181** defendants during the course of the book, distinguishing between the commission of the criminal act and the operation of the criminal justice system. Under English law, responsibility for an offence will either be with the 'principal offender' or an 'accessory'. The types of person involved in such activities may differ considerably within the different branches and categories identified in the taxonomies discussed above. Perpetrators are often considered to fall more often within the general class of 'white-collar' criminals,[298] although whether such a classification is apposite is itself disputed.[299]

While there is no typical cybercriminal, any more than there is a typical cybercrime, certain common characteristics are likely to be found among those that commit particular **2.182**

---

[298] See eg Jordan, T and Taylor, P, 'A sociology of hackers', 46(4) *Sociological Review* 757 (1998) . This is how computer crime literature is classified in the library at the Institute of Criminology, University of Cambridge, where the author carried out some of his research.

[299] See Wasik, M, *Crime and the Computer*, Clarendon Press, 1991, at 24 et seq and Smith, above, n 43, at 10.

kinds of offence. For the computer-related crimes examined in Chapter 3, primarily crimes of acquisition, the characteristics are likely to be the same as those for such crime in a traditional environment. As an inevitable consequence of ICTs facilitating content-related crimes, more people are likely to engage in the commission of such crimes, potentially from a broader spectrum of society. The range of people investigated and prosecuted in connection with child pornography offences under Operation Ore,[300] for example, included a naval commander, a judge, a doctor, a police officer, a teacher, and a rock star.[301] From a criminological perspective, a particularly interesting area for study in computer crime has been of those engaged in the new forms of crime, where the computer is the target.

2.183 A term prevalent in any discussion about cybercrime is that of 'hacker', the archetypal cybercriminal, portrayed to the public through films, such as 'War Games' (1983), 'Sneakers' (1992), 'The Net' (1995), 'Hackers' (1995), and 'Swordfish' (2001), and books, such as William Gibson's seminal *Neuromancer* (1984). Hackers are generally associated with computer-integrity crimes, the 'new' crimes, rather than the 'old wine' of computer and content-related crimes, as Coupland writes:

> So maybe that's why people are so interested in computer 'hackers'—because they've invented a new sin.[302]

According to Levy, the term 'hackers' has its origins in the Tech Model Railroad Club at MIT, where people used their skills, determination, and patience to make the early computer systems operate free of errors.[303] The term then evolved to encompass those involved in the hardware and the games industry. As such, the phrase did not originally have criminal connotations. Indeed, many in the industry and academia, keen to maintain its noncriminal meaning, distinguish hackers from 'crackers', or qualify use of the term between 'white-hat' and 'black-hat' hackers. While understanding the origins of the 'hacker' is important, we are also forced to accept that the term has been effectively hijacked by the media, and in the public mind, to mean computer criminals or 'electronic highwaymen',[304] rather than simply clever techies.

2.184 The three widely accepted variables said to drive criminal activity are motivation, opportunity, and skill.[305] A consideration of these three variables can better enable us to understand the range of persons involved. These variables will obviously vary over time, more so in areas such as cyberspace where the environment itself is evolving so rapidly.

2.185 What motivates cybercriminals? As Grabosky et al note, cybercriminals are driven 'by time-honoured motives, the most obvious of which are greed, lust, power, revenge, adventure, and the desire to taste "forbidden fruit"'.[306] Alternatively, Kilger has summarized the

---

[300] Operation Ore was based on a list of 7,272 credit card subscribers potentially residing in the UK, which was found on the Landslide site in Texas in 1999.

[301] This is based on a Google search of publicity surrounding the operation, carried out in January 2006. Inevitably, such prosecutions are more likely to receive publicity where they involve persons occupying particular positions.

[302] Coupland, D, *Microserfs*, Flamingo, 1995, at 357.

[303] Levy, S, *Hackers*, Penguin, 1984, at 23.

[304] Hollinger, R, 'Hackers: Computer heroes or electronic highwayman?', 21 *Computers and Society* 6 (1991).

[305] Cohen, L and Felson, M, 'Social change and crime rate trends: A routine activity approach', 44 *American Sociological Review* 588 (1979).

[306] Grabosky et al, above, n 48, at 2.

motives by the acronym 'MEECES', which stands for money, entertainment, ego, cause, entrance to social groups, and status.[307] Examples abound of all these motivations, and we already have a considerable body of literature exhibiting this variety, some written by perpetrators themselves.[308] Attempts have even been made to reduce cybercriminal activity to a cost-benefit calculus, where $M_b + P_b > O_{cp} + O_{cm}P_aP_c$![309]

2.186 Whatever initially motivates a person to commit a certain criminal act, the activity may, in certain circumstances, develop into a mental illness in the form of an addiction, dependency, or obsession.[310] While mental illness has always been present in some cases of child abuse, and therefore child pornography, claims of compulsion and obsession have also been utilized by defence counsel and accepted by the courts in computer-integrity cases in the US[311] and the UK,[312] both as a defence and as a mitigating factor in sentencing.[313]

2.187 As with other forms of criminal activity, there will often be a variety of perpetrators with varying motives. So, for example, a hacker may engage in an act for money, on a commercial basis, paid for by an individual, nation state, or political organization motivated by personal vendetta,[314] espionage,[315] or terrorist motivations. Indeed, UK law enforcement strategy is focusing more attention and resources on the perpetrator as a member of an organized crime syndicate or terrorist cell than as an individual.

2.188 As Wall writes, '[s]ince crime tends to follow opportunity and the Internet provides many new opportunities, then new crimes will certainly emerge'.[316] As well as new crimes, however, the Internet clearly facilitates traditional crimes, or as Levi notes, it 'democratizes criminal opportunities'.[317] Content-related crimes in particular would seem to have been facilitated by the digitization of information and the ease by which it can be copied, accessed, and communicated. In terms of copyright, while there may be an on-going debate about the business impact of infringement activities, that infringement is rife in cyberspace is undisputed. As pornography has become one of the key content industries in cyberspace, so there has been a proliferation of the illegal and extreme end of the market, particularly in respect of child pornography, while crimes of fraud and forgery involving computers and communications technologies have become the norm, as the technologies have been integrated into our daily lives.

---

[307] Kilger, M, Arkin, O, and Stutzman, J, 'Profiling', in Honeynet Project, *Know Your Enemy: Learning about Security Threats*, 2nd edn, Addison-Wesley Professional, 2004, Chapter 16.

[308] See eg Mitnick, K and Simon, WL, *Art of Intrusion: The real stories behind the exploits of hackers, intruders and deceivers*, Hungry Minds, 2005. See also Xu, Z, Hu, Q, and Zhang, C, 'Why computer talents become computer hackers', 56(4) *Communications of the ACM* 64 (2013).

[309] Kshetri, N, 'The simple economics of cybercrimes', 4(1) *IEEE Security and Privacy* 33 (2006), available at <http://ssrn.com/abstract=881421>.

[310] Shotton, M, *Computer Addiction?: A Study of Computer Dependency*, Taylor & Francis, 1989.

[311] eg in the case of Kevin Mitnick, see Hafner, K and Markoff, J, *Cyberpunk: Outlaws and Hackers on the Computer Frontier*, Simon and Schuster, 1991, at 343.

[312] eg in *Bedworth*, Southwark Crown Court, 17 March 1993, see para 3.293.

[313] See also Smith, above, n 43, at 78 and 140.

[314] See eg *Debnath* [2005] All ER (D) 49, discussed at para 3.212.

[315] eg Hans Huebner ('Pengo') and Karl Koch sold defence secrets to the KGB during the Cold War.

[316] Wall, above, n 68, at xv.

[317] Levi, M, 'Between the risk and the reality falls the shadow', in Wall, DS (ed), *Crime and the Internet: Cybercrimes and Cyberfears*, Routledge, 2001, at 44.

2.189 Opportunity has been created by the manner in which the technology has been designed, at both a system and network level. Digitization is the language of convergence because all types of information can be represented that way. The Internet Protocol, which underpins the Internet as the network of networks, was designed to be platform-independent, decentralized, and robust, which in turn mitigates against attempts to exercise control and enforcement. Computers are by nature social beings: 'Say "hello" to a computer and its response will be "hello, who are you?" ' Such ease and flexibility has underpinned the development of cyberspace, but has a cost in terms of providing opportunities to the perpetrators of criminal activities.

2.190 In Levy's description of the early hackers, the level of skill and determination required by those wanting to make and break computer and communications technologies was somewhat awe-inspiring. Indeed, the difficulty of breaking into systems clearly continues to be one of the motivations for perpetrators of integrity offences. Inevitably, the spread of the technology has resulted in a decline in the level of skill required by perpetrators and hence, in one sense, opportunities have increased.

2.191 However, perceptions of skill are intimately linked to popular perceptions of the culprits, ie the teenage nerd working away in the attic of his parents' house, the parents being ignorant of what their son is up to. Such an image does not chime with numerous early surveys that indicated that the majority of unauthorized access was committed by persons within, or associated with, the victim organization. As such, insiders generally require a lower level of skill and they are adult employees, rather than teenagers.

2.192 Again, however, a distinction must be made between the skills required to commit different computer and cybercrimes. As noted above, content-related crimes generally require the least skill, since the copying, communication, and storage of data is a basic function of ICTs. For fraud and forgery, the required skill will vary according to the nature of the act; for example, a programming fraud requires greater skills than inputting fraudulent data.

2.193 In terms of computer-integrity offences, a primary division must be made between insiders and outsiders, since the former will obviously often have greater opportunities and require less skill. Among outsiders, external hackers, at one end of the spectrum we see the proliferation of 'joyriders', or 'script kiddies', who use off-the-shelf and widely available tools to exploit known weaknesses in systems; at the other end, we have the so-called 'überhackers', who discover the 'zero-day exploits' for sale or release to others.

Criminal organizations

2.194 Much of the current focus of UK policy and law enforcement on computer and cybercrime revolves around the use and abuse of ICTs in organized crime, a position shared by many developed nations. Concerns about the spotty teenager hacking into military systems motivated by mere curiosity have been largely transferred to concerns about the criminal organization, mafia-style, involved in every sector of profitable criminality, from counterfeiting to child pornography, malware to spam, and operating on a transnational basis. One consequence of this shift is that computer crime is increasingly viewed at a policy and enforcement level simply as a subset of organized crime, a particular technique, rather than a distinct category of activity. While disputing the merit of such a characterization, this book must also address this policing reality and consider the policy and legal responses to organized crime.

While criminal organizations or gangs may engage in most of the types of crime examined **2.195**
in this book, favoured activities are thought to include the following:

- *Extortion*—for example threatening to disrupt an organization's online presence unless
  a fee is paid, and carrying out the threat using a Distributed Denial-of-Service (DDoS)
  attack from a 'botnet' of zombie computers.[318] In 2004, for example, a German betting site was bombarded by email for 16 hours after it refused to pay a demand for
  $15,000.[319]
- *Fraud*—for example, 'pump and dump' share scams, where the price of a stock is artificially inflated through false disclosures made through online share trading chat rooms.
- *Information acquisition*—from identity theft and 'phishing',[320] to industrial espionage
  carried out to order or used for blackmail purposes. In so-called 'ransomware' cases,
  the perpetrators gain access to the victim's system and encrypt files, leaving a message
  demanding some form of payment.[321]
- *Information supply*—as well as acquisition, the value of certain content may promote
  industrialized information production or reproduction, as in the case of child abuse
  images. Such crimes have been described as 'market-based' crimes, as distinct from
  acquisition offences, or 'predatory' crimes.[322]
- *Money laundering*—either directly through online banking and financial services operations or indirectly through the sale of stolen merchandise via the Internet.[323]

As in the case of computer and cybercrime, there is a debate about the true scale and nature
of organized cybercrime.[324] The existence of a significant and substantial link between
organized crime and terrorism is also somewhat controversial.[325]

The concept of a criminal organization is not clearly defined under English law. At one end **2.196**
of a continuum, it is a recognizable legal person, incorporated as a company or other form
of commercial entity, and capable of being held directly liable for the criminal activities carried out on its behalf. So, for example, under EU law, the main harmonizing instruments
on substantive law make express reference to the liability of legal persons, defined in the
following terms:

---

[318] See paras 3.294–3.303 for a discussion about DDoS attacks.

[319] Libbenga, J, 'European betting sites brace for attack', *The Register*, 28 June 2004, available at <http://www.theregister.co.uk/2004/06/28/betting_sites_attack/>.

[320] See para 3.73 for a definition.

[321] eg 'CryptoLocker', which encrypts files and then presents the victim with a pop-up win-
dow stating what has occurred and requesting a ransom in Bitcoin. See National Crime Agency
(NCA), 'Two-week opportunity for UK to reduce threat from powerful computer attack', Press
Release, 2 June 2014, available at <http://www.nationalcrimeagency.gov.uk/news/news-listings/
386-two-week-opportunity-for-uk-to-reduce-threat-from-powerful-computer-attack>.

[322] See Naylor, R, *Wages of crime: Black markets, illegal finance, and the underworld economy*, Cornell
University Press, 2004.

[323] See McAfee, *Virtual criminology report: North American study into organised crime and the Internet*,
July 2005, available at <http://www.softmart.com/mcafee/docs/McAfee%20NA%20Virtual%20
Criminology%20Report.pdf>.

[324] See eg Levi, M, 'The organisation of serious crimes', in Maguire, M and Morgan, R (eds), *The Oxford
Handbook of Criminology*, 3rd edn, Oxford University Press, 2002, at 878–913.

[325] Council of Europe, *Organised Crime Situation Report 2004: Focus on the threat of cybercrime*, December
2004, at 172 et seq, available at <http://www.coe.int/t/dghl/cooperation/economiccrime/organisedcrime/
Organised%20Crime%20Situation%20Report%202004.pdf>.

... means any entity having the status of legal person under the applicable law, but does not include States or other public bodies acting in the exercise of State authority, or public international organisations.[326]

2.197   Historically the law has struggled to address the criminal liability of legal persons, since the conduct and mental elements of crimes are carried out by individuals, not a legal entity, although modern criminal law has evolved means of providing for corporate liability[327] and new statutory measures have been adopted.[328] At the other end of the continuum, the organization may simply constitute, from an English law perspective at least, a conspiracy of persons with an agreed criminal objective.[329] Between these two extremes, we see widely differing levels of formality, coordination, and permanency.

2.198   To a limited extent, an analogy can perhaps be drawn between the variety of criminal organizations and the diversity of networks that comprise and connect to form the Internet. Indeed, we can obviously go further and note that the flexibility and possibilities offered by cyberspace as a networked environment have facilitated the development of innovative organizational forms, criminal or otherwise. Seiber, for example, suggests that 'cybercrime may favour those organizations which are already based on flat-structured networking', rather than a classic hierarchical structure,[330] a view shared by Brenner, who views the ability to automate many of the processes of 'large-scale, complicated entrepreneurial' criminal activities as a key driver behind the emergence of such new organizational forms.[331] Naylor, by contrast, suggests that ICTs have tended to 'democratize the commission of crimes by rendering large organizations uncompetitive'.[332] Whatever the reality, the variety of forms that may comprise a criminal organization creates obvious problems for policy-makers and legislators in terms of crafting a legal framework to address such forms, let alone for law enforcement agencies trying to investigate them.

2.199   Despite a shared concern to address criminal organizations, states have adopted differing legal treatments and responses to such organizations. Jurisdictions have recast individual criminal conduct or extended individual liability when carried out in the context of a criminal organization, primarily in terms of harsher penalties. Criminal procedure may also be amended to provide for new organizational structures and special powers to tackle the problem. In 2005, the Serious Organised Crime Agency (SOCA) was established to address this area, although it has since been superseded by the National Crime Agency in 2013. In 2007, the UK introduced new civil law enforcement orders, called 'serious crime prevention orders', which are designed to disrupt organized crime activities, by imposing prohibitions on certain types of behaviour.[333] It is also argued, however, that tackling criminal

---

[326] Directive 2013/40/EU, above, n 8, Art 2(c). On EU law generally, see paras 5.158–5.202.

[327] See generally *Blackstone's Criminal Practice 2016*, above, n 43, Chapter 10; and Pinto, A and Evans, M, *Corporate Criminal Liability*, Sweet & Maxwell, 2003.

[328] Corporate Manslaughter and Corporate Homicide Act 2007. The Convention on Cybercrime, Art 12, requires signatory states to provide for corporate liability in respect of the offences detailed in it.

[329] See paras 2.215–2.217 for a discussion of conspiracy.

[330] *Situation Report 2004*, above, n 324, at 124. The section on cybercrime was written by Professor Ulrich Seiber, Director of the Max Planck Institute for Foreign and International Criminal Law, Freiburg, Germany.

[331] See Brenner, S, 'Organised cybercrime? How cyberspace may affect the structure of criminal relationships', 4(1) *North Carolina Journal of Law and Technology* 49 (2002).

[332] Naylor, above, n 322, at 6.

[333] Serious Crime Act 2007, Pt 1.

organizations does not require such new laws, as existing offences are sufficient; rather these reform initiatives are simply pandering to public demands for action to be taken.[334]

Two broad and overlapping approaches have been taken to criminal organizations. In the **2.200** first, offences are established that relate to certain patterns of behaviour, which are considered to evince the presence of a criminal organization. Such behaviour may relate to actual criminal conduct or the benefits that flow from such conduct, ie the proceeds of crime. In the UK, for example, the concept of a 'criminal lifestyle' has been introduced.[335] While in the US, the Racketeer Influenced and Corrupt Organizations Act (RICO)[336] is focused on a 'pattern of racketeering activity',[337] which comprises at least two criminal acts that evidence 'continuity plus relationship'.[338]

A second approach is to define the nature of the organization and then criminalize partici- **2.201** pation or other conduct that takes place in relation to that organization. This is the approach adopted in the United Nations Convention Against Transnational Crime (UNTOC)[339] in 2000, which adopted the following definition:

> 'Organized criminal group' shall mean a structured group of three or more persons, existing for a period of time and acting in concert with the aim of committing one or more serious crimes or offences established in accordance with this Convention, in order to obtain, directly or indirectly, a financial or other material benefit.[340]

The Convention then defines certain conduct in relation to an 'organised criminal group', such as conspiracy, which signatory states are expected to criminalize.[341] The UK ratified the Convention in February 2006,[342] through provisions in the Serious and Organised Crime and Police Act 2005.[343] The Convention has been approved by the European Community and therefore the same approach is taken in its Framework Decision on organized crime.[344]

For the purposes of our analysis, the rise of the criminal organization has a number of **2.202** important implications. In terms of substantive law, it provides an alternative means of characterizing and criminalizing the conduct carried out using, or against, computers or other ICT resources. Rather than focusing on the perpetrator's conduct in relation to a specific computer, it widens the perspective out to focus on the context within which the conduct was carried out. In terms of procedural law, the investigation of a criminal organization will generally require the deployment of more sophisticated covert investigative

---

[334] Freedman, D, 'The New Law of Criminal Organizations in Canada', 85(2) *Canadian Bar Review* 171 (2007).

[335] Proceeds of Crime Act 2002, s 75.

[336] Pub L No 92-452, 84 Sat 922 (codified as 18 USC ss 1961 et seq).

[337] 18 USC s 1961(5).

[338] *Sedima, SPRL v Imrex Co*, 473 US 479 (1985).

[339] UNTOC, above, n 262.

[340] ibid, Art 2(a).

[341] ibid, Art 5 'Criminalization of participation in an organised criminal group'.

[342] See UNTOC, above, n 262, which entered into force for the UK on 11 March 2006.

[343] Serious and Organised Crime and Police Act 2005 (SOCPA), s 95.

[344] Council Framework Decision 2008/841/JHA on the fight against organised crime, OJ L 300/42, 11 November 2008.

techniques, over longer periods of time, in order to identify the multitude of organizational participants, often evidenced through their communications activities.[345]

Accessories

2.203 While the figure of the lone perpetrator fits classic media representations of a hacker, the reality seems far from that. As well as criminal organizations, another form of criminal involvement is that of the person who somehow assists the offender to engage in criminal conduct, from employees supplying passwords enabling access to a system to a person offering software tools that enable viruses to be written.

2.204 Under English criminal law, an accessory is liable as a principal offender,[346] although the liability is generally referred to as 'secondary liability'. An accessory is a person who aids, abets, counsels, or procures the commission of an offence. Generally the four constituent terms are used as a whole, although they may be different depending on the circumstance, sometimes requiring a common purpose, or 'meeting of minds' or, alternatively, the establishment of a causal link between the conduct of the accessory and the commission of the offence by the principal.[347]

2.205 Although the liability is identical as between principal and accessory, the fault element, or *mens rea*, for an accessory is different. It is both more limited, generally requiring knowledge or intent, rather than recklessness or negligence, as well as being dual in nature, requiring intent in respect of the aiding and abetting, and knowledge in respect of the 'essential matters which constitute the offence'.[348] As such, *mens rea* must be present even where the principal commits an offence of strict liability.[349] Under the Computer Misuse Act 1990, for example, although it is now possible to commit the offence of impairing the operation of a computer through recklessness,[350] it would have to be shown that a person prosecuted as an accessory had the required knowledge that an unauthorized act leading to impairment was, or was likely to be committed, and an intention to aid in the achievement of that result.

2.206 A person may be found liable as an accessory even where the principal cannot be identified. So, for example, a person who operates an online forum offering malware and other tools designed to compromise the integrity of computers could be tried as an accessory in a situation where a clear forensic link exists between a tool made available via the forum and an actual offence of hacking or modification, even though the actual perpetrator can either not be identified or, as is often the case, is located in a foreign jurisdiction and cannot be prosecuted. Although the Computer Misuse Act now contains a separate offence in respect of supplying such tools,[351] prosecution as an accessory to the commission of the primary offence is an alternative charge and the available tariff is greater. Another potential scenario would be where two people shared a computer, or a user account, and it could be

---

[345] See generally Bacigalupo, E, 'The use of technical means in interception and surveillance of private communications', in Militello, V and Huber, B (eds), *Towards a European Criminal Law Against Organised Crime*, Edition Iuscrim, 2001, at 131–42.
[346] See the Accessories and Abettors Act 1861, s 8 (for indictable offences) and the Magistrates' Courts Act 1980, s 44(1) (for summary offences).
[347] *Blackstone's Criminal Practice 2016*, above, n 43, at A4.5 et seq.
[348] *Johnson v Youden* [1950] 1 KB 544, at 546.
[349] *Callow v Tillstone* (1900) 83 LT 411.
[350] CMA, s 3. See paras 3.282–3.293.
[351] CMA, s 3A. See para 3.346.

shown that both were engaged in trying to break into a system, but not which person was at the keyboard when entry was achieved and the damage done or confidential information obtained. As such, the role of accessory can assist prosecutors and helps avoid defendants 'escape criminal liability by blaming one another'.[352]

The role of accessory is present in the criminal code of other jurisdictions and has been expressly addressed in harmonization instruments on computer crime. Both the Convention on Cybercrime and the EU Directive 2013/40/EU, for example, expressly require states to criminalize 'aiding and abetting'.[353]   **2.207**

The characterization of a person's participation in a crime as an accessory must be distinguished from the person being considered a co-principal, in a conspiracy to defraud for example, or as a person who encourages or assists another. An offence of encouragement or assistance may still be committed even where the principal offence has not been committed;[354] while this is generally not the case for accessory liability. The boundaries between each are often blurred, especially with respect to encouragement or assistance, and will have to be determined in the particular circumstances of the case and, perhaps, on the basis of the available evidence. Aiding and abetting should also be distinguished from situations where the person's perceived involvement in a crime is a distinct offence in itself. The Terrorism Act 2006, for example, creates a form of speech offence of encouraging terrorism, distinct from any actual act of terrorism. For the offence to be committed, a person has to have intentionally 'directly or indirectly encouraged or otherwise induced by the statement' others to prepare or commit acts of terrorism,[355] which has similarities with the concept of counselling a criminal act.   **2.208**

Inchoate acts

While responsibility for a criminal offence rests with the principal offender and any accessory, English criminal law also criminalizes certain acts that, while not the main offence, are considered to comprise a step towards the commission of the main or substantive offence. Such offences are known as 'inchoate' offences, which means 'just begun, not yet fully developed',[356] although the term is commonly used in a wider context than simply that of incomplete crimes.[357] The three classic inchoate offences are attempt, conspiracy and incitement.   **2.209**

While attempt and conspiracy were placed on a statutory footing some while ago,[358] incitement only became statutory under Part 2 of the Serious Crime Act 2007, and renamed 'encouraging or assisting the commission of an offence'.[359] Each offence is used, however, in relation to a particular substantive offence, whether statutory or otherwise, and they attract a comparable tariff. In addition, various statutory offences have addressed specific   **2.210**

---

[352] Ashworth and Horder, above, n 87, Chapter 10.
[353] Convention on Cybercrime, Art 11(1) and Directive 2013/40/EU, above, n 8, Art 8(1). See Appendices II and III, respectively.
[354] Serious Crime Act 2007, s 49(1).
[355] TA 2006, s 1. See para 3.198.
[356] Garner, BA, *Garner's Dictionary of Legal Usage*, 3rd edn, Oxford University Press, 2011.
[357] eg Law Commission, *Fraud*, Report No 276, Cm 5569, HMSO, 2002, para 7.54: 'Fraud as an inchoate offence'.
[358] Criminal Attempts Act 1981 and Criminal Law Act 1977, respectively.
[359] Serious Crime Act 2007, s 45.

forms of inchoate assistance, such as 'facilitation' under the Computer Misuse Act 1990,[360] 'permitting' under the Forgery and Counterfeiting Act 1981,[361] and 'encouragement' under the Terrorism Act 2006.[362] Both the Convention on Cybercrime and the EU Directive 2013/40/EU expressly require states to criminalize attempt.[363] The other forms of inchoate offence are not referred to, although the Framework uses the phrase 'the instigation of ... an offence', which would seem to be applicable both to situations of conspiracy and incitement.

2.211　To be prosecuted, all three offences require evidence of an intention to commit the substantive offence, although one distinct feature is that they can be committed even though the substantive offence is not actually completed, for whatever reason, and no harm results. Attempt is generally an act carried out by the perpetrator and can be seen as forming part of our earlier discussion of principal and accessory liability. Conspiracy comprises an agreement to engage in an unlawful act, potentially involving both principals and accessories. With encouragement or assistance, while a person could potentially be characterized as an accessory for counselling or procuring the offence, they would never be a principal offender of the substantive offence.

2.212　From a law enforcement perspective, an obvious advantage of conspiracy and incitement in a transnational cyberspace environment of diverse and uncertain locations and competing jurisdictions is that communication-based offences provide a comparatively straightforward enforcement strategy, focusing on the act of communication rather than the substantive criminal conduct. This is particularly the case for conspiracy, since it can be committed even if the substantive act is impossible;[364] while for the offences of encouragement and assistance, impossibility is not intended as a defence.[365]

2.213　Such inchoate offences are also likely to have an enhanced role in an 'intelligence-led' law enforcement strategy, as called for in the 'war on terrorism', where prevention and intervention before the substantive crime is committed and harm inflicted is clearly preferable to a reactive or coercive strategy.[366] Conversely, however, the commission of crimes through the mere communication of words may be seen in certain circumstances as over-criminalization, potentially raising human rights issues in respect of the right to freedom of expression under Art 10.[367]

2.214　This section briefly considers the acts of conspiracy and incitement, since they are essentially communicative in nature, as are the activities that take place in cyberspace.

Conspiracy

2.215　The agreement that comprises the basic element of a conspiracy requires a certain mental state, a meeting of minds, rather than any physical manifestation. Such an agreement may often be inferred from behaviour, rather than the actual recording of a meeting or terms

---

[360] CMA, s 2(1)(b).
[361] Forgery and Counterfeiting Act (FCA) 1981, s 17(1).
[362] Terrorism Act 2006 (TA 2006), s 1.
[363] Convention on Cybercrime, Art 11(2) and Directive 2013/40/EU, above, n 8, Art 8(2).
[364] Criminal Law Act 1977, s 1(1)(b), except for common law conspiracy.
[365] *Smith & Hogan Criminal Law*, above, n 43, s 13.5.2.3.
[366] ibid, s 13.1.
[367] eg *Rusbridger v Attorney General* [2002] EWCA Civ 397.

of an agreement.[368] Patterns derived from communications data, for example, detailing persons contacted, frequency, times, and duration may provide a valuable forensic source, using a form of social network analysis.[369] In *Singh*,[370] for example, the defendant was convicted of conspiracy to kidnap partly on the basis of evidence of his phone numbers being found in the memories of the telephones of his co-accused.

While the agreement may be purely mental, the criminal conduct is the agreement that **2.216** a 'course of conduct will be pursued which, if the agreement is carried out in accordance with their intentions ... will necessarily amount to or involve the commission of an offence or offences by one or more of the parties to the agreement'.[371] The offence of conspiracy is complete even if the offence that forms the substance of the agreement is never carried out. In terms of *mens rea*, there are effectively three separate elements.[372] First, the person must have the mental state to be able to enter into an agreement. Second, he must have an intention that the substantive offence be carried out. Third, he must 'intend or know' that the material facts and circumstances relevant to the commission of the offence will exist.[373]

Conspiracy is currently based both in common law, primarily in the form of conspiracy to **2.217** defraud, as well as statute, under the Criminal Law Act 1977. Although they may be used concurrently,[374] there is dissatisfaction with the current position, coupled with an on-going unwillingness to comprehensively codify the situation.[375]

Incitement, encouragement, and assistance

As noted above, the common law offence of incitement was replaced by three statutory **2.218** offences of encouragement or assisting, although supplemented by various statutory offences.[376] Encouragement and assistance can be seen as forms of communication, where person A encourages through words or actions person B to commit a criminal act, although such communication may be direct, using words of persuasion, or indirect, such as advertising items that are clearly targeted at those wishing to commit the substantive offence.[377] From a jurisdictional perspective, acts of encouragement or assistance trigger liability in England and Wales if the person knows or believes that the conduct being encouraged or assisted might take place wholly or partly in England and Wales.[378] A person could be found liable for an attempt to encourage or assist, although such circumstances are likely to be rare.[379] It has been held that where a person attempts to subscribe to a website, but fails

---

[368] eg *Murphy* [1837] 8 C & P 297.

[369] Davis, RH, 'Social network analysis: An aid in conspiracy investigations', 8 *FBI Law Enforcement Bulletin* 11 (1981) . See also Haggerty, J et al, 'A framework for the forensic investigation of unstructured email relationship data', 3(3) *International Journal of Digital Crime and Forensics* 1 (2011) .

[370] [2006] 2 Cr App R 12. In this decision, the court held that such evidence constituted implied assertions that were admissible under the Criminal Justice Act 2003. See further paras 6.54–6.58.

[371] Criminal Law Act 1977, s 1(1).

[372] *Saik* [2006] UKHL 18.

[373] Criminal Law Act 1977, s 1(2).

[374] Criminal Justice Act 1987, s 12.

[375] See eg the debate concerning the Fraud Act 2006 and conspiracy to defraud, discussed at paras 3.71–3.72.

[376] eg Terrorism Act 2000, s 59.

[377] eg *Invicta Plastics Ltd v Clare* [1976] RTR 251.

[378] Serious Crime Act 2007, s 52(1). For computer-related crimes, the Criminal Justice Act 1993 addresses jurisdiction for conspiracy and incitement offences ('Group B offences'). See also the Sexual Offences (Conspiracy and Incitement) Act 1996.

[379] *Smith & Hogan Criminal Law*, above, n 43, s 13.4.4.5.

in that attempt, that failure having been recorded by the system, communication has still been achieved, therefore incitement rather than attempt should be the specified offence.[380]

2.219 The inchoate acts of encouragement or assistance are of particular interest to the subject matter of this book in four areas; based on how the common law offence of incitement was used in the past. First, charges of incitement have been used against those involved in content-related crimes, such as child pornography, where demand for illegal content generates its supply. In *Goldman*,[381] for example, the defendant wrote a letter to a Dutch company, ESV, expressly asking for pornographic images of children, in response to their advertisement. The court accepted the prosecution's case that the request was an attempt to incite, through inducement, the distribution of images, contrary to s 1(1)(b) of the Protection of Children Act 1978.

2.220 *Goldman* has been criticized on the grounds that the initiative to commit the offence was taken by ESV, inciting the defendant to become an accessory to its commission.[382] This is analogous to contract formation in a retail environment, where the availability of the products is an invitation to treat, an inducement to the customer to make an offer. A second concern about the use of incitement in a cybercrime environment is where the communication is made solely with a machine (eg the web server), which raises potentially similar issues to the problems of deceiving a machine in fraud. Such an argument was rejected by the courts in *O'Shea*,[383] concerning the 'Landslide' child pornography website operated out of Texas, where the court held that the messages exchanged with the server incited the business that operated through that server.

2.221 Second, with content-related cybercrimes, a charge of incitement is often only resorted to when investigators are unable to find evidence of illegal content, such as child abuse images, on the data media seized from the suspect. In such cases, as illustrated by *O'Shea*, the relevant evidence will then become the payment data, such as credit card details, used in the subscription process for accessing the illegal online resource. However, proving that the nominated individual was the actual user of those details, beyond reasonable doubt, may become increasingly difficult as the scale of Internet credit card fraud grows, along with public awareness of the problem.

2.222 The third area of our interest in incitement is in respect of the supply of 'devices' or tools that enable others to commit cybercrimes, such as hacking. As Ashworth notes, possession offences may also be considered 'inchoate' in nature, since criminalization is predicated on the basis of what 'the possessor might do with the article or substance'.[384] One such consequence is to incite others to commit an offence. In a cybercrime environment, such incitement-related possession has been subject to distinct criminalization in respect of 'devices'.[385] Such 'devices' may obviously also be supplied by an accessory, in an attempt or conspiracy. However, the nature of the market for such cybercrime tools seems most appropriately characterized as an act of encouragement or assistance.

---

[380] *Grout*, Hull Crown Court, 21 April 2004, unreported.
[381] [2001] EWCA Crim 1684; (2001) Crim LR 822.
[382] Smith, JC, 'Case Comment', *Criminal Law Review* 823 [2001] .
[383] [2004] EWHC 905 (Admin); [2004] Crim LR 948.
[384] Ashworth and Horder, above, n 87, at 487.
[385] See paras 3.336–3.350.

A fourth area concerns acts of encouragement or assistance carried out by law enforcement **2.223** agencies in the course of their investigations. Proactive policing techniques in cyberspace may include, for example, the establishment of an undercover website offering illegal devices for the commission of integrity offences, or participation in a P2P network offering access to illegal content. Such acts may result in the commission of an offence of incitement by the investigator, as well as resulting in a stay of proceedings by a court for abuse of process through entrapment.[386]

Intermediaries

In two of our three categories of computer crime, the technology is an instrument used for **2.224** the commission of the crime. In a networked environment, such as the Internet, connectivity and transmission capacity are the instruments or tools, as much as the computers used and targeted by the perpetrators at the edges of a network. The provision of such connectivity, and related services, could therefore be seen as a key facilitating role in such cybercriminality. This view would potentially render communications service providers (CSPs) criminally liable for aspects of the services they provide. It would also operate as a significant disincentive to provision of such services, which would have a detrimental impact on the development and exploitation of such technologies, related services, and our Information economy in general. To address such concerns, *sui generis* liability rules have therefore been adopted in many jurisdictions, providing certain types of CSPs, as intermediaries in the cybercrime supply chain, with defences from both civil and criminal liability in certain circumstances.

The first part of this section examines these *sui generis* liability rules, particularly those **2.225** provided for under European Union law. In the second part, consideration is given to the possibility that the rapid liberalization of the telecommunications market, coupled with the *sui generis* liability rules, may create opportunities for criminals to enter the market for the provision of intermediary communication services.

Liability rules

A key public policy issue addressed by countries trying to facilitate the development of the **2.226** Internet and electronic commerce is that of the liability of the intermediary CSPs for the content that they provide access to and transmit to and from their customers. How can we promote electronic commerce if those that provide access and communication services are liable for the content that is made available through, or activities carried out using, those services? If liability is imposed, then CSPs may be less willing to provide the services or may impose certain controls on the types of access and services that are offered. The need to offer certain liability limits has also been seen as critical to ensure the continuing free flow of information and expression, such a feature of the online environment.

In response to concerns about the impact of intermediary CSP liability on the growth of **2.227** electronic commerce, as well as Internal Market concerns from some EU Member States already legislating in the area,[387] the eCommerce Directive[388] provides safe harbours for

---

[386] See paras 6.35–6.48.

[387] eg in Germany, s 5 of the Act on the Utilization of Teleservices (Gesetz über die Nutzung von Telediensten) Federal Law Gazette (Bundesgesetzblatt) I 1870 (1997), enacted as Art 1 of the Information and Communication Services Act.

[388] EU Directive 2000/31/EC on certain legal aspects of information society services, in particular electronic commerce, in the Internal Market, OJ L 178/1, 17 July 2000 ('eCommerce Directive'). The Directive has been transposed into UK law by the Electronic Commerce (EC Directive) Regulations 2002 (SI No 2013) ('2002 Regulations').

certain activities carried out by those that provide access to Internet-based services, so-called 'information society services providers' (ISSPs):

> 'service', any Information Society service, that is to say, any service normally provided for remuneration, at a distance, by electronic means and at the individual request of a recipient of services.[389]

These statutory protections are not available to those that only provide 'electronic communication services', which 'consist wholly or mainly in the conveyance of signals on electronic communications networks',[390] because historically such protections have been widely accepted for such 'common carriers',[391] and on the basis that criminal liability is not imposed on a strict liability basis, unless expressly provided for in statute.

2.228 The uncertainty in an Internet environment arose because the nature of the access and communication services being provided goes beyond the simple carriage of third party content that took place when using traditional voice telephony services. In particular, the nature of IP-based networks and the types of services made available over the Internet involves acts of storage and distribution of content that potentially change the nature of the acts that a CSP is engaged in, from 'common carrier' to that of supplier or publisher.

2.229 In respect of storage, the store-and-forward nature of IP-based networking means that a CSP will temporarily store a communication in the course of its transmission, since each individual packet of information is copied, stored, and then sent on to the next designated node in the communications chain.[392] In addition, CSPs offer storage capacity to their customers to enable them to offer content via services, such as the World Wide Web and cloud computing. In respect of distribution, the accessibility and availability of content transmitted by CSPs is of a qualitatively and quantitatively different nature from traditional communication services. While one-to-one was the standard model for voice telephony, one-to-many and many-to-many have become common alternative modes of communication. While information was traditionally sent from sender to recipient, communications now include the 'making available'[393] of information for a recipient to download from the sender or another online resource.

2.230 Where content is held by a person, for whatever period, two potential consequences arise: knowledge and control. First, the person may become aware of the nature of the content being held, whether illegal in itself, such as child abuse images, or as evidence

---

[389] Directive 98/34/EC laying down a procedure for the provision of information in the field of technical standards and regulations, OJ L 204/37, 21 July 1998, as amended by Directive 98/48/EC, OJ 217/18, 5 August 1998, Art 1(2).

[390] Directive 2002/21/EC on a common regulatory framework for electronic communications networks and services, OJ L 108/33, 24 April 2002 ('Framework Directive'), Art 2(c).

[391] While originating in England, the application of the 'common carrier' doctrine to the telecommunications sector has been a US development. See generally Noam, E, 'Beyond liberalization II: The impending doom of common carriage', 18(6) *Telecommunications Policy* 435 (1994) .

[392] Although a copy of the information is made at each node, it will generally only be stored until onward transmission, which usually occurs immediately.

[393] This terminology is used in the World Intellectual Property Organization (WIPO) Copyright Treaty, adopted 20 December 1996, WIPO Doc. CRNRIDC/94, Art 8 'Right of Communication to the Public'. The footnote to this article makes it clear that 'the mere provision of physical facilities for enabling or making a communication does not in itself amount to communication' within the meaning of the Treaty.

of illegality. Second, with that knowledge, the possibility exists that the content can be removed or acted upon in some other manner and/or passed on to the appropriate authorities, in cases of criminality, or others, where such material causes harm capable of giving rise to civil suit. Knowledge may therefore be a sufficient condition to attract criminal liability, while control may confer responsibilities and obligations. In an Internet environment, CSPs face a significantly enhanced risk of both consequences arising, compared with the provider of traditional conveyance services.

To reduce such risk, thereby facilitating the provision of such services, liability rules have **2.231** been introduced to address some of the activities of an ISSP, specifically 'mere conduit', 'caching', and 'hosting'. 'Mere conduit' services are akin to a CSP's traditional conveyance services, but are a subsidiary component of an ISSP's overall service offering[394] and will involve storage elements:

> the automatic, intermediate and transient storage of the information transmitted in so far as this takes place for the sole purpose of carrying out the transmission in the communication network, and provided that the information is not stored for any period longer than is reasonably necessary for the transmission.[395]

'Caching' is used as a means to limit the need for the retransmission of information from **2.232** the point of origin, therefore reducing network congestion and improving information provision.[396] In an Internet environment, caching occurs at two primary places, 'on' the network, by an ISSP in the course of providing services to its customer, and 'off' network on the end-user's equipment. An ISSP will cache the most popular pages of information requested by its users on a 'proxy server', while an end-user's browser software caches pages recently visited. As well as storage in the course of transmission, the service itself may consist 'of the storage of information provided by a recipient of the service', known as 'hosting'.[397]

For each activity, however, the protection from liability is subject to certain conditions, **2.233** designed to reflect the absence of knowledge or control.[398] The protection from liability for 'mere conduit' is only available on satisfaction of three conditions in respect of the content. First, that the ISSP does not initiate the transmission, ie that the decision to transmit or access the content is not taken by the ISSP, even though it may be determined in part by the operational parameters of the service.[399] So, for example, when a user sends an email message it may not immediately coincide with when the ISSP transmits the email to the intended recipient. Second, the ISSP does not select the recipient of the transmission.[400] Third, that the ISSP does not select or modify the information contained in the transmission.[401] The exercise of such editorial control over the information would render it a 'content

---

[394] If a CSP's services consist 'wholly or mainly' in conveyance, that service would comprise an 'electronic communication service'.

[395] eCommerce Directive, above, n 388, Art 12(2).

[396] ibid, Art 13(1).

[397] ibid, Art 14(1).

[398] ibid, Recital 42.

[399] ibid, Art 12(1)(a) and the 2002 Regulations, above, n 388, reg 17.

[400] eCommerce Directive, above, n 388, Art 12(1)(b).

[401] ibid, Art 12(1)(c).

service',[402] although this would not encompass technical manipulations of data in the course of its transmission or access that does not impact on the integrity of the contents.[403]

2.234 To be able to rely on the 'caching' provision, an ISSP will need to meet seven conditions, which means it will effectively have an evidential burden to discharge in the event of a claim.[404] First, any storage will have to occur automatically, and be intermediate and temporary. Human intervention will presumably be involved at the outset, setting the parameters for the caching attribute of the service, but there should be no on-going intervention on a case-by-case basis. An issue may also arise in respect of storage for back-up purposes, which may mean more permanent storage than that strictly required for the operation of the caching process. Second, there is a purposive requirement, ie the copy must have been made for the 'sole purpose' of improving transmission to service recipients. Third, the provider does not modify the information.[405] Fourth, any conditions placed on the ISSP concerning access to the information are complied with, such as under a copyright licence.[406] Fifth, any rules concerning the updating of information, such as a requirement to refresh the data on a periodic basis, are complied with.[407] Sixth, any mechanisms utilized by the supplier of the information to monitor its usage, from 'cookies' to digital rights management systems, must not be interfered with.[408] Finally, the ISSP must remove or disable access to the information where the provider has 'actual knowledge' that the source information has been removed, disabled, or is subject to a court order requiring such removal or disablement.[409]

2.235 Where any of the conditions are not met, then the ISSP may become exposed to liability. For example, with regard to hosting, as long as the service provider is not aware or does not have 'actual knowledge of the illegal activity or information and, as regards claims for damages, is not aware of facts or circumstances from which the illegal activity or information is apparent' then it is exempt from liability.[410] Once an ISSP has been put on notice of the illegal nature of the information, action will have to be taken 'expeditiously' to mitigate any possible liability.[411] This is generally referred to as 'notice-and-take-down'[412] or 'notice and action'.[413]

2.236 Under the eCommerce Directive, the need for intermediaries to adopt notice and take-down procedures may be imputed from the attribution of liability provision; although such procedures will vary in terms of legal nature and operation. Most service providers will self-provide through 'abuse report teams', to which users are directed to report material they have concerns about. Additionally, reporting may be directed through a third-party

---

[402] Framework Directive, Art 2(c). Such as an 'audiovisual media service' under Directive 2010/13/EU, OJ L 95/1, 15 April 2010 or a newspaper website: see *Papasavvas v O Fileleftheros Dimosia Etairia Ltd and others* [2015] 1 CMLR 24.

[403] eCommerce Directive, above, n 388, Recital 43.

[404] ibid, Art 13 and the 2002 Regulations, above, n 388, reg 18.

[405] eCommerce Directive, above, n 388, Art 13(1)(a).

[406] ibid, Art 13(1)(b).

[407] ibid, Art 13(1)(c).

[408] ibid, Art 13(1)(d).

[409] ibid, Art 13(1)(e).

[410] ibid, Art 14(1)(a) and the 2002 Regulations, above, n 388, reg 19(a)(i).

[411] eCommerce Directive, above, n 388, Art 14(1)(b), and 2002 Regulations, above, n 388, reg 19(a)(ii).

[412] See eg Reed, C, *Internet Law: Text and Materials*, 2nd edn, Cambridge University Press, 2004.

[413] Commission Staff Working Document, E-commerce Action Plan, 2012–15, Brussels, 23 April 2013, s 3.4.

organization, such as the IWF, which is industry-funded and self-regulatory in nature. Alternatively, as noted above,[414] reporting to a law enforcement agency may lead to notification to a service provider. Under the Terrorism Act 2006, the notice and take-down regime is given statutory expression; although failure to comply does not give rise to direct liability, but the loss of a defence against liability.[415]

A key question for an ISSP will therefore be: What constitutes 'actual knowledge'? Under the UK regulations transposing the eCommerce Directive, it is made clear that an ISSP shall 'not be liable for damages or for any other pecuniary remedy *or for any criminal sanction*'.[416] To endow such protection with procedural support, it is provided that in any criminal proceedings against an ISSP, where any of the defences made available under the 2002 Regulations is raised, with sufficient evidence adduced, 'the court or jury shall assume that the defence are satisfied unless the prosecution proves beyond reasonable doubt that it is not'.[417] 'Actual knowledge' would be a fact to be determined by the court. In *Bunt v Tilley*,[418] for example, the court noted that in order to be able to characterize something as 'unlawful' a person would need to know something of the strength or weakness of available defences.[419] To provide the court with guidance, and to effectively bolster legal certainty for the ISSP, the 2002 Regulations detail factors that would be considered relevant, including whether the notice identifies its sender, provides the location of the information in question, and indicates the illegal nature of such information or related activity.[420] **2.237**

However, an ISSP's liability for the third-party content may not end at that point. For certain content-related offences, such as child pornography, mere possession is considered a basis for criminal liability. In such circumstances, additional defences may need to exist to prevent the ISSP's employees or agents from being exposed to liability in the course of their legitimate activities.[421] **2.238**

Reflecting the capability of an ISSP to control content in certain circumstances, as noted above, the eCommerce Directive and implementing regulations also provide that an ISSP may be required by a court or administrative authority to terminate or prevent an infringement.[422] This would include, for example, complying with an injunction or notice not to publish or remove certain information from a website,[423] to disclose the identities of subscribers to a service,[424] or to block access to certain resources accessible over the Internet.[425] **2.239**

---

[414] See paras 2.91 et seq.

[415] TA 2006, s 3.

[416] 2002 Regulations, above, n 388, regs 17–19. For other jurisdictions, see the Commission-funded report, 'Study on the Liability of Internet Intermediaries', November 2007, available at <http://ec.europa.eu/internal_market/e-commerce/docs/study/liability/final_report_en.pdf>.

[417] 2002 Regulations, above, n 388, reg 21.

[418] [2006] EWHC 407 (QB).

[419] ibid, para 72.

[420] 2002 Regulations, above, n 388, reg 22.

[421] eg in 2003, the POCA was amended to provide a defence that: 'it was necessary for him to make the photograph or pseudo-photograph for the purposes of the prevention, detection or investigation of crime, or the purposes of criminal proceedings, in any part of the world' (s 1B, inserted by the Sexual Offences Act 2003, s 46).

[422] eCommerce Directive, above, n 388, Arts 12(3), 13(2), and 14(3); and the 2002 Regulations, above, n 388, reg 20(1)(b) and (2) respectively.

[423] eg the *Tomlinson* case concerning the list of MI6 agents. Discussed at para 3.23.

[424] See paras 3.187–3.213.

[425] *Cartier International AG and others v British Sky Broadcasting Ltd and others* [2014] EWHC 3354 (Ch).

2.240 ISSPs are exempt from any general obligation to monitor the information they transmit or store,[426] since any such obligation would effectively undermine the basis for the statutory protection. However, with increasing governmental demands for filtering of certain content at a network level, such as child pornography,[427] there is a potential conflict with such provisions. The 'mere conduit' provision, for example, states that the ISS provider is not liable where it:

(a) does not initiate the transmission;

(b) does not select the receiver of the transmission; and

(c) does not select or modify the information contained in the transmission.[428]

Where filtering is carried out on a user's egress traffic, for example preventing access to a requested URL, then this would seem to be effectively selecting the recipient, at (b), by dictating that the requested recipient does not receive the request, and the ISSP's web proxy becomes the effective recipient, returning a '403'—'forbidden' or '404'—'error or not found' response. Where filtering is carried on ingress traffic, for example blocking spam, then this would seem to be a selection of information, as provided at (c). The provision is drafted in terms of the transmission being 'provided by the recipient of the service', which would imply that the conditions are only applicable to egress, not ingress network traffic. However, while such an interpretation may address the filtering problem, it also exposes the ISSP to potential liability for interfering with egress transmissions.

2.241 The provisions provide liability safe harbours to encourage the provision of third party access to everything. They were, in part, a response to case law such as *Godfrey*[429] in the UK, where the ISP Demon Internet were found liable for making available a defamatory statement about Lawrence Godfrey; and *Yahoo*[430] in France, where Yahoo was found liable for providing access to information about buying and selling Nazi memorabilia. Both are examples where national rules imposed liability upon those that facilitated access to certain content, which under the eCommerce Directive would potentially be subject to limitation.[431]

2.242 Under the EU Copyright Directive,[432] the adverse result of broadening the scope of the reproduction right to all temporary reproductions of a work would have been to render those that provide Internet access services, for example ISSPs, potentially liable for copyright infringement, since the mere provision of access results in the creation of a temporary

---

[426] eCommerce Directive, above, n 388, Art 15. See C-70/10 *Scarlet Extended SA v SABAM*, [2011] ECR I-11959 and C-360/10 *SABAM v Netlog NV*, [2012] 2 CMLR 18. This has not been transposed through the 2002 Regulations, above, n 388, but is effectively achieved under the prohibitions contained in the Regulation of Investigatory Powers Act 2000, Pt I, Chapter I.

[427] eg BT's 'Cleanfeed' initiative.

[428] eCommerce Directive, above, n 388, Art 12(1), and the 2002 Regulations, above, n 388, reg 17(1).

[429] *Godfrey v Demon Internet Limited* (1999) EMLR 542.

[430] *League Against Racism and Antisemitism (LICRA), French Union of Jewish Students, v Yahoo! Inc (USA), Yahoo France*, Tribunal de Grande Instance de Paris, 20 November 2000.

[431] It is debatable whether mere notification by Godfrey about the defamatory statement would have constituted 'actual knowledge' on behalf of Demon, since under UK law a making of a defamatory statement is subject to a number of defences that would render the statement legal.

[432] Directive 2001/29/EC on the harmonisation of certain aspects of copyright and related rights in the information society, OJ L 167/10, 22 June 2001 ('Copyright Directive').

copy. To avoid such a result, the Copyright Directive creates a safe harbour in certain circumstances:

> transient or incidental and an integral and essential part of a technological process and whose sole purpose is to enable:
> (a) a transmission in a network between third parties by an intermediary, or
> (b) a lawful use
> of a work or other subject matter to be made and which have no independent economic significance . . .[433]

This provision effectively complements the protections granted under the eCommerce Directive, particularly that concerning 'mere conduit'.[434]

Similar statutory safe harbour provisions have been adopted under US law, although **2.243** only in relation to civil liability[435] and copyright infringement.[436] The US Digital Millennium Copyright Act of 1998 provides limitations of liability for an even broader range of activities than that provided for under European law: transitory copying, system caching, material stored at the direction of users and information location tools (eg hypertext links).

The eCommerce Directive provides for a period of re-examination every two years, **2.244** which includes 'the need for proposals concerning the liability of providers of hyperlinks and location tool services'.[437] To date, four Member States (Spain,[438] Portugal,[439] Hungary,[440] and Austria[441]) and Liechtenstein have adopted some form of extended protection from liability. In the UK, in June 2005, the then Department of Trade and Industry engaged in a consultation exercise, to seek views on whether liability protection should be extended to 'hyperlinking', 'location tools', and 'content aggregation services'.[442] The consultation document did not take a position on the issue, although

---

[433] ibid, Art 5(1); Copyright Designs and Patents Act 1988, s 28A. See also C-360/13 *Public Relations Consultants Association Ltd v Newspaper Licensing Agency Ltd* [2014] AC 1438.

[434] Under the Copyright Designs and Patents Act 1988, s 97A, a court can grant an injunction against a 'service provider' to stop providing service to the customer, where the 'service provider has actual knowledge of another person using their service to infringe copyright'. See *Paramount Home Entertainment International v British Sky Broadcasting Ltd* [2013] EWHC 3479 (Ch).

[435] 47 USC s 230(c). See *Zeran v America Online*, 129 F 3d 327 (4th Cir 1997). Otherwise known as the 'Communications Decency Act of 1996', the majority of which was struck down by the Supreme Court, as unduly restricting protected speech under the First Amendment: see *Reno v ACLU*, 521 US 844 (1997).

[436] 17 USC s 512(a)–(d), otherwise known as the 'Digital Millennium Copyright Act of 1998'.

[437] eCommerce Directive, above, n 388, Art 21(2). To date, however, only one such report has been published and no change was proposed: see First Report from the Commission on the application of Directive 2000/31/EC of the European Parliament and of the Council of 8 June 2000 on certain legal aspects of information society services, in particular electronic commerce, in the Internal Market (Directive on electronic commerce), COM (2003) 702(final), 21 November 2013.

[438] Law on Information Society Services and E-Commerce, No 34/2002, Art 17 (links and search engines).

[439] Decree-Law No 7/2004, DR No 5, series I-A, 7 January 2004, Art 17 (content aggregation services).

[440] Act CVIII on certain aspects of electronic commerce services related to the information society, 2001, ss 7–12

[441] Federal Act on Certain Legal Aspects of Electronic Commerce and Legal Transactions [2001] Bundesgesetzblatt (Austria) I 1977, 21 December 2001, ss 14 (search engines) and 17 (links).

[442] DTI, 'On the Electronic Commerce Directive: The liability of hyperlinkers, location tool services and content aggregators', Consultation Document, June 2005, available at <http://webarchive.nationalarchives. gov.uk/20090609003228/http://www.berr.gov.uk/files/file13986.pdf>.

the Government subsequently decided that 'there is insufficient evidence to justify any extension to these limitations'.[443]

2.245 Under Australian law, CSPs are not granted broad common carrier immunity, since they are under a general obligation to do their *best* 'to prevent telecommunications networks and facilities from being used in, or in relation to, the commission of offences', as well as give such help as is 'reasonably necessary' to law enforcement authorities.[444] However, in respect of Internet-based services, CSPs are offered certain protections from liability when engaged in hosting or transmitting Internet content:

> Liability of Internet content hosts and Internet service providers under State and Territory laws etc.
>
> (1) A law of a State or Territory, or a rule of common law or equity, has no effect to the extent to which it:
>
> (a) subjects, or would have the effect (whether direct or indirect) of subjecting, an Internet content host to liability (whether criminal or civil) in respect of hosting particular Internet content in a case where the host was not aware of the nature of the Internet content; or . . .
>
> (c) subjects, or would have the effect (whether direct or indirect) of subjecting, an Internet service provider to liability (whether criminal or civil) in respect of carrying particular Internet content in a case where the service provider was not aware of the nature of the Internet content.[445]

However, these protections are subject to strict obligations in respect of obscene material, which has been classified by the Australian Communications and Media Authority.

2.246 While the statutory liability protections discussed above are a *sui generis* policy response to the development of the Internet as an environment, at heart they do not represent a radical departure from traditional English law principles of criminal liability. Strict liability, except through statutory dictate, is very rarely imposed, while knowledge is a standard fault requirement conferring liability in certain circumstances. The provisions in fact represent a form of 'omissions liability', placing CSPs under a duty to act, but only where 'actual knowledge' can be shown, reflecting the principle of 'fair warning',[446] and only to expeditiously remove or disable access to the offending material, not to further report it to any law enforcement agency.

Participation

2.247 While the preceding analysis has focused on CSP liability for content provided by a third party outside their control, an alternative basis for criminal liability would obviously be if the CSP were considered to be an active participant in the criminal act, such as an accessory or conspirator; as stated in the eCommerce Directive:

---

[443] DTI, *Government response and summary of responses*, December 2006, available at <http://webarchive. nationalarchives.gov.uk/20090609003228/http://www.berr.gov.uk/files/file35905.pdf>.

[444] Telecommunications Act 1997, s 313(1) and (3), respectively.

[445] Broadcasting Service Act 1992, at 91, Sch 5, Pt 9.

[446] Ashworth and Horder, above, n 87, at 55.

A service provider who deliberately collaborates with one of the recipients of his service in order to undertake illegal acts goes beyond the activities of 'mere conduit' or 'caching'.[447]

In a traditional communications environment, such a scenario has not, to the author's knowledge, arisen. However, with market liberalization, we have begun to see such a possibility becoming reality. As the barriers to market entry have been lowered, there is an obvious opportunity for criminals to enter the CSP market, effectively moving down the supply chain to control facilities that comprise a component of the criminal activity, in a similar manner to the operation of banks and transportation networks by criminal organizations.[448]

In a UK context, such a situation has seemingly arisen in the market for premium rate **2.248** services (PRS). Premium rate services are content services, such as 'chatline' services and ring-tone downloads, made available over a communications service where the charge for the content is levied by the CSP which provides the communication service.[449] The monies generated from PRS are collected by the originating operator, are passed on to the terminating operator and then paid to the provider of the content service, minus the carriage fees retained by the operators.[450] The industry has expanded rapidly in the UK over recent years, which makes it an obvious target for criminality. Such criminality takes a variety of forms, such as competition lines without prizes and auto-diallers redirecting your Internet connection to a premium rate number.

Regulation of the industry is based on a co-regulatory model, with an industry-funded **2.249** regulator, PhonepayPlus taking lead responsibility for monitoring and enforcement. The regulation is applicable against the content providers, although the terminating CSP, with whom the content provider has a contract, has responsibilities to assist in compliance and enforcement.[451] The maximum penalty for a breach of the rules is currently £250,000.[452] However, reflecting the position on intermediary liability discussed above, the terminating CSP cannot generally be held liable, since they are not responsible for the content.

In May 2005, however, we saw the first arrests of people involved in the provision of an **2.250** allegedly fraudulent PRS, including persons controlling and operating the terminating CSP.[453] While this case has not resulted in the prosecution of those associated with the CSP, it does highlight the possibility that CSPs may be established specifically to assist in the commission of criminal conduct. Under the UK regime, a person wishing to establish a CSP is not required to obtain a licence, can obtain numbers from OFCOM on application and without discrimination, and does not need to own the circuits, switches, and other apparatus

---

[447] eCommerce Directive, above, n 388, Recital 44.

[448] In September 2006, the police moved against the First Curaçao International Bank, when it was found that every person charged with carousel fraud over the past two years had had an account with the bank.

[449] PRS is subject to a complex and convoluted definition under the Communications Act 2003, s 120.

[450] To assist enforcement, the terminating CSP is required to retain any payment due the content provider for a minimum thirty-day period: PhonepayPlus, Code of Practice, 10th edn, January 2004, s 3.5.1.

[451] ibid, Pt 3 'Registration and Responsibility'.

[452] The Communications Act 2003 (Maximum Penalty and Disclosure of Information) Order 2005 (SI No 3469). Such a penalty can be imposed for a breach of conditions made under s 120 of the Communications Act 2003, as provided for under s 96.

[453] See Richardson, T, 'Four arrested in £6m phone scam probe', *The Register*, 26 September 2005, available at <http://www.theregister.co.uk/2005/09/26/premium_rate/>.

that comprise a network.[454] While this clearly facilitates market entry, it also presents the unscrupulous with an opportunity to control a facility critical to their criminal conduct, as well as providing additional revenues and even statutory protections from liability!

F. Policing Cyberspace

2.251　One key issue in computer crime and cybercrime is the ability and availability of law enforcement resource to pursue those perpetrating illegal acts. The inability of governments to enforce laws in cyberspace is a widely held perception, seen as both a source of its strength and dynamism as an environment, as well as facilitating criminality. As always, the reality is more varied, with numerous examples of successful law enforcement initiatives being taken against Internet-based activities. However, the extent to which the perception of lawlessness is held can have an impact on computer crime policy, deter reporting by victims, and the allocation, and therefore the availability, of law enforcement resource. Availability can also be impacted by the potentially industrial scale of criminal activities in cyberspace, resulting in overload for those resources that do exist in a jurisdiction. In the area of child abuse images, for example, the UK authorities at all levels of the criminal justice system were swamped when required to handle the more than 7,000 suspects generated by the Landslide investigation in the US.[455]

2.252　Traditional law enforcement is generally thought of as a two-stage process, the investigation of illegal activities and the prosecution of perpetrators. Investigative activities obviously consume a greater proportion of the time and resource of law enforcement agencies than prosecutorial activities, as relatively few cases are ever prosecuted. The lack of prosecutions should be seen as a systemic feature of the criminal justice system, however, rather than necessarily a failure of law.

2.253　In reality, modern law enforcement strategies embrace a range of different approaches. Preventative measures would include encouraging computer users to take steps to better protect their devices and systems, so-called 'target hardening'; the issuance of public warnings about specific cybercrime threats,[456] as well the post-conviction treatment of offenders, designed to reduce the likelihood of re-offending. Disruption is also seen as an effective law enforcement strategy, especially when tackling organized criminal activities,[457] as well as those with a transnational dimension. Disruption measures can include so-called 'hackback' tactics, whereby online criminal resources are targeted by law enforcement through the use of similar techniques used by criminals to compromise the integrity of victims systems.[458] Another example is the disruption of criminal communications through 'DNS sinkholing', whereby a domain name associated with criminal activity is reassigned to a requesting law enforcement agency by a domain name registrar, and is then reconfigured

---

[454] Regulation is applied to 'providers' of an electronic communications network, which includes where the network or service is provided 'under the direction or control of another person' (Communications Act 2003, s 32(4)(b)).

[455] Interview with Peter Robbins, Internet Watch Foundation, 21 February 2006.

[456] eg in June 2014, the NCA issued a warning about two forms of malware, GoZeuS and CryptoLocker. See NCA, 'Two-week opportunity for UK to reduce threat from powerful computer attack', 2 June 2014, available at <http://www.nationalcrimeagency.gov.uk/news/news-listings/386-two-week-opportunity-for-uk-to-reduce-threat-from-powerful-computer-attack>.

[457] See HM Government, *Serious and Organised Crime Strategy*, Cm 8715, October 2013.

[458] eg evidence leaked by Edward Snowden suggests that Government Communications Headquarters (GCHQ) engaged in a Distributed Denial of Service (DDoS) attack against the Anonymous hacktivist

to issue non-routable addresses in response to requests, thereby preventing traffic communicating with the target resource.[459] The use of such techniques can generate significant issues in terms of the legality of such conduct, as well as the need for safeguards designed to prevent their abuse, which are examined further in subsequent chapters.[460]

Law enforcement is traditionally perceived as comprising tasks carried out by public author‐ **2.254** ities. However, the reality is that the 'policing' of computer crime involves a diverse range of public and private sector entities. Wall identifies four different levels at which policing activity takes place: Internet users and user groups; Internet service providers; state-funded non-public police organizations; and state-funded public police organizations.[461] For our purposes, therefore, use of the terms 'law enforcement' and 'investigators' applies equally to public and private entities or persons.

Public law enforcement

When we think about public law enforcement agencies, we tend to think primarily in **2.255** terms of the police, as well as the intelligence services where issues of national security are involved. That is clearly not the full picture in respect of criminal law enforcement, since in most jurisdictions a wide range of public authorities are granted powers to investigate and/ or prosecute persons for offences within their regulatory jurisdiction.

Such multiplicity of organizations was highlighted in the UK when the Government **2.256** issued regulations allowing designated public authorities the right to request 'commu‐ nications data' from communication service providers.[462] The first draft, issued in June 2002, attracted substantial public criticism for seeming to grant rights of access to so many authorities, such that the Government eventually withdrew the proposal. However, most of the public authorities listed in the draft already had existing statutory powers under which such data could be requested, although with little public recognition. These authorities have functions to investigate and prosecute specific conduct and offences, some that may involve a computer and cybercrime aspect, such as the Financial Conduct Authority (eg in an Internet securities fraud), the Serious Fraud Office and local authority trading standards bodies (eg in the sale of illegal signal decoders).

This section examines some of the key public sector entities at a national and international **2.257** level involved in the investigation and prosecution of computer and cybercrimes. The existence of appropriate institutional arrangements is a critical element in an effective law enforcement strategy.

Investigation

While there is a multiplicity of public law enforcement agencies, for general criminal **2.258** activities the police do take a leading role. The organizational structure of policing in a

---

group. See Schone, M et al, 'Snowden docs show UK spies attacked Anonymous, hackers', NBC News, 5 February 2014, available at <http://www.nbcnews.com/feature/edward-snowden-interview/exclusive-snowden-docs-show-uk-spies-attacked-anonymous-hackers-n21361>.

[459] Paganini, P, 'Sinkholes: Legal and technical issues in the fight against botnets', 28 May 2014, available at <http://resources.infosecinstitute.com/sinkholes-legal-technical-issues-fight-botnets/>.

[460] See further Chapters 3 and 4.

[461] Wall, DS, 'Policing and the regulation of the Internet', in Walker, C (ed), *Crime, Criminal Justice and the Internet* (special edn, *Criminal Law Review*), Sweet & Maxwell, London, 1998, at 79–91.

[462] See paras 4.206–4.207.

jurisdiction obviously has an important influence on all forms of enforcement, including the subject matter of this book. In England, there is a two-tier model, with currently forty-three local police forces and a number of national agencies with specialist expertise.[463]

2.259 At a national level, the institutional handling of computer and cybercrimes has evolved over the last two decades. The first dedicated agency was the National Hi-Tech Crime Unit (NHTCU), created in April 2001 as part of the National Crime Squad. At local level, each local police force has established specialized units. While such initiatives show recognition of the unique features of computer and cybercrime, they are sometimes undermined by traditional police procedures, such as the policy of rotating personnel on a regular basis, which erodes any skill base and expertise established.[464] In addition, even when skilled internal resource is developed, the discrepancy between public and private sector salaries and career structures will often result in a drain of personnel away from the public sector, such that some nations 'have more policemen with experience of running major computer crime investigations working for industry than in their law enforcement agencies'.[465]

2.260 Despite its successes at an operational level and in raising the profile of computer crime issues, in April 2006 the NHTCU disappeared as an entity and was subsumed into the SOCA, established under the Serious Organised Crime and Police Act 2005.[466] This development was indicative of the evolving nature of cybercrime, with organized crime dominating policing priorities in the UK. SOCA lasted less than ten years before being transformed into the National Crime Agency (NCA), within which sits the National Cyber Crime Unit (NCCU).[467] The NCCU was established from specialists in the SOCA Cyber unit and the Police Central e-Crime Unit of the Metropolitan Police.[468]

2.261 Within SOCA, 'hi-tech crime' was viewed as a criminal technique, rather than a category of criminal activity in its own right.[469] As a consequence, the general public profile of computer and cybercrime at a national level diminished and was subsumed into the broader, more secretive fight against organized crime. A new national agency was established to address child abuse over the Internet: the Child Exploitation and Online Protection Centre (CEOP).[470] Initially, CEOP was operationally independent, although subject to scrutiny by SOCA. It has since been subsumed into the NCA and rebranded 'CEOP Command'. While such institutional turnover may be justifiable from a policy perspective, it must also present an obstacle to effective law enforcement in the area.

2.262 As well as impacting public awareness about computer crime, the disappearance of the NHTCU raised concerns about law enforcement coverage. While the NHTCU was

---

[463] In the US, special divisions have been established within the FBI, the 'Cyber Division', available at <http://www.fbi.gov/cyberinvest/cyberhome.htm>; Department of Justice, 'Computer Crime and Intellectual Property Section', available at <http://www.justice.gov/criminal-ccips>; and within some of the US Attorney's offices, 'Computer Hacking and Intellectual Property' (CHIP) units.

[464] Wall, above, n 68, at 170.

[465] EURIM, *Policing the Internet*, Submission to the Internet Governance Forum, July 2006, available at <http://www.eurim.org.uk/activities/ecrime/eurim_IGF06paper.pdf>.

[466] Serious Organised Crime and Police Act 2005 (SOCPA), s 1.

[467] Established under the Crime and Courts Act 2013, Pt 1.

[468] NCA, 'National Cyber Crime Unit', available at <http://www.nationalcrimeagency.gov.uk/about-us/what-we-do/national-cyber-crime-unit>.

[469] Interview with Kevin McNulty, Home Office, 28 September 2005.

[470] See <http://ceop.police.uk>.

established to address both level 2 (national) and level 3 (international) crimes, SOCA was to focus only on level 3 crimes.[471] Such developments were likely to open up gaps in UK law enforcement activities, such that computer or cybercrime that has a regional element, beyond the capacity of a local force, or involves an international element but not carried out on an organized basis, may fall outside the current policing structure.[472] As a consequence, the Metropolitan Police established its own specialized unit, the Police Central e-Crime Unit (PCeU) in April 2008, which has since become part of the NCA.[473]

As well as national structures, international public law enforcement institutions and **2.263** cooperative initiatives between national forces have become an increasingly critical element in the strategic response to the policing of cyberspace. The most important international body is the International Criminal Police Organization (Interpol), which has established regional working groups on hi-tech crime.[474] Among its activities in the area, Interpol has compiled an 'Information Technology Crime Investigation Manual' to guide best practice in law enforcement, offers training courses to share expertise, and has established a 'rapid information exchange system' consisting of expert reference points in over eighty-five countries and computer crime message formats, ensuring certain minimum information is provided with a request for assistance.

In 2005, Interpol, together with national forces in the UK, Canada, the US, and Australia, **2.264** established the Virtual Global Taskforce (VGT) to address child pornography on the Internet.[475] The initiative is part-funded by industry, such as the PayPal. One purpose of this Taskforce is to provide policing on a level that reflects the 24/7 nature of Internet-based activities. With the countries involved, when one national police force 'goes to sleep', another will be beginning the day and can continue to police cyberspace.

Traditional policing involves varied modes of activity to prevent and detect criminality, **2.265** and apprehend perpetrators to be dealt with by the criminal justice system. Reactive investigations may be commenced in response to events, such as a denial-of-service attack, or information received, 'tip-offs', that a future event is going to occur or where persons are located. The police are increasingly expected to use 'intelligence-led' techniques to enable early intervention and apprehension. Police also engage in patrols, moving around an area as both a deterrent to potential criminals, as well as to reassure the public about their safety. In an online environment, such locational modes of policing continue to be relevant, as illustrated by the cyber-patrolling activities of the VGT.

Another mode of policing in a cyber-context is the possibility of actively interfering with an **2.266** online resource associated with a perpetrator, in order to inhibit the person from engaging in future such illegal activities. As noted above, such interventions may involve working with

---

[471] Statement by Caroline Flint, Home Office Minister, during consideration by Standing Committee D, 11 January 2005, Col 10.

[472] Interview with Peter Robbins, CEO of the IWF, 21 February 2006.

[473] Although PCeU has disappeared, it has become infamous for becoming the front for distributing a 'ransomware' virus! See eg Yoo Security, 'Police Central E-Crime Unit (PCEU) Virus Locked Computer? Removal Guide', 16 January 2014, available at <http://guides.yoosecurity.com/computer-locked-by-police-central-e-crime-unit-pceu-virus-how-to-remove/>.

[474] Interpol, 'Cybercrime', available at <http://www.interpol.com/Public/TechnologyCrime/default.asp>. The organization comprises 190 Member States.

[475] See <http://www.virtualglobaltaskforce.com>.

intermediary service providers, such as web hosts, to get the online resource taken down or rendered inoperable. Alternatively, the resource itself may be directly accessed and modified. Following the July 2005 terrorist attacks on London, for example, chief police officers called for new powers 'to attack identified websites'.[476] Edward Snowden revealed that the NSA engaged in such offensive activities through its 'Tailored Access Operations' group;[477] while the Government Communications Headquarters (GCHQ) has recently been openly recruiting 'white-hat' hackers to carry out 'computer network operations against terrorists, criminals, and others posing a serious threat to the UK'.[478]

2.267 The deliberate causing of damage by a law enforcement agency against a person's computer system or online resource would clearly constitute the commission of a criminal offence by the agency, such as an 'unauthorized act' under the Computer Misuse Act, potentially in multiple jurisdictions. A statutory defence or immunity from prosecution is therefore required, coupled with an authorization and supervision regime addressing such interference.[479]

2.268 It could be argued that such an approach was justifiable on the basis of a claim of self-defence. Where carried out by a private victim, such as an automated attack response by an Intrusion Detection System (IDS), any claim of self-defence would be based on traditional criminal law principles.[480] In the context of such an attack being a police action, however, the basis would likely be the right of a nation to defend itself.

2.269 Over recent years an increasing number of incidents have been reported of attacks against military and corporate systems, where the attackers have been identified as operating from within, and possibly sponsored by, potential enemy states.[481] As discussed earlier, such attacks have focused governments and policy-makers on the vulnerabilities of societies due to their dependence on computer and communication systems.

2.270 Under public international law, the United Nations Charter provides a Member State with the right of self-defence:

> Nothing in the present Charter shall impair the inherent right of individual or collective self-defense if an armed attack occurs against a Member of the United Nations . . .[482]

---

[476] See ACPO, 'Chief Police Officers recommend changes to counter the terrorist threat', Press Release 55/05, 21 July 2005.

[477] See Gellman, B and Nakashima, E, 'U.S. spy agencies mounted 231 offensive cyber-operations in 2011, documents show', *Washington Post*, 30 August 2013, available at <http://wapo.st/17sEENT>.

[478] GCHQ, 'GCHQ recruits Computer Network Operations Specialists', 12 May 2015, available at <http://www.gchq.gov.uk/press_and_media/news_and_features/Pages/GCHQ-recruits-CNO-Specialists.aspx>.

[479] In terms of immunity, see CMA, s 10; Copyright Designs and Patents Act 1988, s 296ZB(3); and Police Act 2007, s 92. In terms of authorization, see the Police Act 2007, s 93 and Intelligence Services Act 1994, s 5. See further paras 4.68 et seq.

[480] See further McGee, S, Sabett, R, and Shah, A, 'Adequate attribution: A framework for developing a national policy for private sector use of active defense', 8 J Business & Technology Law 1 (2013), available at <http://digitalcommons.law.umaryland.edu/jbtl/vol8/iss1/3>.

[481] eg DoJ, 'US charges five Chinese military hackers with cyber espionage against US corporations and a labor organization for commercial advantage', Press Release, 19 May 2014, available <http://www.justice.gov/opa/pr/us-charges-five-chinese-military-hackers-cyber-espionage-against-us-corporations-and-labor>. See generally Terry, J, 'The lawfulness of attacking computer networks in armed conflict and in self-defense in periods of short of armed conflict: What are the targeting constraints?', 169 *Military Law Review* 70 (2001) .

[482] Charter of the United Nations, 24 October 1945, 1 UNTS 16, Art 51.

While the drafters of the provision could not have envisaged the concept of computer-based attacks against national critical infrastructure, such a broad interpretation would seem reasonable, as noted by the US Department of Defense:

> If the international community were persuaded that a particular computer attack or a pattern of such attacks should be considered an 'armed attack', or equivalent to an armed attack, it would seem to follow that the victim nation would be entitled to respond in self-defense . . . by computer network attack . . .[483]

However, public international law obliges nation states to show necessity and proportionality in their response to any such attack, as would any private individual's action.[484]

2.271 The use of aggressive measures as a policing response against perpetrators of computer crime is an issue fraught with difficulties, on grounds of principle, legality, and practicality. It is another area, however, where the current environment, reflecting the language of a 'war on terrorism', may result in measures that in other contexts and at other times would not be considered acceptable.

Prosecution

2.272 The two leading prosecution authorities in the UK are the Crown Prosecution Service (CPS),[485] established in 1986 and headed by the Director of Public Prosecutions;[486] and the Serious Fraud Office (SFO), established in 1988.[487] The relationships between the police and other investigating authorities and the CPS and other prosecuting authorities have changed over recent years to become less distinct and separate in their functions and responsibilities.[488] This development has been led, in part, by the need to improve the workings of the criminal justice system in the face of new challenges, such as organized crime and the 'war on terrorism'.

2.273 When deciding to prosecute, the CPS is required to go through two distinct stages in determining whether to prosecute: the evidential stage and the public interest stage.[489] In terms of the former, the 'Full Code Test' standard is that there is objectively sufficient evidence for a 'realistic prospect of conviction', taking into account what the defence case may be.[490] When examining the evidence, two key considerations are whether the evidence can be used (questions of admissibility) and whether it is reliable (questions of probative value). These issues are examined further in respect of computer and network-derived evidence in Chapter 6. The second stage is described in the following terms:

> It has never been the rule that a prosecution will automatically take place once the evidential stage is met. A prosecution will usually take place unless the prosecutor is satisfied that

---

[483] General Counsel, Department of Defense, 'An Assessment of International Legal Issues in Information Operations', 1999, at 22.

[484] See generally Schmitt, M (ed), *Tallinn Manual on the International Law Applicable to Cyber Warfare*, Cambridge University Press, 2013.

[485] See <http://www.cps.gov.uk>. There was a third authority, the Revenue and Customs Prosecutions Office, which merged with the CPS in 2010.

[486] Under the Prosecution of Offences Act 1985.

[487] Under the Criminal Justice Act 1987.

[488] Ashworth and Redmayne, above, n 196, at 198.

[489] Crown Prosecution Service, *Code for Crown Prosecutors*, January 2013, available at <http://www.cps.gov.uk/publications/docs/code_2013_accessible_english.pdf>.

[490] ibid, para 4.4. There is also a 'Threshold Test', where it is not considered appropriate to release the suspect on bail after charge, but not sufficient for the Full Code Test (ibid, para 5.1).

there are public interest factors tending against prosecution which outweigh those tending in favour.[491]

There is therefore a pro-prosecution stance, once evidential sufficiency has been met. However, a prosecutor may decide that the public interest can be served through the use of out-of-court measures, such as cautions and conditional cautions, which serve to reduce the volume of cases entering the system.[492] The manner and timing for making determinations of evidential sufficiency and public interest clearly require the exercise of discretion on behalf of the prosecutor and, as discussed previously, is another point in the criminal justice system at which demands for legal certainty may conflict with the need for procedural fairness.

2.274 In 2012, in the wake of the phone hacking scandal and the revelations before the Leveson Inquiry of payments being made by journalists to public officials, the CPS issued guidelines for prosecutors when assessing the public interest in prosecutions involving the media.[493] The issue is particularly pertinent to phone hacking, because the offences being committed, under the Regulation of Investigatory Powers Act 2000 and the Computer Misuse Act 1990, do not contain a public interest defence, in contrast, for example, to the offence of unlawfully obtaining personal data under the DPA.[494] From an accused's perspective, the absence of a statutory defence substantially increases the risk of liability, being forced to rely on the discretion of the prosecution, rather than being able to present an argument before the tribunal of fact.[495]

2.275 In terms of prosecuting those that commit cybercrimes, the main policy concern is whether prosecutors have the necessary expertise and resources to support a police investigation and facilitate any subsequent prosecutions. As with the police, the CPS therefore initiated a training and awareness programme aimed at ensuring that personnel within each CPS region are given specialist training, while all prosecutors are given a minimum exposure to the technical and legal issues surrounding prosecuting such cases, such as liaising with expert witnesses. In addition, an international network of prosecutors has been established to share resource and expertise.[496] In some countries, such as India and Bangladesh,[497] specialized courts or tribunals have been established to hear computer crimes. This is designed to address the lack of experience and knowledge within the judiciary, sitting at the apex of the criminal justice system.

Private law enforcement

2.276 The origins and nature of the Internet has meant that self-regulation and private law enforcement mechanisms have been a central component of the regulatory response to

---

[491] ibid, para 4.8.

[492] ibid, paras 7.1 and 7.2. See also Ashworth and Redmayne, above, n 196, Chapter 6.

[493] Director of Public Prosecutions, CPS, *Guidelines for prosecutors on assessing the public interest in cases involving the media*, September 2012, available at <http://www.coe.int/t/DGHL/cooperation/CCPE/opinions/Travaux/OP_8_England_Wales_CPS.pdf>.

[494] DPA, s 55. See further para 3.35.

[495] In *R v Shayler* [2002] UKHL 11, the House of Lords held that no public interest defence would be implied into the Official Secrets Act 1989, which the guidance states is indicative that no such interest need be considered by the CPS (para 23).

[496] Global Prosecutors E-Crime Network, available at <http://www.iap-association.org/GPEN/Home.aspx>.

[497] eg Bangladesh, Information & Communication Technology Act 2006, Pt 2.

criminal activities in cyberspace. Such regulation operates along a continuum, substantially overlapping with public law enforcement activities at one end, and encompassing not only users and interest groups, but crucially the intermediaries that provide the infrastructure through which users access the Internet, ie communication service providers. As with public law enforcement, we can distinguish between the processes of investigation, where varying degrees of interaction with public authorities take place, and the possibility of pursuing a private prosecution.

Investigation

In terms of criminal investigations, industry may assist public law enforcement through **2.277** self-regulatory initiatives, such as the establishment and funding of entities with a specific remit to receive complaints, investigate criminal activities, and report illegal activities to the appropriate public authorities. In the UK, for example, the IWF was established in 1996 by Internet service providers to monitor and report on the availability of child abuse images hosted anywhere in the world and obscene and racist material hosted in the UK.[498] When notified of the presence of offending material, members have an obligation to remove such material from their service. While the IWF has strong support from the Government, its work is only legally sanctioned to the extent that a Memorandum of Understanding between the CPS and ACPO recognizes that it is a 'relevant authority' for the purposes of third parties wanting to report the existence of child abuse images.[499]

In the US, the CERT exists within a publicly funded institution, Carnegie Mellon **2.278** University, although with significant private revenues.[500] CERT alerts Internet users to security vulnerabilities, as well as engaging in research, providing resources and training. The CERT, or CSIRT,[501] model has been copied in numerous jurisdictions, including the UK[502] and Australia.[503]

In an age of ever-tighter public sector finances, the private sector provides an obvious alter- **2.279** native source of funding for the investigative activities of public law enforcement agencies. Organized credit card fraud in the UK, for example, is primarily led by a force, the Dedicated Cheque and Plastic Crime Unit (DCPCU), which is fully funded by the banking industry.[504] In the US, Microsoft has established, and part funded, a 'Botnet Task Force' to tackle the growth of malicious 'botnets' through providing training to law enforcement officials.[505]

---

[498] See <http://www.iwf.org.uk>.
[499] See CPS and ACPO, 'Memorandum of Understanding Between Crown Prosecution Service (CPS) and the Association of Chief Police Officers (ACPO) concerning Section 46 Sexual Offences Act 2003', first signed October 2004, available at <https://www.iwf.org.uk/assets/media/hotline/CPS%20ACPO%20 S46%20MoU%202014%202.pdf>. See further para 3.181.
[500] See <http://www.cert.org>.
[501] Computer Security and Incident Response Team.
[502] ie CERT-UK, <https://www.cert.gov.uk>, established in March 2014, and JANET-CSIRT, <https://www.ja.net/products-services/janet-connect/csirt>.
[503] AusCERT, <http://www.auscert.org.au>, located at the University of Queensland. For a list of national CSIRTs, see <http://www.cert.org/incident-management/national-csirts/national-csirts.cfm>. See also the members of the Forum of Incident Response and Security Teams (FIRST), available at <http://www.first.org/members/teams>.
[504] DCPCU, <http://www.financialfraudaction.org.uk/Police-The-dcpcu.asp>.
[505] Charney, S, 'Combating cybercrime: A public–private strategy in the digital environment', Paper written for the Eleventh United Nations Congress on Crime Prevention and Criminal Justice, 18–23 April 2005, Bangkok, Thailand.

2.280 In addition to the actions of recognized entities, cybercrimes may be reported to the police by individuals or groups operating as online or digital vigilantes. In *US v Jarrett*,[506] for example, a Turkish hacker supplied evidence to Alabama Police Department about two US citizens whose computers he had hacked and found child pornography, leading to their convictions.[507] To encourage online reporting, Microsoft established an 'Antivirus Reward Program' in 2003, offering financial rewards to persons who provide information leading to the arrest and prosecution of those responsible for releasing malicious code, such as worms.[508] Sometimes, groups take action against the perpetrators themselves, rather than involve the police, although such actions will themselves likely be criminal. The Metropolitan Police have admitted relying on cyber-activists to help tackle online fraudsters. A group, named 'Artists Against 419', takes action against fraudulent banking and lottery sites, including interfering with the bandwidth of such sites.[509]

2.281 Whether such initiatives are actively encouraged by governments and public authorities, or are a self-defence response by industry and users concerned about the risks and liabilities they are exposed to, the development of a so-called 'unholy alliance'[510] between the state and the private sector to enhance criminal law enforcement is an inevitable feature of cyberspace. However, such collaboration can raise important concerns in terms of vigilantism, infringement of rights and a blurring of accountability.

2.282 One particular area of concern is the information sharing that inevitably accompanies cooperative enforcement initiatives between public and private sector entities. While the disclosure of information from the private to the public sector may be considered a normal element of a crime prevention and investigation process, disclosure of certain information by public authorities to private entities raises more complex issues in terms of balancing the rights of the persons involved. With respect to intellectual property, disclosure of intelligence to a rights-holder can assist them to protect and enforce their statutory rights against infringers.[511] In the area of child abuse images, disclosure of conviction data to payment card companies can enable them to terminate any account used in the purchase of illegal images.[512] To combat fraud, public authorities can disclose to specified anti-fraud organizations, which includes the Telecommunications United Kingdom Fraud Forum Limited.[513]

---

[506] 338 F 3d 339 (Va, 2003).

[507] The case concerned the defendant's application to have evidence suppressed on the grounds that his Fourth Amendment rights had been infringed. The court held that searches carried out by private persons, unless acting as agents of government, did not engage Fourth Amendment protections. For a similar analysis under English law see *Rosenberg* [2006] EWCA Crim 6, discussed at para 4.56.

[508] See Microsoft, 'Microsoft Announces Anti-Virus Reward Program', Press Release, 5 November 2003, available at <http://news.microsoft.com/2003/11/05/microsoft-announces-anti-virus-reward-program/>. This initiative appears to have since been discontinued.

[509] See Espiner, T, 'Police maintain uneasy relations with cybervigilantes', CNet, 18 January 2007, available at <http://news.cnet.com/Police-maintain-uneasy-relations-with-cybervigilantes/2100-7348_3-6150817.html>. See also Artists against 419, <http://wiki.aa419.org/index.php/Main_Page>.

[510] Birnhack, MD and Elkin-Koren, N, 'The invisible handshake: The reemergence of the state in the digital environment', 8 *Virginia Journal of Law & Technology* 6 (2003) .

[511] Enterprise Act 2002, s 241A.

[512] The Data Protection (Processing of Sensitive Personal Data) Order 2006 (SI No 2068).

[513] Serious Crime Act 2007, s 68. See also Serious Crime Act 2007 (Specified Anti-fraud Organisations) Order 2008 (SI No 219) and Serious Crime Act 2007 (Specified Anti-fraud Organisations) Order 2014 (SI No 1608).

While each is justifiable on different policy grounds, restorative justice and crime preven- **2.283**
tion respectively; in each case, the effective consequence of the disclosure is to substitute
or supplement any state sanction imposed for the criminal conduct with a private remedy, which raises further policy issues concerning the proper limits of such an approach.
As examined already, one form of state sanction would be to restrain an offender from
using computers or accessing the Internet. An alternative approach, however, would be
for the police to send a report to the offender's CSP, who may choose to close his account
and, potentially, notify other industry players not to accept him as a customer; which has
been referred to as the 'e-death penalty'.[514] However, while restraining orders are subject to
judicial review and consideration in terms of human rights, disclosure mechanisms would
not be and could clearly be open to abuse. To try and address such concerns, European
rules governing the protection of personal data processed for the purposes of cooperation
between Member State law enforcement agencies expressly provides for the onward transmission of data to private parties, subject to certain controls.[515]

Prosecutions

Private persons may be involved in the investigative process, as well as any subsequent pros- **2.284**
ecution. They may be a victim of the cybercrime, or representative for, such as an industry
association, or will be a third party, such as an expert witness. Such persons generally act
in conjunction with public law enforcement agencies. However, under English law, private
persons have a general right, unless a statutory provision provides otherwise, to instigate
their own criminal proceedings.[516]

The Director of Public Prosecutions (DPP) has the right to take over the conduct of any **2.285**
private proceedings.[517] A court may also stay such proceedings for abuse of process, where
a person has already been formally cautioned by the police in respect of the criminal conduct.[518] Once private proceedings have commenced, public law enforcement agencies may
be compelled to supply any evidence they possess in respect of the alleged wrongdoing.[519]
In addition, it has been held that the police have the power to retain seized evidence for
the purpose of a private prosecution, even where public prosecutors have decided not to
proceed.[520]

In some areas of criminal law enforcement, private prosecutions may be a significant com- **2.286**
ponent of the enforcement regime. In the area of copyright infringement, for example,
rights-holders may lead the investigation and prosecution of perpetrators. In the UK, for
example, the Federation Against Copyright Theft (FACT) and the Federation Against
Software Theft (FAST)[521] engage in such activities. In respect of computer-integrity
offences, in June 2004, the All Party Parliamentary Internet Group recommended that the

---

[514] EURIM, above, n 465.
[515] Council Framework Decision 2008/977/JHA on the protection of personal data processed in the
framework of police and judicial cooperation in criminal matters, OJ L 350/60, 30 December 2008, Art 14.
[516] eg Prosecution of Offences Act 1985, s 6(1).
[517] ibid, s 6(2), which could then be subsequently discontinued on evidential grounds.
[518] *Jones v Whalley* [2006] UKHL 41.
[519] Under the Criminal Procedure (Attendance of Witness) Act 1965.
[520] *Scopelight Ltd and others v Chief of Police for Northumbria and others* [2009] EWCA Civ 1156.
[521] See <http://www.fast.org.uk>.

DPP adopt a 'permissive policy' towards private prosecutions under the CMA in order to encourage such actions.[522]

G. Concluding Remarks

2.287 Computer crime is a phrase that conveys little other than the involvement of a computer, while cybercrime simply denotes the Internet as the environment in which such activities are carried out. The extent and nature of the involvement of ICTs will vary widely according to the particular activities in question. Such criminality has evolved, with new forms emerging and disappearing, as fast as the technologies themselves have developed.

2.288 Computer crime has inevitably grown substantially over the years, as ICTs permeate ever more aspects of our lives. As we have also seen, the true scale of the problem can be difficult to measure and therefore trends can be hard to discern. Over recent years, however, the attention of policy-makers, governments, and legislators on the issue has moved beyond that of the technology itself, to an agenda that focuses on the problems of tackling organized crime and pursuing the 'war on terrorism'.

2.289 Computer crime can challenge existing criminal law, both the criminal code detailing substantive offences and procedural rules governing the investigation and prosecution of perpetrators. These challenges have required a re-examination and amendment of the criminal law framework to adequately reflect the needs of law enforcement and to better protect the victims of such criminality and society as a whole. The first element of that legal framework is the existence of an appropriate criminal code, which is the subject of Chapter 3.

---

[522] APIG, 'Revision of the Computer Misuse Act', Report, June 2004, para 112.

3

COMMITTING CRIMES:
SUBSTANTIVE OFFENCES

A. Introduction

In Chapter 2, we considered the various possible classification schemes for computer crime, **3.01** choosing to adopt a slightly amended version of the categorization used in the Council of Europe Convention on Cybercrime: computer-related crimes, content-related crimes, and computer-integrity offences. This chapter considers some of the offences under English law that are relevant to crimes carried out under those three headings, involving information, computers, and networks, particularly where cyberspace is the environment.

The analysis does not intend to be a comprehensive examination of all forms of criminal **3.02** conduct that may be engaged in or offences that may be applicable, rather it examines in detail aspects of all the major types of computer and cybercrimes committed, broken down into the three categories. Comparable offences in comparative jurisdictions are considered, where they provide alternative approaches to a particular activity, offence, or element of an offence. Particular attention will be given to common law countries, such as the US and Australia.

It should always be borne in mind that while the analysis proceeds on the basis of three **3.03** distinct categories, a person may obviously engage in a range of acts, in parallel or series, which encompass offences from all three categories. As much as criminals are creative in the opportunities they find to commit traditional crimes in innovative ways and new activities not previously conceived, so prosecutors often have to be creative in framing the charges against a suspect. Not creative in the unlawful and corrupt sense (hopefully), but in terms of prosecuting under a range of offences intended to capture adequately the criminal nature of the activity in the specific facts and circumstances of the case.

3.04 In recent years, the fight against organized crime has seen governments and law enforcement agencies shifting their attention towards the targeting of the proceeds of crime through money-laundering laws. Such laws consider criminality from a slightly broader perspective than other conduct-based crimes, focusing on the overriding purpose of the activity, ie making money, rather than a series of individual events, for example an unauthorized modification. As computer and cybercrime has become an element of organized crime, so such laws have increasingly been used.

3.05 While the objective of the criminal code is to capture specific wrongs, the nature of the real world may mean that the offence purportedly designed to address an activity may not always be suitable. Two seemingly similar cases of hacking, for example, may involve differing charges depending on specific circumstances, such as the means by which the perpetrator communicated with the accessed computer or the motivation of the perpetrator. An Internet fraud may be prosecuted on the basis of the financial element, the use of false credentials, the modification made to the system, or any combination of these or others that may be relevant. The 'patchwork' reality of criminal law must qualify our structured analysis of the substantive offences relevant to computer crime. The schematic adopted for this chapter does not describe the world as it is; it simply provides a framework for analysis.

B. Computer-related Offences

3.06 It is obvious that computers may play a part in the commission of nearly every form of criminal activity, from fraud to murder. It is beyond the scope of this book to review the broad range of English criminal law that may involve computers and networks, but instead this section focuses on the misappropriation or manipulation of information in order to cause loss to the victim or benefit to the perpetrator. In particular, we examine those areas of law which have given rise to particular problems where computers and networks are involved, either because the legislation was drafted in an era before such technology was envisaged, or because statutory drafting has failed to be robust enough to appropriately address the use of information and communication technologies (ICTs).

3.07 Fraud and forgery are the only two forms of computer-related crime addressed in the Convention, based on a perception that the legal interests represented under such crimes were not sufficiently protected against new forms of interference.[1] Forgery was tied to tangible documents, not intangible data, while property represented or administered by data facilitated fraudulent manipulations in a multitude of new ways.[2] These areas of law are often closely related, although we consider them as discrete topics. We also examine some particular activities that have flourished in modern times, such as 'identity theft', which are generally simply variations on forms of fraud and forgery. First, however, we look at the more complex issue of the treatment of information under English law.

---

[1] Explanatory Report to the Convention on Cybercrime, 23 November 2001, para 80, available at <https://rm.coe.int/CoERMPublicCommonSearchServices/DisplayDCTMContent?documentId=09000016800cce5b>.

[2] ibid.

Appropriating and misusing information

In acts of cyber fraud and forgery, the computers, networks, and processed information are **3.08** all simply being used as tools for the commission of a traditional form of offence. However, information may also be the *object* of the crime, analogous to the appropriation of computer or network components. While the theft of memory chips and laptops is beyond the scope of this book, appropriating and misusing information is an important area for consideration as information becomes an ever more valuable asset in our post-industrial economy.[3]

However, our starting point must be to ask whether 'information' is a sufficiently clear con- **3.09** cept to be capable of being an object in respect of which a criminal act can be committed. As Hammond succinctly warns:

> Lawyers everywhere have demonstrated a rather naïve acceptance of the utility of the term 'information' as the foundation of a legal concept. To every other discipline, information is not a thing or a commodity, it is a process.[4]

Even if we were able to define the concept, its breadth of scope would inevitably mean that criminalizing the appropriation of 'information' per se, without further qualification, would interfere disproportionately with other rights, particularly the right to freedom of expression.

So what conditions should be associated with information to render it susceptible to pro- **3.10** tection from misappropriation or misuse under criminal law? The general approach is to identify and articulate some form of 'entitlement'[5] in relation to the information, using criteria such as its subject matter, the investment involved in its creation, the relationship of the person holding, possessing, or controlling the information, or its locational setting. The range of offences examined in this book evidences each of these distinct but overlapping rationales for national legal regimes to grant criminal law protection to information.

Personal data, for example, may divulge details about a person to others, potentially **3.11** impinging on the individual's right to privacy. The law therefore entitles an individual to exercise certain controls over the uses made of his personal data, separate from any legal protections granted to the owner of such information. Trade secrets, on the other hand, embody commercial value, the investment of the owner in its creation (or acquisition) and maintenance as a secret. The law protects such investments, to facilitate the production of future information assets.

In respect of the information holder, we include rules that criminalize the disclosure of **3.12** information by persons in possession of that information as a consequence of their position. Under English law, for example, a number of offences have been established in respect of unauthorized disclosures in a regulatory context,[6] while in the US, it may be an offence for a federal officer or employee to disclose 'critical infrastructure information', 'individually

---

[3] For a general treatment of information in the modern economy, see Shapiro, C and Varian, H, *Information rules: A strategic guide to the network economy*, Harvard Business School Press, 1998.

[4] Hammond, RG, 'Theft of information', 100 *Law Quarterly Review* 263 (1984).

[5] See Calabresi, G and Melamud, AD, 'Property rules, liability rules and inalienability: One view of the Cathedral', 85 *Harvard Law Review* 1089 (1971).

[6] eg Data Protection Act (DPA) 1998, s 59(1) and Communications Act 2003, s 393.

identifiable information', or 'trade secrets'.[7] This is similar in kind to the treatment of information governed under contractual or equitable principles, except that the nature of the relationship that exists between the information and the person in possession is considered to be such as to warrant the imposition of criminal law remedies.

3.13 Computer-integrity offences can be seen as falling into a fourth criterion, location, since the information is only seen as being entitled to the protection of criminal law because of where the information is located, ie in a computer. Such offences do not simply extend existing legal principles to the new environment of ICTs, they are *sui generis* in that they offer protection to information not available in other locational settings. The analogous legal remedy for unauthorized access, or hacking, is the civil action for trespass. It is the perceived value of ICTs in modern society that establishes a public interest in protecting them and the information they process through criminal sanction.[8]

3.14 English law grants the protection of criminal law to particular categories of information, such as certain governmental information, under the Official Secrets Acts, and personal information, under data protection laws. However, except in the regulatory context referred to above and in respect of certain forms of intellectual property rights infringements,[9] English law does not grant any criminal protection to commercial information per se, such as trade secrets and confidential information. This section will give brief consideration to each of these categories in turn.

Official secrets

3.15 Espionage has always been a feature on the landscape of international relations. Governments, terrorists, and others use spies and other persons to find out what foreign governments and other entities are up to, particularly in relation to defence and national security matters. Cyberspace simply provides an alternative route for obtaining access to such secret information. A classic example of cyber-espionage was that of Markus Hess, who during the 1980s accessed some 400 US military computers from his base in Hanover, Germany, using ARPANET, the precursor to the Internet, to obtain information for the Soviet Union.[10] In terms of state-based foreign intelligence gathering, the Snowden disclosures have indicated the extent of US signals intelligence (SIGINT) activities, as well as those of the UK and others, against both its enemies and allies.[11]

3.16 Governments have long criminalized the acquisition and disclosure of certain types of governmental secrets. Equally, open and transparent government is a prerequisite quality of liberal democratic societies, which creates an obvious potential tension in terms of achieving an appropriate balance and determining workable rules. Under English law, the Official Secrets Acts 1911, 1920 and 1989 criminalize the acquisition and disclosure of certain types of information, although the nature of that information differs, as do the persons capable of committing an offence.

---

[7] 6 USC s 133(f), 5 USC s 552a(i)(1), and 18 USC s 1905, respectively.
[8] Wasik, M, *Crime and the Computer*, Clarendon Press, 1991, at 75.
[9] See paras 3.105–3.128.
[10] See further Stoll, C, *Cuckoo's Egg*, Pocket Books, 1998.
[11] See the Snowden Surveillance Archive, available at <https://snowdenarchive.cjfe.org/greenstone/cgi-bin/library.cgi>.

The Official Secrets Acts do not define what comprises an 'official secret', rather a primary **3.17** distinction is between persons external to government, who engage in 'spying' activities to obtain certain information, and those internal to government, who obtain information in the course of their duties, but may disclose such information inappropriately. In respect of the former, the offence focuses on the process of acquiring the information, while in the latter, on the act of disclosure to others.

In respect of 'spying' or espionage, any person may commit an offence where they obtain, **3.18** collect, record, publish, or communicate information 'which is calculated to be or might be or is intended to be directly or indirectly useful to an enemy'.[12] The concept of 'obtaining' includes copying, while 'communication' includes the transmission of the information.[13] The *mens rea* element is that the purpose or intention for the obtaining is 'prejudicial to the safety or interests of the state'. While it is for a jury to decide whether the *actus reus* has been prejudicial, the courts have recognized that the Crown has the right to decide what is in the 'safety or interests of the state'.[14] It is also an offence for a person to disclose information which he knows, or has reasonable cause to believe, has come into his possession through a breach of the primary offence.[15]

One means used to prevent the acquisition of an official secret is to criminalize the *actus* **3.19** *reus* of entering a 'prohibited place',[16] where such secret information may be located. The expression 'prohibited place' is defined broadly under the Act[17] and has been extended to protect non-governmental places, in particular 'any electronic communications station or office belonging to, or occupied by, the provider of a public electronic communications service'.[18] Such an explicit recognition of communication networks as part of the nation's critical infrastructure is illustrative of the shift in attitudes consequent on the 'war of terror', as well as government perceptions of its relationship with the communications industry.

While the concept of a 'prohibited place' would have been originally conceived in terms of **3.20** physical entering, there is nothing in the wording of the statute that would seem to prevent this being interpreted to include the 'virtual' entering of the computer and communication systems operated from a prohibited place, through hacking and associated intrusion techniques. Indeed, the use of various means to 'gain admission' to a prohibited place is expansively defined and would seem to potentially encompass any form of new or existing privilege or credential.[19]

In targeting conduct in respect of a location, the law protecting official secrets can be seen **3.21** as analogous to the indirect protection given to information held in computers, under the computer-integrity offence of unauthorized access. Indeed, in the US, the main statute governing computer-integrity offences, the Computer Fraud and Abuse Act, was initially directed primarily at the protection of classified information or information held on

---

[12] Official Secrets Act 1911, s (1)(c).
[13] ibid, s 12.
[14] *Chandler v DPP* [1964] AC 763.
[15] Official Secrets Act 1989 (OSA 1989), s 5(6).
[16] Official Secrets Act 1911, s 1(1)(a).
[17] ibid, ss 3 and 12.
[18] Modified by the Communications Act 2003, Sch 17, para 2.
[19] Official Secrets Act 1920, s 1(1).

computers 'operated for or on behalf of the Government of the United States',[20] before it was amended to protect a very broad range of public and private computer systems.[21]

3.22 In terms of controlling the disclosure of 'official secrets' by those operating in some manner from within government, there is a wide range of offences relating to different forms of disclosure, of which two are key. It is an offence for a member of the 'security or intelligence'[22] services to disclose without lawful authority information 'relating to security or intelligence' in his possession by virtue of his position.[23] With respect to the issue of lawful authority, it is a defence if the accused can prove that he believed he had the necessary authority, or had no reasonable cause to believe that he did not have such authority.[24] In *Shayler*,[25] the House of Lords rejected an assertion that there existed an additional defence of disclosure in the public interest, although the Court of Appeal in the same case held that the common law defence of necessity or duress of circumstance was potentially available to a defendant prosecuted under the Official Secrets Act 1989.[26] As a consequence, the Home Office stated an intention to amend the 1989 Act to remove the common law defence, as well as further detail the issue of authorization[27]; although such amendments have not yet been made.

3.23 It is also an offence for a Crown servant or government contractor to make a 'damaging disclosure'[28] without lawful authority of information falling into one of four categories:

(a) security or intelligence,
(b) defence,
(c) international relations[29] or confidential information obtained from a foreign state or international organization, and
(d) the commission of, or prevention and detection of, an offence.[30]

An example of the potential role of the Internet in such disclosure cases is that of Richard Tomlinson. In 1997, Tomlinson was convicted and imprisoned for a breach of the Official Secrets Act 1989, when he tried to publish a book concerning his career in MI6.[31] He was subsequently alleged to have published a list of MI6 agents on a website, which was reproduced widely across the Internet before government lawyers could get the information taken down, although Tomlinson's involvement was never proved.

---

[20] Computer Fraud and Abuse Act, Pub L No 98-473, Title II, Chapter XXI, s 2102(a), 98 Stat 1837, at 2190 (1984).

[21] Defined as 'protected computers' at 18 USC s 1030(e)(2).

[22] OSA 1989, s 1(9).

[23] ibid, s 1(1).

[24] ibid, ss 1(5) and 7(4). For a discussion of authorization in respect of computer-integrity offences, see paras 3.235–3.257.

[25] [2003] 1 AC 247.

[26] [2001] 1 WLR 2206. The Lords held that the issue had not properly arisen in the case and should not therefore have been the subject of a ruling.

[27] Intelligence and Security Committee, *Annual Report 2005–6*, Cm 6864, June 2006, at 31.

[28] OSA 1989, s 1(4).

[29] In *R v Keogh (David)* [2007] EWCA Crim 528, the Court of Appeal held that ss 2(3) and 3(4) should be read down and not in accordance with the natural meaning of the words used, since they imposed a reverse burden of proof, which was incompatible with Art 6 of the European Convention on Human Rights, adopted 4 November 1950, entered into force 3 November 1953, 213 UNTS 222.

[30] OSA 1989, ss 1(3), 2(1), 3(1), and 4 respectively.

[31] Reid, AS and Ryder, N, 'The case of Richard Tomlinson: The spy who emailed me', 9(1) *Information and Communications Technology Law* 61 (2000).

The operation of the regime protecting official secrets has been impacted by the coming into **3.24** force of the Freedom of Information Act 2000, which establishes a disclosure regime for governmental information based on proactive publication requirements and an obligation to respond to individual requests for information.[32]

The 2000 Act addresses official secrets through a number of different mechanisms. First, **3.25** the various security and intelligence service bodies are not considered a 'public authority' subject to the publication and disclosure obligations under the Act, which prevents direct disclosure.[33] Second, information held by a 'public authority' that has been supplied directly or indirectly by one of the security bodies is subject to an absolute exemption from the obligation to disclose.[34] Finally, information may be withheld by a 'public authority' where it considers that it is necessary to 'safeguard national security', is 'likely to prejudice' the defence of the UK or its relations with foreign states, international organizations, or interests abroad,[35] and no public interest in disclosure overrides the public interest in maintaining such an exemption.[36]

In the past, the regime for the protection of 'official secrets' has been criticized for being so **3.26** widely drafted that information only remotely related to the security of the state could give rise to criminal liability.[37] However, reform of the regime and changes to administrative law and practice, most notably the Freedom of Information Act, have diminished many of the concerns of those who felt that governmental information was overly protected by the criminal law. The Internet can be seen as further undermining the efficacy of such rules, since the global availability of secrets once published on the Internet can render national legal controls at best temporary, with the Wikileaks site being the most high profile example of this.[38] In the UK, this was also the situation the Thatcher Government faced with the publication of Peter Wright's book, *Spycatcher*, in the mid 1980s, when the government was initially able to obtain an injunction preventing publication, but once it had become widely available over the Internet after publication in other jurisdictions, a permanent injunction was refused.[39]

Personal information and data protection law

Widespread concern exists about the potential threats to our privacy in cyberspace. Such **3.27** threats can be broadly divided into two kinds: personal data being made available over the Internet and the monitoring of an individual's Internet-based activities. In the first scenario, whether or not an individual uses the Internet, personal data may be processed and made available over the Internet. From online telephone directories to Google Earth, information about us is now available to the world, exposing us to potential scrutiny of a

---

[32] See generally Coppel, P (ed), *Information Rights: Law and Practice*, 4th edn, Hart Publishing, 2014.
[33] The public authorities which are subject to the Act are listed in Sch 1, are designated by order under s 5, or are a 'publicly owned company' as defined by s 6.
[34] Freedom of Information Act 2000 (FOI Act), s 23.
[35] ibid, ss 24, 26, and 27. See eg the decision of the Information Commissioner in respect of a request to the Foreign and Commonwealth Office for information that was refused under s 27(1): Case Ref FAC0069504, 5 January 2006, available at <https://ico.org.uk/media/action-weve-taken/decision-notices/2006/359492/ DECISION_NOTICE_FS50069504.pdf>.
[36] ibid, s 2(2)(b).
[37] Williams, D, *Not in the Public Interest*, Hutchison, 1965.
[38] See <https://wikileaks.org/index.en.html>.
[39] *Attorney-General v Guardian Newspapers* [1987] 1 WLR 1286.

qualitatively different nature than that present in a traditional environment. The second category of threat concerns the ability to obtain personal data arising from our online activities. On the one hand, users are often not fully aware of the risks associated with disclosing information, such as credit card details, over the Internet, while the collation of 'clickstream data', recording sites visited, pages read, and links followed, enables a detailed profile of an individual to be constructed. On the other hand, the massive explosion in the use of social networking websites, such as Facebook and YouTube, illustrates the willingness of people to publicize intimate details about their lives over the Internet.

3.28 Intangible information has become a key asset, the fuel driving the 'information economy'. Personal data is one category of such information assets. During the dot.com boom at the end of the twentieth century, much of the value ascribed by stock markets to companies, such as eBay and lastminute.com, was based on the personal data they held: millions of registered users (*read* 'future customers'), rather than the products and services they had sold. However, personal data reveals our lives to others and, as such, its use and abuse engage and impinge on our right to privacy. As information increases in value, so the appropriateness of the legal regime protecting personal data and privacy becomes increasingly important, balancing the needs of individuals, commerce, and society as a whole.

3.29 In some jurisdictions, an infringement of a person's privacy is subject to direct criminal sanction;[40] however, this is not generally the case under UK law. Currently, personal information is protected under either the Data Protection Act 1998, as a tort of misuse of private information[41] or an equitable action for breach of confidence.[42] The Data Protection Act 1998 provides for a range of criminal and administrative sanctions, as well as civil remedies, while the latter are purely civil in nature.[43] This section therefore considers the criminal aspects of the data protection regime.

3.30 The UK's data protection regime was first enacted under the Data Protection Act 1984, to meet the UK's obligations under a Council of Europe convention.[44] The 1984 Act was subsequently repealed and replaced by the Data Protection Act 1998, which transposed the EU Directive 95/46/EC.[45] The 1984 Act had its roots in concerns about the impact of computerization and was solely concerned with 'automatically processed' personal data. By contrast, Directive 95/46/EC and the Data Protection Act 1998 extend the scope of protection to manual records as well as computer records, provided they comprise a 'relevant filing system'.[46]

3.31 Under data protection law, the protection offered to a data subject is on the basis of his or her 'personal data', defined in the following terms:

---

[40] Israel, Protection of Privacy Law 5741-1981, s 5.

[41] eg *Judith Vidal-Hall and others v Google* [2014] EWHC 13 (QB).

[42] eg *Campbell v MGN Ltd* [2004] UKHL 22.

[43] See generally Aplin, T and Bently, L (eds), *Gurry on Breach of Confidence: The Protection of Confidential Information*, 2nd edn, Oxford University Press, 2012.

[44] Convention for the Protection of Individuals with regard to Automatic Processing of Personal Data, ETS No 108, 28 January 1981.

[45] Directive 95/46/EC on the protection of individuals with regard to the processing of personal data and on the free movement of such data, OJ L 281/31, 23 November 1995.

[46] The DPA 1998 also protects certain 'accessible records' (s 1(1)(d)), as well as other unstructured manual records held by a 'public authority', as defined under the Freedom of Information Act 2000.

data which relate to a living individual who can be identified—
(a) from those data, or
(b) from those data and other information which is in the possession of, or is likely to come into the possession of, the data controller,
and includes any expression of opinion about the individual and any indication of the intentions of the data controller or any other person in respect of the individual.[47]

As such, the regime does not extend protection to information relating to legal persons, such as companies, even though legal persons have been recognized as having rights of privacy[48] and, as 'subscribers', are given rights in respect of electronic communication services.[49] In addition, the data protection laws of some European countries do grant protection to legal persons.[50]

The definition of 'personal data' is generally considered to involve an objective question of **3.32** fact in each particular case, ie that which identifies directly or indirectly an individual.[51] However, in *Durant v Financial Services Authority*,[52] the Court of Appeal recast the concept of 'personal data' under the Data Protection Act 1998 more narrowly, such that the mere mention of an individual within a document or, by implication, in any collection of data does not render it 'personal data' as defined by the Act.

In *Durant*, there was no question that the data identified an individual; instead, however, **3.33** the court focused on the meaning of 'relates to' in the definition, stating that data that relates to a person 'is information that affects [a person's] privacy, whether in his personal or family life, business or professional capacity'.[53] To assist, the court suggested two criteria for assessment. First, whether the data is biographical in nature, ie the more concerned it is with the person's private life and, second, its focus, whether on the person or someone or something else.[54] In taking this stance, the court has seemingly introduced a subjective privacy filter over the objective statutory definition. As a result of the *Durant* decision, the UK Government was involved in infraction correspondence with the European Commission,[55] although proceedings were never brought.

While data protection law objectifies personal information through the criterion of being **3.34** able to 'identify' a person, either directly or indirectly (although subject to the stance taken in *Durant*), the scheme of the Data Protection Act 1998 clearly indicates that data subjects have no proprietal interest in the 'personal data' processed by a data controller.[56] First, the

---

[47] DPA 1998, s 1(1).
[48] See *R v Broadcasting Standards Commission ex parte BBC* [2000] 3 All ER 989.
[49] The Privacy and Electronic Communications (EC Directive) Regulations 2003 (SI No 2426), Art 2(1).
[50] eg Italian Personal Data Protection Code, Legislative Decree No 196, 30 June 2003.
[51] This is the wording used in Directive 95/46/EC, above, n 45, Art 2(a).
[52] [2003] EWCA Civ 1746.
[53] ibid, para 28.
[54] See Information Commissioner, 'The "Durant" Case and its impact on the interpretation of the Data Protection Act 1998', Guidance, 4 October 2004, available at <http://www.nhsgrampian.org/grampianfoi/files/DurantCase.pdf>. The approach taken in *Durant* has been followed in *Johnson v Medical Defence Union* [2004] EWHC 347 (Ch) and *Smith v Lloyds TSB Bank* [2005] EWHC 246 (Ch).
[55] See Thomas, D, 'UK to respond to EU data demands', *Computing*, 20 October 2004, available at <http://www.computing.co.uk/ctg/news/1838724/uk-respond-eu-demands>.
[56] A 'data controller' is the person who 'determines the purposes for which and the manner in which any personal data' are processed (s 1(1)).

data protection regime does not grant a data subject a general right to prevent a data controller from processing personal data about him, contrary to popular perceptions.[57] Under the Data Protection Act 1998, provided the data controller legitimately processes the data in compliance with the data protection principles, a data subject can only prevent the processing of his personal data in two specific circumstances: where the processing is likely to cause damage or distress,[58] or where the purpose of the processing is for direct marketing.[59] Second, the remedies available against the unlawful obtaining of personal data from a data subject are only civil or administrative in nature, while such unlawful obtaining from a data controller is subject to criminal sanction, analogous to property-based crimes such as theft or fraud.

3.35 Under the Data Protection Act 1998, it is an offence to 'knowingly or recklessly' obtain or disclose, or procure the disclosure of, personal data or information contained in personal data without the consent of the data controller.[60] The offence was designed to address the growth of private investigation agencies in the mid 1990s offering services based on the acquisition of such personal information. The provision is clearly conceived in terms of obtaining data 'at rest', contained in some database residing on a computer system. However, the phraseology is wide enough to encompass obtaining through interception, ie data 'in transmission', such as was carried out by, and for, journalists during the 'phone hacking' scandal.

3.36 There are a number of defences that may be argued, including that the obtaining or disclosure was for the purpose of preventing or detecting a crime, or that the act was in the public interest.[61] It is also an offence to advertise that such information may be for sale.[62] The penalty is not custodial in nature, but a potential unlimited fine,[63] although to date such fines have been relatively low.[64] However, where the conduct involves a public official, the offence may form the basis for a prosecution for misconduct in public office, an offence at common law that carries a maximum sentence of life imprisonment.[65] Where the conduct has generated significant monies from the sale of unlawfully obtained data, a confiscation order under s 6 of the Proceeds of Crime Act 2002 may be obtained.[66]

---

[57] The key right granted data subjects under the DPA 1998 is that of access to personal data (s 7).

[58] DPA 1998, s 10. With regard to what constitutes 'damage' capable of compensation under s 13, see *Google Inc v Judith Vidal-Hall and others* [2015] EWCA Civ 311.

[59] DPA 1998, s 11. 'Direct marketing' means the communication (by whatever means) of any advertising or marketing material which is directed to particular individuals (ibid, s 11(3)).

[60] ibid, s 55(1).

[61] ibid, s 55(2). See eg *Rooney* [2006] EWCA Crim 1841.

[62] DPA 1998, s 55(4)–(6).

[63] ibid, s 60(2). Maximum fine of £5,000 in a Magistrates' Court and unlimited in a Crown Court.

[64] eg *Dhanju*, Information Commissioner's Office, 13 November 2014, available at <https://ico.org.uk/about-the-ico/news-and-events/news-and-blogs/2014/11/pharmacist-who-unlawfully-spied-on-family-and-friends-medical-records-prosecuted/>.

[65] *Attorney-General's Reference No 140 of 2004* [2004] EWCA Crim 3525. A Crown Prosecution Service (CPS) legal guidance notes that, while statutory offences should normally form the basis of any case, one reason for prosecuting for the common law offence is where 'the maximum offence for the statutory offence would be entirely insufficient for the seriousness of the misconduct'. See CPS, 'Misconduct in Public Office', available at <http://www.cps.gov.uk/legal/l_to_o/misconduct_in_public_office/>.

[66] In June 2011, two ex-employees of T-Mobile, Hames and Turley, obtained and sold customer information and were found guilty of twenty s 55 offences. They were ordered to pay £28,700 and £45,000 respectively within six months, with periods of fifteen and eighteen months' custody in default of such payment.

The insufficiency of the applicable penalties in the face of a rapidly expanding market in   **3.37**
the obtaining of personal data prompted the Information Commissioner to call upon the
Government to increase the level of penalty to a maximum of two years' imprisonment.[67]
An amendment was introduced in the Criminal Justice and Immigration Bill 2007.[68]
However, in the face of lobbying by the newspaper industry, concerned that such rules
could operate as a chilling effect on investigative journalism, the provision was amended
to grant the Secretary of State the power to issue an order raising the tariff at some point in
the future.[69] A new statutory defence under s 55 is also provided for in the Criminal Justice
and Immigration Act 2008:

> (ca) that he acted—
>   (i) for the special purposes,
>   (ii) with a view to the publication by any person of any journalistic, literary or artistic
>   material, and
>   (iii) in the reasonable belief that in the particular circumstances the obtaining, disclosing
>   or procuring was justified as being in the public interest.[70]

One can suggest that this addition was unnecessary, given the existing public interest
defence, but again shows the power of the media.

While the s 55 offence is intended to protect the privacy interests of the subject of the   **3.38**
personal information, such protection is indirect, since a similar offence does not arise
where personal information is unlawfully obtained from the data subject himself (unless
he could be considered a data controller). In the latter scenario, the entity obtaining the
personal data will be acting in breach of the first data protection principle, that data
be processed 'fairly and lawfully', which may give rise to administrative action by the
Information Commissioner in the form of an 'enforcement notice'[71] or a claim for compensation by the data subject if damage has resulted.[72] The criminal provisions therefore
seem to focus on the commercial interests of the data controller in the personal data
as an information asset, rather than personal data as an element of the data subject's
private life.

Trade secrets and confidential information

Industrial espionage is a feature of modern business, as processes and know-how have   **3.39**
become increasingly valuable assets. Today, such activities will almost certainty involve the
use of ICTs, whether as a means of accessing information, through hacking, spyware,[73] or
electronic eavesdropping,[74] or as a tool for removing the appropriated information, such

---

[67] Information Commissioner, 'What price privacy? The unlawful trade in confidential personal information', 10 May 2006, available at <https://ico.org.uk/media/about-the-ico/documents/1042393/what-
price-privacy.pdf>.
[68] Criminal Justice and Immigration Bill 2007, s 75.
[69] Criminal Justice and Immigration Act 2008 (CJIA 2008), s 77. Before issuing such an order, the
Secretary of State has an obligation to consult, including with 'media organisations'.
[70] ibid, s 78. Not yet in force.
[71] DPA 1998, s 40.
[72] ibid, s 13. On the scope of s. 13, see *Google Inc. v Vidall-Hall* and ors [2015] EWCA Civ 311.
[73] See *Ashton Investments Ltd and another v OSJC Russian Aluminium and others* [2006] All ER (D) 209
(Oct), where a Russian company was accused of remotely accessing the IT systems of the English claimant to
obtain privileged information relevant to ongoing litigation involving the parties.
[74] eg where emissions from a computer VDU screen are surreptitiously received and reconstituted for
viewing on external equipment.

as a USB memory stick. Espionage may be carried out by competitors or at a state level.[75] It may be achieved with the complicity of someone within the victim organization, with rights to access the information, or by external persons acting illegally either directly for themselves, or as a commercial service for others. Realizing the value of trade secrets is a complex process, which generally means that such information is obtained to order rather than on a speculative basis.

3.40 A high-profile example of cyber-industrial espionage is that concerning Mr and Mrs Haephrati, Israeli and German citizens operating out of the UK. In May 2005, in a coordinated operation, the Haephratis and a large number of major businessmen in Israel were arrested on charges of industrial espionage, carried out against competing Israeli businesses.[76] The Haephratis were accused of developing and deploying a 'Trojan horse' virus designed to penetrate the computer systems of the victim company and provide covert access to the systems for private investigators hired to investigate business rivals. The virus was deployed either as an attachment to an email or on a disk sent to the victim that appeared to contain a legitimate business proposal.[77] The illicitly obtained documents were stored on FTP servers located in Israel and the US. The Haephratis were subsequently extradited to Israel, entered into plea-bargain agreements with the authorities, and received reduced custodial sentences in return for providing evidence against the private investigators.[78]

3.41 From a legal perspective, a distinction must be made between protections granted to trade secret information itself and protections triggered by the means of obtaining the information. In the Haephrati case, for example, the extradition proceedings were carried out on the basis that the suspects had potentially committed offences under the laws of conspiracy to defraud and computer misuse, the former addressing the value inherent in the information and the motivation of the perpetrator, the latter concerned with its location and means of obtaining.

3.42 In most legal systems, the primary means of protecting trade secret information is through civil remedies, protections similar in kind to that granted to other forms of intellectual property.[79] Under the World Trade Organization (WTO) Agreement on Trade-related Aspects of Intellectual Property Rights ('TRIPS Agreement'), for example, the general obligation on Member States in respect of 'undisclosed information' is to provide natural and legal persons with the possibility of preventing disclosure,[80] only requiring state-based

---

[75] eg US Department of Justice (DoJ), 'U.S. Charges Five Chinese Military Hackers with Cyber Espionage Against U.S. Corporations and a Labor Organization for Commercial Advantage', Press Release, 19 May 2014, available at <https://www.fbi.gov/pittsburgh/press-releases/2014/u.s.-charges-five-chinese-military-hackers-with-cyber-espionage-against-u.s.-corporations-and-a-labor-organization-for-commercial-advantage>.

[76] Urquhart, C, 'London couple remanded in Israel's biggest industrial espionage case', *The Guardian*, 31 May 2005, available at <http://www.theguardian.com/world/2005/may/31/israel>.

[77] 'Court remands top Israeli execs in industrial espionage affair', *Haaretz*, 30 May 2005, available at <http://www.haaretz.com/news/court-remands-top-israeli-execs-in-industrial-espionage-affair-1.159878>.

[78] Leyden, J, 'Israel jails spyware-for-hire couple', *The Register*, 27 March 2006, available at <http://www.theregister.co.uk/2006/03/27/israeli_spyware_duo_jailed/>.

[79] See Freedman, CD, 'Criminal misappropriation of confidential commercial information and cyberspace: comments on the issues', 13 *International Review of Law, Computers and Technology* 147 (1999).

[80] Agreement on Trade-Related Aspects on Intellectual Property Rights, adopted 15 April 1994, entered into force 1 January 1995), 1869 UNTS 299; (1994) 33 ILM 1197 (TRIPS), Art 39(2).

protection for data relating to pharmaceuticals and agricultural chemicals that has been submitted to government agencies.[81]

However, as the value of commercial information has increased, many developed nations **3.43** have adopted criminal sanctions to supplement civil rules protecting the information itself. In the US, trade secrets are granted the protection of criminal law at a federal level.[82] An example of the type of case brought under the Act is *US v Lange*,[83] where the defendant, a disgruntled former employee, was convicted for offering for sale over the Internet trade secret information taken from his former employer.

Under English law, the primary means for protecting trade secrets is under the law for **3.44** breach of confidence, which is also used to protect governmental information[84] and personal information.[85] However, in common with data protection law, the courts have made it clear that confidential information does not constitute a proprietary interest in the information, with corresponding rights of control.[86] In *Douglas*, for example, the court noted that the plaintiff's right to protection 'does not arise because they have some form of proprietary interest ... that could be exercised against a third party regardless of whether he ought to have been aware that the information was private or confidential'.[87] In *Source*,[88] the issue at stake was the disclosure by pharmacists of anonymous patient prescription data. Lord Justice Brown, in considering the nature of the patient's right in information contained in a prescription, stated that it gave 'the patient no property in the information and no right to control its use provided only and always that his privacy is not put at risk'.[89] Confidential information is endowed with some proprietary characteristics, most especially in respect of remedies, but the grounds for equitable intervention to protect confidential information are not due to its proprietary nature.

English law of theft would also seem not to view information per se as 'property'. In the **3.45** leading case, *Oxford v Moss*,[90] a student took a forthcoming examination paper from a lecturer's desk drawer, photocopied it, and returned the original. The High Court when considering the appeal addressed two questions: first, was the confidential information a form of 'intangible property', as defined under the Theft Act, s 4(1):

> 'Property' includes money and all other property real or personal, including things in action and other intangible property.

Second, if the information was property, had the owner been permanently deprived of it?

---

[81]   ibid, Art 39(3). A relational rationale according to the scheme outlined previously.

[82]   The Economic Espionage Act of 1996, Pub L No 104-294, 110 Stat 3488 (1996), codified at 18 USC s 1832. Maximum penalty is fifteen years' imprisonment.

[83]   312 F 3d 263 (7th Cir 2002).

[84]   *A-G v Guardian Newspapers (No 2)* [1990] 1 AC 109.

[85]   *Douglas and others v Hello! and others* [2005] EWCA Civ 595, para 126. However, with the development of the tort of misuse of private information, breach of confidence has become less relevant in respect of personal information.

[86]   However, for a contrasting view, see Lord Hodson's comment in *Boardman v Phipps* [1967] 2 AC 46: 'I dissent from the view that information is of its nature something which is not properly to be described as property' (at 107B).

[87]   *Douglas* [2005] EWCA Civ 595, para 126.

[88]   *R v Department of Health, ex parte Source Informatics* [2000] 1 All ER 786.

[89]   ibid, at 796.

[90]   [1979] 68 Cr App R 183.

3.46 The court held that the offence of theft had not been committed because the information did not constitute 'property' under the Theft Act.[91] This decision has not been subsequently re-examined, although it has since been held that export quotas[92] and an electronic funds transfer[93] were forms of 'intangible property', which suggests that *Oxford v Moss* should not be applied too broadly.

3.47 Although the court was not required to decide the second question, Justice Wein noted *obiter* that the victim had not been permanently deprived of the asset, a copy had simply been taken. This view has received support from the Canadian courts in *Stewart*, where Judge Lamer for the Supreme Court held: 'one cannot be deprived of confidentiality, because one cannot own confidentiality. One enjoys it.'[94] However, in a subsequent English court decision, it has been held that a person can be 'permanently deprived' of something where the value of an object has been significantly affected,[95] which echoes the criminal damage decisions discussed below.[96]

3.48 The concept of 'property' used in the Theft Act is also reflected in other provisions of English criminal law, effectively extending the exclusion of information.[97] Under the Proceeds of Crime Act 2002, for example, the money laundering offences centre on the concept of 'criminal property', where property is defined in the following terms:

> Property is all property wherever situated and includes—
> (a) money;
> (b) all forms of property, real or personal, heritable or moveable;
> (c) things in action and other intangible or incorporeal property.[98]

In other jurisdictions, property has been defined more expansively to expressly encompass data held in ICTs. Under the Computer Crimes Act in the US state of Virginia, for example, 'property' is defined broadly to include 'computers and computer networks' and 'computer data, computer programs, computer software',[99] regardless of whether they are in tangible or intangible form, which leaves little room for doubt that information is subject to the protection of criminal law. This example offers a possible approach for English law, creating an offence of 'data theft' using a tailored definition of 'property' and locating the data within a computer, rather than expanding the general concept of theft.

3.49 The issue of granting commercial information the protection of the criminal law has been the subject of a Law Commission consultation paper, which has proposed the establishment of an offence of the unauthorized use or disclosure of a trade secret.[100] Such an offence would require that the concept of a 'trade secret' be clearly defined, and it has been proposed that such a definition should comprise a number of criteria. First, that the owner

---

[91] See generally Hammond, RG, 'Theft of Information', 100 *Law Quarterly Review* 252 (1984).

[92] *Attorney-General of Hong Kong v Nai-Keung* (1988) 86 Cr App R 174.

[93] *Crick*, The Times, 18 August 1993.

[94] *Stewart* (1988) 50 DLR (4th) 1, at 14.

[95] *Lloyd* (1985) 2 All ER 661.

[96] See paras 3.279–3.280.

[97] In civil law, the courts are similarly cautious about recognizing data as property; see *Your Response Ltd v Datateam Business Media Ltd* [2014] EWCA Civ 281 (concerning possession of a database).

[98] Proceeds of Crime Act 2002 (PCA 2002), s 340(9).

[99] Virginia Code, ss 18.2–152.2.

[100] Law Commission, *Legislating the Criminal Code: Misuse of Trade Secrets*, Consultation Paper No 150, 1997.

has 'indicated, expressly or impliedly, a wish to keep it secret'.[101] A conduct obligation is therefore placed upon an owner, similar in kind to that required in respect of authorization under computer-integrity offences. Second, the information must not be generally known, akin to the requirement that confidential information has the 'necessary quality of confidence'.[102] The third element is that the information has economic value arising from it being kept secret, which is the entitlement rationale for granting the protection of criminal law.

To commit an offence, a person would have to use or disclose the trade secret, knowing both that the information is a trade secret belonging to another, and that he does not have the consent of the owner to use or disclose it.[103] Such an offence would place the UK in a similar position to that existing in other industrialized countries.[104] **3.50**

To date, the Law Commission's initiative has not progressed, although one form of fraud under the Fraud Act 2006 may be applicable in certain situations: 'fraud by abuse of position'. **3.51**

(1) A person is in breach of this section if he—
   (a) occupies a position in which he is expected to safeguard, or not to act against, the financial interests of another person,
   (b) dishonestly abuses that position, and
   (c) intends, by means of the abuse of that position—
      (i) to make a gain for himself or another, or
      (ii) to cause loss to another or to expose another to a risk of loss.[105]

An example would seem to be where a departing employee is able to use his access rights to copy valuable data from his employer's IT systems, such as customer lists, in knowing contravention of company policy and for the purpose of disclosing to his future employer. Such a scenario is familiar in an employment context, giving rise to claims for breach of contract and confidence.[106]

Fraud

The range of fraudulent activity is not substantially altered by the use of computers, although they may facilitate certain forms, such as securities fraud (eg 'pump and dump' schemes[107]) or revive other forms that were previously in decline, such as 'long firm fraud' (now known **3.52**

---

[101] ibid, para 4.18.
[102] *Coco v AN Clark (Engineers) Ltd* [1969] RPC 41.
[103] Law Commission, above, n 100, paras 5.3 and 5.8.
[104] See Commission Staff Working Document, SWD(2013) 471 final, 28 November 2013, accompanying a proposal for a Directive on the protection of undisclosed know-how and business information (trade secrets) against their unlawful acquisition, use and disclosure, Annex 9, A9.3 notes that the UK is one of only four Member States that do not have a specific criminal framework for trade secret violations.
[105] Fraud Act 2006 (FA), s 4.
[106] eg *Shepherds Investments Ltd v Walters* [2006] EWHC 836; *Corporate Express Ltd v Day* [2004] EWHC 2943; *Gabem Group Ltd v Mahatma* [2002] EWHC 2221; and *Intelsec Systems Ltd v Grech Cini* [2000] 1 WLR 1190.
[107] When the price of a stock is artificially inflated through false statements made on Internet investment sites. See eg Lewis, M, 'Jonathan Lebed: Stock manipulator, S.E.C. Nemesis—and 15', *New York Times*, 25 February 2001, available at <http://www.nytimes.com/2001/02/25/magazine/25STOCK-TRADER.html>.

as 'break-out fraud'[108]). Computers may be involved in any aspect of the fraudulent process, from the information being input into a system, such as 'click fraud',[109] manipulating the operation of programs processing the information, such as 'salami' frauds,[110] to altering the information output derived from the system.[111] In each scenario, the computer is simply a modern tool by which the perpetrator's actions are carried out. Indeed, since nearly all forms of commercial transaction utilize the computer as a tool, it has been suggested that 'computer fraud' is 'no longer useful as a distinctive category'.[112]

3.53   Fraudulent activity may be designed to obtain money or other property, or to obtain the benefit of services. The intangible nature of services has meant that English criminal law addresses the obtaining of the services under a separate offence. Until 2006, a charge for fraud was generally brought under the Theft Act 1968, s 15, where property was involved, or the Theft Act 1978, s 1, for services.

3.54   In the majority of cases involving computers, the Theft Act provisions had been adequate to prosecute. In *Thompson*,[113] for example, an employee of a bank in Kuwait manipulated the bank's computers to debit certain customer accounts and credit accounts under his control. Later, when in the UK, he sent a request to transfer the monies to accounts in the UK, at which point the fraud was discovered. However, as with other areas of the criminal law, traditional statutory terminology gave rise to problems of application not anticipated before computers appeared. In certain jurisdictions, including the UK's Theft Act provisions, it is a requirement to show that a 'person has been deceived' for a fraud to be deemed to have occurred.[114]

3.55   English case law had further defined 'deception' to mean 'to induce a man to believe a thing which is false, and which the person practising the deceit knows or believes to be false'.[115] Where an innocent person was involved at some moment in a fraud, such as the processing of computer output, there did not appear to be any problem with prosecuting under s 15; however, where the process was completely automated, the courts had indicated that an offence may not be deemed to have taken place. In *Moritz*,[116] for example, it was held that the automated processing of VAT returns meant that 'deception' could not be evidenced in the obtaining of fraudulent repayments. Where a machine was deceived to obtain property, such as a withdrawal of notes from an ATM, then the offence of theft was generally

---

[108] Where the fraudster builds a reputation as a legitimate Internet trader, but then 'breaks out' by offering high value goods and requiring payments direct into a controlled bank account with no intention of delivering. See eg *Shuman Ullah* [2009] EWCA Crim 2397.

[109] When revenue is generated from the number of clicks an advertising link receives, there is an opportunity to artificially inflate the number of clicks. See 'Google click-fraud deal approved', *BBC News*, 28 July 2006, available at <http://news.bbc.co.uk/2/hi/business/5223330.stm>.

[110] Where software is programmed to round down accounting data, placing the surplus monies, representing small denominations, into a third account controlled by the fraudster.

[111] This categorization was proposed in the Audit Commission, *Survey of Computer Fraud and Abuse*, Her Majesty's Stationery Office, 1987.

[112] *Fraud: Law, Practice and Procedure*, LexisNexis, 2004, para 13.1.

[113] [1984] 3 All ER 565.

[114] eg Strafgesetzbuch (German Penal Code) (StGB), s 263, although a separate offence of 'computer fraud' has since been adopted (ibid, s 262a).

[115] In the words of Buckley J in *Re London and Globe Finance Corpn Ltd* [1903] 1 Ch 728, at 732.

[116] Acton Crown Court, 19 June 1981, unreported, quoted in Wasik, M, *Crime and the Computer*, Clarendon Press, 1991, at 105. See also *Clayman*, Times Law Reports, 1 July 1972.

also applicable, which rendered the 'deception' issue secondary. However, where a service is obtained from a machine, the absence of 'deception' was often fatal to the founding of a criminal prosecution under s 1 of the Theft Act 1978.[117] This was a reported problem in an Internet environment, where people gave false credit card details during the online registration process for accessing Internet services.[118]

The Law Commission first examined how to address this lacuna in English criminal law **3.56** in response to a request from the then Home Secretary to consider, among other matters, whether existing law 'meets the need of developing technology including electronic means of transfer'.[119] In 1999, the Commission published a consultation paper that recommended that, rather than taking the approach of extending the concept of 'deception' to include machines,[120] a new offence related to theft should be established.[121] This approach received general support and therefore became a recommendation in the Law Commission's subsequent 2002 Fraud Report.[122]

The Report noted that since the wrong is the dishonest obtaining of a service, such as **3.57** information, then the means by which the benefit was obtained should be irrelevant. In an Internet context, for example, a person may engage in some form of 'identity theft' in order to masquerade as a legitimate subscriber, using another's *existing* privileges. Alternatively, he may circumvent or exploit a weakness in the system, such as through a 'buffer overflow' attack,[123] in order to obtain *new* privileges to the service.

The recommendation made was for a new offence of dishonestly obtaining services where **3.58** payment is required, with intent to avoid such payment,[124] as well as repeal of s 1 of the Theft Act 1978. The 'dishonest' element of the offence, also present in the existing offence, follows the test established in *Ghosh*,[125] that it be found that the defendant's behaviour was dishonest according to the 'standards of ordinary decent people' and that the defendant realized his behaviour was contrary to those standards. For services where payment may not be required, 'in the hope of future gains rather than payment for the services themselves',[126]

---

[117] Under the Criminal Appeal Act 1968, s 3, it is possible for an appeal court to substitute an offence where 'the jury could on the indictment have found him guilty of some other offence'. eg a conviction under Theft Act 1968, s 15(1) could be substituted for an offence under Theft Act 1978, s 1, eg *Smith (Wallace Duncan) (No 4)* [2004] 3 WLR 229.

[118] Law Commission, *Fraud*, Report No 276, Cm 5569, HMSO, 2002 ('2002 Fraud Report'), para 3.35. In civil proceedings, a court found no difficulty in holding that a fraudulent misrepresentation could be made to a machine: see *Renault UK Ltd v Fleetpro Technical Services* [2007] EWHC 2541 (QB).

[119] Written Answer, *Hansard* (HC) 7 April 1998, vol 310, cols 176–7.

[120] As adopted in the Value Added Tax Act 1994, s 72(6):

... making use of a document which is false in a material particular, with intent to deceive, includes a reference to furnishing, sending or otherwise making use of such a document, with intent to secure that a machine will respond to the document as if it were a true document.

See also the concept of 'induce' in the offence of forgery, at para 3.91.

[121] See Law Commission, *Legislating the Criminal Code: Fraud and Deception*, Consultation Paper No 155, 1999, paras 8.36–8.58.

[122] 2002 Fraud Report, above n 119, Pt VIII.

[123] ie where an attacker inputs excess data into the buffer of a vulnerable program enabling him to take control of the program and, depending on the privileges of the program, take control of the host machine.

[124] 2002 Fraud Report, above n 119, Recommendation 3.

[125] [1982] QB 1053. For a criticism of *Ghosh*, see Palfrey, T, 'Is fraud dishonest? Parallel proceedings and the role of dishonesty', 64(5) *The Journal of Criminal Law* 518 (2000).

[126] Law Commission, above, n 121, para 8.15.

a common business model on the Internet, the Law Commission's other proposals for an offence of fraud by misrepresentation would generally be applicable, provided that such a misrepresentation could be made to a machine as well as a person, which it does:

> a representation may be regarded as made if it (or anything implying it) is submitted in any form to any system or device designed to receive, convey or respond to communications (with or without human intervention).[127]

3.59 In May 2004, the Home Office published a consultation document in response to the Law Commission's report.[128] It broadly followed the Law Commission's recommendations for reform of fraud law, including the proposed 'theft of services' offence.[129] The Fraud Act 2006 establishes a new offence of obtaining services dishonestly:

> (1) A person is guilty of an offence under this section if he obtains services for himself or another—
>   (a) by a dishonest act, and
>   (b) in breach of subsection (2).
> (2) A person obtains services in breach of this subsection if—
>   (a) they are made available on the basis that payment has been, is being or will be made for or in respect of them,
>   (b) he obtains them without any payment having been made for or in respect of them or without payment having been made in full, and
>   (c) when he obtains them, he knows—
>   (i) that they are being made available on the basis described in paragraph (a), or
>   (ii) that they might be,

but intends that payment will not be made, or will not be made in full.[130]

3.60 As well as a 'dishonest act', three other elements must be present. First, focusing on the conditions of service provision, the services must have been made available on the basis that payment has been, or will be, made. Second, the perpetrator must have obtained the services without making such payment. Third, the second *mens rea* element, the person knows that the services will be made available, or might be, but intends not be pay.

3.61 Another aspect of English fraud law that has given rise to problems in a cyberspace era is that of what constitutes 'property', a topic discussed already in respect of theft. The need to obtain property 'belonging to another' in the commission of a fraud gave rise to a serious lacuna in English law in the House of Lords decision in *Preddy*.[131] Here the court acquitted the defendants of mortgage fraud on the basis that the process of altering the accounting data recorded in the accounts of the lending institution and the mortgagor, by the amount representing the loan, did not constitute the obtaining of property 'belonging to another'. Instead, the court characterized the process as one where property, as a chose in action, is extinguished in one place and a different chose in action is created in another place. This

---

[127] FA, s 2(5). The terms 'system' and 'device' are not further defined.
[128] See Home Office, *Fraud Law Reform: Consultation on Proposals for Legislation*, May 2004 ('2004 Consultation').
[129] ibid, para 34.
[130] FA, s 11.
[131] [1996] 3 All ER 481.

decision required the government to push through emergency legislation creating a new offence of 'obtaining a money transfer by deception' to cover such activities.[132] However, *Preddy* illustrates the types of problem raised when trying to apply traditional criminal concepts to acts involving intangible information.[133]

The Fraud Act 2006 repeals the 'deception' offences under the Theft Act 1968 and replaces **3.62** them with three new fraud offences:

- fraud by false representation,
- fraud by failing to disclose information, and
- fraud by abuse of position.[134]

In each case, both dishonesty and intention to make gain or cause loss must be present, although an actual gain or loss does not need to be shown. The tariff remains at a maximum of ten years' imprisonment,[135] despite significant tariff inflation in other areas of cybercriminality, such as child pornography and copyright infringement, and the computer-integrity offences.

Gain or loss relate only to money or other property, whether temporary or permanent. **3.63** Property is defined broadly as 'any property whether real or personal (including things in action and other intangible property)',[136] which replicates that under the Theft Act 1968, and will not therefore extend to information per se.[137] By contrast, ss 6 and 7 of the 2005 Act address the possession and supply of 'articles' for use in fraud, but define the concept of an 'article' expansively as including 'any program or data held in electronic form', in order to 'future-proof' it.[138] It would appear possible, therefore, that a person may dishonestly obtain certain information, which does not constitute a fraud as it is not a gain or loss of 'property', but then uses that same information in a manner that does constitute an 'article' for use in a fraud. Such an asymmetric treatment of information would seem wrong both as a matter of principle and at a practical level.

While prior to the Fraud Act 2006, the offence of fraud faced problems when ICTs **3.64** were involved, the process of reform did not involve the inclusion of express provisions referring to such technologies, except in respect of the making a misrepresentation. The current law of fraud can therefore be seen as technology-neutral, remedying the previous regime, which discriminated against ICT-based fraud. By contrast, international legal instruments in the field of computer and cybercrime have chosen to recommend

---

[132] Theft Act 1968, s 15A. For an example of its application, see *Holmes v The Governor of Brixton Prison and another* [2004] EWHC 2020 (Admin); [2004] All ER (D) 111.

[133] See also *Smith (Wallace Duncan) (No 4)* [2004] 3 WLR 229. A decision similar to *Preddy* from New Zealand, *R v Wilkinson* [1999] 1 NZLR 403, held that electronic funds were not a thing 'capable of being stolen'.

[134] FA, ss 2–4, respectively.

[135] ibid, s 1(3)(b).

[136] ibid, s 5(2).

[137] 2004 Consultation, above, n 128, para 31.

[138] FA, s 8(1); Home Office, *Fraud Law Reform: Government Response to Consultations*, November 2004, para 50 ('2004 Response'). FA, s 6 replicates the 'going equipped' provision in the Theft Act 1968, s 25, although without the requirement that the person be 'not at his place of abode'.

specific fraud offences in respect of computers. The Council of Europe Convention on Cybercrime, for example, has formulated an offence of computer-related fraud in the following terms:

> Each Party shall adopt such legislative and other measures as may be necessary to establish as criminal offences under its domestic law, when committed intentionally and without right, the causing of a loss of property to another by:
> (a) any input, alteration, deletion or suppression of computer data,
> (b) any interference with the functioning of a computer system,
> with fraudulent or dishonest intent of procuring, without right, an economic benefit for oneself or for another.[139]

As with the Fraud Act 2006, this formulation focuses on the intent of the perpetrator rather than the mind of the victim, as required under the concept of 'deception'. In (a), it attempts to detail the different means by which data may be manipulated.[140] The possibilities of hardware manipulations are covered by (b).[141] Jurisdictions may have differing conceptions of 'property', although it was conceived as a 'broad notion', including 'intangibles with an economic value'.[142] However, English law remains somewhat hostile to the treatment of information as property.

3.65 Under the Convention, a state may choose whether to meet its obligations through its general rules of fraud or through specific provision. The UK has opted for the former approach. The potential disadvantage of the latter approach is that it can be seen as inappropriately focusing attention on the mechanics of the fraudulent act, rather than the overriding objective, the obtaining of economic benefits.

3.66 As an example of the latter approach, focusing on the means of committing the fraudulent act, under US law there is an offence of 'wire fraud':

> any scheme or artifice to defraud, or for obtaining money or property by means of false or fraudulent pretenses, representations, or promises, transmits or causes to be transmitted by means of wire, radio, or television communication . . . any writings, signs, signals, pictures, or sounds for the purpose of executing such scheme or artifice.[143]

This offence reflects the role of the communication of information in describing the criminal act, and has proved invaluable against cyber-frauds.[144] In the UK, the only similar offences are that of conspiracy to defraud, where communication between the parties is central to evidencing the agreement, and money laundering, where the movement of money is key.

---

[139] Convention on Cybercrime, signed 23 November 2001, entered into force 1 July 2004, ETS No 185, Art 8. See also Council Framework Decision 2001/413/JHA of 28 May 2001 combating fraud and counterfeiting of non-cash means of payment, OJ L 149/1, 2 June 2001, Art 6.

[140] See also the Belgian Computer Crime Act 2000, [2000] CLE 280, which defines different types of act: 'by entering in a computer system, altering or erasing data which are stored, processed or transmitted by a computer system, or by altering by any technological means the possible use of data in a computer system' (ibid, Art 5(1)).

[141] Explanatory Report to the Convention on Cybercrime, above, n 1, para 87.

[142] ibid, para 88.

[143] 18 USC s 1343.

[144] In *Carpenter*, 484 US 19 (1987), at 25, it was held that wire fraud extended to intangible property rights, which includes confidential business information.

False accounting

As well as fraud, theft, and forgery, the nature of English criminal law means that there **3.67**
may be alternative or supplementary charges that may be brought against a person engaged
in computer-related fraud, such as false accounting. False accounting is defined in the
following terms:

(1) Where a person dishonestly, with a view to gain for himself or another or with intent to
cause loss to another—
 (a) destroys, defaces, conceals or falsifies any account or any record or document made
 or required for any accounting purpose; or
 (a) destroys, defaces, conceals or falsifies any account or any record or document made
 or required for any accounting purpose; or
 (b) in furnishing information for any purpose produces or makes use of any account,
 or any such record or document as aforesaid, which to his knowledge is or may be
 misleading, false or deceptive in a material particular;
 he shall, on conviction on indictment, be liable to imprisonment for a term not exceeding seven years.[145]

It therefore comprises two distinct offences. The first concerns actions carried out in respect
of information contained in the account, record, or document, akin to forgery, while the
second is concerned with the use of information possessed by the perpetrator. A perpetrator
will generally be involved in the commission of both forms of conduct, although he may
not be. The terms 'account', 'record', and 'document' are given the meanings associated
with their normal usage and would certainly encompass digital formats. Whether a record
or document is required for an accounting purpose will be a question of fact that the prosecution will need to prove.

While false accounting offences are often used in conjunction with fraudulent transactions, **3.68**
they will often also overlap with other offences, such as forgery, in respect of s 17(1)(b) and
the computer-integrity offence of unauthorized acts, under s 3 of the Computer Misuse Act
1990 (CMA), in respect of s 17(1)(a).

Conspiracy to defraud

One of the most frequently used charges in cases of fraud is the common law offence of **3.69**
conspiracy to defraud. There are two main forms, although we are concerned with that
described by Viscount Dilhorne in *Scott v Metropolitan Police Commissioner*:[146]

 . . . an agreement by two or more [persons] by dishonesty to deprive a person of something
 which is his or to which he is or would be or might be entitled [or] an agreement by two
 or more by dishonesty to injure some proprietary rights of his suffices to constitute an
 offence . .

The offence overlaps with the offence of statutory conspiracy,[147] although its advantage **3.70**
is that specific substantive offences do not have to be identified in the indictment, where
uncertainty exists.[148] While evidence of an agreement is required, the agreement does not
need to involve the commission of a substantive offence. So, for example, communications

---

[145] Theft Act 1968, s 17.
[146] [1975] AC 819.
[147] See paras 2.215–2.217.
[148] Ormerod, D (ed), *Blackstone's Criminal Practice 2016*, 26th edn, Oxford University Press, 2015, paras
A5.64 et seq.

between hackers agreeing to establish a bulletin board for distributing malware or cracking tools would be sufficient for the offence of conspiracy to defraud to be made out, even though no evidence may exist that the perpetrators intended to use the tools themselves.[149]

3.71 The offence continues in existence despite various attempts to abolish it. Arguments in favour of its retention are the uncertainty created by 'developing technology', its use in intellectual property cases and situations where no economic loss has been inflicted.[150] As a result, the Government decided to maintain the offence.[151]

3.72 However, the courts have also made it clear that 'conduct falling within the terms of a specific statutory provision should be prosecuted under that provision', rather than a common law offence, such as conspiracy to defraud, where the penalty is unlimited and may not provide the same defences.[152] Such judicial sentiment should further constrain reliance on the offence of conspiracy to defraud against cybercrimes in favour of more specific offences.[153]

'Identity theft'

3.73 One aspect of fraud which has received considerable publicity over recent years has been the phenomenon of so-called 'identity theft', where a person's identification[154] details are obtained through various surreptitious methods, from rifling through the contents of household dustbins to 'phishing', where emails are sent to individuals falsely claiming to originate from their financial institutions and asking them to re-register their account details at a replica website,[155] or contain a virus which surreptitiously obtains and discloses an individual's confidential details.[156] In a 2005 case, a gang operated a phishing scam against eBay retail accounts, netting over £200,000 from fraudulent sales;[157] while in another, one of the perpetrators obtained the details of some 765 bank accounts, which he then sold on to other criminals for a fee of 3–5 per cent of the value of the respective credit balances.[158] However achieved, the objective is to obtain details about a person in order to enable a fraudulent operation to be carried out, either using the person's existing privileges or creating new privileges under that person's identity. Identity theft can therefore be viewed as a form of preliminary conduct in the course of committing fraud; although obviously other criminal acts may be the ultimate objective. Alternatively, it may be considered an aggravating circumstance in respect of the other criminal act, resulting in an enhanced sanction against the perpetrator.[159]

---

[149] See eg *Hollinshead* [1985] AC 975, which concerned devices that falsified utility meters.

[150] 2004 Response, above, n 138, paras 40 et seq.

[151] See Attorney General's Office, 'Guidelines for prosecutors on the use of the common law offence of conspiracy to defraud', 29 November 2012, available at <https://www.gov.uk/use-of-the-common-law-offence-of-conspiracy-to-defraud--6>.

[152] See the comments of Lord Bingham in *Rimmington* [2005] UKHL 63; [2006] HRLR 3, at 30.

[153] This may have implications for extradition cases.

[154] The details involved may not always identify a person (ie who you are); rather they may authenticate (ie are you genuine) or authorize (ie what you can do) a person without necessarily identifying a specific individual. See further Schneier, B, *Beyond Fear*, Copernicus Books, 2003, Chapter 13.

[155] See written answer from Caroline Flint, Home Office Minister, to Mr Brian Gardiner MP, 18 November 2003, House of Commons Hansard. A new technique, known as 'pharming' involves placing a Trojan program on the user's machine, which diverts the user's web browser when logging on to the user's online bank account.

[156] eg the Mimail.J virus used against the PayPal payment service. See 'Virus tries to con PayPal users', BBC News, 19 November 2003, available at <http://news.bbc.co.uk/1/hi/technology/3281307.stm>.

[157] *Daniel Levi & others* [2005] ECLR 5(5).

[158] *Jabeth and Babatunde* [2014] EWCA Crim 476.

[159] eg EU Directive 13/40/EU on attacks against information systems, OJ L 218/8, 14 August 2013, Art 9(5).

The vulnerability of personal information in an Internet environment and the growth of **3.74** 'identity theft' have led to calls for specific legislative measures to be adopted. In the US, for example, the Identity Theft and Assumption Deterrence Act of 1998, establishes a range of offences related to the abuse of identification documents, including:

> Knowingly transfers or uses, without lawful authority, a means of identification of another person with the intent to commit, or to aid and abet, any unlawful activity . . .[160]

The tariffs under the Act range from five years' to fifteen years' imprisonment.[161] In 2004, the Act was amended to insert an offence of 'aggravated identity theft',[162] which imposes additional prison terms on those who knowingly transfer, possess, or use a means of identifying another person in the course of the commission of a felony or terrorist offence.[163]

Under English criminal law, there is a range of potentially applicable offences being com- **3.75** mitted depending on the form of 'identity theft' carried out. The term 'identity theft' is generally a misnomer, since information itself is not generally capable of being stolen. Theft would only be applicable where the identification details are contained in some tangible property, such as a payment card, which is also taken. Forgery may be applicable, where the identification is incorporated into some form of 'instrument'.[164] The offences under the Fraud Act 2006 will be applicable in most circumstances, especially fraud by false representation, as well as conspiracy to defraud. Finally, since the obtaining of the identification details is generally a precursor to some fraudulent act, such as unauthorized transactions, then the person may be also charged with attempt to commit the applicable misappropriation offence, provided there exists a clear evidential link.[165]

Under a previous Labour administration, one element of its strategy to tackle the rise in **3.76** identity theft was the introduction of a national identity card. However, part of the controversy surrounding the introduction of ID cards was whether they would facilitate or reduce identity theft.[166] The Identity Cards Act 2006 contained a number of offences concerning the possession of false 'identity documents'[167] and providing false information.[168] While the national identity card scheme was terminated by the Coalition administration in 2010, most of the offences were re-enacted under the Identity Documents Act 2010. It is an offence to be in possession of false identity documents[169] or possess apparatus, an article, or materials which the person knows are or have been designed or adapted to make false identity documents.[170] These two offences attract a potential tariff of ten years' imprisonment.[171] A third offence relates to the mere possession 'without reasonable excuse' of

---

[160] 18 USC s 1028(a)(7).
[161] 18 USC s 1028(b).
[162] Identity Theft Penalty Enhancement Act, HR 1731, 2003, Public Law No 108-275.
[163] Codified at 18 USC s 1028A.
[164] See paras 3.88–3.93.
[165] Criminal Attempts Act 1981.
[166] See London School of Economic and Political Science (LSE), *The Identity Project: an assessment of the UK Identity Cards Bill and its implications*, Report Version 1.09, 27 June 2005, Chapter 8, available at <http://eprints.lse.ac.uk/29117/1/identityfullreport.pdf>.
[167] Identity Cards Act 2006, s 25.
[168] ibid, s 28.
[169] Identity Documents Act 2010, s 4 'Possession of false identity documents etc with improper intention'.
[170] ibid, s 5.
[171] ibid, ss 4(4) and 5(3) respectively.

identity documents that are false, have been improperly obtained, or relate to someone else; or the offence may relate to apparatus, articles, or materials.[172]

Obtaining communication services

3.77 Exploiting networks to obtain free telephone service, or 'phone phreaking', was one of the earliest activities of the hacker community, based on the emission of tones at the required 2600 Hz and the manipulation of phone company switches.[173] While the ability to manipulate networks to obtain free service was initially driven by the curiosity of engineers, it was soon taken up by a broader spectrum of users to avoid the then high per-minute tariffs, particularly for long-distance and international calls.

3.78 With the increasing sophistication and security of modern networks, communications fraud has since spread from manipulation of the network itself to acts carried out against the equipment used at the edges of a network, possessed by users. 'Dial-through-fraud', for example, involves the routing of unauthorized calls through the PBX of a business user,[174] while the cloning of the electronic serial numbers of mobile phones is also a major form of communications fraud.[175] With the growth of wireless networking (eg 'WiFi' and 'Bluetooth'), the problem of unauthorized obtaining of communication services has assumed a new dimension, as households install wireless solutions without the wherewithal to protect such access mechanisms from visitors, whether neighbours or drive-by hackers.[176]

3.79 While the obtaining of services fraudulently is subject to general criminal provision, English law also separately criminalizes the obtaining of communication services, ie the unlawful use of networks. The offence first appeared in conjunction with the commencement of the process of liberalizing the UK telecommunications market, under the British Telecommunications Act 1981. The Act criminalized the dishonest use of a 'public telecommunication system' with intent to avoid payment.[177] On enactment, British Telecommunications, as a public corporation, had an exclusive privilege to provide such systems,[178] although this was subsequently extended to Mercury, under powers granted to the Secretary of State.[179] The offence was subsequently re-enacted in the Telecommunications Act 1984, which replaced the British Telecommunications Act 1981 and established the regulatory framework for the next phase in the liberalization process.[180]

3.80 The Telecommunications Act 1984 was replaced by the Communications Act 2003, further liberalizing the provision of 'electronic communication services'.[181] However, the offence

---

[172] ibid, s 6.

[173] See Levy, S, *Hackers*, Penguin, 1984.

[174] See *The Simkins Partnership v Reeves Lund & Co Ltd*, [2003] All ER (D) 325 (Jul), where civil proceedings were pursued against a company that improperly installed the equipment used for such a crime.

[175] See paras 3.84–3.87.

[176] In the US, such activities are referred to as 'wardriving' or 'warchalking'. See Ryan, PS, 'War, peace or stalemate: Wargames, wardialing, wardriving and the emerging market for hacker ethics', 9(7) *Virginia Journal of Law & Technology* 3 (2004).

[177] British Telecommunications Act 1981 (BTA 1981), s 48.

[178] ibid, s 12.

[179] ibid, s 15.

[180] British Telecommunications Act 1984 (BTA 1984), s 42.

[181] Communications Act 2003 (CA), s 32(2):

> In this Act 'electronic communications service' means a service consisting in, or having as its principal feature, the conveyance by means of an electronic communications network of signals, except in so far as it is a content service.

has again been re-enacted, using different phraseology, as 'Dishonestly obtaining electronic communication services':

> A person who—
> (a) dishonestly obtains an electronic communications service, and
> (b) does so with intent to avoid payment of a charge applicable to the provision of that service,
> is guilty of an offence.[182]

The maximum tariff, on indictment, is five years' imprisonment.[183] While the 2003 Act was designed to establish a single regulatory framework for telecommunication and broadcasting networks, reflecting developments at an EU level,[184] the offence does not encompass the dishonest obtaining of a broadcasting service, such as a subscription TV channel, which is subject to a much lesser offence.[185]

It is an offence for a person to have in his possession, or under his control, 'anything' that **3.81** may be used to obtain an electronic communication service.[186] The provision goes on to state that 'references, in the case of a thing used for recording data, to the use of that thing include references to the use of data recorded by it'.[187] Such wording implies that the thing must be tangible and would not encompass intangible information, such as knowledge of a code. The supply or offering to supply 'anything' with the intention of obtaining a communications service dishonestly is also an offence.[188] These preparatory offences attract the same tariff as the main offence.[189]

The range of activities to which this offence could apply is broad, and it has been **3.82** successfully used against a person accessing the Internet through a local resident's unsecured wireless broadband access point.[190] The offence will usually be prosecuted by the police, although service providers themselves could potentially initiate proceedings.

One area in which it has been used is against those engaged in computer-integrity offences, **3.83** specifically hacking. Obtaining access to systems across a network may require a considerable amount of time, for example entering random passwords or codes, which involve a substantial communication element which the perpetrator may want to avoid. Likewise, laundering communications activities through a series of different networks enables the perpetrator to hide his activities. As such, the offence has been used as a supplementary charge to computer-integrity offences,[191] or as an alternative, where problems may exist in pursuing for the integrity offence.

---

[182] ibid, s 125(1).
[183] ibid, s 125(3)(b).
[184] See Directive 2002/21/EC on a common regulatory framework for electronic communications networks and services, OJ L 108/33, 24 April 2002.
[185] Copyright Designs and Patents Act 1988, s 297 'Offence of fraudulently receiving programmes'.
[186] CA, s 126(1).
[187] ibid, s 126(6).
[188] ibid, s 126(2). For an example of such a device, see *Levitz* (1990) 90 Cr App R 33.
[189] CA, s 126(5).
[190] *Straszkiewicz*, Isleworth Crown Court, 17 August 2005. See Wakefield, J, 'Wireless hijacking under scrutiny', BBC News, 28 July 2005, available at: <http://news.bbc.co.uk/go/pr/fr/-/1/hi/technology/4721723.stm>.
[191] eg *Morgans* [1999] 2 Cr App R 99.

3.84   Mobile phones have proved a particular boon to the criminal fraternity, both as a valuable convertible commodity and as a tool of the trade, due to the anonymity available through 'pay-as-you-go' products. Whether for use or trade, the value of a mobile handset is obviously substantially greater when it comes with a free communications service. The main mechanism for obtaining such a service is to clone, or copy, the various pieces of identification information held in a SIM card[192] from a legitimate handset into the fraudulent handset. To address this growing phenomenon, the Government adopted a specific criminal statute in respect of mobile telephones, in the form of the Mobile Telephones (Re-programming) Act 2002.

3.85   The Act establishes two main offences, where a person 'changes a unique device identifier' or 'interferes with the operation of a unique device identifier'.[193] Three ancillary offences under the Act relate to a person in possession, supplying, or offering to supply equipment for the purpose of changing or interfering with a unique device identifier.[194] Mere possession is not sufficient for liability; the person must intend to use the equipment or to allow it to be used unlawfully.[195] On indictment, these offences may carry a maximum five-year prison term.[196]

3.86   The enforcement of the Act has been coordinated through the establishment of a dedicated law enforcement body, the National Mobile Phone Crime Unit, which works closely with industry.[197] However, the Mobile Telephones (Re-programming) Act 2002 is seen as being greatly underused, mainly due to the extensive and costly surveillance operations often required in connection with such investigations.[198] As a consequence, the Government amended the Act, by introducing a new offence of 'offering or agreeing to re-programme' a mobile phone,[199] which would enable action to be taken at an earlier stage in the course of the crime conduct.

3.87   While the Mobile Telephones (Re-programming) Act 2002 may be more appropriately categorized as a form of computer-integrity offence, the overriding objectives of the Act are to reduce the amount of theft in relation to the equipment itself, a major cause of street and violent crime. Also, by tackling re-programming, a preliminary stage in the fraudulent obtaining of communication services is addressed.

Forgery

3.88   We make use of a wide range of documentation in our daily lives, from £20 notes to driving licences and insurance certificates. Many of these documents either identify or authenticate us in a particular context. Creating forged versions of these physical documents is an obvious area of crime that has benefited from developments in computer technology. Most genuine documents are now created using computers, therefore computers provide

---

[192]   The Electronic Serial Number (ESN) in an analogue phone and the International Mobile Electronic Identity (IMEI) number of a digital phone.

[193]   Mobile Telephones (Re-programming) Act 2002 (MTRA), s 1(1).

[194]   ibid, s 2.

[195]   ibid, s 2(1)(b).

[196]   ibid, ss 1(4)(b) and 2(6)(b) respectively.

[197]   See <http://www.nmpcu.police.uk>.

[198]   Home Office, *Regulatory Impact Assessment: Violent Crime Reduction Bill–Mobile Phone Re-programming*, 18 October 2005.

[199]   Violent Crime Reduction Act 2006, c 38, s 62.

the opportunity to amend them in an often-undetectable manner. Current software-based digital manipulation applications provide a powerful tool for even the most amateur of forgers.[200]

In a cyberspace environment, a perpetrator is either going to create new privileges, on the **3.89** basis of false credentials, or exploit existing privileges, through the use of information obtained from a range of sources. Such information may come from the victims themselves, through the use of 'social engineering' techniques, which rely on human interaction to trick people into disclosing information that helps overcome data security mechanisms and procedures. The success of such techniques is being facilitated, in part, by people's readiness to disclose private details about themselves over the Internet, through social networking sites for example. Alternatively, a person may hack into the customer database of an electronic commerce website to obtain credit card details and other identity data. Both acts may constitute an offence of forgery under the Forgery and Counterfeiting Act 1981.

Section 1 of the Forgery and Counterfeiting Act 1981 states: **3.90**

> A person is guilty of forgery if he makes a false instrument with the intention that he or another shall use it to induce somebody to accept it as genuine . . .

As legislation drafted in the age of computing, one could expect the Act to avoid the interpretative issues raised by the use of computer technology in respect of fraud, discussed above. However, the leading English case concerning the use of computers to commit forgery, *Gold*,[201] illustrates the potential problems faced by legislative draftsmen.

In *Gold*, the defendants gained unauthorized access to BT's Prestel service and discovered the password codes of various private email accounts, including the Duke of Edinburgh's! The defendants were prosecuted under the Forgery and Counterfeiting Act 1981 for creating a 'false instrument', by entering customer authorization codes to access the system.

The Act defines an 'instrument' in two ways: generically and broadly to include 'any disc, **3.91** tape, sound track or other device on or in which information is recorded or stored by mechanical, electronic or other means',[202] as well as distinguishing specific instruments that are subject to a separate offence.[203] The broad definition was expressly designed to reflect developments in technologies.[204] In addition, the meaning of 'induce' expressly avoids the need for a real person, as required in respect of 'deception':

> . . . references to inducing somebody to accept a false instrument as genuine . . . include references to inducing a machine to respond . . .[205]

However, the House of Lords held that the electronic signals that comprised the identifica- **3.92** tion codes could not be considered tangible in the sense that a disk or tape were. It also held

---

[200] eg Adobe Photoshop CC.

[201] *R v Gold (Stephen William); R v Schifreen (Robert Jonathan)* [1988] 2 All ER 186.

[202] Forgery and Counterfeiting Act 1981 (FCA), s 8(1)(d).

[203] ibid, s 5: the list of instruments is detailed in subsection (5), including share certificates and money orders.

[204] Law Commission, *Report on Forgery and Counterfeit Currency*, Report No 55, HMSO, 1973, paras 24–25.

[205] FCA, s 10(3).

that the signals were present in the system for such a fleeting moment that they could not be considered to have been 'recorded or stored':

> The words 'recorded' and 'stored' are words in common use which should be given their ordinary and natural meaning. In my opinion both words . . . connote the preservation of the thing which is the subject matter of them for an appreciable time with the object of subsequent retrieval and recovery.[206]

In respect of the issue of whether somebody had been 'induced', the Court of Appeal in *Gold* recognized that the prosecution's case could be rendered absurd because the machine being induced was also claimed to be the false instrument.[207]

3.93 It is also interesting to note that the Court of Appeal was highly critical of the application of the Act to such a set of circumstances:

> The Procrustean attempt to force these facts into the language of an Act not designed to fit them produced difficulties for both judge and jury which we would not wish to see repeated.[208]

Such an explicit determination by the judiciary of the need to draft new legislation rather than try to extend traditional terminology to fit computer technology was criticized by commentators,[209] but lent significant pressure to the calls for reform of the criminal law in respect of computer-integrity offences.

C. Content-related Offences

3.94 When considering content-based crimes, a distinction needs to be made between the acts carried out in relation to certain subject matter, which comprise the *actus reus* of the offence, from the subject matter itself. In terms of conduct, we are generally either concerned with issues of supplying illegal content, whether through making, publishing, or distributing material, or the possession of such content. In addition, we criminalize certain acts related to the process of supply, for example, the manufacture of circumvention devices. Such matters tend to be relatively uncontroversial, although cyberspace can blur the line between acts of supply and possession, and debate exists about whether it is always appropriate to criminalize the consumption as well as production of such material.[210]

3.95 By contrast, classifying certain subject matter as criminally illegal can be a highly contentious matter, raising complex definitional issues, questions of causation, and human rights concerns, specifically rights to privacy, freedom of expression, assembly, and association.[211]

3.96 The issue of illegal content is also often tied, both at a policy level and in the minds of the general public, to the broader topic of harmful and unwanted content, such as children

---

[206] *Gold*, n 203, at 192c per Lord Brandon.

[207] [1997] 3 WLR 803, at 809G per Lord Lane CJ. This question was not considered by the House of Lords.

[208] ibid, at 809H. Such sentiment was echoed by Lord Brandon in the House of Lords: [1988] 2 All ER 186, at 192d.

[209] See Tapper, C, *Computer Law*, 4th edn, Longman, 1989, at 292.

[210] Rowbottom, J, 'Obscenity laws and the Internet: Targeting the supply and demand', *Criminal Law Review* 97 [2006].

[211] See generally Emmerson, B, Ashworth, A, and Emmerson, A, *Human Rights and Criminal Justice*, 3rd edn, Sweet & Maxwell, 2012, Chapter 17.

accessing pornography and the general problem of 'spam'.[212] This blurring of subject matter further exacerbates debate and polarizes views about the right approach to address illegal content on the Internet. In respect of harmful content, for example, the focus of control is the end-user, through 'user empowerment'[213] mechanisms such as filtering software; while for illegal content, communication service providers, as intermediaries, are viewed as the focus for law enforcement control.[214]

3.97 Illegal content may be 'taken down' by an Internet service provider (ISP), for example, where the material is located in the jurisdiction, ie the material is either removed, where held by the ISP on a 'hosted' basis, or the subscriber's service is terminated, where the ISP only supplies Internet connectivity. Alternatively, access to the resource may be blocked, where the material is sourced from abroad, ie filtering egress user requests against a database of addresses where illegal material is located. However, the sheer volume of available material and the speed and flexibility with which it can be moved can undermine enforcement actions.

3.98 Yet despite the complexities surrounding content regulation, in recent years we have witnessed substantial policy and legislative activity in the area, in terms of both expanding the subject matter considered illegal and raising the tariff applicable to such offences. Indeed, over the past five years, content-related crimes have risen from the bottom to the top half of the league table in terms of the maximum tariff available. Such activity would seem to reflect, in part, the impact of the Internet as a pre-eminent facilitator of communications, coupled with public disquiet stoked by media representations.

3.99 The following section examines three categories of content-related crime: intellectual property, pornography, and speech and communication crimes, such as hate speech and harassment.

3.100 Computers and communication technologies are designed to process information or data. Such technologies have had a fundamental impact on national economies, particularly in the developed world, shifting them from a traditional industrial base towards an information base. Companies are increasingly valued not on their tangible assets, such as plant and materials, but their intangible assets, in the form of information. Such information is protected under a range of intellectual property laws, including copyright, patent, trademarks, and database right. Some aspects of these laws, such as copyright, have criminal sanctions as part of their enforcement regime, which require examination.

3.101 Another form of information that has increased in economic value in our networked environment is pornography. The pornography industry contributes huge sums to the global economy, although as with cybercrime estimates tend to vary greatly and are the subject of much debate.[215] The distribution of certain forms of pornography, primarily child pornography over the Internet, is one of the most prevalent forms of content-related computer

---

[212] eg Decision No 854/2005/EC of the European Parliament and of the Council of 11 May 2005 establishing a multiannual Community Programme on promoting safer use of the Internet and new online technologies, OJ L 149/1, 11 June 2005.

[213] ibid, at 6.

[214] eg the Internet Watch Foundation.

[215] eg Chalabi, M, 'Pornography: what we know, what we don't', *The Guardian*, 24 May 2013, <http://www.theguardian.com/news/datablog/2013/may/24/missing-statistics-pornography>.

crimes, attracting a high public profile, the attention of politicians and, as a consequence, law enforcement activity.

3.102   Despite the children's chant of 'sticks and stones', it is widely accepted that certain forms of speech can hurt and harm those against whom they are directed. Racial abuse, for example, has been criminalized in the UK for many years. In 2006, legislation criminalized speech that stirs up religious hatred[216] and encourages terrorism.[217] Such laws have proved difficult to draft and enforce, generating substantial controversy, not least because of the nature and perceptions of cyberspace as an open environment.

3.103   As a general principle, an act is subject to criminal sanction where it causes a certain degree of harm to a victim(s), directly or indirectly, and to the wider interests of society. In the field of content-related crimes, there is often controversy concerning the existence of an 'operating and substantial'[218] causal link between the content and the perceived harm, whether intellectual property, pornography, or hate speech. Empirical evidence is scant, while research is often inherently problematic.[219] However, legislators are inevitably wary of delaying action simply due to the absence of conclusive research results. This is coupled with the reality of law-making, which is often less a strictly evidence-based process than precautionary or anecdotal, driven by events and artful lobbying. As such, content-related crimes generate substantially more public and political debate than computer-related and computer-integrity offences, both as substantive offences as well as in terms of enforcement regimes.

3.104   Finally, it should be noted that the political culture of the US has a dominant influence on the international enforcement agenda in terms of content-related crimes, particularly concerning pornography and hate speech. The US, as the progenitor of the Internet, has such a strong constitutional tradition of free speech that it impacts directly and indirectly on the enforcement practice of other countries. US law enforcement agencies tend to be more conservative about taking action, while the strength of resource free speech organizations such as the American Civil Liberties Union (ACLU) can bring to bear on an issue can render international cooperation in the field difficult. By making this comment, it is not the intention to criticize the prevalent free speech discourse of the Internet; it is simply to highlight the impact that such discourse and culture can have on content-related crime issues.

Intellectual property crimes

3.105   As noted in respect of computer-related crimes, information is subject to a range of discrete but overlapping forms of legal protection depending on its nature. In terms of information with commercial value, the primary source of legal protection is that offered under the various strands of intellectual property (IP) law: patents, copyright, trade marks, and related regimes. While a comprehensive examination of intellectual property laws are beyond the scope of this book,[220] most legal systems grant criminal as well as civil remedies to certain rights-holders in certain circumstances, and therefore these elements are of concern to us.

---

[216]   Racial and Religious Hatred Act 2006, c 1, which amended the Public Order Act 1986.
[217]   Terrorism Act 2006 (TA 2006), c 11.
[218]   *Smith* [1959] 2 QB 35.
[219]   See eg Home Office, *Consultation: on the possession of extreme pornographic material*, August 2005, paras 28–31, available at <http://www.gov.scot/resource/doc/57346/0017059.pdf>.
[220]   For a general treatment, see Bently, L and Sherman, B, *Intellectual Property Law*, 4th edn, Oxford, 2014.

Computers, networks, and cyberspace have been widely recognized as key factors gener-   **3.106**
ating substantial infringement and enforcement problems for rights-holders, as the ease
of reproduction and distribution of digital information challenges historical methods of
doing business and traditional limitations and controls. While, for example, the software
industry grew up in this environment and has had to address large-scale piracy and counterfeiting from its inception; the music and movie industry has had to tackle the problem
in the context of a rapidly changing marketplace resulting in large part from these technological developments. Criminal IP activities continue to involve the mass production and
distribution of pirate CDs and DVDs.

Such growth has slowed and changed in nature, however, as producers increasingly dis-   **3.107**
tribute pirate content over the Internet, such as 'warez'[221] groups that reverse-engineer
newly issued software to crack the copyright protection mechanisms and then release
the content, as well as consumers shifting to virtual products and unauthorized services
downloaded, file-shared, or streamed over broadband networks.[222] In 2001, for example,
a coordinated operation between authorities in the US, Australia, UK, Canada, Finland,
Norway, and a number of other countries was carried out against a international 'warez'
piracy group known by the name 'Drink or Die'.[223] The group was estimated to have been
responsible for the illegal reproduction and distribution, via FTP sites, of pirated software, music, and movies worth $50 million.[224] Operation 'Blossom', as it was known in
the UK, resulted in six convictions in the UK with prison sentences of up to two and a half
years. One of the group's leaders, Hew Griffiths, a British national living in Australia, was
eventually extradited to the US in February 2007 and pleaded guilty before a US District
Court on one count of conspiracy to commit criminal copyright and one count of criminal
copyright infringement, after a three-year struggle while in a detention centre in Australia.
He was sentenced to fifty-one months' imprisonment. The case represents one of the first
ever extraditions for an IP offence, as noted by Assistant Attorney General Alice Fisher:

> This extradition represents the Department of Justice's commitment to protect intellectual
> property rights from those who violate our laws from the other side of the globe.[225]

More recently, however, the US has been trying, unsuccessfully to date, to obtain the   **3.108**
extradition of Kim Dotcom from New Zealand for online piracy connected with his
Megaupload service, which was claimed to be worth some $175 million in criminal pro-
ceeds.[226] The case has spawned numerous court decisions in New Zealand, including at

---

[221] See 'Wares', Wikipedia, available at <https://en.wikipedia.org/wiki/Warez>.

[222] International Federation of the Phonographic Industry (IFPI), *The Recording Industry 2005: Commercial Piracy Report*, July 2005, at 16, available at <http://www.ifpi.org/content/library/piracy2005.pdf> ('IFPI Piracy Report 2005').

[223] 'Arrests uncover global software piracy ring', *The Guardian*, 12 December 2001, available at <http://www.theguardian.com/technology/2001/dec/12/piracy.news>.

[224] DoJ, 'Defendant indicted in connection with operating illegal Internet software piracy group', Press Release, 12 March 2003, available at <http://www.justice.gov/archive/criminal/cybercrime/press-releases/2003/griffithsIndict.htm>.

[225] DoJ, 'Extradited software piracy ringleader sentenced to 51 months in prison', Press Release, 22 June 2007, available at <http://www.justice.gov/archive/opa/pr/2007/June/07_crm_444.html>.

[226] Federal Bureau of Investigation (FBI), 'Justice Department charges leaders of Megaupload with wide-spread online copyright infringement', Press Release, 19 January 2012, available at <https://www.fbi.gov/news/pressrel/press-releases/justice-department-charges-leaders-of-megaupload-with-widespread-online-copyright-infringement>.

least two Supreme Court hearings,[227] but any final decision on extradition is likely to take many more months.

3.109 Criminal sanctions are generally imposed where the infringement is carried out on a commercial scale, commonly referred to as 'counterfeiting', in respect of trade mark infringement,[228] and 'piracy', in respect of copyright infringement. The leading international instrument on intellectual property rights, the TRIPS Agreement,[229] imposes the following obligation on signatories:

> Members shall provide for criminal procedures and penalties to be applied at least in cases of wilful trademark counterfeiting or copyright piracy on a commercial scale.[230]

Other international IP instruments do not, however, require the imposition of criminal sanctions.[231] Under TRIPS, states have the freedom to extend criminal sanctions to encompass infringements of other rights, such as patent, which is the case in a number of European countries, as well as Japan.[232]

3.110 The Convention on Cybercrime only addresses one category of IP infringement: copyright and related rights. The Convention requires a party to criminalize the infringement of copyright and related rights 'where such acts are committed wilfully, on a commercial scale and by means of a computer system', except in respect of moral rights.[233] The use of the term 'wilful', rather than 'intentional', as used in the other Convention offences, is designed to reflect the wording of the TRIPS provision.[234] The parties are, however, granted the possibility of not imposing criminal sanctions, in limited circumstances, provided that 'other effective remedies are available', such as civil and administrative.[235] Examples given of such 'limited circumstances' are parallel imports and rental rights,[236] where the nature of the infringement presents more complex policy issues—in both cases because the work has been lawfully distributed, rather than copied, and is simply being used in an unauthorized manner.

3.111 As intellectual property assets have increased in value in industrialized economies, rightholders have lobbied policy-makers and legislators, successfully arguing that intellectual property crime can have a serious economic impact on national economies, innovation, and global trade.[237] Intellectual property piracy has also moved up the public policy and law

---

[227] eg *Dotcom v United States of America* [2014] NZSC 24.

[228] This must be distinguished from the offence of 'counterfeiting' under the FCA, s 14, which applies to notes and coins.

[229] TRIPS, above, n 80.

[230] ibid, Art 61.

[231] eg the Berne Convention for the Protection of Literary and Artistic Works, enacted 9 September 1886, entered into force 5 December 1887, 828 UNTS 221, S Treaty Doc No 99-27; the World Intellectual Property Organization (WIPO) Copyright Treaty, adopted 20 December 1996, WIPO Doc CRNRIDC/94; and the WIPO Performances and Phonograms Treaty, adopted 20 December 1996, WIPO Doc CRNR/DC/95.

[232] See International Association for the Protection of Intellectual Property (AIPPI) 'Summary Report. Question 169: Criminal law sanctions with regard to the infringement of intellectual property rights', 2002. available at <http://www.aippi.org/download/commitees/169/SR169English.pdf>.

[233] Convention on Cybercrime, Art 10(1), (2).

[234] Explanatory Report to the Convention on Cybercrime, above, n 1, para 113.

[235] Convention on Cybercrime, Art 10(3).

[236] Explanatory Report to the Convention on Cybercrime, above n 1, para 116.

[237] In 2009, an Organisation on Economic Co-operation and Development (OECD) report, *Magnitude of Counterfeiting and Piracy of Tangible Products* (November 2009, available at <http://www.oecd.org/sti/ind/44088872.pdf>), estimated the market for counterfeit and pirated goods to be some $250 bn, about 1.95% of the value of world trade, in 2007.

enforcement agenda as organized crime has become increasingly involved in the practice, as well as becoming a financing mechanism for terrorist organizations.[238] In a communiqué adopted by the G8 states in 2005, all these concerns were reflected, as well as a specific commitment to '[e]nhance detection and deterrence of the distribution and sale of counterfeit goods through the internet and combat online theft'.[239] As a result of these developments, there has been a broadening of the scope of infringement activity attracting criminal sanction, a rise in the level of sanction, and an attempt to expand public authority involvement in enforcement activities.

Under UK law, criminal sanctions for infringement only arise in respect of copyright, performers' rights, trade mark law, and registered designs,[240] not under patent law.[241] The primary means by which a rights-holder enforces his copyright or trade mark is through civil proceedings, seeking protective remedies, such as an injunction or order to destroy or deliver up infringing works; or through compensatory remedies, such as damages or an account of profits. In terms of legal process, such proceedings are obviously advantageous to the rights-holder due to the lower standard of proof required to be met.[242] There would also seem to be strong public policy grounds for requiring that those granted exclusive economic rights have primary responsibility to police and enforce those rights. Conversely, criminal proceedings tend to generate greater publicity and a stronger deterrent effect; as well as having potential cost benefits.[243] **3.112**

Criminal sanctions have been linked with copyright since its origins, which lie in a desire within the executive branch of government to control the publishing industry. The first statutory embodiment of copyright law under English law, the Copyright Act of 1710, recognized that remedies extended to criminal as well as civil, although the first specific criminal sanction did not appear until the Musical Copyright Act 1906.[244] General criminal liability then formed part of the first consolidation of copyright legislation in the Copyright Act 1911. **3.113**

Under the Copyright, Designs and Patents Act 1988, s 107, certain forms of copyright infringement are criminalized. Such acts can be broadly divided into those carried out 'in the course of business' and those carried out 'otherwise than in the course of business to such an extent as to affect prejudicially the owner of the copyright'.[245] In *Lewis*,[246] for example, the defendant operated a pirate bulletin board, known as 'the pool', which **3.114**

---

[238] See eg Union des Fabricants, *Counterfeiting and Organised Crime*, 2003, available at <http://www.gacg.org/Content/Upload/Documents/rapport_uk.pdf>. See also Interpol Press Release, 'INTERPOL acts against intellectual property crimes', 28 July 2002, available at <http://www.interpol.int/News-and-media/News/2002/PR016>.

[239] G8, 'Reducing IPR piracy and counterfeiting through more effective enforcement', Gleneagles, July 2005, available at <https://www.eff.org/files/filenode/EFF_PK_v_USTR/foia-ustr-acta-response1-doc46.pdf>.

[240] Registered Designs Act 1949, c 88, ss 35ZA–35ZD, as amended by the Intellectual Property Act 2014, c 18, s 13.

[241] However, criminal sanctions do exist under patent law in respect of the registration process (eg Patent Act 1977, c 37, ss 109–11).

[242] ie on the balance of probabilities, rather than beyond reasonable doubt. See generally Chapter 6.

[243] Under the Prosecution of Offences Act 1985, a private prosecutor may apply for an order to be granted by the court for payment of expenses out of central funds (s 17(1)), or by the convicted person (s 18).

[244] See Tapper, CB, 'Criminality and copyright', in Vaver, D and Bently, L (eds), *Intellectual Property in the New Millennium*, Cambridge University Press, 2004, at 266–79.

[245] Copyright, Designs and Patents Act 1988 (CDPA 1988), s 107(1), (2), and (3).

[246] [1997] 1 Cr App R(S) 208.

facilitated the exchange of infringing versions of computer games. He pleaded guilty to the distribution of infringing articles contrary to s 107(1)(d)(iv). Under the CDPA 1988, there are also a number of offences in relation to a performer's rights, such as the 'making available' right, which would include the placing of a recording on a website for downloading or transferring over a peer-to-peer (P2P) network.[247]

3.115 The criminal provisions under the CDPA 1988 have been amended twice in recent years, addressing both the depth and breadth of criminal copyright infringement. In terms of depth, the Copyright, etc and Trade Marks (Offences and Enforcement) Act 2002 raised the tariff under s 107(4) from two to ten years.[248] Such a substantial increase indicates how intellectual property has come to be viewed as being vital to UK plc. However, raising the tariff on such offences may have minimal impact on the average length of sentence handed down by the courts for the commission of such offences. While the courts have expressed strong sentiments in respect of such acts, seeing them as analogous to 'stealing other men's property',[249] as well as being 'difficult, time consuming and expensive to detect',[250] such crimes have tended to attract lower sentences due to perceptions that IP crimes are in some sense victimless.[251]

3.116 In terms of breadth, the Copyright and Related Rights Regulations 2003 (SI No 2498)[252] has created new criminal offences in respect of the following acts:

- communicating a work to the public in the course of a business or otherwise to such an extent as to prejudice the copyright owner; and
- the manufacture, sale, or related acts of devices and services designed to circumvent 'effective technological measures'.[253]

With respect to first offence, criminalizing online infringement, the maximum tariff is two years' imprisonment,[254] which contrasts starkly with that applicable to physical copying. In 2006, the Gowers Review recommended that this discrepancy be removed, by increasing the penalty for online infringement.[255] Although the then Government accepted the recommendation, it subsequently decided to focus instead on increasing the applicable financial penalties,[256] conceding that 'prison should be used mainly for serious and dangerous offenders'.[257] The current Government has decided that the discrepancy between

---

[247] CDPA 1988, s 198(1).

[248] Applicable to s 107(1)(a), (b), (d)(iv), and (e).

[249] *Dukett* [1998] 2 Cr App R(S) 59. See also *Gibbons* (1995) 16 Cr App R(S) 398.

[250] *Kemp* (1995) 16 Cr App R(S) 941.

[251] See Intellectual Property Office (IPO), *Penalty Fair? Study of criminal sanctions for copyright infringement available under the CDPA 1988*, Report, February 2015, available at <https://www.gov.uk/government/organisations/intellectual-property-office> ('1988 Report'), which found no evidence of custodial sentences being imposed of over five years.

[252] This Regulation transposes EU Directive 2001/29/EC on the harmonisation of certain aspects of copyright and related rights in the information society, OJ L 167/10, 22 June 2001, which itself was partly an implementation of the WIPO Copyright Treaty of 1996.

[253] CDPA 1988, ss 107(2A) and 296ZB, respectively.

[254] ibid, s 107(4A).

[255] *Gowers Review of Intellectual Property*, December 2006, Recommendation 36, available at <https://www.gov.uk/government/publications/gowers-review-of-intellectual-property>.

[256] The Digital Economy Act 2010, s 42, increased the maximum fine from £5000 to £50,000.

[257] *Taking forward the Gowers Review of Intellectual Property: Report on the outcome of consultation on penalties for copyright infringement*, available at <http://webarchive.nationalarchives.gov.uk/20140603093549/http://www.ipo.gov.uk/consult-gowers36.pdf>.

the treatment of physical and online infringement is no longer defensible and has issued a consultation paper as part of a process towards future reform.[258]

Under the second offence, a 'technological measure' is defined as 'any technology, device or component which is designed, in the normal course of its operation, to protect a copyright work other than a computer program'; while 'effective' means: **3.117**

> the use of the work is controlled by the copyright owner through—
> (a) an access control or protection process such as encryption, scrambling or other trans-formation of the work, or
> (b) a copy control mechanism,
> which achieves the intended protection.[259]

In *Shahzad*,[260] a shopkeeper was imprisoned for possessing R4DS devices that circumvented anti-piracy technology built into Nintendo DS games consoles. However, in *Higgs*,[261] the court was asked to consider whether 'modchips', which when fitted to computer games consoles enabled them to play pirated DVDs and CD-ROMs, were an 'effective technological measure'. It held that any such measure must be more than 'a discouragement or general commercial hindrance to copyright infringement'.[262] However, on very similar facts, in *Gilham*,[263] the prosecution proved that data was copied into the memory of the games console when playing a game from a counterfeit DVD, which was sufficient to address the lacuna identified in *Higgs*. As with online infringement, the maximum penalty is two years' imprisonment.[264]

Under the Trade Marks Act 1994, it is an offence for a person to use a registered mark of another 'with a view to gain for himself or another, or with intent to cause loss to another'.[265] This could be applicable where a website owner directly used the mark on a public web page, as well as use of the mark in a meta-tag or through 'word stuffing' techniques, which are hidden from the general user but are visible to search engines examining the site to find relevant information.[266] In addition to IP-specific laws, a common charge used against commercial-scale counterfeiting is the common law offence of conspiracy to defraud.[267] It is considered particularly useful in intellectual property cases, where no economic loss has been suffered. **3.118**

Under the Proceeds of Crime Act 2002, the offences under the Copyright, Designs and Patents Act 1988, and the Trade Marks Act 1994 are categorized as a 'criminal lifestyle',[268] **3.119**

---

[258] IPO, *A consultation on changes to the penalties for offences under sections 107(2A) and 198(1A) of the Copyright Designs and Patents Act (Penalties for Online Copyright Infringement*, 18 July 2015, available at <https://www.gov.uk/government/uploads/system/uploads/attachment_data/file/446515/Changes_to_penalties_for_online_copyright_infringement.pdf>.

[259] CDPA 1988, s 296ZF(1) and (2), respectively.

[260] *Shahzad (Umar)* [2013] EWCA Crim 389.

[261] [2008] EWCA Crim 1324.

[262] ibid, para 35.

[263] [2009] EWCA Crim 2293.

[264] CDPA 1988, s 296ZB(4).

[265] Trade Marks Act 1994, c 26 (TMA), s 92(1).

[266] See eg *Roadtech Computer Systems Ltd v Mandata (Management and Data Services) Ltd* [2000] ETMR 970.

[267] See eg *Stanley* [2003] EWCA Crim 2498 (re: copying music, films, and games on to CDs) and *Alibhai and others* [2004] EWCA Crim 681.

[268] PCA 2002, s 75 and Sch 2, para 7.

which means that a court is able to make a confiscation order against the convicted person for the assessed benefits accrued as a result of such general criminal conduct.[269] Any determination made about whether the person has benefited from his criminal conduct and what is a recoverable amount is done to a civil standard of proof, on the balance of probabilities, rather than in accordance with the criminal standard.[270]

3.120 In respect of the role of public law enforcement agencies in pursuing intellectual property crimes, the rising profile of such crimes has inevitably required an appropriate response from such agencies. In 2004, for example, the then Patent Office (now the Intellectual Property Office, IPO) established an IP Crime Group to develop and pursue a national strategy on intellectual property crime.[271] The strategy extended from changing public perception of such crimes as 'victimless' to engaging in joint operations.[272] Historically, much IP crime enforcement activity in the UK has been carried out by customs authorities, concerned with the revenue loss from illegally imported products, and local trading standards bodies, sometimes operating under an express statutory duty.[273] However, both agencies are primarily focused on physical products, shipped in, or sold at local markets, and are therefore less relevant when tackling cyberspace piracy. In September 2013, the City of London Police launched a specialist national police unit, the Police Intellectual Property Crime Unit (PIPCU).[274] Among its various activities, in July 2014, PIPCU started 'Operation Creative', an ad replacement initiative in which sites that supply infringing material have their banner ads 'hijacked' by the police and replaced with messages notifying visitors that the site is under criminal investigation.[275] The scheme, carried out with the cooperation of the UK advertising industry, is only applicable to visitors accessing the site through UK IP addresses, but is designed to disrupt the revenue flows to such sites.[276]

3.121 Rights-holders have increasingly looked to communication service providers to help control online copyright infringement. Following successful lobbying, new measures to enhance enforcement were adopted under the Digital Economy Act 2010.[277] Under the Act, ISPs[278] are obliged to send notifications to their subscribers when in receipt of an infringement report from a rights-holder; as well as the provision of 'copyright infringement lists' to rights-holders indicating subscribers (anonymously) that have been the subject of a number of reports.[279] The latter was designed to facilitate legal action by the rights-holder against

---

[269] ibid, s 6.

[270] ibid, s 6(7).

[271] Patent Office, *Counter Offensive: An IP Crime Strategy*, 10 August 2004.

[272] eg 'Raids net £1.5m pirate discs haul', *BBC News*, 30 December 2005, available at <http://news.bbc.co.uk/2/hi/uk_news/england/london/4567362.stm>.

[273] eg Trade Marks Act 1994, s 93 'Enforcement function of local weights and measures authority'.

[274] City of London Police, Advice and Support—Fraud and Economic Crime—PICPU, available at <http://www.cityoflondon.police.uk/advice-and-support/fraud-and-economic-crime/pipcu/Pages/default.aspx>.

[275] City of London Police, 'Operation Creative and IWL', available at <http://www.cityoflondon.police.uk/advice-and-support/fraud-and-economic-crime/pipcu/Pages/Operation-creative.aspx>.

[276] Kamen, M, 'UK Police double pirate site "ad highjacking" scheme', Wired, 25 August 2015, available at <http://www.wired.co.uk/news/archive/2015-08/25/uk-police-double-pirate-site-ad-hijacking>.

[277] The Act inserted provisions into the Communications Act 2003, ss 124A–124N.

[278] CA, s 124N, defines an internet service provider as a person providing an 'internet access service', which is defined as an 'electronic communication service that (a) is provided to a subscriber; (b) consists entirely or mainly of the provision of access to the internet; and (c) includes the allocation of an IP address or IP addresses to the subscriber to enable that access'.

[279] ibid, ss 124A and 124B.

the infringer. In addition, the Digital Economy Act 2010 made provision for the possibility that ISPs could be required to implement 'technical measures' against persistent infringers, which could include suspension of the service.[280] All these measures have been highly controversial, especially the idea of service disconnection, and have been subject to legal challenge.[281] The implementation details of the notification scheme were to be set out in an 'initial obligations code', which the Office of Communications (Ofcom) was tasked with drafting.[282] While the provision of technical measures would require an order from the Secretary of State, which cannot be made until twelve months after the code is in place.[283] However, in July 2014, rights-holders' representatives and the four largest ISPs agreed to a voluntary scheme, to be known as Creative Content UK, which is expected to remove the need for the mandatory scheme, except as a backstop power.[284]

UK law permits private prosecutions for copyright infringement. As a consequence, indus- **3.122**
try bodies have been established, such as the Federation Against Software Theft (FAST)[285] and the Federation Against Copyright Theft (FACT)[286] that act as both investigators, passing intelligence on to the police, as well as prosecutors in their own right in certain situations. A leading example of this dual role arose in the *Scopelight* case.[287] The claimants were operating a website, 'SurfTheChannel.com', which provided links to third-party video-hosting websites. Having identified this site, FACT complained to the police, who obtained a search warrant for the premises of the couple operating the website, in relation to the offences of conspiracy to defraud and money laundering. When the warrant was executed, FACT investigators accompanied the police and assisted in the seizure of various materials, including servers and electronic storage media. The Crown Prosecution Service (CPS) subsequently decided not to pursue a prosecution, so the claimants demanded the return of their property. Some of the property was held by the police and some by FACT, pending a decision to pursue a private prosecution, which was duly commenced. The issue for the court was whether further retention by the police was justifiable, once they had decided not to prosecute. The judge at first instance cast doubt on the right to retain;[288] but the Court of Appeal held that it was for the police to make a determination whether 'it was necessary in all the circumstances' that the material be retained for further use, including for a private prosecution. In the vast majority of cases, however, rights-holders will look to utilizing civil procedures to stop infringing activities and seize related profits.

One issue that arises from the close relationship between civil and criminal remedies in the **3.123**
IP field is the exchange of information between private and public law enforcement agencies. While it is perfectly legitimate for organizations, such as FAST, to report infringers to

---

[280] ibid, s 124G.

[281] *R (British Telecommunications Plc) v BPI (British Recorded Music Industry) Ltd and others* [2012] EWCA Civ 232.

[282] CA, s 124D. See Ofcom consultations in May 2010 and June 2012, available at <http://stakeholders.ofcom.org.uk/consultations/>.

[283] CA, s 124H(2).

[284] Department for Culture, Media & Sport, 'Government response to CMS Select Committee Report on Supporting the Creative Economy: Third Report of Session 2013–14', 11 December 2013, available at <https://www.gov.uk/government/uploads/system/uploads/attachment_data/file/265089/v3.7_final.pdf>.

[285] See <http://www.fast.org.uk>.

[286] See <http://www.fact-uk.org.uk>.

[287] *Scopelight Limited and others v Chief of Police for Northumbria and FACT* [2009] EWCA Civ 1156.

[288] *Scopelight Limited and others v Chief of Police for Northumbria* [2009] EWHC 958 (QB).

the police and other authorities, restrictions exist on the flow of information in the other direction, from the authorities to rights-holders and their representatives. Under Part 9 of the Enterprise Act 2002, for example, controls are placed on the disclosure of information obtained by authorities exercising consumer and competition law regulatory functions.[289] The provisions provide for disclosure through designated 'gateways' or where the information is already public. The Act was amended in 2006, to enable disclosure to a private person for the purpose of civil proceedings.[290]

3.124 Initiatives have been taken at a European Union level to address issues of IP enforcement. In 2004, a Directive was adopted 'on the enforcement of intellectual property rights',[291] which harmonizes and facilitates civil law enforcement by rights-holders. In the initial draft proposal, a provision stated that 'responsible authorities', such as police and customs, would have the right to disclose any identification information in their possession to rights-holders to enable them take enforcement action:

> Apart from the cases referred to in paragraph 1, Member States shall lay down that, when the responsible authorities are in possession of the information referred to in paragraph 2, they may so inform the right-holder, provided the latter is known, while complying with the rules on the protection of confidential information, in order to allow the right-holder to institute proceedings leading to a decision on the merits of the case or to obtain provisional or precautionary measures.[292]

However, this provision did not make it into the final text. The Directive has been implemented into UK law through amendments to the Civil Procedure Rules[293] and the Intellectual Property (Enforcement, etc) Regulations 2006.[294]

3.125 The European Commission has pursued further harmonization in the field, publishing proposals for a Directive 'on criminal measures aimed at ensuring the enforcement of intellectual property rights' and a Framework Decision 'to strengthen the criminal law framework to combat intellectual property offences' in July 2005.[295] The main objective of these proposals was to harmonize the penalties available against infringers, while issues concerning information exchange from public authorities to rights-holders were not addressed. The proposed Directive was subsequently formally withdrawn, while the Framework Decision was also abandoned.[296]

3.126 In the US, criminal copyright infringement historically required that an infringer obtain financial gain from his acts. This limitation was illustrated in *United States v LaMaccia*,[297]

---

[289] Enterprise Act 2002, ss 237–47.

[290] ibid, s 241A and Enterprise Act 2002 (Disclosure of Information for Civil Proceedings etc) Order 2007 (SI No 2193).

[291] Directive 2004/48/EC of the European Parliament and of the Council of 29 April 2004 on the enforcement of intellectual property rights, OJ L 195/16, 2 June 2004.

[292] COM(2003) 46 final, 30 January 2003, Art 9(4).

[293] By the 41st update of the Civil Procedure Rules (CPR), effective 1 April 2006, Rule 25 and Practice Direction 63 have been amended.

[294] Intellectual Property (Enforcement, etc) Regulations 2006 (SI No 1028).

[295] Proposal for a European Parliament and Council Directive on criminal measures aimed at ensuring the enforcement of intellectual property rights and Proposal for a Council Framework Decision to strengthen the criminal law framework to combat intellectual property offences, COM(2005)276 final, 12 July 2005.

[296] Withdrawal of obsolete Commission proposals, OJ C 252/7, 18 September 2010.

[297] 871 F Supp 535 (D Mass 1994).

where a student operated a bulletin board for the free exchange of commercial software products. The student was acquitted on the grounds that he had obtained no financial gain from his activities. US copyright law was subsequently amended by the No Electronic Theft Act of 1997 to address such situations:

> Criminal Infringement.—Any person who infringes a copyright willfully either—
> (1) for purposes of commercial advantage or private financial gain, or
> (2) by the reproduction or distribution, including by electronic means, during any 180-day period, of 1 or more copies or phonorecords of 1 or more copyrighted works, which have a total retail value of more than $1,000,
> shall be punished as provided under section 2319 of title 18, United States Code. For purposes of this subsection, evidence of reproduction or distribution of a copyrighted work, by itself, shall not be sufficient to establish willful infringement.[298]

However, to trigger the applicability of these provisions, the rights-holder is required to have registered the copyright work, a formality not present under UK law.[299]

3.127 As in Europe, US copyright law has been extended in recent years to criminalize those that circumvent physical and logical copy protection mechanisms or interfere with rights management information,[300] where carried out 'willfully and for purposes of commercial advantage or private financial gain'.[301] The first prosecution under these provisions was brought against a Russian, Dmitry Sklyarov, and his software company Elcomsoft Ltd, who produced a software tool that was claimed to circumvent the eBook software produced by Adobe. The case generated much controversy at the time, although at trial the jury acquitted on the grounds that the defendants had not been acting wilfully.[302]

3.128 The trend towards increasing criminalization of intellectual property infringement has come about partly through heavy lobbying by rights-holders, combined with an association being made between piracy and counterfeiting and other criminal activities, specifically organized crime and terrorism.[303] Such developments have met with substantial criticism from civil liberties groups and organizations representing rights-users, who are concerned that the traditional balance of interests present in intellectual property laws has shifted too far in the favour of the rights-holder.

Pornography

3.129 In terms of legal treatment, a distinction must be made between general pornographic imagery and specific sub-categories of pornographic material, particularly child pornography, which has been the focus of much law enforcement activity in cyberspace. The laws against child pornographic images are primarily concerned with the child abuse that occurs

---

[298] 17 USC s 506(a). Title 18 USC s 2319 states that the maximum tariff is five years' imprisonment and/or a $250,000 fine.

[299] 17 USC s 411(a).

[300] 17 USC ss 1201, 1202 respectively.

[301] 17 USC s 1204(a). The maximum tariff is five years for a first offence and ten for any subsequent offences.

[302] Brenner, S, 'Defining cybercrime: A review of state and federal law', in Clifford, R (ed), *Cybercrime: The Investigation, prosecution and defence of a computer-related crime*, 2nd edn, Carolina Academic Press, 2006, at 74–7.

[303] See eg IFPI Piracy Report 2005, above, n 222, at 6: 'Behind Music Piracy: Organised Crime'.

in the course of creating the image and, to a lesser extent, that which may result from the consumption of such images. As such, child pornography crimes must be recognized as being fundamentally different in kind from other obscene material, where the focus is on the effect on the consumer of such material, in terms of potential future offences, from sexual depravity to violence or drug-taking.[304]

General

3.130　Under the Obscene Publications Act 1959, it is an offence to publish an obscene article or to have an obscene article for publication for gain, attracting a maximum tariff of five years.[305] Obscenity need not have a sexual context, as the test for determining whether an article is obscene is wider in scope:

> . . . if its effect or (where the article comprises two or more distinct items) the effect of any one of its items is, if taken as a whole, such as to tend to deprave and corrupt persons who are likely, having due regard to all relevant circumstances, to read, see or hear the matter contained or embodied in it.[306]

The intention of the author or publisher is irrelevant to a finding of obscenity. Over the years there has been much criticism made against this formulation, from all sides of the free speech debate. The threshold can be viewed as breaching the principle of legal certainty and fair warning, or as having the necessary flexibility to evolve 'with contemporary moral standards'.[307] However, reform has not been seriously pursued within government and, the Home Office has stated about the Act that they 'are satisfied that it continues to provide a benchmark for society's tolerance of certain material at a given time, as expressed through the courts …'.[308]

3.131　Determining whether material is obscene is for a jury to decide, without the admission of expert testimony. While the threshold of obscenity is higher than that for indecency, applicable to child pornographic images, the obscenity threshold is based on the likely audience for the material. Where that audience comprises children, the threshold is likely to be met more easily, on the basis that children are more vulnerable to being corrupted and depraved. As noted by Lord Wilberforce in *DPP v Whyte*,[309] 'to apply different tests to teenagers, members of men's clubs or men in various occupations or localities would be a matter of common sense'.

3.132　While the issue of child access to obscene material may not be a major issue in a traditional environment, where access controls can be exercised by those operating a physical outlet, such age-verification controls may not be present or adequate in an Internet environment. It could be envisaged, therefore, that a site which aggressively promoted pornographic material to Internet users, through search engines and associated techniques such as meta-tags, without placing controls on access to its material, could be found liable on the basis that

---

[304] *Blackstone's Criminal Practice 2016*, above, n 148, s B18.

[305] Obscene Publications Act 1959 (OPA 1959), s 2(1). Under the CJIA 2008, s 71, the maximum tariff was raised from three to five years imprisonment.

[306] OPA 1959, s 1(1). See *John Calder (Publications) Ltd v Powell* [1965] 1 QB 509, as an example of a non-sexual obscene publication.

[307] Ormerod, D and Laird, K (eds), *Smith & Hogan Criminal Law*, 14th edn, Oxford University Press, 2015, s 31.1.2.4.

[308] Home Office, above, n 219, para 21.

[309] [1972] AC 849, at 863B.

children are 'likely' to be visitors attracted to the site. Such an argument would seem even stronger in the case of those that send unsolicited emails that contain potentially obscene material.

This is an objective issue for the jury to decide not a quantitative issue; the prosecution not **3.133** being required to show how many and what types of persons actually visited the site, but rather that vulnerable people such as children are 'likely' to have visited the site. However, this still raises the question of what numerical threshold the jury should have in mind when deciding whether children would 'likely' constitute the audience. In *Calder and Boyars Ltd*, Salmon LJ felt that it required 'a significant proportion',[310] although such an approach was rejected by Lord Pearson in *DPP v Whyte*, who felt that it was sufficient that 'some persons' were affected, subject to a *de minimis* principle.[311] In *Perrin*,[312] a case involving material depicting coprophilia and coprophagia in the form of a preview page made available to anyone with access to the Internet from a website based in the US (<sewersex.com>), the court rejected a claim based on 'significant proportion' in favour of a 'more than a negligible number' standard.[313] Subsequent to *Perrin*, the government stated that they considered the threshold for obscenity where children are likely to access material to be a 'degree of sexual explicitness equivalent to what is available to those aged 18 and above in a licensed sex shop'; while such access is considered 'likely' where material is 'not behind a suitable payment barrier or other accepted means of age verification, for example, material on the front page of pornography websites and non-commercial, user-generated material'.[314]

The sheer scale of the potential audience in cyberspace effectively increases the risk that **3.134** a publication may be held to be obscene in respect of a particular societal group, whether determined by age, culture, or other relevant characteristic. In such a case, expert evidence may be submitted in respect of the nature of the audience that is likely to view particular material, even though the only evidence before the jury of someone having actually seen it may be from the law enforcement officer involved in the investigation, who is not susceptible to corruption and depravity.[315]

Publication of an obscene article is defined in the following terms: **3.135**

(a) distributes, circulates, sells, lets on hire, gives, or lends it, or who offers it for sale or for letting on hire or;
(b) in the case of an article containing or embodying matter to be looked at or a record, shows, plays or projects it, or, where the matter is data stored electronically, transmits that data.[316]

What constitutes an act of publication in a cyberspace context? Does making an obscene article available for download from a website, or transfer via a P2P network, constitute

---

[310] [1969] 1 QB 151, at 168.
[311] [1972] AC 849, at 866F. See also *O'Sullivan* [1995] 1 Cr App R 455, at 466G, where the two were conjoined: 'such as to tend to deprave and corrupt a significant proportion, that is more than a negligible number of those who were likely'.
[312] [2002] EWCA Crim 747.
[313] ibid, para 31.
[314] Vernon Coaker, Home Office Minister, in a response to a question from Dr Brian Iddon MP, 13 December 2006.
[315] *Perrin* [2002] EWCA Crim 747, para 22.
[316] OPA 1959, s 1(3).

'transmission'? Transmission has connotations of information being pushed from the sender to the recipient, while in the examples given the process is more akin to information being pulled by the recipient from the sender. A similar semantic issue has arisen in the copyright field, giving rise to legal reform making it clear that the exclusive right to communicate a copyright work to the public included 'the making available to the public of their works in such a way that members of the public may access them from a place and at a time individually chosen by them'.[317] The courts took a robust approach to interpretation on this point in *Fellows and Arnold*,[318] rejecting an argument that publication requires some form of active conduct, rather than the passive conduct of making information available for access.

3.136 In *Waddon*,[319] the defendant operated a website entitled 'xtreme-perversion', which was accessed by a police officer through subscription enabling material to be downloaded that was considered obscene. In the course of appeal proceedings, defence counsel conceded that the defendant was responsible for the transmission of the material to the website, as well as its subsequent transmission to the police officer. However, the court was also asked to rule on what the position would be were the person uploading the material not to have the intention to enable subsequent downloading into the jurisdiction. While the court refused to rule, it did opine that publication should not be considered as a single act, but multiple acts, further acts of publication taking place each time the material was downloaded. As such, the *actus reus* of the offence is carried out by the perpetrator in the first instance, when uploading the material, but subsequently by the victim(s), or jointly with the perpetrator, when downloading the material. In addition, by conceiving the act broadly, the *obiter* in *Waddon* consequently multiplied the possible places of publication and therefore the jurisdictional scope of the offence, which was subsequently applied in *Perrin*,[320] examined in Chapter 5.[321]

3.137 In *Smith (Gavin)*,[322] the defendant was tried for explicit conversations on Internet relay chat concerning various sexual fantasies, including sadistic sex acts against children. At trial, he successfully argued that transmission to a single person, without the recipient being expected to publish onwards, did not constitute an act of publication. This interpretation was overturned on appeal, with the court holding that not only can there be publication when there is only a single recipient, but also that this one person can be the only one corrupted and depraved by the material.

3.138 In respect of the offence of having an article that is 'for publication for gain', a preparatory offence of prospective publication introduced by the Obscene Publications Act 1964, reference should be made:

> . . . to such publication for gain of the article as in the circumstances it may reasonably be inferred he had in contemplation and to any further publication that could reasonably be expected to follow from it.[323]

---

[317] Directive 2001/29/EC on the harmonisation of certain aspects of copyright and related rights in the information society, OJ L 167/10, 22 June 2001, Art 3(1).
[318] [1997] 2 All ER 548.
[319] [2000] All ER (D) 502.
[320] [2002] All ER (D) 359.
[321] See paras 5.22–5.25.
[322] [2012] EWCA Crim 398.
[323] Obscene Publications Act 1964, c 74 (OPA 1964), s 1(3)(b).

In the case of digital information, especially where it could be shown that a person was intending to distribute the obscene material via a file sharing application, the extent of further publication that could be 'reasonably expected' must be of a different degree in terms of propagation than that for a physical text.

While the Obscene Publication Acts may be seen as standing the test of time, including the **3.139** emergence of cyberspace, numerous supplementary statutory regimes have been established to address the supply of pornographic material in different contexts. It is to these matters that we now turn.

Video recordings In addition to the Obscene Publications Acts, there are other offences that **3.140** may be applicable to the provision of pornographic material over the Internet or via other communications services, such as mobile telephony. The Video Recordings Act 1984,[324] for example, establishes a classification system for video works and video games and a number of offences relating to their supply, including supplying unclassified videos[325] and supplying video recordings classified as 'R18'[326] material, except from licensed premises.[327] As well as being applicable to the distribution of pornographic material, the Video Recordings Act 1984 has also been relevant in intellectual property counterfeiting cases[328] and child abuse images.[329]

Under the Act, a 'video recording' is defined in the following terms: **3.141**

> any disc, magnetic tape or any other device capable of storing data electronically containing information by the use of which the whole or part of a video work may be produced.[330]

While this would clearly seem to capture the shift from video cassettes to DVDs, and the distribution of such material through web-based transaction engines,[331] the focus on the existence of a 'device' would seem to preclude pure digital video products, where the 'video work' is downloaded as a stream of data to the customer's equipment, such as a computer or mobile handset. In the latter scenario, however, the data may instead fall under broadcasting laws, depending on the manner in which it is distributed, ie simultaneously or on demand through selections made by customers.[332]

The application of the Act in a distance-selling context was examined in *Interfact Ltd and others v Liverpool City Council*,[333] which has implications for web-based transaction sites distrib- **3.142** uting physical products. Here the defendants operated licensed sex shops, but also supplied

---

[324] The Act was repealed and re-enacted by the Video Recordings Act 2010, after being considered unlawful by virtue of having not been notified to the European Commission as a technical standard under Directive 83/189/EEC.

[325] Video Recordings Act 1984 (VRA 1984), s 9.

[326] ibid, s 7(2)(c), as classified by the British Board of Film Classification.

[327] ibid, s 12(1).

[328] eg *Passley* [2004] 1 Cr App R (S) 70.

[329] eg *Farquhar* [2002] EWCA Crim 1633.

[330] VRA 1984, s 1(3). A 'video work' is 'any series of visual images (with or without sound)—(a) produced electronically by the use of information contained on any disc magnetic tape or any other device capable of storing data electronically, and (b) shown as a moving picture' (s 1(2)).

[331] eg from Amazon.co.uk.

[332] Communications Act 2003, s 361.

[333] [2005] EWHC 995 (Admin). The defendants applied to have the decision quashed, following the government's admission that the Act was unenforceable, but the Court of Appeal upheld the conviction as safe: [2010] EWCA Crim 1486.

such products in response to orders received by post, telephone, or email. On appeal, the issue for the court was the meaning of 'supply' and offering to supply under the Act. The defendants argued that since the process of supply commenced in a licensed shop, the fact that the person was not required to be physically present in the shop to receive the goods was not relevant. The court rejected this interpretation, holding that the requirement for persons to be supplied at a specific physical location was a critical aspect of the control regime established under the Act. However, the purposive approach taken by the court towards 'supply' would not likely enable the scope of the Act to be extended beyond device-based distribution schemes.

3.143 The Act provides a defence where the commission of the offence was due to the act of another person and the defendant has taken 'all reasonable precautions and exercised all due diligence' to avoid the offence.[334] Despite the wording, the standard of care that an innocent reputable retailer is required to exercise has been held to be relatively minimal.[335]

3.144 Certain types of 'video works' are exempt from the regime, such as educational and music videos.[336] Video works and video games are not exempted where they depict certain types of content, such as violence, mutilation, or torture.[337] The regime is also applicable where the content 'depicts techniques likely to be useful in the commission of offences',[338] which could include, for example, videos showing hacking techniques and related matter.[339]

3.145 **Indecent displays** Under the Indecent Displays (Control) Act 1981, it is an offence to 'publicly display' 'indecent matter',[340] subject to a potential maximum two-year term of imprisonment.[341] As discussed below in respect of child abuse images, 'indecent' is a lower standard from that of 'obscene' material under the Obscene Publications Acts.

3.146 In a cyberspace context, the key concept is that of 'public place', defined in the following terms:

> means any place to which the public have or are permitted to have access (whether on payment or otherwise) while that matter is displayed except—
> (a) a place to which the public are permitted to have access only on payment which is or includes payment for that display; or
> (b) a shop or any part of a shop to which the public can only gain access by passing beyond an adequate warning notice,
> but the exclusions contained in paragraphs (a) and (b) above shall only apply where the persons under the age of 18 years are not permitted to enter while the display in question is continuing.[342]

3.147 The terms and nature of the 'warning notice' are also detailed:

> WARNING
> Persons passing beyond this notice will find material on display which they may consider indecent. No admittance to persons under 18 years of age.[343]

---

[334] VRA 1984, s 14A.
[335] eg *Bilon v WH Smith Trading Ltd* [2001] EWHC Admin 469.
[336] VRA 1984, s 2(1).
[337] ibid, s 2(1ZA) and 2(2) respectively.
[338] ibid, s 2(3). See also TA, s 2 ('Dissemination of terrorist publications').
[339] See further para 3.336 concerning illegal devices.
[340] Indecent Displays (Control) Act 1981 (IDC), s 1(1).
[341] ibid, s 4(1).
[342] ibid, s 1(3).
[343] ibid, s 1(6)(a).

There are certain types of subject matter that are excluded for the Act's provisions, such as television programmes, museums, art galleries, plays, and films,[344] but nothing that would protect a website or other online resource that failed to implement appropriate access controls and notices.

However, the paucity of prosecutions under the Indecent Displays (Control) Act 1981 suggests that it is not going to be used by law enforcement agencies as a key weapon against the distribution of pornographic material online.[345] There have also been calls from child protection agencies for a 'cyber equivalent' of the Indecent Displays (Control) Act 1981,[346] which is surprising given the breadth of its provisions. There would seem to be nothing in the definition of 'public place' that restricts its applicability to physical locations, rather than cyberspace. **3.148**

Extreme pornography In August 2005, the Home Office published a consultation paper 'On the possession of extreme pornographic material'. The initiative was driven, in part, by some disturbing evidence presented in *Coutts*.[347] One element of the evidence presented against Graham Coutts in his trial for the murder of Jane Longhurst was that, around the relevant time, he had visited various websites concerned with sexual violence related to rape, murder, and necrophilia.[348] **3.149**

In the consultation paper, it noted that while the Obscene Publications Act 1959 was applicable to such material, its focus on those that supply such material was problematic in an Internet era, where publishers are generally located abroad. Therefore, it put forward proposals to mirror the arrangements for child pornography, by criminalizing possession of such material, thereby attempting to address the demand side. **3.150**

The proposal differed from the Obscene Publications Act approach of examining the effect such material may have on the viewer, criminalizing instead specific types of content, similar to the Video Recordings Act 1984. Given the vague nature of the 'deprave and corrupt' standard, the addition of a possession offence to the 1959 Act would lack sufficient clarity and certainty.[349] It was proposed to criminalize, through a separate offence, possession of material containing actual or 'realistic depictions' of the following: **3.151**

- intercourse or oral sex with an animal;
- sexual interference with a human corpse;
- serious violence in a sexual context; and
- serious sexual violence.[350]

However, this change of focus created problems for legislators in terms of adequately defining such content without encroaching on existing legitimate activities, such as certain **3.152**

---

[344] ibid, s 1(4).

[345] See House of Commons Written Answers for 16 February 2006, from Home Office Minister Fiona Mactaggart, which showed that between 2002 and 2004 only eleven proceedings had been commenced and only three convictions obtained (Col 2352W).

[346] The Children's Charities' Coalition on Internet Safety (CHIS), *Child safety online: Digital manifesto summary*, November 2004, at 2.

[347] [2005] EWCA Crim 52.

[348] ibid, at 39–43.

[349] Rowbottom, above, n 210, at 102.

[350] Such violence would be subject to prosecution for grievous bodily harm in England and Wales.

sadomasochist practices and the film industry. The proposal generated particular controversy in respect of the last two categories of content. The penalty for possession would be three years, although a distinction would be maintained from that of publication, by raising the tariff under the Obscene Publications Act to five years.

3.153 Despite opinion among respondents being 'sharply divided', the Government proceeded with its proposals and introduced the new offence under the Criminal Justice and Immigration Act 2008.[351] The new offence criminalizes the possession of an 'extreme pornographic image'.[352] An image is 'pornographic' if 'it must reasonably be assumed' to have been produced for the purpose of sexual arousal.[353] The offence originally addressed four categories of content: acts that threaten a person's life; which results (or is likely to) in serious injury to a person's anus, breasts, or genitals; which involves sexual intercourse with a corpse or sexual acts with an animal.[354] The list was extended in 2015 to include scenes of rape.[355] As for obscenity and indecency, it will be for a jury to find that the material is 'pornographic', as well as involving real acts or a depiction of apparently real acts. The statutory defences mirror those available under the Criminal Justice Act 1988 (CJA 1988) in respect of child abuse images.[356] In addition, there is a defence where the acts, other than those involving animals, can be proved to have been consensual in nature.[357] The three-year maximum prison tariff will only be sought for material depicting serious violence, with lesser maximums for the other categories.[358] As with other speech-related offences, proceedings can only be brought with the consent of the Director of Public Prosecutions.[359]

Child abuse and pornography

3.154 If any topic is unequivocally associated in the minds of politicians, the media, and the public with the 'dark side' of the Internet, it is that of child pornography. The Internet has facilitated the supply of this form of illegal content to such an extent that it is now considered a multi-billion dollar industry,[360] primarily through a proliferation of pay-per-view sites, while at the same time cyberspace engenders broader child protection concerns about the harms children can suffer from the content and contact available over the Internet.[361] As a consequence, child protection is currently at the forefront of Government policy on cybercrime.[362]

---

[351] CJIA 2008, ss 63–8.

[352] Although the offence is for possession, in *Oliver (Philip)* [2011] EWCA Crim 3114, the court held that it was aggravating feature that the defendant had downloaded file-sharing software, called 'TeamViewer', which made the images available to others.

[353] CJIA 2008, s 63(3).

[354] ibid, s 63(7).

[355] ibid, s 63(7A) and (7B), inserted by the Criminal Justice and Courts Act 2015, c 2.

[356] CJIA 2008, s 65. See *Ping Chen Cheung* [2009] EWCA Crim 2965.

[357] CJIA 2008, s 66.

[358] ibid, s 67, which distinguishes between images portraying a 'relevant act' (ibid, s 67(5)), ie involving violence, and other images for which the maximum is two years (ibid, s 67(3)).

[359] ibid, s 63(10)

[360] International Center for Missing and Exploited Children, 'Financial and Internet industries to combat Internet child pornography', Press Release, 15 March 2006, available at <http://www.icmec.org/press/financial-and-internet-industries-to-combat-internet-child-pornography-european-news-release/>.

[361] See generally Millwood Hargrave, A and Livingstone, S, *Harm and Offence in Media Content*, Intellect, 2006.

[362] Interview with Tim Wright, Head of Computer Crime Team, Home Office, 1 February 2006.

Some of the images are taken surreptitiously without direct interference with the child; **3.155** however, the vast majority of hard-core images involve the direct abuse of children. Indeed, it has been noted that the term 'pornography' is inappropriate in the context of children, since the term embraces a semi-legitimate industry and creates confusion in the minds of the public, especially where the images involve pubescent children.[363] The more appropriate term is simply child abuse. While supporting such a view, for the purpose of this book, the examination of the issue has been placed within the section on pornography, with which it is more popularly associated. This section is concerned primarily with the production, distribution, and possession of indecent photographs of children.

While the majority of children are abused by those related to them, such as fathers and uncles, **3.156** or in some form of relationship, such as a priest, the Internet provides a new environment for potential abusers to form intimate relationships with children at a distance, eventually leading to the arrangement of a physical meeting with the child. Broader child protection issues are beyond the scope of this book, although the new offence of 'Internet grooming', as a preparatory communications offence, is the exception and is briefly discussed below.

The two principal statutory provisions under UK law in respect of child pornographic **3.157** images are in relation to the supply of such images, under the Protection of Children Act 1978 (POCA 1978), and the possession of such images, under the CJA 1988.[364] Supply is distinguished into four different types of activity: (a) taking and making; (b) distributing or showing; (c) possession with a view to distribution; and (d) publishing an advertisement suggesting that the advertiser distributes or shows indecent photographs.[365]

As with other areas examined in this chapter, one issue policy-makers and the courts have **3.158** been required to address is the extent to which offences detailed in statutes drafted in a pre-cyberspace age can be applied to Internet-based activities. While the relevant legislation has proved largely robust, it has also been subject to a series of amendments over the years, designed to address the evolving nature of the criminal conduct, as well as to enhance the penalties applicable to such conduct. In *Fellows and Arnold*,[366] the court was asked to consider whether the legislation prior to the 1994 amendment would enable computer data to be considered a 'copy of an indecent photograph' and whether making images available for downloading from a website constituted material being 'distributed or shown'. The court held that the statutory wording was drafted in sufficiently wide terms to encompass the use of technology that was 'either not anticipated or was in its infancy' when the statute was adopted.[367] Importantly, the mere fact that the wording of the statute was amended in 1994 was not itself indicative that the terms should be construed narrowly.[368] By contrast, US federal criminal law has been amended to expressly include the use of computers as a means of sending, distributing, or receiving child pornography.[369]

---

[363] Stated by Jim Gamble, Deputy Director General, National Crime Squad, at a conference, 'Child pornography on the Internet: investigation and prosecution', London, 19 October 2005.
[364] Criminal Justice Act 1988 (CJA 1988), s 160.
[365] PCA 2002, s 1(1)(a)–(d), respectively.
[366] [1997] 1 Cr App R 244.
[367] ibid, at 254.
[368] ibid, at 253.
[369] 18 USC s 2252A.

3.159 **Child** While child pornography is a distinct offence under English law, an international survey has highlighted the fact that in fifty-three jurisdictions, such as Pakistan and Ghana, there is no specific legal regime to address child pornography.[370]

3.160 In terms of what constitutes a child, the POCA 1978 states that '... a person is to be taken as having been a child at any material time if it appears from the evidence as a whole that he was under the age of 18'.[371] This is critically important, since the identity of the child is generally unknown, a phenomenon exacerbated in an Internet environment. The age threshold was raised from sixteen by the Sexual Offences Act 2003.[372] UK law is in line with EU law,[373] US law,[374] and the Convention of Cybercrime, although a party may stipulate a lower age not less than sixteen years.[375] In *Land*,[376] the court held that the determination of the age of a child in an image was to be made exclusively by the jury, and was something for which expert testimony was not normally required. However, in reality, prosecution activity tends to focus on pre-pubescent children, thereby avoiding any significant argument about age.[377]

3.161 **Indecent image** Under English law, both the supply and possession of 'indecent images' of children is criminalized, which contrasts with the regime governing 'obscene' publications, both in terms of the applicable standard and the nature of the illegal activity.[378] 'Indecent' is not defined in the legislation, but is a question of fact to be determined by the jury, applying normal standards of propriety,[379] which may include account of the age of the child, where known.[380] Indeed, as with obscenity, the intention of the person making the image is irrelevant to a finding of indecency.[381]

3.162 However, from a prosecutorial perspective, it is necessary to categorize the nature of the images when preparing the indictment. Until April 2014, there was a five-point scale, established by the Sentencing Advisory and endorsed with amendment by the Court of Appeal,[382] which was originally based on the COPINE scale developed by researchers in Ireland.[383] Since 1 April 2014, the Sentencing Council has adopted a new three-tier categorization:

Category A: Involving penetrative activity or sexual activity with an animal or sadism,
Category B: Non-penetrative sexual activity,

---

[370] International Centre for Missing and Exploited Children, *Child Pornography: Model Legislation & Global Review*, 7th edn, 2012, available at <http://www.icmec.org/en_X1/pdf/Child_Pornography_Model_Law_English_7th_Edition_2012.pdf>. However, this represents a significant reduction from the position in 2006, when some 95 countries had no such legislation.

[371] Protection of Children Act 1978 (POCA 1978), s 2(3).

[372] Sexual Offences Act 2003 (SOA 2003), s 45.

[373] Directive 2011/92/EU on combating the sexual abuse and sexual exploitation of children and child pornography, OJ L 335/1, 17 December 2001.

[374] 18 USC s 2256(1).

[375] Convention on Cybercrime, Art 9(3). Only Switzerland has taken up the option.

[376] (1998) 1 CAR 301.

[377] See Gillespie, AA, 'Child pornography: Balancing substantive and evidential law to safeguard children effectively from abuse', 9(1) *International Journal of Evidence & Proof* 36 (2005).

[378] Although see the possession offences in respect of 'extreme pornographic images', detailed at paras 3.149–3.153.

[379] *Murray* [2004] EWCA Crim 2211; [2005] Crim LR 386.

[380] *Owen* (1986) 86 Cr App R 291.

[381] *Smethurst* [2002] 1 Cr App R 50; [2001] 1 Crim LR 657.

[382] In *Oliver, Hartrey and Baldwin* [2003] 2 Cr App R 28, para 10.

[383] See Taylor, M, Holland, G, and Quayle, E, 'Typology of paedophile picture collections', 74 *Police Journal* 97 (2001).

Category C: Indecent images not falling within the other categories.[384]

The nature of material falling into Category C has created some controversy in the past, **3.163** because of the potential for innocent behaviour on the part of the child to be wrongfully construed, yet result in liability for the maker or possessor of the image.[385] In the US, federal law requires that the child be involved in some form of 'sexually explicit conduct', which includes 'lascivious exhibition of the genitals or pubic area of any person'.[386] This focus on specific areas of the body reasserts the responsibility of the image-maker for the indecent nature of the image and raises the threshold of criminality in the US from that contained in Category C. In practice, the difference between the two regimes is unlikely to be substantial, since UK prosecuting authorities will generally be cautious about commencing a prosecution based solely on images of an uncertain erotic nature, unless the volumes involved or the conduct of the defendant supports any such assertion.

The offence was originally limited to indecent 'images' in the form of photographs, rather **3.164** than other forms of publication, such as text or drawn pictures. This was partially addressed in 2008 by the inclusion of 'a tracing or other image' derived from a photograph.[387] The term 'image' is not defined, although the Sexual Offences Act 2003 defines it in the following terms: 'a moving or still image and includes an image produced by any means and, where context permits, a three-dimensional image'.[388]

For other non-photographic material, the only alternative offence would have been under **3.165** the Obscene Publications Act 1959. This perceived gap was closed through provisions in the Coroners and Justice Act 2009, which criminalized the possession of 'prohibited images of children'.[389] Here the definition of an 'image' includes 'a moving or still image (produced by any means)', but excludes photographs and pseudo-photographs.[390] An image should be treated as an 'image of a child' if either the impression conveyed, or the predominant impression, is that or a child, whether real or imaginary.[391] A 'prohibited' image is one that is pornographic, defined in equivalent terms to the 'extreme pornography' offence; falls within a list of images or acts;[392] and is 'grossly offensive, disgusting or otherwise of an obscene character'.[393] The defences replicate those of the other possession offences.[394] As with the extreme pornography, an exclusion was crafted for films that have been classified by the British Board of Film Classification.[395] The maximum term is only three years; below

---

[384] Sentencing Council, *Sexual Offences: Definitive Guideline*, 2013, at 76, available at <https://www.sentencingcouncil.org.uk/wp-content/uploads/Final_Sexual_Offences_Definitive_Guideline_content_web1.pdf>.

[385] eg the case concerning ITN news reader Julia Somerville: see Toynbee, P, 'The voyeurs have won', *The Guardian*, 13 March 2001, available at <http://www.theguardian.com/society/2001/mar/13/childprotection.pollytoynbee>.

[386] 18 USC s 2256(2)(A)(v).

[387] POCA 1978, s 7(4A), inserted by CJIA 2008, s 69(3).

[388] SOA 2003, s 79(4).

[389] CJA 1988, ss 62–8.

[390] ibid, s 65(2) and (3).

[391] ibid, s 65(6) and (8).

[392] ibid, s 62(6) and (7).

[393] ibid, s 62(2).

[394] ibid, s 64.

[395] ibid, s 63.

that applicable to the possession of indecent photographs, which reflects the perception that they are not of the same gravity, on the presumption that no child was abused in the making of the image.[396]

3.166 As with computer-related offences such as fraud, English indecency laws have sometimes struggled to adequately address computer-based activities and the unique features of computer-generated pornography. As a result, such laws have been subject to legislative amendment to close particular lacunae. In 1994, for example, the POCA 1978 and the CJA 1988 were amended to extend offences in relation to the distribution and possession of indecent photographs of children to the concept of 'pseudo-photographs', created through the manipulation of digital images:

> an image, whether made by computer-graphics or otherwise howsoever, which appears to be a photograph.[397]

However, what if the 'pseudo-photograph' image is a composite of a child and an adult. Would this still be a photograph of a child? The amendment also addressed this situation, stating:

> If the impression conveyed by a pseudo-photograph is that the person shown is a child, the pseudo-photograph shall be treated for all purposes of this Act as showing a child and so shall a pseudo-photograph where the predominant impression conveyed is that the person shown is a child notwithstanding that some of the physical characteristics shown are those of an adult.[398]

This amendment has, however, been strictly construed. In *Goodland*,[399] the court held that two photographs that were taped together in a hinge effect did not 'appear to be a photograph' even though a photocopy of the same probably would have been.

3.167 The Convention on Cybercrime would seem to adopt an even broader formulation:

> 'child pornography' shall include pornographic material that visually depicts:
> (a) a minor engaged in sexually explicit conduct;
> (b) a person appearing to be a minor engaged in sexually explicit conduct;
> (c) realistic images representing a minor engaged in sexually explicit conduct.[400]

The second category does not directly result in harm to a child, as potentially with the third category where an image can be entirely generated by a computer. However, the concern is that such images 'might be used to encourage or seduce children into participating in such acts, and hence form part of a subculture favouring child abuse'.[401] Signatories can reserve the right not to criminalize categories (b) and (c); an option that has been taken by a number of Member States, including Switzerland and the UK, on the basis that Article 9(2)(b)

---

[396] ibid, s 66. See *Palmer (Richard)* [2011] EWCA Crim 1286, which involved 'stylised fantasy images in a graphic cartoon-type format'.

[397] POCA 1978, s 7(7) and CJA 1988, s 160(4), inserted by the Criminal Justice and Public Order Act 1994, s 84. See also the recommendations made in the House of Commons, Home Affairs Committee, *Computer Pornography*, 1st Report, Session 1993–94 HC No 126.

[398] POCA 1978, s 7(8).

[399] *Goodland v DPP* [2000] 2 All ER 425; [2000] 1 WLR 1427.

[400] Convention on Cybercrime, Art 9(2).

[401] Explanatory Report to the Convention on Cybercrime, above, n 1, at para 102.

'is incompatible with domestic law regarding indecent photographs of children'.[402] The EU Directive 'on combating the sexual exploitation of children and child pornography' defines child pornography in terms that reflect the Convention formulation.[403] Although the UK Government has opted-in to this measure, it has not made any pronouncements concerning its compatibility with UK law.

In the US, similar legislation, the Child Pornography Prevention Act of 1996,[404] also ini-   **3.168** tially extended the concept of an image of a child to include a 'computer-generated image' that 'is, or appears to be, of a minor engaging in sexually explicit conduct';[405] and defined child pornography to include images that 'convey the impression' of a minor engaged in sexually explicit conduct.[406] However, the Supreme Court has struck down these provisions as over-broad and therefore unconstitutional under the First Amendment.[407] In respect of the first provision, the court rejected the assertion made by Congress that such images threaten children in a number of indirect ways, although they do not in themselves involve or harm children.

In Canada, the Supreme Court was asked to rule on whether the prohibition on the pos-   **3.169** session of child pornography was a constitutional restriction on freedom of expression.[408] In the course of its judgment, which concluded that the provision was substantially consti- tutional, the court considered the fact that the prohibition extended to 'imaginary human beings' as well as actual children. First, the court accepted that the 'available evidence suggests that explicit sexual materials can be harmful whether or not they depict actual children'.[409] It then went on to note that the inherent difficulties in distinguishing real from 'a computer creation or composite' justify a broad conception of what constitutes a porno- graphic image.[410]

Mens rea While the *actus reus* of the offences of supplying and possessing child abuse images   **3.170** are clearly specified in the statutory provisions, the *mens rea* component is not. The issue has therefore fallen to the courts for determination. However, the nature of cyberspace and the technologies involved has provided complex issues for the courts to consider.

In *Atkins & Goodland v Director of Public Prosecutions*,[411] the court was required to address   **3.171** a situation where the offending images, upon which the prosecution was based, were con- tained in the cache memory of the defendant's machine.[412] Such copies are generally created and stored automatically by the browser software used to access the Internet, for reasons of efficiency. Expert evidence was submitted which indicated that most computer users are unaware of the operation of the cache memory feature on their machines.

---

[402] List of declarations made with respect to Treaty No 185, available at <http://www.coe.int/en/web/ conventions/full-list/-/conventions/treaty/185/declarations?p_auth=pFU8ehfk>.
[403] Directive 2011/92/EU, above, n 373, Art 2(c).
[404] 18 USC s 2251.
[405] ibid, s 2256(8)(B).
[406] ibid, s 2256(8)(D).
[407] *Ashcroft v Free Speech Coalition* 535 US 234 (2002), at 244.
[408] *R v Sharpe* [2001] 1 SCR 45.
[409] ibid, para 38.
[410] ibid.
[411] [2000] 2 All ER 425.
[412] Images were also found in a separate directory; however, charges relating to those saved images were dismissed for being brought out of time.

3.172 Two issues for the court, therefore, were whether the cache copies could be said to have been 'made' under the POCA 1978, s 1(1)(a) or 'possessed' under the CJA 1988, s 160(1). In a previous decision, *Bowden*,[413] a court held that the downloading and printing images from the Internet fell within the concept of 'making', since the term 'applies not only to original photographs but ... also to negatives, copies of photographs and data stored on computer disc'.[414] However, in *Atkins*, the prosecution could not prove that the defendant was aware of the cache copies and therefore liability for 'making' or 'possession' could only be found if s 1(1) or s 160, respectively, were construed as offences of strict liability rather than requiring knowledge. The general presumption of the courts when construing criminal legislation is that Parliament does not intend to punish a blameless individual and therefore *mens rea* must be read into a statute.[415] The court therefore held that knowledge was required and the appeal succeeded on this point. If the prosecution could have proved that the defendant was aware of the cache memory, perhaps by showing that the individual had altered the default settings for the caching function, then the conviction may have been upheld.[416]

3.173 While in *Atkins* the courts accepted that subjective knowledge was required for the offence of 'possession' to be made out; in *Warwick*,[417] the appeal court was required to further consider what comprises 'possession' in a computer environment. The defendant had been charged with two counts of possession in respect of some 3,000 still images and forty movie files. However, for the period in respect of which the charge related, it was agreed that the images and files had been either placed in the operating system's 'recycle bin' and the bin emptied; were viewable only in thumbnail format;[418] or were only present in the computer cache. As such, except in respect of the cached files, they were recoverable only with the use of specialized software, which it was accepted the defendant did not have.[419] At trial, the judge had directed the jury that the fact that the files were deleted did not have any bearing on the fact that the defendant was in possession of the indecent images, and he was subsequently convicted.

3.174 On appeal, defence counsel argued that the offence of possession was not committed where the material was no longer 'readily accessible', especially when a person has taken all reasonable steps to delete them and render them inaccessible.[420] In deciding this issue, the court referred to one of the defences provided under s 160, where an indecent photograph has been received 'without any prior request made by him or on his behalf and he did not keep it for an unreasonable time'.[421] This defence, the court stated, would be effectively undermined in a computer context if 'possession' was interpreted on the basis that a person possesses images simply through having custody or control of the computer on which deleted files resides. The court held that 'if a person cannot retrieve or gain access to an

---

[413] [2000] 1 Cr App R 438.

[414] ibid, at 444E per Otton LJ.

[415] *Sweet v Parsley* [1970] AC 132, at 148H.

[416] eg *Neil John Harrison v R* [2007] EWCA Crim 2976, where the appellant admitted he knew that automatic 'pop-ups' or redirections to other sites would occur when accessing legal pornographic sites.

[417] [2006] EWCA Crim 560.

[418] Comprising a subset of the image, not the full image itself; this would be stored as a separate file elsewhere, but had been deleted.

[419] The thumbnail images could only have been retrieved with very specialist software supplied only with the authorization of the US Federal Government!

[420] [2006] EWCA Crim 560, para 9.

[421] CJA 1988, s 160(2)(c).

image, in our view he no longer has custody or control of it', and therefore can not be said to be in possession for the purposes of the s 160 offence.[422] Whether in a particular set of circumstances a defendant could be found to remain in control of deleted files, due to his level of technical skill and ability, will be a matter for the jury to decide in each case.[423] The court recognized that this introduced a second subjective element into the offence, together with that of knowledge.

Another technical defence that has been successfully advanced in child pornography cases **3.175** concerns the presence of a 'Trojan horse' virus, an apparently benign program, which executes functions without the user being aware. In *Schofield*, the defendant claimed that a 'Trojan horse' virus found on his computer had downloaded the pornographic images without his knowledge. Expert testimony confirmed that such a scenario was possible, and the prosecution offered no evidence.[424]

In *Westgarth Smith* and *Jayson*,[425] a similar argument to *Atkins* was advanced in respect of **3.176** the receipt of an email with an attachment containing a pornographic image. Here Smith's counsel argued that the 'making' involved in the receipt of an unsolicited email was similar to that of the cache copy in *Atkins*. The court accepted this assertion in general terms, but held that this was not the situation before the court. In *Jayson*, the prosecution was able to prove that the defendant was aware of the caching function within his browser software. However, the court also held that the mere 'act of voluntarily downloading an indecent image from a web page on to a computer screen is an act of making',[426] whether or not there was an intention to store the images for subsequent retrieval.

While *Jayson* addressed in part the *Atkins* problem of reliance on technical ignorance as **3.177** a defence, it did so at the cost of treating the most basic electronic act in a cyberspace environment, downloading information, as a form of 'making'. The Protection of Children Act offences are addressed at those that supply child pornography, criminalizing the taking, making, distribution, showing, or publishing of an advertisement.[427] By contrast, the Criminal Justice Act is concerned with the demand for such material, criminalizing mere possession. While the two are clearly interrelated, demand creates supply, the nature of the link, particularly in terms of the extent to which possessors are likely to become hands-on abusers, is not well known.[428] Despite this, Parliament has perceived the latter, possession, to be of a lesser seriousness, attracting a substantially lower tariff. However, under *Jayson*, the process of obtaining possession is itself being viewed as an act of supply. Prosecutors have also charged those involved with purchasing such material with incitement to supply, again blurring the line between supply and possession.[429]

---

[422] [2006] EWCA Crim 560, para 21.

[423] ibid, para 24. For similar reasoning in respect of deleted files under the Freedom of Information Act 2000, see Information Tribunal decision in *Harper v Information Commissioner*, [2005] UKIT EA_2005_0001.

[424] *Schofield*, The Times, 18 April 2003.

[425] [2002] EWCA Crim 683.

[426] ibid, para 33 per Dyson LJ.

[427] POCA 1978, s 1(1). Advertising under subsection (d) includes 'any advertisement likely to be understood as conveying that the advertiser distributes or show', which could be broadly interpreted to include the publication of a URL or hypertext link.

[428] See NCH, *Out of sight, out of mind: Tackling child sex abuse images on the internet—a global challenge*, Report, July 2006, at 11–12, available at <http://www.chis.org.uk/file_download/13/67-OutSightExSum.pdf>.

[429] eg *Goldman* [2001] EWCA Crim 1684, where a prosecution was successfully brought against a person possessing child pornography for incitement to commit an offence of supply under the POCA 1978.

3.178   Another example of the blurred line between supply and possession arose in respect of the offence of possession 'with a view to their being distributed or shown'.[430] In *Dooley*,[431] the defendant had obtained the indecent images using the P2P software KaZaA. Such images were downloaded to the defendant's 'My Shared Folder' and were subsequently transferred to other parts of the defendant's system that were not accessible to others using the same software. The defendant was charged with the subsection (c) offence on the basis of six images found in his 'My Shared Folder'. The defence case was that the defendant did not have any intention to distribute or show the images, but rather intended and, indeed, was in the process of moving the images to a non-public part of his machine, although the images remained accessible by others until that process was complete. At first instance, the Crown Court held that the phrase 'with a view to' did not equate with the defendant's intention and therefore mere knowledge that the images were accessible was sufficient. On appeal, the court held that the correct issue for a jury to determine was whether one of the reasons for the defendant leaving the images in his 'My Shared Folder' was to enable further distribution.[432] Since such an intention was not being argued by the prosecution, the court felt the need to quash the conviction.

3.179   To address the drift from possession to production represented by *Jayson*, in May 2002 the Sentencing Advisory Panel issued sentencing guidelines in respect of child pornography, which stated:

> 23. . . . the downloading of indecent images onto a computer for personal use should be treated, for sentencing purposes, as equivalent to possession . . . Our reason for this was that 'making' in the sense of making or taking an original indecent film or photograph of a child is clearly a more serious matter than downloading an image from the Internet, which is more akin to buying a pornographic magazine from a shop or mail order service.

This position is now contained in the Sentencing Council's guidelines.[433] However, the intention of Parliament to clearly distinguish between production and possession can be subverted through judicial interpretation and prosecutorial charging policy. However abhorrent such material is, it would seem more appropriate to address such issues through legislative amendment, rather than through sentencing policy and the discretion of the judiciary.

3.180   Until 2003, the only express defences available in respect of supply applied to distribution and showing or possession with a view to distribution.[434] A defence could be made out if the defendant could prove either a 'legitimate reason', or that he had not seen the photographs and did not know, or have any cause to suspect their nature, ie an absence of knowledge. However, when 'making' a photograph was inserted into the POCA 1978 in 1994,[435] no similar statutory defence was provided for, leaving a defendant with only the possibility of showing an absence of the necessary *mens rea*.

---

[430] POCA 1978, s 1(1)(c).
[431] [2005] EWCA Crim 3093.
[432] Quoting favourably from *Smith & Hogan Criminal Law*, above, n 307, at 1075 fn 70.
[433] *Sexual Offences: Definitive Guideline*, above, n 384, at 76.
[434] POCA 1978, s 1(4).
[435] By the Criminal Justice and Public Order Act 1994, s 84(2)(a), (b).

However, as a consequence of the courts more broadly defining the concept of 'making' **3.181** as something akin to simple possession, they inadvertently criminalized a range of activities and actors beyond that anticipated by Parliament when the legislation was adopted. For example, a system administrator or ISP may discover an indecent image and decide to report its presence to the law enforcement authorities. However, the act of reproducing the image to make the report was itself a criminal offence. While a prosecution would unlikely result, as the prosecution authorities would exercise their discretion, this exposure to liability was perceived as an unsatisfactory state of affairs. To remedy this situation, the Sexual Offences Act 2003 inserted a new defence into the POCA 1978 that the defendant is not guilty if he can prove that:

> it was necessary for him to make the photograph or pseudo-photograph for the purposes of the prevention, detection or investigation of crime, or the purposes of criminal proceedings, in any part of the world.[436]

The operation of this provision has been the subject of a Memorandum of Understanding between the CPS and the Association of Chief Police Officers (ACPO).[437] In it, major factors are listed that shall be taken into account when considering the intentions of an individual who has 'made' an image and wishes to rely on the s 46 defence, including how the images were handled, the number of copies 'made' and the timeliness of the reporting.

In respect of possession, there is a defence of 'legitimate reason': that the image had not **3.182** been seen and the person did not know or have cause to suspect the nature of such material, or that the material had been received without prior request and had not been kept for an unreasonable time.[438]

Tariff and sentence As well as reforming the legal framework to prevent lacunae, there is **3.183** also evidence that computer and communications technologies have facilitated the distribution of child pornography, with a subsequent rise in the numbers of people involved in the trade and the volume of material. This rise is evidenced, in part, by the significant rise in the number of prosecutions in the UK.[439]

In an attempt to counter such developments, governments have substantially raised the **3.184** penalties that such offences attract. In the US, sentencing guidelines provide for enhanced penalties where 'the offense involved the use of a computer or an interactive computer service',[440] on the basis that extra deterrent is required where the activity is more difficult to detect and prosecute.[441] In the UK, the maximum penalty for the s 1 offences under the

---

[436] SOA 2003, s 46, inserting a new section POCA 1978, s 1B(1)(a) 'Exception for the criminal proceedings, investigations etc.'. Other defences are available for those working in the Security Service, Secret Intelligence Service, and Government Communications Headquarters (GCHQ) (POCA 1978, s 1B(1)(b) and (c)).

[437] CPS, 'Memorandum of Understanding between Crown Prosecution Service (CPS) and the Association of Chief Police Officers (ACPO) concerning Section 46 Sexual Offences Act 2003', October 2004, available at <https://www.cps.gov.uk/publications/agencies/mouaccp.html>.

[438] CJA 1988, s 160(2)(a)–(c) respectively. See *Collier* [2005] 1 WLR 843.

[439] Home Office, *Cybercrime: A review of the evidence*, Research Report 75, October 2013, Chapter 3 'Cyber-enabled crimes—sexual offending against children', available at <https://www.gov.uk/government/uploads/system/uploads/attachment_data/file/246754/horr75-chap3.pdf>.

[440] US Sentencing Guidelines Manual, s 2G2.2(b)(6), available at <http://www.ussc.gov/guidelines-manual/guidelines-manual>.

[441] *United States v Fellows*, 157 F 3d 1197 (9th Cir 1998), at 1202.

Protection of Children Act has been raised from three years to ten years; while the tariff for possession under the Criminal Justice Act, s 160, was raised from six months to five years.[442]

3.185 The s 1 offences are also each considered a 'specified sexual offence' for the purpose of the Criminal Justice Act 2003, and therefore a person may be sentenced to imprisonment for an indeterminate period for the purpose of public protection.[443] In addition, the courts have been advised that they *must* consider public protection sentences for the most serious kinds of involvement in the supply of child abuse images, ie the offences of causing or inciting a child to become involved in child pornography, controlling a child involved in child pornography, and arranging or facilitating child pornography,[444] for which the maximum penalty could be either a life sentence or an extended sentence.[445]

3.186 Generally, cases will involve the supply and/or possession of multiple images, often numbering in the thousands. Indeed, one mechanism by which offenders commonly control access to such material is by requiring that a person attempting to join the group submit a minimum number of images as the price of admission. The volume of images involved can cause difficulties when an indictment is being drafted, since it may be inappropriate to detail every single image. As a consequence, the courts have laid down some standard practice guidelines:[446]

- the indictment should include both a comprehensive count as well as a specimen count;
- the specimen count should be 'broadly representative of the images' in the comprehensive count;
- if such a specimen count is impractical, the images should be divided into different categories of indecency … which can be reviewed by the defence;
- the specimen count should distinguish between real images and pseudo-images …;
- each image should be individually referenced; and
- the estimated age range of the child in each specimen count should be indicated.

3.187 It can be seen, therefore, that the courts take into account four key factors when assessing the seriousness of a case: the number of images; the age of the child; the subject matter of the image; and whether it is real or pseudo.

3.188 **'Grooming'** Historically, the vast majority of cases of sexual abuse involved a member of the family, ie someone known to the child. However, the Internet provides a new means by which a paedophile can contact children for the purposes of sexual abuse, so-called 'Internet grooming'. Such activities may include using the Internet as a medium to contact and entice children, through chat rooms, for example,[447] with the intention of arranging a physical meeting, as well as showing child pornography to a child in order to 'normalize' such acts and encourage the child to engage in sexual activities.

---

[442] Inserted by the Criminal Justice and Court Services Act 2000, s 41.
[443] Criminal Justice Act 2003, c 44 (CJA 2003), Sch 15, Pt 2, at 99.
[444] SOA 2003, ss 48, 49, and 50 respectively.
[445] CJA 2003, ss 224A and 226A respectively. See *Sexual Offences: Definitive Guideline*, above, n 384, at 79 (Step Five).
[446] *Thompson (Richard)* [2004] 2 Cr App R 16, para 11.
[447] eg *Mansfield* [2005] EWCA Crim 927.

To tackle such activities, the Sexual Offences Act 2003 creates an offence of 'meeting a child **3.189** following sexual grooming', which involves the following forms of conduct:

A has met or communicated with another person (B) on one or more occasions and subsequently—
  (i) A intentionally meets B,
 (ii) A travels with the intention of meeting B in any part of the world or arranges to meet B in any part of the world, or
(iii) B travels with the intention of meeting A in any part of the world.[448]

The maximum tariff is ten years' imprisonment,[449] although it is also an offence for which an indeterminate prison sentence may be conferred on the grounds of public protection.[450] The offence is similar in concept to that used in the context of harassment,[451] although it targets preparatory steps taken by a potential abuser, where such acts fall short of an attempt. While the offence is widely drafted, covering all forms of communication, the Government's stated intention was to criminalize such Internet-based activities.[452] Where the offence has not progressed sufficiently to charge with attempt, an application may be made for a sexual offences prevention order, which could prevent the defendant from continuing to communicate with persons via a chat room or a similar environment.[453]

Speech and communication crimes

In content-related computer crimes, it is the nature of the content being processed that is **3.190** the crime, rather than as a tool or instrument of some other criminal act. As such, content-related crimes may encompass any offence involving writing, speech, or publication, such as criminal libel, blasphemy, sedition, obscene publications, performances, and displays. An examination of all these areas of law is, however, beyond the scope of this book.[454]

The following sections examine four distinct areas of speech crime: sexual communica- **3.191** tions, hate speech, improper communications, and harassment. Some of these may be considered as falling on the border with the computer-related crime category, since the content is only sometimes illegal in itself. Alternatively, they could be viewed as forming a new category of computer crime, 'contact-related crime', which focuses on the use of Internet-related communication services, such as social media, as a means of contacting a person, whether directly and indirectly, in an abusive manner.

Sexual communications

Grooming is focused on the intention of the abuser to meet with the targeted child. In some **3.192** circumstances, however, the intention may simply be to obtain sexual gratification through the communication process itself, without intending to physically meet the child. In 2015, a new offence of 'sexual communication with a child' was inserted into the Sexual Offences

---

[448] SOA 2003, s 15.
[449] ibid, s 15(4)(b).
[450] See eg *Attorney-General's Reference (No 3 of 2006), Re* [2006] EWCA Crim 695, where the defendant met a girl of fourteen over the Internet and, after graphic exchanges, met with the girl.
[451] See paras 3.212–3.226.
[452] See Sexual Offences Act 2003, Explanatory Notes, at para 27, available at <http://www.legislation.gov.uk/ukpga/2003/42/notes/contents>.
[453] SOA 2003, s 107.
[454] See generally *Blackstone's Criminal Practice 2016*, above, n 148, s B18.

Act 2003.[455] The communication must relate to a 'sexual activity', which would be what a reasonable person considers it to be.[456] The communications must be between an adult and a child under sixteen.[457] The offence has a maximum tariff of two years imprisonment,[458] although it is interesting to note that, unlike other speech-related offences, proceedings do not require the consent of the Director of Public Prosecutions.

Hate speech

3.193 As a communications medium par excellence, the Internet provides an obvious opportunity to publish and distribute material that is considered capable of either generating 'hatred against a group of persons', by reference to their colour, race, nationality, ethnic origin, or religious beliefs; or by advocating acts of violence.[459] Historically, governments have been cautious about criminalizing such material. However, as part of the 'war on terrorism', coupled with growing public disquiet about the availability of dangerous content over the Internet, the Government has introduced new hate speech offences.

3.194 Under English law, hate speech is categorized as an offence affecting public order, as the law is concerned with behaviour as much as words, and is criminalized under the Public Order Act 1986.[460] Part 3 of the Act criminalizes speech intended to stir up 'racial hatred', defined by reference 'to colour, race, nationality (including citizenship) or ethnic or national origins'.[461] Although concerned with public order, the use of 'threatening, abusive or insulting words'[462] or displays of 'written material' may be committed in a public or private place.[463] In a cyberspace context, therefore, an offence could be made out whether the environment, such as a social media service or chat room, was subject to access controls or not.[464] It is also an offence to publish or distribute such material;[465] although it is unclear whether putting information on a website would be considered an offence of display or publication, a defendant may simply be charged under both offences. The distinction is not relevant, however, to the offence of possession with a view to it being displayed, published, or distributed.[466]

3.195 To limit the scope for the provisions to be abused, unduly restricting free speech, a prosecution can only be brought with the consent of the Attorney-General.[467] As with the other content-related offences examined above, the maximum tariff has been raised substantially, from two to seven years' imprisonment.[468] However, the paucity of prosecutions for racial

---

[455] SOA 2003, s 15A. Inserted by the Serious Crime Act 2015, s 67. Not in force at the time of writing.

[456] SOA 2003, s 15A(2).

[457] ibid, s 15A(1)(c).

[458] ibid, s 15A(3)(b).

[459] See generally White, M, 'Far right extremists on the Internet', in Thomas, D and Loader, B (eds), *Cybercrime: Law Enforcement, Security and Surveillance in the Information Age*, Routledge, 2000, at 234–50.

[460] Public Order Act 1986, c 64 (POA), Pt 3 'Racial Hatred'. Offences were first introduced under the Race Relations Act 1965.

[461] POA, s 17.

[462] Not defined in the POA, but is a question of fact to be determined: see *Brutus v Cozens* [1973] AC 854.

[463] POA, s 18(2).

[464] The only defence based on location is when the act is between persons in a 'dwelling' (ibid, s 18(4)), which would not be applicable to such examples.

[465] ibid, s 19.

[466] ibid, s 23.

[467] ibid, s 27(1). This would also extend to charges of conspiracy to commit such offences: see *Pearce* (1981) 72 Cr App R 295.

[468] ibid, s 27(3)(a), amended by the Anti-Terrorism Crime and Security Act 2001, Pt 5, s 40.

hatred, a total of sixty-five over a twenty-year period,[469] would not seem to justify such a shift. Such low levels of prosecutions are despite both Government and the police targeting action against the publishing of racist material on the Internet over recent years.[470] As with other cybercrimes, the perpetrators often use online resources located outside the jurisdiction, leaving law enforcement with no other option but to simply pass information on to the relevant national authority in countries where both the law and policing priorities may be significantly different.

In 2006, the Public Order Act was amended by the Racial and Religious Hatred Act 2006, **3.196** to insert a new offence of stirring up 'religious hatred', defined by reference to 'religious belief or lack of religious belief'.[471] In response to concerns about the 'chilling effect' that the amendment could have on free speech, in addition to the requirement for consent from the Attorney-General for prosecutions, the following provision was inserted:

> Nothing in this Part shall be read or given effect in a way which prohibits or restricts discussion, criticism or expressions of antipathy, dislike, ridicule, insult or abuse of particular religions or the beliefs or practices of their adherents, or of any other belief system or the beliefs or practices of its adherents, or proselytising or urging adherents of a different religion or belief system to cease practising their religion or belief system.[472]

Experience to date in respect of the offences relating to racial hatred does not augur well for **3.197** the application of the new offence, although a Government minister has stated that lack of prosecutions is not necessarily indicative of bad law-making, but rather reflects the law as an effective mechanism to change people's behaviour.[473]

As discussed in the next section, words themselves are sometimes capable of causing actual **3.198** harm to a person, so the idea that words that advocate violence may be criminalized as a form of hate speech would seem reasonable in certain circumstances. Words or written material are capable, for example, of causing fear of, or provoking, 'immediate unlawful violence'.[474] In such cases, however, there is a strong temporal relationship between the speech and the possible violence. Under the Terrorism Act 2006, a new offence has been established of publishing a statement 'as a direct or indirect encouragement or other inducement to them to the commission, preparation or instigation of acts of terrorism or Convention offences'.[475] The person publishing such a statement must either intend to encourage or induce, or be reckless as to such a consequence.[476] However, the tenuous nature of the causal and temporal relationship between the speech and any eventual terrorist conduct would seem to challenge traditional principles of English criminal law.[477]

---

[469] House of Lords Hansard, statement by the Attorney-General, Lord Goldsmith, 31 January 2005, Col WA5.

[470] See 'UK crackdown on Internet racism', *BBC News*, 15 September 1998, available at <http://news.bbc.co.uk/2/hi/uk_news/171484.stm>.

[471] Racial and Religious Hatred Act 2006, Schedule, inserting a new Part 3A in POA, ss 29A–29N.

[472] POA, s 29J.

[473] Comment by Paul Goggins, then a Home Office Minister, quoted in Rozenberg, J, 'Now you face jail for being nasty to Satanists', *The Telegraph*, 10 June 2005, available at <http://www.telegraph.co.uk/news/uknews/1491742/Now-you-face-jail-for-being-nasty-to-Satanists.html>.

[474] POA 1986, s 4.

[475] TA 2006, s 1.

[476] ibid, s 1(2).

[477] See Ashworth, A, *Principles of Criminal Law*, 4th edn, Oxford University Press, 2003, para 4.6.

3.199   At a European level, in January 2003, the Council of Europe adopted an additional protocol to the Convention on Cybercrime (2001) 'concerning the criminalisation of acts of a racist and xenophobic nature committed through computer systems'. The Protocol requires the establishment of a range of substantive offences concerning 'racist or xenophobic material', including the dissemination of such material, threats and insults, and denial of genocide and crimes against humanity. However, owing to the complexities of legislating against such material, Member States have considerable autonomy not to adopt such measures, where, for example, issues of freedom of expression conflict.[478] However, the UK is not a signatory to this Protocol.

3.200   The tension between hate speech and free speech is most apparent in the US, with its constitutional elevation of free speech under the First Amendment.[479] The US stance has special resonance in terms of Internet-based activities due to the Internet's US origins and continuing dominance. It is widely accepted that the libertarian culture found in most aspects of the Internet derive, in large part, from US liberal traditions.

Malicious and improper communications

3.201   While the control of hate speech on the Internet is an area fraught with controversy and difficulties, criminalizing the use of communication technologies, such as the Internet, to communicate a threat directed at a specific person does not generally raise a free speech challenge, provided such threats are real.[480] Communication technologies can be used as a means of transmitting content that constitutes a threat, or as a tool in itself to harass, stalk and cause harm to a person. Words and even silence are capable of causing actual bodily harm;[481] therefore computers and networks are simply another medium through which harm may be inflicted on others. In an unreported case in Northern England, for example, a defendant was successfully prosecuted for causing a woman psychiatric harm as a result of a series of insulting postings made on the website 'Friends Reunited'.[482] These offences are considered as content-related computer crimes because both the manner and content of the communications are elements of the offence.

3.202   In the UK, the three principal statutory instruments addressing such harmful conduct are the Malicious Communications Act 1988, the Communications Act 2003, and the Protection of Harassment Act 1997.[483] The first two are very similar, although the former is broader in scope, embracing postal services and other physical delivery mechanisms, as well an 'electronic communication'.[484] The nature of the distinction between these two pieces of legislation was addressed by Lord Bingham, in *Collins*.[485] He noted that the object of the

---

[478]   See paras 5.119–5.141 for an examination of the Protocol.

[479]   The First Amendment states: 'Congress shall make no law respecting an establishment of religion, or prohibiting the free exercise thereof; or abridging the freedom of speech, or of the press; or the right of the people peacefully to assemble, and to petition the Government for a redress of grievances'.

[480]   *Watts v United States* 394 US 705 (1969).

[481]   *Ireland* [1998] 1 Cr App R 177.

[482]   Case reported to the author at a CPS training course. In such a case, expert evidence would be required about the nature of the illness suffered and the causal link with the actions of the defendant.

[483]   There is also the possibility of the common law offence of public nuisance. See *Goldstein* [2004] 2 All ER 589.

[484]   Malicious Communications Act 1988 (MCA), s 1(2A) includes 'any oral or other communication by means of an electronic communications network; and … any communication (however sent) that is in electronic form'.

[485]   [2006] UKHL 40.

1988 Act was 'to protect people against receipt of unsolicited messages which they may find seriously objectionable', while the object of the 2003 provision was 'to prohibit the use of a service provided and funded by the public for the benefit of the public for the transmission of communications which contravene the basic standards of our society'.[486]

While this latter statement of purpose reflects the historical context of the specific pro- **3.203** vision, which can be traced back through the Telecommunications Act 1984, the British Telecommunications Act 1981, and the Post Office Acts 1953 and 1969, to the Post Office (Amendment) Act 1935,[487] it does not appropriately describe our modern liberalized, competitive and largely non-publicly funded communications industry and therefore seems an unsatisfactory basis upon which to distinguish the two statutes and to interpret the latter. Lord Brown, in the same decision, while endorsing Lord Bingham's words, also describes the offence as protecting 'the integrity of the public communications system',[488] which would seem the better description, on the basis that integrity is given its moral meaning, rather than a term of data security, as used in respect of computer-integrity offences below.

The Malicious Communications Act 1988 was enacted to give effect to a Law Commission **3.204** Report on 'Poison-Pen Letters'.[489] Under the Act, it is an offence to send a communication that conveys an indecent or grossly offensive message, a threat, or information that is false and is known to be or thought to be by the sender.[490] A relevant example in the context of cyber-terrorism is the making of a hoax bomb claim.[491] In terms of *mens rea*, the message sender must have the intention, at least in part, of causing 'distress and anxiety' to the recipient.[492] The sending of the communication is therefore sufficient for the offence to be committed, without the recipient having received it. So, for example, if such a message was removed in the course of transmission by filtering software, the offence could still be made out. Originally, the s 1 offence was summary-only, with a maximum penalty of six months' imprisonment and a six-month time limit for proceedings to be brought. This was amended in 2015 to become an offence triable either way, with a maximum sentence of two years and no time limit.[493] In proposing this amendment, the Government noted that as originally drafted it could 'hamper police investigations into internet related offences that might be charged under section 1, for example in the context of "trolling"'.[494]

The Malicious Communications Act 1988 is complemented by the Communications Act **3.205** 2003, under which the act of sending certain material across an 'electronic communications

---

[486] ibid, para 7.
[487] ibid, para 6.
[488] ibid, para 27.
[489] Law Commission, 'Report on Poison-pen Letters', No 147 (1985).
[490] MCA, s 1(1).
[491] *Morgans v Essex Magistrates' Court* [2004] EWHC 2478; although a specific communication offence in relation to bomb hoaxes also exists under the Criminal Law Act 1977, s 51(2).
[492] *Connolly v DPP* [2007] EWHC 237 (Admin), para 9. In *Elonis v United States*, 575 US (2015), the US Supreme Court held that for the offence of sending a threatening communication, under 18 USC s 875(c), it is necessary to evidence specific intent on the part of the defendant, not how the communication would be viewed by a reasonable recipient.
[493] MCA, s 1(4), amended by the Criminal Justice and Courts Act 2015, s 32(1).
[494] Ministry of Justice, 'Making the offence in section 1 of the Malicious Communications Act 1988 a triable either way offence', Impact Assessment No MoJ019/2014, available at <https://www.gov.uk/government/uploads/system/uploads/attachment_data/file/321285/malicious-communicationss-impact-assessment.pdf>.

network'[495] may constitute an offence of 'improper use of an electronic communications network':

> (1) A person is guilty of an offence if he—
>   (a) sends by means of a public electronic communications network a message or other matter that is grossly offensive or of an indecent, obscene or menacing character; or
>   (b) causes any such message or matter to be so sent.
> (2) A person is guilty of an offence if, for the purpose of causing annoyance, inconvenience or needless anxiety to another, he—
>   (a) sends by means of a public electronic communications network, a message that he knows to be false;
>   (b) causes such a message to be sent; or
>   (c) persistently makes use of a public electronic communications network.[496]

The scope of this provision makes it a potential supplementary charge in the pornography and child abuse cases over the Internet discussed previously.

3.206 As discussed in respect of child pornography, where a court is required to construe a criminal statute, the presumption is that it contains *mens rea* elements. However, it was not clear where on a continuum from intention, recklessness to negligence the subsection (1) offence would reside, although intention or knowledge was necessary for the acts of sending or causing a message to be sent.

3.207 The nature of the s 127 offence was first extensively examined in *DPP v Collins*.[497] In this case, the defendant regularly phoned his constituency office to complain about a range of matters and used offensive terminology in respect of ethnic minorities. At trial, it was held that his words were merely offensive, but not 'grossly offensive'. This issue was then taken on appeal to the Divisional Court, which upheld the lower court's decision, and then to the House of Lords, which overturned the original decision.

3.208 In the Divisional Court, while recognizing that the words were clearly offensive, Lord Justice Sedley noted that the differential standard was indicative of Parliament's intention to minimize the impact that such a provision would have on an individual's freedom of expression,[498] a common feature of many content-related computer crimes. He also noted, *obiter*, that the four classes of message, 'grossly offensive', 'indecent', 'obscene', and 'menacing', varied in respect of being conduct or result crimes, as well as between evaluation on objective or subjective criteria. Their common characteristic was that the context in which they appeared was critical to a finding of liability in the circumstances under consideration.

3.209 Whether a message is menacing will focus on the 'intended or likely effect on the recipient', as does indecency and obscenity, although 'the law has historically treated them as a matter of objective fact to be determined by contemporary standards of decency'.[499] In respect of

---

[495] CA 2003, s 32(1).
[496] ibid, s 127.
[497] In the Divisional Court [2005] EWHC 1308 (Admin), and subsequently in the House of Lords [2006] UKHL 40.
[498] [2005] EWHC 1308 (Admin), para 5.
[499] ibid, para 10.

'grossly offensive', Lord Justice Sedley felt that the defendant's evident lack of care about his use of certain words was a factor for consideration, which suggested recklessness or negligence as to the *mens rea*, as well as an objective consideration of what reasonable people would consider grossly offensive.

On appeal to the House of Lords, the decision was overturned, holding that the defendant's **3.210** messages were 'grossly offensive' and therefore finding in favour of the DPP.[500] Concerning the necessary culpable state of mind, Lord Bingham held that the defendant must intend that his words be 'grossly offensive' to those to whom they are made, or be aware that they may be.[501] This sets a higher threshold than that suggested by the Divisional Court and academic commentators.[502] Lord Brown also noted that, in contrast to the Malicious Communications Act 1988 where the intention to offend depends on the recipient of the communication, the intention under s 127(1)(a) need only be in respect of the 'grossly offensive' terms of the message, not the intended recipient.[503] He also noted, however, that such an interpretation places messaging services, such as chat-lines, in a potentially invidious position, since the essence of some such services is an exchange of messages that are intended to be at least indecent in nature.[504]

Since *Collins*, s 127 of the Communications Act has become the subject of considerable **3.211** attention and usage, particularly in the context of 'trolling', where various forms of communication service are used to insult and attack others. By 2014, the numbers convicted under s 127 had risen to 1,209, from 143 a decade earlier.[505] The potential scope of the provision first came to public attention in the case of the 'Robin Hood' Tweet. In 2010, Paul Chambers tweeted the following message to his some 600 followers:

> Crap! Robin Hood Airport is closed. You've got a week and a bit to get your shit together otherwise I am blowing the airport sky high!!

He was convicted by a Magistrates Court for sending a message of a 'menacing character', contrary to s 127(1)(a). His appeal was upheld before the Crown Court before finally being overturned by the High Court.[506] The central question for the High Court was whether the act of sending a message of a 'menacing character' had occurred. It concluded that because it was clear from all the evidence that none of the recipients considered the message 'menacing', it could not have a 'menacing character'.[507] Given this finding, the issue of *mens rea* was not considered relevant, although the High Court opined that the offence only required a showing of basic intent, rather than specific intent directed towards the person to whom

---

[500] [2006] UKHL 40.

[501] ibid, para 10. Endorsed by Lord Carswell, ibid, para 21.

[502] Ormerod, D [2005] Crim LR 795.

[503] [2006] UKHL 40, para 26.

[504] ibid, para 27.

[505] Ministry of Justice source quoted in 'Five internet trolls a day convicted in the UK as figures show ten-fold increase', *The Telegraph*, 24 May 2015, available at <http://www.telegraph.co.uk/news/uknews/law-and-order/11627180/Five-internet-trolls-a-day-convicted-in-UK-as-figures-show-ten-fold-increase.html>.

[506] [2012] EWHC 2157.

[507] ibid, paras 30 et seq. In response to this decision, the CPS notes that 'as a general rule' menacing communications should be dealt with as credible threats of violence that may constitute an offence under s 16 of the Offences Against the Person Act 1861 or under the Protection from Harassment Act 1997. See *Guidelines on prosecuting cases involving communications sent via social media*, para 29, available at <http://www.cps.gov.uk/legal/a_to_c/communications_sent_via_social_media/>.

it was sent or was likely to receive it; but even that state of mind was unlikely to have been established in this case.[508]

3.212 The s 127 offence is summary only, with a maximum six-month term.[509] As with the Malicious Communications Act, the time limit was amended in 2015, to permit proceedings up to three years after the offence was committed.[510]

3.213 The subsection (2) offence is only concerned with 'false' messages, although it is not clear whether this would include messages that are true in terms of content, but were sent under 'false' pretences, to cause the annoyance, inconvenience, or anxiety. A 'denial-of-service' (DOS) attack, for example, involves the mass sending of 'true' messages, but the motivation can be characterized as 'false' in the sense that each transmission is intended only to use up resource of the target machine, not communicate information. However the phrase is conceived, subsection (2) is only considered a 'penalty offence',[511] and therefore subject to a fixed penalty of £80,[512] unlikely to excite either prosecutors or the courts!

3.214 Another variant of a content-related cybercrime with a communication component has been the emergence of so-called 'revenge porn', where images are posted of individuals engaged in sexually explicit acts, generally by ex-partners. While such conduct may fall within existing forms of criminal conduct,[513] concerns were raised that such harmful conduct may not always meet the required thresholds. In 2015, a new offence of 'disclosing private sexual photographs and films with intent to cause distress' was adopted.[514] The term 'sexual' is defined either in terms of specific parts of the body (ie genitals or pubic area) or what a 'reasonable person' would consider sexual.[515] The disclosure must occur without the consent of the person appearing in the picture or film and there must be intention to cause distress.[516] The offence can give rise to maximum tariff of two-year imprisonment.[517]

Harassment

3.215 The manner in which we communicate with someone can, in itself, constitute a form of harassment, regardless of the content of what is being communicated. Under the Protection from Harassment Act 1997, any 'course of conduct' which amounts to harassment and which the person knows 'or ought to know'[518] amounts to harassment may comprise an offence. This could, of course, and has involved the use of computer and network technologies as a manner in which the harassing conduct has been carried out. In *Debnath*,[519]

---

[508] [2012] EWHC 2157, paras 35 et seq.

[509] CA, s 127(3). See eg the sentencing comments in *Nimmo and Sorley*, 24 January 2014, available at <https://www.judiciary.gov.uk/wp-content/uploads/JCO/Documents/Judgments/r-v-nimmo-and-sorley.pdf>.

[510] CA, s 127(5), amended by the Criminal Justice and Courts Act 2015, s 51(1).

[511] As specified under the Criminal Justice and Police Act 2001, s 1(1).

[512] The Penalties for Disorderly Behaviour (Amount of Penalty) Order 2002 (SI No 1837), Sch 1(1), Pt 1.

[513] eg as an indecent or obscene communication (CA, s 127); as an indecent image of a child (see paras 3.205 et seq) or as harassment (see paras 3.215 et seq).

[514] Criminal Justice and Courts Act 2015, s 33.

[515] ibid, s 35(3).

[516] Intention would not be made out where distress was a 'natural and probable consequence of the disclosure' (ibid, s 33(8)).

[517] ibid, s 33(9).

[518] An objective standard of whether 'a reasonable person in possession of the same information would think' (Protection from Harassment Act 1997 (PHA), s 1(2)).

[519] [2005] All ER (D) 49.

for example, the defendant pursued a campaign against the complainant that included establishing a website; the unauthorized registration of the complainant with a web service; the sending of emails to the complainant's fiancée and employer; as well as paying hackers to sabotage the complainant's email service and send unauthorized emails.[520] The concept of harassment includes 'alarming the person or causing the person distress',[521] therefore a malicious or improper communication of the type discussed above could become a form of harassment. As well as a fine or custodial sentence, the court may impose a restraining order.[522] The victim may also bring a claim for compensation.[523]

In *Thomas v News Group Newspapers*,[524] it was held that harassment could occur through **3.216** the publication of articles in a newspaper, such as inciting racial hatred against a specific individual, although 'in only very rare circumstances', bearing in mind the right to freedom of expression under Art 10 of the European Convention on Human Rights (ECHR). However, in an age of widespread 'blogging' and other forms of cyberspace publication, which lack the editorial control of traditional journalistic endeavours, the possibility of personal vendettas being pursued through publication is likely to be greater. Indeed, in *Debnath*, the defendant raised an appeal based on Art 10 against the terms of the restraint order imposed upon her prohibiting the publication of any information about the complainant, whether true or not, which the courts rejected.[525]

An action for harassment through repetitive communications has been successfully pursued in Singapore, in *Malcomson v Naresh*.[526] The case concerned a former employee of the **3.217** plaintiff's company who bombarded the plaintiff with a combination of unsolicited SMS messages, emails, and phone calls in an attempt to obtain re-employment. In this case, the court was required to establish a new tort of intentional harassment in Singapore.[527]

In the US, federal law contains a series of offences in relation to the making of a telephone **3.218** call or using a 'telecommunications device' to communicate obscene or related material or to harass the recipient of the communication.[528] As originally drafted, the concept of a 'telecommunications device' did not include an 'interactive computer service', which encompasses Internet access services.[529] In January 2006, this provision was therefore amended by a provision 'preventing cyberstalking', inserted by an act addressing violence against women.[530] The provision amends the definition of a 'telecommunications device' to expressly include communications over the Internet, but only in respect of the offence of communicating 'without disclosing his identity and with intent to annoy, abuse, threat or

---

[520] As well as a conviction under PHA, the defendant was charged under the Computer Misuse Act 1990 (CMA), s 3.

[521] PHA, s 7(2).

[522] ibid, s 5. A restraining order may also be obtained against a person even though they have been acquitted of an offence (s 5A).

[523] ibid, s 3.

[524] The Times, 25 July 2001.

[525] See also *Law Society v Kordowski* [2011] EWHC 3185.

[526] [2001] 4 SLR 454.

[527] See generally Keng Feng, T, 'Harassment and intentional tort of negligence', *Singapore Journal of Legal Studies* 642 [2002].

[528] 47 USC s 223 'Obscene or harassing telephone calls in the District of Columbia or in interstate or foreign communications'. Maximum two-year jail term.

[529] 47 USC s 230(f)(2).

[530] Violence Against Women and Department of Justice Reauthorization Act of 2005, HR 3402, 109th Congress, enacted 5 January 2006, s 113.

harass'.[531] However, the amendment has been criticized for potentially chilling free speech through anonymous 'blogs' and Usenet.[532]

3.219 Existing law governing harmful communications remains based in an era of one-to-one communication techniques, specifically voice telephony. However, the variety of one-to-many communication techniques in cyberspace, such as personal websites, may challenge the suitability of existing rules. The distress and anxiety caused to a target of malicious, improper, or harassing communications is likely to be of a considerably greater magnitude where the communications are of a public rather than private nature.

D. Computer-integrity Offences

3.220 When considering computer crime or cybercrime, most people think in terms of 'hacking' into systems and the distribution of 'viruses'. Such activities target the computers themselves, as the subject, rather than as an instrument to commit other crimes. With the spread of computerization and our consequential dependency, the adequacy of criminal law to deter such activities has had to be addressed by policy-makers and legislators. In most jurisdictions, the application of traditional criminal law has been often uncertain, such as forgery, or completely inappropriate, such as theft of electricity.[533] As such, *sui generis* legislation has been adopted to tackle the threat to the security of computer and communication systems.

3.221 The three primary activities we are concerned with are access, modification, or interference, and interception; examining the suitability and sufficiency of these concepts to safeguard the confidentiality, integrity, and availability of the systems themselves (both hardware and software) and the data they process. Obtaining access and interception are primarily means by which the confidentiality of data may be compromised, whether 'at rest' or 'in transmission'; while interference is primarily centred on issues of system and data integrity and availability. Although access under UK law is primarily conceived in terms of computers and networks, the information being processed as data is the underlying object of protection. Access protection may be supplemental where the information is subject to other protective regimes, such as laws on confidentiality, but may be the exclusive criminal remedy for many forms of information crime. Criminalizing interference with systems and data, as distinct from traditional criminal damage, can be viewed as recognition of the enhanced status of incorporeal property in our modern information society.

3.222 Another consideration when examining these offences is the level of sanction such acts should attract. Does the scale of harm resulting from, and/or societal concern with breaches of confidentiality equate with a breach of integrity or availability? Such questions could be answered strictly on an empirical basis, using crime statistics. However, as discussed in Chapter 2, such an approach depends on the existence of information that is often not currently available. As a consequence, we rely on policy-makers and legislators to make such an assessment as to maximum appropriate tariffs, based on somewhat opaque criteria,

---

[531] 47 USC s 223(a)(1)(C).

[532] McCullagh, D, 'Create a e-annoyance, go to jail', *CNet*, 9 January 2006, available at <http://www.cnet.com/news/create-an-e-annoyance-go-to-jail/>.

[533] Theft Act 1968, s 13.

and the judiciary to provide some reasoning in the specific case. For example, when examining a proposal to create an offence specifically targeted at DOS attacks, the All Party Parliamentary Group felt that such activities were more akin to an act of unauthorized access in terms of seriousness than that of modification, and hence should be subject to a comparable tariff.[534] However, determinations of seriousness may also be made subject to the presence of aggravating circumstances, such as being part of a criminal organization, which alters the applicable tariff whatever the form of conduct.[535] As we shall see under current UK law, access and interception are considered of lesser seriousness than interference, ie breaches of integrity and availability rank higher in terms of harm than breaches of confidentiality.

Before analysing the different integrity offences, access, interference, and interception, it **3.223** is necessary to examine two questions generic to all three categories of criminal activity. First, we must consider the nature of the subject matter being protected by law, ie information and communication technologies and the data they process; and second, the concept of authorization in relation to our subject matter, which comprises a line that divides that which is criminal from that which is not.

Of computers, systems, and devices

In Chapter 2, we began by defining the various technologies that comprise our subject mat- **3.224** ter, unencumbered by any legal constraint. We now need to consider precisely how such technologies are defined in law, as the basis for our subsequent analysis. Such definitions may, for example, betray a failure to fully understand the nature of what is being regulated, thereby creating legal uncertainty and potential lacunae.

The CMA does not define a 'computer', therefore potentially extending its scope to every- **3.225** day domestic appliances, cars and any object that incorporates computer technology. It has been argued that a narrow view of what constitutes a computer should be adopted;[536] although this looks less appropriate as we enter the age of the 'Internet of Things', where domestic appliances can become targets for attack.[537] In 1988, the Law Commission found general support for the view that to attempt such a definition would be 'so complex, in an endeavour to be all-embracing, that they are likely to produce extensive argument';[538] and therefore recommended that 'the word should be given its ordinary meaning'.[539] Indeed, this is the approach commonly taken in UK legislation when addressing technology.[540] When the issue was subject to re-examination in 2004, by the All Party Parliamentary Internet Group (APIG), it recommended that the Government resist any temptation to define the term.[541] The UK Government is not obliged to depart from the English law

---

[534] Interview with Richard Clayton, specialist advisor to the APIG inquiry on 'Revision of the Computer Misuse Act', 31 January 2006.

[535] eg Directive 13/40/EU, above, n 159, Art 9(4).

[536] See Ormerod, D and Laird, K (eds), *Smith & Hogan Criminal Law*, 14th edn, Oxford University Press, 2015, s 30.2.1.1.

[537] eg 'Your FRIDGE is Full of SPAM: Proof of An IoT-driven Attack', 16 January 2014, available at <https://www.proofpoint.com/us/threat-insight/post/Your-Fridge-is-Full-of-SPAM>.

[538] Law Commission, *Computer Misuse*, Report No 186, Cm 819, London, HMSO, 1989, para 3.39.

[539] ibid, para 6.23.

[540] eg Copyright, Designs and Patents Act 1988, c 48, in respect of a 'computer program'.

[541] All Party Parliamentary Internet Group (APIG), 'Revision of the Computer Misuse Act', June 2004, para 17, available at <https://www.cl.cam.ac.uk/~rnc1/APIG-report-cma.pdf> ('APIG Report').

approach to definitions by the Convention on Cybercrime and the Directive[542] and, to date, the courts have not struggled to interpret the scope of such terms.[543] A similar position has been taken in other jurisdictions, such as France and Germany.

3.226 However, the absence of a definition does not mean that the CMA contains no implicit treatment of the concept. In respect of modification, the Act distinguishes the legal treatment of any 'storage medium' when in the computer and when removed.[544] This clearly implies that the mere storage of programs or data on a DVD or USB memory stick is not sufficient to constitute a computer. Some further functionality or processing capability would seem to be a necessary feature of a computer, which conforms both to general definitions and common usage within the IT community.[545] However, such an interpretation does not match concepts of 'processing' in other contexts, where mere storage is sufficient to trigger application of the law.[546] In addition, a narrow perspective may create problems at the edges of technological development. Over the years, for example, 3¼ inch floppy disks have given way to CDs, DVDs, and USB memory sticks as a storage medium for portable computing. However, as such devices evolve from 'dumb' towards 'smart' storage solutions, which incorporate some processing capacity in the memory stick, we can easily envisage the uncertainty a court may have about interpreting s 17(6), which could be aided by a definition that listed the minimum functionality required of a computer.

3.227 Numerous other countries do feel the need to define the term. In the US, for example, the federal Computer Fraud and Abuse Act provides the following definition:

> . . . an electronic, magnetic, optical, electrochemical, or other high speed data processing device performing logical, arithmetic, or storage functions, and includes any data storage facility or communications facility directly related to or operating in conjunction with such device, but such term does not include an automated typewriter or typesetter, a portable hand held calculator, or other similar device.[547]

The attempt to distinguish between storage as a function of a 'processing device' and storage as a 'facility' does not appear to resolve the legal status of a USB stick.

3.228 The exclusions in the final part of the US definition very much reflect the period when the provisions were first adopted, ie the early to mid 1980s. Today, nearly all typewriters and calculators would fall within the concept of a computer, and contain no distinguishing features that enable us to discern what would be a 'similar device', other than the absence of those features defined in relation to a computer. In *US v Mitra*,[548] the court stated that the choice of exclusions meant that 'other devices with embedded processors and software are covered. As more devices come to have built-in intelligence, the effective scope of the statute grows.' It should also be noted, however, that US law constrains the scope of the majority

---

[542] Directive 13/40/EU, above, n 159.
[543] eg in *DPP v McKeown, DPP v Jones* [1997] 2 Cr App R 155, Lord Hoffmann simply notes that 'a computer is a device for storing, processing and retrieving information'.
[544] CMA, s 17(6).
[545] eg Encyclopaedia Britannica Online: 'device for processing, storing, and displaying information'. See also ISO, 'Information Technology—Cloud Computing—Overview and vocabulary, which refers to 'processing, storage or networking resources', Draft International Standard, ISO/IEC 17788: 2013(E), available at <http://infostore.saiglobal.com/store/PreviewDoc.aspx?saleItemID=2670417>.
[546] eg DPA 1998, s 1(1), defining 'processing'.
[547] 18 USC s 1030(e)(1).
[548] 405 F 3d 492 (7th Cir 2005).

of offences under s 1030 to cases involving a 'protected computer', which is due in part to the federal nature of the US legal system, but also reflects a specific policy concern with the vulnerability of computers used by the US Government and financial institutions.[549] The Singapore Computer Misuse and Cybersecurity Act adopts a virtually identical definition of 'computer' to that found in US federal law, except that it provides that a 'similar device' is that which is either 'non programmable or which does not contain any data storage facility',[550] which implies that mere storage would not be sufficient to be a computer.

The Council of Europe Convention of Cybercrime utilizes the following definition for a **3.229** 'computer system':

> any device or a group of inter-connected or related devices, one or more of which, pursuant to a program, performs automatic processing of data.[551]

While refreshingly brief compared with the US definition, substantial clarification is provided in the Explanatory Report.[552] It states that parties are not 'obliged to copy *verbatim* into their domestic laws the four concepts defined in Article 1, provided that these laws cover such concepts in a manner consistent with the principles of the Convention and offer an equivalent framework for its implementation'.[553] In 2006, the Cybercrime Convention Committee (T-CY) issued a Guidance Note on the term, confirming that the common understanding of the parties to the Convention on Cybercrime is that it extends beyond traditional notions of the mainframe and desktop computer to include smart phones, tablets, and other developing technologies.[554]

The EU Directive uses a different term, 'information system', although with a broadly simi- **3.230** lar definition to that of the Convention:

> a device or group of interconnected or related devices, one or more of which, pursuant to a programme, automatically processes computer data, as well as computer data stored, processed, retrieved or transmitted by that device or group of devices for the purposes of its or their operation, use, protection and maintenance.[555]

Echoing the Convention, the Directive distinguishes between an 'information system' and 'computer data', the former acting upon the latter, referred to as 'processing'. An attempt is made to draw a bright line between the two concepts, although such an approach would seem to be based on a fundamental difficulty.

A computer or information system comprises 'devices', a term not further defined in the **3.231** Directive, although the commentary to the draft 2005 Framework Decision stated that the

---

[549] 18 USC s 1030(e)(2).

[550] Singapore's Computer Misuse and Cybersecurity Act (Chapter 50A), s 2(1)(c). Subsection (d) also grants the Minister the power to designate other devices.

[551] Convention on Cybercrime, Art 1(a). The Commonwealth Model Law on Computer and Computer Related Crime, LMM(02)17, October 2002, Art 3 adopts a virtually identical definition.

[552] Explanatory Report to the Convention on Cybercrime, above, n 1, paras 23–4.

[553] ibid, para 22.

[554] Cybercrime Convention Committee (T-CY), 'On the notion of "computer system"—Article 1.a Budapest Convention on Cybercrime', Guidance Note No 1, T-CY(2012) 21, 5 December 2012, available at <https://www.coe.int/t/dghl/cooperation/economiccrime/Source/Cybercrime/TCY/TCY2012/T-CY%282012%2921E_guidanceNote1_article1_final.pdf>.

[555] Directive 13/40/EU, above, n 159, Art 2(a).

term 'covers both the hardware and the software of the system',[556] and the Convention's Explanatory Report provides that a device consists of 'hardware or software developed for automatic processing of digital data'.[557] These devices process data 'pursuant to a program'. The Explanatory Report conceives a 'program' as being a 'set of instructions that can be executed by the computer', which would seem to equate to software, given its ordinary meaning. Thus, a device may be software, which then acts pursuant to software to process data. Presumably a distinction being made is between operating systems, such as Windows, and applications, such as Word and PowerPoint. The former operates to enable a 'group of inter-connected or related devices' to execute instructions upon the data, while the latter interpret and present the data so manipulated.

3.232 However, such a distinction would seem to raise further problems. First, a single program may contain both an operating system and various applications.[558] Second, the program may take the form of data input into the computer or may be physically hardwired into a device within the computer, such as a ROM, generally referred to as 'firmware'. However, 'computer data' is defined to include a 'program':

> means any representation of facts, information or concepts in a form suitable for process-
> ing in an information system, including a programme suitable for causing an information
> system to perform a function.[559]

While this would seem semantically correct, it creates definitional uncertainty in respect of the nature of 'firmware' programs, whether as a device comprising part of the 'information system' or as a form of 'computer data'. A third problem is that the term 'device' is also used by the Convention in a different context, external to the computer, as a tool that is capable of enabling acts of unauthorized access and interference to be carried out. This latter concept is examined further below.[560]

3.233 However, do these definitional uncertainties create a problem of law and, if so, how could the problem be resolved? The potential problem would seem to be that both the Convention on Cybercrime and the Directive 13/40/EU create an offence in respect of accessing an information system, but not the data held on it, as well as creating separate offences of system and data interference. In the former case, the offence occurs when 'the whole or any part' of the system is accessed, which means that the unauthorized use of a program may or may not constitute an offence, depending on whether it is viewed as part of the system or the data. In the latter case, where the offences are viewed as being of different levels of seriousness,[561] and therefore attracting different penalties, a determination of software as system or data could again be critical. An example of the latter can be found in an *ex parte* temporary restraining order obtained by Microsoft in June 2014. In it, Microsoft made the following statement:

---

[556] Proposal for a Council Framework Decision on attacks against information systems, OJ 203 E/109, 27.8.2002, at Art. 2(d).

[557] Explanatory Report to the Convention on Cybercrime, above, n 1, para 23.

[558] In the Commission's anti-trust action against Microsoft, this was seen as 'tying'. See Commission adopted Decision 2007/53/EC against Microsoft Corp, Case COMP/C-3.37.792—*Microsoft*, OJ L 32/23, 2007.

[559] Directive 13/40/EU, above, n 159, Art 2(d).

[560] See paras 3.336–3.350 for a discussion of unlawful devices.

[561] The Convention on Cybercrime, eg permits signatories to only criminalize data interference resulting in 'serious harm' (Art 4(2)).

The installation of malware by deceiving consumers and without Microsoft's authorization is an intrusion into the Microsoft Windows operating system (which is licensed to Microsoft's customers), without Microsoft's authorization.[562]

The court granted the order, although the dispute was eventually settled.[563] However, it illustrates the potential for such criminal statutes to be interpreted broadly by IP rights-holders.

In terms of addressing the problem, the issue would seem to be that of the perception of **3.234** computers as distinct physical, singular objects, separate from the data which they process, rather than as virtual machines, integrating hardware, firmware, software, and data in an effectively indistinguishable manner. The criminal law should be able to protect the confidentiality, integrity and availability of these virtual machines without the need to distinguish the component elements. Unauthorized access to, or interference with, the whole or part of this virtual machine is the mischief being addressed, and differential treatment can be addressed on the basis of the nature of the act carried out, harm suffered, and/or culpability of the perpetrator, not some uncertain and unsustainable technical distinction.

Of authorization, right, and lawful excuses

Central to the legislative response to activities threatening the integrity of computers, net- **3.235** works, and the information they process has been the issue of determining whether a person has the right to do the thing that they do, primarily in terms of access, use, modification, interference, or interception. Under common law jurisdictions, the pertinent term is 'authorization'[564] or 'without lawful excuse or justification',[565] while European legal instruments refer to a 'right'.[566] Since the absence of such 'authorization', 'excuse', or 'right' triggers exposure to criminal liability, we must carefully examine the nature and appropriateness of these concepts, before considering the integrity offences arising from them.

Determination of authorization in respect of a computer or network resource generally **3.236** resides with the person that controls the resource (the 'controller'), the right to control being distinguished from legal ownership. The granularity of authorization in respect of a particular resource can vary from obtaining access to the computer to detailed rules governing the use of particular resources available on, or from, the computer once initial access has been obtained. This freedom of the controller to determine levels of authorization has led to concerns being expressed about the over-criminalization of users' activities in cyberspace, where legal statements are routinely ignored.[567] A leading example of this potential problem arose in *US v Drew*,[568] which involved the defendant establishing a fake profile on the social media service MySpace in order to cause harm to a thirteen-year-old classmate of her daughter. As a result of the actions of the defendant and others, the child ended

---

[562] *Microsoft Corporation v Naser Al Mutari and others*, US District Court in Nevada, Case No 2:14-cv-00987-GMN-GWF, 19 June 2014, para 58.

[563] See Goguen, N, 'Update: Details on Microsoft takeover', *no-ip*, 10 July 2014, available at <http://www.noip.com/blog/2014/07/10/microsoft-takedown-details-updates/>.

[564] eg the UK, US, Australia, and New Zealand. Some civil law countries, such as Belgium, also use this term.

[565] eg Commonwealth 'Model Computer and Computer-related Crimes Bill'.

[566] ie Directive 13/40/EU, above, n 159, and Convention on Cybercrime.

[567] Kerr, O, 'Cybercrime's scope: interpreting "access" and "authorization" in computer misuse statutes', 78(5) *New York University Law Review* 1596 (2003).

[568] *US v Drew*, 259 FRD 449 (CD Cal 2009).

up committing suicide. The defendant was prosecuted under the Computer Fraud and Abuse Act (CFAA)[569] on the basis that her acts were an intentional breach of the terms of service (TOS) applicable to the site, which therefore rendered her conduct either unauthorized or exceeding her authorization. She was found guilty by the jury on this basis, but appealed. On appeal, the court struck down the verdict on the grounds that by enabling criminal liability to turn on a website's TOS, the CFAA contravened the US doctrine of 'void-for-vagueness', one element of which concerns whether ordinary people would understand that such conduct is subject to criminal prohibition, as well as the clarity of the TOS themselves.[570]

3.237 English law would also generally curtail any attempt to overly restrict authorization through statements by imposing obligations upon the relying party, primarily in respect of transparency and practice. When considering the applicability of a legal notice, a court will have regard to the adequacy of the steps taken by the relying person to bring the terms of the notice to the attention of those against whom it is being asserted; an obligation to communicate. Second, consideration will be given to the actual practice of the relying party, especially where such practice differs from the terms of the notice. Therefore, while the controller retains the freedom to set the terms of authorization, in the event of dispute, such terms will likely be subjected to an objective assessment by the court.

3.238 In the course of a court's objective assessment of the controller's authorization policy; the prosecution will also be required to show that the perpetrator had the subjective knowledge that his actions were without, or exceeded, the terms of any authorization policy in relation to the resource. Indeed, if the latter *mens rea* can be shown then there may not be any need to evidence the controller's authorization policy at all. The extent to which the question of authorization will need to be addressed from the controller's perspective would, in a traditional computing environment, often correlate with the status of the perpetrator vis-à-vis the controller. Where the perpetrator operates from within the controller's organization, such as an employee, greater attention will likely need to be given to the specificity of the controller's authorization policy,[571] while for external persons, the absence of authorization would often be assumed. Two problem areas are likely to be where a person operates on the periphery of the controller's organization, such as an independent contractor, and where systems are designed to interact with external persons.

3.239 In a cyberspace environment, this second problem arises from the nature of the interactions taking place. Two cases illustrate this point: *Lennon*[572] and *Cuthbert*.[573] The first case concerns a DOS attack. The perpetrator admitted sending millions of email messages, but successfully argued at first instance that, as each message was of a kind that the recipient machine was designed to receive and respond to, and was therefore authorized, this rendered the totality of messages sent authorized. Here the manner in which the machine was

---

[569] ie 18 USC ss 1030(a)(2)(C) and 1030(b)(2)(A).

[570] The court noted that virtually all previous CFAA decisions based on terms of service were civil actions under 18 USC s 1030(g).

[571] Compare, eg, two employment cases involving computer misuse: *Denco v Joinson* [1991] 1 WLR 330 and *British Telecommunications plc v Rodrigues* (1995) Employment Appeal Tribunal, EAT/854/92, 20 February 1995.

[572] *Lennon* [2005] ECLR 5(5), 3.

[573] *Cuthbert (Daniel)*, Horseferry Road Magistrates' Court, 6 October 2005, unreported.

set up, essentially the authorization policy as coded, was initially considered fatal to the prosecution, irrelevant of the perpetrator's *mens rea*.[574]

In *Cuthbert*, the accused, known as the 'Tsunami hacker', tried to access the non-public parts **3.240** of the web server via the directory structure by entering a URL with a string of /../../, referred to as a 'directory traversal' attack.[575] While such practices may be common among users trying to locate information on a website, which must be considered to be implicitly authorized, such practices become criminal when the perpetrator has the necessary *mens rea*.

A third example is P2P networks, where the user effectively opens a part of his system (eg **3.241** 'My Shared Folder' with KaZaA) to anyone else connected to the network. In all three situations, the nature of the interaction between person and computer or computer and computer blur traditional conceptions of authorization.

In some jurisdictions, specific obligations have been placed upon controllers concerning the **3.242** manner in which they operate their systems, as a means of encouraging good security practices, as well as limiting criminal liability. In Germany, for example, data must be 'specially protected' against unauthorized access.[576] A similar provision existed under Norwegian law, with liability arising where any person obtains access 'by breaking a protective device or in a similar manner'.[577] This resulted in the Supreme Court finding that simply 'probing computers connected to the Internet for the purpose of disclosing the lack of security measures was not illegal'.[578] A failure by a controller to implement such measures would undermine the prosecution's ability to characterize any unauthorized access as criminal. The Council of Europe Convention on Cybercrime provides that a party 'may require that the offence be committed by infringing security measures',[579] as an optional qualifying element for commission of the offence. In the EU, such a qualification was optional under the EU Framework Decision,[580] but has become mandatory under the Directive.[581] The Commission's original proposal did not contain the need to infringe a security measure and indeed specifically warned against 'the introduction of additional constitutive elements';[582] however, the European Parliament, on the initiative of Jan Albrecht MEP representing the Greens/European Free Alliance, disagreed and inserted the qualification.[583] In particular,

---

[574] For a fuller discussion of the legal issues raised by DOS attacks, see paras 3.294–3.303.

[575] Sommer, P, 'Computer misuse prosecutions', 16(5) *Computers and Law* (2006), available at <http://www.scl.org/site.aspx?i=ed832>.

[576] StGB, Art 202a. See also Brazil's Código Penal, Art 154-A ('by means of undue violation of a security mechanism') and Japan's Unauthorized Computer Access Law, Art 3(2)(1) ('restricted by an access control function').

[577] Norwegian General Civil Penal Code, s 145. The provision was enacted in 1987, but was amended in April 2005 and now reads: 'Any person who unlawfully opens a letter or other closed document or in a similar manner gains access to its contents, or who breaks into another person's locked repository'. See also Criminal Code of Finland, s 8(1) ('breaking a protection').

[578] Case No 83 B, RT-1998-1971, 15 December 1998.

[579] Convention on Cybercrime, Art 2.

[580] Council Framework Decision on attacks against information systems, OJ L 69/67, 16 March 2005, Art 2(2) '(Framework Decision').

[581] Directive 13/40/EU, above, n 159, Art 3.

[582] European Commission, 'Proposal for a Directive on attacks against information systems and repealing Council Framework Decision 2005/222/JHA', COM(2010) 517 final, 30 September 2010, at 7.

[583] See Committee on Civil Liberties, Justice and Home Affairs (Rapporteur M Hohlmeier), Report on the proposal for a directive of the European Parliament and of the Council on attacks against information systems and repealing Council Framework Decision 2005/222/JHA', A7-0224/2013, 19 June 2013.

there was a concern that employees using their work computers for 'unauthorised' private purposes may be exposed to criminal liability.[584]

3.243 During passage of the Computer Misuse Bill in the UK, an attempt was made to add a provision whereby hackers would be able to offer a defence if computer users had not implemented security measures:

> For the purposes of this section, it shall be a defence to prove that such care as was in all the circumstances reasonably required to prevent the access or intended access in question was not taken.[585]

The imposition of a 'security measure' threshold would seem likely to generate greater legal uncertainty, however, were a court required to make an assessment of the appropriateness or reasonableness of any security measure, as well as providing defence counsel with plenty of scope to challenge prosecutors and raise doubts in the minds of the jury. While the proposed amendment was rejected, the issue of the existence of security measures would seem implicitly relevant in the context of establishing whether an access was 'unauthorized'.[586] Commentators continue to argue the case that criminal liability for unauthorized access should only be triggered when it involves the 'circumvention of code-based restrictions'.[587] While Directive 13/14/EU states in its recitals that 'contractual obligations or agreements to restrict access to information systems by way of a user policy or terms of service' should not be the sole basis for criminal proceedings for unauthorized access.[588]

3.244 When computer misuse statutes were first proposed, during the 1980s, prior to the Internet, comparisons were made with seemingly analogous concepts from the traditional criminal code: the act of trespass with unauthorized access; criminal damage with unauthorized interference. These comparisons have coloured the subsequent debate about the question of authorization, particularly the law of trespass. Indeed, trespass is used as a descriptive term for unauthorized access in the literature, as in 'cybertrespass';[589] is used in statutory provisions,[590] and has been argued as a basis for legal action in cybercrime cases in the US.[591] Entering an open house may be unlawful, but will not be criminal unless the trespasser has been adequately warned; therefore, the argument runs, an unsecured computer is akin to an open house. However appealing the analogy, it should also be borne in mind that computer crime statutes were adopted as a response to the failure of property-based solutions, such as trespass, to address the types of misuse being carried out against computer systems.[592]

---

584 See Directive 13/40/EU, above, n 159, recital 17. Also an email from Ralf Bendrath, Senior Policy Advisor to Jan Albrecht, received on 7 July 2015.

585 Amendment proposed by Harry Cohen MP, at Standing Committee C, 'Computer Misuse Bill' HC (1989-90) col 15 (14 March 1990).

586 The APIG Report, above, n 541, paras 41–8, also examined the issue, but rejected any statutory provision.

587 Kerr, above, n 567, at 1600.

588 Directive 13/40/EU, above, n 159, recital 17.

589 See Wall, DS, 'Policing the Internet: Maintaining order and law on the cyberbeat', in Walker, C, and Wall, D (eds), *The Internet, Law and Society*, Longman, 2000, Chapter 7, at 157.

590 eg Brazil Código Penal, Art 154-A 'Trespass of a computer-related device'.

591 *Intel Corp v Hamidi*, 71 P 3d 296 (Cal 2003), where a claim was pursued under the tort of trespass to chattels in respect of unwanted emails. The claim was unsuccessful.

592 Kerr, above, n 567, at 1602 et seq.

The question of authorization under interception laws is more complex than that for access **3.245** and interference, involving three different dimensions. First, there is the authority of the person controlling the network.[593] This dimension is most similar in nature to that for the other integrity offences. Second, there is the authority or consent of the communicating parties, those utilizing the network. It is the protection of the privacy of these users that is the primary objective of interception laws. Finally, as an investigative tool, there is the authorization required to legitimize, in terms of *vires*, the conduct of public law enforcement agencies when engaged in an act of interception.[594]

An issue that intersects and overlaps the boundary that must exist between authorized **3.246** and unauthorized is the distinction between public and private space. Indeed, many of the problems discerning authorization in cyberspace arise, in part, from the manner in which the Internet challenges and disrupts traditional concepts of public and private spheres. The popular conception of the Internet is as the World Wide Web, a particular service available over the 'network of networks', which in large part operates as a public space, governed by implied authorizations underpinning the availability and exchange of information.[595] Concurrently, public consciousness of the Internet has often involved a perception of anonymity, an environment of private relationships and space, unmonitored and unencumbered by state oversight. Taken together, these notions may challenge reliance on authorization in integrity offences.

Under the CMA, access is considered to be unauthorized access if: **3.247**

    (a) he is not himself entitled to control access of the kind in question to the program or data; and

    (b) he does not have consent to access by him of the kind in question to the program or data from any person who is so entitled;

but this subsection is subject to section 10.[596]

Where the accused is external to the victim's organization, showing knowledge of an absence of entitlement or consent is not generally an issue, subject to the scenarios discussed above. However, where the accused is an employee of the organization, the burden is upon the prosecution to show that the accused knew that 'access of the kind in question' was unauthorized, rather than a misuse of express or implied rights of access, for example an accounts clerk entering false expenses claims. As noted by the Law Commission:

> An employee should only be guilty of an offence if his employer has clearly defined the limits of the employee's authority to access a program or data.[597]

US federal law does not criminalize mere unauthorized access, akin to the s 1 offence, such **3.248** access has to be linked to some further purpose, such as obtaining national security information or financial records.[598] Also in contrast to the UK, US federal law expressly addresses two distinct scenarios in respect of authorization: 'knowingly accessed a computer without

---

[593] See further paras 3.328–3.331.
[594] See further paras 4.167–4.178.
[595] Reed, C, *Internet Law: Text and Materials*, 2nd edn, Cambridge University Press, 2004, at 66 et seq.
[596] CMA, s 17(5).
[597] Report No 186, above, n 538, para 3.37.
[598] 18 USC s 1030 'Fraud and related activity in connection with computers'.

authorization or *exceeding* authorized access'.[599] The latter term is intended to cover 'insiders', such as employees,[600] and is defined in the following terms:

> means to access a computer with authorization and to use such access to obtain or alter information in the computer that the accesser is not entitled so to obtain or alter.[601]

3.249 There have been conflicting decisions, however, as to when the entitlement threshold is reached in the case of departing employees. In *International Airport Centers LLC v Citrin*,[602] a departing employee installed a program on his employer-owned laptop and securely deleted all the company's proprietary data. The court held that Citrin lost his entitlement as an agent of the company the moment he breached his duty of loyalty as an employee. This sets a very low threshold, placing the onus primarily on the employee to act appropriately, rather than upon the employer to clearly set out those acts which are permitted and those that are not. In *Lockheed Martin Corporation v Speed*[603] such a broad approach was explicitly rejected by the court. The case concerned the copying on to various data media of Lockheed's proprietary information by three departing employees prior to joining a competitor. The court considered that the 'breach of loyalty' test effectively places an employee in a position of being 'without authorization', rather than that of exceeding such authorization. This latter reading would seem more logical and principled in terms of creating a meaningful distinction between the two concepts, 'without' and 'exceeding', but will require approval from a higher court and in the context of criminal rather than civil proceedings.

3.250 The interpretation of 'authorization' under the CMA in an employment context was first considered in detail in *DPP v Bignell*.[604] The case concerned two serving police officers who had accessed the Police National Computer (PNC), via an operator, for personal purposes. They were charged with offences under s 1 of the CMA and convicted in the Magistrates' Court. They successfully appealed to the Crown Court against their conviction, and this decision was the subject of a further appeal before the Divisional Court, which was dismissed.

3.251 The central issue addressed to the court was whether a person authorized to access a computer system for a particular purpose (eg policing) can commit a s 1 offence by using such authorized access for an unauthorized purpose (eg personal). The Crown Court asserted that the CMA was primarily concerned 'to protect the integrity of computer systems rather than the integrity of the information stored on the computers ...', therefore such unauthorized usage was not caught by the Act. The Divisional Court upheld this view. First, Justice Astill stated that the phrase in s 17(5)(a): 'access of the kind in question' was referring to the types of access detailed in s 17(2): alteration, erasure, copying, moving, using, and

---

[599] ibid, s 1030(a)(1). Similarly, under Belgian law a separate offence exists where a person 'exceeds his power of access to a computer system' (Art 6(2)).

[600] eg *EF Cultural Travel BV v Explorica, Inc*, 274 F 3d 577 (1st Cir 2001), at 583–84.

[601] 18 USC s 1030(e)(6).

[602] 440 F3d 418 (7th Cir 2006). Following an earlier decision in *Shurgard Storage Centers, Inc v Selfguard Self Storage, Inc*, 119 F Supp 2d 1121 (WD Wash 2000).

[603] 2006 US Dist LEXIS 53108, 1 August 2006.

[604] [1998] 1 Cr App R. In an earlier case, *Bennett*, unreported, Bow Street Magistrates' Court, 10 October 1991, a police superintendent pleaded guilty to a s 1 offence, after checking the PNC to discover who his former wife was now seeing.

obtaining output. Second, the phrase 'control access' was referring to the authority granted to the police officers to access the PNC. He concluded that this did not create a lacuna in the law as the then Data Protection Act 1984 contained appropriate offences in relation to the use of personal data for unauthorized purposes.[605]

A near identical scenario to *Bignell* has been considered before a US state court, with a similar result. In *State v Olson*,[606] the officer was convicted of computer trespass for accessing a police computer database in order to find car licence plate details for female students at the local college. His initial conviction was overturned on appeal after the court concluded that while 'certain *uses* of retrieved data were against departmental policy, [the record] did not show that permission to *access* the computer was conditioned on the uses made of the data'.[607] Here, the concept of access is strictly distinguished from what may be done once access has been gained, although in this case the court had no statutory definition to assist them. In New Zealand, the relevant provision expressly states that an offence of unauthorized access is not committed when 'a person who is authorized to access a computer system accesses that computer system for a purpose other than the one for which that person was given access',[608] although other provisions may be relevant.[609] **3.252**

The *Bignell* decision attracted significant criticism and, as with *Sean Cropp*, was seen as significantly limiting the scope of the Act.[610] However, key aspects of the decision were re-examined by the House of Lords in *Allison*.[611] The case concerned an extradition request by the US Government of an individual accused in a fraud involving an employee of American Express, who was able to use her access to the computer system to obtain personal identification numbers to encode forged credit cards. As in *Bignell*, defence counsel argued that a s 1 offence had not been committed since the employee was authorized to access the relevant computer system. The House of Lords, while agreeing with the decision in *Bignell*, rejected the subsequent interpretation of s 17(5) made by Justice Astill.[612] **3.253**

On the first issue, 'access of the kind in question', Lord Hobhouse stated that this phrase simply meant that the authority granted under s 17(5) may be limited to certain types of programs or data, and is not referring to the kinds of access detailed in s 17(2). Evidence showed that the employee at American Express accessed data in accounts for which she was not authorized, therefore the access she obtained was 'unauthorized access'. Second, 'control access' did not refer to the individual authorized to access the system, but the organizational authority granting authority to the individual. In the *Bignell* case, it was the Police Commissioner who exercised such control and, through employee manuals, specified that access was for police purposes only. As a result of the decision in *Allison*, a subsequent case **3.254**

---

[605] Data Protection Act 1984, s 5(6). This has been replaced by an offence of unlawful obtaining under the DPA 1998, s 55 (see paras 3.35–3.38). See also *Rooney* [2006] EWCA Crim 1841, where an employee of the Staffordshire Police accessed the PNC for personal reasons.

[606] 735 P 2d 1362 (Wash Ct App 1987).

[607] ibid, at 1365 (emphasis added).

[608] Crimes Act 1961, s 252(2).

[609] eg accessing a computer to dishonestly obtain a pecuniary benefit (ibid, s 249).

[610] eg Bainbridge, D, 'Cannot employees also be hackers?', 13(5) *Computer Law and Security Report* 352 (1997); and Spink, P, 'Misuse of Police Computers', 42 *Juridical Review* 219 (1997).

[611] *Bow Street Magistrate and Allison (AP), ex parte US Government (HL(E))* [1999] 4 All ER 1.

[612] This interpretation had been followed by the Divisional Court from which the appeal had been made: see *R v Bow Street Magistrates' Court, ex parte Allison* [1999] QB 847.

of misuse of the PNC by a police officer did result in a successful conviction for unauthorized access.[613]

3.255 While the decision in *Allison* clarifies the interpretation of 'control' under s 17(5), the court's acceptance of *Bignell* would seem to perpetuate the uncertain jurisprudence under the CMA. First, Lord Hobhouse stresses the point that in *Bignell* 'the computer operator did not exceed his authority' and therefore did not commit an offence (at 627G). This would seem irrelevant to the question of whether the Bignells were committing a s 1 offence, since the operator is simply an innocent agent[614] and does not break the chain of causation between the Bignells' request and the 'unauthorized access'. Second, Lord Hobhouse recognizes that the concept of authorization needs to be refined, as 'authority to secure access of the kind in question', and the example given is where access 'to view data may not extend to authority to copy or alter that data' (at 626F–G). On this reasoning, it seems incongruous that the court should hold, by implication, that authority to view the data may not also be limited to particular circumstances. The Bignells knew that they were only authorized to access the PNC for policing purposes and knowingly misrepresented the purpose for their request.

3.256 The 'without right' concept used in the Convention and Directive appears to reflect a fundamental difference between a common law approach, whereby that which is not specified is lawful, and a civil law approach, in which that which is specified is lawful. The Explanatory Report to the Convention suggests that 'without right' can either refer to conduct 'undertaken without authority', such authority being derived from a multiplicity of sources including legislation and consent; or conduct not covered by 'established legal defences, excuses, justifications or relevant principles under domestic law'.[615] For our purposes, the former shall be referred to as 'positive' authority and the latter as 'negative' authority. The drafters were particularly keen to ensure that the conduct of law enforcement agencies when investigating a cybercrime was not affected by these new offences.[616]

3.257 Law enforcement officers may require 'positive' authority to engage in certain forms of investigative conduct, such as interception,[617] but will also require 'negative' lawful authority in terms of a defence against commission of any integrity offences. Addressing the latter aspect of law enforcement conduct under the CMA has proved complicated and has evolved over time. In the original statute, a saving provision was inserted in respect of the offence of unauthorized access, rendering it inapplicable where officers were exercising powers of inspection, search and seizure.[618] However, where an officer was not exercising such powers, then potential exposure to liability remained. Indeed, certain websites began specifically stating that law enforcement officers were not authorized to access the site, which was designed to exploit this lacuna. To address this, the saving provision was amended in 1994 to state:

---

[613] *Begley*, Coventry Magistrates' Court, referenced by Turner, MJL, 'Computer Misuse Act 1990 cases', available at <http://www.computerevidence.co.uk/Cases/CMA.htm>. See also a related appeal for judicial review of her dismissal for misconduct, *R (on the application of Begley) v Chief Constable of the West Midlands* [2001] EWCA Civ 1571.

[614] eg *R v Manley* (1844) 1 Cox 104.

[615] Explanatory Report to the Convention on Cybercrime, above, n 1, at para 38.

[616] ibid.

[617] See further Chapters 4 and 5.

[618] CMA, s 10 (as of 1990).

... nothing designed to indicate a withholding of consent to access to any program or data from persons as enforcement officers shall have effect to make access unauthorised for the purposes of the said section 1(1).[619]

More recently, further amendment has been made to the saving provision, extending both its scope to encompass all of the integrity offences under the CMA, thereby providing a defence for more proactive policing conduct,[620] as well as the relevant powers that may authorize such conduct.[621]

There would also seem to be a particular problem with the 'without right' concept as **3.258** detailed in the EU Directive. In the Convention, entitlement to control refers to the system as a whole as well as the kind of access being granted. In the Directive, however, entitlement extends beyond the owner of the system to any 'another right-holder of the system or of part of it'.[622] The scope of this depends, in part, on the distinction between system and data, as discussed above. To what extent is data 'part' of the system? If data is part of a system, then a work protected by intellectual property laws (eg copyright, design right, chip protection) that is being used without the authorization of the right-holder would potentially give rise to the offence. Such criminalization of IP infringement through the back door of computer-integrity offences can surely not have been the intention of the drafters.

The phrase used in the Commonwealth Model Law, 'without lawful excuse or justifica- **3.259** tion', also appears to be a problematic formulation. It is not further defined in the text of the Model Law. However, the phrase 'without lawful excuse' does appear in English law in respect of criminal damage, with two types of excuse being detailed: where there is a belief that consent does, or would, exist; or where it is considered necessary in order to protect property.[623] The question of belief is subjective, not concerned with whether the belief is either justified or reasonable.[624] Defence counsel could be expected to argue, for example, that the justification for the perpetrator's actions was to expose the frailties of the security measures in place. This was in fact argued in *Grey*:[625] 'Your claimed motivation was to expose and publicize the fact that the e-commerce retailers were not security conscious ...' One can imagine such 'justifications' having a strong 'Robin Hood' appeal to juries! Although 'consent' shares a common thread with the 'authorization' approach, the wording is couched in the style of a defence, rather than the requirement to show 'knowledge' in respect of authorization. This latter requirement can be viewed as a positive characteristic, since it is likely to reduce the scope of criminal law in respect of computer-integrity offences.

---

[619] Inserted by the Criminal Justice and Public Order Act 1994, s 162(1). An 'enforcement officer' is defined as:

> a constable or other person charged with the duty of investigating offences; and withholding consent from a person 'as' an enforcement officer of any description includes the operation, by the person entitled to control access, of rules whereby enforcement officers of that description are, as such, disqualified from membership of a class of persons who are authorised to have access.

[620] See further paras 2.267 and 4.68 et seq.
[621] CMA, s 10 (as of 2015, see Appendix I). The amendment was made by the Serious Crime Act 2015, s 44(2).
[622] Directive 13/40/EU, above, n 159, Art 1(d).
[623] Criminal Damage Act 1971, s 5(2).
[624] ibid, s 5(3).
[625] [2001] Swansea Crown Court, 6 July 2001, para 4C.

Unauthorized access

3.260 Obtaining unauthorized access into a person's system, also popularly referred to as 'hacking' or 'cybertrespass', may be carried out simply for the challenge of doing it, or may be the preliminary step to compromising the system and the information held on it. Access takes the perpetrator from the public domain into the private realm, a space sometimes subject to criminal law protections. Indeed, there has been much discussion about whether it is appropriate to use the criminal law against mere unauthorized access, since the most commonly used physical world analogy is that of trespass, a primarily civil area of law.[626] During the debates on the CMA, a decisive factor distinguishing access from trespass was perceived to be the cost to a system owner from the breach of confidentiality and integrity, and the consequential remedial work required.[627]

3.261 Under the CMA, s 1 establishes the basic offence of unauthorized access. Commission of the offence requires the *actus reus* of causing 'a computer to perform any function'. Some form of interaction with the computer is required, but actual access does not need to be achieved. This broad formulation means that simply turning on a computer could constitute the necessary act, while stealing a computer with the intention of simply selling it on would be unlikely to constitute a s 1 offence.

3.262 Access is not defined in terms of the computer itself, but the information, as 'program' or 'data', held in the computer. Section 17(2) broadly defines 'function' to include alterations or erasure, copying, or moving data, using it or producing output, such as displaying it on a screen. As such, 'function' is akin to the concept of 'processing' under the Data Protection Act 1998.[628] The concept of access has been equated with the process of acquiring information,[629] although access is broader than that of acquisition', since a person may use information, such as a program, without acquiring it in any meaningful sense.

3.263 The *mens rea* of the s 1 offence comprises two elements. First, there must be 'intent to secure access to any program or data held in any computer'. This was subject to amendment in 2006 to encompass also acts which 'enable any such access'[630] which criminalizes those that go beyond the mere provision of 'hacking' tools to others, an offence under s 3A, and interfere, directly or indirectly, with the target computer, such as disabling an access control mechanism without then attempting to penetrate the system to access programs or data, but leaving it for other persons, or for entry at some later date.[631] Second, the person must know at the time that he commits the *actus reus* that the access he intends to secure is unauthorized. The intent does not have to be directed at any particular program, data, or computer (CMA, s 1(2)). The offence is also not concerned with any ulterior motivation that

---

[626] However, the Criminal Justice and Public Order Act 1994, Pt V, created a number of new offences in respect of various forms of trespass considered to threaten public order, such as aggravated trespass (s 68). In addition, the Serious Organised Crime and Police Act 2005 established an offence of 'trespassing on designated site' (s 128).

[627] See comments from Mr Douglas Hogg, Minister for Industry, during the debate on the Second Reading of the Computer Misuse Bill, Hansard (Commons), Col 1181, 9 February 1990.

[628] DPA 1998, s 1(1).

[629] Christie, AL, 'Should the law of theft extend to information?', 69(4) *The Journal of Criminal Law* 350 (2005).

[630] CMA s 1(1)(a), as inserted by the Police and Justice Act 2006 (PJA), s 35(2).

[631] See statement of Lord Bassam, Home Officer Minister, Lords Hansard, 11 July 2006, Col 604.

a defendant may have for obtaining access, whether nefarious or otherwise. Any such 'third' intent would be relevant to the s 2 offence discussed below.

The first prosecution under the new Act addressed the nature of the *actus reus* under s 1. In **3.264** *R v Sean Cropp* (Snaresbrook Crown Court, 4 July 1991), the defendant returned to the premises of his former employer to purchase certain equipment. At some point when the sales assistant was not looking, the defendant was alleged to have keyed in certain commands to the computerized till granting himself a substantial discount. During the trial, the judge accepted the submission of defence counsel that s 1(1)(a) required 'that a second computer must be involved'. He believed that if Parliament had intended the offence to extend to situations where unauthorized access took place on a single machine, then s 1(1) (a) would have been drafted as 'causing a computer to perform any function with intent to secure access to any program or data held in *that or any other computer*'.

Such an interpretation would have seriously limited the scope of the Act, especially since **3.265** the majority of instances of hacking are those carried out within organizations.[632] The critical nature of this distinction led the Attorney-General to take the procedure of referring the decision on a point of law to the Court of Appeal.[633] The Court of Appeal subsequently rejected the lower court's interpretation, stating that the 'plain and natural meaning is clear'.[634] It is interesting to note, however, that the Council of Europe Convention offence of 'illegal access' does permit Member States to limit the offence to 'exclude the situation where a person physically accesses a stand-alone computer without any use of another computer system'.[635] This is the position adopted under Japanese law.[636]

In *Farquharson*, the defendant was prosecuted for obtaining mobile telephone numbers **3.266** and codes necessary to produce cloned telephones.[637] The computer system containing this information was actually accessed by his co-defendant Ms Pearce, an employee of the mobile telephone company, who was charged with the s 1 offence.[638] Farquharson was found to have committed the 'unauthorized access' required for the s 2 offence even though he never touched the computer himself, but had simply asked Pearce to access the information.

The s 1 offence was originally only punishable on summary conviction by a fine of up to **3.267** £2,000 or six months in jail (s 1(3)).[639] The original penalty was already double that recommended by the Law Commission.[640] In 2006, the Act was amended and the penalty was raised for summary convictions to a twelve-month jail term, while on indictment, a term of up to two years' imprisonment could be imposed.[641] The stated purpose of this amendment was to 'ensure that there are adequate and more effective penalties available for the offence of unauthorized access to computer material, to reflect the seriousness of the

---

[632] See Audit Commission Report, 'Ghost in the Machine: An Analysis of Fraud and Abuse' (1998), which found that nearly 25% of frauds were committed by staff in managerial positions.

[633] Criminal Justice Act 1972, s 36.

[634] *Attorney-General's Reference (No 1 of 1991)* [1992] 3 WLR 432, at 437F.

[635] Explanatory Report to the Convention on Cybercrime, above, n 1, at para 50.

[636] Unauthorized Computer Access Law, Art 3, which provides that each unauthorized act is committed against a 'specific computer … via a telecommunications line'.

[637] Croydon Magistrates' Court, 9 December 1993.

[638] ibid. A £300 fine was imposed on Pearce, while Farquharson received a six-month prison sentence.

[639] The maximum fine is level 5 on the standard scale, and has risen over the intervening years to £5,000.

[640] 1988 Report, above, n 251, Pt V.

[641] CMA, s 1(3), as amended by the PJA, s 35(3).

criminal activities which can be involved in committing this offence'.[642] In terms of effectiveness, the amendment changes the procedural nature of the s 1 offence in a number of ways: rendering it capable of being subject to an attempt;[643] a magistrate's search warrant;[644] and extradition proceedings.

3.268 With regard to attempt, it seems hard to imagine in what circumstances attempt would be the most appropriate charge because the person has done more than that which is 'merely preparatory', for example the possession of a person's password,[645] but less than that of causing, directly or indirectly, the target computer to 'perform any function', which is sufficient for the offence to be made out.

3.269 Under the EU Framework Decision on 'attacks against information systems', Member States were required to provide for a maximum available penalty of between two and five years, where the illegal access involves 'infringing security measures' and is committed by in the 'framework of a criminal organization'.[646] However, in Directive 13/40/EU, a minimum two-year term has been imposed,[647] but no aggravated circumstances pertain to the illegal access offence.

3.270 Prior to its repeal by the Police and Justice Act 2006, a prosecution under s 1 was subject to certain time limits. First, proceedings had to be brought within six months 'from the date on which evidence sufficient in the opinion of the prosecutor to warrant the proceedings came to his knowledge'.[648] The provision was examined by the courts in *Morgans v DPP*,[649] where it was held that the 'prosecutor' includes the policeman in charge of the investigation, which meant that in this case the charges had to be quashed for falling out of time. In addition, the phrase 'evidence sufficient in the opinion of' was construed as being descriptive of the state of the evidence, rather than requiring the prosecutor to have formed an opinion about the adequacy of the evidence.[650] The second time limit was that proceedings cannot be brought more than three years after commission of the offence.[651] This was an exception to the normal rule, whereby proceedings must be brought within six months of them taking place.[652] The extension was granted to reflect the fact that it may take time for such acts to come to the notice of a victim, as well as to assist investigators faced with the forensic challenges of such cases.[653]

3.271 Those that distribute passwords, codes, or other tools designed to facilitate hacking activities could have been subject to prosecution in relation to the s 1 offence, the appropriate charge being dependent on the circumstances and nature of their activities. Under

---

[642] Police and Justice Bill, Pt 5, s 35 Explanatory Note, para 297, available at <http://www.legislation.gov.uk/ukpga/2006/48/notes/division/5/1/5/2>.

[643] Under the Criminal Attempts Act 1981, s 1(4), attempt is only possible for indictable offences.

[644] Previously under the CMA, a s 14 warrant could only be granted by a circuit judge, which was generally perceived as a more demanding process than obtaining a warrant from a Magistrates' Court.

[645] See Lord Justice Taylor's comments in *Jones* [1990] 1 WLR 1057, at 1062.

[646] Framework Decision, above, n 580, Art 7(1) with respect to the optional offence under Art 2(2). No minimum term was set for the Art 2(1) offence.

[647] Directive 13/40/EU, above, n 159, Art 9(2).

[648] CMA, s 11(2), which was not complied with in *Morgans v DPP* [1999] 1 WLR 968, DC.

[649] [1999] 1 WLR 968, DC.

[650] ibid, at 982.

[651] CMA, s 11(3).

[652] Magistrates' Courts Act 1980 (MCA), s 127(1).

[653] Report No 186, above, n 538, paras 3.46–3.48.

the Magistrates' Courts Act 1980, they could be charged as a person who 'aids, abets, counsels or procures the commission by another person of a summary offence';[654] alternatively, a charge could be brought of incitement[655] or conspiracy with others to commit an offence of unauthorized access. When the CMA was enacted the publishers of the 'Hackers Handbook', a popular guide to current developments in this area, decided to withdraw the book from circulation to avoid potential legal action.[656] Incitement was successfully used in *Maxwell-King*,[657] where the defendant supplied on a commercial basis a device, known as a 'multimode board', which enabled people to gain access to encrypted satellite television channels by modifying in an unauthorized manner the set-top box.[658] However, such acts would now be subject to prosecution under s 3A offence, 'making, supplying or obtaining articles for use in computer misuse offences', discussed later in this chapter.

When mere unauthorized access was first criminalized, the debate centred on the appropriateness of the application of criminal law to such circumstances. Indeed, as noted above, that debate continues to be present in the international instruments. However, in the UK, arguments against criminalization would seem to be mute; instead, the act is being seen to be of greater seriousness.[659] The harm to a system owner from an act of unauthorized access, other than those intended by the perpetrator, would seem to fall into one of three broad types. First, there is the cost of investigatory work required to check the compromised system and any impact on data confidentiality, integrity, and availability. Second, there is the cost of remedial work to the system to prevent future access being obtained. Third, there is the cost of restoring the system and any data that may have been damaged or modified inadvertently by the actions of the perpetrator. However, all the examples used to justify a more serious treatment of unauthorized access seem to fall into the third type, inadvertent damage or modification.[660] Addressing such loss under an unauthorized access offence would seem to be confusing issues of access with issues of interference; the latter offence being the more serious and not requiring the access to be unauthorized.. **3.272**

Across Europe, Member States have adopted similar unauthorized access offences.[661] In the US, however, federal law does not contain an equivalent to the CMA s 1 offence. Unauthorized access is only criminal where a certain threshold is met, ie where the authorized use of the computer reaches more than $5,000 in a twelve-month period.[662] **3.273**

Under s 2 of the CMA, it is an offence to commit a s 1 offence together with the intent to commit, or facilitate the commission of, a further offence. The distinction between this offence and that of mere access is therefore one of differing motivations or, as stated by the Law Commission, the presence of an 'ulterior intent'.[663] The linkage between an act of **3.274**

---

654 MCA, s 44(1).

655 Now itself repealed and put on a statutory basis under the Serious Crimes Act 2007.

656 See Dumbill, E, 'Computer Misuse Act 1990—recent developments', 8(4) *Computer Law and Practice* 107 (1992).

657 The Times, 2 January 2001.

658 See also *Parr-Moore* [2003] 1 Cr App R (S).

659 ie the amendments made under the PJA and the Serious Crime Act 2015.

660 See the APIG Report, above, n 541, para 98.

661 eg France, Penal Code Art 323-1: 'Fraudulently penetrating or maintaining access to an information system'. See generally UNODC Cybercrime Repository, available at <https://www.unodc.org/cld/index-cybrepo.jspx>.

662 18 USC s 1030(a)(4).

663 Report No 186, above, n 538, para 3.49.

unauthorized access and some additional purpose is a common feature in other jurisdictions. Indeed, the Convention on Cybercrime gives signatories the option of requiring the additional 'intent of obtaining computer data or other dishonest intent'.[664] The relevant further offence under s 2 is one for which the sentence is fixed by law, for example life imprisonment for murder, or where imprisonment may be for a term of five years or more, for example a computer fraud.[665] The access and the further offence do not have to be intended to be carried out at the same time,[666] and it also does not matter if the further offence was in fact impossible.[667] Upon conviction, a person could be sentenced to imprisonment for up to a five-year term on indictment; while the penalty for a summary conviction was raised from six months to twelve months.[668]

3.275 The following cases illustrate a range of situations that have arisen under the s 2 offence:

- In *Pearlstone*, an ex-employee used his former company's telephone account and another subscriber's account to defraud the computer-administered telephone system and place calls to the US.[669]
- In *Borg*, an investment company analyst was accused of establishing dummy accounts within a 'live' fund management system.[670] The alleged 'further offence' was expected to be fraudulent transfers into the dummy accounts.
- In *Grey*,[671] the defendant exploited a weakness in electronic commerce sites using Microsoft's Internet Information Server application to access customer databases and obtain the credit card and other personal details of at least 5,400 customers, which were then published on the Internet; as well as purchasing various goods and services.
- In *Brown*,[672] the defendant had obtained stolen bank and credit card details and used them to change account details online and impersonate the account holder to obtain a new card and PIN and then withdraw funds.

3.276 Prosecutions under s 2 are likely to be relatively infrequent or concurrent with other charges, since in many cases prosecutors will pursue a prosecution for the further offence rather than the unauthorized access, even though the individual may be initially charged with the s 2 offence. In addition, the perpetrator's act of unauthorized access may be sufficient to found a prosecution for an attempt to commit the further offence,[673] although it is more likely to be of use where the steps taken were 'merely preparatory'.[674]

---

[664] Convention on Cybercrime, Art 2. Only the US has declared that it has included this additional requirement. See 'Reservations and Declarations for Treaty No. 185—Convention on Cybercrime', available at <http://www.coe.int/en/web/conventions/search-on-treaties/-/conventions/treaty/185/declarations>.

[665] CMA, s 2(2), ie for a first offender at twenty-one or over.

[666] ibid, s 2(3).

[667] ibid, s 2(4).

[668] ibid, s 2(5), as amended by the PJA, s 52, Sch 14, para 17.

[669] Bow Street Magistrates' Court, April 1991; described in Battcock, R, 'Prosecutions under the Computer Misuse Act 1990', 6(6) *Computers and Law* 22 (1996).

[670] March 1993; see Battcock, above, n 669.

[671] [2001] Swansea Crown Court, 6 July 2001.

[672] [2014] EWCA Crim 695.

[673] See Criminal Attempts Act 1981, s 1: 'If, with intent to commit an offence to which this section applies, a person does an act which is more than merely preparatory to the commission of the offence, he is guilty of attempting to commit the offence.'

[674] Wasik, above, n 8, at 84.

An effective criminal code may require what can be called 'facilitative' offences, offences **3.277** which facilitate the investigation and prosecution of a criminal, but which are not generally used as the main or leading charge. Both s 1 and s 2 offences under the CMA could be characterized as such 'facilitative' offences. However, as with other attempt or preparatory offences, the fact that they may have limited application or actual use would not seem to, per se, render them worthless as a tool in the armoury of law enforcement.

Unauthorized interference

Obtaining access to a computer system clearly threatens the confidentiality of any infor- **3.278** mation residing in it. However, the greater concern is often that having accessed a system, the perpetrator may affect the integrity and availability of the information being processed, by interfering with the data or the hardware on which it resides. Such interference may be the result of deliberate action, a form of electronic vandalism, or the unwitting by-product of the hacker's actions when operating within the system. Indeed, one argument used in favour of criminalizing mere unauthorized access to a system is that such access can result in non-intentional damage. The consequences of unauthorized modifications can range from simple inconvenience to life-threatening incidents, such as *Rymer*,[675] where a hospital nurse hacked into a hospital computer system and altered patient drug prescriptions.

Criminal damage

The offence of criminal damage may obviously be relevant in many situations where a com- **3.279** puter is the subject of the crime. The value of a computer system normally resides in the information it contains, software, and data, rather than the physical hardware.[676] However, as with the concept of theft, to what extent does the unauthorized deletion or modification of computer-based information constitute 'damage' to property, as required under the Criminal Damage Act 1971?[677] The question was examined in *Cox v Riley*,[678] where an employee deleted computer programs from a plastic circuit card that was required to operate a computerized saw. The court stated that the property (ie the plastic circuit card) had been damaged by the erasure of the programs to the extent that the action impaired 'the value or usefulness' of the card and necessitated 'time and labour and money to be expended' to make the card operable again.

This interpretation was upheld in *R v Whiteley*,[679] where the defendant was convicted of **3.280** causing damage through gaining unauthorized access into the Joint Academic Network, used by UK universities, and deleting and amending substantial numbers of files. It was argued, on his behalf, that the defendant's activities only affected the information contained on a computer disk, not the disk itself. However, the court stated:

> What the Act [Criminal Damage Act 1971] requires to be proved is that tangible property has been damaged, not necessarily that the damage itself should be tangible.[680]

---

[675] Referenced by Turner, above, n 613. See also 'Nurse alters hospital prescriptions', 2 *Computer Fraud and Security Bulletin* (1994), at 4–5.

[676] Although the theft of computers for their processor chips has been significant during periods where market demand has exceeded supply.

[677] Criminal Damage Act 1971, s 1(1). Under s 10(1), 'Property' means 'property of a tangible nature, whether real or personal'.

[678] (1986) 83 Cr App R 54.

[679] (1991) 93 Cr App R 25.

[680] ibid, at 28.

The alteration of the magnetic particles contained on a disk, while imperceptible, did impair the value and usefulness of the disk and therefore constituted damage. However, if the disk had been blank, any alteration would not necessarily be 'damage'.

3.281 Despite these successful prosecutions, the Law Commission considered that uncertainty continued to exist when prosecuting computer misuse under the Criminal Damage Act and, therefore, proposed the creation of a new offence under the CMA. One concern was the possibility of situations where it would be difficult to identify the tangible 'property' that had been damaged when altering data, for example deleting information being sent across the public telephone network. A second major concern was that police and prosecuting authorities were experiencing practical difficulties 'explaining to judges, magistrates and juries how the facts fit in with the present law of criminal damage'.[681]

Section 3

3.282 The third substantive offence under the CMA was originally that of 'unauthorised modification of computer material':

> A person is guilty of an offence if—
> (a) he does any act which causes an unauthorised modification of the contents of the computer; and
> (b) at the time when he does the act he has the requisite intent and the requisite knowledge.[682]

The offence was principally promoted by the spate of publicity and fear surrounding the use of computer viruses and other malware, as well as concerns about what hackers do once they obtain access to a machine. The provision was amended in 2006 and re-titled 'unauthorised acts with intent to impair, or with recklessness as to impairing, operation of computer, etc.':

> (1) A person is guilty of an offence if—
>   (a) he does any unauthorised act in relation to a computer;
>   (b) at the time when he does the act he knows that it is unauthorised; and
>   (c) either subsection (2) or subsection (3) below applies.
> (2) This subsection applies if the person intends by doing the act—
>   (a) to impair the operation of any computer;
>   (b) to prevent or hinder access to any program or data held in any computer;
>   (c) to impair the operation of any such program or the reliability of any such data; or
>   (d) to enable any of the things mentioned in paragraphs (a) to (c) above to be done.
> (3) This subsection applies if the person is reckless as to whether the act will do any of the things mentioned in paragraphs (a) to (d) of subsection (2) above.

As discussed below, the amendment arose primarily in response to concerns about the original provision's suitability to address denial-of-service attacks. However, while the scope of the provision has been significantly widened, not least by its extension to include reckless conduct, much of the original wording was retained. In 2015, a further amendment to the interference provisions in the CMA saw the insertion of an additional offence of 'unauthorised acts causing, or creating risk of, serious damage'.[683]

---

681 Report No 186, above, n 538, para 2.31.
682 CMA, s 3(1).
683 ibid, s 3ZA.

The concept of damage in the Criminal Damage Act 1971 is amended by s 3 to the extent **3.283** that 'a modification of the contents of the computer' shall not be regarded as damage, and therefore an offence under the 1971 Act, 'unless its effect on that computer or computer storage medium impairs its physical condition'.[684] In the case of removable data media, such as a USB memory stick or CD-ROM, deletion of data would only be an offence under s 3 if the storage medium were in the computer.[685] Once removed, any subsequent damage to the data media would be subject to the terms of the 1971 Act, if it were damage to its physical condition. Despite these changes, data held on a computer may still be subject to judicial examination as to whether 'damage' has occurred under the terms of the Data Protection Act 1998.[686]

The original offence created a substantial discrepancy with the situation prior to the 1990 **3.284** Act, since conviction under the Criminal Damage Act could be punishable by imprisonment for up to ten years,[687] twice that available for an offence under s 3.[688] In addition, liability for criminal damage could arise through the defendant 'being reckless as to whether any such property would be destroyed',[689] without the requirement for the prosecution to show intent. Such reckless damage is often a feature of 'hacking' cases, where a hacker inadvertently deletes or alters files and data during the course of his activities, causing the victim substantial loss.[690] However, the Law Commission considered that the s 3 offence should be limited to those engaged in intentional acts of sabotage and noted that those causing inadvertent damage would already be guilty of the s 1 offence, which should be a sufficient deterrent. Under the 2006 amendments, the maximum tariff for the offence was raised to ten years[691] and reckless-ness is sufficient to commit the offence,[692] thereby restoring the pre-1990 position on liability.

The offence comprises the *mens rea* of intent or recklessness, as well as knowledge that the **3.285** act was unauthorized. The conduct element is broadly defined to include the causing of an act and a series of acts.[693] In respect of the former, a person would still have committed the act where an innocent agent, such as a system operator inadvertently triggering a virus, executed the actual keystrokes. As with the other CMA offences, the issue of authorization is further defined:

> An act done in relation to a computer is unauthorised if the person doing the act (or causing it to be done)—
> (a) is not himself a person who has responsibility for the computer and is entitled to deter-mine whether the act may be done; and
> (b) does not have consent to the act from any such person.[694]

---

[684] Criminal Damage Act 1971, s 10(5), as amended by the PJA, s 52, Sch 14, para 2.

[685] CMA, s 17(6). Similarly, under Australian law, data held on a 'data storage device' is subject to the offences where 'for the time being held in a computer' or 'on a computer network of which the computer forms a part': Criminal Code Act 1995, s 476.1(1). In addition, a separate offence has been established to address impairment to data held on a stand-alone computer disk or data storage device (ibid, s 478.2).

[686] DPA 1998, Sch 1, Pt I, Principle 7.

[687] CDA, s 4.

[688] CMA, s 3(7)(b).

[689] ibid, s 1(1).

[690] Report No 186, above, n 538, para 3.62.

[691] CMA, s 3(6)(c).

[692] ibid, s 3(3).

[693] ibid, s 3(5).

[694] ibid, s 17(8).

This differs from the original provision by the inclusion of the concept of 'responsibility' in addition to that of entitlement. It is not expressly stated what the purpose of the additional phrase is; although one can speculate that it is designed to clarify that 'insiders', such as employees, who are given responsibility for a computer, such as a laptop, can still be held to have engaged in an unauthorized act in respect of that computer if they do not have the requisite entitlement.

3.286 The nature of any 'act' may be permanent or temporary.[695] Also, as with the s 1 offence, the intent or recklessness need not be directed at any particular program, data, or computer.[696] Knowledge only relates to the issue of authorization, not the scale of the act being committed. This was illustrated in the first prosecution of a virus writer, Christopher Pile, aka the 'Black Baron', in 1995.[697] When arrested, Pile had initially denied any involvement with computers, let alone writing the viruses; however, during the course of his police interview, carried out in parallel with a forensic expert examining computers that had been seized, he eventually admitted his activities.[698] Pile was found guilty of the offence even though he had no knowledge of which computers were affected by his viruses, called 'Pathogen' and 'Queeg', and he had not targeted any specific computer. He was sentenced to eighteen months' imprisonment. Similarly, in *Vallor*,[699] the defendant committed a series of offences over the course of a number of weeks, sending out three different viruses attached to email messages. By the time a search warrant was executed at his home, his first virus, named 'Gokar', had been detected in some forty-two countries.

3.287 Under the original provision, there was requirement for the presence of dual intention, in respect of causing a modification and of causing impairment:

> . . . the requisite intent is an intent to cause a modification of the contents of any computer and by so doing—
> (a) to impair the operation of any computer; . . .

This was illustrated in the *Sean Cropp* case. In the Crown Court, the judge had agreed with the defence counsel's argument that the defendant's actions more appropriately fell under the unauthorized modification offence rather than that of unauthorized access. However, in the Court of Appeal, Lord Taylor put forward the opinion that the only form of modification that could be applicable to the defendant's actions was with respect to the impairment of the reliability of the data, and went on to note:

> That would involve giving the word 'reliability' the meaning of achieving the result in the printout which was intended by the owner of the computer. It may not necessarily impair the reliability of data in a computer that you feed in something which will produce a result more favourable to a customer than the store holder intended.[700]

---

[695] ibid, s 3(5)(c).
[696] ibid, s 3(4).
[697] Plymouth Crown Court, 1995.
[698] See 'The sad tale of Chris Pile's 15 seconds of fame', available at <http://vxheaven.org/lib/static/vdat/lgguilt2.htm>.
[699] [2004] 1 Cr App R (S) 319.
[700] *Attorney-General's Reference (No 1 of 1991)* [1992] 3 WLR 432, at 438A.

This statement clearly recognizes the requirement for dual intention and also seems to support the Law Commission's stance that 'the offence should not punish unauthorized modifications which improve, or are neutral in their effect'.[701]

However, the meaning of the term 'reliability' was revisited in *Yarimaka v Governor of HM* **3.288** *Prison Brixton; Zezev v Government of the United States of America*.[702] The case concerned the hacking into the systems of the financial information company Bloomberg, and the subsequent attempt to blackmail the founder Michael Bloomberg. In the course of extradition proceedings, defence counsel for Zezev challenged the validity of the s 3 charge. It was submitted that the purpose of s 3 was confined to acts which 'damage the computer so that it does not record the information which is fed into it' (para 14). In this case, the defendant fed false information into the system concerning the source of certain information and as such he did not alter or erase the data, the apparent mischief against which the section was directed.

A clear similarity could be drawn between this situation and the position in *Sean Cropp*. In **3.289** the former, false information was also input into the computer to benefit the perpetrator, and yet Lord Taylor was of the opinion that this does not 'necessarily impair the reliability of the data in a computer'. In *Yarimaka*, Lord Woolf did not feel inclined to make a distinction between an intention to modify and an intention to impair, stating '[i]f a computer is caused to record information which shows that it came from one person, when it in fact came from someone else, that manifestly affects its reliability'.[703] Such an approach, while chiming with common sense, potentially generated uncertainty regarding the scope of the original s 3 offence.[704] Under the new s 3, the intent is simply in relation to the listed forms of interference, not the unauthorized act itself.

Prosecutions under s 3 can be distinguished into two broad categories: those where the **3.290** perpetrator often has no knowledge at all about the identity or number of victims against whom his crime is committed, as in *Pile* and *Vallor*, which can be labelled 'remote crimes'; and those involving persons having some pre-existing relationship with the victim, so-called 'insider crimes'.

The first major prosecution brought under s 3 was an insider crime, *Goulden*.[705] In this case, **3.291** Goulden installed a security package on an Apple workstation for a printing company, Ampersand. The package included a facility to prevent access without use of a password. Goulden made use of this facility as part of his claim for fees totalling £2,275. Owing to the computerized nature of their printing operations, Ampersand were unable to function for a period of a few days. They claimed £36,000 lost business as a result of Goulden's actions, including £1,000 for a specialist to override the access protection. The court imposed a two-year conditional discharge on Goulden and a £1,650 fine. The judge also commented that Goulden's actions were 'at the lowest end of seriousness'! By contrast, in *Carey*,[706] a software

---

[701] Report No 186, above, n 538, para 3.72.

[702] [2002] EWHC 589 (Admin). Zezev was eventually sentenced to a four-year jail term: see DoJ, 'Kazakhstan hacker sentenced to four years prison for breaking into Bloomberg systems and attempting extortion', Press Release, 1 July 2003, available at <http://www.justice.gov/archive/criminal/cybercrime/press-releases/2003/zezevSent.htm>

[703] [2002] EWHC 589 (Admin), para 18.

[704] See Tausz, D and Smith, JC, Case Comment, *Criminal Law Review* 648 [2002].

[705] The Times, 10 June 1992.

[706] Hove Crown Court, 19 September 2002.

engineer deleted three years' worth of design drawing in another payment dispute with a company and was sentenced to an eighteen-month prison sentence.

3.292 In *Whitaker*,[707] the courts were required to consider the extent to which the unauthorized modification offence could be applied against an owner of intellectual property. The case concerned a software developer and his client, and arose when the developer initiated a logic bomb designed to prevent use of the software following a dispute over payment. The defendant programmer argued that since under the contract he had retained all intellectual property rights in the software (title transferred upon payment), he had the requisite right to modify the software. The court held that, despite the existence of copyright in the software, the nature of the development contract constituted a limitation on the exercise of the developer's rights. The court did recognize, however, that such an action would have been permitted if it had been explicitly provided for in the contract, ie the licensee was made aware of the consequences of a failure to pay. He was therefore found guilty of an offence under s 3. This was an important decision, since the software industry has resorted to such techniques as a means of ensuring payment for their services.[708]

3.293 In May 1993, the first classic 'hackers' were given six-month jail sentences for conspiracy to commit offences under s 1 and s 3 of the CMA.[709] The defendants, known as the 'Eight Legged Groove Machine' (8LGM), hacked computer systems ranging from the Polytechnic of Central London to National Aeronautics and Space Administration (NASA), causing damage valued at £123,000. In passing sentence, the judge said:

> There may be people out there who consider hacking to be harmless, but hacking is not harmless. Computers now form a central role in our lives, containing personal details . . . It is essential that the integrity of those systems should be protected and hacking puts that integrity in jeopardy.

Such judicial sentiment is critical if the Act is to have a significant deterrent effect. However, the jury acquitted one of the co-defendants in the same case, Bedworth, because defence counsel successfully argued, with testimony from an expert medical witness, that the necessary *mens rea* for a charge of conspiracy was absent because the defendant was an 'obsessive' hacker.[710] This case was widely publicized and was seen by many as a potential 'hacker's charter'.[711] However, the decision seems to have arisen partly from a mistaken choice by the prosecuting authorities to pursue an action for conspiracy, rather than a charge under the CMA.

Denial-of-service attacks

3.294 One issue that arose concerning the original s 3 offence of unauthorized modification was its applicability to the carrying out of DOS attacks launched against websites and other online resources, particularly commercial operators such as eBay and Amazon. Such attacks are designed to disrupt the operation of a site by deliberately flooding the host server

---

[707] Scunthorpe Magistrates' Court, unreported, 1993; see Battcock, above, n 669.

[708] For a civil case under similar circumstances, see *Rubicon Computer Systems Ltd v United Paints Ltd* (2000) 2 TCLR 453. In the US, the Uniform Computer Information Transactions Act (1999) expressly provides for the use of such 'electronic self-help' mechanisms, at s 816, although it was amended in 2000 to exclude mass-market products.

[709] *R v Strickland, R v Woods*, Southwark Crown Court, 21 May 1993.

[710] Southwark Crown Court, 17 March 1993.

[711] See eg 'Bedworth case puts law on trial', *Computing*, 25 March 1993, at 7.

with multiple requests for information.[712] Sometimes the DOS attacks succeed by causing congestion in the communications links, rather than the target machine; which was the case in October 2002 when the thirteen domain name system (DNS) root name servers were subjected to an attack.[713] Whether the attack impacts on connection capacity or bandwidth, the primary objective is to compromise the availability of the online resource, rather than its confidentiality or integrity. Motivations range from extortion attempts, such as against gambling sites,[714] to political protest, such as anti-globalization activists against the WTO site[715] or against companies.[716]

To achieve the necessary volumes and to conceal the location of the perpetrator, 'distributed **3.295** denial-of-service' (DDOS) attacks are usually the normal mode of attack. To mobilize the multiple computers required, the perpetrator will generally surreptitiously seize control of what are known as 'zombie' computers, or 'botnets', computers acting under the control of the perpetrator without the owner's knowledge. Indeed, there is a black market in 'botnets', where computers, in sets of hundreds, thousands, or even hundreds of thousands, can be hired for criminal activities;[717] as one security professional has noted: 'Hackers don't want to damage computers any more, they want to own them'.[718]

In terms of criminal conduct, a distinction should be made between the obtaining control **3.296** of the individual systems that comprise the 'botnet', which will generally involve illegal access, and the launching of a DDOS attack against the target systems, which is usually designed to impact its availability.[719] Prior to the amendment of the s 3 offence, attempts to prosecute those considered responsible for launching DDOS attacks encountered problems from two sources, in relation to both the conduct and fault elements. First, in respect of conduct, as discussed further in Chapter 6,[720] one avenue of defence is to deny that you

---

[712] Such actions should be contrasted with the sending of multiple requests for supposedly legitimate purposes, eg a competitor checking current prices. See eg *eBay v Bidders Edge*, 100 F Supp 2d 1058 (ND Cal 2000), where eBay successfully obtained an injunction on the basis of a claim for trespass to chattels.

[713] Vixie, P, Sneeringer, G, and Schleifer, M, 'Events of 21 Oct 2002', 24 November 2002, available at <http://d.root-servers.org/october21.txt>.

[714] eg Ward, M, 'Bookies suffer online onslaught', *BBC News*, 19 March 2004, available at <http://news.bbc.co.uk/2/hi/technology/3549883.stm>.

[715] eg DJNZ and The Action Tool Development Group of the Electrohippies Collective, 'Client-side Distributed Denial-of-Service: Valid campaign tactic or terrorist act?', 34(3) *Leonardo* 269 (2001).

[716] On 22 May 2006, a German Higher Regional Court held that an online demonstration by 13,000 demonstrators against Lufthansa's corporate website, through a two-hour DDOS attack, was not unlawful coercion or data modification.: Case against *Andreas Thomas Vogel*, Case No 1 Ss 319/05 991 Ds 6100 Js226314/01-1009, see further at <http://post.thing.net/node/1370>.

[717] See DoJ, 'Computer virus broker arrested for selling armies of infected computers to hackers and spammers', Press Release, 3 November 2005, available at <http://www.justice.gov/archive/criminal/cyber crime/press-releases/2005/anchetaArrest.htm>. See also Cullen, D, 'Dutch smash 100,000-strong zombie army', *The Register*, 7 October 2005, available at <http://www.theregister.co.uk/2005/10/07/dutch_police_smash_zombie_network/>.

[718] Johnson, B, 'Of worms and woodpeckers: The changing world of the virus-busters fighting rise in internet crime', *The Guardian*, 6 February 2006, available at <http://www.theguardian.com/uk/2006/feb/06/russia.security>.

[719] See T-CY, 'Provisions of the Budapest Convention covering botnets', Guidance Note No 2, T-CY (2013) 6E Rev, 5 June 2013, available at <https://www.coe.int/t/dghl/cooperation/economiccrime/Source/Cybercrime/TCY/TCY%202013/TCY_2013_6REV_GN2_botnets_V7adopted.pdf> and T-CY, 'DDOS attacks', Guidance Note No 5, T-CY (2013) 10E Rev, 5 June 2013, available at <https://www.coe.int/t/dghl/cooperation/economiccrime/Source/Cybercrime/TCY/TCY%202013/T-CY%282013%2910REV_GN5_DDOS%20attacks_V7adopted.pdf>.

[720] See paras 6.95–6.96.

were the person responsible for initiating the attack from the source machine, even if you own it! In an environment where there is a prevalence of 'zombie' machines, establishing the required evidential link between a machine and the conduct of its owner may prove difficult. In *Caffrey*,[721] the defendant successfully argued that the DOS attacks launched from his machine, which brought the Port of Houston in the US to a standstill, had been initiated by a 'Trojan horse' virus operating on his machine without his knowledge. This was despite the absence of evidence of the presence of such malware. As he was held not to have done the *actus reus* causing the modification, there was no need for the question of fault to be addressed.

3.297 Because of the different means of carrying out a DDOS attack, there was concern that the unauthorized modification offence may be unable to address all such activities. With direct attacks, the nature of the communications sent to the target machine will often fall within a class of transmission which the target machine was designed to receive. As such, while there may be the necessary intent to cause a modification and impairment, the modification itself may not be considered unauthorized. Such an argument was accepted in a written judgment in *Lennon*[722] given by District Judge Grant at Wimbledon Magistrates' Court in November 2005, a case involving a teenage boy. The defence had been argued after the teenager had admitted to carrying out a DOS attack against his former employer, Domestic and General Group, using a specialist email-bomber program called Avalanche. Some five million emails had been sent, causing the company's servers to crash. On the issue of authorization, Judge Grant stated:

> the individual emails caused to be sent each caused a modification which was in each case an 'authorized' modification. Although they were sent in bulk resulting in the overwhelming of the server, the effect on the server is not a modification addressed by section 3 (of the CMA) . . . On the narrow issue of an authorized or unauthorized modification, I concluded that no reasonable tribunal could conclude that the modification caused by the e-mails sent by the defendant were unauthorized within the meaning of section 3.[723]

In this decision, the court adopted a limited perspective on the perpetrator's activities. If it is clear that the defendant caused the modification and had the 'requisite intent', to treat each message in isolation when addressing the issue of authorization, rather than as a totality, seemed to be unnecessarily literal. If each message is treated as separate, it is inevitably logically difficult to argue that at a certain increment all the messages, those already received and those to be received, become unauthorized. However, if the perpetrator's initial act is viewed as triggering the sending of a sum *x* of messages that are designed to overwhelm the recipient system, then a lack of authorization could be found by implication.

3.298 Such an approach was indeed taken on appeal by the Director of Public Prosecutions, by way of case stated.[724] The Divisional Court allowed the appeal, stating:

---

[721] Southwark Crown Court, 17 October 2003.

[722] *L* [2005] ECLR 5(5), 3 (the defendant was under eighteen at the initial trial, hence his name was not disclosed).

[723] See Espiner, T, 'British teen cleared in "email bomb" case', ZDNet (UK), 2 November 2005. See also 'Teen cleared over e-mail salvo', *BBC News*, 3 November 2005, available at <http://news.bbc.co.uk/1/hi/technology/4402572.stm>.

[724] An appeal by way of 'case stated' may be made by the prosecution or defence, and is made under the Magistrates' Courts Act 1980, s 111(1). See also Criminal Procedure Rules 2005 (SI No 384), Pt 64.

The owner of a computer able to receive emails would ordinarily be taken to have consented to the sending of emails to the computer. However, such implied consent was not without limits, and it plainly did not cover emails that had been sent not for the purpose of communication with the owner but for the purpose of interrupting his system.[725]

While the amended definition of 'unauthorised' would not necessarily remove the problem raised at first instance in *Lennon*, an 'act' is now explicitly defined as including a 'series of acts',[726] which enables DOS traffic to be treated as a sum rather than as individual messages. On returning to the Magistrates' Court, Lennon pleaded guilty and was given a two-month suspended sentence with a curfew order.

With DDOS attacks, offences under ss 1 and 3 are likely to have been committed against the 'zombie' computers, by the person surreptitiously installing the malware, even if uncertainty existed about the nature of what is carried out against the target computer. Where a DOS or DDOS attack effectively disabled the communication links to the target computer through congestion, rather than the target itself, the original s 3 offence may not have been applicable, since it may not be possible to show any modification of the 'contents of any [ie the target] computer'. Obviously, the computers comprising the congested network, such as routers, would have been modified and a prosecution could focus on the act of compromising these resources, although the issue of authorization arises here as well. As a result of the legal uncertainty, there were a number of proposals to address the potential lacuna.[727] In June 2004, the All Party Parliamentary Internet Group proposed the creation of a new offence of 'impairing access to data', which would have a similar tariff to the CMA s 1 offence.[728] **3.299**

In July 2003, the Government announced its intention to review the 1990 Act,[729] in part to address existing lacunae, such as the need to tackle certain DOS activities, as well as to comply with its international commitments. The provisions to amend the CMA were contained in the Police and Justice Act 2006.[730] Rather than establishing a supplementary offence, the amendment replaced the s 3 offence. **3.300**

The offence of 'unauthorised acts' shifts the locus of the crime from the 'contents of the computer' to potentially any point in a network which is held to be 'in relation to' the target computer, a phrase not further defined. The wording thus further weakens the conceptual link between the s 3 offence and criminal damage. While *Cox v Riley* and *Whiteley* extend the meaning of damage to include impairment of value or function, both are located in the property itself. By shifting the locus away from the computer, such provisions become more analogous to the common law offence of public nuisance,[731] similar in kind to the **3.301**

---

[725] *DPP v Lennon* [2006] All ER (D) 147 (May).

[726] CMA, s 3(5)(b).

[727] Private members bills were proposed by the Earl of Northesk (2002), Derek Wyatt MP (2005), and Tom Harris MP (2005).

[728] APIG Report, above, n 541, para 75.

[729] Caroline Flint MP, Parliamentary Under-Secretary, Home Officer Minister in speech made at a EURIM meeting, 14 July 2003.

[730] PJA, s 36.

[731] Although see the House of Lords' judgment in *Rimmington* [2005] UKHL 63; [2006] HRLR 3, which while recognizing that such an offence was sufficiently clear, precise and rational to be consistent with Art 7 of the European Convention on Human Rights (ECHR) (4 November 1950, entered into force 3 November 1953, 213 UNTS 222) was severely limited to use against conduct that was not subject to express statutory provision.

obstruction of a highway,[732] especially where the communications links are congested and collateral damage in the form of loss of connectivity is extensive. The wording also has some similarities with the US formulation of a 'protected computer' in that both recognize that it is the networked quality of computers where the 'integrity' threat resides, as much as other features of a computer.

3.302   The new provision was intended to comply with the 'illegal system interference' offences under the Convention on Cybercrime and 2005 Decision.[733] However, the terms of these offences are not identical. Both list a series of possible intentional acts against a system, 'deletion, damaging, deterioration, alteration, suppression'; but the Decision also refers to 'rendering inaccessible'. While the common list would seem to be located within the system, akin to damage, the latter phrase takes us away from the computer, akin to obstruction. The only instrument that expressly uses the language of obstruction is the Commonwealth Model Law, in respect of data interference:

> 6(1)   A person who, intentionally or recklessly, without lawful excuse or justification, does any of the following acts:
> (a) destroys or alters data; or
> (b) renders data meaningless, useless or ineffective; or
> (c) *obstructs*, interrupts or interferes with the lawful use of data; or
> (d) *obstructs*, interrupts or interferes with any person in the lawful use of data; or
> (e) denies access to data to any person entitled to it.[734]

3.303   To date, DOS attacks have been primarily discussed in terms of an external attack against a website, in contrast to the unauthorized access, which often involves insiders. However, other forms of availability attacks may occur. For example, it was reported in 2006 that Second Life,[735] an online gaming environment, passed on details of a group of its users to the FBI accusing them of a DOS attack by repeatedly causing the 'virtual world' to crash.[736]

3.304   As noted earlier, in April 2015, a new offence was inserted in the CMA: that of 'unauthorised acts causing, or creating risk of, serious damage'.[737] It is designed to address 'the most serious cyber attacks'[738] against critical national infrastructure, such as transport and financial systems, which can result in damage of a 'material kind'.[739] The perpetrator must know that his conduct is unauthorized, and either intend to cause serious damage or be reckless as to whether such damage is caused.[740] Where the serious damage is caused to human welfare or national security, the maximum tariff is life imprisonment; while for damage to the

---

[732] Now a statutory offence under the Highways Act 1980, s 137.

[733] See Police and Justice Act 2006, Explanatory Note, para 301, available at <http://www.legislation.gov.uk/ukpga/2006/48/notes>. See also the Convention on Cybercrime, Art 5 and Framework Decision, above, n 580, Art 3, respectively.

[734] Commonwealth Model Law, Art 6(1).

[735] See <http://secondlife.com>

[736] See Krotoski, A, 'Population explosion puts our virtual worlds at risk', *The Guardian*, 12 January 2006, available at <http://www.theguardian.com/technology/2006/jan/12/games.guardianweeklytechnologysection>.

[737] CMA, s 3ZA.

[738] Home Office, *Serious Crime Act 2015*, Circular 008/2015, 25 March 2015, para 8, available at <https://www.gov.uk/government/publications/circular-0082015-serious-crime-act-2015>.

[739] CMA, s 3ZA(2).

[740] ibid, s 3ZA(1)(b) and (d), respectively.

economy or the environment, it is up to fourteen years.[741] This represents a very substantial increase in the potential tariff available for a computer-integrity offence in the UK and is recognition within government of the scale of damage and disruption that can result from successfully targeting such systems.

Terrorism

In our post-11 September world, a major concern of policy-makers is the 'blended threats' that terrorists may pose.[742] Combining a series of explosions with attacks against the availability of the local phone system, for example, would create greater terror, disruption, and impact than either act on its own. Cyberterrorism is simply a means of labelling the offences examined already in this chapter with a specified motivation. **3.305**

In the UK, legislation has defined the concept of what constitutes an act of terrorism to include actions 'designed seriously to interfere with or seriously disrupt an electronic system',[743] akin to 'unauthorised acts'. However, to be an offence under the Terrorism Act 2000, as opposed to a CMA s 3 offence, the other constituent elements for an 'act of terrorism' would also have to be present: **3.306**

- that the 'use or threat is designed to influence the government or an international governmental organisation or to intimidate the public or a section of the public'; and
- the use or threat is made 'for the purpose of advancing a political, religious or ideological cause'.[744]

Once all the elements are present, there are a number of discrete offences that a person may commit, such as possessing an article for a purpose 'connected with the commission, preparation or instigation of an act of terrorism',[745] or collecting or possessing information likely to be useful for the commission of an act of terrorism.[746] So, for example, a person found with keystroke logging software or an access code, following an investigation into a DDOS attack, could be charged with terrorist offences if the other elements were present. The maximum tariffs for such offences were considerably greater than under the CMA, prior to the introduction of the s 3ZA offence discussed above.[747]

At a broader level, terrorism and the threat of terrorism is impacting on criminal law in a number of different ways. One example is the concept of 'incitement' to commit an offence. Under the Terrorism Act 2006, indirect acts of encouragement and inducement have been criminalized, as well as direct acts of incitement,[748] as discussed above in respect of hate speech crimes.[749] **3.307**

In the Directive 13/40/EU, it states that Member States shall provide that attacks that have caused 'serious damage or ... are committed against a critical infrastructure information system' be considered an aggravating circumstance giving rise to greater criminal penalties **3.308**

---

[741] ibid, s 3ZA(7) and (6), respectively.
[742] Interview with Tim Wright, Head of Computer Crime Team, Home Office, 1 February 2006.
[743] Terrorism Act 2000 (TA 2000), s 1(2)(e).
[744] ibid, s 1(1)(b) and (c) respectively, as amended by the TA 2006, s 34.
[745] TA 2000, s 57(1).
[746] ibid, s 58(1).
[747] eg fifteen years under TA 2000, s 57(4)(a) and ten years under s 58(4)(a) respectively.
[748] TA 2006, s 59.
[749] See paras 3.192–3.200.

of a least five years' imprisonment.[750] The term 'critical infrastructure information system' is not further elaborated in the Directive, which leaves considerable discretion to Member States, which can be seen in s 3ZA of the CMA. The concept of 'critical infrastructures' is subject to harmonization measures at an EU level, although they are currently limited to energy and transport networks.[751]

Unauthorized interception

3.309 The integrity offences discussed so far in this section are directed at data 'at rest', ie data residing in a system that is accessed or modified by a perpetrator. However, the criminal law also protects data 'in transmission' across networks from being intercepted by others. While the motivations for attacking data in transmission may be the same as when the data is 'at rest', ie to impact on the confidentiality, integrity, and availability of the data, the primary harm has traditionally been perceived to be the breach of the confidential or private nature of communications. This bias is reflected in the relevant legislative instruments, for example:

> This provision aims to protect the right of privacy of data communication.[752]

> Measures should be taken to prevent unauthorised access to communications in order to protect the confidentiality of communications . . .[753]

This privacy focus has meant that illegal interception has often been viewed primarily as a component of an individual's private life that requires protection from interference by the state,[754] rather than as a form of computer-integrity offence. Although interception offences are concerned with access to the content of a person's communications, it is not categorized as a form of content-related offence because the law protects the right to confidential communications, irrelevant of whether the content itself is private or public, legal or illegal.

3.310 As with the other computer-integrity offences, such as 'hacking', interception may be carried out in the course of criminal conduct or by law enforcement agencies as a tool of criminal investigation, although current law and policy-making is more concerned with the latter situation. The following discussion focuses on the commission of the offence; the operation of the legal framework in respect of computer forensics and criminal procedure is examined further in Chapter 4.

Regulation of Investigatory Powers Act 2000

3.311 The primary governing statute in the UK is Part I, Chapter I of the Regulation of Investigatory Powers Act 2000 (RIPA). Part I is sub-divided into two chapters, concerned respectively with the interception of the content of a communication and the acquisition and disclosure of communications data. The Act is primarily addressed at law enforcement activities, regulating the exercise of investigatory powers in accordance with human

---

[750] Directive 13/40/EU, above, n 159, art 9(4).

[751] Council Directive 2008/114/EC on the identification and designation of European critical infrastructures and the assessment of the need to improve their protection, OJ L 345/75, 23 December 2008.

[752] Explanatory Report to the Convention on Cybercrime, above, n 1, para 51.

[753] Directive 02/58/EC of the European Parliament and of the Council concerning the processing of personal data and the protection of privacy in the electronic communications sector, OJ L 201/37, 31 July 2002, Recital 21.

[754] eg ECHR, Art 8(1) and Charter of Fundamental Rights of the European Union, Art 7.

rights,[755] rather than members of the general public. However, the first prosecution under RIPA was against a private individual in September 2005,[756] while persons from a private detective agency were charged with intercepting phone calls in January 2006;[757] it therefore demands consideration as a form of integrity offence.

There are two offences under s 1 of RIPA. It is an offence for a person 'intentionally and without lawful authority to intercept ... any communication in the course of its transmission by means of ... a public telecommunication system'. Where the same act is carried out by means of a 'private telecommunication system', it is also an offence.[758] The maximum penalty is a two-year prison term.[759] An administrative penalty, known as a 'monetary penalty notice', was added in 2011 to cover unintentional acts of interception.[760]   **3.312**

Both these offences use terminology that requires further consideration and clarification. First, in similar fashion to computer misuse, we are concerned with the issue of 'lawful authority'. The RIPA comprehensively defines those circumstances where such lawful authority is present.[761] They are primarily detailed in the Chapter, at ss 3, 4, and 5, and generally concern the exercise of powers by law enforcement agencies. The only circumstances where a private person[762] may engage in an intercept with 'lawful authority' are when the interceptor has the consent of both parties,[763] or when it is authorized under regulations issued by the Secretary of State.[764]   **3.313**

'**Interception**' An interception is defined in the following terms: **3.314**

> ... a person intercepts a communication in the course of its transmission by means of a telecommunication system if, and only if, he—
> (a) so modifies or interferes with the system, or its operation,
> (b) so monitors transmissions made by means of the system, or

---

[755] Regulation of Investigatory Powers Act 2000, Explanatory Notes, para 3, available at <http://www.legislation.gov.uk/ukpga/2000/23/notes/division/2>.

[756] 'Email hackers sentenced following NHTCU investigation', *Police Oracle*, 19 September 2005, available at <http://www.policeoracle.com/news/Email-Hackers-Sentenced-Following-NHTCU-Investigation_8343.html>.

[757] '18 charged in "snoop" probe', *BBC News*, 28 January 2006, available at <http://news.bbc.co.uk/1/hi/uk/4656780.stm>.

[758] Regulation of Investigatory Powers Act 2000 (RIPA), s 1(1) and (2) respectively.

[759] ibid, s 1(7): the possible penalties are, on indictment, imprisonment for a maximum two-year term or fine; or, on summary conviction, a fine not exceeding the statutory maximum, ie £5,000 (Magistrates' Courts Act 1980, s 32).

[760] RIPA, s 1(1A) and Sch A1. Such notices may be imposed by the Interception of Communications Commissioner.

[761] ibid, s 1(5).

[762] Other than a person who provides a telecommunication service (ibid, s 3(3)) which is related to their role in law enforcement. Prior to the Communications Act 2003, a specific offence existed against disclosure by those providing communication services (Telecommunications Act 1985, s 45, and previously British Telecommunications Act 1981, s 50).

[763] RIPA, s 3(1). The original provision stated that the interceptor only required 'reasonable grounds for believing' that he had such consent. See *Chand v Commissioner of Police of the Metropolis* [2006] Po LR 301 (IPT), where it was accepted that awareness of the likelihood of monitoring and continued use of the system was sufficient to constitute consent. The wording was considered by the European Commission to be non-compliant with EU data protection law, who threatened infringement proceedings: see European Commission, 'Digital Agenda: Commission refers UK to Court over privacy and personal data protection', Press Release IP/10/1215, 30 September 2010, available at <http://europa.eu/rapid/press-release_IP-10-1215_en.htm>). As a consequence, the provision was amended by reg 3 of the Regulation of Investigatory Powers (Monetary Penalty Notices and Consents for Interception) Regulations 2011 (SI No 1340).

[764] RIPA, s 4(2). The applicable regulations are the Telecommunications (Lawful Business Practice) (Interception of Communications) Regulations 2000 (SI No 2699).

(c) so monitors transmissions made by wireless telegraphy to or from apparatus comprised in the system,

as to make some or all of the contents of the communication available, while being transmitted, to a person other than the sender or intended recipient of the communication.[765]

3.315   The concern is with the 'contents' of the communication, rather than any related 'traffic data', which details certain attributes of the communication, such as identification (eg number) of the source or destination of the communication.[766] The concept of transmission is conceived partly in terms of the technical process, ie the use of a 'telecommunication system', and partly by reference to the parties to the transmission, particularly the 'intended recipient'.

3.316   Where the 'system' stores the data for subsequent access or collection by the intended recipient, such as a voice mailbox, then it is considered to still be 'in the course of transmission'.[767] The meaning of this provision was subject to extensive examination in *Edmondson*,[768] which concerned the phone hacking by journalists from the News of the World. The defendants argued that where a voice mail message residing on the service provider's server had been read by the intended recipient, it was no longer 'in the course of its transmission'. The court rejected this interpretation, finding that the 'natural meaning' of the provision does not support the proposition that 'the first receipt of the communication should be considered as bringing the transmission to an end'.[769] The court thought it significant that with voice mail, the intended recipient was 'totally dependent' on the service provider for access to the message. It would seem arguable, therefore, that a distinction could be made between voice mail, which are 'accessed' and email systems, where the intended recipient 'collects' messages on the intended recipient's device, whether a computer or smart phone.

3.317   Such storage is a facility of the system, which should be distinguished from the transient storage that occurs in course of transmission using communication protocols, such as IP, that operate on a store-and-forward basis.[770] Section 2(7) storage must also be distinguished from a call recorded on the intended recipient's apparatus, or an unread email on a person's computer, which fall outside the 'telecommunication system'.

3.318   'Telecommunication system' What constitutes a 'telecommunication system'? The term is defined as follows:

---

[765] RIPA, s 2(2).

[766] 'Traffic data' is defined in ibid, s 2(9). See further paras 4.182–4.194.

[767] RIPA, s 2(7). By contrast, under US law, an intercept does not occur if the communication is retrieved from storage: see *United States v Steiger*, 318 F 3d 1039 (11th Cir), cert denied, 538 US 1051 (2003).

[768] *Edmondson and others v R* [2013] EWCA Crim 1026.

[769] ibid, para 27. It is worth noting that a narrow interpretation of RIPA, s 2(7) was taken by Lord Woolf CJ in *R (on the application of NTL) v Ipswich Crown Court* [2002] EWHC 1585 (Admin), paras 18–19, where he stated: 'Subsection (7) has the effect of extending the time of communication until the intended recipient has collected it.' This was initially endorsed by the DPP, when giving evidence to the Culture, Media and Sport Committee (November 2009); although he subsequently adopted a 'robust attitude' when advising the police that they 'should not be inhibited by a narrow approach to the provisions' (Correspondence from Keir Starmer, QC, Director of Public Prosecutions to the Chair of the Committee, 11 July 2011).

[770] Such transient storage has also been addressed in respect of intermediary liability, see paras 2.233–2.253.

any system (including the apparatus comprised in it) which exists (whether wholly or partly in the United Kingdom or elsewhere) for the purpose of facilitating the transmission of communications by any means involving the use of electrical or electro-magnetic energy.[771]

In terms of criminal liability, as well as evidentially,[772] an important distinction exists   **3.319** between a 'public' and 'private' telecommunication system. Where a 'private' telecommunication system is being used, then an interception carried out with the 'express or implied consent of a person having the right to control the operation or the use of' the system is not an offence, but is a statutory tort.[773] This provision therefore raises two key definitional issues: what comprises a 'private telecommunication system' and what constitutes 'control'? The former is defined under the RIPA:

> 'private telecommunication system' means any telecommunication system which, without itself being a public telecommunication system, is a system in relation to which the following conditions are satisfied—
> (a) it is attached, directly or indirectly and whether or not for the purposes of the communication in question, to a public telecommunication system; and
> (b) there is apparatus comprised in the system which is both located in the United Kingdom and used (with or without other apparatus) for making the attachment to the public telecommunication system.[774]

Such a negative definition in turn requires us to consider what a 'public telecommunication system' is, which is elaborated through two further definition in s 2(1):

> 'public telecommunications service' means any telecommunications service which is offered or provided to, or to a substantial section of, the public in any one or more parts of the United Kingdom;
>
> 'public telecommunication system' means any such parts of a telecommunication system by means of which any public telecommunications service is provided as are located in the United Kingdom.

Taken together, the only bright line afforded by these definitions would seem to be that a   **3.320** completely stand-alone network within an organization, not connected by any means to the outside world (and therefore extremely unlikely or rare!) does not fall within the regime.[775] Otherwise, we are faced with two boundary issues:

(a) When does a communication leave a 'system'?
(b) When does a communication pass from a public to a private telecommunication system?

The answer to (a) has been touched upon already in our consideration of whether a communication is 'in the course of transmission'. Under EU communications law, the regulatory boundary of the network (ie system) is the 'network termination point', to which

---

[771] RIPA, s 2(1).
[772] See generally Chapter 6.
[773] RIPA, s 1(3) and (6).
[774] ibid, s 2(1).
[775] See Regulation of Investigatory Powers Act 2000, Explanatory Notes, above, n 755, para 27.

'telecommunication terminal equipment'[776] is attached.[777] To answer (b), the determinant would appear to be whether the communication service is 'public', since any part of a system used in the provision of that service is also 'public'. Both questions may need to be addressed during criminal proceedings, and will be a question of fact to be determined by reference to all the circumstances of the case.[778]

3.321 The difficulty with distinguishing between what may be considered public and private is not a debate unique to cybercrime, but is one that has become more complex in our integrated and networked society. The concept underpins the liability protections historically conferred on 'common carriers' in the telecommunications industry.[779] The Communications Act 2003 also struggles with the distinction, defining a public service in terms of being 'available for use by members of the public'.[780] This was elaborated by the then sector regulator, Oftel, to mean 'available to anyone who is both willing to pay for it and to abide by the applicable terms and conditions'.[781] In an Internet environment, the problem is how to label the various network components utilized in the course of transmitting a communication. For example, BT FON is an initiative that enables BT customers to securely share a portion of their WiFi bandwidth with other members within range of their signal through a separate channel on their home router.[782] The router would normally be considered a 'private' telecommunication system, but when sharing capacity, it would seemingly become part of a 'public' telecommunication system.

3.322 The cumulative lack of clarity in these definitions, as well as the nature of the consequence of falling on the 'public' side, could be said to breach Ashworth's principle of 'maximum certainty'[783] and may fall foul of the European Court of Human Rights jurisprudence that requires laws to be 'formulated with sufficient precision to enable the citizen to regulate his conduct'.[784]

3.323 The requirement that some or all of the content be made available to a third party 'while being transmitted' has been interpreted by the Court of Appeal, in *Hardy*,[785] as meaning that the recording of a conversation by one party to the communication, so-called 'participant monitoring', does not constitute an 'interception', but rather 'surveillance', for which authorization may be required under Part II of the RIPA. However, such an interpretation

---

[776] Radio Equipment and Telecommunications Terminal Equipment Regulations 2000 (SI No 730), reg 2(1): 'means a product enabling communication or a relevant component thereof, which is intended to be connected directly or indirectly by any means whatsoever to interfaces of public telecommunications networks'.

[777] See Directive 2002/22/EC on universal service and users' rights relating to electronic communications networks and services, OJ L 108/7, 24 April 2002, Recital 6.

[778] See *Allen and Bunting* [2001] EWCA Crim 1027, para 50.

[779] See generally Noam, E, 'Beyond liberalization II: The impending doom of common carriage', 18(6) *Telecommunications Policy* 435 (1994).

[780] Communications Act 2003, s 151. Note that the Act uses the term 'network' rather than 'system', the former originating in EU law, while the latter was used in the BTA 1984.

[781] Office of Telecommunications (Oftel), *Guidelines for the Interconnection of Public Electronic Communication Networks*, 23 May 2003, s 6.1, available at <http://www.ofcom.org.uk/static/archive/oftel/publications/eu_directives/2003/intercon0503.htm>.

[782] See <http://www.btwifi.com/help/about-bt-fon.jsp>.

[783] Ashworth, above, n 477, at 75 et seq.

[784] *Sunday Times v UK* (1979) 2 EHRR 245, para 49.

[785] (2003) 1 Cr App R 494. See also *Hammond, McIntosh, Gray* [2002] EWCA Crim 1423, for a similar finding under the Interception of Communications Act 1985, although the recording party was not a law enforcement officer.

would seem to somewhat contradict s 3(2), which implies that such an act remains an 'interception', even if it requires an authorization under Part II to be lawful, as does s 48(4):

> References in this Part to surveillance include references to the interception of a communication in the course of its transmission by means of a postal service or telecommunication system if, and only if—
>
> (a) the communication is one sent by or intended for a person who has consented to the interception of communications sent by or to him; and
>
> (b) there is no interception warrant authorising the interception.

The Home Office Explanatory Report also gives an example of the police recording a call from a kidnapper.[786] However, whichever is correct, the suspect would appear to be protected by at least one RIPA authorization regime in respect of the actions of law enforcement officers, although neither is judicial in nature and the Part II regime is particularly open to criticism.[787]

In addition to 'participant monitoring', there have been various attempts to have the use **3.324** of bugging devices reclassified as a form of interception. In *E*, for example, a device was placed in the accused's car which recorded conversations carried out over a mobile phone. In response to an argument from the defence that the evidence was a form of 'interception' and therefore inadmissible, the court stated:

> In our view, the natural meaning of the expression 'interception' denotes some interference or abstraction of the signal, whether it is passing along wires or by wireless telegraphy, during the process of transmission. The recording of a person's voice, independently of the fact that at the time he is using a telephone, does not become interception simply because what he says goes not only into the recorder, but, by separate process, is transmitted by a telecommunications system.[788]

However, were the *Hardy* approach to 'participant monitoring' to be followed where the recording was carried out by a private person, then the remedies available under s 1, whether criminal (s 1(2)) or civil (s 1(3)), may not be available depending on the mechanism of recording. While the analysis tends to be couched using voice telephony examples, such as holding a recording device to the earpiece of a telephone,[789] email represents a substantial share of modern communications and may create more difficult technical distinctions. If, for example, the participant monitoring was carried out while the communication is still in the 'system', such as through the intended recipient's proxy server, then it may be considered 'in the course of transmission', since the server will comprise part of a 'private telecommunication system', and an 'interception' under RIPA, as it would seem to potentially fall within s 2(8):

> For the purposes of this section the cases in which any contents of a communication are to be taken to be made available to a person while being transmitted shall include any case in which any of the contents of the communication, while being transmitted, are diverted or recorded so as to be available to a person subsequently.

---

[786] See Regulation of Investigatory Powers Act 2000, Explanatory Notes, above, n 755, para 39.

[787] See Ormerod, D, 'Telephone intercepts and their admissibility', *Criminal Law Review* 15 [2004].

[788] *E* [2004] EWCA 1243, para 20. See also *MacDonald*, Woolwich Crown Court, 23 April 2002, and *Allsopp and others* [2005] EWCA Crim 703.

[789] See also Lord Bassam's explanation of the phrase 'in the course of transmission': Hansard HL Vol 613, Col 1435, 12 June 2000.

However, if the recording occurs on the intended recipient's PC, then it has left the 'system' and is not considered interception.

3.325   It has been suggested that such a narrow technical interpretation fails to provide the privacy protections required under the European Convention on Human Rights and court jurisprudence in respect of the Art 8 right to privacy.[790] Instead, the determinant of an 'intercept' should be the purpose for which it was carried out, ie to breach the confidential nature of a communication, which is the protective objective of such legislation. Support for this approach can be found in the RIPA itself, where a purposive approach is adopted when intercepts are carried out for a lawful business practice.[791] Under the Home Office Code of Practice on Covert Surveillance, issued in 2002, the following statement was made:

> The use of a surveillance device should not be ruled out simply because it may incidentally pick up one or both ends of a telephone conversation. . . . However, its use would not be appropriate where the sole purpose is to overhear speech which, at the time of monitoring, is being transmitted by a telecommunications system. In such cases an application should be made for an interception of communication warrant under section 5 of the 2000 Act.[792]

This clearly endorses a conception of 'interception' based on purpose, rather than technical means. However, this approach was dropped in the revised versions of the Code in 2010 and 2014. The current advice is as follows:

> The recording or monitoring of one or both ends of a telephone conversation by a surveillance device . . . will not constitute interception . . . provided the process by which the product is obtained does not involve any modification of, or interference with, the telecommunications system or its operation.[793]

The Council of Europe Cybercrime Convention may also be viewed as supportive of a broad interpretation of 'intercept', since it includes 'electromagnetic emissions from a computer system' as a means of interception,[794] although such techniques may be simply used as a sophisticated means of eavesdropping, similar in nature to a bugging device.

3.326   'Intended recipient' While, on first consideration, it would seem obvious that the 'intended recipient' is the initial called party, this must be seen as capable of variation in certain circumstances, specifically when a communication leaves a 'telecommunication system'. In the classic voice mail scenario, the sender sends a communication using his telecommunications service from a telecommunication system to the intended recipient's telecommunications service, operated on a telecommunication system.[795] In this scenario, any storage within the system is covered by s 2(7). However, once a communication leaves a 'telecommunication system', any further processing of the communication would not be 'interception', as discussed above. An example would be a secretary who picks up the phone when his boss is otherwise engaged and notes down a message. The communication has not yet reached the initial 'intended recipient', but it is no longer 'in the course of transmission by

---

[790] See Ormerod, above, n 787.
[791] RIPA, s 4(2).
[792] Home Office, *Covert Surveillance: Code of Practice*, The Stationery Office, 2002, para 4.32.
[793] Home Office, *Covert Surveillance and Property Interference: Revised Code of Practice*, The Stationery Office, 2014, para 2.10
[794] Convention on Cybercrime, Art 3.
[795] The telecommunication system may be the same or different, and may pass through more than one intermediary telecommunication system, although this is not relevant to the analysis.

means of a telecommunication system'. In addition, when the sender chooses to leave the message with the secretary, he effectively changes the 'intended recipient' of the communication to the secretary, acting as agent for the 'intended recipient', in the expectation that the message will be passed on in due course. It is clear in this scenario that, by taking the message, the secretary is not engaged in an act of interception.

The 'intended recipient' of a communication could be determined by a court on the basis **3.327** of evidence about the subjective intention of the sender, ie who was the person intending to communicate with; or, alternatively, on an objective technical basis, ie the virtual identity of the recipient supplied by the sender, or the terminal equipment to which the network directed the transmission. From a law enforcement perspective, the former approach would create significant problems, such as where the recipient is an undercover officer engaged in a surveillance operation.[796] To date, however, the issue has not been addressed by the courts.

'Right to control' The final concept that determines the criminality of an interceptor's **3.328** conduct is the question of whether the person has the 'right to control' the private telecommunication system. If the person does have such a right, or has the 'express or implied consent' of such a person, then the act of interception is transformed from being an offence to a statutory tort.[797] The concept is not subject to further definition in the RIPA, although the concept of a 'system controller' is defined in the 'Lawful Business Practice' regulations:

> 'system controller' means, in relation to a particular telecommunication system, a person with a right to control its operation or use.[798]

For further elucidation, we may look elsewhere for an indication of how this concept may be interpreted. Three possible candidates are the CMA in relation to entitlement to control access; the 'data controller' under the Data Protection Act 1998[799] and the Communications Act 2003. In respect of the latter regime, the Communications Act clearly distinguishes the concept of 'control' from that of ownership, reflecting the liberalized nature of the telecommunications market. A person may control a system, whether private or public, without necessarily owning any part of it.[800]

The question of control was central to the first prosecution under s 1, when Cliff Stanford, **3.329** founder of Demon and Redbus, and George Liddell pleaded guilty to the offence after the judge ruled that they were neither a person with a right of control, nor had they the express or implied consent of such a person. Stanford had been able to intercept the emails of three staff members at Redbus Interhouse plc, where he had previously worked, including the company Chairman. He induced an employee at the company to obtain access to the email system by using the user name and password given to him by a senior employee. A program was then installed on the system that automatically copied emails to a Hotmail

---

[796] See paras 4.73–4.77.
[797] RIPA, s 1(6).
[798] Telecommunications (Lawful Business Practice) (Interception of Communications) Regulations 2000, reg 2(d).
[799] ie 'a person who (either alone or jointly or in common with other persons) determines the purposes for which and the manner in which any personal data are, or are to be, processed' (DPA 1998, s 1(1)).
[800] Communications Act 2003, s 32(4)(b): '… where one or more persons are employed or engaged to provide the network or service *under the direction or control* of another person …' (emphasis added).

account operated by George Liddell, a private investigator.[801] Stanford had argued that the employee who obtained access had the right to control under s 1(6)(a).

3.330 On appeal, the court upheld the decision of the judge, taking the meaning of 'control' adopted by Lord Hobhouse in *Allison*[802] under the CMA, ie that 'control' means the right to 'authorise or forbid' use of a computer, not merely the ability to use it.[803] In addition, the Court of Appeal agreed with the lower court's decision to impose a six-month custodial sentence, coupled with a substantial fine, since the objective of the interception was to procure a 'substantial commercial advantage'.[804] However, as with unauthorized access and modification, the issue of authorization is likely to cause most problems where an insider is involved in the act.

3.331 In respect of the acquisition of communication data, under Part I, Chapter II of the RIPA, there is no equivalent offence of obtaining without lawful authority or consent of the 'system controller'; rather the provisions are solely concerned with granting law enforcement agencies the power to obtain such data.[805] Such conduct could, however, be prosecuted under the Data Protection Act 1998.[806] Under the Telecommunications Act 1984, there were specific offences where an employee of a telecommunications company intercepted and disclosed either content or communications data 'otherwise than in the course of his duty', ie without authority,[807] although similar offences were not enacted in the Communications Act 2003.

Wireless telegraphy

3.332 Under UK law, the provision of communication services is primarily governed by the Communications Act 2003. However, where a provider utilizes a portion of the electromagnetic spectrum in the provision of its services, such as mobile operators or WiFi providers, then the Wireless Telegraphy Act 2006 (WTA) is also applicable. In addition to the RIPA regime, the WTA prohibits a range of activities, including the use of wireless telegraphy apparatus with intent to 'obtain information as to the contents, sender or addressee of a message'.[808] In contrast to RIPA, acquisition of communications data is encompassed by the offence.

3.333 An example would be the operation of a so-called 'IMSI catcher', which is capable of capturing the content of a wireless communications session and related traffic data.[809] Such a process is achieved by scanning a frequency to find an unoccupied channel and when found, establishing itself as a local base station. It then either interrupts a handset's existing connection with a mobile operator's base station, or is the initial base station which the

---

[801] See Walker, C, 'Email interception and RIPA: the Court of Appeal rules on the "right to control" defence', 11(1) *Communications Law* 22 (2006).

[802] *Bow Street Magistrate and Allison (AP), ex parte US Government (HL(E))* [1999] 4 All ER 1. See further paras 3.254–3.255.

[803] *Stanford*, Times Law Reports, 7 February 2006.

[804] Quoted in Walker, above, n 801.

[805] See paras 4.197–4.213 for a discussion of the regime.

[806] See para 3.35.

[807] BTA 1984, s 45. It was also an offence for such persons to modify or interfere with the content of a communication (ibid, s 44).

[808] Wireless Telegraphy Act 2006 (WTA), s 48(1)(a).

[809] eg the International Mobile Subscriber Identity (IMSI) and International Mobile Equipment Identity (IMEI).

phone then connects to. The IMSI catcher can operate in two modes. Mode one results in the obtaining of communications data, specifically the IMSI and IMEI. Once these details have been logged, the IMSI catcher then terminates the connection and the user then has to re-instigate the original call. In mode two, the call is forwarded by the IMSI catcher on to the original mobile operator's base station, enabling the interception of the content of the call.[810]

Under the Wireless Telegraphy Act, an offence is not committed where such activities occur **3.334** 'under the authority of a designated person'. A 'designated person' is very narrowly defined and only includes the Secretary of State, the Commissioners for Her Majesty's Revenue and Customs and any other person designated by the Secretary of State by regulation.

There are complex rules governing those circumstances where such a designated person may **3.335** give authority to 'obtain information as to the content, sender or addressee of any message'. First, the designated person may only give an 'interception authority' where he considers it necessary for one of a number of specified purposes.[811] Strangely, these purposes are practically identical to those applicable to the acquisition of communications data, under RIPA Part I Chapter II,[812] rather than those for interception. Second, it must be proportionate to what is being sought to be achieved.[813] However, this authorization procedure is not applicable where the conduct is unlawful under RIPA, Chapter I of Part I, or which may be authorized under Chapter II of Part I, in respect of communications data, or Part II, in respect of surveillance activities.[814]

Unlawful devices

A primary distinction being made between computer-integrity offences and computer- and **3.336** content-related offences is that the latter two use computer and communication technologies as a tool to commit criminal acts that preceded such technologies; the technology is merely an instrument for the commission of the crime, rather than the subject of the crime. However, a common strand through all three categories is the criminalization of the supply and/or possession of items that are tools specifically designed to assist in the commission of an offence. Such devices may typically include items such as software designed for password cracking, cryptography, or keylogging.

In fraud, it is an offence to possess or supply an 'article' for use in a fraud,[815] or to possess or **3.337** supply apparatus enabling the dishonest obtaining of electronic communication services.[816] In forgery, it is an offence to make or have or control a 'machine or implement, or paper or any other material' which has been 'specially designed or adapted for the making of a specified instrument'.[817] Under copyright law, it is an offence to supply 'devices' designed to

---

[810] A form of 'man-in-the-middle' attack.
[811] WTA, s 49(4).
[812] RIPA, s 22(2).
[813] WTA, s 48(3)(b).
[814] ibid, s 48(2).
[815] FA, ss 6 and 7 respectively. See eg *Charles Brown* [2014] EWCA Crim 695, where the defendant was found to have stolen bank and credit card details on his computer.
[816] CA, s 126.
[817] FCA, s 5(3), (4).

circumvent technological protection measures.[818] Likewise, computer-integrity laws criminalize the supply and possession of 'devices'.

3.338 All these offences may be characterized as 'preliminary' or 'inchoate' offences, since they
address a casual component in the commission of the substantive offence. They also sit
somewhere on the boundary between the computer as the object and subject of the crime.
Possession being the *actus reus*, similar in kind to the theft of a machine, while the *mens rea*
is directed elsewhere, ie at the confidentiality and integrity of a system and the data it holds.

3.339 Under Art 6 of the Cybercrime Convention, Member States are obliged to criminalize the
supply and possession of a 'device', computer password, access code, or similar data. This
would include, for example, information about a known weakness or vulnerability in a software application, such as the Windows operating system, generally referred to as 'exploits'
and which are commonly used to introduce 'malware' into another person's system. The
provision is designed to criminalize the market for 'hacker tools', referred to as the 'malicious marketplace',[819] which has become an inevitable feature of cybercrime.

3.340 The term 'device' is not further defined in the Convention, although it includes a 'computer
program' and it is used in the definition of a 'computer system'.[820] The Explanatory Report
to the Convention notes that a device consists of 'hardware or software developed for automatic processing of digital data'.[821] The provision therefore seems to make a distinction
between devices and data, although a computer program is obviously a particular manifestation of data, which creates a potential confusion. In addition, the list of data components,
'computer password, access code, or similar data', would not necessarily be interpreted as
including data about a known exploit in a system, since such data would not seem to be of
a similar nature to passwords and access codes that actually enable access in themselves,
rather than either facilitating access or modification, depending on the precise nature of the
'exploit'.[822] To the extent that a 'device' is in the form of data, criminalizing the supply or
possession of such information is similar in kind to the content-related crimes discussed in
section C of this chapter.

3.341 Supply is broadly conceived in terms of 'the production, sale, procurement for use, import,
distribution or otherwise making available',[823] the latter term encompassing the placing of
such material on a website for download, via a P2P network or the provision of hyperlinks
to facilitate access.[824] For liability to attach there must be a general intent to supply and a
specific intent that the device be used to commit any one of the integrity offences. In terms

---

[818] CDPA 1988, s 296ZB.

[819] See comments by Roger Cummings, Director of the UK National Infrastructure Security Coordination Centre (NISCC) in Espiner, T, 'Foreign powers are main cyberthreat, UK says', CNET News.
com, 23 November 2005, available at <http://www.cnet.com/news/foreign-powers-are-main-cyberthreat-
u-k-says/>.

[820] Convention on Cybercrime, Art 1(a).

[821] Explanatory Report to the Convention on Cybercrime, above, n 1T>, para 23.

[822] eg under the English law rule *eiusdem generis* ('of the same kind') of statutory interpretation, which
provides that general words, ie 'similar data', which follow particular words, ie 'password', must be limited to
meanings analogous to those of the particular words.

[823] Convention on Cybercrime, Art 6(1)(a).

[824] Explanatory Report to the Convention on Cybercrime, above, n 1, para 72. See eg *Universal City
Studios, Inc and others v Corley and others*, SD Cal, 17 August 2000, in respect of links to a 'DeCCS' program
which decrypts DVDs' regional protection mechanism.

of English criminal law, therefore, a person engaged in supply would have to be characterized as either an accessory, a conspirator, or engaged in encouraging or assisting, depending on the circumstance.

For added certainty, the offence is further supplemented by a provision stating that the **3.342** article 'shall not be interpreted as imposing criminal liability where [the supply] is not for the purpose of committing any of the offences ..., such as for the authorised testing or protection of a computer system'.[825] This provision would seem to go to the question of intent, although the Explanatory Report relates it solely to the concept of being 'without right', focusing on the intended use.[826] The qualifying phrase was seen as necessary to protect those involved in data security issues, whether from an academic or commercial perspective, which may utilize such devices in the course of their legitimate activities.

The provision also requires that the device has been 'designed or adapted primarily' for the **3.343** purpose of committing one of the integrity offences, which may be a significant evidential burden for the prosecution, and is ultimately a question of fact to be objectively determined by the court. Generally, however, regard will be had to the acts or statements made by the person engaged in the supply. In *Invicta Plastics Ltd v Clare*, for example, the incitement was considered implicit in the advertisement used to sell devices that detected the use of police radar traps, despite the inclusion of a warning that their operation was contrary to the Wireless Telegraphy Act 1949.[827] Similarly, in the US[828] and Australia,[829] the courts have held that companies distributing P2P software are liable for copyright infringement on the basis of 'evidence of intent' to promote such illegality. While we are concerned here with devices used for the commission of computer-integrity offences, similar issues arise in respect of devices used for copyright infringement. As noted previously, the manner in which computers and networks facilitate copyright infringement has led to the adoption of new offences against devices used to circumvent copy-protection measures[830] and in respect of conditional access devices.[831]

In terms of possession, there is again a dual intention requirement, the first requiring that **3.344** the person intends to possess the item, rather than accidentally being found to be in possession; second, that there is an intention to use the item, without right, to commit one of the offences. The Convention on Cybercrime allows signatory states to require that a certain number of items are in a person's possession before attributing criminal liability.[832] This would seem to go to the issue of intent, on the basis that possession of a minimum number of items enables an inference to be drawn about intent to use for illegal activities; although such intent seems more likely to be directed towards supplying the item to others, rather than personal use. Member States are also free not to criminalize possession at all.[833]

---

[825] Convention on Cybercrime, Art 6(2).

[826] Explanatory Report to the Convention on Cybercrime, above, n 1, para 77.

[827] [1976] RTR 251.

[828] *MGM Studios and others v Grokster and others*, 545 US 913, 125 S Ct 2764 (2005). On 7 November 2005, Grokster agreed to halt offering its P2P service and pay $50 m in compensation.

[829] *Universal Music Australia Pty Ltd v Sharman License Holdings Ltd* [2005] FCA 1242, which referred to 'exhortations to users'.

[830] Copyright, Designs and Patents Act 1988, s 296ZB.

[831] ibid, s 297A.

[832] Convention on Cybercrime, Art 6(1)(b). See also Commonwealth Model Law, Art 9(3). eg under US law, 18 USC s 1029(a)(3), possession is only an offence where it involves fifteen or more counterfeit or unauthorized access devices.

[833] Art 6(3). Azerbaijan, Germany, Japan, Norway, Switzerland, Ukraine, and the US have made declarations concerning this article.

3.345 The inclusion of the 'without right' requirement in the offence obviously needs to be viewed from the perspective of a lawful excuse or justification, rather than in a positive sense, in terms of authority being granted or withheld. Where proceedings are being brought against a person for supplying an item, the prosecution would not only have to prove the dual intention, the general intention being relatively straightforward, but also that the use for which the device is being supplied is 'without right' or lawful excuse. This was intended to prevent over-criminalization, particularly in respect of dual-use devices.

3.346 The EU Directive also contains a provision concerning 'tools used for committing offences',[834] which was absent from the 2005 Framework Decision. The provision is limited to supply-related conduct in relation to two types of tool: a computer programme 'designed or adapted primarily', similar to the Convention, and 'a computer password, access code, or similar data' that enables access to an information system. The offence requires that the conduct should be 'without right' and with intent to be used to commit the computer-integrity offences.

3.347 The CMA did not originally contain provisions in relation to 'devices'; although a supplier could have been prosecuted as an accessory or for incitement.[835] However, to meet its commitment under the Cybercrime Convention, the Government introduced such a provision into the Act in 2006; further amending it in April 2015:

> 3A. Making, supplying or obtaining articles for use in offence under section 1, 3 or 3ZA
>
> (1) A person is guilty of an offence if he makes, adapts, supplies or offers to supply any article intending it to be used to commit, or to assist in the commission of, an offence under section 1, 3 or 3ZA.
> (2) A person is guilty of an offence if he supplies or offers to supply any article believing that it is likely to be used to commit, or to assist in the commission of, an offence under section 1, 3 or 3ZA.
> (3) A person is guilty of an offence if he obtains any article –
>   (a) intending to use it to commit, or to assist in the commission of, an offence under section 1, 3 or 3ZA, or
>   (b) with a view to its being supplied for use to commit, or to assist in the commission of, an offence under section 1, 3 or 3ZA.[836]

The provision addresses the supply of 'articles', including presumably both tangibles and intangibles, although only the latter are expressly referred to in the section: 'any program or data held in electronic form'.[837] The making, adaptation, or supply of an article is an offence only if the person intends that it be used in the course of an unauthorized access or unauthorized act offence, a potentially high threshold to be met when bringing a prosecution.[838] The second offence, however, has a different *mens rea*, that of believing that the article is likely to be used for hacking or unauthorized acts. The third offence is the obtaining of such an article, either intending to use it or with a view to it being supplied, which

---

[834] Directive 13/40/EU, above, n 159, Art 7.
[835] See para 3.271.
[836] PJA, s 42, inserting s 3A in the CMA.
[837] CMA, s 3A(4).
[838] See *Lewys Stephen Martin* [2013] EWCA Crim 1420.

targets prospective middlemen in the distribution of such articles. When this third offence was inserted in 2006, it only addressed the supply of the article to a third party. This was considered too narrow, so was extended to 'capture the *personal use* of tools'[839] to commit the integrity offences. All three offences are subject to a maximum tariff of two years,[840] which compares unfavourably with the supply or possession of articles for use in fraud, where the terms are ten and five years respectively.

These offences are designed to address the growth of 'malicious marketplaces', such as bulle-   **3.348**
tin boards, where people make available devices for sale to others, with no specific intention concerning when, where, or how they are used.[841] However, the second offence of supplying 'believing' it likely the articles will be so used has been criticized for potentially criminal-izing, and therefore generating legal uncertainty, for researchers in information security, penetration testers, and other professionals in the field, who may develop and make available such tools in the course of their study or business.[842] The nature of the fault where 'belief' is required is not currently clearly defined under English law; while 'likely' suggests a probability in favour of such abusive usage, rather than mere suspicion or even possibly knowledge that some proportion of articles downloaded will fall into the wrong hands and be used for nefarious purposes.[843]

To address concerns about so-called 'dual-use' articles, the Government asked that the   **3.349**
Director of Public Prosecutions publish guidance regarding its policy on prosecuting under this section.[844] The guidance states that when considering what is 'likely', prosecutors should consider 'the functionality of the article and at what, if any, thought the suspect gave to who would use it'.[845] Other relevant factors include whether the article is available on a commercial basis and through legitimate channels and has a 'substantial installation base'.

Under US federal law, provision is made for the fraudulent use of an 'access device',   **3.350**
which would encompass all categories of computer and cybercrime, as the term is defined expansively:

> any card, plate, code, account number, electronic serial number, mobile identification num-ber, personal identification number, or other telecommunications service, equipment, or instrument identifier, or other means of account access that can be used, alone or in con-junction with another access device, to obtain money, goods, services, or any other thing of value, or that can be used to initiate a transfer of funds (other than a transfer originated solely by paper instrument).[846]

---

[839] Home Office, Circular 008/2015, above, n 738, para 13.

[840] CMA, s 3A(5)(c). A maximum twelve months on summary conviction.

[841] See eg Europol, 'Cybercriminal Darkode forum taken down through global action', Press Release, 15 July 2015, available at <https://www.europol.europa.eu/content/cybercriminal-darkode-forum-taken-down-through-global-action>.

[842] See the comments of the Earl of Northesk, Lords Hansard, Col 611, 11 July 2006. However, see also Hazel Blears, Home Office Minister, Hansard, Standing Committee D, 7th Session, Col 265, 28 March 2006.

[843] See *Smith & Hogan Criminal Law*, above, n 307, at 855. See also Lord Bassam, Home Office Minister, Lords Hansard, Col 615, 11 July 2006.

[844] Lord Bassam, Home Office Minister, Lords Hansard, Col 217, 10 October 2006.

[845] CPS, Legal Guidance to Computer Misuse Act 1990, at 'Section 3A CMA—Making, supplying or obtaining articles', available at <http://www.cps.gov.uk/legal/a_to_c/computer_misuse_act_1990/#an10>.

[846] 18 USC s 1029(e)(1).

3.351 A further distinction is made between 'counterfeit access device' and an 'unauthorized access device'; the former being false, while the latter is genuine but is not in the possession of the rightful user (eg lost or stolen), or is no longer valid (eg expired or revoked). The production, trafficking, use, and possession of such a device is an offence, with sanctions of up to twenty years' imprisonment.[847]

Unsolicited communications

3.352 'Spam' or unsolicited email is an activity with which all Internet users are very familiar. The constant receipt of messages trying to sell us things, show us things and engage us in various nefarious practices is both well known and much written about. The scale of the problem in recent years, believed to comprise a substantial proportion of all email traffic, combined with the perceived threat such activities pose to the future of cyberspace has resulted in numerous initiatives being taken both by industry and governments to tackle the problem. Similar techniques have also spread to other messaging services, such as weblogs and instant messaging, known as 'spimming'.[848]

3.353 Governments are concerned not only with unsolicited email, but also other means of communications, specifically voice calls and facsimiles. Historically, the sending such communications was not considered a criminal offence, unless the content itself was illegal (eg child pornography) or the manner in which such messages were sent (eg harassment). However, with its increasing prevalence and abuse through the ability to initiate communications in bulk, effectively on an industrial scale, there have been attempts in various jurisdictions to criminalize aspects of the activity. The legal response has often varied between different means of communications, reflecting the differing forms of intrusion and therefore harm caused. Voice calls require the person to engage directly in the communication; unsolicited facsimiles utilize the recipient's machine and paper, while emails may cost the recipient to receive and congest his mailbox.[849]

3.354 Although unsolicited communications could be classified as a content-related crime, the content itself is only sometimes criminal in nature. As noted by the Spamhaus Project, 'spam is an issue about consent, not content',[850] and consent is closely associated with the issue of authorization, which is central to the criminalization of conduct threatening the confidentiality, integrity, and availability of ICTs. The public policy objectives articulated for such legislation also reflect concerns about the impact such traffic may have on the integrity and availability of the Internet and email services, as well as the integrity of information contained in such messages, such as the source of the message. The distinction that can be made between unsolicited communications and the other integrity offences discussed in this section is generally one based on the degree of interference with the victim's ICT resource. The more direct and substantial the threat to the confidentiality, integrity, and availability of the resource, the more likely such acts will be criminalized.

---

[847] ibid, s 1029(c)(1). See *US v Brewer* (1987) 835 F 2d 550.

[848] In the US, in March 2005, Anthony Greco pleaded guilty to threatening to damage the computer systems of MySpace.com with the intent to extort: see <http://www.usdoj.gov/usao/cac/pr2005/050.html>.

[849] See Koops, B-J, 'Should ICT regulation be technology-neutral?', in Koops, B-J, *Starting points for ICT Regulation: deconstructing p[r]evalent policy one-liners*, Asser, 2006.

[850] See <http://www.spamhaus.org/definition.html>.

Under UK law, the problem of unsolicited communications is directly addressed through **3.355**
two legal instruments, both transposing EU measures and providing only civil not criminal remedies. Under the Electronic Commerce (EC Directive) Regulations 2002 a statutory duty is placed upon service providers to ensure that unsolicited emails are 'clearly and
unambiguously identifiable' as such.[851] While the nature of the obligation is extremely
mild, the Directive on which it is based recognizes that such communications have the
potential to threaten the integrity and availability of networks, noting that they 'may disrupt the smooth functioning of interactive networks'.[852] The second measure is concerned
with the privacy threats created by modern communications technology: the Privacy and
Electronic Communications (EC Directive) Regulations 2003.[853] The provisions regulate
unsolicited communications by automated calling systems, facsimile, voice telephony, and
email, prohibiting such activities under certain conditions.[854] In respect of email, the concealment of the identity of the sender or an address where the sender may be contacted is
an additional prohibition,[855] which is an attempt to address the problem of anonymity in
cyberspace. As with the other measure, in justifying the prohibition, the Directive makes
reference to the fact that large volumes of unsolicited messages may 'cause difficulties for
electronic communication networks and terminal equipment'.[856] Breach of these obligations again only attracts civil sanction, although the Information Commissioner has the
power to impose a monetary penalty of up to £500,000.[857]

In seeming contrast to the UK, criminalization of aspects of the process of sending unsoli- **3.356**
cited communications has occurred in the US, in both state and federal legislation. At a federal level, the primary measure is the Controlling the Assault of Non-Solicited Pornography
and Marketing Act of 2003 (the 'CAN-SPAM Act').[858] As with the EU Directives, the
congressional findings make reference to the impact that unsolicited email may have on the
integrity and availability of the communications infrastructure and services used over it.[859]

As well as utilizing traditional criminal terminology in its title, referring to such acts as **3.357**
a form of 'assault', the CAN-SPAM Act specifically criminalizes the following activities:

- Accessing a computer without authorization for the purpose of sending unsolicited
emails; this would include the creation of 'zombie' computers.
- Sending messages designed to deceive or mislead as to the origin of such messages, by
using techniques such as 'open relays' and 'open proxies'.[860] This is similar to the provision in the UK's 2003 privacy regulations.

---

[851] SI No 2013, reg 8.
[852] Directive 2000/31/EC on certain legal aspects of information society services, in particular electronic
commerce, in the Internal Market, OJ L 178/1, 17 July 2000, Recital 30.
[853] SI No 2426.
[854] ibid, regs 19–22.
[855] ibid, reg 23.
[856] Directive 02/58/EC of the European Parliament and of the Council concerning the processing of
personal data and the protection of privacy in the electronic communications sector, OJ L 201/37, 31 July
2002, Recital 40.
[857] SI No 2426, reg 31 and the DPA 1998, s 55A. This power was amended by SI 2015/355 to lower the
threshold for a finding of a 'serious breach' in respect of the unsolicited communication provisions.
[858] Public Law 108–87, 108th Congress, 15 USC s 7701.
[859] ibid, s 7701(a)3.
[860] An 'open relay' is a mail server that enables unauthorized users to launder email through it. An 'open
proxy' is a network server that allows unauthorized users to connect through it to other hosts.

- Falsifying 'header'[861] information and sending messages; this is distinguished from the deception offence above.
- Registering falsified identity information for email, user accounts, or domain names and intentionally sending messages. This is an alternative to using 'zombie' computers, by signing up to numerous accounts using false credentials.
- Falsely representing oneself as the registrant, or successor, or an IP address and intentionally sending messages. The object is to obtain use of blocks of IP addresses that have not been 'blacklisted'.

These represent activities carried out by spammers in order to evade the filters implemented by communication service providers and avoid detection by law enforcement agencies. The provisions have been inserted into the same part of the US criminal code that addresses other forms of computer and cybercrimes,[862] and prosecutions are handled by the Computer Crime and Intellectual Property Section in the Criminal Division of the Department of Justice.[863]

3.358　A number of prosecutions have been brought under the Act, with guilty pleas being entered in the majority of cases.[864] The penalties include a possible maximum prison term of five years, where the activity is carried out as part of a felony[865] or the person has been previously convicted under this or similar provisions.[866] The penalties vary according to other factors, such as the volume of messages sent or the number of false accounts registered. The US Sentencing Commission's guidelines include sentencing enhancements in certain circumstances, such as the harvesting of email addresses.[867] Finally, forfeiture may also be ordered, in respect of either the proceeds from such activities, or the ICTs used to commit the offence.[868]

3.359　While the stance taken by the US on the criminal nature of unsolicited communications appears to differ starkly from that of the UK, and indeed most other European countries and countries such as Australia, the differences may be less significant than they first appear. Under UK law, hacking into a machine to establish a 'zombie' for the sending of unsolicited communications would generally be addressed by the CMA, ss 1 and 2. The offences of fraud and forgery may be applicable against the deception and falsification practices of spammers, especially the new fraud offences under the Fraud Act 2006: fraud

---

861　Defined as: 'the source, destination, and routing information attached to an electronic mail message, including the originating domain name and originating electronic mail address, and any other information that appears in the line identifying, or purporting to identify, a person initiating the message': see 15 USC s 7702(8).

862　18 USC, Pt I 'Crimes', Chapter 47 'Fraud and False Statements', s 1037 'Fraud and related activity in connection with electronic mail'.

863　The Act is enforced by the Federal Trade Commission (FTC), see further <http://www.ftc.gov>.

864　eg Jason Smathers, the 'AOL spammer', Nicholas Tombros, the 'wi-fi spammer', and Peter Moshou, the 'timeshare spammer'. See generally press releases issued by the DoJ, available at <http://www.usdoj.gov>.

865　ie a crime that carried a sentence of imprisonment for more than one year or the death penalty.

866　18 USC s 1037(b). In April 2005, Jeremy Jaynes was sentenced to nine years' imprisonment for breaching anti-spamming legislation in Virginia (Title ss 18.2–152.3: 1): see Hancock, D, 'Spammer gets 9 years', CBS News, 8 April 2005, available at <http://www.cbsnews.com/news/spammer-gets-9-years/>.

867　US Sentencing Commission, *Guidelines Manual* (effective 1 November 2014), s 2B1.1, available at <http://www.ussc.gov/guidelines-manual/guidelines-manual>: 'the unauthorized harvesting of electronic mail addresses of users of a website, proprietary service, or other online public forum'.

868　18 USC s 1037(c).

by false representation and fraud by failing to disclose information. This latter offence provides that a person acts in breach if he 'dishonestly fails to disclose to another person information which he is under a legal duty to disclose'. Such a duty can be found in the 2003 Privacy Regulations.[869] The advantage of the US approach, however, is the attendant publicity that such a dedicated measure generates—both among the general public and potential spammers—as well as the political commitment and resultant law enforcement resources that are promised to tackle such activities.

E. Concluding Remarks

This chapter has examined substantive offences in three categories: computer-related, content-related, and computer-integrity. These categories are open to criticism and debate, but have been adopted to reflect the approach taken by the leading international legal instrument in the field, the Council of Europe Cybercrime Convention. The analysis under the first two categories was not intended to be comprehensive in respect of specific offences, such as fraud, since that is beyond the scope of this book; rather areas were highlighted where problems and controversies have arisen when computers and networks played a particular central role in the criminal conduct. **3.360**

In terms of the *sui generis* computer-integrity offences, the concern was to examine in detail the scope and nature of such offences. It has been argued that the nature of our current integrity offences reflects a computing environment that has been fundamentally altered by the Internet and the novel ways in which persons and computers interact with each other. As with other areas of ICT law, the rules currently in place can inevitably lag behind the state of technological development or the pace of innovation within the criminal fraternity. Our *sui generis* integrity offences seem as susceptible to obsolescence as other areas of the criminal code. **3.361**

In most jurisdictions, computer-integrity offences are drafted in a manner that reflects an aspiration to minimize the range of conduct being criminalized, tying concepts of access, modification, and interference to more complex determinations of authorization and harm. Kerr suggests that such a 'one-size-fits-all' approach may no longer be suitable; that authorization as the standard integrity threshold should perhaps be replaced by integrity offences more tailored to specific results and types of misconduct carried out by the perpetrator.[870] **3.362**

Defining appropriate offences is obviously only one element of a strategy to tackle the growth of computer and cybercrime. As a deterrent to criminal conduct, offences are recognized as being of limited value where the likely sanction is relatively low and/or the perceived risk of being apprehended is minimal. As we have seen, there has recently been substantial tariff inflation for certain offences, particularly in relation to illegal content and illegal interference. We will have to wait and see whether these changes feed through to sentencing decisions and the level of criminality in these areas. **3.363**

---

[869] Privacy and Electronic Communications (EC Directive) Regulations 2003 (SI No 2426).
[870] Kerr, above, n 567, at 1642–3.

3.364 In terms of apprehension, computer and cybercrimes raise a raft of policing and investigative issues. Policing issues, such as resource, expertise, and organization, were considered in Chapter 2. The next stage is therefore to examine the ability of law enforcement agencies to adequately investigate such offences in order to obtain the necessary evidence to enable criminal proceedings to be brought. The process of evidence gathering is referred to as forensics and is the topic of Chapter 4.

4

ADDRESSING THE DATA PROBLEMS:
CYBER-FORENSICS
AND CRIMINAL PROCEDURE

A. Introduction

Digital information or data, zeros and ones, is the form in which our emerging 'Information **4.01** Society' carries out its activities, whether through software applications, emails, data feeds, or the Web. The global economy has become increasingly dependent on the processing and transmission of such data across networks to support its infrastructure and carry out many of its functions. When cybercrimes are carried out, the ability of law enforcement agencies (LEAs) to investigate and prosecute the perpetrators will be driven, in part, by the availability and accessibility of such data or information to the investigators, whether in the context of intelligence gathering, evidential retrieval, or subsequent analysis and presentation in court.

Law enforcement investigative techniques can be subdivided into ordinary, coercive, and **4.02** covert techniques. 'Ordinary' refers to the use of techniques that are available to any person, police or otherwise, such as searching for material on the Internet;[1] 'coercive' techniques involves the exercise of such powers that force a subject to disclose information, such as search and seizure, while covert techniques involves interception, surveillance, and human intelligence sources. Ordinary and covert techniques are generally used at an earlier stage in the investigative process, for the gathering of intelligence as much as evidence, while coercive techniques are used primarily to gather evidence once the relevant ICT resources have been identified. A particular technique used, or investigative power exercised, at

---

[1] However, as discussed below at paras 4.50 et seq, in some situations 'ordinary' techniques may not be permitted of public law enforcement agents or are subject to prior authorization.

different points in an investigation may therefore form part of an ordinary, covert, or coercive investigative process. Law enforcement access to data about whom a person has called, for example, may be used to identify persons to be placed under surveillance, or post-arrest to establish evidential links between defendants.

4.03 Any criminal investigation interferes with the rights of others, whether the person is the subject of an investigation or a related third party. In a democratic society any such interference must be justifiable and proportionate to the needs of society to be protected. However, the growth of network-based crime has raised some unique and difficult issues in respect of the appropriate balance between the needs of those investigating and prosecuting such crime, and the rights of network users, particularly privacy. While attempting to resolve such conflicts is beyond the remit of this book, the intention is to contribute to the on-going debate[2] by critically analysing current rules and examining aspects of the environment in which they operate.

4.04 There are also the interests of communication service providers (CSPs), the intermediaries that build and/or operate the networks and communication services through which data is communicated. Law enforcement agencies will be looking towards such intermediaries to assist them in the investigative process, either in terms of gathering data transmitted by the suspects themselves or by providing data generated by the CSPs about the communication activities of suspects. Such assistance may be provided on either a voluntary or mandatory basis, which also raises important legal issues for consideration.[3] This chapter examines legislative measures that have been adopted in the UK and other jurisdictions to address some of these problems of criminal procedure and the manner in which such measures impact on CSPs, from a legal, technical, and operational perspective.

4.05 First and foremost, however, this chapter is concerned with the problems raised by data for law enforcement agencies investigating network-based crime. It begins with a review of the field of computer and network forensics. As a law text, it is not within the scope of this book, or indeed the competence of the author, to engage in a detailed examination and critical analysis of the various forensic techniques employed in computer and cybercrime investigations.[4] Instead, attention is given to the two key elements of the activity: identifying the suspect(s) and obtaining data related to the suspect's activities. It is the second of these that comprises the majority of the discussion in this chapter.

4.06 For the purpose of our analysis, we are going to distinguish between the three main avenues for obtaining forensic data. First, data obtained from, or about, the suspect through 'open source' intelligence gathering or covertly through various forms of surveillance. Second, data obtained from a CSP, whether in the course of a covert investigation or otherwise.

---

[2] See further Intelligence and Security Committee (ISC), *Privacy and Security: A modern and transparent legal framework*, Report, HC 1075, March 2015, available at <http://fas.org/irp/world/uk/isc-privacy.pdf> ('ISC Report 2015'); Anderson, D, *A Question of Trust*, Independent Reviewer of Terrorism Legislation Report, June 2015, available at <https://terrorismlegislationreviewer.independent.gov.uk/wp-content/uploads/2015/06/IPR-Report-Print-Version.pdf> ('Independent Reviewer Report'); and the Royal United Services Institute (RUSI) Independent Surveillance Review, *A Democratic Licence to Operate*, Report, July 2015, available at <https://www.rusi.org/downloads/assets/ISR-Report-press.pdf> ('RUSI Report').

[3] For the purposes of this chapter, a mandatory requirement for a CSP to provide assistance is not being classified as a coercive policing technique.

[4] See eg *Digital Investigation: The International Journal of Digital Forensics & Incident Response*, available at <http://www.journals.elsevier.com/digital-investigation/>.

Third, data obtained coercively from the suspect, through the exercise of search-and-seizure powers. These are currently the primary sources of evidence in cybercrime investigations and they are going to be considered in the order in which they will generally arise.

As noted above, covert policing is a common feature of cybercrime investigations, and **4.07** therefore consideration is given to the legal rules governing such activities, both as a purely investigative activity, as well as through the involvement of CSPs. Coercive policing generally follows on from the intelligence and evidence obtained through ordinary and covert policing and the fourth section addresses such issues. The problems of seizing intangible data without undue interference is the initial challenge; however, being able to access and make sense of the data once seized is likely to present the greater difficulties in the future.

Finally, it should be reiterated that the issues discussed in this chapter have a wider applic- **4.08** ability and resonance than those offences examined in Chapter 3. Issues of criminal procedure examined in this chapter are not limited to cybercrime investigations, but are relevant to any crime that involves computers and cyberspace, while the challenges of digital investigations can be as relevant in the context of civil proceedings as they are for criminal.

B. Computer and Network Forensics

The investigation of cybercrime and the gathering of appropriate evidence for a criminal **4.09** prosecution, the science of 'forensic computing', 'digital forensics', or 'cyber-forensics', can be an extremely difficult and complex issue. This is primarily due to the intangible and often transient nature of data, especially in a networked environment. The technology renders the process of investigation and recording of data for evidence extremely vulnerable to defence claims of errors, technical malfunction, prejudicial interference, or fabrication. Such claims may lead to a ruling from the court against the admissibility of such evidence.[5]

A lack of adequate training of law enforcement officers, prosecutors, and, indeed, the judi- **4.10** ciary, will often exacerbate these difficulties. In the UK, as in many countries, substantial efforts have been made over recent years to address this training need, with the establishment of specialized facilities and courses,[6] supplemented by training courses offered by the vendors of forensic applications and services.[7] In addition, computer forensics has become a recognized academic discipline, leading to a range of qualifications at higher education institutions.[8]

Until recently, the practice of digital or cyber-forensics had developed in a rather haphazard **4.11** manner, often based on expediency and circumstance; reflecting, in part, the story of the ICT industry itself. However, attempts are being made to impose greater professionalism in the field, to better serve the needs of the market, both public and private sector, and to improve the quality of evidence being used in criminal prosecutions.

---

[5] See generally Chapter 6.
[6] See the College of Policing courses on 'Cyber crime' and 'Hi-Tech Training' available at <http://www.college.police.uk/What-we-do/Learning/Curriculum/Investigation/Pages/default.aspx>.
[7] eg <http://www.sapphire.net>.
[8] eg the University of Glamorgan offers a BSc or HND in Computer Forensics; Canterbury Christchurch University College offers an MSc in Cybercrime Forensics, and Cranfield University has a Centre for Forensic Computing.

4.12 The experience garnered by law enforcement agencies over the years has also been formalized through the issuance of guidance on the forensic treatment of computer-derived evidence. In the UK, the Association of Chief Police Officers (now the National Police Chiefs' Council)[9] and the National Hi-Tech Crime Unit, as was, published a 'Good Practice Guide for Computer-based Electronic Evidence', which is now in its fifth edition.[10] In the United States, the Department of Justice has guidance on law and practice in the field: 'Searching and Seizing Computers and Obtaining Electronic Evidence in Criminal Investigations'.[11] Such guidance becomes a de facto benchmark against which the practices of law enforcement officers and other investigators are likely to be evaluated. In addition, more formal forensic standards have been developed and promulgated in the field, which are designed to bolster the use of digital evidence.[12]

4.13 This section briefly considers two key challenges in a digital investigation, identifying the suspect and obtaining data relevant to the suspect's criminal activities. However, first, consideration is given to some of the problems that handling data creates for investigators, some of which the law has expressly tried to address or mitigate.

Some data problems

4.14 This chapter is entitled 'addressing the data problems', which obviously begs the question: what are some of the data problems in a cybercrime investigation? Data in our digital environment raises a range of problems for investigators, many of which require not only specialist technical skills, but also an appropriate procedural framework designed to tackle these problems. This section introduces some of the key data problems in a digital investigation, most of which are generic to cyberspace and recur in the context of other parts of the book.

4.15 The first of these is the 'identity problem': how to establish an adequate forensic link between an item of data and the virtual identity of the person to whom the data relates; and then between the virtual identity and a real-world person. Establishing identity is widely recognized as being one of two key problems in a cybercrime investigation that is likely to become worse over time;[13] in part because the development and proliferation of anonymization techniques and services.[14]

4.16 A second problem may be referred to as the 'location problem', although this really covers three distinct issues arising from where the data is to be found. Related to resolving the 'identity problem' is the obvious need to identify the physical location of the suspect. In a mobile phone context, for example, cell site analysis may determine whether the suspect in possession of an identified handset was present in the locality at the relevant time. Location

---

⁹ Since 1 April 2015, see <http://www.npcc.police.uk/Home.aspx>.

¹⁰ Association of Chief Police Officers (ACPO), 'Good Practice Guide for Computer Based Evidence' ('ACPO Guide'): see Appendix IV in this volume.

¹¹ Office of Legal Education, *Searching and seizing computer and obtaining electronic evidence in criminal investigation*, available from <http://www.justice.gov/sites/default/files/criminal-ccips/legacy/2015/01/14/ssmanual2009.pdf>.

¹² eg 'Information technology—Security techniques—Guidelines for identification, collection, acquisition, and preservation of digital evidence', ISO/IEC 27037: 2012, available at <http://www.iso.org>.

¹³ See eg Barrett, N, *Traces of Guilt*, Bantam Press, 2004, at 373.

¹⁴ eg the TOR project and software <https://www.torproject.org> and the service Hide my Ass!, at <https://www.hidemyass.com>.

also has jurisdictional implications, since cyberspace activities cross state borders requiring investigators to seek data residing outside their national jurisdiction and their legal competence.[15]

A third aspect of the location problem arises from the fact that forensic data may also be **4.17** present within a network forming part of, or connected to, the Internet, and/or may be found on terminal equipment operating at the edges of the network. The law sometimes treats data obtained within a network differently from that same data when it is at the edges of a network. In addition, data may reside, or be at rest, on the ICT resources of the victim, the suspect, or some third party, such as a CSP or online service provider (eg cloud provider, credit card company, or search engine). Alternatively, the same data may be obtained in the process of it being transmitted across a network, generally referred to as intercepted data. Specific rules of criminal procedure address law enforcement access to these different sources of evidence: data 'at rest' and data 'in transmission'. Indeed, such a situation has been recommended, in order to facilitate cybercrime investigations:

> [t]he legal distinction between searching computer systems and seizing data stored therein and intercepting data in the course of transmission should be clearly delineated and applied.[16]

The nature of ICTs bestows upon data the duality of being notoriously vulnerable to loss **4.18** and modification, as well as being surprisingly 'sticky', at one and the same time. These characteristics may be referred to respectively as the 'integrity problem' and the 'stickiness problem'. The former means the process of obtaining forensic data is a significant technical challenge for investigators, since it may modify the source data or its related meta-data, fatally undermining the evidential value of the forensic material.

The 'stickiness' of data is attributable, in part, to the multiple copies generated by the com- **4.19** munications process, particularly in an Internet environment, as well as the manner in which data is held and removed on electronic storage media. While the 'stickiness' of data will generally work to the advantage of an investigator, as we saw in Chapter 3, the availability of data may not enable a successful prosecution where the defendant is unaware of its existence. Conversely, the widely held perception that data held on an ICT resource is transient may work to the advantage of a defendant, where he can raise doubt as to the existence or otherwise of relevant forensic data. In *Caffrey*,[17] for example, defence counsel was able to create sufficient doubt in the minds of the jury as to the existence of a Trojan horse virus on the defendant's PC at the relevant time for the defendant to be acquitted, despite expert testimony to the contrary.

Related to the 'stickiness' problem is the 'analysis' problem created by the volume and **4.20** nature of the data that an investigator may be required to handle in the course of an investigation. Modern data media, such as SSDs, hard drives, DVDs, and memory sticks are capable of storing vast amounts of data, while networks are capable of transmitting vast bit-streams of data over channels and across nodes. While an investigator may be able to obtain and preserve such data in a relatively straightforward manner, through the exercise of seizure or interception powers, the ability to access, manage, and analyse it for subsequent

---

[15] See generally Chapter 5.
[16] Council of Europe Recommendation No R(95) 13 concerning problems of procedural law connected with information technology, 11 September 1995, Principle 1.
[17] Southwark Crown Court, 17 October 2003.

presentation in court can present very significant problems, from the need to overcome protection mechanisms, to the availability of appropriate resource within any time limits imposed by law.[18]

4.21 Digital evidence may comprise the content of a transmission or, more frequently, the attributes of a communications activity, or 'meta-data', that identifies and describes the content of a transmission and its management by an ICT resource. The digitization of information also means that traditionally distinct forms of data are represented in a common language: binary machine code. Taken together, these features create a 'data type' problem, where existing legal rules treat the obtaining of different types of forensic data differently; the law governing interception, for example, being only applicable to the obtaining of communications content. Distinguishing different types of data and determining the applicable procedural regime governing the obtaining of such data can be an increasingly significant challenge for investigators.

4.22 An inability to adequately address some or all of the data problems can have a direct impact on the prosecutorial process, especially evidential admissibility and the probative value of any forensic data.[19] Under English law, investigators are under a duty to pursue 'all reasonable lines of inquiry';[20] however, discharging this duty in the face of the data problems just outlined may no longer be realistically possible. As noted by a police representative in evidence given before a Home Affairs Committee in 2006:

> Traditional, good detective work is that you follow the evidence wherever it takes you and that is the purity. You keep an open mind from the beginning of an investigation and follow the evidence where it takes you. However, with the weight of material we are now seeing, what we actually have to do is to set clear priorities at a very early stage and we have to make choices around which material we are going to try and access on computers or through mobile phones or overseas and hope, and it really does come down to hope, that that will yield the evidence we need . . .[21]

This chapter considers both the technical challenges and the legal rules that relate to these data problems.

Traceability

4.23 One of the classic aphorisms of the Internet age is that 'On the Internet, nobody knows you are a dog'.[22] However, in the course of an investigation, the investigator will want to identify the person carrying out the illegal activity, whether canine or not! The process of establishing a real-world person's identity from their Internet-related identity creates a significant forensic and legal hurdle.

4.24 Broadly speaking, there are two initial sources of forensic data to assist in the identification process: that created by a suspect's use of communication services; and the content of a person's communications activities. In the former case, we are concerned to identify the

---

[18] eg Magistrates' Courts Act 1980, s 127 and the Prosecution of Offences (Custody Time Limits) Regulations 1987 (SI No 299).

[19] See generally Chapter 6.

[20] Criminal Procedure and Investigations Act 1996, s 23(1)(a). See paras 6.09–6.23.

[21] Evidence presented by DAC Clarke and published in the Home Affairs Select Committee, *Fourth Report: Terrorism Detention Powers*, HC 910–11, 3 July 2006 ('Home Affairs Report'), para 62.

[22] Steiner, P, cartoon, *New Yorker*, 5 July 1993, at 61.

source, and often the recipient, of a communication, based on some form of unique identifier. The identifier will generally identify the terminal equipment or device from which the communication originated, such as a telephone number or PC, and may identify a specific user, such as an email address. However, where the terminal equipment resides in an environment where multiple persons have access, whether at home, the office, or a public place, proving that a specific person was using the equipment or account at the relevant time is an obvious problem, and potential defence. Successfully completing this forensic trail to a real person, therefore, raises substantial challenges for investigators.

In the second scenario, investigators may be able to obtain various data elements that a **4.25** suspect has disclosed in the course of his activities, which can be traced back to the suspect. Such content may be disclosed knowingly, but unwittingly, or inadvertently, such as 'cookies'.[23] In *Vallor*,[24] for example, the virus writer was identified through postings he made to various Internet bulletin boards boasting about his activities, under the name of 'Gobo'. One common means of identification is through payment data, such as credit card details, used to access and purchase online services. In the child abuse case *Landslide*[25] and subsequent 'Operation Ore' in the UK, for example, the primary source of identification evidence was credit card details given by subscribers.[26] Also, in the cyber-espionage case, *Haephrati*,[27] the suspects were traced, in part, through the use by one of the accused of his American Express credit card to open an email account used to send messages with a virus attached.[28] In June 2006, it was revealed that SWIFT, the international electronic funds transfer network based in Brussels, had transferred transactional financial data contained in millions of records to the US Government, as well as enabling US authorities direct access.[29] Indeed, such payment details may not only be valuable in the investigative stage, but may subsequently be used as a component of a crime prevention strategy, enabling a payment service provider to close an account used in the course of criminal conduct.[30]

While it is beyond the scope of this book to examine the full range of technical means **4.26** available to identify persons in a cybercrime environment, it is valuable to briefly examine some of the complexities that arise when an investigator needs to resolve an IP address to an individual.

When utilizing any Internet-based service, such as email, the originator and recipient of **4.27** a message require an IP address, a unique number that identifies the relevant resources.[31]

---

[23] 'Cookies' can be configured to include user names, passwords, and other identification data.

[24] [2004] 1 Cr App R (S) 319.

[25] US Department of Justice (DoJ), 'Thomas Reedy Sentenced to Life Imprisonment in Child Porn Case', Press Release, 6 August 2001. See also *US v Reedy*, 304 F 3d 358, 60 Fed R Evid Serv 133 (5th Cir (Tex) 2002).

[26] See 'Operation Ore: Can the UK cope?', BBC News, 13 January 2003, available at <http://news.bbc.co.uk/2/hi/uk_news/2652465.stm>.

[27] See further para 3.40.

[28] See Government Opening Note in *The Government of Israel v Michael and Ruth Haephrati*, drafted by John Hardy, Counsel, delivered at Bow Street Magistrates' Court, 26 August 2005, para 10.

[29] Lichtblau, E and Risen, J, 'Bank data is sifted by US in secret to block terror', *New York Times*, 23 June 2006.

[30] eg the Data Protection (Processing of Sensitive Personal Data) Order 2006 (SI No 2068).

[31] IPv4, uses 32 bit addresses written in dot.decimal notation comprising four octets, eg 38.111.64.2. The new IPv6 uses 128 bit addresses written as eight groups of hexadecimal digits, eg 1002:0db8:0770:003c:0 546:0000:1428:57ab. Once fully migrated to IPv6, we may see less dynamic IP allocation, especially in the context of the 'Internet of Things', which may alter this process.

That IP address is then logically linked to the originator's pseudonym and domain name, for example i.n.walden@qmul.ac.uk. However, while the IP address is unique, the person to whom it is linked will usually vary. Internet service providers (ISPs) and corporate networks will generally, for reasons of efficiency, dynamically assign an IP address to a user, or be shared between multiple users, each time they log onto a service or at the commencement of each communication session.

4.28 Identification in a cyberspace environment may therefore be a four-stage process.[32] First, it is necessary to identify the IP address(es) that needs to be resolved to a machine or person. These will generally be found on logs generated by the specific application utilized by the suspect, such as the web or mail server of the victim or an intermediary CSP.[33] The recorded source IP address may, however, have been 'spoofed', where a false source IP address is inserted in the packet headers. While 'spoofing' may be carried out at an individual user level, it may also be done on a commercial level, as a service offered to users wanting to use the Internet anonymously, sometimes referred to as a 'darkweb' service.[34]

4.29 Second, one has to establish the entity, such as a CSP, to whom the IP address has been assigned. This can be relatively straightforward, for example using 'whois' software to interrogate one of the regional, national, or local registry databases, detailing IP address allocation.[35] However, since the registries do not have a requirement to verify such information, a large proportion of it is often inaccurate, either because false information was supplied in the first instance, or because the information is not kept up to date. An alternative or supplement to registry lookup is to use a 'traceroute' application to follow the route of the packets across the Internet.[36] In either case, if accurate, an IP address holder will be found. Generally, this will be a service provider or organization, although an individual may be identifiable if he has a fixed IP address, then the registry may effectively identify the owner of the machine.

4.30 Where a block of IP addresses belongs to a service provider or organization, the third stage will be to approach the IP holder to match the target IP address to a specific user at the relevant time.[37] This may be achieved by studying one or more historic logs, such as a Proxy, DHCP, or NAT log, each of which provides different types of data of varying value.[38] Such a process will clearly not be possible where the IP holder is an anonymous public service such as a cyber café; or the user has logged on to an unsecured wireless network, or, most commonly, the IP holder does not maintain or retain a complete or sufficiently detailed log of IP address allocation.

---

[32] Clayton, R, 'Anonymity and traceability in cyberspace', University of Cambridge, Computer Laboratory, Technical Report, UCAM-CL-TR-653, November 2005, s 2.2, available at <http://www.cl.cam.ac.uk/TechReports/UCAM-CL-TR-653.html>. See also LINX, 'Best Current Practice—Traceability', 18 May 1999, available at <https://www.linx.net/good/bcp/traceability-bcp-v1_0.html>.

[33] Clayton, above, n 32, at 28.

[34] eg <http://www.anonymizer.com> and <https://www.hidemyass.com>.

[35] See Nikkel, B, 'Domain name forensics: a systematic approach to investigating an internet presence', 1 *Digital Investigation* 247 (2004).

[36] eg <http://www.monitis.com/traceroute/>. Traceroute data may also be misleading; see Clayton, above, n 32, para 3.5.3.

[37] Determining time can itself be difficult, due to machine errors and time values (eg time zones and daylight saving).

[38] See MacGregor, R, 'Needle in a haystack', PWC Cyber security updates, 27 January 2015, available at <http://pwc.blogs.com/cyber_security_updates/2015/01/needle-in-a-haystack-network-logs.html>.

The final stage is to obtain the subscriber's account details, such as home address, from the **4.31** CSP's administrative records. As with the third stage, the existence of administrative records will depend, in part, on the nature of the connection being provided, as well as the method of payment for the service (eg direct debit). For 'free' Internet communication services, scant subscriber data may be held by the service provider; while as 4G phones increasingly become the standard device for mobile broadband access to the internet, administrative records may not exist for that proportion of subscribers using 'pay-as-you-go' services.

It should be noted that a fifth stage of the process will also increasingly arise, where the sub- **4.32** scriber, such as a landlord, has multiple devices utilizing the same access service through a wireless router, which may or may not log the devices connecting to it.

The above illustrates that the ability to trace a person from their IP address is dependent **4.33** on the input of different entities, often based in different jurisdictions, and the existence of various logs and records. As will be discussed later in this chapter, the forensic value of such logs and records has recently prompted governments to impose data retention requirements on CSPs operating at stages 3 and 4, in order to preserve the identification data, rather than depend on the vagaries of individual CSP practices and procedures.[39]

Having considered the complexities involved in tracing and identifying a suspect, the next **4.34** forensic challenge concerns the capability of law enforcement agencies to appropriately obtain the required intelligence or evidential data.

Obtaining data

The digital forensic process for obtaining data generally involves a number of different **4.35** stages: (a) identifying what data may be available and where it may reside; (b) preserving such data in a manner that minimizes interference with the original data; (c) analysis of the data for intelligence and evidential purposes; and (d) presentation of the data and evidence derived from it in a court of law.[40] There are also certain widely accepted rules or principles that govern each of these processes. The ACPO Guide, for example, promulgates standard forensic practices for obtaining data on the basis of four key principles:

> Principle 1: No action taken by law enforcement agencies or their agents should change data held on a computer or storage media which may subsequently be relied upon in court.
>
> Principle 2: In exceptional circumstances, where a person finds it necessary to access original data held on a computer or on storage media, that person must be competent to do so and be able to give evidence explaining the relevance and the implications of their actions.
>
> Principle 3: An audit trail or other record of all processes applied to computer based electronic evidence should be created and preserved. An independent third party should be able to examine those processes and achieve the same result.
>
> Principle 4: The person in charge of the investigation (the case officer) has overall responsibility for ensuring that the law and these principles are adhered to.

As noted above, forensic data may be obtained from numerous sources, victim, suspect, or **4.36** third party; either in the course of its transmission or when residing on a source-controlled

---

[39] See paras 4.224 et seq.
[40] McKemmish, R, 'What is forensic computing?', *118 Australian Institute of Criminology Trends & Issues in crime and criminal justice*, June 1999, available at <http://www.aic.gov.au/media_library/publications/tandi_pdf/tandi118.pdf>.

resource, medium, or device. This section briefly considers some of the pertinent technical features concerning the different ICT resources from which digital evidence may be obtained. It should also be borne in mind that every incidence of cybercrime, as for any other crime, will have a unique life cycle, from first detection and reporting to any eventual proceedings.[41]

4.37 Data may be held on a huge variety of types of data media. Such media varies in respect of its mobility and ease of use, from the SSDs and HDDs on a computer, to tapes and removable USB flash drives. However, all such storage media are becoming cheaper, have greater storage capability, and operate at greater speeds, all of which directly feeds into the 'analysis' problem in terms of the volumes of data potentially involved in the forensic process.

4.38 Most media have a basic four-way functionality, in terms of enabling data to be written to, read, modified, and deleted from the media, while some, such as CD-Rs, only enable data to be written and read. The latter have been designed to address the integrity problem for individual and commercial users, but would also be beneficial from an investigatory perspective.

4.39 Digital media store data in different ways at a physical level, such as magnetic particles and laser-created pits, as well as at a logical level, in terms of partitions, drives, and sectors. The way in which a device logically handles the data it processes has direct implications for any subsequent forensic analysis. Microsoft's FAT and NTFS file systems and Unix's FFS system, for example, utilize space on the storage media in very different ways, which require the use of different analytical techniques to examine data stored by such systems. However, under all file systems, data is not necessarily stored in a contiguous manner, but rather will often be fragmented across one or more media or services, in blocks, which are only logically associated through addressing information.

4.40 The deletion of data from digital media may take different forms. The deletion of files in standard desktop applications will generally only result in the removal of the addressing information associated with each block of data, which logically links the various blocks comprising the contents of the file; or the files are simply treated as deleted and are renamed in another directory, such as the 'Recycle Bin' or 'Trash'. As such, the data remains on the media, and is potentially recoverable, until it has been either completely overwritten by new data, or been deleted by other means. This residual physical representation of erased data is sometimes referred to as 'data remanence',[42] and is one cause of the 'stickiness' data problem.

4.41 As well as the organization of files in terms of the characteristics of the digital media, the operating system and applications that utilize the media also use systems for identifying and organizing the data they operate upon, in terms of file names, extensions, folders, and directories. Such systems will often maintain a wide range of valuable forensic details about the attributes of a data file, in terms of its size and usage. Usage data, such as the date and

---

[41] See Sommer, P, *Digital Evidence, Digital Investigations and E-Disclosure*, 4th edn, Information Assurance Advisory Council (IAAC), November 2013, s 3, available at <http://www.iaac.org.uk/media/1347/iaac-forensic-4th-edition.pdf>.

[42] eg Bennett, DW, 'The challenges facing computer forensic investigations in obtaining information from mobile devices for use in criminal investigations', *Forensic Focus*, 20 August 2011, available at <http://wp.me/p1F8Sz-8y>.

time at which actions were carried out on a data file,[43] is obviously an extremely valuable forensic source, but is also highly vulnerable to claims of inaccuracy, modification, and interference. As such, it will often require some form of corroboration using other data sources, including the contents of the data file, such as a date placed in a digital photograph or the actual commission of the offence.

To address the 'integrity' problem discussed above, an investigator needs to be able to obtain **4.42** the data in a manner which is complete, yet minimizes the interference with the target data. Such data may simply be printed and copied, although this may result in alterations to the meta-data associated with the target data, which may create evidential vulnerabilities. Therefore, for most types of digital media, the most common technique used to obtain forensic data is that of 'imaging'.[44]

Imaging involves the acquisition and creation of a complete bitstream image of the **4.43** digital media, such as hard drive or smart card, in a non-invasive manner and including those areas which are not occupied by data elements. The imaging process itself will obviously generate data, such as a cryptographic hash function, that may be required at a later stage to verify the authenticity and integrity of the acquisition process and any subsequent copies. A number of copies of the image are generally created, a master copy for evidential purposes, a copy on which the analysis is carried out, and a third that is provided to the suspect for his own verification and analysis purposes.[45] The images are widely accepted as an accurate representation of the original digital media, and the use of such images never appears to have been successfully challenged before the UK courts. Another advantage of 'imaging' is that it can allow the original digital media to be returned to the owner, such as a business, who can then continue to use the resource, thereby minimizing the degree of collateral disruption and interference caused to a victim or innocent third party.

One critical element of the process of forensic analysis is the capability to map the **4.44** events recorded on the various devices from which data is derived to real time, in terms of establishing an accurate chronology of the events relating to the criminal conduct. Most of the ICTs that operate within a network and at its edges will time record; yet such multiplicity, coupled with their susceptibility to inaccuracy, makes mapping events in cyberspace to the real world a considerable forensic challenge. This problem is obviously exacerbated by the transnational context and different time zones within which such networks operate.

The nature of networks, such as the Internet, means that forensic and evidential data is **4.45** often present in foreign jurisdictions, which raises complex jurisdictional issues when law enforcement need to obtain such remote material. These issues are examined in detail in Chapter 5.

---

[43] The three primary date systems are creation date, last modified date, and last accessed date.

[44] See eg EnCase (<http://www.encase.com>) used by the majority of law enforcement agencies in the UK; but see also Salvage Data (<http://www.salvagedata.com>).

[45] See generally Sommer, P, 'Digital footprints: Assessing computer evidence', *Criminal Law Review*, Special edn 61 (December 1998).

C. Cyber-surveillance

4.46 It is an oft-made statement that we live increasingly in a surveillance society, primarily manifest in the public's mind through the proliferation of CCTV cameras in our public and private spaces. Surveillance is a crime prevention and detection measure, and has been greatly facilitated by developments in information and communication technologies. The nature of cybercrimes means surveillance is an important law enforcement tool in their detection and investigation, which makes it of concern to this book.

4.47 Surveillance may be carried out on a specified person's, or persons', communication *activities*, such as emails or file transfers; or of a 'virtual' *location* in cyberspace where communications are exchanged, such as a chat room or 'Hangout'. The surveillance may be put into operation at the edges of a network, ie on a suspect's terminal equipment, such as computer or mobile phone; or within the network, such as a mail server, physically remote from the suspect.

4.48 From a legal perspective, a clear distinction needs to be made between surveillance activities carried out by public law enforcement agencies in the course of an investigation and those carried out by private entities, such as employers and landowners. As a state-based activity, the former is governed by rules of criminal procedure designed to protect individual rights, including a person's right to privacy under Art 8 of the European Convention on Human Rights (ECHR). The latter, on the other hand, generally engage a range of civil rights, such as confidentiality and employment law, which are topics beyond the scope of this book.[46] However, while the focus of this section will be on state-based surveillance, the role of private surveillance in computer and network forensics, and its interaction with public law enforcement, will also be considered where relevant.

4.49 State-authorized or controlled surveillance may be carried out by personnel of the law enforcement agency itself, through the use of an informant, or require the involvement of a third-party communication service provider to provide access to the forensic data, whether stored or in transmission and either created by the surveillance target or generated by the communication service itself. The obtaining of data from a CSP is examined separately in the following section, since data obtained from, or with the direct involvement of a CSP, may not always comprise a form of surveillance subject to regulatory control. Obtaining data from CSPs has also required a distinct legal framework and raises unique issues of concern.

4.50 This section examines two categories of surveillance. First, targeted surveillance, carried out by, or under the authority of, a public LEA in the course of a specific investigation or operation, and subject to a distinct regulatory regime. Second, the more pervasive non-targeted bulk surveillance, here referred to as 'monitoring' and 'filtering', which is carried out by the state and private entities as a generic security measure, and is subject to a more opaque set of legal rules. As well as considering general monitoring and filtering activities, specific attention will also be given to the use of 'honeypots', as a location-based surveillance

---

[46] eg Information Commissioner's Office (ICO), *The employment practices code*, Pt 3: 'Monitoring at Work', available at <https://ico.org.uk/media/for-organisations/documents/1064/the_employment_practices_code.pdf>.

tool; and issues arising from the monitoring of 'peer-to-peer' (P2P) network activity, which has attracted a considerable reputation as an environment for unlawful behaviour over the years, from copyright infringement to child abuse images.

Regulated activities

Surveillance activities by public authorities in the course of a criminal investigation are **4.51** primarily governed by Part II of the Regulation of Investigatory Powers Act 2000 (RIPA), supplemented by a series of codes of practice. The RIPA was designed to bring UK law into line with the ECHR, although it does not create a unified regime, since complementary rules and procedures exist under other legislation, such as the Intelligence Services Act 1994 (ISA) and the Police Act 1997 (PA).[47]

Under the RIPA, 'surveillance' is defined in the following terms:

(a) monitoring, observing or listening to persons, their movements, their conversations or their other activities or communications;

(b) recording anything monitored, observed or listened to in the course of surveillance; and

(c) surveillance by or with the assistance of a surveillance device.[48]

All these activities are clearly potentially applicable to investigative activities carried out in a cybercrime environment, from the use of keystroke loggers, to password 'sniffers' and 'honeypots'. Some of these activities will involve interference with a person's property, such as placing a surreptitious logging application on a suspect's personal computer.[49] In such cases, while the surveillance is governed by RIPA, the interference is authorized either under the Intelligence Services Act or the Police Act.[50] While it is beyond the scope of this book to engage in a comprehensive review of all the relevant provisions and related codes,[51] it is necessary to examine some of the key features of the regulatory regime and their potential operation in a cybercrime context.

Surveillance under the RIPA is subdivided into three main categories: 'directed surveil- **4.52** lance', 'intrusive surveillance', and the use of a 'covert human intelligence source'.[52] In respect of each category, there is a procedure by which such activities must be authorized by certain designated persons within the relevant investigating authority,[53] as well as restricted purposes for which such an activity may be authorized. An investigation may obviously involve a combination of activities, including property interference, which will then require multiple or combined authorizations.[54]

---

[47] On the 4 November 2015, the UK Government published its Draft Investigatory Powers Bill (IPB) (available at <https://www.gov.uk/government/uploads/system/uploads/attachment_data/file/473770/Draft_Investigatory_Powers_Bill.pdf>), which would reform the current regime, replacing Part I of the RIPA, but retaining Parts II and III. While the Bill and its implications are beyond the scope of this edition, brief references are made to some of its provisions at relevant points.

[48] Regulation of Investigatory Powers Act 2000 (RIPA), s 48(2).

[49] This includes interfering with 'wireless telegraphy'.

[50] Intelligence Services Act 1994 (ISA), s 5 and Police Act 1997 (PA), Pt III.

[51] For detailed coverage see, McKay, S., *Covert Policing: Law and Practice*, 2nd ed., OUP, 2015.

[52] RIPA, s 26.

[53] Although by virtue of s 80, it is not unlawful to engage in the forms of surveillance governed by the RIPA without an authorization unless explicitly stated to be unlawful under the Act or under other law, eg the Human Rights Act 1998 or Computer Misuse Act 1990 (CMA).

[54] Where all three forms of authorization are required, then the Secretary of State may be the authorizing officer: RIPA, s 30(2). See also Home Office, *Covert Surveillance and Property Interference: Code of Practice*,

4.53 When embarking on and authorizing surveillance, the relevant persons are required to consider issues of necessity and proportionality before engaging in such activities.[55] The relevant persons are required to make a judgment that the proposed action is necessary to achieve the identified purpose (eg prevention or detection of crime), and that the nature and scale of the intrusion, both in terms of the target suspect and any third parties ('collateral intrusion'), is proportionate to the anticipated operational benefits, in terms of intelligence and evidence. To be able to make that judgment, the person needs to be fully aware of all the circumstances surrounding the authorized activities, which requires care and candour on the part of the requesting investigating officer. In *Chatwani*,[56] the investigating officer from the National Crime Agency (NCA) was held to have failed in this duty, by not disclosing that the 'main objective' behind a series of arrests and search was to enable the installation of covert listening devices and 'to provoke the behavioural reaction' of causing the released suspects to discuss their conduct. This resulted in the authorization being quashed.[57]

Directed surveillance

4.54 Directed surveillance is the most common form of surveillance activity used for detecting crime.[58] It is defined by reference to four express characteristics.[59] First, it is covert but not intrusive, in the sense that it takes place in a public or quasi-public space or location, such as a cybercafé; or where the surveillance occurs using a network resource remote from the physical location of the suspect, such as an ISP-hosted web server.

4.55 The second characteristic is that the surveillance be carried out in respect of a specific investigation or operation, rather than on a general basis.[60] So, for example, the surveillance of persons using a privately installed, unconcealed CCTV camera system in a shopping centre would only seem to require Part II authorization were the system to be used as part of a planned police operation.[61] Analogous scenarios would be the investigation of a hacker identified by an Intrusion Detection System (IDS) operating on a private network or regularly visiting a person's page on a social network site.[62] Each raises a boundary question: what criteria determine the point at which police involvement in an act of surveillance renders it subject to regulatory control and oversight? This question is effectively a fifth implied characteristic of directed and, indeed, intrusive surveillance, i.e. that the activity should be carried out by the police, or some other public law enforcement authority.

December 2014 ('CSPI Code'), paras 3.12–3.14, available at <https://www.gov.uk/government/uploads/system/uploads/attachment_data/file/97960/code-of-practice-covert.pdf>.

[55] eg under the PA, the relevant persons are the 'Authorising Officer' (eg s 93(5)) and the 'Commissioner' (s 91(1)(b)).

[56] [2015] UKIPTrib 15_84_88-CH.

[57] However, the obtained material could be retained (although not listened to) and no compensation was awarded. With respect to the legally of the search warrant, see *R (on the application of Chatwani) v National Crime Agency* [2015] EWHC 1283 (Admin).

[58] RIPA, s 81(5)(a): 'establishing by whom, for what purpose, by what means and generally in what circumstances any crime was committed'.

[59] ibid, s 26(2).

[60] ibid, s 26(2)(a).

[61] CSPI Code, above, n 54, para 2.5. Overt use of CCTV is governed by the Home Office, *Surveillance Camera Code of Practice*, June 2013, available at <https://www.gov.uk/government/publications/surveillance-camera-code-of-practice>, issued under the Protection of Freedoms Act 2012, s 30(1)(a).

[62] See Office of the Surveillance Commissioners, *Annual Report 2013–14*, HC 343, SG/2014/92, paras 5.30–5.33. See also O'Floinn, M and Ormerod, D, 'Social networking sites, RIPA and criminal investigations', 10 *Criminal Law Review* 766 (2011).

Calling in the police when a crime is detected and providing them with access to data gen- **4.56**
erated by a surveillance tool would not seem to be sufficient, since the data was generated
without police involvement. However, once the police are involved, what degree of participation in on-going surveillance renders it a regulated activity? The answer would appear to
be one for the courts to address in the particular circumstances. In *Rosenberg*,[63] for example,
the admissibility of video evidence was challenged by defence counsel on the basis that the
police were aware that a neighbour of the defendant was using a CCTV system to record the
illegal drug-dealing activities of the defendant. However, absent any initiative or encouragement from the police, mere knowledge was held to be insufficient to convert the act into
police surveillance.[64] This suggests that the exercise of some degree of control over the surveillance activity would be the relevant criterion. In the shopping centre CCTV example,
were the police to request that the direction of the cameras be altered to better capture an
activity, this would seem to be sufficient to convert the surveillance into a regulated activity.
Likewise, in the IDS example, were the police to request that certain features of the IDS be
altered to record specified data. This approach reflects similar considerations in respect of
entrapment and the applicability of the abuse of process jurisdiction.[65]

The third characteristic of 'directed surveillance' is that it is likely to result in the obtaining **4.57**
of 'private information about a person', which is defined as 'any information relating to his
private or family life'.[66] This wording reflects Art 8 of the ECHR, although its scope may
raise particular definitional complexities in a cyberspace context, where the boundaries
between private and public life blur. It is also only a subset of the objective concept of 'personal data' utilized in data protection law, which imposes controls over the processing of
personal data in whatever context the data subject operates.[67]

The final characteristic is temporal, in the sense that the surveillance is not an immediate **4.58**
response to external events.[68] This would not be applicable, for example, where the police
actively searched out websites or bulletin boards to engage in surveillance, but could be
applicable to investigative activities arising in the course of cyber-patrolling, such as that
carried out by the Virtual Global Taskforce against child pornography on the Internet.[69]

'Directed surveillance' may only be carried out where it is a necessary and proportionate **4.59**
response for achieving certain specified purposes, including in the interests of national
security and the prevention and detection of serious crime.[70] The range of permitted purposes is essentially the same as those for the use of a 'covert human intelligence source'
and access to communications data, which implies an equality in terms of interference
in a person's private life; although supported by little if any empirical research or other
reasoning.

---

[63] [2006] EWCA Crim 6.
[64] ibid, para 18.
[65] See paras 6.30–6.48.
[66] RIPA, s 26(2)(b) and (10). See CSPI Code, above, n 53, para 2.4. Also note that under the Data
Protection Act 1998 (DPA 1998), personal data about an 'individual's personal, family or household affairs
(including recreational purposes)' is exempt from the majority of the Act's provisions (s 36).
[67] See further paras 3.27–3.38.
[68] RIPA, s 26(2)(c).
[69] See <http://www.virtualglobaltaskforce.com>.
[70] RIPA, s 28(3).

4.60   Directed surveillance may only be carried out by those authorities listed in Schedule 1 of the RIPA, while responsibility for the grant of an authorization within any such authority is specified in secondary regulation.[71] The authorization lasts for a three-month period, unless renewed. Under the Code, an application for authorization should include the identities of those subject to the surveillance, any potential collateral intrusion and any confidential information that is likely to be obtained.[72] However, such information would seem difficult to acquire without some prior surveillance having been carried out.

Intrusive surveillance

4.61   'Intrusive surveillance' is distinguished from 'directed surveillance' on a spatial basis by reference to 'anything taking place on any residential premises or in any private vehicle'.[73] Intrusive surveillance is only likely to arise in a cybercrime context, therefore, when the surveillance is carried out at the edges of the network, on the suspect's computer or other form of terminal device.

4.62   As noted in Chapter 2, the nature of cyberspace can challenge our reliance on the use of such locational concepts as 'residential premises'.[74] A person may utilize processing capacity on a remote machine, for example, but the installation of software by a LEA to record the same activity that could have been carried out locally would not be considered 'intrusive', solely on the basis of the location of the processing operation; although it may render it unlawful by virtue of being outside the jurisdiction of the LEA.[75] Such activities might also then comprise a form of directed surveillance or interception, depending on the circumstances and the nature of information recorded. The distributed nature of cyberspace activities clearly renders our private lives more exposed.

4.63   The second characteristic of intrusive surveillance is that either the person engaged in the surveillance is present or use is made of a surveillance device.[76] A 'surveillance device' is defined as 'any apparatus designed or adapted for use in surveillance',[77] which would encompass logical mechanisms, such as a keystroke logger or other types of 'spyware' placed on a suspect's machine to record and disclose information.

4.64   Since intrusive surveillance is considered to present a greater interference in a person's private life than directed surveillance, the purposes for which it may be utilized are limited to circumstances where either the interests of national security, serious crime and the economic well-being of the UK are involved, which corresponds to the grounds on which interception may be used.[78] In addition, authorization for such activities may only be granted by the Secretary of State, similar to a warranted intercept, or a 'senior authorising officer'.[79]

---

[71] The Regulation of Investigatory Powers (Directed Surveillance and Covert Human Intelligence Sources) Order 2010 (SI No 521). A copy of the standard application form is available at <https://www.gov.uk/government/collections/ripa-forms--2>.

[72] CSPI Code, above, n 54, Chapter 3.

[73] RIPA, s 26(3)(a).

[74] Defined ibid, s 48(1). See *Walters* [2004] EWCA Crim 987, para 56, where the court noted that a space that afforded a person a certain degree of privacy was an irrelevant consideration in a determination of whether the space was 'residential premises'.

[75] CSPI Code, above, n 54, paras 6.9–6.10.

[76] RIPA, s 26(3)(b).

[77] ibid, s 48(1).

[78] ibid, s 32(3).

[79] ibid, s 32.

Where such an authorization has been given by a relevant officer from the police, NCA, Revenue and Customs, immigration, or the Competition and Markets Authority, then it will ordinarily not become effective without the prior approval of an ordinary Surveillance Commissioner.[80]

Interference with property

Sometimes in the course of a covert surveillance operation concerning a cybercriminal, **4.65** particularly in a case of intrusive surveillance, it will be necessary for the investigating agency to interfere directly with a person's property, either the suspect or a related third party. The classic example is the installation of a 'bugging' device in a person's phone; although in the current environment it would seem more likely that an agency may install some form of malware application on a suspect's computer, such as a 'Trojan horse' virus. In 2001, the Federal Bureau of Investigation (FBI) in the United States publicly confirmed that it was developing a technology, codenamed 'Magic Lantern', which could be installed remotely on a suspect's system, using a Trojan horse-style delivery mechanism.[81] Following the Snowden revelations, we now know that the US National Security Agency has an Office for Tailored Access Operations, whose staff are tasked with breaking into information systems, which presumably includes the use of tools such as 'Magic Lantern'.[82]

Such techniques may be used to listen in to voice conversations, record the use of messaging **4.66** applications, from emails to chat sessions, or to capture passwords to enable access to protected data.[83] In a US case, *Scarfo*,[84] for example, the FBI implemented a 'keylogger system' on the suspect's personal computer to obtain access to the password required to access data held in an encrypted form using the program PGP (Pretty Good Privacy).

Such interference may obviously often involve trespass onto a person's private property, may **4.67** involve the commission of criminal damage, or unauthorized access to, and modification of, the contents of a computer. The interference may be inadvertent, in the course of installing the device, or deliberate, such as circumventing technical protection mechanisms or concealing the fact of the system intrusion.[85] Such actions could expose the investigating agency to the risk of both a tortious claim and prosecution, unless the agency was acting under some form of authorization, or granted a statutory defence or immunity from prosecution. Under UK copyright law, for example, the use of circumvention devices or services to overcome copy-protection mechanisms has been rendered lawful when done by, or on behalf of, LEAs for the purpose of preventing or detecting crime.[86] The Computer Misuse Act 1990 (CMA) has been amended to enable an 'enforcement officer' to obtain

---

[80] ibid, s 36. There are also obligations to notify the Surveillance Commissioners of all grants, renewals, or cancellations of an authorization, ibid, s 35. See the Regulation of Investigatory Powers (Notification of Authorisations etc) Order 2000 (SI No 2563); see generally <http://www.surveillancecommissioners.gov.uk/>.

[81] 'FBI confirms "Magic Lantern" project exists', *Reuters*, 12 December 2001.

[82] See 'Inside TAO: Documents reveal top NSA hacking unit', *Der Spiegel*, 29 December 2013, available at <http://spon.de/ad6W5>.

[83] See further paras 4.291–4.300.

[84] *United States v Scarfo*, 180 F Supp 2d 572 (DNJ 2001).

[85] In Australia, a warrant may be granted to the intelligence services authorizing, where access to a computer is involved, 'any thing reasonably necessary to conceal the fact that any thing has been done under the warrant' (Australian Security Intelligence Organisation Act 1979 (Cth), s 25A).

[86] Copyright, Designs and Patents Act 1988, s 296ZB(3).

unauthorized access to a computer or carry out an unauthorized act without committing an offence.[87] Any interference can, however, obviously also undermine the evidential value of any forensic product, unless such actions can be fully accounted for.[88]

4.68 As an interference with the rights of the suspect, or third party, it is also necessary to place such interference on a statutory footing to protect those being investigated and in order to comply with the requirements of the ECHR. As well as surveillance activity requiring authorization under the RIPA, any interference with property will therefore also require authorization under the Intelligence Services Act 1994[89] or Part III of the Police Act 1997[90] to render such actions lawful.

4.69 Under the Police Act, such authorization should only be granted where it involves the prevention or detection of a serious crime, which is defined in the following terms:

(a) it involves the use of violence, results in substantial financial gain or is conduct by a large number of persons in pursuit of a common purpose, or
(b) the offence or one of the offences is an offence for which a person who has attained the age of twenty-one and has no previous convictions could reasonably be expected to be sentenced to imprisonment for a term of three years or more.[91]

Such surveillance techniques would not therefore be available for use in the investigation of a number of the offences examined in Chapter 3, especially an act of unauthorized access under the Computer Misuse Act 1990.

4.70 Under the Police Act, an 'authorising officer', generally at chief constable level or above,[92] may authorize the taking of any action that he specifies, which is an extremely broad formulation.[93] That action may include the maintenance or retrieval of any equipment, device, or apparatus that has been authorized under Part II of the RIPA.[94] However, where the property concerned is a home, hotel bedroom, or office, or the information likely to be obtained is subject to legal privilege, confidential personal information, or confidential journalistic information,[95] then the authorization must have the prior approval of the independent Surveillance Commissioner, unless it is an urgent matter.[96]

4.71 Neither the Police Act, nor the Intelligence Services Act, defines what constitutes 'property' for which interference may be authorized, although it is required to be specified in an application for authorization.[97] This creates inevitable uncertainty in respect of intangible

---

[87] CMA, s 10. See further paras 3.257 and 5.68.

[88] See generally Chapter 6.

[89] ISA, s 5. Note that under the IPB, the Government proposes to establish distinct warranty regimes for 'equipment interference' and 'bulk equipment interference'.

[90] PA, s 93. In *SL* [2001] EWCA Crim 1829, the court examined the compatibility of Part III of the PA with the ECHR, rejecting an assertion that the Act is not compliant.

[91] PA, s 93(4).

[92] ibid, s 93(5); although the Director General of the National Crime Agency may designate any member of his staff as an 'authorising officer' (ibid, s 93(5)(f)).

[93] ibid, s 93(1)(a). See also Ashworth, A, Macdonald, A, and Emmerson, B, *Human Rights and Criminal Justice*, 3rd edn, Sweet & Maxwell, 2012, Chapter 6.

[94] PA, s 93(1A).

[95] Defined at PA, ss 98, 99(1), and 100(1), respectively.

[96] ibid, s 97. The position of the Commissioner is established under s 91.

[97] CSPI Code, above, n 54, para 7.18.

property, such as computer data; particularly bearing in mind the decision in *Oxford v Moss* and the exclusion of modifications to such data from the Criminal Damage Act 1971.[98] In addition, both Acts expressly extend the authorization scheme to include interference with 'wireless telegraphy',[99] which may be the intangible medium over which data is transmitted in a wireless network.

While 'interference' is not defined in respect of property, it is in respect of 'wireless telegraphy', being taken from the Wireless Telegraphy Act 2006 (WTA): **4.72**

> . . . if the fulfilment of the purposes of the telegraphy is prejudiced . . . by an emission or reflection of electromagnetic energy.[100]

On this basis, the use of a surveillance device to monitor emissions from a wireless network may not be considered to 'interfere', since it may not be considered to be prejudicing the emission, even though it would still constitute a form of interception governed by Part I of the RIPA or the WTA, s 48.[101] Further, the installation of a logical surveillance device on to a suspect's computer, via the computer's wireless port, could also be seen as falling outside the regimes established under the 1994 and 1997 Acts. As such, this seems like another example of the criminal law failing to reflect the possibilities created by developments in ICTs.

Covert human intelligence source

A 'covert human intelligence source' (CHIS) may be a law enforcement person, such as an **4.73** undercover officer or, more commonly, a private person who is either a perpetrator themselves or is in some manner associated with one or more of the perpetrators of a criminal activity, turned informant. The key characteristics are that the activity is covert and that 'a personal or other relationship' exists between the CHIS and the person, or persons, about whom he is providing information.[102] In a cybercrime context, an example of the use of a CHIS would be the participation of an agent or informer in a network for the exchange of malware or illegal content.[103] Alternatively, a disaffected member of a hacking group could become an informer.

The use of a CHIS is subject to a distinct authorization procedure and may only be granted **4.74** by specified authorizing officers.[104] An authorization should only be granted where necessary for the purposes of national security; the prevention and detection of crime or disorder; the economic well-being of the United Kingdom; public safety; public health; revenue related; or as specified by the Secretary of State[105] Once granted, an authorization lasts for a minimum twelve-month period, unless renewed, which is four times the duration of the other types of authorization,[106] reflecting the longer term nature of CHIS activity.

---

[98] See paras 3.45 and 3.283 respectively.

[99] PA, s 92 and ISA, s 5(1).

[100] Wireless Telegraphy Act 2006 (WTA), s 115(3).

[101] In *E* (2004) 2 Cr App R 484, the court held that 'the expression "interception" denotes some interference or abstraction of the signal' (para 20), which would clearly encompass the monitoring of emissions from a wireless network.

[102] RIPA, s 26(8).

[103] The 'Drink or Die' warez piracy group was exposed by an informant (see para 3.107).

[104] The Regulation of Investigatory Powers (Directed Surveillance and Covert Human Intelligence Sources) Order 2010 (SI No 521).

[105] RIPA, s 29(3).

[106] See Home Office, *Covert Human Intelligence Sources: Code of Practice*, December 2014, para 5.14 ('CHIS Code').

4.75 The Home Office Code of Practice on the use of a CHIS contains additional controls where the CHIS is expected to obtain confidential information, in the form of legally privileged material and confidential personal or journalistic material.[107] Similar controls are applicable to the use of juvenile sources, under the age of eighteen,[108] which could be expected to be a more common scenario in a cyberspace environment, where the age profile of users is low and their capacity to engage in criminal conduct is high.[109] In such circumstances, the authorizing officer must be of a higher rank or position within the authority,[110] and, where juveniles are involved, the authorization only lasts for a month.[111]

4.76 As well as the person who authorizes the use of a CHIS, the authority will also be required to designate a person who has responsibility for dealing with the CHIS on a regular basis, generally determining the tasks that the CHIS is asked to carry out, and a different person who will exercise an oversight role.[112] Where the tasks being undertaken begin to differ in nature from that for which authorization was originally obtained, a new authorization may need to be sought; for example, changing from operating a P2P node exchanging file requests to obtaining illegal material as a test purchase.[113]

4.77 The nature of the relationship that a CHIS often has with the perpetrators of the criminal conduct means that such activities may often result in the commission of an offence by the CHIS, directly as an accessory or indirectly through encouragement, as well as the possibility that the case may be thrown out by a court for abuse of process on the grounds of entrapment. However, the RIPA renders certain conduct lawful 'for all purposes', for example where otherwise it would be unlawful under civil or criminal law, if it has been authorized and the conduct is in accordance with, or is incidental to, that authorization.[114] In addition, where an informant is involved, the Serious and Organised Crime and Police Act 2005 provides for the possibility of an offender being offered immunity from prosecution and/or other benefits.[115]

Monitoring and filtering

4.78 Monitoring and filtering the traffic that is received via, or submitted to, the Internet is a common security measure taken to address cyberspace-based criminality, as well as a wide range of other risks and vulnerabilities. It may be carried out at a network level or at the edges of a network, such as on an individual's personal computer. While a form of surveillance, it differs from the types discussed above in two key respects. First, rather than being targeted at a specific suspect under investigation, monitoring and filtering is targeted at types of undesirable content without reference, generally, to a specific person or investigation. Second, such surveillance will often be transparent, rather than covert, since the object may be as much to deter the sending of particular types of

---

[107] ibid, Chapter 4.

[108] ibid, para 4.24. See also the Regulation of Investigatory Powers (Juveniles) Order 2000 (SI No 2793).

[109] See Smith, R, Grabosky, P, and Urbas, G, *Cyber Criminals on Trial*, Cambridge University Press, 2004, at 44–5.

[110] CHIS Code, above, n 106, Annex A.

[111] SI 2000/2793, at 6.

[112] RIPA, s 29(5)(a) and (b) respectively.

[113] CHIS Code, above, n 106, para 6.2.

[114] RIPA, ss 26(7), (8), and 27(1).

[115] Serious and Organised Crime and Police Act 2005 (SOCPA), Pt 2, Chapter 2, ss 71 et seq.

communications, as to prevent their receipt. In some cases, such transparency is mandated by law.[116] Obviously, as revealed by Snowden, where bulk surveillance is carried out by the state, the degree of transparency and accountability will clearly be a controversial issue itself.[117]

Different terms of art are used in relation to monitoring and filtering technologies, but the **4.79** term 'firewall' is widely recognized as encompassing hardware and/or software devices that monitor and prevent communications between different networks, or parts of a network.[118] Within a network, a firewall may operate at different layers. At the network layer, packet filtering may operate to prevent packets being sent or received based on their source or destination address, or the port[119] being used. Application level firewalls generally operate on proxy servers[120] and interrogate the actual content of the traffic.

Monitoring and filtering may be carried out by a number of different entities or persons. **4.80** At a regime or state level, it may be used as a repressive measure designed to curb content considered undesirable on political, religious, or national security grounds. Monitoring and filtering will be carried out by a CSP providing access to the Internet and related services, both for purposes of self-protection from potential liability or loss, as well as part of a service to its customers. An individual user or subscriber who controls the access offered to individual users, such as a company or parent, may also engage in monitoring and filtering.

As the Internet has matured as a communications environment, and the technology **4.81** improved, we have seen an increase in the use of content filtering as a security and crime prevention measure. Governments in particular are enthusiastic proponents of filtering as a tool to support their regulatory response to public concerns about the 'dark side' of cyberspace. In the area of child abuse images, for example, the Internet Watch Foundation (IWF)[121] has created a database of URLs to sites containing illegal images, which has been used as the basis for network level filtering by CSPs such as BT, with its 'CleanFeed' initiative.[122] However, filtering is still very much an inexact science and technology, blocking material that should not be, while permitting undesirable material through, vulnerable to attack and exploitation,[123] as well as being effective in certain online environments, such as the web and email, but not in others, such as P2P networks and message forums.

---

[116] eg the Telecommunications (Lawful Business Practice) (Interception of Communications) Regulations 2000 (SI No 2699), s 3(2)(c) ('Telecommunications Regulations 2000').

[117] See ISC Report 2015, above, n 2; Independent Reviewer Report, above, n 2; RUSI Report, above, n 2.

[118] See generally 'Firewall (computing)', Wikipedia, available at <https://en.wikipedia.org/wiki/Firewall_(computing)>.

[119] A network port is a number recognized by the transmission control protocol (TCP) and user datagram protocol (UDP) protocols to map incoming data to particular processes operating on a computer. Port 80 is the standard for web-based connections. Ibid.

[120] A proxy server sits between networks, providing an indirect connection, and supplying various services, from filtering to the caching of data. Ibid.

[121] See <http://www.iwf.org.uk>.

[122] See <https://wiki.openrightsgroup.org/wiki/Cleanfeed>. See also Cybercrime Convention Committee, *Strengthening Co-operation between Law Enforcement and the Private Sector—Examples of how the Private Sector has Blocked Child Pornographic Sites*, T-CY (2006) 04, 20 February 2006, available at <http://www.coe.int/t/dg1/legalcooperation/economiccrime/cybercrime/T-CY/T-CY_2006_04-e-child pronographic sites_en.pdf>.

[123] Clayton, above, n 32, Chapter 7. He shows how the 'Cleanfeed' system could be manipulated to become an 'oracle', enabling lists of undesirable sites to be extracted.

4.82 The following sections consider monitoring and filtering instigated by different actors, the state, CSPs, and by users. For the state and users, the primary motivation is likely to be security, however broadly conceived; while for CSPs, monitoring will be driven by a broader range of commercial considerations. First, however, it is necessary to consider the legal treatment of such activities.

Legal treatment

4.83 In terms of cyber-surveillance, monitoring and filtering generate a number of questions, of which four are central to our analysis of the legal nature of such activities:

- Who carries it out?
- For what purpose?
- What methodology is used?
- At what point is the filtering carried out?

The first question concerns whether the activity is carried out by or with the involvement of public law enforcement agencies. The outcome of any legal analysis depends significantly on whether the monitoring and filtering is being carried out by a public and private sector person. As discussed above, for example, the regulatory regime under the RIPA is only applicable where the participation of public authorities takes place.

4.84 For public sector entities, the purpose of the monitoring relates to the legality of the conduct, since such conduct is only permissible under limited circumstances.[124] While for all entities, filtering may involve the processing of personal data of the user and therefore only processing for 'one or more specified and lawful purposes' is a requirement under data protection law, as well as purpose restrictions under applicable laws.[125]

4.85 In terms of methodology, a distinction must be made between techniques based on monitoring the content of a transmission, as opposed to monitoring the related traffic data. 'Packet filtering' is a term often used to describe the latter situation, where packets in transmission are either passed or dropped according to a set of criteria, such as the source or destination IP address. Such techniques should not constitute 'interception' as defined under the RIPA, since the content of the transmission is not subject to the monitoring activity. However, such filtering could constitute a form of surveillance under Part II of the RIPA and also raises privacy concerns, for example, where a network operator engages in packet filtering in order to block a particular type of service being used over its network, such voice over Internet Protocol (VoIP). While the content is not being directly monitored, in the sense that the substance of the communication is being scrutinized, the person is being prohibited from engaging in a particular form of communication activity.

4.86 As discussed in detail in Chapter 3, 'interception' is defined by reference to the system or network over which the transmission is carried. Once the communication leaves the network, its subsequent treatment, such as eavesdropping, is not considered a form of interception. Therefore, the implementation of filtering software by parents on a home computer to govern what content their children may access is not a form of interception subject to

---

[124] eg national security or serious crime.
[125] ie Data Protection Act 1998, Sch I, Pt I, Principle 2. See also the Lawful Business Practice Regulations 2000, outlined below at paras 4.98–4.99.

the RIPA. Second, the RIPA establishes an important distinction between a 'public' and 'private' telecommunication system. Where the interception occurs on a private telecommunications system, and it is initiated by, or with the consent of, the 'system controller',[126] then it is not criminal in nature.

A question that naturally flows out of the analysis proposed above, which is partly legal in nature, concerns what action is taken in response to any material that may have been 'captured' through the filtering exercise or meta-data generated by the filtering application, such as traffic data. In the former scenario, the material may evidence illegality or be illegal itself. The recipient may therefore be under an obligation to report and remove it, as is the case with child abuse images in some jurisdictions,[127] and/or continued possession may attract liability.[128] With filtering meta-data, the recipient may want to trace the sender, in the course of a civil or criminal investigation, or may choose to take some form of direct action against the purported source or report it for others to act upon. These issues are beyond the scope of our current discussion, however, but are considered elsewhere in the book.   **4.87**

State-instigated

As noted above, the state may engage in large-scale non-targeted monitoring of communications traffic for a range of purposes, many of which can be loosely grouped under the heading 'national security'. While countries such as China and Saudi Arabia may be notorious for such activities for the purpose of censoring material considered by their governments to be inappropriate and subversive,[129] there are also similar monitoring activities being carried out by the UK and its allies for intelligence purposes, including under an interception system widely referred to as 'Echelon'.   **4.88**

Echelon was established after the Second World War to monitor the communications of the former Soviet Union and its allies. Participants in the system are the so-called 'Five Eyes', ie the United States, the United Kingdom, Canada, Australia, and New Zealand.[130] Following the end of the Cold War, it has continued to operate as a tool for investigating criminal and terrorist activities, although claims have also been made that it has been used for more political or economic purposes, such as industrial espionage. In 2001, the Echelon system was subjected to an investigation by a temporary committee of the European Parliament,[131] and formed the basis of a Parliamentary Resolution condemning the system.[132] Following the Snowden revelations, further details about this particular monitoring system, as well as numerous others, have become public.[133]   **4.89**

---

[126] See paras 3.328–3.330.

[127] eg 42 USCs 13032 ('Reporting of child pornography by electronic communications service providers').

[128] eg Criminal Justice Act 1988, s 160.

[129] See generally the OpenNet case studies on Internet filtering in various countries: available at <http://www.opennetinitiative.net/>. See also Reporters Without Borders, *Annual Report 2006*, at 107–34, available at <http://www.rsf.org/IMG/pdf/report.pdf>.

[130] See Keefe, P, *Chatter: Dispatches from the Secret World of Global Eavesdropping*, Random House, 2005.

[131] European Parliament, Report on the existence of a global system for the interception of private and commercial communications (ECHELON interception system), 2001/2098(INI), 11 July 2001, available at <http://www.europarl.europa.eu/sides/getDoc.do?pubRef=-//EP//TEXT+REPORT+A5-2001-0264+0+DOC+XML+V0//EN>.

[132] Resolution of 5 September 2001 on the existence of a global system for the interception of private and commercial communications (ECHELON interception system), OJ C 72E/221, 21 March 2002 ('Echelon Resolution').

[133] Campbell, D, 'GCHQ and me: My life unmasking British eavesdroppers', The Intercept blog, 3 August 2015, available at <https://theintercept.com/2015/08/03/life-unmasking-british-eavesdroppers/>.

4.90   In terms of legality, large-scale interception of UK residents by the state is subject to a distinct regulatory regime.[134] It has been alleged that such rules are circumvented by national agencies using the system to intercept foreign communications and transferring any intelligence back to the domestic agency, so-called 'solicited intercept'.[135] However, such procedures should not prevent the system from being held to be incompatible with the ECHR.[136]

4.91   It is beyond the scope of this book to examine in detail the Echelon system and other monitoring activities carried out on national security grounds. It is important, however, to acknowledge that such practices exist and form part of the state's response to the growth of criminality in cyberspace.

4.92   While monitoring schemes such as Echelon are composed largely of state-owned and operated listening stations, it must also be true that such systems are dependent on communications traffic being sent to and from such facilities over network capacity provided by the major CSPs. Such dependency raises a broader point about the role of CSPs in state-instigated monitoring. In countries such as China, the major CSPs are often seen as simply an arm of the state, tasked to support and implement state policies concerning the monitoring and filtering of cyberspace. In the Western democracies, however, you have largely privately owned operators, providing services to governments, as to any end-user, on an arm's-length commercial basis. This, of course, is an idealized picture that ignores the on-going informal cooperation that tends to exist between governments and the major national network CSPs, particularly the ex-incumbent operators, such as BT, France Telecom, and Deutsche Telekom. An illustration of this relationship is the exposure of the role that AT&T played in the large-scale monitoring of the communications of US citizens by the National Security Agency.[137]

4.93   However, while governments may use CSPs covertly to support monitoring on national security grounds, they also publicly look to CSPs to support other government policies concerning cyberspace activities. A key ground upon which some governments have justified the instigation of large-scale monitoring by CSPs and others is that of child protection. In the US, for example, there have been a number of attempts to control the availability of material considered harmful to children. While legislative attempts to criminalize the supply of such material have been struck down or enjoined by the Supreme Court, as unduly restricting protected speech under the First Amendment,[138] the imposition of filtering obligations on federal-funded schools and libraries, under the Children's Internet Protection Act of 2000,[139] has been upheld by the Supreme Court.[140] In addition, some US ISPs have

---

[134] See paras 4.167–4.178.

[135] See *Liberty and others v GCHQ and others* [2014] UKIPTrib 13_77-H.

[136] Echelon Resolution, above, n 132, Arts H–K.

[137] eg Agwin, J et al, 'AT&T helped U.S. spy on Internet on a vast scale', *New York Times*, 16 August 2015, available at <www.nytimes.com/2015/08/16/us/politics/att-helped-nsa-spy-on-an-array-of-internet-traffic.html>. See also the documents made available by the Electronic Frontier Foundation (EFF) concerning multi-district litigation against the NSA, at <http://www.eff.org/legal/cases/att/>.

[138] See *Reno v ACLU*, 521 US 844, 117 S Ct 2329 (1997) (in respect of the Communications Decency Act) and *Ashcroft v ACLU*, 535 US 564, 122 S Ct 1700 (2004) (in respect of the Children's Online Protection Act).

[139] 114 Stat 2763A-335, codified at 47 USC s 254 (re: schools and libraries) and 20 USC s 9134 (re: libraries).

[140] *United States and others v American Library Association, Inc and others*, 539 US 194, 123 S Ct 2297 (2003).

chosen to self-regulate in the area, implementing the UK-based IWF list of sites into their search engines, effectively circumventing domestic First Amendment restraints.[141]

In the United Kingdom, while no similar legislative initiatives have yet been taken, a private **4.94** member's bill was introduced into the Commons during the 2005–06 session that would have obliged CSPs to make annual public declarations 'whether or not they have taken, or are taking, appropriate technical steps to block access to websites that contain child pornography'.[142] While the Government failed to support such an approach, the subsequent coalition Government gave strong support to initiatives which encourage monitoring and filtering as a child protection measure, whether at a network level, such as the IWF initiative, or at a user level.[143] In 2006, the Home Office set a target 'that by the end of 2007, all ISPs offering broadband internet connectivity to the UK general public put in place technical measures that prevent their customers accessing websites containing illegal images of child abuse identified by the IWF', which if it is not achieved on a voluntary basis through cooperation with CSPs, may be placed on a mandatory footing.[144] In July 2013, the leading ISPs agreed with the Government to establish a system whereby all subscribers would be asked to choose whether their services allow access to such material, but for those that fail to exercise an option, filters would be activated by default.[145]

As noted in Chapter 3, controlling access to harmful content over the Internet is currently **4.95** a lead priority of the UK Government, whether it is child abuse images, extreme pornography, or terrorist publications. As such, the Government views CSPs as a gateway through which control mechanisms can be applied, protecting the general public from the dark side of the Internet. The Government is inevitably wary about the image created by the mandatory imposition of monitoring and filtering obligations on CSPs, hence the enthusiasm for, and promotion of, industry self-regulatory schemes, such as the IWF. However, from a civil liberties perspective, concerns can be raised about such an approach in terms of transparency and accountability.[146] In addition, at some point, on some issue, the CSPs may simply refuse to voluntarily comply with the policy desires of governments, driven both by benevolent concerns for their customers' rights as well as concerns about exposure to potential liability. An example of such an issue has been the voluntary retention of communications data.[147]

CSP-instigated

While CSPs have to respond to demands from governments and legislators about Internet **4.96** content, as commercial entities they are inevitably also interested in using monitoring and filtering techniques in the course of providing a commercial service. CSPs will be concerned

---

[141] See witness testimony by Yahoo! and Google before the US House of Representatives, Subcommittee on Oversight and Investigations, of the Committee on Energy and Commerce, 27 June 2006.

[142] Control of Internet Access (Child Pornography) Bill, 26 October 2005.

[143] eg Get Safe Online <http://www.getsafeonline.org>.

[144] House of Commons Written Answer from Home Office Minister, Vernon Coaker, Hansard, 15 May 2006, Col 716W.

[145] 'The Internet and pornography: Prime Minister calls for action', Speech by David Cameron, 22 July 2013, available at <https://www.gov.uk/government/speeches/the-internet-and-pornography-prime-minister-calls-for-action>.

[146] See European Digital Rights, 'Euro ISPA warns against BT web block-list', 4 August 2004, available at <https://edri.org/edrigramnumber2-15webblock/>.

[147] See paras 4.228–4.243.

to protect their network and the machines of their customers from a range of undesirable content, from spam to viruses. A CSP may also be pursuing self-interest when filtering to restrict the use of its network for certain types of services, such as Internet telephony, which may be considered as competing with its own service.

4.97 At one level, a CSP may use its ability to control or mediate access to the cyberspace as a marketing tool, in terms of offering customers a protected, walled-garden experience. This has been the approach of operators such as AOL and Disney Mobile. At another level, however, the ability to know your customer, through a more covert monitoring of his communications activities, presents a very powerful tool in terms of tailoring the provision of services to individual customer profiles.

4.98 In Europe, CSP monitoring is subject to data protection laws,[148] while in the UK it is governed under both data protection rules and the RIPA. As noted previously, the applicable rules vary somewhat depending on whether the monitoring and filtering activity is carried out against the content of a communication or data about its attributes. Where control is exercised against the content being communicated, 'interception monitoring', the primary governing instrument is the Lawful Business Practice Regulations (LBPRs).[149] This instrument governs the interception of any telecommunication system, whether public or private, by the 'system controller'. As such, it would be applicable to non-CSPs, such as private business systems, as well as CSPs.

4.99 Under the LBPRs, an interception may be rendered lawful depending on the stated purpose of such filtering. An explicit list of those purposes considered permissible is laid down, which includes the following of relevance in the context of a cybercrime investigation:

- 'for the purpose of preventing or detecting crime', and
- 'for the purpose of investigating or detecting the unauthorised use of that or any other telecommunication system'.[150]

Both of these grounds would seem to potentially legitimize wide-scale network-based filtering for spam, viruses, and other illegal content, as well as the more dubious service restrictive monitoring referred to earlier.

4.100 While the LBPRs authorize interception monitoring, the 'system controller' does have transparency obligations in respect of such monitoring, being required to make 'all reasonable efforts to inform every person who may use the telecommunication system',[151] although consent of the person using the system is not required. Where the monitoring or record-keeping is carried out for one purpose under the LBPRs, the information gleaned cannot be used for another further purpose,[152] which differs from normal data protection

---

[148] See generally Working Party 29 Opinion 2/2006 on privacy issues related to the provision of email screening services, WP 118, 21 February 2006.

[149] The Telecommunications (Lawful Business Practice) (Interception of Communications) Regulations 2000 (SI No 2699) (LBPR), made under the RIPA, s 4(2).

[150] LBPR, above, n 149, reg 3(1)(a)(iii) and (iv) respectively.

[151] ibid, reg 3(2)(c). This obligation is not considered to extend to all parties to a communication, as was originally proposed, but only the users of the particular telecommunication system. See Department for Business Innovation and Skills (DTI), 'Lawful Business Practice—Response to Consultation', Report, available at <http://webarchive.nationalarchives.gov.uk/+/http:/www.dti.gov.uk/industries/ecommunications/lawful_business_practice_regulations__response_to_consultation.html>.

[152] RIPA, s 3(2)(a).

rules that permit processing for further purposes that are not incompatible with the original purpose. Under data protection law, CSPs are also required to be transparent in respect of such monitoring activities, however obliquely, through contractual reference in respect of its subscriber, and through notice for its non-subscriber users.[153]

One potential adverse consequence of engaging in filtering at a network level is that it potentially renders a CSP liable for the content it blocks, since the act of filtering may be said to give the CSP knowledge about the illegal nature of the communication, which could be sufficient to incur liability.[154]   **4.101**

User-instigated

Users will be concerned to monitor cyberspace activities for a variety of motivations. A business will want to protect its systems from external threats, such as unauthorized intrusions, and internal threats, whether malicious or inadvertent but both exposing the business to loss and liability. A domestic user will want to protect his home devices and, as a parent, may control the access and use that his children have. Monitoring and filtering are therefore one element of a spectrum of preventative security measures taken in response to the increased incidence of cybercrime.   **4.102**

Users may, however, engage in more proactive cyber-surveillance techniques, designed to investigate specific instances of criminal activity, rather than reactive protection against general criminality. The following sections examine two such proactive techniques: honeypots and P2P infiltration. The former is a locational tool, designed to attract cybercriminals to utilize a particular online resource. The latter is a relational tool, similar in kind to the use of covert intelligence sources, where the investigator participates in the network of communicating parties. Both techniques raise the same questions in respect of their legal treatment under the RIPA regime.   **4.103**

Honeypots A 'honeypot', or deception host, is a designated area within a computer network that has been designed specifically with the expectation that it will be attacked by unauthorized users, whether internal or external to the organization.[155] The functions of a honeypot may vary. It can serve as a decoy to deflect hackers from breaking into the real system, as a research tool for systems administrators merely to observe and learn how hackers operate and about weaknesses in their systems, or to monitor communications in a criminal investigation.   **4.104**

The term 'honeypot' has also been used to describe decoy websites established to attract those seeking out child abuse images. 'Operation PIN', an initiative of the Virtual Global Taskforce launched in December 2003, comprised a series of websites that purportedly offered such illegal images. Visitors to the site who attempted to download images were informed that the site was operated by LEAs and that their details had been captured and passed on to the appropriate national authorities.[156] In July 2006, a man was convicted after sending images to a bogus website established by police from the UK and US, thinking that   **4.105**

---

[153] Under the Data Protection Act 1998 and the Privacy and Electronic Communications (EC Directive) Regulations 2003 (SI No 2426) ('2003 Privacy Regulations').
[154] See further paras 2.226 et seq.
[155] See Spitzner, L, *Honeypots: Tracking Hackers*, Addison-Wesley, 2002.
[156] See Virtual Global Taskforce, 'What we do', available at <http://217.64.233.220/what_we_do.asp>.

he had found people with similar interests.[157] For the purposes of this section, however, we are concerned with the former type of honeypot, designed to deceive hackers.

4.106 An intruder may use the honeypot for the storage of data or programs, such as viruses or pornographic images, or the traffic may comprise communications between various parties. Once the attacker has gained entrance to the honeypot, it is hoped that the organization will be able to gather additional information about the identity of the attacker and his activities.[158] For example, an individual may be intending to use the network as a platform from which to launch a denial-of-service (DOS) attack against another system. Trying to secure a network against such unauthorized access may clearly be the sole objective of an organization. However, simply preventing the attacker from entering the network will not, necessarily, generate sufficient evidence to take legal action against the attacker and, second, will not provide any information about the nature of the activities that the attacker was intending to engage in once the network had been compromised.

4.107 As a surveillance technique, a first question to be addressed is whether a honeypot may be considered a form of 'interception monitoring', subject to Part I, Chapter 1 of the RIPA. As discussed previously, 'interception' only takes place where a 'communication' is 'in the course of its transmission'. Once the communication has reached the intended recipient, any subsequent monitoring is no longer considered interception, although it would be surveillance.[159] The question of when a communication is 'in the course of its transmission' has interesting implications in the context of honeypots.

4.108 Activities within a honeypot can be broadly divided into two categories:

- accessing the network for the purpose of further intrusion into the systems associated with the network; or
- accessing the network to utilize the resources for the perpetrator's own purposes, such as data storage, execution of programs, communications with others, etc.

4.109 In the first scenario, the transmissions initiated by the perpetrator to interrogate or 'crack' the network are clearly 'communications' as defined under the RIPA:

> (b) anything comprising speech, music, sounds, visual images or data of any description; and
> (c) signals serving either for the impartation of anything between persons, between a person and a thing or between things or for the actuation or control of any apparatus.[160]

However, data recorded by the network components that have been the subject of the interrogation, such as password attempts, are not 'communications in the course of transmission' since the component, or 'thing' in the context of the definition above, is the intended recipient.

4.110 In the second scenario, a further distinction must be made. Where data is placed on the honeypot network for later retrieval by the user himself, does this constitute a 'communication'? Such an act would not be strictly 'between' persons or things, unless

---

[157] See 'Man sent child porn to police', *IC Croydon*, 11 July 2006.
[158] See generally Walden, I and Flanagan, A, 'Honeypots: A sticky legal landscape', 29(2) *Rutgers Computer and Technology Law Journal* 317 (2003).
[159] Subject to authorization under the RIPA, Pt II.
[160] ibid, s 81(1).

the network itself was considered the 'intended recipient', which would seem unlikely given s 2(7), which envisages intermediate storage. However, people may send messages to themselves for a whole host of reasons, such as reminders or as a security measure. Were such communications to be considered to fall outside the RIPA regime, it would open a considerable lacuna in the protection offered to individuals and would seem to go against the broadly stated objectives of the Government when adopting this legislation.[161] It is presumed, therefore, that communications to oneself do fall within the regime. If the person places a message on the honeypot network for later retrieval by another person, then monitoring such messages must be considered interception subject to the Act.[162]

If the activity is interception, to what extent may it be considered lawful, under the RIPA?[163] **4.111**
If the honeypot is operated within a 'private telecommunication system', which would seem likely, the critical issue is whether the person 'having the right to control the operation or the use'[164] of the system is either the party carrying out the interception or has consented to the interception. The general position under the Act is that such an interception is actionable as a statutory tort.[165] However, regulations have been adopted pursuant to the Act that render the interception of communications over telecommunication systems lawful to the extent that they are considered:

> [A] legitimate practice reasonably required for the purpose, in connection with the carrying on of any business, of monitoring or keeping a record of—
> (a) communications by means of which transactions are entered into in the course of that business; or
> (b) other communications relating to that business or taking place in the course of its being carried on.[166]

Such practices have been further elaborated in the LBPR, which detail a broad range of applicable purposes. Those most applicable to monitoring in the course of operating a honeypot are '(iii) for the purpose of preventing or detecting crime, or (iv) for the purpose of investigating or detecting the unauthorised use of that or any other telecommunication system'.[167]

However, if a public law enforcement agency were to intercept communications in the **4.112**
course of operating a honeypot, either on a 'private telecommunication system' with the consent of the 'system controller'[168] or on a 'public telecommunication system', then the agency will need to seek an 'interception warrant'. Under US law, as amended in 2001, such 'participant monitoring' has been specifically rendered a lawful form of intercept, where the owner or operator of a computer has been subject to an unauthorized access by a 'computer

---

[161] See Home Office, *Interception of Communications in the United Kingdom*, Consultation Paper, Cm 4368, June 1999, para 4.5.
[162] RIPA, s 2(7).
[163] ibid, s 1(5).
[164] ibid, s 3(3).
[165] ibid, s 1(3).
[166] ibid, s 4(2). A business includes 'any activities of a government department, of any public authority or of any person or office holder on whom functions are conferred by or under any enactment' (ibid, s 4(7)).
[167] Telecommunications Regulations 2000, above, n 116, reg 3(1)(a).
[168] ibid, reg 2(d).

trespasser' and authorizes investigators, 'lawfully engaged in an investigation', to intercept the contents of the communications sent or received by the trespasser.[169]

4.113 Where the honeypot has been established by, in cooperation with, or at the instigation of public law enforcement agencies, there is also the possibility that it could be characterized as a form of 'entrapment'. A finding of entrapment may either prevent legal proceedings from being pursued or fatally undermine the success of a prosecution. As a legal concept, entrapment and its treatment under abuse of process jurisdiction concerns the involvement of public law enforcement authorities and their agents in the inducement or commission of a crime.[170]

4.114 **P2P infiltration** P2P networks comprise a significant portion of communications traffic over the Internet, commonly used for transferring content such as audio and video files, but also increasingly other services such as voice telephony. Such networks can be distinguished from traditional models by their reliance on the processing capacity of those at the edges of the network, ie its users, referred to as 'peers' or 'nodes', rather than centralized resources provided by a CSP to its users, operating on the 'client-server' model. A vast number of P2P networks are in existence, using software applications such as KaZaA and BitTorrent, each differing significantly in the way they operate on a continuum reflecting the extent to which centralized resources are utilized in the service.

4.115 P2P networks became notorious during the 'dot.com' boom for their use in the illegal sharing of music files, most famously through the Napster service.[171] In response, the music industry commenced a series of legal actions, around the world, aimed at shutting down similar such services, the most significant perhaps being the US Supreme Court decision in *MGM Studios, Inc v Grokster, Ltd*,[172] as well as pursuing large-scale users, sometimes through civil proceedings[173] and others for criminal copyright infringement.[174]

4.116 The versatility of P2P networks, based around their decentralized structure, and their greater anonymity, has also inevitably attracted criminals, such as paedophiles[175] and terrorists. As with many areas addressed in this book, claims about the scale of criminal activity are sometimes based more on rumour and gossip rather than verifiable empirical data; however, whatever the extent of such activities, P2P networks present an obvious environment for criminality and present investigators with unique issues in terms of cyber-surveillance.

4.117 In a decentralized P2P network, a person 'A' sends a search request to the nearest node, 'B', which will then send it on to other nodes, 'C', 'D', and 'E', with whom 'B' is connected. Once the requested file is found, for example on node E, a direct connection is established between A and E for downloading of the file. In such environment, there is no central

---

[169] 18 USC s 2511(2)(i), as inserted by the USA Patriot Act, s 217.

[170] In the UK, entrapment is viewed as a threat to the integrity of the judicial system (*R v Loosely (Attorney General's Reference No 3 of 2000)* (2001) 4 All ER 897). See paras 6.35–6.48.

[171] See *A & M Records, Inc v* Napster, Inc, 239 F 3d 1004, 1013 (9th Cir 2001).

[172] 545 US, 125 S Ct 2764 (2005).

[173] eg *Polydor Ltd and others v Brown and others* [2005] EWHC 3191 (Ch).

[174] In May 2006, the German authorities charged some 3,500 users of a file sharing network: see 'Police act on German file-sharing', BBC News, 23 May 2006, available at <http://news.bbc.co.uk/2/hi/entertainment/5009224.stm>.

[175] See Fournier, R et al, 'Comparing pedophile activity in different P2P systems', 3 *Social Sciences* 314 (2014).

location that can be monitored, like a bulletin board or FTP server; rather the communication activities of the network participants will be the target of surveillance. However, in contrast to traditional interception, capturing the traffic passing between two nodes will not necessarily capture the full scale of the conspiracy or nature of the content being communicated.

One mechanism for investigating P2P networks, therefore, is for an investigator to infil- **4.118** trate the network, establishing himself as a peer, node, or 'supernode',[176] becoming part of the network, with the specific objective of monitoring communications of illegal content, such as infringing copyright material or pornographic material. Where such participation is carried out by a public LEA, it raises a number of legal issues, such as entrapment, incitement, and the person's status.[177] For a private investigator, the nature of the material being transferred and the investigator's role in its distribution raises obvious issues about illegal behaviour.

However, to what extent may surveillance through participation be characterized as an act **4.119** of interception? A broad range of traffic passes through the numerous computers linked into a P2P network. Such traffic will constitute communications, the monitoring of which may be considered a form of interception, such as a search request for an MP3 music file held on one of the shared directories of the members of the P2P network. However, it could be argued that the person operating the node is an intended recipient of the communication, together with everyone else that is connected to the P2P network, even if they are not the final recipient, ie the person with the MP3 file. An issue for a court to consider is whether 'intention' in this context is considered as meaning the final recipient, rather than the intermediaries in the communications process. Such an interpretation would seem counter to the nature of how P2P networks operate, although it would perhaps be arguable were the sender able to show ignorance of this mode of operation, and therefore a reasonable expectation of privacy.

If such 'participant monitoring' is not considered to avoid the application of the RIPA on **4.120** the basis of 'intended recipient', then similar to 'honeypots', the investigator may still avoid liability due to the characterization of *where* the interception takes place. The investigator operating the node will generally either be utilizing a 'private telecommunication system' or terminal equipment outside of a 'telecommunication system'. In the former scenario, the investigator may avoid criminal liability as the 'system controller',[178] and civil liability if his activities are considered to be for a 'lawful business practice'.[179] In the latter scenario, once the message has left a 'system' it falls outside the regime, as was held in *Hardy*.[180]

This section has considered a range of covert cyber-surveillance techniques and the legal **4.121** framework applicable to their deployment, in the course of both private and public investigations. The next section examines an overlapping but distinct aspect of digital investigations, obtaining intelligence and evidence from CSPs. The topic overlaps with other forms

---

[176] Under the 'FastTrack P2P stack', a 'supernode' is a peer that indexes the IP addresses of peers to whom it is connected and, sometimes, the available files.

[177] eg as a CHIS.

[178] RIPA, s 1(6).

[179] eg 'to establish the existence of facts': Telecommunications Regulations 2000, above, n 116, reg 3(1)(a)(i)(aa).

[180] *Hardy* (2003) 1 Cr App R 494. See further para 3.323.

of cyber-surveillance to the extent that such activities are generally carried out covertly, prior to a suspect being apprehended. However, assistance may also be sought from CSPs post-arrest, in the course of further evidence gathering. A second reason for distinguishing CSP-sourced surveillance from other forms is that a unique legal and regulatory framework has been established to govern such law enforcement activities.

D. CSP-derived Data

4.122 As well as data obtained from the suspect and the victim, in a cybercrime environment a very significant source of evidence will be obtained from the intermediaries providing the communication services used by perpetrators in the course of their conduct (CSPs). Such evidence may comprise the content of a communication ('content data'), such as a list of passwords; the attributes of a communication session, such as the duration of a call or the location of the caller ('communications data'); and subscriber data, such as the person's billing address and credit card details. Some such data may be considered as being 'at rest', in the sense that it is stored by the CSP in the course of the provision of its services; other data will be available 'in transmission' across or through the communication networks, through a process generally referred to as interception.[181] The value of CSP-derived data is such that obtaining access is subject to a distinct regulatory framework.

4.123 One dominant feature of the modern communications environment is the proliferation of CSPs utilizing alternative access and core network technologies, both wireline and wireless. As a consequence, it can be assumed that most data will be transmitted across a number of different networks owned and/or operated by different legal entities. As such, relevant evidence may need to be obtained from various CSPs involved in a communication's transmission.

4.124 In a traditional voice telephony environment, the general principle was that an interception would be carried out as physically close to the suspect as possible, which usually meant at a 'local loop'[182] or exchange level. In the current communications environment, the principle is no longer necessarily applicable as the proliferation of 'intermediary service providers'[183] within the network hierarchy structure, as well as alternative network structures from traditional Public Switched Telephone Network (PSTN) to IP-based, presents a range of alternative points of interception, particularly in respect of certain types of communications, such as a web-based email service and cached web pages. However, whatever the form of network, the availability of evidence for an investigation is predicated on the CSP having the technical capability to obtain and preserve the requested data, as well as a legal obligation to obtain, retain, and deliver-up such data to the requesting LEA.

Communication services

4.125 As noted above, the critical role that CSPs can have in the provision of forensic material in cybercrime investigations has resulted in the development of a distinct regulatory

---

181 In the US, it is commonly known as 'wiretap'.

182 The wire between the subscriber and the CSPs local exchange.

183 See Directive 2000/31/EC on certain legal aspects of information society services, in particular electronic commerce, in the Internal Market, OJ L 178/1, 17 July 2000, Recital 45 and s 4.

framework governing the obtaining of such data. The need for such a regime was also inextricably linked to the seismic changes that have occurred in the communications industry over the past thirty years as a consequence of market liberalization and technological developments. In an environment where there was a single (usually) state-owned provider of telecommunication services, the relationship between that entity and LEAs was often close and opaque in nature. With liberalization and the development of mobile telephony and the Internet, there has been a vast influx of private sector suppliers into the market, both domestic and foreign, from a broad spectrum of backgrounds. As a consequence, from an investigative perspective, there was a need to put in place a clear set of rules governing LEA–CSP relationships in the new industry to ensure that the necessary procedures and practices are in place to enable access to CSP data. In addition, such rules were also necessary to protect the rights of users of such communications services, especially concerning privacy.

As with any regulatory framework, an initial issue is the scope of coverage, ie what con- **4.126**
stitutes a regulated communications service and who are subject to the data obligations?
Given the rapidly changing nature of communications technologies, addressing these questions can be inevitably fraught and controversial.

A substantial component of the Cybercrime Convention deals with LEA–CSP relations. **4.127**
Under Art 1(c) of the Convention, the concept of a 'service provider' is broadly defined:

(i) any public or private entity that provides to users of its service the ability to communicate by means of a computer system, and

(ii) any other entity that processes or stores computer data on behalf of such communication service or users of such service.

The Explanatory Report notes that the relevant service may be provided to the public or **4.128**
on a private basis to a closed user group, such as a multinational corporation.[184] The second
limb extends the scope to encompass those that simply store data, without necessarily providing a communication service; reference is made to 'hosting and caching services', while excluding those that are a 'mere provider of content'.[185] While a broad-brush approach may be inevitable in such an international instrument, national rules need to be more precise.

Under the RIPA, a 'telecommunications service' was defined in the following terms: **4.129**

> any service that consists in the provision of access to, and of facilities for making use of, any telecommunication system (whether or not one provided by the person providing the service).[186]

Understanding the boundaries of this definition has given rise to debate and uncertainty. It would seem arguable, for example, that the phrase should be interpreted in accordance with European telecommunication law, since the relevant provisions were said to be a transposition of a European Directive.[187]

---

[184] Explanatory Report to the Convention on Cybercrime, 23 November 2001, para 26, available at <https://rm.coe.int/CoERMPublicCommonSearchServices/DisplayDCTMContent?documentId=09000 016800cce5b>.
[185] ibid, para 27.
[186] RIPA, s 2(1).
[187] Explanatory Notes to the Regulation of Investigatory Powers Act, para 9 ('RIPA Explanatory Notes'). The provisions in Part I are said to implement Art 5 of Directive 97/66/EC of the European Parliament and of the Council concerning the processing of personal data and the protection of privacy in the telecommunications sector, OJ L 24/1, 30 January 1998, which has since been replaced by Directive 02/58/EC of the

4.130   The terminology used in this Directive is transposed into UK law by the Communications Act 2003. Under this Act, the corresponding term to 'telecommunications service' was an 'electronic communication service', defined as follows:

> a service consisting in, or having as its principal feature, the conveyance by means of an electronic communications network of signals, except in so far as it is a content service.[188]

Adopting this definition as interpretive guidance, a service will only fall within scope if its principal feature is that of conveyance. Where a service simply has communications functionality, enabling it to exchange data with a user, such as a Software as a Service (SaaS) application, that would seem not be sufficient to bring it within the scope of Part I of the RIPA.

4.131   A counter-argument can be made that when interpreting domestic criminal procedure laws, reference to European law is inappropriate given that such laws extend to conduct beyond that subject to European jurisdiction. Such an issue was addressed in a decision in Belgium involving Yahoo!. In this case, a public prosecutor requested the disclosure of certain data from Yahoo! regarding certain fraudulent conduct carried out using Yahoo! webmail accounts, under Art 46bis of the Belgium Criminal Procedure Code. Yahoo! refused to disclose on two grounds: (a) Yahoo! Inc, being based in the US, was not subject to Belgian jurisdiction, and therefore the request should have been made through mutual legal assistance procedures; and (b) the service was not an 'electronic communication service' and therefore not subject to the relevant order. The lower court held that Yahoo! had unlawfully refused to disclose and imposed a €55k fine, with an additional €10k for every day they continued to refuse to comply.[189] On appeal, the court held that Yahoo! was not a 'provider of an electronic communication service' and could not therefore be required to cooperate.[190] The Supreme Court, however, held that the Court of Appeal had been wrong to exempt Yahoo! from the application of the criminal procedure provisions on the basis that the service was not an 'electronic communication service' under the Belgian Electronic Communications Act 2005, as the scope of the concept under criminal law was broader than that under regulatory law.[191] An English court could take a similar approach, holding that the concept being used under the RIPA should be given a broader interpretation to that provided for under the Communications Act 2003. Indeed, the Court of Appeal touched on such matters when interpreting the concept of 'interception' under the RIPA in *Edmondson and others v R*,[192] where it held that the scope of the concept need not be constrained by European Union law, provided that it is not prohibited under such laws.

4.132   In 2014, such uncertainties led the Government to amend the RIPA to further elaborate the definition:

> For the purposes of the definition of 'telecommunications service' in subsection (1), the cases in which a service is to be taken to consist in the provision of access to, and of facilities for making use of, a telecommunication system include any case where a service consists in or

---

European Parliament and of the Council concerning the processing of personal data and the protection of privacy in the electronic communications sector, OJ L 201/37, 31 July 2002, although the relevant provisions are identical.

   [188]   Communications Act 2003, s 32(2).
   [189]   Court of Dendermonde, Not. No DE 20.95.16/08/26, 2 March 2009.
   [190]   Court of Appeal of Ghent of 30 June 2010.
   [191]   Supreme Court, No P.10.1347.N, 18 January 2011.
   [192]   [2013] EWCA Crim 1026.

includes facilitating the creation, management or storage of communications transmitted, or that may be transmitted, by means of such a system.[193]

By redefining the term, the Government has expressly declared its desire to include 'companies who provide internet-based services, such as webmail'.[194] The amendment would also seem to bring it closer to the broad concept of 'service provider' under the Cybercrime Convention.

However, there remains one area of uncertainty with respect to the imposition of an obligation to maintain an intercept capability (discussed below). Section 12(4) states that a person shall not be liable to have an obligation imposed

    by reason only that he provides, or is proposing to provide, to members of the public a telecommunications service the provision of which is or, as the case may be, will be no more than:

    (a) the means by which he provides a service which is not a telecommunications service; or

    (b) necessarily incidental to the provision by him of a service which is not a telecommunications service.

There would seem to be an argument that either option is applicable to many Internet-based services, where the telecommunications component is necessarily incidental. For it to be held otherwise, it would raise serious questions as to how to give effect to this provision in respect of many, if not all, Internet-based services, especially given how broadly the RIPA defines a 'communication', including 'anything comprising speech, music, sounds, visual images or data of any description'.[195]

Intercept capability

Historically, in order to enable law enforcement agencies to intercept communications, the state-owned incumbent operator had obligations to maintain a technical capability to intercept communications, although not generally governed under express statutory provision.[196] Following progressive liberalization of the telecommunications sector from the early 1980s, one on-going issue for policy-makers, presented by the rapidly evolving communications environment, was whether such obligations should be formalized and extended to the expanding range of entities that offer communication services, from VoIP providers to airports offering wireless access, as well as the scope of any such obligation.

Most jurisdictions[197] now explicitly address the issue of intercept capability, although despite harmonization initiatives,[198] significant differences between national regimes exist across a number of issues:

- Should 'intercept capability' be imposed upon all providers of communication services and networks, or only providers of 'public' services and networks?

4.133

4.134

4.135

---

[193] RIPA, s 2(8A), inserted by s 5 of the Data Retention and Investigatory Powers Act 2014 (DRIPA).
[194] RIPA Explanatory Notes, above, n 187, para 71.
[195] RIPA, s 81(1).
[196] See *Interception of Communications*, above, n 161, s 2 'The history of interception'.
[197] eg Germany: Telecommunications Law, para 88; Netherlands: Telecommunications Act 1998, s 13; Australia: Telecommunications Act 1997, Part 15.
[198] Council Resolution of 17 January 1995 on the lawful interception of telecommunications, OJ C 329/1, 4 November 1996, Annex.

- Should an 'intercept capability' be imposed upon providers of communication networks, rather than providers of communication services?
- Should the 'intercept capability' enable law enforcement agencies direct access to the point of intercept, without the involvement of CSP personnel?
- Who should bear the cost of implementing an 'intercept capability'?

4.136 The term 'intercept capability' is traditionally used in reference to the capture of data, content, and associated communications data, 'in transmission'. However, as examined later in this chapter, communications data 'at rest' is also an extremely important forensic source for law enforcement, and CSPs will generally need to establish technical and operational capabilities in respect of the retrieval and delivery of such data upon lawful request. Therefore, for the purposes of this section, 'intercept capability' is used in a broad sense to encompass CSP systems that enable access both to content and communications data, when in transmission and at rest.

4.137 One aspect of the issue of intercept capability is that of industry standards. In Europe, the European Telecommunications Standards Institute (ETSI) has developed technical standards that are designed to address the needs of law enforcement agencies.[199] However, while de jure standards-making bodies, with significant historical governmental participation, have developed so-called 'LI' standards; the de facto standards body for the Internet, the Internet Engineering Task Force (IETF),[200] has in the past expressed itself to be opposed to the introduction of a 'functionality designed to facilitate wiretapping'.[201] These contrasting positions are illustrative of the changing nature of the communications industry and reconciling such attitudes may be a policy issue for the future.

4.138 The Convention on Cybercrime obliges the parties to adopt measures to enable the competent authorities to carry out an interception directly themselves, as well as compel a service provider to do the task.[202] However, this dual obligation was unacceptable to the legal systems of some members, so they need only provide for indirect access through service providers.[203] The obligation upon service providers is limited to their 'existing technical capability', therefore not requiring them 'to acquire or develop new equipment, hire expert support or engage in costly re-configuration of their systems'.[204] It also only applies when infrastructure is located in the territory even if the business is legally established elsewhere.

Scope of duty

4.139 In the United Kingdom, the issue of capability is addressed under the Regulation of Investigatory Powers Act 2000, Part I, Chapter I. Under s 11, a person has a duty to give effect to a warrant if they provide a 'public telecommunication service'[205] to the public in

---

[199] eg 'Lawful Interception (LI); Handover interface for the lawful interception of telecommunications traffic', ETSI TS 101 671 V3.12.1 (2013–10), available at <http://www.etsi.org/deliver/etsi_ts/101600_101699/101671/03.12.01_60/ts_101671v031201p.pdf>.

[200] See <http://www.ietf.org>.

[201] Network Working Group, 'IETF Policy on Wiretapping' (May 2000), available at <ftp://ftp.isi.edu/in-notes/rfc2804.txt>. In 2004, Cisco submitted a draft architecture for 'Lawful Intercept Control' to the Internet Engineering Task Force (IETF), although it has not been taken up.

[202] Convention on Cybercrime, Art 20(1) for communications data, and Art 21(1) for content data.

[203] ibid, Arts 20(2) and 21(2) respectively. See also Explanatory Report to the Convention on Cybercrime, above, n 184, para 224.

[204] Explanatory Report to the Convention on Cybercrime, above, n 184, para 221.

[205] RIPA, s 2(1). See paras 3.318–3.321.

the United Kingdom or where they 'control' a telecommunication system that is located in the UK.[206] In the first scenario, a person may provide a service, although the infrastructure relevant to effecting an interception warrant is located outside the United Kingdom. The territorial trigger in this case is the provision of services to the UK public, rather than the service provider's place of establishment or the use of equipment—an approach that is consistent with existing national, European, and international telecommunications law. In such a case, the obligation would have an extraterritorial effect and may give rise to a conflict with the laws of the jurisdiction where the infrastructure is located.[207] In the second scenario, the obligation is applicable where part of a telecommunication system is located in the UK, such that a CSP established outside the UK would have compliance obligations were it to control a 'system' within the UK, even if it does not provide a public telecommunication service in the UK.[208]

Uncertainties about the extraterritorial reach of the RIPA resulted in a series of amendments in 2014. First, it was expressly stated that an interception warrant could be served on a person 'outside the United Kingdom (and may relate to conduct outside the United Kingdom)'.[209] Second, it was made explicit that a s 12 notice may be served on a person providing 'public telecommunications services' that is located 'outside the United Kingdom (and may be so imposed or given in relation to conduct outside the United Kingdom)'.[210] Third, a request for communications data can be given to a person outside the UK.[211]   **4.140**

The question of what constitutes 'control' over a network, system, or service in a single jurisdiction has also become considerably more complex in a modern communications environment. The rise of Mobile Virtual Network Operators (MVNOs) and Internet telephony are two prominent examples of market and technological developments that create significant problems for law enforcement in terms of the implementation and delivery of an intercept capability. In both cases, law enforcement may address a request for access to data to one CSP only to find that fulfilment of the request can only be met by a third party provider of network infrastructure. Such fulfilment may be governed by contract between the service provider and the network, which may or may not be construed as 'control' from a regulatory perspective. Such a scenario is anticipated under the RIPA, and where a warrant or notice is addressed to one person, ie a CSP, it also authorizes conduct by a third party, which is required in order to comply with the terms of the warrant or notice, without the third party incurring potential liability.[212]   **4.141**

Compliance with a warrant is subject to a defence that the CSP is not required 'to take any steps which it is not reasonably practicable for him to take'.[213] This defence would only   **4.142**

---

[206] RIPA, s 11(4)(b) and (c). In the latter case, it is conceivable that a 'telecommunication system' exists without the person in control being fully aware of its function. For example, a provider may offer hosting or cloud services. The customer, without the provider's knowledge, may utilize the capacity to operate an email/voice server in the provision of an email service to third parties. As such, the server would constitute part of a 'telecommunication system' over which they exercise control.

[207] Unless it is subject to mutual legal assistance procedures.

[208] This is similar to the applicable law provisions under the Data Protection Act 1998, s 5(1)(b).

[209] RIPA, s 2(2A), inserted by the DRIPA, s 4(2).

[210] RIPA, s 12(3A).

[211] ibid, s 22(5A) and (5B).

[212] ibid, ss 5(6)(c) and 11(4) in respect of interception and ss 21(2) and (3) and 22 in respect of communications data.

[213] ibid, s 11(5).

seem to permit technical and organizational considerations, rather than the financial costs involved. If, following negotiations between the requesting agency and the CSP, agreement cannot be reached as to what is 'reasonably practicable', the Secretary of State may enforce through civil proceedings[214] or instigate criminal proceedings against the CSP, as a person 'who knowingly fails' to comply with his duty.[215] It is unlikely, however, that a dispute between a UK-based CSP and the Home Office would ever result in civil or criminal remedies being sought, with both parties keen to avoid any publicity. The default position under RIPA, therefore, is that law enforcement agencies have to take CSPs as they find them. However, this is further qualified by s 12 of the RIPA, which provides for a process whereby the Home Office can impose on a CSP a requirement to establish and maintain a specific 'intercept capability'.

Section 12 notices

4.143 The purpose of s 12 is to ensure that providers of 'public telecommunications services' are able to assist law enforcement agencies in the carrying out of interceptions under a warrant issued by the Secretary of State. The basis for the giving of such assistance is through the implementation and maintenance of an 'interception capability', through which the required activities would be carried out.

4.144 The Secretary of State's powers under s 12 have been detailed in an order, which was adopted following a consultation process and which came into force on 1 August 2002.[216] The Order grants the Secretary of State the power to issue a notice to a specified service provider detailing the measures that the service provider is required to implement in order to establish an interception capability and the timescales within which the requirement must be met.

4.145 The Order expressly excludes two categories of service provider: those that do not intend to provide a public telecommunication service to more than 10,000 persons in the United Kingdom; and those that are only providing such services to the banking and financial services sector.[217] The latter would be applicable, for example, to SWIFT, the international communications network operated as a cooperative by its member banking organizations.[218] This exclusion is likely designed to protect the reputation of the City as a global financial centre, by preventing claims being made that such networks are insecure.

4.146 The Home Office will always discuss the notice with the service provider prior to its issuance, to agree the process by which its terms will be effected.[219] However, if no agreement is reached and a notice is issued, the service provider has an opportunity, within a period of twenty-eight days from the date of the notice, to refer the notice to the Technical Advisory Board (TAB) for consideration.[220] The TAB has the remit to examine only the 'technical

---

[214] ibid, s 11(8).

[215] ibid, s 11(7). See also the Interception of Communications Code of Practice (8 September 2010), para 2.7 <https://www.gov.uk/government/uploads/system/uploads/attachment_data/file/97956/interception-comms-code-practice.pdf> ('Interception Code of Practice'). A revised was adopted in January 2016.

[216] The Regulation of Investigatory Powers (Maintenance of Interception Capability) Order 2002 (SI No 1931).

[217] ibid, reg 2(3).

[218] See <http://www.swift.com>.

[219] Interception Code of Practice, above, n 215, para 2.9.

[220] RIPA, s 13. See also Technical Advisory Board, at <https://www.gov.uk/government/organisations/technical-advisory-board>. The TAB would be retained under the IPB.

requirements and the financial consequences' of the notice and report their conclusions to the Secretary of State.[221] It comprises balanced representation from industry and law enforcement interests.[222] After consideration, the Secretary of State is required to either withdraw the notice or give a further notice, although he is not bound to modify the terms of the initial notice.[223] To date, no referral has been made to the TAB. However, when the Home Office starts looking to bring a wider range of service providers under the regime, one could expect this to change.

Once a notice has been served, a service provider has a statutory duty to comply with the notice. Civil proceedings may be instigated by the Secretary of State to ensure compliance, for example through an order for specific performance.[224] **4.147**

Part II of the Schedule to the Order details those capabilities that are considered reasonable to impose on providers of public telecommunication services: **4.148**

- To be able to implement an interception within one working day of being informed of an appropriately authorized request.
- To be able to obtain, in their entirety, all communications and related communications data[225] and be able to ensure their simultaneous (ie copied in near real time for stream-based services, while emails will need to be forwarded as soon as available within the service provider's infrastructure) transmission to a hand-over point within the service provider's network.
- The intercepted data should be capable of being transmitted in a manner in which they can be unambiguously correlated.
- The hand-over interface should comply with any standards notified to the service provider by the Secretary of State.[226]
- To be able to filter out and supply only the 'traffic data'[227] associated with the warranted telecommunications identifier.
- To enable the removal of any electronic protection applied to the data by the service provider.[228]
- To enable the simultaneous interception of the communications of up to one in 10,000 persons to whom the service provider provides a service.
- To ensure that the reliability of the intercept capability matches that of the public telecommunication service.
- To ensure that the intercept capability may be audited to ensure that the intercepts were from or intended for the interception subject or premises specified in the warrant.
- To ensure that the capability is operated in a manner which prevents the interception subject or any other unauthorized person becoming aware of any interception.

---

[221] RIPA, s 12(6).
[222] ibid, s 13(2).
[223] See further Regulation of Investigatory Powers (Technical Advisory Board) Order 2001 (SI No 3734)..
[224] RIPA, s 12(7).
[225] ie attributes of the communications session, as defined in RIPA, s 21(4).
[226] eg the European Telecommunications Standard Institute (ETSI) standards for 'lawful intercept' (LI), available at <http://www.etsi.org/technologies-clusters/technologies/security/lawful-interception>.
[227] As defined in RIPA, s 2(9).
[228] See paras 4.291 et seq. A similar provision can be found in US law, at 47 USC s 1002(b)(3).

4.149 As noted at the start of this section, in some jurisdictions, the requirement to provide an 'intercept capability' includes enabling law enforcement direct access to the required data, without the mediation of the CSP's personnel. Under UK law, while the RIPA, s 12, does not make express reference to such functionality, the 'hand-over point within the service provider's network' could obviously be an automated interface, without the active involvement of CSP personnel. Justifications for adopting such an approach are to expedite law enforcement access, particularly given the industrial-scale of requests for communications data; to minimize the possibility of a security breach in respect of the investigation; and to reduce the CSP's operational costs involved in responding to requests. However, a concern with direct access is the absence of any opportunity for the CSP to review the legitimacy of an investigator's actions, through verification that the authorization procedures have been complied with. Conversely, it can be argued that it is inappropriate for oversight of a public function to be carried out by a private entity, such as a CSP, such supervisory and compliance functions having been given to a statutory entity: the Interception and Surveillance Commissioners.[229]

4.150 There may be circumstances where a law enforcement agency wishes to employ its own tools to carry out the collection of data 'in transmission', although implemented on a CSP's network. In the US, for example, the FBI developed a special filtering tool known as 'Carnivore', which was able to track information requested under a court order; although it was subsequently abandoned in favour applications developed by commercial software providers.[230] From a UK perspective, the deployment of such a tool would need to be expressly addressed in the s 12 notice.

4.151 CSPs have expressed numerous concerns in relation to the obligation to ensure an 'intercept capability'. Considerable reservations have been expressed about the feasibility of achieving a stable 'intercept capability' solution in a rapidly evolving communications environment. 'Intermediary service providers' in particular are concerned that their freedom to design, build, and operate innovative data communications networks and services, in accordance with the dictates of newly available technologies and commercial imperatives, may be significantly restrained by the need to meet an on-going obligation to ensure an 'intercept capability'. In addition, at the level of the traditional circuit-switched local access network, significant change will be experienced as a result of the regulatory drive within Europe for local loop unbundling, to encourage the roll-out of broadband communication facilities. It is generally accepted that a single technological solution to the requirement for 'intercept capability' is not going to be available, which will have associated cost implications for CSPs and potentially procedural implications for law enforcement agencies.

Costs

4.152 The costs arising from compliance with an obligation to provide 'intercept capability' is obviously an important issue for CSPs. Such costs can be subdivided into fixed costs or capital expenditure, in relation to building the 'capability' into the network (eg switches with intercept functionality), and variable costs or operational expenditure, arising from the operational aspects of carrying out an interception (eg personnel). It is beyond the remit of this book to suggest the most appropriate division of costs between governments, as holders

---

229 Established respectively under the RIPA, s 57, and the Police Act 1997, s 91.
230 'FBI abandons Carnivore wiretap software', *NBC News*, 18 January 2005.

of public funds, and the providers of communication networks and services. However, in a study commissioned by the Home Office in 2000, during the passage of the RIPA, it was recommended that the Government cover the full costs involved.[231] In many jurisdictions, fixed costs are borne by the CSP, while variable costs are covered by the relevant public authority.[232] Where an interception is carried out in response to a request from a foreign state, under a mutual assistance agreement, the operational costs will generally be covered by the foreign state.[233]

Issues of cost can obviously impact both CSPs and its LEA customers, ie the requesting agencies. Placing the burden with the CSP is likely to lead to greater resistance from the business, while overly generous grant giving could render CSPs willing to go beyond that which is required of them by law. Conversely, while shifting some of the financial cost arising from an investigation on to the enforcement agency may act as an effective restraint on the use of such techniques, it may also mean that certain crimes are effectively ignored by the agency, where either the value of the data as evidence is viewed as less than the cost of obtaining or simply because there are no remaining funds available. It has been reported, for example, that BT's surveillance service has been designed to a high specification to meet the quality of service criteria of the intelligence services, but which has detrimental cost implications for the high volumes of requests generated by normal policing activities, which effectively cross-subsidize the needs of the intelligence community.[234] **4.153**

To address industry concerns about the costs related to interception in modern communication networks, some jurisdictions have made statutory reference to the issue of the division of such costs. In the United Kingdom, the RIPA provides that the Secretary of State has a duty to ensure that a CSP 'receives such contribution as is, in the circumstances of that person's case, a fair contribution towards the costs incurred', which would include obligations incurred under a s 12 notice.[235] In respect of the Part I, Chapter II regime governing access to communications data, the Secretary of State has to make 'appropriate contributions towards the costs incurred' by CSPs in responding to requests for information,[236] such as the employment of persons or upgrading technology to handle such requests. Figures about the amount of monies paid to industry as grants and fees under RIPA are not currently available.[237] **4.154**

In the Netherlands, the Telecommunications Act 1998 enables CSPs to 'claim compensation from the national treasury for the administrative and personnel costs incurred by them **4.155**

---

[231] The Smith Group Ltd, 'Technical and cost issues associated with interception of communications at certain Communication Service Providers', 19 April 2000, available at <http://www.dis.org/gessel/IS2K/British Home Office RIP report.pdf>.

[232] In Belgium and Finland, the costs involved in a criminal investigation may ultimately be recovered from the perpetrator, if found guilty.

[233] See eg Convention on Mutual Assistance in Criminal Matters between the Member States of the European Union established by Council Act of 29 May 2000, OJ C 197/1, 12 July 2000, Art 21 and Explanatory Memorandum.

[234] Rowland, T, 'Ringing up the wrong numbers', *The Guardian*, 18 May 2006, available at <http://www.theguardian.com/media/2006/may/18/newmedia.technology>.

[235] RIPA, s 14(1) and (2)(c).

[236] ibid, s 24(1).

[237] See eg HPM Britain, 'RIPA Section 14 Payments—Grants to cover interception', What do they know, 3 May 2001, available at <https://www.whatdotheyknow.com/request/ripa_section_14_payments_grants>.

directly'.[238] In the US, the Communications Assistance to Law Enforcement Act of 1994 provides that the Attorney General will pay 'for the additional reasonable costs of making compliance with such assistance capability requirements reasonably achievable'[239] and $500m was initially appropriated for such financial support.[240] By contrast, in Germany, an operator of a telecommunications system must maintain the necessary technical configuration 'at his own expense'.[241]

4.156 Were the costs associated with the provision of 'intercept capability' to be placed exclusively upon the communication service providers, this may impact on the commercial viability of certain small and medium-size enterprises (SMEs) entering the market for the provision of communication services and networks. The imposition of onerous 'intercept' obligations upon CSPs within Europe, in comparison with other jurisdictions, may also have an adverse effect on where CSPs choose to establish their business in the medium to long term. Conversely, the provision of an overly generous compensation scheme could be viewed as an unlawful state aid, in breach of Community law.[242]

Communications content

4.157 When considering law enforcement access to data 'in transmission', a distinction must be made between the targeted interception of the communications of a specific person or location, and the on-going wholesale monitoring and filtering of communications, which is targeted by reference to the content itself, rather than the persons or locations to and from which it is transmitted. Non-targeted interception is carried out at various levels within and outside the network, by CSPs, organizations, and by national security agencies.

4.158 In the former 'targeted' scenario, the interception activity is triggered in the course of an investigation, from a tip-off perhaps, as a forensic tool to assist the investigation and prosecution of the target. In the latter situation, the monitoring is carried out as a proactive tool for security protection, prevention, and detection of criminal activity by persons unknown, except possibly as a class, such as employees or subscribers. While both may form legitimate parts of a law enforcement strategy for cyberspace, it is the policy issues and legality of targeted interception activities that are of primary concern to us in this section.

4.159 Interception of the content of a communication is primarily governed in the UK under Part I, Chapter I of the Regulation of Investigatory Powers Act 2000 (RIPA), supplemented by a Code of Practice.[243] The Act makes it an offence to intercept a communication being

---

[238] Telecommunications Act 1998, Art 13.6.2.

[239] Pub L No 103-414, 108 Stat 4279, codified 47 USC ss 1008(b)(2)(A). See also 28 Code of Federal Regulations (CFR), Chapter 1, Pt 100 'Cost recovery regulations, Communications Assistance for Law Enforcement Act', available at <http://www.ecfr.gov>.

[240] See Office of the Inspector General, DoJ, 'Implementation of the Communications Assistance for Law Enforcement Act by the Federal Bureau of Investigation', Audit Report 08-20, March 2008, available at <https://oig.justice.gov/reports/FBI/a0820/final.pdf>.

[241] Telecommunications Act 1998, s 88.

[242] This issue was explicitly recognized by the Commission in a declaration to the European Council in February 2006, when it noted that '[i]n assessing the compatibility of such aids with the Treaty, the Commission will, inter alia, take due account of such necessity and of the benefits in terms of public security impact on society in general ...' (quoted in Home Office, 'Transposition of Directive 2006/24/EC', Consultation Paper (August 2008), para 5.8, available at <http://www.statewatch.org/news/2008/aug/uk-ho-consult-mand-ret-internet.pdf>).

[243] Interception Code of Practice, above, n 215.

transmitted over a public telecommunications system without a warrant issued by the Secretary of State, or over a private telecommunication system without the consent of the system controller.[244]

The RIPA regime is not, however, primarily designed to tackle the activities of those inter- **4.160** cepting communications in the furtherance of their criminal activities; rather its purpose is to control the interception, surveillance, and other investigative practices of law enforcement agents consistent with the ECHR:

> We recognise that, by its nature, interception of communications is highly intrusive activity, affecting the privacy of the individual . . . The Government is committed to ensuring that interception of communications complies fully with the ECHR.[245]

The European Court of Human Rights (ECtHR) has on numerous occasions found UK **4.161** law to be in fundamental breach of the Convention in respect of protecting the right of privacy of those who have been subject to interception by public authorities, including for not having a governing statutory scheme at all,[246] and for its limitation to interceptions carried out on a public telecommunication system.[247] The RIPA also enables the Government to comply with Art 5(1) of the European Union Directive on communications privacy, which states:

> Member States shall ensure the confidentiality of communications and the related traffic data by means of a public communications network and publicly available electronic communications services, through national legislation. In particular, they shall prohibit listening, tapping, storage or other kinds of interception or surveillance of communications and the related traffic data by persons other than users, without the consent of the users concerned, except when legally authorised to do so in accordance with Article 15(1).[248]

The grounds detailed in Art 15(1) reflect those derogations listed in Art 8(2) of the ECHR.

Lawful intercept

As discussed in Chapter 3, the RIPA comprehensively details conduct in respect of an **4.162** interception which has 'lawful authority', elaborated in ss 3, 4, and 5. Section 3 details circumstances where an interception warrant is not required; s 4 details circumstances where the Secretary of State may adopt regulations authorizing interception, or such conduct is authorized by virtue of the location where the interception takes place;[249] while s 5 concerns interception warrants granted by the Secretary of State. The only other ground where an interception would be lawful is in the following circumstance:

> . . . it is in exercise, in relation to any stored communication, of any statutory power that is exercised (apart from this section) for the purpose of obtaining information or of taking possession of any document or other property.[250]

---

[244] RIPA, s 1.

[245] *Interception of Communications*, above, n 161, at 1.

[246] *Malone v United Kingdom* [1984] 7 EHRR 14.

[247] *Halford v United Kingdom* (1997) IRLR 471.

[248] This wording is taken from Directive 02/58/EC, above, n 187, which superseded the original instrument, Directive 97/66/EC, above, n 187. The wording is substantially identical.

[249] ie in a prison, hospital providing high security psychiatric services and state hospitals in Scotland: RIPA, s 4(4), (5), and (6) respectively. See *Mahmood (Asad) and Khan (Majid)* [2013] EWCA Crim 2356, which concerned interception of prisoners calls and considered the scope of RIPA, s 4(4), as well as Prison Rules 1999/728, r 35A.

[250] RIPA, s 1(5)(c).

Under RIPA, an 'interception' occurs when some or all of the content of a communication is made available, during its transmission, to a person other than the sender or the intended recipient.[251] This includes any storage of the communication in the telecommunications system prior to its receipt, such as voice mail or an unread email.[252]

4.163 The operation of this provision was subject to judicial scrutiny in *R (NTL Group Limited) v Ipswich Crown Court*.[253] Here the communications company, NTL, had been subject to a court order made under s 9 and Schedule 1 of the Police and Criminal Evidence Act 1984, after an application from the Chief Constable to access 'special procedure material'.[254] NTL applied for judicial review of the order on the grounds that compliance would require NTL to commit an interception offence under the RIPA. The issue arose due to the manner in which NTL's email system operated. In order to comply with the court order, and retain copies of the emails of the customer under investigation, the system would need to copy the targeted emails to a different address from that of the intended recipient. This, NTL argued, would result in an unlawful interception. The court agreed with NTL's characterization of the process as one of interception, although expressing reservations as to whether this was the intention of the drafters.[255] The court then went on to consider whether such interception was lawful by virtue of s 1(5)(c). NTL argued that since the conduct was theirs, they lacked the lawful authority granted the police under the s 9 procedure. However, the court held that this police procedure would be rendered unworkable with such an interpretation and, therefore, an implicit power must exist to render NTL's conduct lawful.[256]

4.164 Another example of communications stored in the course of their transmission that has come to light is a practice referred to as the 'virtual dead drop'.[257] Rather than send a message direct to the recipient, the sender prepares the message in his web-based email account and saves it to the 'drafts' folder on his account. The intended recipient is then able to access the shared account, review the message, and save a draft reply. By utilizing a single account, the conspirators reduce the digital footprint created by such communications. This was apparently a method used by those involved in the Madrid train bombings in March 2004[258] and by Kafeel Ahmed, the man who drove a car bomb into Glasgow airport.[259] Similar practices have also been observed in respect of honeypots, where compromised resources are effectively used to establish a bulletin board for hackers to exchange messages.[260] As a consequence, court orders will often specify that draft emails, especially those with attachments, should be disclosed.

---

[251] ibid, s 2(2).

[252] ibid, s 2(7).

[253] [2002] EWHC 1585 (Admin), [2003] 1 Cr App R 14.

[254] Under Police and Criminal Evidence Act 1984, Sch 1, para 4, a court may grant access to material subject to certain access conditions (ibid, para 2).

[255] *R (NTL Group Limited) v Ipswich Crown Court* [2002] EWHC 1585 (Admin), [2003] 1 Cr App R 14, para 21.

[256] See also para 3.316, for a discussion of *Edmondson and others v R* [2013] EWCA Crim 1026, in which the court distinguished its interpretation of RIPA, s 2(7) from that made by Lord Woolf LJ in *NTL* (para 14).

[257] McLean, R, 'Unsent email helped plotters coordinate Madrid bombings', *New York Times*, 30 April 2006, available at <http://www.nytimes.com/2006/04/30/world/europe/30spain.html>.

[258] ibid.

[259] See 'Doctor admits car bomb charge', *BBC News*, 11 April 2008, available at <http://news.bbc.co.uk/2/hi/uk_news/7342379.stm>, which states that the terrorist's brother had been alerted 'to a draft e-mail available to read online'.

[260] See Spitzner, above, n 155.

In the US, federal 'wiretap' law contains no express reference to the temporary storage of **4.165** communications in the course of their transmission, although the issue was subject to judicial consideration in *US v Councilman*.[261] In this case, the defendant owned an online rare and out-of-print book-listing service, which also provided an email service for its customers. In 1998, the defendant directed his employees to modify the operation of the email service, so that any messages sent from the online retailer Amazon.com to a customer using the defendant's service would be copied to a separate mailbox that was accessible to the defendant. The defendant argued, successfully on the first two occasions, that such actions were not an offence under US wiretap law,[262] since the definition of an 'electronic communication' does not refer to electronic storage, in contrast to other related definitions in the statute. However, the court rejected such an interpretation, finding instead that 'electronic communication' 'includes transient electronic storage that is intrinsic to the communication process for such communications'.[263]

Under the RIPA, s 3, an interception is lawful where both the sender and recipient have con- **4.166** sented to the interception,[264] or it is carried out by a communications service provider 'for purposes connected with the provision or operation of that service or with the enforcement ... of any enactment relating to the use of ... telecommunications services'.[265] As noted in Chapter 3, the first exemption provision was amended in 2011 to comply with EU data protection law.[266] The second exemption must be broken down into two distinct purposes, ie connected with the provision or operation of the service and for enforcement of relevant enactments. The latter would seem relatively straightforward and would render lawful an interception carried out by a telecommunications operator to prevent fraudulent use of a telecommunication service or its improper use, under the Communications Act 2003, ss 125[267] and 127.[268] The former, however, could be interpreted extremely broadly, which has significant implications in terms of surveillance practices for commercial purposes. The issue came to public attention in relation to a company called Phorm, who was trying to market a system for online-targeted advertising. The system operated by monitoring a user's browsing activities and enabling relevant adverts to be generated on visited web pages. In the course of on-going discussions about the legality of Phorm's system, the Home Office issued 'informal guidance' as to the meaning of s 3(3), which concluded: 'targeted online advertising can be regarded as being provided in connection with the telecommunication service'.[269] Such a broad interpretation has inevitably been challenged, while accusations were levelled at the Home Office.[270] From a data protection perspective, one issue that

---

[261] *US v Councilman*, 418 F 3d 67 (1st Cir 2005).

[262] 18 USC ss 2510–22.

[263] *Councilman*, 418 F 3d 67, at 26, II A 3.

[264] RIPA, s 3(1).

[265] ibid, s 3(3).

[266] See para 3.313.

[267] See *Mariusz Mikolajczak v District Court in Kalisz, Poland* [2013] EWHC 432 (Admin), where the judge queried whether the accused's conduct constituted an offence under this section. See also *Morgans v DPP* [1999] 1 WLR 968, DC, which involved hacking through the dishonest obtaining of services in breach of s 42 of the Telecommunications Act 1984, the previous version of this offence.

[268] See further paras 3.201 et seq.

[269] Home Office, 'Targeted Online Advertising: Interception of communications or not? If it is, is it lawful interception?', Opinion, January 2008, para, 22, available at <http://cryptome.org/ho-phorm.htm>.

[270] eg Waters, D, 'Home Office "colluded with Phorm"', BBC News, 28 April 2009, available at <http://news.bbc.co.uk/2/hi/technology/8021661.stm>.

would require consideration is whether the interceptor's conduct was compliant, especially the purpose limitation principle. One could also expect the courts to adopt a narrow reading of s 3(3), on the basis that it represents an exception to an individual's right to privacy under Article 8(2) of the ECHR. Conversely, when interpreting criminal fault, the courts also adopt a narrow interpretation, so the result may be a finding that the provision itself is incompatible,[271] rather than the conduct of the interceptor.

Warranted intercept

4.167 In stark contrast to the position in most other jurisdictions, the power to authorize the interception of a person's communications resides not with the judiciary but with the executive branch of government, usually in the form of the Secretary of State at the Home Office or the Foreign Office.[272] An interception warrant may only be issued by the Secretary of State where he considers it necessary on the following grounds:

- in the interests of national security;
- the prevention or detection of 'serious crime',[273] which represents the great majority of cases;[274]
- safeguarding the 'economic well-being of the United Kingdom';[275] or
- in response to a request under mutual legal assistance procedures.[276]

In addition, an application for a warrant to the Secretary of State may only be made by those persons listed on the face of the statute, such as the Director General of the National Crime Agency or the Commissioner of the Metropolitan Police.[277]

4.168 While the executive authorization procedure under RIPA is generally viewed as a unique feature of UK law, compared with the norm of judicial authorization, the US presidency was mired in controversy in December 2005 when it was revealed that following the terrorist outrages of 11 September 2001, President Bush authorized the on-going surveillance of the international communications of a large number of US residents for national security purposes. The cited legal basis for such action was a Congressional resolution, the 'Authorization for the Use of Military Force', which granted the President authority 'to use all necessary and appropriate force against those nations, organizations, or persons he

---

[271] Human Rights Act 1998, s 4(2).

[272] RIPA, s 5(1). In the event that a Secretary of State is absence, a senior official would issue the warrant, under the Secretary of State's authority, it would not go to another Secretary of State (ibid, s 7(1)(b)).

[273] ie RIPA, s 81(3):

> (a) . . . an offence for which a person who has attained the age of twenty-one and has no previous convictions could reasonably be expected to be sentenced to imprisonment for a term of three years or more; (b) that the conduct involves the use of violence, results in substantial financial gain or is conduct by a large number of persons in pursuit of a common purpose.

[274] See Report of the Interception of Communications Commissioner (IoCC), March 2015, at 28 ('IoCC Report 2014').

[275] This was amended by the DRIPA, s 3(2), to state that the circumstances must be relevant to the interests of national security, which was already the position adopted in the Interception Code of Practice, above, n 215, para 4.4. The IoCC notes in his 2015 Report (above, n 274, paras 5.60–5.10) that this link is required to comply with the terms of Directive 02/58/EC, above, n 187, Art 15(1). A warrant shall not be issued for this purposes unless the information relates 'to the acts or intentions of persons outside the British Islands' (RIPA, s 5(5)).

[276] RIPA, s 5(2)(a) and (3). See further paras 5.96–5.107.

[277] RIPA, s 6(2). Any application made on behalf of the persons listed must be made by a person holding office under the Crown (ibid, s 6(3)).

determines planned, authorized, committed, or aided the terrorist attacks that occurred on September 11, 2001'.[278] In addition, reference was made to an inherent authority in the President as commander in chief.[279]

As a consequence of the disclosure, various legal challenges were mounted, including a **4.169** class action launched by the Electronic Frontier Foundation against the communications company AT&T, seeking damages on behalf of AT&T customers for its alleged breaches of state and federal law by facilitating such interception.[280] The first Federal Court ruling on the matter, in an action commenced by the American Civil Liberties Union among others, held that the programme was in breach both of statutory and constitutional provisions.[281] However, in December 2011, a federal judge dismissed all the lawsuits against AT&T,[282] citing the retroactive immunity granted CSPs under controversial amendments passed in 2008.[283]

Under RIPA, the conduct authorized by the warrant must be proportionate to the objective **4.170** being sought, including whether the information 'could reasonably be obtained by other means'.[284] Considerations of proportionality must not only be assessed by the Secretary of State when granting the warrant, but must also inform management of the implementation of the warrant, the implicit assumption being that interception is an investigative technique of last resort. Under US law, a similar sentiment has been expressed as a matter for a judge to consider when determining whether to issue a warrant: 'whether normal investigative procedures have been tried and have failed or reasonably appear to be unlikely to succeed if tried or to be too dangerous'.[285] To assist the Secretary of State in making a judgement on proportionality, the applicant is required to indicate any circumstances that should be taken into account, such as the extent of collateral intrusion likely to result, or where material relating to confidential, religious, medical, journalistic, or legally privileged material may be involved.[286]

Two forms of warrant may be issued under RIPA, under s 8(1) and 8(4). A s 8(1) warrant **4.171** must identify a particular subject or a set of premises against which the interception is being carried out.[287] This is commonly referred to as 'targeted' intercept and is primarily an investigative tool used by domestic law enforcement agencies against known threats or people.[288] Where an individual is the subject of a s 8(1) warrant, interception may be carried out against any communication services used by that person, such as landline, mobile,

---

[278] Senate Joint Resolution 23 (2001), s 2(a).

[279] Johnston, D and Greenhouse, L, "01 Resolution is central to '05 Controversy', *New York Times*, 20 December 2005, available at <http://www.nytimes.com/2005/12/20/politics/01-resolution-is-central-to-05-controversy.html>.

[280] See further <https://www.eff.org/nsa/hepting>.

[281] *ACLU and others v NSA*, Case No 06-CV-10204, US District Court, Eastern District of Michigan, 17 August 2006.

[282] *In re: National Security Agency Telecommunications Records Litigation*, Case No 09-16676, 29 December 2011. The Supreme Court declined a petition for a writ of certiorari on 9 October 2012.

[283] Foreign Intelligence Surveillance Act of 1978 (FISA) Amendments Act of 2008, Title II, s 201, codified at 50 USC s 1885a 'Procedures for implementing statutory defenses'.

[284] RIPA, s 5(2)(b) and (4).

[285] 18 USC s 2518(3)(c).

[286] Interception Code of Practice, above, n 215, s 4.

[287] RIPA, s 8(1).

[288] See ISC Report 2015, above, n 2, Chapter 3.

and Internet account, provided such services are detailed in the schedule to the warrant; in the form of 'addresses, numbers, apparatus or other factors ... used for identifying the communications' to be intercepted.[289]

4.172 Such identity information does not need to appear in a s 8(4) warrant, where the interception is of an 'external communication' in the course of its transmission by a telecommunication system.[290] Instead of identifying persons or premises, a s 8(4) warrant will list 'selectors' that either relate to individual targets or more general enquiries, operating either through simple matching or more complex selection rules, against which flows of communications traffic will be monitored.[291] This is commonly referred to as 'bulk' intercept and is primarily used by MI6 and GCHQ for foreign intelligence gathering purposes.[292] An 'external communication' is defined as 'a communication sent or received outside the British Islands',[293] which would include communicating with a web server based in the US, but would not cover a communication sent and received in the UK, but which was routed via a foreign server or network, such as a Gmail account.[294] This provision would enable, for example, a warrant to be issued in respect of traffic transiting through the UK where no identifiable person or premises were located here, triggered perhaps by the receipt of foreign intelligence.[295]

4.173 Given the 'bulk' nature of s 8(4) warrants, they are subject to a second layer of procedure requiring a ministerial certificate, which governs the examination of the material collected under the warrant.[296] The provisions governing certificated warrants have been criticized for being impenetrable and creating a 'third kind' of warrant.[297] In essence they require the minister to certify that the material needs to be examined for one of the statutory purposes[298] and does not refer to a person known to be in the British Islands at the time.[299] The latter restriction is not absolute, however, since an examination may relate to a person known to be in the British Islands where either the minister certifies in respect of the 'individual in question' that it is necessary for the statutory purposes,[300] or a senior official authorizes examination of the material for a short period in respect of a person who was thought to be abroad when he is in fact in the British Islands.[301]

4.174 A procedure for *ex post* judicial scrutiny of warrants exists through two different mechanisms. First, the Act established the office of the Interception Commissioner,[302] currently

---

[289] RIPA, s 8(2). See also Interception Code of Practice, above, n 215, para 5.2.
[290] RIPA, s 8(4) and (5).
[291] See ISC Report 2015, above, n 2, paras 60–73.
[292] ibid, Chapter 4. The IPB will retain this distinction between targeted and bulk interception warrants.
[293] RIPA, s 20.
[294] See Interception Code of Practice, above, n 215, para 6.5.
[295] This provision could provide a basis for authorizing the types of intercept that are thought to be carried out under the Echelon system.
[296] RIPA, ss 8(4)(b) and 16.
[297] eg Bowden, C, 'Submission to the Intelligence and Security Committee of Parliament', 7 February 2014, paras 26–33, available at <http://blog.privacystrategy.eu/public/published/Submission_ISC_7.2.2014_-_Caspar_Bowden.pdf>.
[298] RIPA, s 8(4)(b).
[299] ibid, s 16(2). See also the Report of the Interception of Communications Commissioner for 2013, HC 1184, April 2014, paras 6.5.33–6.5.38.
[300] RIPA, s 16(3).
[301] ibid, s 16(4) and (5).
[302] ibid, s 57. See generally <http://www.iocco-uk.info>.

Rt Hon. Sir Stanley Burnton, who reviews the exercise and performance of the powers and duties granted to persons under the RIPA and prepares a half-yearly report.[303] Over the years, the Commissioner has raised concerns about a range of matters; from the level of resource required to operate an effective oversight regime,[304] to recommendations about the retention, storage, and destruction of intercept material.[305]

The second scrutiny procedure is through persons having the right to bring proceedings,[306] **4.175** or make a complaint or reference[307] to the Investigatory Powers Tribunal (IPT).[308] The Tribunal has assumed responsibility for the jurisdiction previously held by the Interception of Communications Tribunal, the Security Service Tribunal and the Intelligence Services Tribunal. Of those cases dealt with by the IPT, to date, only a very small minority of decisions have found in favour of the complainant.[309] An appeal against a decision of the IPT would need to be made to the ECtHR.[310]

In addition to the warrant regime, there is a non-warrant authorization procedure to **4.176** engage in surveillance, under Part II of the RIPA. This procedure may be relevant to interception since, as discussed previously,[311] an interception carried out with the consent of one of the parties to the communications is lawful if so authorized.[312] Such an authorization may be granted by a prescribed officer, such as a superintendent.[313] However, the stark contrast between the different levels of authorization required for surveillance and interception, ie the applicable criteria, the status of the applicant, as well as the absence of any *ex ante* judicial scrutiny, have all been the subject of much well-deserved criticism.[314]

One important feature of the UK interception regime is that it does not generally permit **4.177** information obtained through an interception to be adduced as evidence in legal proceedings.[315] Such evidence is for the purpose of an investigation, not for any subsequent prosecution. The reasoning behind such a provision is to protect from disclosure information about the investigative activities of law enforcement agencies. Such activities would enter the public domain if intercept evidence was used in court and became subject to challenge

---

[303] RIPA, s 58(4), as amended by DRIPA, s 6(2). The report is made to the Prime Minister, who lays copies before the Houses of Parliament, except those portions considered sensitive material in accordance with s 58(7).

[304] Report of the Interception of Communications Commissioner for 2004, HC 549, November 2005 ('IoCC Report 2004'), para 22.

[305] IoCC Report 2014, above, n 274, 42.

[306] RIPA, s 65(2)(a) or (d).

[307] ibid, s 65(2)(b) or (c).

[308] ibid, s 65. See also the Investigatory Powers Tribunal Rules 2000 (SI No 2665). See also <http://www.ipt-uk.com>.

[309] See IPT Annual case statistics. See eg *Liberty and others v Secretary of State for Foreign and Commonwealth Affairs and others* [2015] UKIPTrib 13 77-H.

[310] Under the IPB, a right of appeal on a point of law would be possible.

[311] See further paras 4.51–4.77.

[312] RIPA, s 3(2).

[313] Regulation of Investigatory Powers (Directed Surveillance and Covert Human Intelligence Sources) Order 2010 (SI No 521).

[314] See eg Ormerod, D, 'Telephone intercepts and their admissibility', *Criminal Law Review* 15 [2004]. See also the ISC Report 2015, above, n 2; Independent Reviewer Report, above, n 2; and RUSI Report, above, n 2.

[315] RIPA, s 17.

by a defendant's counsel. Rendering the product of interception inadmissible can also operate as a disincentive to interception activity.[316]

4.178   The interception rules would not cover the practice of 'electronic eavesdropping', where emissions from computer screens are surreptitiously received and reconstituted for viewing on external equipment,[317] since they are not in the course of transmission to a recipient. Such techniques are primarily used as a mechanism for industrial espionage, but they could be used by law enforcement agencies. As a forensic technique, 'electronic eavesdropping' would probably constitute a form of 'surveillance', which is governed under Part II of RIPA.[318] However, where electromagnetic emissions are used as the wireless transmission path, such as a WiFi link, capturing such emissions would constitute a form of interception requiring a warrant.[319] Hence, under the Cybercrime Convention, the concept of 'illegal interception' has been explicitly extended to include 'electromagnetic emissions from a computer system carrying such computer data'.[320]

Communications data

4.179   Establishing the identity of a suspect is obviously the starting point for commencement of criminal proceedings and a key aspect of cybercrime forensics. However, network users are often not readily identifiable from the naming and addressing information processed in the course of a communications session. There will generally be a need, therefore, for the investigator to map or trace a user's electronic identity to his real-world identity. The difficulties associated with this task have encouraged a popular perception of the Internet as a realm of anonymity, where we can engage in conduct without fear of exposure, which in itself has encouraged criminality. In the *Landslide* case, for example, the fact that some 7,000 UK residents felt they could register their credit card details for a child pornography service with impunity indicates a strong perception of anonymity when using the Internet.

4.180   However, anonymity is not the default setting in cyberspace, although law enforcement agencies will face a number of practical difficulties. In particular, a third party, the user's CSP, will generate and store substantial amounts of data in relation to the provision of services to the user, which may enable identification of the user. CSPs will often have a shared interest with law enforcement in detecting certain forms of criminality, since its continuance may harm the commercial interests of the CSP, although CSPs will be primarily concerned with identifying accounts rather than actual persons, which are the concern of law enforcement.[321] However, law enforcement access to such information will mean interfering with the interests of the CSP, the person being investigated, as well as collateral intrusion into the lives of others.

---

[316]   See further paras 6.70 et seq.

[317]   See generally Lewis, O, 'Information Security & Electronic Eavesdropping—A perspective', 7(4) *Computer Law and Security Report* 165 (1991); and Steele, D, 'Eavesdropping on electromagnetic radiation emanating from video display units', 32 *Criminal Law Quarterly* 253 (1989–90).

[318]   RIPA, Pt II 'Surveillance and Covert Human Intelligence Sources'.

[319]   Under either RIPA, Pt I, Chapter I or the Wireless Telegraphy Act 2006, ss 48–9.

[320]   Convention on Cybercrime, Art 3 and Explanatory Report to the Convention on Cybercrime, above, n 184, para 57.

[321]   See Clayton, above, n 32, at 60.

This section will first review the range and types of forensic data that are generated con-   **4.181**
cerning the attributes of a user's communications activities, and other data related to the
provision by a CSP of communication services. Second, the legal regime governing access
to such data by law enforcement agencies and other persons will be examined. While it
is recognized that such data can be extremely valuable in a digital investigation, its value
depends on the data being available as and when law enforcement agencies require access.
The retention of such data beyond the period needed to support the provision of services
represents both a cost to the CSP and a threat to the privacy interests of its customers. Prior
to the terrorist attack on New York in September 2001, it was widely accepted that any
benefits from requiring data retention for law enforcement purposes was outweighed by the
potential costs involved. However, this balance has now shifted in favour of greater security, requiring not only new powers for law enforcement, but new capabilities in terms of the
retention of potential forensic data. These developments will be considered in the third part
of this section.

Data types

While we intuitively know that data about a person's communications activities will be   **4.182**
valuable in a digital investigation, it is important to consider the different types of data that
may be involved, especially in our modern communications environment. Broadly speaking, when a CSP provides services to its customers and users,[322] data is obtained from three
main sources:

- Customers and users will disclose information to the CSP.
- Data will be generated by the ICT systems and resources used by the CSP in the provision
  of its services.
- Data will be obtained from third parties, such as other CSPs with whom the CSP is
  connected.

However, in order to establish a regulatory regime governing access to such data, it is necessary to give these different sources of data statutory expression. Part I, Chapter II of the
RIPA uses the term 'communications data' to encompass these diverse sources of forensic
material.

'Communications data' encompasses three categories of data: **4.183**

   (a) any traffic data comprised in or attached to a communication (whether by the sender or
      otherwise) for the purposes of any postal service or telecommunication system by means
      of which it is being or may be transmitted;
   (b) any information which includes none of the contents of a communication (apart
      from any information falling within paragraph (a)) and is about the use made by any
      person—
        (i) of any postal service or telecommunications service; or
        (ii) in connection with the provision to or use by any person of any telecommunica-
      tions service, of any part of a telecommunication system;

---

[322] For the purposes of our analysis, a distinction needs to be made between those with whom the CSP
has a direct contractual relationship, also referred to as 'subscribers', and those to whom it supplies services,
also referred to as 'users'.

(c) any information not falling within paragraph (a) or (b) that is held or obtained, in relation to persons to whom he provides the service, by a person providing a postal service
or telecommunications service.[323]

4.184 Understanding the nature and scope of each of these categories is important for the CSP
that generates and retains such data, the requesting law enforcement agencies, and any
other investigative entity that may be seeking access to such data. Under s 71(4) of RIPA,
the Home Office has adopted a code of practice governing the exercise of the powers granted
under Part I, Chapter II.[324] Another source of guidance can be found in related legislation
concerning the retention of communications data. The code of practice adopted under the
Anti-terrorism, Crime and Security Act 2001 (ATCSA) indicates the various types of communications data that the Government would like to see retained for specified minimum
periods, which primarily reflects the perceived needs of law enforcement agencies ('ATCSA
Code').[325]

4.185 The first category, 'traffic data', is further defined in the following terms:

(a) any data identifying, or purporting to identify, any person, apparatus or location to or
from which the communication is or may be transmitted,
(b) any data identifying or selecting, or purporting to identify or select, apparatus through
which, or by means of which, the communication is or may be transmitted,
(c) any data comprising signals for the actuation of apparatus used for the purposes of a
telecommunication system for effecting (in whole or in part) the transmission of any
communication, and
(d) any data identifying the data or other data as data comprised in or attached to a particular communication,
but that expression includes data identifying a computer file or computer program access to
which is obtained, or which is run, by means of the communication to the extent only that
the file or program is identified by reference to the apparatus in which it is stored.[326]

The first sub-category would include the telephone number of a calling and called party,
and the IP address of the sender and recipient of an Internet transmission. This category
is exclusively concerned with the persons and apparatus[327] operating at the edges of a network. As noted earlier, in respect of traceability such naming and addressing schemes may
identify a person, but more usually will identify a CSP, IP holder, and/or an item of terminal
equipment connected to the network. Establishing the forensic link between such data
and an actual person will generally require corroborative data from other sources. As the
Explanatory Notes to the RIPA note, category (a) data provides 'subscriber information',
but this may not be the actual user.[328]

---

[323] RIPA, s 21(4). Under the IPB, the Government would replace these 3 categories with 2: 'entity data'
and 'event data'.
[324] Home Office, *Acquisition and Disclosure of Communications Data: Code of Practice*, The Stationery
Office, 2015 ('ADCD Code'), available at <http://www.gov.uk>. The most recent version was published in
March 2015.
[325] Retention of Communications Data (Code of Practice) Order 2003 (SI No 3175).
[326] RIPA, s 21(6). This reiterates the definition at s 2(9).
[327] Defined as including 'any equipment, machinery or device and any wire or cable' (ibid, s 81(1)).
[328] RIPA Explanatory Notes, above, n 187, para 33.

Reference is also made to the location to or from which a transmission may be made. As **4.186** noted above, one of the data problems faced by cybercrime investigators is the issue of 'location': where is the perpetrator physically rather than virtually? Location has always been an issue in criminal investigations, as portrayed in numerous films where the police try to keep the suspect, such as a kidnapper, on the line while their location is traced. However, the forensic value of 'location data' has grown exponentially with the development of mobile communication services, which has fundamentally altered our access to and use of ICTs. In terms of mobile services, we are not only concerned with devices, such as the ubiquitous mobile phone, but also our greater mobility of access, which enables us to gain access to communication services, such as email, from any publicly available access point, such as a cybercafé, anywhere in the world. Under the ATCSA Code, location data includes the latitude and longitude reference, where available, of the start and completion of a call, and the cell site data from the time the cell ceases to be used.[329]

The second sub-category is concerned with the networks themselves. It would include the **4.187** IP addresses of the routers or 'hops' taken by message packets transmitted over the Internet, as well as the networks over which traffic is carried, which may arise under interconnection arrangements. Such data about a communication's path can be extremely valuable in an investigation, potentially enabling the real origin of the message to be determined where the sender has attempted to spoof his identity. So, for example, a hacker in the UK may 'launder' his communications through foreign networks simply to mask his location. Such data may be held by and obtained from the CSP under the RIPA regime, or it may be sought by the investigators directly themselves, using a widely available network tool, known generically as 'traceroute', which is able to determine the route that packets have taken across an IP network, such as the Internet.[330]

The third sub-category is intended to cover communications made between an end-user **4.188** and a network, rather than another end-user. It was primarily designed to address 'dial-through fraud', where an end-user manipulates a network to route his communication across the system.[331] Hackers, for example, often engage in such activities, accessing private exchange systems in order to re-route their communications, generally for the purpose of obtaining free services.[332]

The final sub-category (d) was the subject of considerable controversy during the pas- **4.189** sage of the RIPA Bill. It was specifically included to address a feature present in packet-switched networks, rather than traditional circuit-switched networks. In order for the packets that comprise a transmission to be reassembled at the edge of a network, each and every packet will comprise data that enables them to be correctly associated with each other, such as a sequence number. However, each packet also contains the content

---

[329] Home Office, 'Retention of Communications Data under Part 11: Anti-Terrorism Crime and Security Act 2001 – Voluntary Code of Practice' ('ATCSA Code'), Appendix A, available at <http://www.opsi.gov.uk/si/si2003/draft/5b.pdf>. A CSP would also be expected to provide collateral data required to interpret such locational data, such as mapping data between cell site identifiers and their location (eg OS Landranger reference).

[330] eg <http://ping.eu/traceroute/>; <http://www.monitis.com/traceroute/>; and <http://tracert.com/traceroute>.

[331] RIPA Explanatory Notes, above, n 187, para 33.

[332] See *The Simkins Partnership (A Firm) v Reeves Lund & Co Ltd* [2003] EWHC 1946.

of the communications, either in whole or in part. The concern expressed at the time the Bill was going through Parliament was that law enforcement access to the former, communications data, should not inadvertently grant access to the latter content, which falls under the Interception regime, Part I, Chapter I of the RIPA. The provision, read in conjunction with the tailpiece, was intended to clearly distinguish between content and communications data; as stated by the Home Secretary, Charles Clarke, during the passage of the Bill:

> . . . traffic data stop at the apparatus within which files or programmes are stored, so that traffic data may identify a server but not a website or page.[333]

This 'data type' problem, distinguishing between content and communication data, is an issue to which we shall return later in this chapter.

4.190 The second category of 'communications data' is that concerning the usage of a service. This would include any time- and date-related data, including time/date stamps; duration data generated from recorded events, such as log-in and log-out connection data for an Internet service and itemized telephone call records; information about the amount of data downloaded or uploaded; information concerning connections, disconnections, and reconnections; information relating to forwarding or redirection services; and information relating to the use of specific communication services subscribed to, such as instant messaging, web storage capacity, or call barring services.[334] One key forensic issue with all time data is the need to take into account any time zone differential arising from the diverse location of network components, the preferred method being the use of Coordinated Universal Time.[335]

4.191 The third category is widely referred to as 'subscriber data', although this is potentially misleading, since a subscriber only describes the person with whom the service provider has a contractual relationship, while the data under (c) is very broadly defined, encompassing data provided by subscribers and users. It would cover, for example, user-disclosed data, such as personal preferences, address information for installation and billing purposes, as well as data obtained from a third party, such as a credit reference agency for credit checks.[336] It could include, for example, a user's log-in password, available in case it is forgotten, which would potentially enable law enforcement access to protected data.[337] While potentially wide ranging, the ATCSA Code only lists those data items that may assist in identifying the subscriber, not other data that may be obtained in the course of providing the services. Subscriber data excludes those data items that fall into the previous two categories. So, for example, an email address is traffic data, although it will also form part of a customer's account details. Data items may also straddle categories, such as a customer's evening telephone number, which would seem to be both traffic data and subscriber data, while the last number a person called would seem to be both traffic data and usage data.

---

[333] Official Report, House of Commons, 26 July 2000, vol 354, Col 1178. See also the statement of the Home Office Minister, Lord Bassam, Official Report, House of Lords, 12 July 2000, vol 615, c 257.

[334] ADCD Code, above, n 324, para 2.29.

[335] Otherwise known as 'Greenwich Mean Time'.

[336] ADCD Code, above, n 324, para 2.31.

[337] ibid, para 2.31, which states that passwords and similar access mechanisms to content should not be disclosed except in the interests of national security.

Whatever the clarity or suitability of the definitions of 'communications data' and 'traf- **4.192**
fic data' under the RIPA, it should also be noted that a potentially competing definition
of 'traffic data' exists in UK law, under data protection rules. Under the data protection
regime, which transposes EU law,[338] 'traffic data' is defined in the following terms:

> . . . means any data processed for the purpose of the conveyance of a communication on an
> electronic communications network or for the billing in respect of that communication and
> includes data relating to the routing, duration or time of a communication.[339]

This definition differs from the RIPA concept in two respects. First, the data protection
definition potentially extends to all three categories of 'communications data', since routing information falls under category (a); duration and time under category (b), and data
required for billing purposes under category (c) data.[340] Second, 'location data' is conceived
as an overlapping but distinct concept from that of 'traffic data', rather than a sub-category:

> 'location data' means any data processed in an electronic communications network indi-
> cating the geographical position of the terminal equipment of a user of a public electronic
> communications service, including data relating to—
> (f) the latitude, longitude or altitude of the terminal equipment;
> (g) the direction of travel of the user; or
> (h) the time the location information was recorded.[341]

The reason why 'location data' may not fall within the broad concept of 'traffic data' under **4.193**
data protection rules is that location data may be generated through the operation of a GPS
chip system within the handset, rather than based on cell site analysis, such that the data is
used neither in the conveyance of the call nor its subsequent billing.

This potential divergence between the RIPA definitions and the data protection terms is **4.194**
only likely to be of interest were the CJEU to be called upon to interpret the provisions of
European data protection law in a manner that created a substantive difference in meaning,
which could impact on individual rights.

Obligations to disclose

From a law enforcement perspective, once an investigator has identified that valuable 'com- **4.195**
munications data' relating to a suspect's criminal conduct may be held by a CSP, the next
question is: what legal obligations does the CSP have to disclose such information to an
investigator?

A CSP will usually be subject to obligations not to disclose data about its subscribers and **4.196**
users, whether in confidence, based on contract or equitable, or under data protection rules.
The default position of a CSP will generally be to refuse a request for disclosure of such
information, to avoid any potential liability, and/or damage to its commercial reputation.
A requesting party will therefore need to have some legal authority to support its request.
The nature of this legal authority will vary according to whether the person making the

---

[338] ie Directive 02/58/EC, above, n 187.
[339] 2003 Privacy Regulations, above, n 153, reg 2(1).
[340] Note that under the previous regime, 'billing data' comprised a category overlapping but distinct from
'traffic data'. See the Telecommunications (Data Protection and Privacy) Regulations 1999 (SI No 2093),
regs 7, 8, and Sch 2.
[341] 2003 Privacy Regulations, above, n 153, reg 2(1).

request is a public authority, and therefore subject to a human-rights-compliant regulatory framework, or a private person engaged in either criminal or civil proceedings.

4.197 **Public LEAs** In 2015, the Interception of Communications Commissioner reported that over 500,000 requests for communications data were made each year by public authorities, of which nearly 90 per cent were from the police and the other main investigative agencies.[342] It is also reported that some 78.5 per cent of requests are made in respect of investigations to prevent and detect crimes or prevent disorder, while 15 per cent relate to national security purposes.[343] The figure of 500,000 does not take into account that a single recorded request often contains requests for data on multiple persons; and it has been stated that the true figure is more in the region of 5 million.[344] A previous Home Secretary has stated that communications data had been 'important evidence in 95% of serious crime cases and in almost all Security Service operations since 2004'.[345]

4.198 Although not stated on the face of Part 1, Chapter II, the ADCD Code notes that 'relevant public authorities' should not request communications data from CSPs under any other statutory powers they may have, or request the voluntary disclosure of such data under exemptions present in the Data Protection Act 1998.[346] A 'relevant public authority' means the police, NCA and others detailed in an order made by the Secretary of State.[347] While the RIPA regime is intended to create a single regime for accessing communications data by these 'relevant public authorities', the legacy production powers have not been repealed. For any other public authority, the ability to request communications data from a CSP will depend on it having the necessary statutory powers, such as those under the Social Security Fraud Act 2001.[348]

4.199 Part I, Chapter II of the Regulation of Investigatory Powers Act 2000 details a regime that enables law enforcement agencies to *require* the disclosure of 'communications data' from a 'telecommunications operator' (CSP)[349]. The request may be made to any person who provides a 'telecommunication service',[350] which would potentially include both publicly and privately provisioned services, as well as situations where the telecommunications service is simply a means for, or is incidental to, the provision of another type of service, such as an a hotel, airport lounge, or web-based retail service.[351] While the first draft of the Code of Practice excluded the latter category of persons, the Government's position had changed by the time the Code was finalized in 2007, with ancillary telecommunications operators being viewed as within the category of those to whom the disclosure obligation may apply.[352]

---

[342] IoCC Report 2014, above, n 274, paras 7.20 et seq.

[343] ibid.

[344] Martin Hoskins, T-Mobile, 2 July 2007.

[345] Home Office, Home Secretary's speech on the threat of international terrorism, given to the Institute for Public Policy Research Commission on National Security, 15 October 2008.

[346] ADCD Code, above, n 324, para 1.3. See the DPA 1998, s 29(3), which permits voluntary disclosure of personal data.

[347] RIPA, s 25(1) and the Regulation of Investigatory Powers (Communications Data) Order 2010 (SI No 480).

[348] Social Security Fraud Act 2001, s 1 amended the Social Security Administration Act 1992, s 109B (power to require information), to include 'any person who provides a telecommunications service' (s 109B(2A)(j)).

[349] RIPA, s 25(1).

[350] ibid, s 2(1) and (8A).

[351] ibid, s 12(4).

[352] Home Office, *Acquisition and Disclosure of Communications Data: Code of Practice*, The Stationery Office, 2007, para 2.15. This position is maintained in the draft 2015 version.

Under the provisions, the police force, certain criminal and intelligence services, Inland **4.200**
Revenue and Customs and Excise, and other persons can, under an appropriate authorization, give a 'notice' to a CSP requiring access to specified communications data.[353] Such
a notice shall only be issued by a 'designated person'[354] within an authority where it is
considered necessary for any of the public interest grounds set out in the Act: national
security; preventing or detecting crime or preventing disorder; the economic well-being of
the United Kingdom; public health and safety; the collection or assessing tax, duty, levy, or
related payment, and preventing death or personal injury.[355] Considerations about whether
requesting such data is proportionate to the purpose for which it is sought must include any
collateral intrusion on the rights of third parties not under investigation.[356]

It is a statutory duty of a CSP to comply with the requirements detailed in a notice,[357] which **4.201**
is enforceable through civil proceedings.[358] A refusal to comply with the provisions of a
Code issued under RIPA would not render a CSP liable to civil or criminal proceedings,[359]
so enabling a person to disagree with an interpretation adopted in the Code, although a
court, tribunal, or Commissioner may have regard to the Code when determining any
question.[360] As with interception, resort to a judicial remedy is likely to be extremely rare,
although problems have inevitably arisen where the request concerns a UK subscriber, using
the services of a provider located in another jurisdiction, where the requested data is held.
As noted above, this was one reason for the insertion of the extraterritorial provisions by the
Data Retention and Investigatory Powers Act 2014.

A leading example of the potential legal conflict that could arise can be seen in an important **4.202**
case examined in Belgium involving Yahoo! Inc. One aspect of this decision was discussed
earlier, concerning Yahoo!'s argument that its service was not an 'electronic communication service' and, therefore, not subject to the relevant order.[361] Yahoo!'s second argument
was that, being based in the US, it was not subject to Belgian jurisdiction and, therefore,
the request should have been made through MLA procedures.[362] Having lost before the
Supreme Court on the first issue,[363] the decision was referred back to the Court of Appeal
for reconsideration, which then decided that the Belgium prosecutor was not empowered to
act outside Belgian territory and therefore a request to Yahoo! in the US was invalid.[364] On
a further appeal to the Supreme Court, the Court of Appeal's decision was again overturned
and the request was considered valid.[365] This resulted in a further referral back to the Court

---

[353] A copy of the standard form of notice is available at <www.gov.uk/government/publications/
specimen-part-i-chapter-ii-notice>.
[354] RIPA, s 25(2) and the Regulation of Investigatory Powers Order 2010, above, n 347.
[355] RIPA, s 22(2). Under s 22(2)(h), the Secretary of State may make an order specifying additional purposes. No such order has yet been issued.
[356] ADCD Code , above, n 324, para 2.6.
[357] RIPA, s 22(6).
[358] ibid, s 22(8).
[359] ibid, s 72(2).
[360] ibid, s 72(4).
[361] At para 4.131.
[362] de Hert, P and Kopcheva, M, 'International mutual legal assistance in criminal law made redundant: A comment on the Belgium Yahoo! case', 27 *Computer Law and Security Review* 291 (2011).
[363] Court of Cassation, Criminal Law Section, No P.10.1347.N, 18 January 2011. This is now also likely to
be the position under UK law in respect of RIPA, especially following the insertion of s 2(8A) by the DRIPA.
[364] Court of Appeal of Brussels, Decision 2011.VJ11.000075, 12 October 2011.
[365] Court of Cassation, Decision, 4 September 2012.

of Appeal, who partially confirmed the original court's decision in 2009, by imposing a fine on Yahoo!, but did not require the disclosure of the identification data, because it was no longer required by the prosecutor.[366] While the length and convoluted nature of these proceedings are unlikely to be repeated when similar circumstances arise, they are likely to be salutary warning to the Home Office were it to consider taking enforcement proceedings against a foreign CSP under RIPA.

4.203   Another example occurred in Brazil in August 2006, when prosecutors sought substantial civil penalties against Google's office in São Paulo for an alleged failure to disclose user information relating to a criminal investigation in respect of one of Google's social networking sites.[367] The judge ruled against Google, threatening a daily fine of $23,000 for continued non-compliance. In its defence, the company claimed that the information was held on servers in the US, where the judicial requests should have been sent. When subsequently redirected, Google's US office disclosed the requested information.[368]

4.204   A request for communications data may include that which is already in the possession of the CSP, as well as data which the CSP is 'capable of obtaining'.[369] This latter gathering obligation is effectively limited to that which is 'reasonably practicable' for the CSP to do.[370] As well as detailing the communications data required, the notice will also indicate the time period for which such data is sought and the timescales within which a response is needed.[371]

4.205   Where the issuance of a notice is inappropriate, communications data may be obtained directly by persons within the law enforcement agency under an 'authorization'.[372] Possible circumstances where such conduct may be appropriate include where the CSP is not capable of obtaining or disclosing the requested data; the investigator believes notification to the CSP may prejudice an investigation or operation; or where arrangements exist with a CSP for direct law enforcement access to the relevant information.[373] The latter arrangement exists with some CSPs in respect of subscriber checks, also referred to as 'reverse look ups', the most commonly requested information.[374] Owing to the nature of an authorization, it is not served on a CSP, although the CSP may request details as assurance that any such conduct is lawful.[375]

4.206   In June 2002, the Home Secretary proposed extending the list of those designated as a 'relevant public authority'[376] under Part I, Chapter II that can access communications data under RIPA, to include numerous public bodies, ranging from local authorities, National Health Service authorities to the Food Standards Agency and the Postal Services Commission.

---

[366]   Court of Appeal of Antwerp, Judgment C/1785/2013, 20 November 2013.

[367]   'Brazilian prosecutors seek lawsuit against Google', *Reuters*, 22 August 2006.

[368]   Nakashima, E, 'Google to give data to Brazilian Court', *Washington Post*, 2 September 2006.

[369]   RIPA, s 22(4).

[370]   ibid, s 22(7).

[371]   There are three grades, from immediate threat to life through to routine matters (ADCD Code, above, n 324, para 3.5). The routine response period is ten working days (ibid, para 3.50).

[372]   RIPA, s 22(3).

[373]   ADCD Code, above, n 324, para 3.34.

[374]   ibid, para 2.31. See IoCC Report 2014, above, n 274, para 7.26.

[375]   ADCD Code, above, n 324, para 3.36.

[376]   RIPA, s 25(1)(g).

This proposal was met with a storm of controversy and the government quickly withdrew these plans, saying that it would consult further with the public before allowing additional authorities to access communications data under the RIPA.

As a consequence, in March 2003, the Home Office issued a public consultation **4.207** paper,[377] prior to the adoption of the final order.[378] Although the consultation paper admitted that the June 2002 proposal was too permissive, the list of authorities in the final order remained extensive. The final order specified over fifty categories of authority as having the right to obtain access to certain categories of communications data, including those referred to in the preceding paragraph, which comprises 510 individual agencies.[379] Before being replaced in 2010, the 2003 Order was amended twice, each time extending the number of 'relevant public authorities'.[380] The 2010 Order initially continued this expansive trend,[381] but with the coming into power of the coalition Government, the process was reversed. First, in 2012, Part I, Chapter II was amended to establish a separate judicial approvals regime for local authorities.[382] This was the result of a number of high profile cases of perceived abuse of the regime by local authorities.[383] Second, in 2015, the 2010 Order was again amended to remove another thirteen public authorities.[384]

The RIPA grants the Secretary of State the power to restrict the types of data that may be **4.208** accessed by a public authority, as well as the purposes for which such data may be used,[385] therefore the 2010 Order restricts the right of access for these additional authorities using both criteria. Currently, the vast majority of requests for data are made in respect of subscriber data, rather than traffic or usage data, therefore the right of access for the majority of authorities, specifically those designated persons within the authority, is limited to subscriber data falling within the third category of 'communications data'.

The March 2003 proposal contained a number of safeguards against the misuse of com- **4.209** munications data.[386] It noted that RIPA contains no explicit offence against the deliberate misuse of communications data by law enforcement agencies, although the Data Protection Act 1998 does contain a limited offence that may be applicable.[387] The final 2003 Order contained none of the proposed safeguards.

While the definition of 'communications data' under the RIPA indicates the potential range **4.210** of information that may be requested from a CSP by a law enforcement agency, two qualifications must be made in respect of the data that may actually be available. First, whether

---

[377] Home Office, 'Accessing Communications Data: Respecting Privacy and Protection the Public from Crime', Consultation Paper, 11 March 2003 ('Consultation 2003').

[378] SI 2003 No 3172 ('2003 Order').

[379] IoCC Report 2004, above, n 304, para 21. This compares with 138 individual agencies under Pt I, Chapter II.

[380] SI No 2005/3335 and SI No 2006/1878.

[381] Regulation of Investigatory Powers (Communications Data) Order 2010 (SI No 480).

[382] RIPA, s 23A, inserted by the Protection of Freedoms Act 2012, s 37.

[383] See Report of the Interception of Communications Commissioner for 2011, HC 496, July 2012, para 7.5.3.

[384] Regulation of Investigatory Powers (Communications Data) (Amendment) Order 2015 (SI No 228).

[385] RIPA, s 25(3)(a) and (b).

[386] See paras 3.6 et seq.

[387] DPA 1998, s 55.

a service does generate communications data will depend on the nature of the particular service being provided and/or the manner in which it is being supplied. As noted already, a 'pay-as-you-go' mobile customer may not generate much data other than traffic and usage data. In addition, the CSP's network may not be designed to collect certain information, or that information may be generated on network components supplied by another CSP, from which the first CSP obtains service, such as under an MVNO arrangement. The second qualification is that not all law enforcement agencies are entitled to all three categories of communications data; some agencies are only permitted to request access to usage and subscriber data, not traffic data.

4.211   In order to rationalize and standardize requests for communications data from public authorities to CSPs, a system of accredited Single Points of Contact (SPoCs) has been established for public authorities exercising law enforcement functions, empowered to and responsible for making requests for information to CSPs.[388] Each authority is required to have a trained individual, or group of individuals, through which any requests for information made under relevant powers must be made. The SPoCs are intended to 'help the public authority to regulate itself, by providing internal advice on quality assurance, and will also provide authentication of the pubic authority'; this is also referred to as a 'guardian and gatekeeper function'.[389] The latter issue is facilitated by the maintenance of a register by the Home Office, to which CSPs may refer when in receipt of a request for information from a person with a SPoC authentication identifier.[390] In addition, a CSP may refuse to accept requests from a person not appropriately registered as a SPoC,[391] and an authority should not try to acquire such data in the absence of an accredited SPoC.[392]

4.212   Together with the other limitations contained in, or adopted under, Part I, Chapter II, the establishment of a system of SPoCs effectively means that a CSP is not required to respond to a request for communications data from a law enforcement agency unless all the following criteria are met:

- the authority is a 'relevant public authority;
- the request is made by a prescribed officer;
- the request relates to the appropriately specified category of communications data, for example subscriber data;
- the request is made for a relevant specified purpose; and
- the request is made through an accredited SPoC.

While the recipient CSP may carry out such procedural checks, it is not for the CSP to assess or make determinations in respect of the necessity and proportionality of the request in terms of the specified purpose. Such a substantive review would lie with the Interception of Communications Commissioner or the Investigatory Powers Tribunal, depending on the circumstance. However, any *ex ante* procedural scrutiny will not arise where the 'intercept capability' built by the CSP grants law enforcement agents remote access to the system

---

[388]   ADCD Code , above, n 324, paras 3.19–3.30.

[389]   Statement made by Caroline Flint, Home Office Minister, at House of Commons Standing Committee on Delegated Legislation, Hansard, 4 November 2003, Col 024. ADCD Code, above, n 324, para 3.21.

[390]   ADCD Code, above, n 324, para 3.19.

[391]   ibid, para 3.25. The Code is admissible as evidence in any proceedings and shall be taken into account when determining any question to which it is applicable (RIPA, s 71(3) and (4)).

[392]   ADCD Code , above, n 324, para 3.24.

interface, enabling the required communication data to be retrieved directly, without the involvement of CSP personnel.

In the US, such compulsory requirements to disclose data are provided for under the **4.213** Electronic Communications Privacy Act of 1986 (ECPA).[393] It is interesting to note, however, that as part of the overhaul of law enforcement powers after the 11 September terrorist attack, the USA Patriot Act included a provision amending the ECPA to enable providers to *voluntarily* disclose communications data if the provider 'believes that an emergency involving immediate danger of death or serious physical injury to any person' justifies disclosure.[394] This provision is drafted in much broader terms than the emergency call service provisions under the Code.[395] Yet again, therefore, we see somewhat divergent approaches being taken between the US and the UK. Prior to the Snowden revelations, Birnhack and Elkin-Koren's 'unholy alliance'[396] between law enforcement and the Internet service providers was much greater than that which existed in the UK, where concerns about privacy and data protection have meant that any powers of intrusion are placed on a clearer statutory footing. Post-Snowden, it has been widely noted that one of the main consequences of the revelations, is that ISPs have become less willing to cooperate, or to be seen to cooperate, with law enforcement in both the UK and the US.[397]

Private investigators As discussed in previous chapters, private persons and entities have a **4.214** general right to investigate criminal activities and prosecute the perpetrators.[398] In terms of requesting communications data from a CSP, existing law makes a clear distinction between the investigative process and the prosecutorial process. In the former situation, it was clearly held in *ex parte Hallas*[399] that a person has no legal entitlement to request and be supplied with relevant evidence, even though this may fundamentally undermine the possibility of bringing a private prosecution. However, once proceedings have commenced, the prosecuting party can apply to the Crown court for a 'witness summons' requiring that the person 'give the evidence or produce the document or thing'.[400] As this is a coercive procedure, when considering an application, the court must be satisfied that the information is 'likely to be material evidence', and that the summons would be 'in the interests of justice'.[401]

In civil proceedings, the ability of a private investigator to retrieve the identity of a person will **4.215** also generally require a court order. However, echoing the s 29(3) procedure used by public LEAs prior to Part I, Chapter II of the RIPA, the Data Protection Act 1998 provides for the disclosure of personal data 'in connection with any legal proceedings (including prospective legal proceedings)' without breaching the Act, and therefore incurring potential liability.[402] The scope of this provision was considered in *Totalise plc v Motley Fool and Interactive Investor*.[403]

---

[393] 18 USC s 2703 'Required disclosure of customer communications or records' (ECPA).
[394] 18 USC s 2702(c)(4).
[395] ADCD Code, above, n 324, paras 5.5 et seq.
[396] Birnhack, MD and Elkin-Koren, N, 'The invisible handshake: The reemergence of the state in the digital environment', 8 *Va JL & Tech* 6 (2003).
[397] eg the Microsoft case, discussed at paras 5.78 et seq.
[398] Prosecution of Offences Act 1985, s 6(1). See paras 2.284–2.285.
[399] *DPP, ex parte Hallas* (1987) 87 Cr App R 340.
[400] Criminal Procedure (Attendance of Witnesses) Act 1965, s 2(2)(b). See *Pawsey* [1989] Crim LR 152.
[401] Criminal Procedure (Attendance of Witnesses) Act 1965, s 2(1).
[402] DPA 1998, s 35.
[403] (2001) 4 EMLR 750. See also *Sheffield Wednesday Football Club Ltd v Hargreaves* [2007] EWHC 2375 (QB) and *Golden Eye (International) Ltd v Telefonica UK Ltd* [2012] EWHC 723 (Ch).

4.216 The claimant, Totalise, complained to the defendants that a person using the nickname 'Zeddust' was posting defamatory statements about Totalise on discussion boards run by the defendants in the course of providing financial information services to individual investors. Totalise requested the disclosure of the identity and registration details of 'Zeddust' in order to pursue a claim. The defendants raised a number of objections, including restrictions on disclosure under the Data Protection Act. The court held that s 35 was sufficiently broad to enable to the voluntary disclosure of personal data to a third party for their prospective legal proceedings. As noted already, a CSP will generally be wary of voluntarily disclosing customer information to a private entity, both in terms of public image and potential liabilities, such as breach of confidence.

4.217 An alternative approach for private entities therefore lies in English law rules of civil procedure. The standard procedure for a claimant to obtain identification information is through a so-called 'Norwich Pharmacal' Order.[404] This order is applicable 'if through no fault of his own a person gets mixed up in the tortious acts of others so as to facilitate their wrongdoing he may incur no personal liability but he comes under a duty to assist the person who has been wronged by giving him full information and disclosing the identity of the wrongdoers'.[405] Clearly, in an Internet environment, an ISP could be viewed as facilitating a subscriber's wrongdoing, merely through the provision of access.

4.218 The application of the 'Norwich Pharmacal' procedure in a communications environment was examined in *Coca-Cola v BT plc*.[406] In this case, BT challenged a 'Norwich Pharmacal' Order requiring them to deliver up the subscriber details of a mobile customer subject to proceedings for infringement of Coca Cola's trade mark rights. The court held that the information held by BT was critical to the successful pursuance of Coca Cola's civil rights and therefore the information had to be disclosed.

4.219 In *Totalise*, the claimant requested the disclosure of Zeddust's identity under the 'Norwich Pharmacal' procedure. The website operators, Motley Fool and Interactive Investor, opposed the order on three grounds. First, that the proceedings upon which the request for the order was made (ie defamation) should be actual rather than prospective. Second, that s 35 of the Data Protection Act 1998 should be construed as only permitting use of the data by the data controller himself (ie Motley Fool) rather than disclosed to a third party. Third, reliance was placed on s 10 of the Contempt of Court Act 1981, which protects the disclosure of the source of information 'contained in a publication for which he is responsible'. The court rejected all three claims and the order was granted.

4.220 With regard to the third claim, Mr Justice Owen stated that the defendants, Motley Fool and Interactive Investor International, could not consider themselves responsible for the publication since they exercised no editorial control; disclaimed liability for the content (in the case of Interactive Investor International); and 'simply provide a facility by means of which the public at large is able publicly to communicate its views'. Such generous judicial

---

[404] So called after the House of Lords' decision in *Norwich Pharmacal Co v Customs and Excise Commissioners* [1974] AC 133. Now formalized in the Civil Procedure Rules, r 31.18 'Rules not to limit other powers of the court to order disclosure'.
[405] *Norwich Pharmacal* [1974] AC 133, at 175.
[406] [1999] FSR 518.

sentiment will generally be greatly welcomed by website operators and ISPs as they try to avoid liability for the content they provide.[407]

In another case, *Grant v Google*,[408] the claimant was concerned to prevent further infringe- **4.221** ments of its copyright in an as yet unpublished work. The work was being made available as a free download generated by Google's search engine. The claimant had failed to identify the owner of the source website, because the owner was registered with a company which offered customer anonymity. The claimant therefore decided to pursue the person advertising the website, the identity of which was known to Google. Google did not oppose the request for the court order, but had refused to disclose such information without recourse to it. Similarly, the record companies, in their pursuit of persons engaged in the sharing of illegally copied music using P2P software, have had recourse to the procedure to identity infringers.[409]

As well as providing access to identification data held by ISPs, a court may also order the **4.222** disclosure and production of material other than that required to identify the wrongdoer, such as 'information showing that he has committed the wrong'.[410] For example, within the definition of 'communications data', detailed above, the communications attributes of a person's use of a communication service may provide important forensic information about the defendant's activities, such as when a message was sent and to whom or what (eg posting an illegal image on a bulletin board). However, as noted by the House of Lords, the 'Norwich Pharmacal' jurisdiction 'is an exceptional one and one which is only exercised by the courts when they are satisfied that it is necessary that it should be exercised'.[411] It does not, therefore, provide an easy alternative forensic source, but is only available where 'the innocent third parties are the only practicable source of information'.[412]

It has been suggested that civil access procedures to CSP-held communications data can **4.223** operate in a manner that disrupts LEA access, since scarce CSP resource may be diverted from responding to the latter to service the former.[413] A failure to comply with a Norwich Pharmacal Order would result in an offence of contempt, while the latter may simply be enforced through civil proceedings.[414]

Preserved or retained data

As already noted, the patterns created by the communications attributes of criminal and **4.224** terrorist networks in cyberspace are extremely valuable to law enforcement agencies for discerning the operational nature of such networks; forming, dissolving, and reforming according to the logic of the opportunities being pursued. Such evidential data will be generated by the networks that comprise the Internet, as traffic passes into, across, and out of

---

[407] See further paras 2.226 et seq.
[408] [2006] All ER (D) 243 (May).
[409] See *Polydor Ltd and others v Brown and others* [2005] EWHC 3191 (Ch). See also the Hong Kong case *Cinepoly Records Co Ltd & others v Hong Kong Broadband Network Ltd & others* [2006] 1 HKLRD 255.
[410] *Aoot Kalmneft v Denton Wilde Sapte* [2002] 1 Lloyds Rep 417, para 17. See also *CHC Software Care Ltd v Hopkins and Wood* [1993] FSR 241.
[411] *Ashworth Security Hospital v MGN Ltd,* [2002] 4 All ER 193, para 57.
[412] *Mitsui & Co Ltd v Nexen Petroleum UK Ltd* (2005) EWHC 625 (Ch), para 24.
[413] Comment made by Simon Watkin, Home Office official, at an ERA meeting held at the House of Lords, 21 May 2007.
[414] RIPA, s 22(8).

each network, and will often be as transient as the communication session itself. To address such transience, governments have looked to the imposition of express preservation and retention obligations upon the providers of communication services.

4.225 Communications data may be retained by CSPs for relatively short periods of time, due to the volumes involved and the related costs of storage, as well as in compliance with data protection rules, which diminish the commercial value of such data to the CSP.[415] However, a criminal investigation may require access to data generated over a considerable period of time, particularly in serious crime cases, such as terrorism or organized crime. In an ACPO survey, carried out in May 2005 over a two-week period, there were 213 law enforcement requests for data relating to communications that had taken place between six and twelve months earlier.[416] Criminal procedure in most jurisdictions enables law enforcement to request the preservation of real-time data by a communications service provider in specified circumstances, generally under judicial order, the so-called 'Quick Freeze-Quick Thaw' model.[417] The Council of Europe Convention on Cybercrime, for example, requires Member States to harmonize procedures for the expedited preservation of data to facilitate the investigative process, providing for a maximum preservation period of ninety days,[418] which reflects the current position in the US.[419]

4.226 However, with heightened concerns about the threat of terrorism, the issue of the potential unavailability of evidence has led to calls for the imposition of a general broad data retention obligation on communication service providers to enable access to historic stored data, as well as the preservation of real-time data. In March 2006, the EU adopted a harmonization measure on data retention. Other jurisdictions, such as the US, have rejected such an approach to date, although other regulatory mechanisms are sometime relied upon.[420]

4.227 Large-scale retention of communications data remains a highly controversial measure. Criticisms range from concerns about the threat to our individual liberties, to the actual utility of such an approach as a tool of criminal investigation. This section reviews the current regime under UK law and at an EU level, examining some of the arguments raised against the legality and cost of such measures.

4.228 **UK law** Prior to the events of 11 September 2001, the issue of data retention had been raised by law enforcement agencies, but had been rejected out of hand by the Government. In August 2000, the then National Criminal Intelligence Service (NCIS) submitted a proposal to the Home Office, on behalf of ACPO, HM Customs & Excise, and the various branches of the security services, calling for legislation mandating large-scale retention of

---

[415] eg under the 2003 Privacy Regulations, above, n 153 , reg 7, data shall be erased or rendered anonymous upon termination of a call, except in specified circumstances.

[416] Home Office, supra n 242, para 5.5.

[417] Sussmann, M, 'The critical challenges from international high-tech and computer-related crime at the millennium', 9 *Duke Journal of Comparative & International Law* 451 (1999).

[418] Convention on Cybercrime, Arts 16–17 in respect of national rules and Arts 29–30 in respect of mutual legal assistance.

[419] 18 USC s 2703(f).

[420] eg in the US, the Federal Communications Commission imposes an eighteen-month record retention requirement on every carrier, under 47 CFR s 42.6; a period that was extended from six months following a 1985 petition from the US DoJ. The forensic value of such records has diminished over recent years, however, as billing models have changed. See 'Petition to Repeal 47 C.F.R. § 42.6 (Retention of Telephone Toll Records)', 4 August 2015, available at <https://epic.org/privacy/fcc-data-retention-petition.pdf>.

communications data.[421] The proposal argued that communications data provided valuable evidence not only in course of an investigation, as intelligence, primary evidence, and corroborative evidence, but also post-trial, as a means of resolving miscarriages of justice and therefore in 'the interests of justice'.[422] It recommended that CSPs be required to retain communications data available for real-time access for a period of twelve months, followed by archiving for a further six-year period.[423] The archiving would be carried out either in-house or outsourced 'to a Trusted Third Party; either a Government-run Data Warehouse or to a private contractor's facility'.[424]

While no formal response to the proposal was published by the Government, the then **4.229** Minister for e-Commerce Patricia Hewitt made the following statement to the Parliamentary Select Committee for Trade and Industry:

> I do not agree with the proposals ... I have not had formal communications with the Home Office, I have discussed it informally with Charles Clarke and I understand it is his view as well that that proposal should not be implemented.[425]

However, following the 2001 terrorist attacks, the Government's position on the issue fun- **4.230** damentally shifted and data retention provisions were incorporated as a key initiative in the ATCSA. Part 11 of the Act establishes a regime for a voluntary code of practice on the retention of communications data. It purports to require communications providers to retain communications data for certain limited purposes:

(a) for the purpose of safeguarding national security; or
(b) for the purposes of prevention or detection of crime or the prosecution of offenders *which may relate directly or indirectly to national security.*[426]

From the Government's perspective, any types of crime may be committed by a terrorist in the course of his activities, which should be within the scope of law enforcement's legitimate investigation when accessing retained data. However, the original wording was seen as creating a blanket power to investigate any crime, whether related to terrorism or national security or not. The amendment in italics was intended to address this concern by narrowing the grounds for the investigation. However, the literal wording would not appear to achieve this objective, since the word 'may' seems to permit of any purpose related to the investigation of crime, as the crime may not relate directly or indirectly to national security. However, in debate, the Government appears to have accepted that the phrase does limit retention to 'those crimes that relate to national security or terrorism'.[427]

The main mechanism enabling the retention of communications data under the ATCSA **4.231** was a voluntary Code of Practice, drafted by the Secretary of State in consultation with

---

[421] 'Looking to the Future, Clarity on Communications Data Retention Law: Submission to the Home Office for Legislation on Data Retention', 21 August 2000, ('NCIS Submission'). The document was leaked to the Observer and is available at <http://cryptome.org/ncis-carnivore.htm>.
[422] ibid, para 1.2.2. See also ibid, para 2.4.1. Indeed, the proposal implies support from the Criminal Cases Review Committee.
[423] ibid, Recommendations 6.1–6.3.
[424] ibid, Recommendation 7.1.
[425] Minutes of Evidence, Question 93, 13 December 2000.
[426] Anti-terrorism Crime and Security Act 2001 (ATCSA), s 102(3) (emphasis added).
[427] Comments made by Beverley Hughes, Parliamentary Under Secretary of State, 12 December, 2001, Commons Hansard, Col 909.

affected CSPs and the Information Commissioner, the supervisory authority under the Data Protection Act 1998. The Code of Practice was brought into force by Order.[428] The Secretary of State was also empowered to enter into contractual agreements with individual CSPs about their data retention and retrieval practices. Such agreements would take the form of a service contract, detailing service levels that the CSP is expected to meet and the charges that can be levied against the requesting agencies.[429]

4.232 Part 11 is applicable to a 'communications provider', which is defined as a person who provides a telecommunications service.[430] This latter term is then defined under the RIPA,[431] and would potentially encompass a huge range of entities, beyond our traditional notion of a telecoms company, such as cybercafés and locations offering WiFi access, such as airports. The Code narrows the applicability of the obligation further to those providing a 'public telecommunication service', although this concept is still broadly conceived and would likely include the examples given above.[432]

4.233 The Secretary of State was accorded reserve powers to introduce a mandatory Code of Practice where the voluntary arrangements are found not to be working or workable,[433] although the powers lapsed in December 2003.[434] Finally, the ATCSA provides for the Secretary of State to make contributions 'as he thinks appropriate' to the expenses incurred by CSPs in retaining communications data under the Act,[435] which could either take the form of a contribution to the capital expenditure costs incurred by the CSP or the operational expenditures.

4.234 The success of the voluntary scheme in Part 11 of the ATCSA depended on the participation of CSPs with a significant proportion of total subscribers. Whether CSPs participated in the scheme depended on whether they were convinced that Part 11 provided a legitimate legal basis for data retention, that the invasion of privacy that data retention will involve is justified and necessary, and that the costs that they bear will not lead to financial underperformance. Unfortunately for the government, questions arose as to the legality and justification of the voluntary scheme. The major CSPs, ie the fixed and mobile network operators and ISPs, largely rejected the voluntary code approach, and the Government was therefore forced to pursue a mandatory regime.

4.235 Following the enactment of the ATCSA, and in anticipation of being consulted about a Code of Practice issued by the Secretary of State, the Information Commissioner sought advice from counsel about the lawfulness of the proposed data retention arrangements.[436] At the centre of the problem identified by counsel lies the fact that communications data may be retained under the ATCSA solely for purposes relating to national security, but may be accessed by law enforcement authorities under RIPA for any one of several public

---

[428] ATCSA, s 103(5). Retention of Communications Data Order 2003, above, n 325.
[429] ATCSA Code, above, n 329, paras 20–2.
[430] ATCSA, s 107(1).
[431] RIPA, s 2(1).
[432] See Oftel, *Guidelines for the Interconnection of Public Electronic Communication Networks*, May 2003, s 6.1.
[433] ATCSA, s 104.
[434] ibid, s 105.
[435] ibid, s 106.
[436] See <http://www.whatdotheyknow.com>.

interest purposes, such as crime prevention and detection and public health and safety, or, indeed, may be accessed by any other person with a lawful right, including civil litigants.[437] Counsel had 'no doubt' that both the retention of communications data and the disclosure of such data to a public authority would constitute an interference with the 'right to respect for private life and correspondence' enshrined in Art 8(1) of the ECHR.

However, an interference with Art 8(1) can be justified if it is in accordance with the law and **4.236** is necessary to one of the legitimate aims detailed in Art 8(2):

> There shall be no interference by a public authority with the exercise of this right except such as is in accordance with the law and is necessary in a democratic society in the interests of national security, public safety or the economic well-being of the country, for the prevention of disorder or crime, for the protection of health or morals, or for the protection of the rights and freedoms of others.

Counsel was of the view that the balance struck by Parliament in the ATCSA is the best test of proportionality. As Parliament chose only to incorporate the narrow purposes of national security for retention of communications data, and not the broader, less pressing, public interest purposes in RIPA, counsel advised that issuing an access notice under RIPA would be arguably 'disproportionate' and therefore incompatible with Art 8.

Any person whose functions are of a public nature and who acts incompatibly with Art 8 **4.237** would, in the United Kingdom, contravene the Human Rights Act 1998. According to counsel's advice, any public bodies accessing communications data under RIPA would risk contravening this legislation. Counsel also went so far as to suggest that CSPs would 'not be safe to assume' that the Human Rights Act would not apply to their functions under the ATCSA. In other words, by retaining and disclosing communications data under the voluntary scheme, CSPs could themselves be contravening the legislation.

At the time of writing the first edition of this book, there was no case law directly address- **4.238** ing the lawfulness of such retention under human rights law. As a consequence, analogies were drawn from *R (on the application of S) v Chief Constable of South Yorkshire and others*.[438] In this test case, the court was asked to consider whether the continued retention of fingerprint samples or DNA profiles under Police and Criminal Evidence Act 1984 (PACE) s 64(1A), obtained lawfully by the police, was an interference with a person's private life, under Art 8(1) of the ECHR. The Law Lords, with one exception (Baroness Hale), held that Art 8(1) was not engaged by such practices, therefore it was not necessary to go on to consider whether it could then be justified under Art 8(2). This approach differed from that of the Court of Appeal, which had held that Art 8(1) was engaged, but that Art 8(2) provided justification.[439]

In addition to the uncertainty about the legal validity of the data retention scheme, doubt **4.239** arose during the course of 2002 about how any compensation to the industry provided for by the ATCSA would be calculated and funded. This doubt eroded the collaborative relationship between the government, law enforcement authorities, and CSPs. In particular, ISPs, who would be likely to bear a great deal of the cost burden, lost confidence in the success of any scheme. The government's estimates of the costs involved were in the vicinity

---

[437] ATCSA Code, above, n 329, para 28.
[438] [2004] UKHL 39; [2005] Crim LR 136.
[439] [2003] 1 All ER 148.

of £9m. Of course, the exact costs depend on what requirements are actually imposed in any voluntary or compulsory Code of Practice, but industry estimates wildly exceeded the Government's. The All Party Parliamentary Internet Group's (APIG) inquiry on data retention reported, in January 2003, that AOL alone estimated set-up costs in the vicinity of $40m, with annual operational costs of $14m, and that total sum across the industry could exceed £100m.[440] Civil libertarians also expressed great concern about the ATCSA and the potential infringement of privacy that it would permit.

4.240   The questions about the legality of the scheme, the costs involved for the industry and the human rights issues led to calls for the government to abandon the scheme altogether. However, a Code of Practice under Part 11 of the ATCSA entered into force in December 2003.[441] To comply with the Code as drafted, CSPs would need to retain subscriber details and 'telephony data' such as cell site information and call records for twelve months, short message service (SMS), media messaging service, email, and ISP data such as log-on records for six months and 'web activity logs' for four days.[442]

4.241   There is nothing in the terms of the ATCSA that expressly addresses the jurisdictional scope of the data retention provisions, although s 102 extends to data 'obtained or held' by a communications provider. The Code states that the retention obligation extends both to UK-based services, as well as subscribers resident in the UK, which would encompass foreign service providers, such as AOL, that hold UK data in the US.[443] However, the Code recognizes that foreign service providers may be subject to conflicting legal obligations in the jurisdiction in which they are based, which may prevent compliance with the Code.

4.242   In respect of costs, the Code states that the Government will 'contribute a reasonable proportion of the marginal cost as appropriate',[444] the marginal costs being the difference between the period communications data is retained for business purposes and the time required under the Code. While the public debate on ATCSA focused on the question of retention, the related but critical matter of *access* to such data received somewhat less attention. Law enforcement access to such data will be made either under Part I, Chapter II of RIPA or through a production order under PACE. This statutory division was the subject of criticism and calls for reform. The Newton Committee, appointed under ATCSA to review its operation,[445] recommended that a unified regime be established.[446] In response, the Government stated that it 'tend[ed] to agree with this recommendation and is considering putting Part 11 in an additional section to RIPA'.[447] This was never done, however, which has perhaps come back to haunt the current Government!

4.243   The whole future of Part 11 of ATCSA as a voluntary regime remains unclear and uncertain. Pressure for reform has come from a number of different sources. The Newton Committee

---

[440] All Party Internet Group (APIG), Report on Communications Data, January 2003, para 145.

[441] Retention of Communications Data Order 2003, above, n 325.

[442] ATCSA Code, above, n 329, Appendix A.

[443] ibid, Appendix, para 12.

[444] ibid, para 24.

[445] ATCSA, s 122.

[446] Privy Counsellor Review Committee (Chaired by Rt Hon. Lord Newton of Braintree), *Anti-terrorism, Crime and Security Act 2001 Review: Report*, HC 100, 18 December 2003, para 406 ('Newton Committee').

[447] Home Office *Counter-Terrorism Powers: Reconciling Security and Liberty in an Open Society*, Discussion Paper, Cm 6147, February 2004, para 141.

recommended that it should be 'part of mainstream legislation and not special terrorism legislation'.[448] At a parliamentary level, the APIG issued a report recommending that the ATCSA retention scheme be dismantled, in favour of a data preservation scheme.[449] However, the debate over data retention changed radically with the adoption of a harmonization measure by the European Union.

EU Directive One of the first references to data retention at an EU level appeared in a   **4.244**
Council Decision on combating child pornography in 2000. The Decision called for a constructive dialogue with industry to tackle the problem, but also called upon Member States to consider measures that would place CSPs under certain duties, including 'to retain traffic-related data, where applicable and technically feasible'.[450]

EU-wide rules on data retention resurfaced during the negotiations on the revision to the   **4.245**
EU directive on data protection in the telecommunications sector. With the events of 11 September 2001 clearly in the minds of policy makers, particularly the UK following the ATCSA, attention turned to the compatibility of data retention with data protection rules. Under the General Data Protection Directive (95/46/EC) and the Telecommunications Sectoral Directive (97/66/EC), provisions either excluded matters of crime and national security from the scope of protection or provided for exemptions from various of the obligations.[451] With the revision of the Sectoral Directive in 2002, there was a call for data retention to be given specific recognition as a reason for derogating from the general protections being granted data subjects:

> Member States may adopt legislative measures to restrict the scope of the rights and obligations provided for . . . when such restriction constitutes a necessary, appropriate and proportionate measure within a democratic society to safeguard national security (ie State security), defence, public security, and the prevention, investigation, detection and prosecution of criminal offences or of unauthorised use of the electronic communication system . . . To this end, Member States may, *inter alia*, adopt legislative measures providing for the retention of data for a limited period justified on the grounds laid down in this paragraph . . .[452]

Thus, data retention obligations were legitimized, but not harmonized among the Member States.

The next step came following the Madrid train bombings in March 2004. The resulting   **4.246**
'Declaration on Combating Terrorism', issued by EU leaders on 25 March 2004, specifically called upon the Council to examine 'proposals for establishing rules on the retention of communications traffic data by service providers', as a necessary tool in the fight against terrorism, with a view to adopting an instrument as a matter of priority by June 2005.[453] In April 2004, the governments of the United Kingdom, Ireland, France, and Sweden proposed a Council Framework decision to harmonize traffic data retention among

---

[448] Newton Committee above, n 446, para 396.
[449] APIG, above, n 440, paras 141, 178, and 189.
[450] Council Decision 2000/375/JHA to combat child pornography on the Internet, OJ L 138/1, 9 June 2000, Art 3(c).
[451] eg Directive 95/46/EC of the European Parliament and of the Council of 24 October 1995 on the protection of individuals with regard to the processing of personal data and on the free movement of such data, OJ L 281/31, 23 November 1995, Art 3(2) and 13(1).
[452] Directive 02/58/EC, above, n 187, Art 15(1).
[453] Available at <http://www.consilium.europa.eu/uedocs/cmsupload/decl-25.3.pdf>.

EU Member States.[454] The legal basis for the proposal was the so-called 'Third Pillar' of the Treaty on European Union, officially Title VI 'Provisions on Police and Judicial Cooperation in Criminal Matters', which includes measures 'ensuring compatibility in rules applicable in the Member States, as may be necessary to improve such cooperation'.[455]

4.247 Concerns were expressed, particularly by the European Parliament, about the legitimacy of such a measure, both in the terms of its substance, as well as the legal basis for its adoption. As a consequence, in September 2005, the Commission published a proposal for a European Parliament and Council directive on data retention.[456] The legal basis for this measure was the then Art 95 of the Treaty establishing the European Community, a 'First Pillar' measure, concerned with promoting the Internal Market. By amending the legal basis, the European Parliament would obtain an effective veto over the adoption of the measure, rather than merely the right to express an opinion, which was seen as an important safeguard for the rights of individuals and the interests of CSPs.

4.248 In terms of substance, the two proposed instruments did not differ significantly in respect of the types of data to be retained; rather it was the length of time such data is to be retained. Under the Council proposal, such data could be held for twelve months, but with the possibility of Member States adopting longer periods, up to forty-eight months. On the other hand, the Commission proposal stated that twelve months is the maximum retention period. A second area of divergence concerned access to the retained data, a matter not addressed under the ATCSA. The Council proposal contained a specific article addressing access, requiring that the data only be accessed for 'specified, explicit and legitimate purposes by competent authorities',[457] while the Commission simply provided that the data should be available for transmission 'upon request to the competent authorities *without undue delay*'.[458] However, neither proposal expressly addressed access by others, such as a data subject or civil litigant. Finally, while the Commission proposal addressed the issue of costs, stating that CSPs should 'receive an appropriate compensation for demonstrated additional costs',[459] the Council proposal was silent on the matter.

4.249 On 14 December, the United Kingdom, then holding the presidency of the Union, obtained agreement among the various EU institutions that the proposal would take the form of a Directive of the Council and European Parliament, on the basis of Art 95 of the EC Treaty,

---

[454] Draft Framework Decision on the retention of data processed and stored in connection with the provision of publicly available electronic communications services or data on public communications networks for the purpose of prevention, investigation, detection and prosecution of crime and criminal offences including terrorism, No 8958/04, 28 April 2004 ('Council Proposal').

[455] Treaty Establishing the European Union, OJ C191/1; 31 ILM 253 (TEU), Art 31(c).

[456] See European Commission, Commission proposes rules on communication data retention which are both effective for law enforcement and respectful of rights and business interests, Press Release, IP/05/1167, 21 September 2005 and European Commission, 'Data Retention Directive', Memo/05/328, 21 September 2005 ('Commission Proposal').

[457] Council Proposal, above, n 454, Art 6.

[458] Based on an 'Interservice Consultation' versions leaked to lobby group European Digital Rights in July 2005 (available at <http://www.edri.org>). However, the provision is also in the Directive 2006/24/EC of the European Parliament and of the Council of 15 March 2006 on the retention of data generated or processed in connection with the provision of publicly available electronic communications services or of public communications networks and amending Directive 2002/58/EC;

OJ L 105/54, 13 April 2006 ('Retention Directive'), Art 8.

[459] Commission Proposal, above, n 456, Art 8.

and amending the Privacy and Electronic Communications Directive (02/58/EC).[460] The Council finally adopted the Directive at the Justice and Home Affairs Council Meeting on 21 February 2006, although the Irish and Slovak delegations voted against the proposal. The final measure was formally adopted in March 2006,[461] and Member States had until September 2007 to transpose it into national law.[462]

The Directive imposed a mandatory minimum retention requirement of six months and a **4.250** maximum of twenty-four months.[463] At the time, the Home Secretary called upon Member States to implement the maximum period, even though it is twice that provided for under ATCSA.[464] However, by the time the UK Government published its consultation paper on the transposition of the Directive, it had concluded that a twelve-month retention period was proportionate in terms of protecting individual human rights,[465] which is what was implemented.[466] According to the Directive's objectives, the retained data shall be available for the 'investigation, detection and prosecution of serious crime',[467] the definition of which is left to Member States to determine. The categories of data covered by the retention requirement are similar to those defined under the RIPA and detailed in the ATCSA code, except in two respects. One additional category concerns data related to an 'unsuccessful call attempt'.[468] Such data has to be retained 'where those data are generated',[469] which implies that CSPs are not required to specifically reconfigure their systems to explicitly retain this data if not already captured. A second category concerns 'pre-paid anonymous services',[470] for which CSPs are required to retain 'the date and time of the initial activation of the service and the cell ID from which the service was activated',[471] as distinct from the cell ID data relating to a specific communication session.

Member States were able to postpone application of the retention requirements in respect **4.251** of 'data relating to Internet access, Internet telephony and Internet email' until 2009.[472]

---

[460] Ireland unsuccessfully challenged the legal basis of the Directive, see Case C-301/06, *Ireland v European Parliament*, Judgment, 10 February 2009, [2009] ECR I-593, [2009] 2 CMLR 37.

[461] Retention Directive, above, n 458.

[462] ibid, Art 15.

[463] ibid, Art 6. Member States may extend retention periods beyond the maximum, when 'facing particular circumstances', for a limited period and upon notification to the Commission and the other Member States (ibid, Art 12).

[464] Travis, A, 'Clarke wins EU pact on storing phone and internet records', *The Guardian*, 15 December 2005, available at <http://www.theguardian.com/politics/2005/dec/15/uk.terrorism>.

[465] Home Office, 'The initial transposition of Directive 2006/24/EC on the retention of data generated or processed in connection with the provision of publicly available electronic communications services or of public communications networks and amending Directive 2002/58/EC', Consultation Paper, March 2007.

[466] The Data Retention (EC Directive) Regulations 2007 (SI No 2199).

[467] Retention Directive, above, n 458, Art 1(1). The original proposal included the word 'prevention', although this disappeared in the course of negotiations, based on an amendment from the Parliament ('Report on the proposal for a directive of the European Parliament and of the Council on the retention of data processed in connection with the provision of public electronic communication services and amending Directive 2002/58/EC', Report of the Committee on Civil Liberties, Justice and Home Affairs, A6-0365/2005, 28 November 2005). One can speculate that making communication data available for the purpose of 'prevention' was viewed as too broad, facilitating the possibility of bulk rather than targeted access.

[468] Retention Directive, above, n 458, Art 2(2)(f), defined as 'a communication where a telephone call has been successfully connected but not answered or there has been a network management intervention'.

[469] ibid, Art 3(2).

[470] ibid, Art 5(1)(e)(2)(vi).

[471] ibid.

[472] ibid, Art 15(3).

The UK Government made a declaration under this provision, as did fifteen other Member States, in order to give them more time to consider the implications further, in conjunction with industry.[473] VoIP calls, or Internet telephony,[474] represent the most significant challenge to existing law enforcement practices, because such services do not necessarily generate sufficient data to identify the parties to the call. In a 2006 Ofcom consultation on the regulation of VoIP services, responses from law enforcement representatives complained that such issues had not been adequately addressed and could encourage criminals 'to propagate their activities by hiding behind a cloak of virtual anonymity'.[475]

4.252 In respect of access, the Retention Directive states that access should be 'provided only to the competent national authorities in specific cases and in accordance with national law'.[476] Two areas of uncertainty arise from this wording. First, to what extent may those national authorities be based in other Member States, ie direct cross-border requests for access? While there is nothing on the face of the measure that prohibits such an interpretation, it is a controversial issue, which has now been partly addressed in the European Investigation Order.[477] Subsequent to adoption of the Retention Directive, it was reported that the US authorities raised the issue of accessing retained data during a high level meeting with EU representatives, being apparently assured that such data would be available under existing agreements governing mutual legal assistance.[478]

4.253 Second, should this provision be read as precluding access by private persons, such as a data subject or third-party litigant? Such a restrictive interpretation does not seem to be supported by the wording of the recital, which also uses the word 'only', but later in the sentence: 'provided to the competent national authorities only in accordance with national legislation'.[479] During lobbying on the proposed measure, representatives of the entertainment industry called for the Retention Directive to 're-affirm that ... civil litigants and similar parties—including rights holders—can get access to connection and traffic data by court order in accordance with the *acquis communautaire*'.[480] Data retention, it was argued, was the 'missing link' supporting the IP enforcement measures adopted by the EU.[481] Such an affirmation was not forthcoming.

4.254 Member States were required to impose sanctions on 'any intentional access to, or transfer of, data retained' under the Directive,[482] either under data protection law or as a form of

---

[473] Initial transposition was made under the Data Retention (EC Directive) Regulations 2007 (SI No 2199), until replaced by the Data Retention (EC Directive) Regulations 2009 (SI No 859), which have since been revoked.

[474] Strictly speaking, Internet telephony are calls routed over the Internet, whereas VoIP calls simply make use of the IP standard as the mode of transmission, but may not actually pass over the Internet. However, the terms are used interchangeably here.

[475] Response from ACPO to the Ofcom consultation, quoted in Warren, P, 'Lifting the veil on internet voices', *The Guardian*, 27 July 2006, available at <http://www.theguardian.com/technology/2006/jul/27/guardianweeklytechnologysection>.

[476] Retention Directive, above, n 458, Art 4.

[477] See further paras 5.98–5.99.

[478] See Spongenberg, H, 'US could access EU data retention information', *EU Observer*, 12 May 2006, available at <http://euobserver.com/9/21580>.

[479] Retention Directive, above, n 458, Recital 17.

[480] Creative and Media Business Alliance (CMBA), 'Position on the forthcoming Commission proposal on data retention', 17 November 2005, available at <http://cmba-alliance.eu/assets/files/Data_Retention_CMBA_June05.pdf>.

[481] ibid.

[482] Retention Directive, above, n 458, Art 13(2).

unauthorized access.[483] Under UK law, the former regime would generally only impose civil liability,[484] while the latter criminal sanction under the Computer Misuse Act 1990 would not be applicable to 'enforcement officers'.[485] The APIG called for explicit criminal penalties under the RIPA for the unauthorized issuance of notices requesting communications data,[486] which the Government accepted 'may need to be addressed', although no such offence was adopted.[487]

As part of an on-going monitoring and evaluation of the Directive, to be completed by the **4.255** Commission in 2010,[488] the Directive required Member States to provide annual statistics to the Commission concerning, in particular, the time between the retention of data and any subsequent request for access to it by law enforcement.[489] During public debates about the data retention issue, much comment has been made about the failure of policy makers to provide sufficient evidence to support the assertion that large-scale retention for specified periods would improve law enforcement capabilities.[490] The generation of statistics under the Directive could have gone some way to meeting this demand, although the Commission reported that the statistics provided differed 'in scope and detail', while seven of the Member States that had transposed the Retention Directive had failed to provide statistics.[491]

Considerable opposition to, and reservations about, the Retention Directive were expressed **4.256** over the years by academics,[492] civil liberties groups,[493] business,[494] and national data protection authorities.[495] Large-scale data retention must itself be seen as vulnerable to abuse, a new security risk, and concerns have been voiced that such provisions breach data protection and human rights laws, as a disproportionate response to an unmeasured threat. Following transposition in a number of Member States, national courts also questioned the legality of the measure.[496] A case eventually reached the Court of Justice of the European Union (CJEU), which decided that the Retention Directive breached Arts 7 and 8 of the Charter of Fundamental Rights and was declared invalid.[497]

---

[483] ibid, Recital 18.

[484] For unlawful processing.

[485] CMA, s 10.

[486] APIG, above, n 440, para 123.

[487] Consultation 2003, above, n 376, para 18. Under the IPB, such an offence has now been proposed.

[488] Retention Directive, above, n 458, Art 14. See European Commission, 'Evaluation report on the Data Retention Directive (Directive 2006/24/EC)', COM(2011) 225 final, 18 April 2011 ('Evaluation Report').

[489] Retention Directive, above, n 458, Art 10.

[490] See eg ECTA, ETNO, EuroISPA, GSM Europe, and ECCA, 'Joint statement to the Informal Justice Council, 8 and 9 September 2005 on Communications Data Retention', available from <http://www.ecta-portal.com/en/upload/File/Press_Releases/Data_Retention/FINAL September industry-statement.pdf>.

[491] Evaluation Report, above, n 488, para 4.7.

[492] eg Feiler, L, 'The Legality of the Data Retention Directive in Light of the Fundamental Rights to Privacy and Data Protection', 1(3) *European Journal of Law and Technology* (2010).

[493] eg Open Rights Group, Data Retention, available at <https://www.openrightsgroup.org/issues/data-retention>.

[494] eg International Chamber of Commerce letter to European President, 26 May 2004.

[495] eg, the Art 29 Working Party Opinion 113/2005, 21 October 2005. See also Opinion of the European Data Protection Supervisor on the Evaluation Report, 31 May 2011, available at <https://secure.edps.europa.eu/EDPSWEB/edps/EDPS>.

[496] eg Bulgaria (2008), Romania (2009), Germany (2010), Czech Republic (2011), and Cyprus (2011). See generally Kosta, E, 'The Way to Luxemburg: National Court Decisions on the Compatibility of the Data Retention Directive with the Rights to Privacy and Data Protection', 10(3) *SCRIPTed* 339 (2013), available at <http://script-ed.org/?p=1163>.

[497] C-293/12 *Digital Rights Ireland Ltd v Minister for Communications, Marine and Natural Resources* [2014] 3 CMLR 44.

4.257 The full consequences of this decision are still being worked through across Europe and by the EU institutions, but are beyond the scope of this book.[498] However, in the UK, the Government's response was to adopt emergency legislation, in the form of the Data Retention and Investigatory Powers Act 2014 (DRIPA), with accompanying regulations.[499] One of the Government's primary concerns was to address the legal uncertainties around the continued retention of communications data by CSPs.[500] The DRIPA essentially re-enacts the Retention Directive, although with some additional safeguards designed to address some of the concerns expressed by the Court of Justice. It also contains a sunset provision repealing the provisions, and the regulations made under them, on 31 December 2016.[501] Despite these assurances, judicial review proceedings were commenced against the data retention regime under DRIPA, on the basis that it was not consistent with EU law, specifically the CJEU's 2014 decision. The claimants succeeded in their action and s 1 of DRIPA was disapplied.[502] However, given the serious nature of the consequences of such a decision, the court ordered that its effect should be suspended until 31 March 2016, in order 'to give parliament the opportunity to put matters right'.[503] As such, the sunset provision has effectively been brought forward.

4.258 Wholesale data retention for law enforcement purposes remains a highly controversial issue of public policy. The current Conservative administration is committed to retaining a retention regime, in one form or another, so new legislation has been brought forward, in the form of the Investigatory Powers Bill. At an EU level, however, it is less certain whether a future instrument will be attempted.

Distinguishing content and communications data

4.259 As discussed above, current UK law establishes different authorization regimes for access to content and communications data, except when the communications data is an integral element of obtaining the content. As such, CSP-derived data raises similar terminology boundary issues to those considered throughout this book, such as that between interception and monitoring. Not only does the dividing line require different procedures to be followed, but the product is treated differently as evidence. This differentiation can be challenged as a matter of principle and from a technical perspective.

4.260 Historically, national legal systems have always distinguished between the interception of the content of a communication and the attributes of the communication session itself,

---

[498] eg Rauhofer, J and Mac Sithigh, D, 'The Data Retention Directive Never Existed', 11(1) *SCRIPTed* 118 (2014); and Boehm, F and Cole, M, 'Data Retention after the judgement of the Court of Justice of the European Union', 30 June 2014, available at <http://www.janalbrecht.eu/fileadmin/material/Dokumente/Boehm_Cole_-_Data_Retention_Study_-_June_2014.pdf>.

[499] Data Retention Regulations 2014 (SI No 2042).

[500] Speech by the Rt Hon Theresa May MP, Secretary of State at the Home Office, 'Communications data and interception', 10 July 2014, available at <https://www.gov.uk/government/speeches/communications-data-and-interception>.

[501] DRIPA, s 8(3).

[502] *R (on the application of Davis) v Secretary of State for the Home Department* [2015] EWHC 2092 (Admin). DRIPA, s 1 grants the Secretary of State the power to issue retention notices and make regulations.

[503] Bowcott, O, 'High court rules data retention and surveillance legislation unlawful', *The Guardian*, 17 July 2015, available at <http://www.theguardian.com/world/2015/jul/17/data-retention-and-surveillance-legislation-ruled-unlawful>.

such as identity and location (however partial). This distinction would seem to be based on a widely held perception that access to the content of a communication represents a more substantial threat to a person's privacy than details concerning the attributes. Such sentiment has informed ECtHR jurisprudence:

> By its very nature, metering is therefore to be distinguished from interception of communications, which is undesirable and illegitimate in a democratic society unless justified.[504]

A similar sentiment appears to have influenced the drafters of the Cybercrime Convention: 'Due to the higher privacy interest associated with content data'.[505] In the UK, this reasoning was given by a previous government when introducing an amendment to the Telecommunications Act 1984:

> The key point is that there is a fundamental difference between the disclosure of the contents of a communication and the disclosure of so-called metering information.[506]

In the US, the Supreme Court has also held that the recording of telephone numbers dialled by a suspect does not engage the protections under the Fourth Amendment, because people do not have a legitimate expectation of privacy in such information.[507] Indeed, US federal law distinguishes between the privacy interests in communications content, communications attributes, and subscriber records, according the first the greatest degree of protection against law enforcement access, which diminishes in degrees for the other two.[508]

The term 'metering' quoted above reflects our past voice telephony environment, where the **4.261** only attributes generated by a call were the calling parties' numbers and duration information required for billing purposes. Developments in telecommunications have led to a substantial qualitative and quantitative shift in the nature of data being generated through the use of communications technologies, from mobile location to 'clickstream' data. New modalities of communications, such as social networks, go beyond our traditional bilateral conception of communications. However, policy makers, often under the guise of the need to be 'technology-neutral' in approach, continue to regulate the different forms of communications data in a similar manner. As stated by the Earl of Northesk during the debates in the RIPA:

> One of the many difficulties I have with this Bill is that, in its strident efforts to be technology neutral, it often conveys the impression that either it is ignorant of the way in which current technology operates, or pretends that there is no technology at all.[509]

While the volume and value of communications data has expanded considerably, obtain- **4.262** ing access to the content of a communication may conversely be hampered through the use of cryptographic techniques, either built into the technology or applied by the user. Such

---

[504] *Malone v United Kingdom* (1985) 7 EHRR 14. Although the court also noted that traffic and usage data were an 'integral element of the communications made by telephone' and therefore could give rise to an issue under Art 8 of the ECHR.

[505] Explanatory Report to the Convention on Cybercrime, above, n 184, para 230.

[506] Quoted in *Morgans* [1999] 2 Cr App R 99, at 110E.

[507] *Smith v Maryland*, 442 US 735 (1979). Although dissenting from this opinion, Justices Stewart and Brennan stated that distinguishing between the treatment of numbers and the conversation itself was erroneous and that numbers are 'an integral part of the telephonic communication ... entitled to constitutional protection' (ibid, at 748).

[508] 18 USC s 2703 'Required disclosure of customer communications or records'.

[509] Hansard, Lords Debates, 28 June 2000, Col 1012.

problems are becoming increasingly common and, therefore, investigators are going to be increasingly reliant on communications data as a forensic source and as evidence.

4.263 As well as the shift in the nature of content and communications data, it can also be argued that people's legitimate expectations of privacy in a communications environment are changing. In an age of filtered transmissions, from CSP industry schemes to employer good practice, carried out in a transparent manner, there is growing public awareness that an individual does not have unmediated access to the Internet. Indeed, such awareness is a key element of a crime prevention strategy for cyberspace.

4.264 It would therefore seem arguable that the threats to individual privacy from obtaining communication attributes data are no longer 'fundamentally different' from content in our emerging 'Information Society', and consequentially should be subject to more equivalent access and usage regimes. Indeed, it can be suggested that by focusing the debate on the protection of content, the real nature of the privacy threat in a modern communications environment has been obscured, enabling the law enforcement and intelligence community to access the forensic data they desire with a minimal authorization regime.

4.265 International legal instruments recognizing an individual's right to privacy do not make any explicit distinction between the content of a person's communications and its attributes. Indeed, many instruments do not refer to 'communications' at all, preferring to use the term 'correspondence',[510] including the Constitution of the International Telecommunications Union,[511] although 'correspondence' has been broadly conceived to embrace telephone conversations.[512]

4.266 Although there would appear to be no current requirement in any jurisdiction's law to treat access to such categories of data under a similar legal regime, the EU Directive addressing data protection issues in the communications sector would seem to explicitly recognize the idea of equality of treatment:

> Member States shall ensure the confidentiality of communications and the related traffic data by means of a public communications network and publicly available electronic communications services, through national legislation . . .[513]

Indeed, the key provisions of the Directive are directed at controlling the processing of communications data, specifically 'traffic data', 'location data', and 'calling line identification' features,[514] rather than the content of our communications. The Directive expressly addresses the privacy implications of communications data in terms of the relationship between a CSP and his customer or 'subscriber'; between a subscriber and the actual user of the service; between users themselves, for example the called and calling parties; and between a user and the state. It recognizes that communications data, as a form of personal data, has considerable potential value to CSPs, if not for law enforcement agencies.

4.267 Another issue raised by differential legal treatment is that in modern communications networks the distinction between communication attributes and content is becoming

---

[510] European Convention on Human Rights, 4 November 1950, entered into force 3 November 1953, 213 UNTS 222, Art 8(1).
[511] Constitution of the International Telecommunications Union, Art 37: 'ensuring the secrecy of international correspondence'.
[512] *Klass v Germany* (1978) 2 EHRR 214, para 41.
[513] Directive 02/58/EC, above, n 187, Art 5(1).
[514] ibid, Arts 6–9.

increasingly blurred at a technical level. With the introduction of touch-tone technology, for example, an individual became capable of using the key pad on his phone to enter his credit card details and engage in other banking transactions, after having first keyed in the number to connect to his telephone banking service. Such so-called 'post-cut-through' data render any categorization based on a technical distinction between signalling and content channels unworkable. With the explosive growth of 'texting', or SMS, in the latter half of the 1990s, using signalling protocols such as SS7, this distinction has been further eroded.

In an Internet context, a web-based Uniform Resource Locator (URL), for example, contains not only details of the IP address of the website being accessed, akin to a traditional telephone number; but will also often contain further information in relation to the content of the requested communication, such as a particular item held on the site or a search string containing the embedded parameters of the search, for example: **4.268**

http://www.google.com/search?hl=en&q=big+bottom+aliens&btnG=Google+Search

Under UK law, the RIPA tries to address such blurring between the content of a communication and related 'traffic data'. Subsection (c) of the definition is designed to cover situations of 'dial-through fraud', where calls are re-routed over circuit-switched networks to avoid service charges. However, it would seem to be so broadly defined that it potentially covers any signals sent using touch-tone technology, such as payment card details that should more appropriately be treated as content. The final phrase of the definition (d) is designed to limit the concept of 'traffic data' in an Internet-context to the apparatus identified by the IP address and not any files or programs stored on the machine.[515] These definitions have been criticized for inadequately distinguishing between the data generated by a telephone call and when accessing the Internet, leading to calls for revisions to be made.[516]

The statutory definition of what constitutes an act of 'interception' under RIPA addresses the boundary distinction between content and communications data, where the conduct is carried out for the purpose of identifying communications data, rather than the content. Section 2(5)(a) provides that conduct in relation to those elements of a communication that comprise traffic data is not interception, which is simply a statement of the obvious. However, this is then broadened in sub-paragraph (b) to state that conduct in relation to any aspect of a communication, which would include its content, is not interception if it 'is necessary for the purpose of identifying traffic data ...'. Such a purposive test would operate as a statutory defence for conduct that, as a matter of fact, resulted in a third party obtaining access to the content of a message in the course of its transmission, such as an ISP engaged in some form of deep-packet traffic analysis. **4.269**

Under US law, a similar distinction is made between communications content and 'call-identifying information', which is defined as follows: **4.270**

> . . . dialing or signaling information that identifies the origin, direction, destination, or termination of each communication generated or received by a subscriber by means of any equipment, facility, or service of a telecommunications carrier.[517]

---

[515] RIPA Explanatory Notes, above, n 187, para 33.
[516] APIG, above, n 440, para 44.
[517] 47 USCA s 1001(2).

From a law enforcement perspective, the communications attribute of primary interest in an investigation is such identifying information. While this would seem a relatively clear statutory definition, a decision by the Federal Communications Commission to encompass 'post-cut-through dialed digit extraction' within this definition was overturned in the Appeals Court partly on the basis that 'there is no way to distinguish between digits dialed to route calls and those dialed to communicate information'.[518]

4.271   Issues arising at a technical level will result in procedural difficulties for both the CSP from which data is requested and the requesting authority. In the URL example given above, how would such 'call-identifying information' or 'traffic data' be technically separated from associated content, such as file details? Reliance on the law enforcement agencies themselves to distinguish such data would seem unacceptable, which requires us to consider the role of the CSP over whose network the data is being sent during the interception process. To safeguard the rights and freedoms of the individual, the relevant CSP would need to be able to identify the relevant data and then automatically separate 'call-identifying' information for forwarding to the appropriate requesting authority. Under US law, such an obligation is enshrined in the law. Carriers are required:

> to facilitat[e] authorized communications interceptions and access to call-identifying information . . . in a manner that protects . . . the privacy and security of communications and call-identifying information not authorized to be intercepted.[519]

However, the technical feasibility of such approach requires further examination, as well as the costs and how they are distributed.

4.272   The potential consequences of the blurring of the boundary between communication data and content in a modern communications environment are significant. An individual's rights in the content of their communications may be significantly eroded. Communication service providers will face legal, procedural, and operational uncertainties with regard to their obligations to obtain and deliver up data that has been requested by an investigating agency. Finally, law enforcement agencies will be faced with greater legal uncertainties in respect of the appropriate procedures to be complied with when carrying out an investigation or risk any data obtained being excluded.[520]

E. Suspect-derived Data

4.273   In the normal chain of events, a cyber-surveillance operation will lead to the identification of one or more suspects and data concerning their illegal conduct. However, the evidential value of the forensic material generated from such surveillance activities will vary depending on the process involved. Lawful intercept product, for example, will not generally be admissible, and is intended only for intelligence purposes.[521] At some point in an investigation, therefore, law enforcement agents will either initiate, or request that others initiate, a search and seizure of certain physical locations relating to the suspect to obtain further

---

[518] *United States Telecom Association et al v Federal Communications Commission*, 227 F 3d 450 (DC Cir 2000), No 99-1442, 15 August 2000.
[519] 47 USCA s 1002(a)(4)(a).
[520] See generally Chapter 6.
[521] See paras 6.70–6.80.

forensic material. The use of such coercive techniques in the context of a digital investigation are examined in this section.

Seized data

When carrying out a search-and-seizure operation, the objective is to obtain any data that **4.274** may be relevant to the investigation, subject to any rules protecting certain categories of material, such as legally privileged; and to obtain it in a manner that does not enable any material subsequently adduced as evidence to be successfully challenged. Such data may be contained in various forms of digital media and/or may comprise physical source documents, such as photographs, or print-outs from the media. Where the digital media form part of, or are connected to, a computing resource, then the process of seizure will vary considerably according to whether the system is in operation at the time, and whether it is connected to a network, since the process of closing down a system and disconnecting it from a network may have serious forensic implications.[522]

Generally, powers to enter and search premises will either be granted by a magistrate,[523] **4.275** which then confers a general power of seizure,[524] or arise in the course of an arrest, which confers certain powers of search and seizure.[525] The statutory framework governing seizure expressly includes 'any information stored in any electronic form'[526] and 'any computer disk or other electronic storage device'.[527]

While an investigating officer has the power to seize material, he also has the option of **4.276** arranging for such material to be imaged or copied,[528] which may be considered the most appropriate course of action to minimize the intrusion and disturbance caused by a search, which an investigating officer is under a duty to do.[529] So, for example, where the search is carried out on business premises, but only in respect of a particular employee, the ability to image may reduce the amount of kit that needs to be taken away for forensic analysis.[530] A classic example of the potentially abusive use of search-and-seizure powers was the US case of *Steve Jackson Games*,[531] when the US Secret Service raided the computer games company seizing vital business systems and failing to return them for a number of months, causing major disruption to the business, when the target was a known employee.

In respect of computer-integrity offences, the offences under ss 2 and 3 of the Computer **4.277** Misuse Act were both indictable, for which a warrant could be granted, as well as 'arrestable'.[532] However, the s 1 offence of unauthorized access was not arrestable and only summary in nature, therefore a special provision was made for a search warrant (with a power of

---

[522] See generally the ACPO Guide, above, n 10, s 9: 'Attending crime scenes'.
[523] Under the Police and Criminal Evidence Act 1984 (PACE), ss 8 and 19–20. See also PACE Code B. Search-and-seizure warrants may be granted under other statutory schemes, eg Proceeds of Crime Act 2002, s 352; SOCPA, s 66; and the Extradition Act 2003, s 156.
[524] PACE, s 19.
[525] ibid, s 32. See also PACE Code A. Alternatively, for extradition offences, the Extradition Act 2003, ss 161–2.
[526] PACE, s 20.
[527] SOCPA, s 66(3)(c).
[528] PACE Code B, s 7.5.
[529] ibid, s 6.10.
[530] See eg *R (on the application of Paul Da Costa & Co) v Thames Magistrates Court* [2002] EWHC 40, where images were taken of the two hard disks on the firm's server.
[531] *Steve Jackson Games Inc v United States Secret Service*, 816 F Supp 432 (WD Tex 1993).
[532] PACE, s 24, which included offences where the sentence could be imprisonment for a five-year period.

seizure) to be granted by a circuit judge.[533] However, the concept of an 'arrestable offence' was abolished by an amendment inserted by the Serious Organised Crime and Police Act 2005 (SOCPA),[534] replacing an objective seriousness threshold with a discretionary 'necessity' threshold. In addition, the PACE post-arrest powers of entry and search only apply where the offence is indictable. However, the s 1 offence of unauthorized access under the Computer Misuse Act has been made an indictable offence[535] and therefore the provision for a s 14 warrant has been repealed.

4.278   The SOCPA also introduced new rules in relation to the scope of a search warrant issued under PACE. A warrant may now authorize entry on multiple occasions,[536] where necessary to meet the purpose of the warrant, and can encompass one or more set of premises (a 'specific premises warrant') or any premises occupied or controlled by a specified person (an 'all premises warrant').[537] 'Premises' is defined broadly to include any place, vehicle, vessel, aircraft, 'offshore installation', tent, or movable structure.[538] Prior surveillance should enable the investigators to identify the premises to be specified in the warrant, although modern networking techniques will continue to create problems for investigators. Domestic wireless networks, for example, may mean that the actual offender is residing in a building next to the property specified in the warrant, using the connection without the knowledge of the owner.

4.279   A search-and-seizure warrant can give rise to problems where the relevant material is held on a computer system being used at the time of the search, since any attempt to seize the material for further examination may result in either the loss or alteration of the evidence. Other problems for law enforcement are the geographical scope of a warrant, where the seized computer is connected to a network, and the volume of data that is generally subject to seizure, especially as the cost of data storage has fallen and capacity increased dramatically over past decades years. The time and expense involved in sifting and scrutinizing seized data can be a serious impediment to a process of investigation.[539]

Data removal

4.280   One procedural issue raised by the volume of data stored on a computer subject to seizure is whether the scope of the warrant extends to all material contained on the disk. In *R v Chesterfield Justices and others, ex parte Bramley*,[540] the potential vulnerability of the police was exposed when the court held that the Police and Criminal Evidence Act 1984 did not contain a defence to an action for trespass to goods in respect of items subject to legal privilege being seized during the execution of a search warrant. The decision placed law enforcement in an invidious position: searching and shifting the data at the premises of the suspect was not feasible, but removal for subsequent examination could give rise to liability. Subsequently, it was held that *Bramley* only extends to situations involving legal privilege material, not any situation where irrelevant material is seized in the course of taking a computer as evidence.[541]

---

[533] CMA, s 14.

[534] SOCPA, s 110, which came into force 1 January 2006. The amendment also removes the concept of a 'serious arrestable offence' (PACE, s 116) and the related police powers.

[535] Police and Justice Act 2006, s 35.

[536] SOCPA, s 114.

[537] ibid, s 113.

[538] PACE, s 23.

[539] See generally Kenneally, E and Brown, C, 'Risk sensitive digital evidence collection', 2 *Digital Investigation* 101 (2005).

[540] (2000) 2 WLR 409.

[541] *H v Commissioners of Inland Revenue* [2002] EWHC 2164 (Admin).

To address the potential liability established by *Bramley*, the Government added provisions **4.281** to the Criminal Justice and Police Act 2001.[542] The Act grants law enforcement agencies the right to remove material, including material potentially outside the scope of a warrant, where it is 'not reasonably practicable' to separate it.[543] An exhaustive list of relevant factors is provided for determining whether it is 'reasonably practicable', including 'the apparatus or equipment that it would be necessary or appropriate to use for the carrying out of the determination or separation',[544] which would presumably encompass the various software tools used in computer forensics. Similar provisions under Australian law provide that regard shall be had 'to the timeliness and cost of examining or processing the thing at another place and the availability of expert assistance'.[545]

The Act also details a number of safeguards for the handling of such data that are designed **4.282** to protect the defendant's rights under the ECHR. First, written notice must be given to the occupier of the premises detailing, among other items, the name and address of a person to whom an application can be made to attend the initial examination of the material.[546] The examination should not then be commenced without due regard to the desirability of enabling the relevant person an opportunity to be represented at the examination.[547] However, any such representative may be excluded from an examination where techniques are employed by the investigators that facilitate the examination, such as decryption, but which are considered confidential or require protection for security reasons.[548] Second, items subject to legal privilege must be returned as soon as reasonably practicable, except where it is not reasonably practicable to separate it from the rest of the property 'without prejudicing the use of the rest of that property'.[549] Third, an application may be made to the appropriate judicial authority for the material to be returned, although the authority could order that the material be examined by an independent third party.[550] Fourth, where an application has been made, the person holding the data may be placed under a duty to secure the data pending the direction of the judicial authority, which includes preventing its examination, copying, or use.[551]

Concern has been expressed that the safeguards do not go far enough to protect the inter- **4.283** ests of the accused. In particular, such is the absolute nature of the rule protecting legal privilege,[552] it has been suggested that by default seized material be subject to independent examination, rather than relying on the discretion of a judicial authority.[553] However, such a procedure could potentially further compromise the ability of law enforcement to operate with the rapidity often required in situations involving network-based crime.

---

[542] These provisions came into force from 1 April 2003 by reason of the Criminal Justice and Police Act 2001 (Commencement No 9) Order 2003 (SI No 708).

[543] Criminal Justice and Police Act 2001 (CJPA), s 50(1)(c).

[544] ibid, s 50(3)(d).

[545] Crimes Act 1914, s 3K(2), as amended by the Cybercrime Act 2001.

[546] CJPA, s 52(1). Under Australian law, the written consent of the occupier of the premises is required (Crimes Act 1914, s 3K(2)(b)).

[547] CJPA, s 53(4).

[548] PACE Code B, s 7.8A.

[549] CJPA, s 54(2)(b).

[550] ibid, s 59.

[551] ibid, ss 60–61.

[552] *Derby Magistrates' Court, ex parte B* [1996] AC 487.

[553] See Ormerod, DC [2000] Crim LR 388, where he suggests off-site sifting be carried out by an independently appointed legal adviser.

4.284   Material that has been seized may be retained only as long as is necessary, which includes the period required for forensic examination (which may be substantial given police resources in the area); where the item is to be used as evidence at trial; or where it is 'inextricably linked' to other material being used in an investigation or proceedings.[554] Inextricably linked material would include, for example, data held on digital media that cannot be separated without impacting on the evidential integrity of the remaining data.[555] Material should also not be retained if a copy or image of the material would be sufficient.[556]

Civil search

4.285   While the exercise of coercive powers of search and seizure are a standard feature of criminal procedure, similar powers may be available to a litigant in the course of civil proceedings. Such powers can facilitate the preservation of digital evidence, where there is a risk that such data may be destroyed by a prospective defendant. Normally in civil proceedings, access to data held on a defendant's system would be subject to standard rules of civil procedure, such as discovery.[557] However, where a claimant can show evidence of a threat to the integrity of such data, the English courts have jurisdiction to grant an order for the purpose of securing evidence. The order, referred to as a 'Search Order' but historically known as an 'Anton Piller' order,[558] is codified under the Civil Procedure Act 1997[559] and Civil Procedure Rules.[560] Similar procedures exist in other common as well as civil law jurisdictions.[561]

4.286   An application for a Search Order is made *ex parte*, without the presence of the defendant, since the basis for it being granted is that there is a real risk that the defendant would destroy relevant material if put on notice. When making an application, the claimant is required to be show that the request is made in respect of 'existing or proposed proceedings',[562] so the procedure should not be available for a speculative 'fishing expedition'. An applicant must also be able to show the court the nature of the risk posed to the evidence, which requires that the court grants such coercive relief. An illustration of this arose in the Australian case, *Universal Music Australia Pty Ltd and others v Sharman License Holdings Ltd and others.*[563] The claimants were commencing an action for alleged copyright infringement against Sharman based on the activities of their KaZaA P2P file-sharing system. The court granted the application, but the defendants appealed the decision and sought to have the orders discharged. In the course of this appeal, reference was made to the reasons given to the court by the claimants when making the initial application. The following four grounds were given:

(a) There is real risk that with notice of the application some, or all of the respondents, and their associates, will destroy documents and data. The first and second respondents are not companies incorporated or registered in Australia. The applicants are

---

[554] PACE Code B, s 7.14. See also CJPA, s 54.
[555] PACE, s 7H Notes for Guidance.
[556] ibid, s 7.15.
[557] eg UK Civil Procedure Rules (CPR), Pt 31 'Disclosure and inspection of documents'.
[558] After *Anton Piller KG v Manufacturing Processes Ltd and others* [1976] FSR 129.
[559] Civil Procedure Act 1997 (CPA), s 7.
[560] eg CPR, r 25.1(1)(h) re: a 'Search Order'.
[561] See generally Mason, S (ed), *Electronic Evidence*, 3rd edn, LexisNexis, 2012.
[562] CPA, s 7(1).
[563] [2004] FCA 183.

entirely unable to identify the persons, other the [sic] fourth and fifth respondents . . . who are in practical control of the company. I therefore have no knowledge of how many unidentified persons may be directing the activities of the first and second respondents and able to direct staff in Australia to destroy or transfer documents out of Australia.

(b) Much of the information to which the applicants seek access for use in the proceedings is inherently vulnerable to destruction or loss. I have significant concerns about the high risk of destruction of crucial evidence given how quickly electronic files can be moved and/or deleted, particularly around the highly complex Kazaa system. I have found in previous Internet piracy investigations that information is frequently overwritten or lost by the ordinary operation of computer systems. Once overwritten it becomes much more difficult to retrieve by computer forensic processes. This is particularly the case with logs of data or electronic transactions which can be overwritten as new data is recorded.

(c) The transient nature of many aspects of the Kazaa system, and the data likely to record its actions. The [sic] I understand from the evidence filed by the forensic experts in this matter that the Kazaa supernodes are transitory, existing for anywhere from hours to days only to disappear without warning. It is not, in my view feasible for evidence about their activity to be gathered without being able to take a snapshot of the system. Any notice of this is likely in my view to enable the operators of the Kazaa system time to remove or alter the processes to prevent the analysis of individual network elements thereby denying the applicants the opportunity of analysis of the information.

(d) The enormous scale of copyright infringement involved and the potentially very large number of people involved in the infringements of copyright (including KMD users on the Kazaa system) means that there are likely to be a large number of participants who would seek to conceal themselves from detection by the applicants by deleting data and changing their behaviour for the period of observation . . .[564]

While from an English law perspective, the reasons given above are unlikely to be specific enough in relation to the likely behaviour of the defendants to be sufficient for a court to grant an order, they are illustrative of the types of concerns that plaintiffs are likely to raise in a cyberspace environment.

A Search Order can permit the claimant to enter the defendant's premises; search and inspect anything described in the Order; and 'make or obtain a copy, photograph, sample or other record'.[565] Non-compliance with an Order can lead to the proceedings being commenced by the claimant for contempt of court, which can result in the imposition of a custodial sentence.[566] However, the person subject to the order can refuse to supply such information where it might incriminate him, exposing him to the possibility of prosecution.[567] In certain situations, a defendant's refusal to comply with an order on the grounds of self-incrimination may undermine the claimant's claim. **4.287**

---

[564] ibid, para 12.
[565] CPA, s 7(3) and (4).
[566] See CPR, Sch 1, RSC Order 52 and Sch 2, CCR Order 29. See also *Adam Phones Ltd v Goldschmidt* [1999] 4 All ER 486, which involved the intentional but mistaken deletion of source code that should have been delivered up.
[567] CPA, s 7(7).

4.288 An example of the potential conflict that can arise between civil search procedures and self-incrimination was considered by the courts in *O Ltd v Z*.[568] Here the claimant obtained a Search Order against the defendant's premises where it was (rightly) believed that the defendant, a former employee, had taken computer data and other material that could be used to the detriment of the claimant's business. In the course of executing the order, relevant data was taken in the form of imaged copies of hard disks in the defendant's computer as well as various storage media, such as CDs. This material was subsequently examined by an expert, who discovered numerous child abuse images of a very serious nature. The court held that the defendant had waived his privilege against self-incrimination during the course of the search, and therefore the material could be handed over to the police.[569]

4.289 Even where self-incrimination is not an issue, it is possible that materials obtained through execution of a Search Order may subsequently be required as evidence in a criminal investigation. In such circumstances, a potential jurisdictional conflict exists, since the terms of the civil order may contradict a requirement under a criminal disclosure order.[570]

4.290 Since civil search orders constitute a serious interference with a person's privacy and are open to abuse,[571] they are granted infrequently and impose significant undertakings upon the applicant. However, where granted, they are often used in technology and intellectual property cases, where the intangible nature of the evidence can give rise to a risk about the integrity of the evidence.[572]

Protected data

4.291 Even when data has been lawfully obtained, the next problem that investigators increasingly face is that the seized data, or device on which the data resides, may be protected by some form of security measure, such as a password or cryptographic mechanism, which renders the data inaccessible, unintelligible or, indeed, undiscovered by investigators.[573] In the US, for example, when the notorious hacker Kevin Mitnick was finally arrested, many of the files found on his computers were encrypted and investigators were never able to access them.[574] Access to protected data is therefore seen by many as one of the biggest future challenges for computer forensics in the twenty-first century.[575]

4.292 In the context of criminal procedure, access issues are not simply binary, the data being attainable or not; law enforcement agencies are also subject to temporal constraints, such as custody and prosecution time limits, which may be missed if the data cannot be accessed within a reasonable period of time.[576] In response to this threat, some jurisdictions have

---

[568] [2005] EWHC 238 (Ch).

[569] See also *C plc v P* [2006] EWHC 1226.

[570] *Gordon v Summers* [2003] FSR 40.

[571] See *Lock International plc v Beswick* [1989] 1 WLR 1268.

[572] See, eg, *Digital Equipment Corp v Darkcrest Ltd* [1984] 3 WLR 617; *Intergraph Corp v Solid Systems CAD Services Ltd*, [1993] FSR 617; and *Gabem Group Ltd v Mahatma* [2002] EWHC 2221.

[573] Home Affairs Report, above, n 21, para 58.

[574] See 'Mitnick not allowed to use computer to review evidence', 31 March 1998, available at <http://tjscott.net/policy/kevin1.htm#COURTDOCS>. For other examples, see Denning, D and Baugh, W, 'Hiding crimes in cyberspace', in Thomas, D and Loader, B (eds), *Cybercrime: Law Enforcement, Security and Surveillance in the Information Age*, Routledge, 2000, at 105–31.

[575] See Barrett, N, *Traces of Guilt*, Bantam Press, 2004, at 373. See also Morris, S, *The future of netcrime now: Part 1— Threats and challenges*, Home Office Online Report 62/04, 31 May 2013, at 24 et seq, available at <http://www.globalinitiative.net/wpfb-file/home-office-the-future-of-netcrime-now-part-1-threats-and-challenges-pdf/>.

[576] eg Prosecution of Offences (Custody Time Limits) Regulations 1987 (SI No 299).

criminalized the use of data protection mechanisms in the course of a criminal activity, distinct from commission of the underlying criminal activity.[577]

For the purposes of our analysis, a distinction is made between protection mechanisms that **4.293** operate at the level of the ICT resource, such as storage media (eg memory stick) or a software application (eg Windows 10); from those that operate on the data or information itself that is the subject of the processing. A password to access a machine, device, directory, or file, for example, differs in nature, and is treated differently in law, from a cryptographic technique that creates unintelligible ciphertext. The former shall be referred to as 'access' protections, while the latter as 'conversion' protections, although the latter should be more properly classified as a subset of the former, rather than a stand-alone category. In addition, protected data should be distinguished from techniques that can conceal data, such as steganography, where investigators may not even aware of the presence of hidden information, let alone able to access it.

Protection measures applied to data may be implemented at an individual user level, by an **4.294** organization with whom the individual is associated or in which he resides, by the provider of the communications service, or at any combination of these or other points within the processing life cycle of data. So, for example, an LEA may obtain access to a person's email account by requesting password data under a communications data request to the CSP, either covertly or post-arrest as an alternative to obtaining cooperation from the suspect.[578] A CSP may also be required to remove any encryption protection applied by it in the course of providing communication services as part of its provision of an intercept capability.[579]

While we are primarily concerned in this section with data seized from a suspect, we must **4.295** be aware of the multiplicity of points at which protection can be applied, when the data is 'at rest' or 'in transmission', which may require different rules concerning access or similar rules applied differently. In 1999, a Cabinet Office report on the issue detailed the 'ideal requirements' law enforcement have in respect of the interception of encrypted communications and access to encrypted stored data.[580] In the case of communications, for example, the real time nature of the process imposes different demands from that applicable to seized data.

In addition, some evidence from the US suggests that the scale of the problem of protected **4.296** data differs depending on the manner in which the data is obtained. US judicial reports on law enforcement wiretap activity since 2000 are required by law to report whether encryption was encountered and whether it prevented access to the plain text of the intercepted communication.[581] The reports consistently record both a low level of instances where encryption was present and few where investigators were then prevented from obtaining access to the plain text.[582] This suggests that while criminals may be utilizing encryption technologies as a means of protecting data held on data media, such protections are still

---

[577] eg State of Virginia (US), Computer Crime Act, ss 18.2–152.15 'Encryption used in criminal activity'.

[578] However, see ADCD Code, above, n 324, para 2.31, which limits this method to cases involving national security.

[579] eg The Regulation of Investigatory Powers (Maintenance of Interception Capability) Order 2002, SI 1931, Sch 1, para 10. See also 47 USC s 1002(b)(3).

[580] Cabinet Office, Performance and Innovation Unit Report, *Encryption and Law Enforcement*, May 1999, Annex B ('PIU Report').

[581] 18 USC s 2519(2)(b)(iv).

[582] See United States Courts, Wiretap Reports, from 1997–2014, available at <http://www.uscourts. gov/statistics-reports/analysis-reports/wiretap-reports>. In 2014, the number of state cases of wiretap where encryption was encountered decreased from forty-one to twenty-two, of which only two were indecipherable; while the issue arose in only three federal cases, of which two could not be decrypted.

not yet being widely utilized in a communications environment. More widespread usage of encryption is, however, inevitable and a trend that was simply accelerated as a consequence of the Snowden revelations.[583] On this point, it is also interesting to note that one reason given by the UK Government against the use of intercept evidence in court is that it would give unwelcome publicity to the practice of law enforcement and encourage targets to use 'more secure means of communications'.[584]

4.297 The nature of data security technologies means that investigating authorities have essentially three options in respect of gaining access to, or conversion of, protected data they have lawfully seized:

- require the person from whom the data has been obtained to access, or convert, the data into an intelligible plain-text format;
- require the person to disclose the necessary information and/or tools, or provide assistance to enable the authorities to access, or convert, the data into a intelligible format themselves; or
- utilize technologies and techniques that enable the data to be accessed, or converted, without the active involvement of the person from whom the data was obtained.

As coercive investigative techniques, the first two options require lawful authority, and UK law contains provisions addressing both situations. The Cybercrime Convention also provides for the adoption of such powers.[585] In the latter case, the issue is primarily one of having the necessary technical resource that can be applied to the task within the relevant timescales. However, hacking systems to access data also requires an appropriate legal framework, which is addressed elsewhere in the book.[586]

4.298 To address the problem of protected data, Part III of the RIPA contains provisions designed to address the first two options outlined above. From a policy perspective, the issues addressed in Part III were initially raised in the context of the promotion of electronic commerce.[587] While the Government was keen to facilitate the use of security technologies, such as encryption, to establish trust and confidence in electronic commerce, it was also recognized that such technologies represented a threat to law enforcement's ability to investigate crime. As such, when the Government published a bill on electronic commerce, which became the Electronic Communications Act 2000, Part III addressed the 'investigation of protected electronic data'.[588] However, controversy concerning the proposal and the political desirability of distinguishing the promotion of electronic commerce from law enforcement issues meant the part was eventually removed from the bill and placed instead in the RIPA. Elements of Part III were highly controversial at the time of adoption, as discussed further below. The provisions entered in October 2007, with the adoption of a code of practice.[589]

---

[583] See ISC Report 2015, above, n 2, para 440, recounting evidence submitted by MI5.

[584] Attorney-General's Guidelines for Prosecutors, 'Section 18 RIPA Prosecutors Intercept Guidelines England and Wales', 29 November 2012, para 2.

[585] Convention on Cybercrime, Art 19(4).

[586] See further paras 3.257 and 4.65 et seq.

[587] See DTI Consultation Document, *Building Confidence in Electronic Commerce*, URN 99/642, March 1999.

[588] DTI Consultation on Draft Legislation and the Government's Response to the Trade and Industry Committee's Report, *Promoting Electronic Commerce*, Cm 4417, July 1999.

[589] The Regulation of Investigatory Powers 2000 (Commencement No 4) Order 2007, (SI No 2196) and Home Office, Code of Practice: 'Investigation of Protected Electronic Information' (2007), made under RIPA, s 71 ('Part III Code').

As with cybercrime in general, the true scale of the protected data problem in the UK is **4.299** unclear. When the Government first raised the issue in 1999, examples were given where encryption was encountered in cases involving child abuse images, attempted murder and sexual assault, fraud and financial crime, and terrorism.[590] However, the Part III provisions were then not implemented, purportedly because 'the development and adoption of encryption and other information protection technologies has been slower than was anticipated';[591] as also noted by the Interception of Communications Commissioner: 'the use of information security and encryption products by terrorist and criminal suspects is not, I understand, as widespread as had been expected'.[592] It has also been reported that during Operation Ore, a major inquiry into child abuse images covering over 7,000 suspects, only twenty cases have encountered encryption as a serious problem.[593] In 2006, the only examples given by the Government to support its decision to finally implement Part III related to child abuse images. To what extent such cases are representative or are simply viewed as more persuasive in terms of gaining public acceptance for such measures is unclear.[594]

Other jurisdictions have adopted similar provisions, such as France[595] and Australia.[596] At **4.300** an inter-governmental level, in 1997, the Organisation for Economic Co-operation and Development (OECD) published guidelines for national governments on cryptography policy, which addressed the issue of lawful access to data converted into an unintelligible form.[597] Within the European Union, the Justice and Home Affairs ministers agreed in 1998 that LEAs may require lawful access to encryption keys where necessary to decrypt seized material.[598]

Supplying intelligible data

Under RIPA, protected data may come into the possession of law enforcement investigators **4.301** through a number of different routes:

- The exercise of any of the search-and-seizure powers, such as a judicial production order under Schedule 1 of PACE.[599]
- The interception of a person's communications, under Part I, Chapter I of the RIPA.[600]
- The acquisition of communications data, under Part I, Chapter II of the RIPA, or through surveillance techniques carried out under Part II.[601]
- Protected data that has been provided or disclosed through the exercise of any statutory duty, such as a requests for information made by a regulatory authority like the Financial Conduct Authority.[602]

---

[590] See DTI Consultation Document, above, n 588, para 50; PIU Report, above, n 580, at 7.

[591] Home Office, *Investigation of Protected Electronic Information*, Consultation Paper, June 2006, para 6.

[592] IoCC Report 2004, above, n 304, para 7.

[593] Home Affairs Report, above, n 21, para 57.

[594] eg 'Punishing silence—Child sex offenders should not be allowed to hide behind their computer', *The Times*, 12 June 2006.

[595] Penal Code 230 (requirement to decrypt) and 434-15-2 (failure to provide decryption key).

[596] Crimes Act 1914, s 3LC ('Person with knowledge of a computer or a computer system to assist access etc').

[597] Organisation for Economic Co-operation and Development (OECD), *Guidelines on Cryptography Policy*, 19 December 1997, Principle 6.

[598] European Council Press Release No 8856/98, 28 May 1998.

[599] RIPA, s 49(1)(a).

[600] ibid, s 49(1)(b).

[601] ibid, s 49(1)(c).

[602] ibid, s 49(1)(d).

- Protected data that has lawfully come into the possession of any of the intelligence services, NCA, the police, or customs authorities, otherwise than through the exercise of a statutory power.[603]

During the process of acquisition, or once in their possession, consideration will need to be given to how the protected data shall be accessed.

4.302 In respect of the first approach outlined above, the RIPA provides that a notice may be served on a person in possession of protected information requiring that they disclose the 'protected information' in an 'intelligible form'.[604] The concept of possession extends to situations where the protected information is held by another person, but who is under the first person's 'control' or the first person has an immediate right of access to it, or have it transmitted or supplied to him;[605] for example, a service provider supplying data archival or storage services.

4.303 A notice may only be given where a series of conditions are met. First, the person must have 'the appropriate permission', as detailed in Schedule 2 of the RIPA.[606] Generally, permission should be granted by a person having the same level of authority as that required when exercising any power to obtain the protected information in the first place; and should normally be the same person that authorized the use of the power.[607] In all other cases, permission may be sought from a Circuit Judge.[608]

4.304 Second, the person giving the notice must believe 'on reasonable grounds' that the key is in the possession of the person subject to the notice,[609] and that the disclosure requirement is necessary on one of four specified grounds: the interests of national security; prevention and detection of crime; the interests of the economic well-being of the United Kingdom; or for the 'purpose of securing the effective exercise or proper performance by any public authority of any statutory power or statutory duty'.[610]

4.305 Third, the disclosure requirement should be a proportionate response to the objective being sought.[611] Finally, the requesting authority has no 'reasonably practicable' alternative means of obtaining the protected information in an intelligible form.

4.306 The notice provision was thought to be necessary because existing coercive powers utilized different phraseology; for example, the Police and Criminal Evidence Act 1984 only requires that information be provided in a 'visible and legible form',[612] as does the Proceeds of Crime Act 2002, in respect of a production order issued against material contained in a computer.[613] Both provisions would, potentially, enable a suspect to deliver up a print-out of ciphertext that is visible and legible to investigators, but unintelligible.

---

[603] ibid, s 49(1)(e).
[604] ibid, s 49(2)(d).
[605] ibid, s 56(2).
[606] See also Part III Code, above, n 589, at Chapter 9, 44 et seq.
[607] ibid, para 9.2.
[608] RIPA, Sch 2(1).
[609] ibid, s 49(2)(a).
[610] ibid, s 49(2)(b) and (3).
[611] ibid, s 49(3). Part III Code, above, n 589, paras 3.25–3.31.
[612] Police and Criminal Evidence Act 1984 (PACE), s 19.
[613] Proceeds of Crime Act 2002 (POCA), s 349.

Under Part III of the RIPA, 'protected information' means: **4.307**

> any electronic data which, without the key to the data—
> (a) cannot, or cannot readily, be accessed, or
> (b) cannot, or cannot readily, be put into an intelligible form.[614]

This definition recognizes the distinction between 'access' and 'conversion' protections. However, the lacuna under the pre-RIPA coercive regime would appear to arise only in respect of 'conversion' measures, rather than 'access' protections. As such, it could be argued that the scope of the measure is 'disproportionate' in human rights terms to the underlying mischief being addressed. Such arguments are rendered somewhat mute, however, to the extent that the penalty for non-compliance is lower than that provided under other laws.

A 'key' comprises 'any key, code, password, algorithm, or other data the use of which (with   **4.308**
or without other keys):

> (a) allows access to the electronic data, or
> (b) facilitates the putting of the data into an intelligible form.[615]

This broad formulation is intended to cover every type of information held in whatever form, including data that has been memorized.[616] The key may also not be singular, but comprise multiple pieces of data, potentially held or under the control of multiple persons, every one of which may require a notice. Where multiple persons hold a single key within a corporate body, such as employees, the notice should generally be given to the most senior officer of the corporate body.[617] Where a person is no longer in possession of a key, and can therefore not comply with the disclosure notice, he is under a duty to supply any information that may facilitate obtaining the key or the protected information in intelligible form.[618]

The one express exception from the disclosure requirement is where the key is intended to   **4.309**
be used solely for the purpose of generating electronic signatures,[619] since electronic signatures are used for reasons of data authenticity and integrity, rather than data confidentiality, which is the situation with protected data.

What constitutes the provision of data in 'intelligible form' is not defined per se, rather   **4.310**
it is stated to include references 'to its being in the condition in which it was before an encryption or similar process was applied to it or, as the case may be, to its being restored to that condition'.[620] Further guidance may be found in the Communications Act 2003, which states that 'something is not to be regarded as in an intelligible form if it cannot readily be understood without being decrypted or having comparable process applied to it'.[621]

---

[614] RIPA, s 56(1).
[615] RIPA, s 56(1).
[616] Part III Code, above, n 589, para 3.11.
[617] ibid, para 3.21–3.24. RIPA, s 49(5)–(6), except where that person is under investigation (s 49(7)).
[618] RIPA, s 50(8)–(9).
[619] ibid, s 49(9). An 'electronic signature' is defined at ibid, s 56(1) and is based, in part, on that provided for under the Electronic Communications Act 2000, s 7(2). See also comments of Lord Bassam, Home Office Minister, during the debate on the bill: Lords Hansard, 13 July 2000, Col 435.
[620] RIPA, s 56(3). Part III Code, above, n 589, para 3.8–3.9.
[621] Communications Act 2003, s 405(9). See also the Electronic Communications Act 2000, s 15(3).

Key disclosure

4.311 To obtain key information, such as a password, required to access protected data, a suspect may be willing to voluntarily cooperate with investigators or may be placed under a legal obligation to assist. In the former case, the suspect may obviously act in his self-interest, in the course of a plea bargain for example. However, where such self-interest is not manifest, then the latter course of action would seem necessary.

4.312 Under RIPA, it states that, where necessary and proportionate, a person may be required by notice to disclose the 'key' that would enable investigators to render the information intelligible themselves.[622] The Act recognizes that such a requirement should only arise when 'special circumstances' are present, specifically that the purpose for the disclosure notice would be defeated, in whole or part, without access to the key,[623] and it is considered proportionate bearing in mind the extent of protected information that would become potentially accessible, other than that subject to the disclosure requirement, ie raising the possibility of exposing such data to collateral intrusion, and the impact on the business of the person subject to the disclosure requirement.[624]

4.313 However, when the Act progressed through Parliament and during the course of the enactment of Part III, there was substantial criticism directed at this part of the RIPA, especially from elements within the business community and ICT profession. Critics have felt that a disclosure requirement could undermine the deployment and reliance on the use of cryptographic techniques as a security technology, as well as damage the UK economy by placing it in an unfavourable position vis-à-vis its trading partners.[625] Security professionals and vendors have also developed techniques that undermine the value of key disclosure as an investigative tool.[626]

4.314 In response to the criticism, the then Home Secretary, Charles Clarke, stated:

> We envisage that the disclosure of the plain text of protected material, rather than a key, will be sufficient in almost all cases responding to a decryption notice and I expect there to be very few cases where disclosure of the keys themselves will be required.[627]

The Part III Code outlines a number of reasons where such cases may arise, such as where trust, credibility, or timeliness is an issue for investigators, or the key itself may have evidential value.[628] Various statutory safeguards were introduced governing the handling of keys by the authorities to whom they are disclosed,[629] breach of which may give rise to civil proceedings for recovery of any loss or damage caused.[630]

4.315 To address concerns raised within the financial services sector, where the use of cryptography is stated as having 'a crucial role' in business operations, the Part III Code states that a key disclosure requirement will not be imposed on a company regulated by the Financial Conduct Authority (FCA) without prior notification to the Chief Executive

---

[622] RIPA, ss 50(3)(c) and 51.

[623] ibid, s 52(4)(a).

[624] ibid, s 52(4)(b) and (5).

[625] See eg Editorial Comment, 'RIP, RIP', *Financial Times*, 14 July 2000. These criticisms have been reiterated with the coming into force of Part III. See eg Wearden, G, 'Anger over encryption key seizure threat', *ZDNet UK*, 19 May 2006, available at <http://www.zdnet.com/article/anger-over-encryption-key-seizure-threat/>.

[626] eg Anderson, R, Needham, R, and Shamir, A, 'The Steganographic File System', in Ausmith, D (ed), *Information Hiding*, Springer-Verlag, 1998, at 73–82.

[627] Hansard (House of Commons), 6 March 2000, vol 345, Col 834.

[628] Part III Code, above, n 589, para 6.7.

[629] RIPA, s 55(2). See also Part III Code, above, n 589, s 8.

[630] RIPA, s 55(4).

of the FCA.[631] By making this concession, however, the Government may in the future face a clamour from other business sectors arguing that cryptography is equally critical to their business activities, particularly those only having an online presence.

However, this second approach raises issues that may need further consideration in terms **4.316** of balancing the different interests involved. First, the data security technique being delivered up may either be specific to an individual or it may be a tool that protects the data of a community of users, such as a company's employee email over an Intranet. In the latter scenario, the obligation to disclose gives rise to potential vulnerabilities both in terms of the individual rights of others, ie other protected users, and the interests of legal entities, ie the corporation. Under European human rights jurisprudence, the potential for collateral infringements of third-party privacy rights must be necessary and proportionate to the object of the interference.[632] The potential exposure of the corporate entity to a breach of its security may have significant consequences for its commercial activities, particularly in relation to adverse publicity and perceptions of trust. Indeed, such concerns have historically meant substantial under-reporting of computer crimes, such as hacking and fraud.[633]

Second, the person subject to the requirement may be the person under investigation or a **4.317** related third party, such as a company or communications service provider. Again, where the requirement is imposed on a third party, adequate consideration needs to be given to the costs, in the widest sense, being imposed on that third party. For example, in terms of communication service providers, a requirement to disclose keys protecting the data of its customers could restrict the growth of the market for services such as 'key escrow', where a third party maintains copies of cryptographic keys as a safeguard against loss or destruction. The needs of law enforcement could, therefore, militate against the use of data security services that are seen as being important to the development of our 'Information Society'.

A key may also grant access to a range of different devices, such that different authorization **4.318** schemes may be applicable to the various sources of data available. In a mobile phone context, for example, a handset may be subject to a personal identification number (PIN), which once entered gives access to data held on the handset itself (eg numbers called, address book), as well as various services provided to the subscriber (eg voice mail). In an investigation, if the suspect is not prepared to provide the PIN, the police can apply to the service provider to request the PIN unlocking key. However, access to the data on the service provider's system is a form of interception, which requires lawful authority under Part I, Chapter I of the RIPA, while the data on the handset may be accessed under the Police and Criminal Evidence Act 1984. In addition, the network data may comprise content and communications data (eg time and date of call), the former being subject to the access regime under the RIPA Part I, Chapter II. The complexities arising in such a scenario may create substantial problems for both law enforcement and CSPs in terms of ensuring that appropriate procedures have been followed and verified, as well as protecting the rights of the suspect.[634]

---

[631] Part III Code, above, n 589, para 6.8.

[632] See *Lambert v France* [1998] HRCD 806, Judgment, 24 August 1998; and *Amann v Switzerland*, Judgment, 16 February 2000).

[633] See paras 2.79 et seq.

[634] In the US, in *Riley v California*, 134 S Ct 2473 (2014), the court discussed how modern phones differ both in qualitative and quantitative terms with respect to the data that may be held on them, which impacts the rights of law enforcement to search such as device.

4.319   Where a legal obligation is imposed upon a person in relation to an investigation, a failure to comply must inevitably result in sanctions. However, the nature of such sanctions may be couched in different forms, justified on alternative grounds. First, the sanction may result from the commission of a distinct offence, where the mischief is considered to cause sufficient harm in itself.

4.320   This is the approach adopted under the RIPA, where it is an offence if a person 'knowingly fails, in accordance with the notice, to make the disclosure required ...',[635] which carries a maximum two-year prison term.[636] Under the Terrorism Act 2006, this penalty was increased in 'a national security case' to five years, defined in the following terms:

> ... a case in which the grounds specified in the notice to which the offence relates as the grounds for imposing a disclosure requirement were or included a belief that the imposition of the requirement was necessary in the interests of national security.[637]

A five-year term has also since been inserted in respect of 'child indecency' cases.[638]

4.321   Prosecutions in these enhanced penalty cases would seem to raise different evidential issues than that for the basic offence. In proceedings for the offence of non-disclosure, a person is presumed to be in possession of the relevant key, for disclosure itself or for rendering the protected information intelligible and disclosing the information, if the prosecution can show, beyond reasonable doubt, that he was in possession of it at any time before the disclosure notice was given.[639] A defendant can challenge this presumption, therefore, if they can adduce sufficient evidence to raise doubt in respect of their possession.[640] It is also a defence to show that it was not reasonably practicable to make the disclosure within the time limit, or it was disclosed as soon as reasonably practicable after the time limit.[641] In a 'national security case', the prosecution will simply assert that the disclosure requirement was 'necessary in the interests of national security'. A defendant is likely to find it very difficult to adduce evidence that raises doubt about such an assertion, in part due to traditional judicial deference towards the executive branch of government on such matters.[642] Conversely, for 'child indecency cases', the prosecution may have significant forensic challenges evidencing beyond reasonable doubt that the protected data constitutes an offence under child sexual abuse laws. An example of the potential complexities can be seen in *US v Hersh, aka Mario*,[643] where the defendant was in possession of a high-capacity Zip disk that was thought to contain child sexual abuse material. Law enforcement were unable to decrypt the images, so they obtained partial source code from the company that wrote the encryption software, F-Secure. The code did not decrypt the images, but provided certain attributes of the files: specifically file names and file size in terms of 'pre-encryption

---

[635]   RIPA, s 53(1).
[636]   ibid, s 53(5)(a) and (5A)(b).
[637]   Terrorism Act 2006, s 15, inserting subsection (5A) and (5B) into RIPA, s 53.
[638]   Policing and Crime Act 2009, s 26(2), amending RIPA, s 53(5A) and inserting subsection (6).
[639]   RIPA, s 53(2).
[640]   ibid, s 53(2) and (3).
[641]   ibid, s 53(4).
[642]   eg the case of Christopher Wilson, who was given a six month term for failing to disclose a password. The prosecutor noted that 'it was believed to be in the interests of national security to apply for a notice': Kennedy, R, 'Computer whizzkid jailed for failing to provide password after cyber attacks on police', *The Journal*, 4 July 2014, available at <http://www.thejournal.co.uk/news/north-east-news/computer-whizzkid-jailed-failing-provide-7375293>.
[643]   297 F 3d 1233 (11th Cir 2002).

computer bytes'.[644] These names and files sizes were then matched with a database held by the government and the database images were adduced as evidence of what was held on the Zip disk.

Under RIPA, there is also an offence of 'tipping-off', where the person subject to the dis- **4.322** closure requirement is required under the terms of the notice to maintain the secrecy of the notice and its contents.[645] The offence is analogous to that provided for in respect of interception warrants.[646] A secrecy requirement should only be imposed where the protected information has, or is likely to, come into the possession of the police or another agency; and the requirement is reasonable to maintain the effectiveness of the any investigation, operation, or technique, or in the interests of the safety and well-being of a person.[647] The maximum penalty for breaching such secrecy is five years' imprisonment.[648] A defence exists where the secrecy breach was the result of software designed to automatically, and entirely free of human intervention, warn, or indicate when a key is no longer secure or operational.[649]

Surprisingly, this offence would appear to be one of strict liability, occurring upon disclos- **4.323** ure, with no express *mens rea* element required. In interpreting this provision, however, a court may import a *mens rea* element unless it is held that Parliament's intention is clear.[650] A factor in favour of interpreting the offence as one of strict liability is the subsequent defence of lack of knowledge granted to persons other than the recipient of the notice.[651] Against such an interpretation, the court may look to the fact that the non-disclosure offence requires knowledge, while for analogous offences, such as obstructing a constable, intent is critical to a finding of liability where a tip-off has occurred.[652]

Indeed, an alternative basis for sanctioning a failure to disclose would be as a form of **4.324** obstruction in relation to the exercise of enforcement powers, an offence committed against the person investigating the crime.[653] Under the Police Act 1996, for example, it is an offence if a person 'resists or wilfully obstructs a constable in the execution of his duty, or a person assisting a constable in the execution of his duty',[654] which could include a failure to comply with a duty to act,[655] such as the obligation to disclose keys under the RIPA. This offence does not extend, however, to a general duty to assist in a police inquiry.[656]

---

[644] ibid, at 1233 fn 4.
[645] RIPA, s 54(4).
[646] ibid, s 19 'Offence for unauthorised disclosures'.
[647] ibid, s 54(3).
[648] ibid, s 54(4)(a).
[649] ibid, s 54(5). See also Part III Code, paras 10.14–10.17.
[650] *Sweet v Parsley* [1970] AC 132, at 148H.
[651] RIPA, s 54(10).
[652] *Green v Moore* [1982] QB 1044.
[653] See comments from Lord Phillips of Sudbury during a debate on the RIP Bill, Lords Hansard, 28 June 2000, Col 1019.
[654] Police Act 1996, s 89(2). The maximum penalty is one month's imprisonment.
[655] *Lunt v DPP* [1993] Crim LR 534.
[656] *Rice v Connolly* [1966] 2 QB 414.

4.325 Non-disclosure could also be viewed as an offence against the administration of justice. Such sentiment was expressed in *Cutler and others*,[657] where the defendant refused to disclose the key in respect of a number of encrypted containers. In passing sentence, the court stated:

> We regard that as being a very serious offence because it interferes with the administration of justice and it prevents the prosecuting authorities and the police finding out what offences somebody has committed (para 35).

At English common law, it is an offence to intentionally pervert the course of justice, for which the maximum penalty is life imprisonment.[658] Under this offence, the destruction, falsification, or concealment of potential evidence has been considered conduct capable of perverting the course of justice,[659] which could obviously be applicable to the non-disclosure of keys protecting data.

4.326 A fourth approach would be to provide that some form of adverse or incriminating inference may be raised in the course of any subsequent related criminal proceedings, for example possession of obscene material. The latter approach may be statutorily based, as in the United Kingdom,[660] or may comprise a factor in civil law jurisdictions where evidence is freely assessed with regard to all relevant circumstances, including the behaviour of the accused.

4.327 Where an offence is committed through non-compliance with a lawful requirement, any penalty will need to act as an appropriate deterrent against such a refusal to comply. It is obviously quite possible that a person may choose not to comply with the request to disclose, thereby accepting the penalty, rather than comply and potentially expose themselves to prosecution for a more serious offence with greater penalties. Conversely, in *Padellec*,[661] it was held that a sentence for non-disclosure could be higher than the admitted illegal images (ie the plea), since the 'whole point is that the failure to provide the key is itself more serious because of what might be in it'. While such a scenario may be unfortunate, it would seem to be a necessary compromise where the rights of the individual are balanced against the need to protect society.

4.328 The raising of an adverse inference against a person in criminal proceedings for a failure to supply certain information raises issues concerning the right to a fair trial, under Art 6 of the ECHR and similar legal protections.[662] In particular, it may be viewed as an infringement of the individual's right to silence, the right not to self-incriminate,[663] and the principle that the prosecution has the burden of proving its case.[664] Convention jurisprudence

---

[657] [2011] EWCA Crim 2781. In *Southwell* [2012] EWCA Crim 2882, the sentence was reduced because 'although the obstruction of justice was serious, it was temporary'.

[658] See generally Ormerod, D (ed), *Blackstone's Criminal Practice*, 25th edn, Oxford University Press, 2015, paras B.14.26–14.31.

[659] *Kiffin* [1994] Crim LR 449.

[660] Criminal Justice and Public Order Act 1994, ss 34–8.

[661] [2012] EWCA Crim 1956.

[662] eg US Constitution, Fifth Amendment: '… nor shall be compelled in any criminal case to be witness against himself'.

[663] *Goddard LJ in Blunt v Park Lane Hotel* [1942] 2 KB 53, at 257:

> No one is bound to answer any question if the answer thereto would, in the opinion of the judge, have a tendency to expose (him) to any criminal charge, penalty or forfeiture which the judge regards as reasonably likely to be preferred . . . .

[664] See generally Koops, BJ, 'Commanding decryption and the privilege against self-incrimination', in Breur, CM et al (eds), *New Trends in Criminal Investigation: Volume 2*, Intersentia, 2000, at 431–45.

indicates that while a conviction may not be based solely or mainly on a refusal to supply such information,[665] an adverse inference may in specified circumstances be drawn from such a refusal when assessing the evidence adduced by the prosecution.[666]

The courts have had an opportunity to consider such issues in *S and A*.[667] The defendants were **4.329** both arrested in connection with terrorist offences. In the case of *S*, he was detained in a room where an encryption key appeared to have been partially entered in the computer. With *A*, computer materials seized subsequent to his arrest included a computer disc that contained an encrypted area. The defendants appealed against the notices issued under s 49 of the RIPA requiring that they disclose the encryption keys on the grounds of self-incrimination. The court noted that the legality of this process had to be addressed in two stages. The first question was to determine whether the principle was engaged at all. Relying upon the ECtHR decision in *Saunders*,[668] the court noted that the right not to self-incriminate does not extend to material that can be lawfully obtained by law enforcement and has 'an existence independent of the will of the suspect'.[669] The key, irrelevant of the form in which it exists, was held to be such an independent fact, similar in nature to a urine sample taken from a driver suspected of driving under the influence. However, in addition, it was noted that the defendant's knowledge of the key could also be an incriminating fact.[670] The second stage for the court, if it is assumed that the principle is engaged, is to consider whether the interference with the right consequent upon the issuance of the s 49 notice is necessary and proportionate. Here the court held that the procedural safeguards and limitations on usage detailed in the RIPA were sufficient to negate any claim of unfairness under the PACE, s 78.[671]

The operation of Part III of the RIPA, as a form of interference with property subject to the proce- **4.330** dures under Part III of the Police Act 1997, falls under the jurisdiction of the Chief Surveillance Commissioner.[672] As such, he reports annually on how this provision has been used by law enforcement. In 2015, the Commissioner reported that eighty-eight applications had been approved by the National Technical Assistance Centre (NTAC), of which thirty-eight were granted by a judge and thirty-seven were eventually served. Of these, nine were complied with, while in twenty-two cases there was a failure to comply, resulting in three convictions.[673] The relevant criminal conduct included threats to kill, child indecency, and domestic extremism.[674]

---

[665] Except for a specific offence of non-disclosure.

[666] See *Murray v United Kingdom* (1996) 22 EHRR 29, paras 41–58. See generally Jennings, A, Ashworth, A, and Emmerson, B, 'Silence and safety: The impact of human rights law', *Criminal Law Review* 879 [2000].

[667] [2008] EWCA Crim 2177.

[668] *Saunders v UK* [1996] 23 EHRR 313, para 69.

[669] However, following the ECtHR decision in *Jalloh v Germany* [2007] 44 EHRR 32, it was also accepted that such material could be obtained through inhuman or degrading treatment, which would fall foul of Art 6.

[670] See *Greater Manchester Police v Andrews* [2011] EWHC 1966 (Admin), where at first instance the s 49 notice was refused on the grounds that there was no 'independent evidence' to indicate if the respondent knew what the key was and therefore to reveal the key would itself be an incriminating fact, ie knowledge of the key, It was overturned on appeal on the basis that the privilege against self-incrimination was engaged 'only to a very limited extent' and the interference was proportionate (under s 49(2)(c)). The court also noted that a judge would have the discretion (under PACE, s 78) to exclude evidence at any subsequent trial.

[671] *S and A* [2008] EWCA Crim 2177, para 25.

[672] The IoCC and the Intelligence Services Commissioner also have oversight responsibilities under Pt III: RIPA, s 57(2)(c) and (d)(ii) and s 59(2)(b) and (c), respectively.

[673] OSC Annual Report for 2014-15, HC 126, paras 4.17–4.22.

[674] eg Leyden, J, 'Animal rights activist hit with RIPA key decrypt demand', *The Register*, 14 November 2007, available at <http://www.theregister.co.uk/2007/11/14/ripa_encryption_key_notice/>.

4.331 Under New Zealand law, the police have been granted the power to require the provision of 'information or assistance that is reasonable and necessary' to allow access to data held on, or accessible from, a computer on the premises being searched.[675] Following concerns about self-incrimination, a specific provision was included in the final clause limiting the obligation to provide *information* where it could incriminate the person concerned.[676] However, criticism has been expressed that the effect of the provision is meaningless, since subsequent provisions distinguish between situations where the information *itself* is incriminating from information and assistance that may *result* in incrimination.[677] Such criticism would also seem justifiable on the basis that a person could be obliged to assist the police, by logging on to the computer, without expressly requiring that the password (as information) be disclosed.

Breaking the protection

4.332 The third approach is for investigators to break the protection mechanism. The totality of seized material may provide the possibility of shortcut attacks, such as keys or passwords being recovered from disk space or memory sticks, or via back doors built into the technology,[678] or investigators will have to engage in brute force attacks, involving heavy computational processing.[679] The viability of the latter course of action, converting the data into an intelligible form through utilizing available techniques, would seem to depend on a number of factors, including the strength of the security technology employed,[680] the multiplicity of protection systems employed, and the period within which the data realistically needs to be converted. During the investigation of the hacker Kevin Poulson, for example, it is reported that evidence maintained in an encrypted form was only accessed after a US Department of Energy supercomputer was used to find the key, over a period of several months and at the cost of several hundred thousand dollars.[681]

4.333 Some governments have recognized the need to establish some such 'in-house' technical capability to assist law enforcement investigations. In 2001, the UK Government established the NTAC that is designed to provide the necessary technical expertise to law enforcement agencies, on a 24-hour basis, to try and access protected data without the involvement of the suspect, at an initial capital cost of £25 million.[682] NTAC also provides a clearing house for liaising with industry in seeking solutions to

---

[675] Search and Surveillance Act 2012, s 130 'Duty of persons with knowledge of computer system or other data storage devices or Internet site to assist access'.

[676] ibid, s 130(2).

[677] See Conte, A, 'Crime and Terror: New Zealand's Criminal Law Reform since 9/11', 21(4) *New Zealand Universities Law Review* 639 (2005).

[678] Over the years, US hardware and software manufacturers, such as Intel, have been accused of discussing with law enforcement agencies about the possibilities of 'building in' certain functionalities into their products to assist criminal investigations.

[679] See Denning and Baugh, above, n 574, at 117 et seq.

[680] eg the key length, such as over 128 bits.

[681] Littman, J, *The Watchman: The Twisted Life and Crimes of Serial Hacker Kevin Poulson*, Little, Brown & Co, 1997.

[682] Home Office, 'Head of NTAC announced', Press Release 096/2001, 30 March 2001. The establishment of NTAC followed a recommendation in the PIU Report, above, n 580, para 7.6. It is currently part of GCHQ, but co-located with the Security Services.

accessing protected material, both seized and intercepted data; while the requesting agencies are not permitted to serve a s 49 notice without prior written approval from NTAC.[683] As much of the material that NTAC handles will be obtained under powers in the RIPA, its operation is subject to review by the Interception of Communications Commissioner and the Intelligence Services Commissioner, as well as the Surveillance Commissioners.[684]

Breaking the protections applied to data will require use of a variety of techniques, from **4.334** brute force to the deployment of hacker tools used by those that commit computer-integrity offences. The use of covert surveillance techniques prior to the seizure of protected material, such as the installation of key loggers on a suspect's machine, has become a common technique deployed in anticipation that data is likely to be protected. In the longer term, law enforcement's ability to access protected data will depend on developments in technology, since techniques may be developed which are essentially incapable of being overcome.[685]

A number of evidential issues may arise where encryption mechanisms have been broken **4.335** by persons working for the investigator. The primary one is whether it will be possible to prove, 'beyond reasonable doubt', that the decryption process worked correctly, ie the provenance of the decrypted product.[686] Explaining the operation of such techniques to the satisfaction of a judge and jury may prove a formidable hurdle for prosecutors and their expert witnesses.

The issue of protected data is one element of a key debate on the regulation of the Internet **4.336** and cyberspace. On the one hand technologies such as encryption are vital to ensure the security and privacy of data both 'at rest' and 'in transmission'. However, such technologies will inevitably be utilized as much by criminal users as by others. From a control perspective, criminal usage of security technologies can be addressed through a combination of *ex ante* and *ex post* measures.

Ex ante regulatory measures attempt to proactively control the manner in which security **4.337** technologies are produced, deployed and used, and include controls over the export of certain strength products to certain jurisdictions.[687] In the past, a range of *ex ante* initiatives has been proposed by governments and policy makers, such as 'key escrow' and the 'Clipper Chip'.[688] The OECD Guidelines on cryptography policy assert that key management systems 'could provide a basis for a possible solution which could balance the

---

[683] Part III Code, above, n 589, para 3.10. This may be given on a case-by-case basis or to a public authority assessed by NTAC as being competent to exercise such powers.

[684] See House of Commons Hansard, Written Answers, for 30 March 2001, from Jack Straw, Secretary of State at the Home Office (Col 848W).

[685] See eg Grover, D, 'Dual encryption and plausible deniability', 20(1) *Computer Law and Security Report* 37 (2004).

[686] Sommer, P, 'Evidence in Internet Paedophilia Cases', 8(7) *Computer and Telecommunications Law Review* 176 (2002).

[687] eg Council Regulation No 428/2009 setting up a Community regime for the control of exports, transfer, brokering and transit of dual-use items. OJ L 281/1, 31 August 2004, Category 2, Part 5 'Information Security'.

[688] A US government proposal. See generally Froomkin, M, 'It came from Planet Clipper: The battle over cryptographic key "escrow"', *University of Chicago Legal Forum* 15 (1996).

interest of users and law enforcement authorities'.[689] To date, however, all such schemes have eventually been rejected under pressure from industry and users as being undesirable and unfeasible.

4.338 This section has examined three *ex post* measures designed to tackle protected seized data, measures reactive to the consequences of criminal usage of security technologies, two of which place duties on a suspect with penalties for a failure to comply. However, the efficacy of these measures and aspects of their legality remains doubtful. As Reitinger notes, to the extent that *ex post* remedies are 'unlikely to meet the needs of public safety', we are likely to see the attention of governments return to *ex ante* measures.[690]

F. Concluding Remarks

4.339 The nature of digital information raises important policy and legal issues, as well as gathering and handling problems for investigators. A potential consequence of digitization is to make it difficult to ensure that the different types of information obtained from different locations, 'on' and 'off' networks, continue to be subject to distinct legal treatment. Traditional legal categorizations can be rendered invalid or effectively unenforceable, sometimes eroding the protections granted to individuals by law.

4.340 Evidence gathering will generally require the deployment of various investigative techniques, covert and coercive. While these techniques are by no means new, as with our consideration of the criminal code, their deployment within an ICT environment can challenge traditional procedural concepts. While uncertainties and lacunae in the criminal code will generally operate to the advantage of a defendant, offering avenues for argument by defence counsel; similar problems in procedural law are more often to the detriment of a defendant.

4.341 The needs of law enforcement, and wider society, have to be balanced against the rights of the perpetrator, the victim, and others caught up in the investigative process. In the post 11 September environment, the complex balancing process shifted decisively in favour of law enforcement; while post-Snowden, there has been significant push back towards the safeguarding of individual rights. Wherever the policy pendulum lies, the needs of law enforcement in a cyberspace investigation has been most forcefully felt by CSPs, with ever greater obligations and demands being placed upon them. The dynamism of a liberalized marketplace for CSPs may, however, place some practical constraints on the strength of relationships that can exist between law enforcement and the communications industry.

4.342 Seizing systems and data may have become a relatively pedestrian exercise, but obtaining access to such data and analysing it within the time and resource constraints imposed on modern policing presents a significant challenge, which is likely to get worse in the

---

[689] OECD, *Guidelines on Cryptography Policy*, 19 December 1997, Principle 6.
[690] Reitinger, PR, 'Encryption, anonymity and markets', in Thomas, D and Loader, B (eds), *Cybercrime: Law Enforcement, Security and Surveillance in the Information Age*, Routledge, 2000, at 151 fn 16.

foreseeable future. Choices inevitably have to be made that can operate in favour of perpetrators of computer and cybercrimes.

Addressing the data problems created by digital investigations requires a variety of **4.343** approaches, legal, procedural, and technical. However, the forensic challenges increase in complexity when the computer crime involves an international dimension, a common feature, and a topic addressed in Chapter 5.

5

INTERNATIONAL ASPECTS: JURISDICTION AND HARMONIZATION

A. Introduction

Computer and cybercrimes inevitably often have a transnational aspect to them, which can **5.01** give rise to complex jurisdictional issues involving persons, things, and acts being present or carried out in a number of different countries. This can be as true for individual acts of criminality as it is for the multinational criminal organization. Even where the perpetrator and victim are located in the same jurisdiction, relevant evidence may reside on a server located in another jurisdiction, such as a 'Hotmail' account. As with most aspects of Internet-based activities, traditional legal concepts and principles are sometimes challenged by the nature of the environment. As a consequence, legislators, law enforcement agencies, and the judiciary have had to address issues of cybercrime jurisdiction at a number of levels.

This chapter first examines issues of material and procedural jurisdiction under English **5.02** criminal law. In respect of substantive offences, a concern of policy makers is that the law effectively captures the offending criminal behaviour, wherever the perpetrator may reside. However, extending jurisdictional reach raises an opposing policy concern, the classic Internet law problem, that lawful behaviour in the domestic jurisdiction may be categorized as criminal in a recipient jurisdiction. The law governing criminal procedure in a transnational investigative environment is designed to legitimize and control the actions of public law enforcement agencies taking place beyond territorial borders. Both sets of rules have sometimes been difficult to apply to the evolving cyberspace environment and specific reform initiatives have been undertaken to address the problem areas.

The second half of the chapter examines intergovernmental reform initiatives designed **5.03** to harmonize and minimize the differences between jurisdictions present in substantive and procedural laws. Such initiatives are one element of a strategy to tackle the limitations of national legal rules addressed in the first half of the chapter. The success of such initiatives inevitably varies considerably; although the position of the UK as a member of the European Union means that more distinct and substantial progress on harmonization is being achieved among the twenty-eight Member States.

5.04 While notions of cyberspace as a distinct legal jurisdiction have evaporated over recent years,[1] law makers and law enforcers are continuing to struggle to establish and operate within a legal framework that adequately reflects cyberspace as an international information medium. Some traditional mechanisms of control have been eroded, yet new mechanisms are still unclear or are only just emerging.

B. Material Jurisdiction

5.05 According to the Code for Crown Prosecutors, the two key criteria in determining whether to prosecute are evidential sufficiency and public interest.[2] However, a third, implied but unstated, criterion is that the offences were committed under English law jurisdiction. While such a consideration may be less common for traditional crimes, in a cybercrime environment such an issue can arise frequently.

5.06 The general principle of international criminal law is that a crime committed within a state's territory may be tried there. Although the territoriality of criminal law does not coincide with territorial sovereignty, it derives from such sovereign powers.[3] Under English common law, the general principle for determining jurisdiction has recently been stated by the courts to be when 'the last act took place in England or a substantial part of the crime was committed here'.[4] Previously, the general principle was drawn more narrowly, as being where the *actus reus* is completed,[5] also referred to as 'result crimes' or the 'terminatory theory'. The 'last act' rule echoes the civil law principle *lex loci delicti commissi*, whereby torts are governed by the law of the place where the act was committed.

5.07 However, an act may be initiated in one jurisdiction and completed or terminated, ie the effect or harm felt, in another jurisdiction. While, with physical crimes, the initiatory and terminatory elements of a crime are generally concurrent, such as murder (unless the person fires the gun from another state!), where criminal activity is information-based, a jurisdictional distinction between the initiation and termination of an act becomes the norm. The courts had previously recognized this, Lord Diplock stating, for example, that 'there is no reason in principle why the terminatory theory should have the effect of excluding the initiatory theory as an alternative ground of jurisdiction'.[6] However, the terminatory

---

[1] eg Barlow, JP, 'A declaration of the independence of cyberspace', 9 February 1996, available at <http://homes.eff.org/~barlow/Declaration-Final.html>; and Johnson, D and Post, D, 'Law and borders—The rise of law in cyberspace', 48 *Stanford Law Review* 1367 (1996).

[2] Available at <http://www.cps.gov.uk/victims_witnesses/code.html>.

[3] Cassese, A et al, *International Criminal Law*, Oxford University Press, 2013, s 15.2.1. See also Law Commission Report No 91, *Report on the Territorial and Extraterritorial Extent of the Criminal Law*, Cm 75, HMSO, 1978.

[4] *Smith (Wallace Duncan) (No 4)* [2004] QB 1418, at 57.

[5] *Manning* [1998] 2 Cr App R 461.

[6] *Treacy* [1971] AC 537.

theory proved remarkably resilient until an expansive approach was adopted by the Court of Appeal in *Smith (Wallace Duncan)*.

An example of the issues that arise in a cybercrime environment are illustrated by the **5.08** Citibank fraud.[7] In 1994, Citibank suffered a significant breach of security in its cash management system, resulting in funds being transferred from customer accounts into the accounts of the perpetrator and his accomplices.[8] The eventual sum involved was $12 million, although the vast majority, $11.6 million, was transferred subsequent to the discovery of the breach as part of the efforts to locate the perpetrators. After significant international cooperation between law enforcement agencies, an individual was identified. Vladimir Levin was eventually arrested in England and, after appeals, was subsequently extradited to the United States.[9]

One jurisdictional issue in *Levin* revolved around the question of *where* the offences were **5.09** held to have taken place. Defendant's counsel claimed that the criminal act occurred in St Petersburg at the moment when Levin pressed particular keys on the keyboard instigating fraudulent Citibank transfers, and therefore Russian law applied. Counsel for the extradition applicant claimed that the place where the changes to the data occurred, the Citibank computer in Parsippany (US), constituted the place where the offence took place. The judge decided in favour of the applicant on the basis that the real-time nature of the communication link between Levin and the Citibank computer meant that Levin's keystrokes were actually occurring on the Citibank computer.[10]

Such an approach might suggest that a message-based system of communication, such **5.10** as email, operating on a 'store-and-forward' basis, might produce a different result if an interval in the course of committing the act could be shown to exist. In *ex parte Osman*,[11] for example, the court held that the sending of a telex constituted the act of appropriation and, therefore, the place from where the telex was sent was where the offence was committed.[12] With the decision in *Smith (Wallace Duncan)* and other subsequent statutory developments, such an issue would likely no longer arise. However, the nature of computer and communications technologies can create legal uncertainty about where an act occurs, which is likely to be a common ground for challenge by defendants.[13]

One consequence of the common jurisdictional dissonance between initiation and ter- **5.11** mination in an Internet environment is that English criminal law has had to be amended to extend the territorial reach of certain offences. In addition, the general concern about the growth and societal impact of computer crime has also led governments to apply extra-territorial principles to cybercrime.

---

[7] *R v Governor of Brixton Prison and another, ex parte Levin* [1996] 4 All ER 350. The decision was appealed unsuccessfully to the House of Lords (1997) 3 All ER 289.

[8] The system, called the 'Financial Institutions Citibank Cash Manager' (FICCM), provided large institutional customers with dial-in access from any geographic location to the online service, based on a system in Parsipenny, New Jersey. Once accessed, customers could carry out a range of financial transactions, including the execution of credit transfers between accounts.

[9] See further paras 5.108–5.111.

[10] *ex parte Levin* [1996] 4 All ER 350, at 363a.

[11] *Governor of Pentonville Prison, ex parte Osman* [1990] 1 WLR 277.

[12] ibid, at 295e–f.

[13] For consideration of jurisdiction in a civil case involving hacking, see *Ashton Investments Ltd and Another v OSJC Russian Aluminium and Others* [2006] All ER (D) 209 (Oct).

Statutory rules

5.12 In terms of ensuring legal certainty, common law principles of criminal jurisdiction have been made concrete or supplanted through express jurisdictional provisions in substantive legislation. Such rules generally claim jurisdiction if one of the elements of the offence occurs within the State's territory. The following outlines the statutory rules under English criminal law applicable to some of the key cybercrime offences examined in Chapter 3.

5.13 The Computer Misuse Act 1990 contains five substantive computer-integrity offences: unauthorized access to computer material; unauthorized access with intent to commit or facilitate commission of further offences; unauthorized acts with intent or reck- lessness; unauthorized acts causing or creating the risk of serious damage; and making or supplying articles for use in the commission of the integrity offences.[14] The Act has had a problematic history, and the fact that it was adopted prior to rapid expansion of the Internet raised concerns about its effectiveness against new forms of criminal activity such as 'denial- of-service' attacks. As a consequence, it has been amended on a number of occasions.[15]

5.14 Under the Act, the offences may be committed by any person, British citizenship being immaterial to a person's guilt.[16] Jurisdiction over transnational activities is asserted through the concept of a 'significant link' being present in the 'home country', ie England and Wales, Scotland, or Northern Ireland.[17] Where an unauthorized access offence has been committed, the following are considered a 'significant link':

  (a) that the accused was in the home country concerned at the time when he did the act which caused the computer to perform the function; or
  (b) that any computer containing any program or data to which the accused by doing that act secured or intended to secure unauthorized access, or enabled or intended to enable unauthorized access to be secured, was in the home country concerned at that time.[18]

5.15 Where a s 2 offence is involved, ie unauthorized access with a further offence, the Act addresses two potential scenarios. First, the need for a 'significant link' is dispensed with in respect of the unauthorized element of the action, as long as the further offence is triable under English law.[19] If the further offence committed under s 2 is extra-territorial in nature, then an offence may be committed which requires no connection with England and Wales at all.[20] Second, in the alternative, if a 'significant link' does exist, and what was intended to be committed would involve the commission of an offence under the law of the country where the act was intended to take place, whether under the laws of England and Wales or elsewhere, then the domestic courts can still seize jurisdiction.[21] In the case of an unauthor- ized act, under s 3, the 'significant link' is either the presence of the accused or that the acts occurred in the UK.[22] Finally, with regard to unauthorized acts causing serious damage, a

---

[14] Computer Misuse Act 1990 (CMA), ss 1–3A respectively.
[15] Most significantly by the Police and Justice Act 2006 and the Serious Crime Act 2015.
[16] CMA, s 9.
[17] ibid, s 4(6).
[18] ibid, s 5(2). Sections 6 and 7 address the territorial scope for the inchoate offences, ie conspiracy, attempt, or incitement.
[19] ibid, s 4(3).
[20] Hirst, M, *Jurisdiction and the Ambit of the Criminal Law*, Oxford University Press, 2003, at 194.
[21] CMA, ss 4(4) and 8(1).
[22] ibid, s 5(3).

'significant link' would either be the presence of the accused, the computer was present, or the 'serious damage of a material kind' was in the home country.[23]

In contrast to the main substantive offences, the new s 3A offence, making and supplying **5.16** articles, does not have extended territorial reach. While such an extension is recognized as being critical for the effective operation of the other offences, the Government deliberately wanted to narrow the application of the potentially broad scope of the s 3A offence.[24] The offence could have been given extended reach by considering it as a form of communication offence. Since a communication is both sent and received, the supplying of an article by posting it on a website, although done outside the jurisdiction, would become an offence through downloading by a person within the domestic jurisdiction. This is the position in respect of obscene publications, discussed below.

The Act also amends the Criminal Attempts Act 1981.[25] Prior to the amendment, s 1(4) lim- **5.17** ited the commission of attempt, ie an act which is 'more than merely preparatory', to those offences that could be tried in England and Wales as an indictable offence.[26] However, the Law Commission recommended that attempts carried out in the UK to commit computer misuse offences abroad should be criminalized, subject to the 'double criminality' con-dition that the attempted act would be an offence in the jurisdiction where it was to take place.[27]

Similar jurisdictional extensions are present in the computer-integrity offences of other **5.18** jurisdictions. In the US, for example, the USA Patriot Act of 2001 amended the Computer Fraud and Abuse Act to extend the concept of a 'protected computer' to include 'a computer located outside the United States that is used in a manner that affects interstate or foreign commerce or communication of the United States'.[28] This effectively extends the territorial scope to the global arena, since any computer connected to the Internet would potentially be encompassed.

Where computer-related offences have been committed, such as fraud or forgery, the **5.19** Criminal Justice Act 1993, Part I, provides for jurisdiction on the basis of a 'relevant event' occurring in England and Wales (s 2(3)). A 'relevant event' means 'any act or omission or other event (including any result of one or more acts or omissions) proof of which is required for conviction of the offence'.[29] This would include, for example, an email message sent as part of a conspiracy. A court can seize jurisdiction if any 'relevant event' occurs in England and Wales even though all other such events may have occurred abroad.

The Criminal Justice Act 1993 also provides for rules to determine the location of certain **5.20** 'relevant events'. In relation to the obtaining of property, the act occurs in England and Wales if it is either dispatched from or received at a place in the jurisdiction. In the case of

---

[23] ibid, s 5(3A).
[24] Email from Tim Wright, Head of Computer Crime Team, Home Office, dated 23 August 2006.
[25] CMA, s 7(3).
[26] ie the person could be charged with the offence.
[27] Law Commission, *Computer Misuse*, Report No 186, Cm 819, London, HMSO, 1989, para 4.3.
[28] 18 USC s 1030(e)(2)(B).
[29] Criminal Justice Act 1993 (CJA 93), s 2(1). This provision was recommended in the Law Commission Report No 180, *Jurisdiction over Offences of Fraud and Dishonesty with a Foreign Element*, Cm 318 (1989), but the phrase was first proposed in a Law Commission, *Territorial and Extraterritorial Extent of the Criminal Law*, Working Paper No 29, 1970.

a conspiracy to commit fraud, a communication of 'any information, instruction, request, demand or other matter' is a 'relevant event', and it takes place in England and Wales if the message is sent or received here.[30] As such, while the UK does not have an offence comparable to wire fraud in the US,[31] a similar result could be achieved to that held recently by the Supreme Court in *Pasquantino*,[32] where the accused were prosecuted in the US for wire fraud in the course of a broader criminal act of smuggling to evade Canadian revenue laws. While in *Pasquantino* two distinct offences were involved, the UK authorities would only be concerned with one offence, of which only the communication element need touch English jurisdiction.

5.21 Under the Fraud Act 2006, the jurisdictional position under the Criminal Justice Act 1993 has had to be amended to reflect the changed nature of the offence.[33] Under the Theft Act 1968, ss 15 and 15A, an offence involved two distinct elements: the deception of the victim and the obtaining of the property. Where either one of these elements occurred in the UK, the courts had jurisdiction. However, the new fraud offences only require evidence of the dishonest intent of the perpetrator, with no need to show deception or obtaining. A potential consequence of this was that property obtained in the UK would no longer be a 'relevant event' for jurisdictional purposes.[34] The Criminal Justice Act 1993 has therefore been amended to state that where the perpetrator causes the gain or loss intended by his actions that constitutes a relevant event.[35]

5.22 In terms of content-related offences, the issue of jurisdiction has been raised in respect of the 'publication' of material prohibited under the Obscene Publications Act 1959.[36] The Act criminalizes the publication of *any* material which intends to 'deprave and corrupt' those persons likely to read or view it,[37] although pornographic images of children are generally subject to prosecution under separate legislative provisions.[38]

5.23 Section 1(3) of the 1959 Act defines 'publication' in the following terms:

(a) distributes, circulates, sells, lets on hire, gives, or lends it, or who offers it for sale or for letting on hire; or
(b) in the case of an article containing or embodying matter to be looked at . . . where the matter is data stored electronically, transmits that data.

In *Waddon*,[39] the court held, in respect of pornographic images made available through a website, that two distinct acts of publication take place (para 12): the first when the data is uploaded to a website, carried out by the perpetrator; the second when it is subsequently downloaded, carried out by the victim. The court was satisfied that such an approach was clearly encompassed by s 1(3)(b). Subsequently, in *Perrin*,[40] in accepting the *Waddon*

---

[30] CJA 93, s 4.
[31] 18 USC s 1343.
[32] 73 USLW 4287 (2005).
[33] See further paras 3.59–3.63.
[34] See the comments of Lord Goldsmith, when moving the amendment: Lords Hansard, vol 678, Col 185, 31 January 2006.
[35] Fraud Act 2006 (FA), Schedule 1, para 25(3), inserting a new subsection (1A) in CJA 93, s 2.
[36] See generally paras 3.130–3.139.
[37] Obscene Publications Act 1959 (OPA), s 1(1).
[38] ie Protection of Children Act 1978, s 1, and the Criminal Justice Act 1988, s 160.
[39] [2000] All ER (D) 502.
[40] *Perrin* [2002] All ER (D) 359.

position, the court drew further support from the different forms of publications recognized in s 1(3)(a), specifically the reference to 'offers it for sale', which as a passive form of 'publication' has obvious parallels with the establishment of a website (para 18). The defendant was a French citizen and claimed that 'where sites were developed abroad they were legal where they were managed' (para 4). However, such an approach was ignored by the court, finding guilt on the basis that the publication through downloading occurred in England.

The issues raised in *Waddon* and *Perrin* contain interesting parallels with the *Yahoo!* case in France.[41] In *Yahoo!*, one of the determining factors in attributing liability was the perceived targeting of French citizens. Counsel in both English cases raised the issue of jurisdiction. In *Waddon*, the court declined a request to rule on a situation where material was placed on a website with no intention for subsequent transmission back to England; although they did opine that it would likely 'depend upon questions of intention and causation in relation to where publication should take place' (para 11). In *Perrin*, counsel for the defendant suggested that 'a prosecution should only be brought against a publisher where the prosecutor could show that the major steps in relation to publication were taken within the jurisdiction of the court' (para 51), a suggestion dismissed by the court. **5.24**

Perrin has been criticized for having 'not adequately addressed' the difficult jurisdictional questions,[42] potentially extending English obscenity laws to all foreign-hosted websites. Alternative approaches would seem to be either no liability for such foreign sites, even if the site seeks to attract English subscribers—a possibly 'unpalatable conclusion',[43] but perhaps best suited to the nature of cyberspace; or the imposition of liability based on localization factors, such as whether the publisher directs his activities to English subscribers, similar in kind to defamation cases and the US 'minimum contacts' doctrine in an Internet context.[44] **5.25**

For computer-integrity and computer-related crimes, we can see a statutory trend towards expanding the jurisdictional reach of English criminal law, which English common law, in *Smith (Wallace Duncan)*, has only recently been willing to follow. It is perhaps both inevitable and appropriate that Parliament responds more rapidly to the increasing internationalization of criminal activity than the judiciary. However, by contrast, in *Perrin*, an expansive judicial interpretation of the *actus reus* may be seen as criminalizing unwitting foreign citizens, simply on the basis of the nature of the technological environment in which they operate. This may be seen as particularly problematic in the area of content-related offences, such as hate speech, where divergent jurisdictional approaches are at their most stark.[45] **5.26**

---

[41] *League Against Racism and Antisemitism (LICRA), French Union of Jewish Students v Yahoo! Inc (USA), Yahoo France*, Tribunal de Grande Instance de Paris, 20 November 2000; EBLR (2001).

[42] Ormerod, D and Laird, K (eds), *Smith & Hogan Criminal Law*, 14th edn, Oxford University Press, 2015, s 13.1.4.1.

[43] See Hirst, M, 'Cyberobscenity and the ambit of English criminal law', 13(2) *Computers and Law* (2002), available at <http://www.scl.org/site.aspx?i=ed451>.

[44] See eg the Australian defamation case, *Dow Jones & Co Inc v Gutnick* [2003] 1 LRC 368, Aus HC, and the US contacts case, *Zippo Mfg Co v Zippo Dot Com Inc* 952 F Supp 1119 (WD Pa 1997). See generally Reed, C, *Internet Law: Text and Materials*, 2nd edn, Cambridge University Press, 2004, para 7.1.3.

[45] See generally Decroos, M, 'Criminal jurisdiction over transnational speech offenses', 13 *European Journal of Crime, Criminal Law and Criminal Justice* 365 (2005).

Extra-territorial criminal law

5.27 While the jurisdictional norm of criminal law is the territorial principle, there are four broadly recognized principles under which extra-territorial jurisdiction is claimed or exercised in cases of international criminal activity:

- The 'active nationality principle', which is based on the nationality of the perpetrator.
- The 'passive personality principle', which is based on the nationality of the victim.
- The 'universality principle', for crimes broadly recognized as being crimes against humanity, such as genocide or piracy.[46]
- The 'protective principle', to safeguard a jurisdiction's national interest, such as the planning of cyber-terrorism.[47]

These principles may also be broadly distinguished between those that reflect an inward focus, protecting national subjects ('passive personality') and national interests ('protective principle'); and those with an external focus ('active nationality' and 'universality'), which operate in support of international cooperation in the fight against certain crimes.[48] The territorial principle has also expanded over the years, extending the locus of the crime to include acts committed abroad which have an effect in the jurisdiction. This has become known as the 'objective territorial principle', although it is obviously related to the 'passive personality principle'.[49]

5.28 Under English law, the general common law position is that the courts will not accept jurisdiction if the offence is committed outside England and Wales, even if the accused is a British subject.[50] However, this position has been altered by statutory provision in respect of certain offences, including indecent images of children, a major form of content-related computer crime.[51] This provision is applicable to both the supply and possession of child pornographic photographs and 'pseudo-photographs'.[52] In the event of proceedings, it is presumed that the subsection 1(a) condition is met, although a defendant can submit a notice or require the prosecution to prove such equivalence, where the offence may be described differently in the foreign country.[53]

5.29 Another piece of legislation having extra-territorial scope is the Offences Against the Person Act 1861, which has been utilized to prosecute a person for manslaughter in respect of a man killed in Guyana many years previously,[54] based on the 'active nationality' principle. However, it also has potential relevance for cyber-terrorist activities, since it creates an offence of 'conspiring or soliciting to commit murder',[55] whoever and wherever the person

---

[46] On 19 July 2005, a former Afghan warlord became the first person to be prosecuted for offences of torture and hostage-taking, following the House of Lords decision in *Pinochet* [2000] 1 AC 147, which expressly accepted the validity of the 'universality principle' under English law.

[47] See generally Cassese, above, n 3, Chapter 15. The Council of Europe Report on 'Extraterritorial Criminal Jurisdiction' (1990) recognizes seven categories, the additional three being the 'principle of the flag', based on vessels and aircraft flying a flag; the 'representation' principle; and a catch-all category of other forms.

[48] See Cassese, above, n 3, s 1.2.5.

[49] See Bantekas, I and Nash, S, *International Criminal Law*, Routledge Cavendish, 2003, at 16 et seq.

[50] See *Harden* [1963] 1 QB 8.

[51] Sexual Offences Act (SOA) 2003, s 72 'Offences outside the United Kingdom'.

[52] See further paras 4.161 et seq.

[53] SOA, s 72(6), (7).

[54] Offences Against the Person Act 1861 (OAPA), s 9. See *Cheong* [2006] EWCA Crim 524.

[55] OAPA, s 4.

may be, which would seem relevant against UK-based websites advocating foreign terrorist acts; although such behaviour would now be likely to fall under the Terrorism Act 2006,[56] which also contains extra-territorial provisions.[57]

However, such extra-territorial provisions remain the exception, not the rule. At the end of **5.30** 2004, for example, the government published a proposal to reform fraud law, driven in part by a desire to address problems prosecuting cyber-fraud due to the existing requirement that a person rather than a machine be deceived.[58] The proposal considered but rejected the suggestion that the active or nationality personality principle should be adopted.[59] It raised four key arguments against such a position. First, the practical difficulties that would arise from the need to gather evidence overseas and the possibility of bringing witnesses from abroad. Second, the potential conflicts with local laws, which may prevent such evidence being garnered, or the accused being extradited. Third, doubts may be raised whether the public interest is served in the prosecution of cases where there is no impact on the UK.[60] Finally, the report asks whether it is appropriate to make UK nationals abroad subject to domestic law as well as local law.

Despite these views, the government as a signatory to the Cybercrime Convention and **5.31** being subject to obligations under EU law has led it to reconsider its position in respect of computer crimes. The Convention has a jurisdictional provision that includes extra-territorial jurisdiction on the basis of the 'active nationality' principle:

> Each Party shall adopt such legislative and other measures as may be necessary to establish jurisdiction over any offence established in accordance with Articles 2–11 of this Convention, when the offence is committed:
> a. in its territory; or
> b. on board a ship flying the flag of that Party; or
> c. on board an aircraft registered under the laws of that Party; or
> d. by one of its nationals, if the offence is punishable under criminal law where it was committed or if the offence is committed outside the territorial jurisdiction of any State.[61]

The principle, which can be seen as supportive of greater international cooperation, has also been adopted in EU measures, specifically in relation to computer-related fraud,[62] child pornography,[63] and computer-integrity crimes.[64] In addition, the Convention requires a Member State to establish jurisdiction over its own nationals and to prosecute them where,

---

[56] Terrorism Act 2006 (TA 2006), s 1, 'Encouragement of terrorism'.

[57] ibid, s 17.

[58] See Law Commission Consultation Paper No 155, *Legislating the Criminal Code: Fraud and Deception*, 1999, paras 8.36–8.58. See further paras 3.52–3.63.

[59] *Fraud Law Reform: Government response to the consultation*, November 2004, paras 57 et seq.

[60] Under English law, prosecutors are required to consider three issues when deciding to proceed within a prosecution: (a) the public interest, (b) evidential sufficiency, and (c) jurisdiction.

[61] Convention on Cybercrime, signed 23 November 2001, entered into force, 1 July 2004, ETS No 185, Art 22(d).

[62] Council Framework Decision 2001/413/JHA of 28 May 2001 combating fraud and counterfeiting of non-cash means of payment, OJ L 149/1, 2 June 2001 ('Fraud Decision'), Art 9(1)(b).

[63] Directive 2011/92/EU of the European Parliament and of the Council of 13 December 2011 on combating the sexual abuse and sexual exploitation of children and child pornography, and replacing Council Framework Decision 2004/68/JHA, OJ L 335/1, 17 December 2011, Art 17(1)(b).

[64] Directive 2013/40/EU on attacks against information systems and replacing Council Framework Decision 2005/222/JHA, OJ L 218/8, 14 August 2013 ('Integrity Directive'), Art 12(1)(b).

as a matter of national law, such persons may not be extradited to a requesting state where the crime was committed. This has been referred to as the '*aut dedere aut judicare*' principle,[65] or the 'representation' principle of extra-territorial jurisdiction, as the state may be deemed to be acting on behalf of another state.[66]

5.32 While the government was not obliged to adopt extra-territorial provisions under the Convention, because it is an optional measure,[67] the Integrity Directive has rendered it mandatory, in contrast to the earlier Framework Decision.[68] As a consequence, the Computer Misuse Act 1990 was amended in 2015 to introduce extra-territorial jurisdiction where the accused was a UK national at the time and the conduct constituted an offence in the country in which it was committed.[69] Despite this jurisdictional extension, however, the Crown Prosecution Service (CPS) will still be required to consider the public interest when deciding whether to proceed on the basis of jurisdiction through 'active personality', which may be unlikely given the arguments outlined above.[70]

Jurisdictional conflicts

5.33 Having examined the different territorial and extra-territorial rules governing criminal jurisdiction, it is inevitable that conflicts arise between states on the basis of competing claims for jurisdiction, following the application of either similar or different rules. Indeed, while the nature of criminal activities in cyberspace often results in connections with multiple jurisdictions, law reforms that extend territorial jurisdiction and establish extra-territorial jurisdiction as a policy response to the phenomenon have a multiplier effect, increasing the likelihood of jurisdictional concurrency and conflict.

5.34 It is a basic principle of criminal and human rights law, however, that a perpetrator should not be prosecuted more than once for the same criminal conduct ('*non bis in idem*', also know as the 'double jeopardy' principle).[71] While the previous sections indicated *whether* English law is applicable, they do not assist us in determining *which* jurisdiction is the most appropriate in a multi-jurisdictional cybercrime context.

5.35 One mechanism for addressing multiple jurisdictional claims is the possibility of transferring proceedings commenced in one state to another, often where the perpetrator resides. Procedures for transferring criminal proceedings have been subject to international agreement, such as the European Convention on the Transfer of Proceedings in Criminal Matters,[72] although the UK is not currently a signatory to any such instrument. This procedure is different in nature from an obligation to extradite or prosecute those whom a state will not extradite, obligations provided for under the Cybercrime Convention.[73]

---

[65] Council of Europe, Convention on Cybercrime, Explanatory Report (ETS No 185), para 251.

[66] European Committee on Crime Problems, 'Computer-related crime', Report, 1990, at 84 et seq ('CoE Report 1990').

[67] Convention on Cybercrime, Art 22(2).

[68] Council Framework Decision 2005/222/JHA of 24 February 2005 on attacks against information systems, OJ L69/67, Art 10(5) ('Framework Decision 2005').

[69] CMA, s 5(1A).

[70] See Crown Prosecution Service, 'Code for Crown Prosecutors' (2004), paras 4.7 et seq, available at <https://www.cps.gov.uk/publications/docs/code_2013_accessible_english.pdf>.

[71] eg Charter of Fundamental Rights, Art 50. In the UK, the principle is subject to the provisions under the Criminal Procedure and Investigations Act 1996, ss 54–7 ('tainted acquittals') and the Criminal Justice Act 2003, ss 75–97 ('retrial').

[72] European Convention on the Transfer of Proceedings in Criminal Matters, ETS No 073 (1972).

[73] Convention on Cybercrime, Art 24.

To resolve multiple claims for jurisdictions, and thereby 'avoid duplication of effort, unneces- **5.36** sary inconvenience for witnesses, or competition among law enforcement officials',[74] it will be necessary for some form of negotiation to take place, and agreement reached, between authorities in the states concerned. As the Cybercrime Convention states: 'When more than one Party claims jurisdiction over an alleged offence ... the Parties involved shall, where appropriate, consult with a view to determining the most appropriate jurisdiction for prosecution.'[75] However, what is the *process* by which that decision is reached? A number of questions concerning process will generally need to be considered:[76]

- At what point should the decision be made, when the investigation starts, during its course, or at completion?
- Which agencies should be involved in the negotiation, the police, the prosecuting authorities or the judiciary?[77]
- What criteria are applicable to the making of the decision?

While in the past attempts to establish a list of priorities in terms of applicable criteria has **5.37** generally proved problematic,[78] the Eurojust College issued some guidelines in 2003.[79] In answer to the first question, that of timing, the Guidelines not surprisingly advise that a decision be reached at the earliest possible point. In particular, embarking on prosecutions in different states of criminals involved in the same criminality is both inefficient and raises the possibility of proceedings undermining each other. In terms of the second question, Eurojust suggest that senior prosecutors from each jurisdiction meet to decide the issue.

In respect of making a determination, the Guidelines suggest that there should be a pre- **5.38** sumption that the prosecution takes place 'where the majority of the criminality occurred or where the majority of the loss was sustained'.[80] They then details a range of factors which may need to be considered as affecting the final decision, including the following:

- the location of the accused, and the possibility of extradition or transferring proceedings;
- the attendance of witnesses;
- the impact of causing any excessive delay in the commencement of proceedings, which could be construed as unfair to the defendant;[81]
- the interests of the victims, which may include the possibility of a claim for compensation;[82]

---

[74] Explanatory Report to the Convention on Cybercrime, above, n 65, para 239.
[75] Convention on Cybercrime, Art 22(5).
[76] These issues are based on comments made by Bill Wheeldon, CPS, in an interview with the author (6 July 2005).
[77] Under the Prosecution of Offences Act 1985, s 3(2)(eb), the CPS have a duty to give 'advice on any matters relating to extradition proceedings or proposed extradition proceedings'.
[78] See the Explanatory Report to European Convention on the Transfer of Proceedings in Criminal Matters ETS No 073, paras 18–19.
[79] See Eurojust College, 'Guidelines for deciding "Which jurisdiction should prosecute?"' in *Annual Report 2003*, at 61 (Annex), available at <http://www.eurojust.europa.eu/doclibrary/corporate/eurojust%20 Annual%20Reports/Annual%20Report%202003/Annual-Report-2003-EN.pdf> ('Eurojust Guidelines').
[80] ibid, at 62.
[81] eg Extradition Act 2003, s 82: 'A person's extradition ... is barred by reason of the passage of time if ... it appears that it would be unjust or oppressive to extradite him ...'.
[82] Either granted by a court in the course of any criminal proceedings, or civil proceedings for recovery or a tortious wrong.

- the availability of evidence, which may be based on where the majority of it resides, as well as its admissibility in court.

Factors that are considered not to be relevant, or should only be secondary considerations, are the avoidance of legal obligations, the relative penalties available, and the ability to recover the proceeds of crime.[83] Finally, where other factors are equally balanced, the resources and costs involved in carrying out the prosecution should be considered.[84]

5.39 The list of factors is not intended to be exhaustive; for example, while the interests of the victim are mentioned, no consideration is given to the interests of the defendant, such as where he is most likely to be rehabilitated. In addition, a general public interest criterion may also be argued, reflecting national prosecutorial policy, as expressed by the Director of the Serious Fraud Office in correspondence relating to *Bermingham*,[85] a case involving fraud related to the Enron scandal, but whose sentiment would be equally applicable to cybercrimes:

> We are dealing with a crime that by its nature is committed over more than one jurisdiction. Prosecuting and investigating authorities competing for the right to try it is unlikely to be in the public interest. On the contrary, it is important that we cooperate and coordinate such investigations and, where possible, they are all tried before the same court.[86]

5.40 While the Eurojust Guidelines are entirely voluntary, there are legislative initiatives being pursued at an EU level that would formalize such rules, imposing obligations on Member States to resolve jurisdictional conflicts in accordance with specified criteria. Under a proposed Framework Decision on combating intellectual property crime, where multiple states could prosecute, Member States shall take the following factors into account, in 'sequential' order:

(a) the Member State in whose territory the acts were committed;
(b) the Member State of which the offender is a national or resident;
(c) the Member State in whose territory the legal person on whose behalf the offence was committed has its registered office;
(d) the Member State in which the victim is resident or has his registered office;
(e) the Member State in whose territory the offender was found.[87]

5.41 Under English law, the only statutory guidance on the third question of applicable criteria is when either a judge or the Secretary of State is required to consider competing claims for extradition; for example, where multiple European Arrest Warrants (EAWs) have been issued. In this situation, account must be taken, 'in particular', of the following factors:

(a) the relative seriousness of the offences concerned;
(b) the place where each offence was committed (or was alleged to have been committed);
(c) the date on which each warrant was issued;

---

[83] Eurojust Guidelines, above, n 79, at 65–6.
[84] ibid, at 66.
[85] See *Bermingham and others v The Director of the Serious Fraud Office and others* [2006] EWHC 200 (Admin).
[86] ibid, para 46.
[87] Proposal for a Council Framework Decision to strengthen the criminal law framework to combat intellectual property offences, COM(2005)276 final, 12 July 2005, Art 5(3).

(d) whether, in the case of each offence, the person is accused of its commission (but not alleged to have been convicted) or is alleged to be unlawfully at large after conviction.[88]

The Extradition Act 2003 fails to provide for the exercise of any general discretion by the Secretary of State where an extradition request has been received and the relevant conditions met, in contrast to the position prior to the 2003 Act.[89] While the court in *Bermingham* accepted that English law does not provide a mechanism for determining in *which* jurisdiction a crime should be investigated and tried, where English jurisdiction could be invoked, it held that there was a need for a means of protecting a defendant's human rights, such as his right to a fair trial under Art 6 of the European Convention on Human Rights (ECHR).[90] However, such protection was found to be present in the provisions of the 2003 Act.[91] Following the *McKinnon* case,[92] the Government called upon the Director of Public Prosecutions to draft guidance for cases where concurrent jurisdiction arises.[93] Such guidance was published in July 2013 and adopted the main principles of the Eurojust Guidelines.[94]

5.42

As noted at outset of this chapter, cybercrime inevitably and increasingly involves parallel and competing jurisdictions, as indeed do civil claims in an Internet environment.[95] As such, determinations of which jurisdiction should prosecute will involve a much more difficult decision-making process than the initial question of whether an offence has been committed. Other than the Eurojust Guidelines, there are no national or internationally agreed criteria for making such determinations, which raises concerns for individual defendants, law enforcement authorities and governments. There is the potential, for example, for the process of negotiation to result in jurisdictional arbitrage, with severity of sentence and its resultant deterrence value being considered relevant factors.[96] Such an arbitrage scenario runs counter to the widely held concern that the Internet is leading to a regulatory arbitrage in a downward direction, with states competing for the least restrictive regulation.[97]

5.43

---

[88] Extradition Act 2003, ss 44(7) and 179(3). Eurojust has also published guidance on this issue: see 'Guidelines for Deciding on Competing EAWs', in *Annual Report 2004*, at 82–6, available at <http://www.eurojust.europa.eu/doclibrary/corporate/eurojust%20Annual%20Reports/Annual%20Report%202004/Annual-Report-2004-EN.pdf>.

[89] See *Bermingham* [2006] EWHC 200 (Admin), paras 57–8.

[90] ibid, para 60.

[91] ibid, paras 71 and 119, specifically referring to the judicial discretion exercised under s 87 of the Extradition Act 2003.

[92] *McKinnon v Government of the United States of America and others* [2007] EWHC 762 (Admin) and [2008] UKHL 59. See paras 5.111 et seq.

[93] Theresa May statement on Gary McKinnon extradition, 16 October 2012, available at <https://www.gov.uk/government/news/theresa-may-statement-on-gary-mckinnon-extradition>.

[94] CPS, Director's Guidance on the handling of cases where the jurisdiction to prosecute is shared with prosecuting authorities overseas, 17 July 2013, available at <http://www.cps.gov.uk/publications/directors_guidance/director_s_guidance_on_concurrent_jurisdiction.html>.

[95] In the defamation context, see eg *Lewis Lennox v Don King* [2004] EWCA Civ 1329 (CA).

[96] Such concerns were expressed in the *McKinnon* case. See 'British "hacker" fears Guantanamo', *BBC News*, 12 April 2006, available at <http://news.bbc.co.uk/2/hi/uk_news/4905036.stm>.

[97] See eg Froomkin, M, 'The Internet as a source of regulatory arbitrage', in Kahin, B and Nesson, C (eds), *Borders in Cyberspace*, MIT Press, 1997; and Reed, above, n 44, Chapter 8, 'Legislative and regulatory arbitrage'.

C. Procedural Jurisdiction

5.44 In the course of a cybercrime investigation, law enforcement agencies will often need to obtain access to data held on systems located in foreign jurisdictions, or where the physical location of the data is unknown. Such data may be held on systems controlled by the suspect, a victim, or a third party service provider, particularly a communication service provider such as an Internet service provider (ISP). This section considers English and international legal rules governing the obtaining of such data for investigative and subsequent prosecutorial purposes, and how such rules may, and do, interact and potentially conflict with foreign laws and rules.

5.45 The forensic process may involve covert investigative techniques, specifically surveillance and interception, as well as the coercive exercise of law enforcement powers to directly gather such data from the foreign jurisdiction; as well as cooperation between domestic and foreign law enforcement bodies, primarily through mutual legal assistance procedures. As potential evidence, the manner in which such foreign data is obtained can impact directly on the ability to pursue a successful prosecution.

5.46 As well as potential evidence being located in a foreign jurisdiction, the suspected cyber-criminal may be located outside English law jurisdiction when committing a criminal act in the jurisdiction, or be located in England, but be wanted in connection with a criminal act committed in a foreign jurisdiction. In both situations, the question of extradition arises: can the suspect be obtained from or sent to another state for prosecution?

Remote surveillance

5.47 As examined in Chapter 4, surveillance by public law enforcement agencies is a regulated activity distinct from the interception of a person's communications. Under UK law, the applicable rules are dependent, in part, on locational issues, although based on identifiable places rather than any generic conception of public and private spaces. However, such activities are also subject to express jurisdictional constraints.

5.48 Under the Regulation of Investigatory Powers Act 2000 (RIPA), as well as the Intelligence Services Act 1994, surveillance activities may be authorized that are conducted outside the UK.[98] However, even within the UK, a separate authorization may be required where the activity is likely to take place in Scotland, subject to the Regulation of Investigatory Powers (Scotland) Act 2000.[99] An authorization granted under the RIPA would be applicable in any proceedings in the UK, although it would not prevent the investigators committing an offence under the laws of the jurisdiction where the surveillance is being carried out.[100]

---

[98] Regulation of Investigatory Powers Act 2000 (RIPA), s 27(3) and Intelligence Services Act 1994 (ISA), s 7.

[99] RIPA, s 46(1)(b), unless the authorization is being sought for the purposes of national security or the economic well-being of the United Kingdom (s 46(2)(a)); or is made by a public authority listed in s 46(3) or in the Regulation of Investigatory Powers (Authorisations Extending to Scotland) Order 2000, SI No 2418 (as amended by SI No 2009/3403).

[100] See Home Office, 'Covert Surveillance and Property Interference: Code of Practice', December 2014, para 1.20.

Surveillance by foreign law enforcement agencies of activities in the UK is governed by the   **5.49**
RIPA, as amended by the Crime (International Co-operation) Act 2003.[101] It provides for
the possibility of what is commonly referred to as 'hot surveillance', when circumstances
require that a foreign law enforcement officer continue an existing surveillance operation of
a person(s), which is lawful in the country in which it was being carried out, but can only be
carried out in the UK. Such powers are strictly limited to surveillance in respect of a person
suspected of having committed a 'relevant crime', which is primarily defined by reference to
a list of offences detailed in the Schengen Convention,[102] such as forgery and extortion.[103]
The right is also limited to a five-hour period.[104] The Director General of the National
Crime Agency (NCA) has to be notified by the foreign law enforcement officer as he enters
the UK, and has the power to require that such activities cease.[105]

Remote interception

As discussed in Chapter 4, the data held by a communications service provider can also be   **5.50**
broadly distinguished into data 'at rest' and data 'in transmission'. This section is concerned
with the latter, data 'in transmission', obtained through the process of interception, where
the entity capable of carrying out the interception is located in a foreign jurisdiction.

Interception of the content of a communication is governed in the UK by the RIPA. The   **5.51**
RIPA regime is not primarily designed to tackle the activities of those intercepting communications in the furtherance of their criminal activities; rather its purpose is to control
the interception practices of law enforcement agents and the use of intercepted material as
evidence. The European Court of Human Rights has found on a number of occasions UK
law to be in breach of the Convention in respect of protecting the right of privacy of those
who have been subject to state-based interception.[106]

The RIPA makes it an offence to intercept a communication being transmitted over a public   **5.52**
telecommunications system without a warrant issued by the Secretary of State, or over a private telecommunications system without the consent of the system controller.[107] An interception warrant should only be issued by the Secretary of State in the interests of national
security, for the prevention or detection of 'serious crime',[108] or 'in circumstances appearing
to the Secretary of State to be relevant to the interests of national security, of safeguarding
the economic well-being of the United Kingdom'.[109] A fourth ground for a *warrant-based*

---

[101]   RIPA, s 76A, as inserted by Competition in Contracting Act 1984 (CICA), s 83.
[102]   Convention implementing the Schengen Agreement of 14 June 1985 between the Governments of the
States of the Benelux Economic Union, the Federal Republic of Germany and the French Republic on the
gradual abolition of checks at their common borders, OJ L 239/19, 22 September 2000.
[103]   ibid, Art 40(7).
[104]   RIPA, s 76A(7).
[105]   The Regulation of Investigatory Powers (Foreign Surveillance Operations) Order 2004 (SI No 1128),
as amended.
[106]   eg *Malone v United Kingdom* [1984] 7 EHRR 14; *Halford v United Kingdom* (1997) IRLR 471; *Copland
v United Kingdom* (2007) 45 EHHR 37; and *Liberty v United Kingdom* (2009) 48 EHRR 1.
[107]   RIPA, s 1.
[108]   ie '(a) … an offence for which a person who has attained the age of twenty-one and has no previous
convictions could reasonably be expected to be sentenced to imprisonment for a term of three years or more;
(b) that the conduct involves the use of violence, results in substantial financial gain or is conduct by a large
number of persons in pursuit of a common purpose' (ibid, s 81(3)).
[109]   ibid, s 5(3)(a)–(c). Subsection (c) was amended by the Data Retention and Investigatory Powers Act
2014, s 3(2).

interception arises where the Secretary of State considers that a situation equivalent to circumstances in which he would issue a warrant to prevent or detect serious crime is required for the purpose of 'giving effect to the provisions of any international mutual assistance agreement'.[110] Therefore, a request from a foreign law enforcement agency to intercept a suspect's data communications can be authorized.

5.53 The Secretary of State has also issued regulations governing *non-warrant-based* interception activities carried out by, or on behalf of, a foreign communications service provider, authorized in accordance with the laws of the foreign jurisdiction, but which require the use of telecommunication systems located in the UK in order to carry out the interception.[111] For example, given the extremely flexible structure of modern communication networks and services, a service provider could be based in a number of EU states, but operate a Europe-wide service utilizing equipment (eg a server) located in a single jurisdiction.

5.54 The RIPA authorizes interception conduct where the interceptor 'has reasonable grounds for believing' the person is outside the UK; the person is using a public telecommunications service;[112] the foreign service provider (whether the interceptor or another person) is required by law to carry out the interception and to comply with the conditions prescribed by the Secretary of State.[113] There are only two such conditions: (a) that the interception is for the purpose of a criminal investigation, and (b) that the relevant foreign jurisdiction is one that is party to an international agreement:

> Where the United Kingdom is a party to an international agreement which—
> (a) relates to the provision of mutual assistance in connection with, or in the form of, the interception of communications,
> (b) requires the issue of a warrant, order or equivalent instrument in cases in which assistance is given, and
> (c) is designated for the purposes of this subsection by an order made by the Secretary of State, it shall be the duty of the Secretary of State to secure that no request for assistance in accordance with the agreement is made on behalf of a person in the United Kingdom to the competent authorities of a country or territory outside the United Kingdom except with lawful authority.[114]

These regulations were designed to enable the UK to comply in part with its obligations under Title III of the 2000 Convention on Mutual Assistance in Criminal Matters.[115] The Convention was the first mutual assistance instrument to directly address the issue of interception. The adoption of specific measures was driven by the need to establish homogenous

---

[110] RIPA, ss 5(3)(d) and 1(4).

[111] ibid, s 4(1)(d). Regulation of Investigatory Powers (Conditions for the Lawful Interception of Persons outside the United Kingdom) Regulations 2004 (SI No 157).

[112] Or equivalent (RIPA, s 4(1)(b)). The Convention on Cybercrime, Art 14(3)(b), provides that a party may reserve the right not to extend interception to non-public networks and systems.

[113] RIPA, s 4(1).

[114] ibid, s 1(4).

[115] The Convention on Mutual Assistance in Criminal Matters between the Member States of the European Union established by Council Act of 29 May 2000, OJ C 197, 12 July 2000, as designated under the Regulation of Investigatory Powers (Designation of an International Agreement) Order 2004 (SI No 158). The Convention entered into force on 23 August 2005, and came into force for the UK on 21 December 2005.

practices in a rapidly evolving communications environment, while balancing the needs of the interceptor and the rights of the intercepted.[116] As from May 2017, the Convention provisions will be replaced by the procedures governing the European Investigation Order.[117]

At the time of drafting, two technical scenarios were of concern: satellite and mobile communication systems. With the former, the footprint of a satellite system extends over multiple jurisdictions, but the available point of interception may be a so-called 'gateway' located in a single jurisdiction.[118] Thus, a lawful intercept of a person located in territory A may require technical assistance from territory B. This may be termed the 'remote assist scenario'. However, as noted above, such a scenario could equally be applicable to a wide range of modern communication services, such as a Voice over Internet Protocol (VOIP) service operating from a single server. In the second scenario, mobile network coverage in border areas may enable an interception authorized in territory A of persons located in territory B with no requirement for technical assistance from territory B. This may be termed the 'spill-over scenario'. **5.55**

The Convention details two different procedures by which extra-territorial intercepts may be carried out in the 'remote assist' scenario. First, the intercepting state can issue a request to the state where the intercept capability is located. Article 18 of the Convention governs the procedure for standard cross-border interceptions. In terms of a UK authority requiring an intercept to be carried out in a foreign jurisdiction, a request can be made through a 'judicial authority' in accordance with the Crime (International Co-operation) Act 2003.[119] Alternatively, the service provider in territory A may carry out the interception by 'remote control'[120] in territory B in accordance with Art 19, which does not require notification to an authority in territory B. The wording used seems to conceive of 'control' in a purely technical sense, although clearly such control may be organizational, when dealing with a single entity with multiple sites, or contractual, where the intercept is carried out by another service provider. The non-warrant approach under the RIPA, s 4(1), adopts this broad conception. A third procedure, under Art 20, is applicable to the 'spill-over scenario', which requires an authority in territory A to notify the relevant authority in territory B, who may permit or refuse the extra-territorial interception. **5.56**

The 'Art 19' procedure represents a surrender of territorial control over interception for the state where the 'gateway' is located, while extending the jurisdictional reach of criminal procedure for the requesting state, so it may only prove an acceptable solution within the context of the European Union, with its broader political and legal remit to establish an 'area of freedom, security and justice'.[121] A similar approach has not been adopted in the Convention on Cybercrime, despite the accommodation reached on the issue of remote search and seizure. In addition, the losses and the gains are unlikely to be shared equally between Member States, since the location of 'gateways' is likely to be driven by business **5.57**

---

[116] Explanatory Report on the Convention on Mutual Assistance in Criminal Matters between the Member States of the European Union, OJ C 379/7, 29 December 2000, at 20 ('Explanatory Report to the MLA Convention').

[117] See paras 5.98 et seq.

[118] The 'gateway' may be the earth station controlling the telemetry, tracking, and operation of the satellite.

[119] Part 1, Chapter 2, s 7.

[120] Explanatory Report to the MLA Convention, above, n 116, at 20.

[121] See Treaty on European Union (TEU), OJ C 83/13, 30 March 2010, Art 3(2).

imperatives, such as favourable tax regimes or low cost infrastructure, which is likely to result in a clustering of 'gateways' in certain states. This is certainly the case with regard to the OTT communication services,[122] offered by companies such as Yahoo!, Microsoft, and Twitter, who have clustered in the Ireland.

5.58   With the increasing complexity and diversity of the communications market, as well as the flexibility available to service providers about locating themselves, the technical scenarios addressed under the Convention are no longer sufficient to address the needs of domestic law enforcement. Within the EU, the European Investigation Order Directive (EIO) establishes a new framework for cooperation on interception between states.[123] Where a choice of locations for intercept exists, the EIO should be sent to the Member State where the subject of the intercept is, or will be, located.[124] Where the subject of an intercept is located in the territory of a different Member State from that where the intercept is being carried out, for example a roaming subscriber, then the competent authority in the 'intercepting Member State' has an obligation to notify the state where the subject is located, so that the 'notified Member State' can assess the legality of such conduct and, if not authorized, request the intercept be discontinued or the intercept material be not used.[125]

5.59   The EIO regime is limited to participating states,[126] so does not assist interception requests to service providers based in other jurisdictions, especially the United States. One approach to this issue is to assert territorial jurisdiction over such service providers, based on the fact that they provide services in the territory, even though the underlying infrastructure, including the intercept capability, is located outside the territory. In this scenario, rather than utilizing formal inter-state cooperation procedures, the requesting state simply approaches the remote service provider, with a domestic authorization. The service provider is then placed in the potentially invidious position of having to assess its obligations under the legal system in which it is located and where it provides services, to determine whether it is able to comply with the request or not. This is the position adopted under the RIPA,[127] although no examples of enforcement have been tested before the courts.

5.60   One unique feature of the UK interception regime is that it does not permit data obtained through an interception being adduced as evidence in legal proceedings.[128] Such data is for intelligence purposes in the course of an investigation, not for use in any subsequent prosecution. The reasoning behind such a provision is to protect from disclosure information about the investigative activities of law enforcement agencies, which would potentially enter the public domain if intercept evidence was used in court and became subject to challenge by defendant counsel. As a consequence, however, there is a lack of reciprocity in terms of mutual legal assistance. While a request by a foreign agency for an interception of communications for evidential purposes would be refused by the UK

---

[122] In this context, 'OTT' refers to over-the-top messaging services, where the service is provided using the transmission network and service of a third party.

[123] Directive 2014/41/EU regarding the European Investigation Order in criminal matters, OJ L 130/1, 1 May 2014 (EIO), Chapter V.

[124] ibid, Art 30(2).

[125] ibid, Art 31.

[126] Which currently does not include Ireland, where many of the US service providers have located their European operations.

[127] See further para 4.139.

[128] RIPA, s 17. See further paras 6.70–6.80.

authorities,[129] such a request may be made by UK agencies, as foreign intercept evidence may be admissible in the UK if the evidence would be admissible in the foreign court, and it would not reveal anything about the activities of UK law enforcement.[130]

One key policy driver behind the adoption of the RIPA was the need to update the regime **5.61** to address the complexities of lawful intercept in a liberalized communications market, where a vast range of different networks and service providers are present. However, while such rules have clarified domestic intercept, cybercriminals will often route their transmissions via multiple jurisdictions, using numerous service providers, to obstruct the process of investigation, a process referred to as 'communications laundering', 'looping', or 'weaving'.[131] In such circumstances, the complexities of lawful intercept, coupled with an absence of harmonized rules, continue to mean a lack of clarity, legal certainty, and transparency.

Remote search and seizure

This section considers the obtaining of data held remotely in a foreign jurisdiction where **5.62** the data is under the control of a suspect, or some person related to the suspect. It reviews the law governing the right of law enforcement agencies to access such remote data, also referred to as 'direct penetration',[132] other than through mutual legal assistance procedures, including international interception, which have already been examined.

The need to access data controlled by the suspect may arise under a number of scenarios, of **5.63** which four are highlighted for the purpose of this analysis:

(1) During the course of an investigation at the suspect's premises, the investigator may request from the suspect, or acting on his own behalf, access to data located abroad that is available from the suspect's system.
(2) Forensic analysis of a suspect's seized computer and data media may reveal information concerning relevant forensic material stored in a foreign location.
(3) The suspect may inform investigators that relevant data is resident in a foreign jurisdiction.
(4) The suspect of an offence committed in the UK is located in a foreign jurisdiction together with an online resource accessible from the UK.

In order to determine the legality of law enforcement action in the scenarios above, con- **5.64** sideration needs to be given to a range of questions, broadly distinguished into three key determinative issues:

- *Exercise of power*: when the agency carries out its actions, will it be characterized as an exercise of powers within the domestic jurisdiction, even though the action has an extra-territorial effect? When a foreign online resource is accessed, the communication is initiated from a system within the jurisdiction. There may be uncertainty over how a court would characterize the process. In the *Citibank*[133] case, for example, the court

[129] See Home Office, *Requests for Mutual Legal Assistance in Criminal Matters: Guidelines for Authorities Outside the United Kingdom*, 12th edn, March 2015, at 30, available at <https://www.gov.uk/government/uploads/system/uploads/attachment_data/file/415038/MLA_Guidelines_2015.pdf>.

[130] See *R v P and others* [2001] 2 All ER 58.

[131] See Reitinger, PR, 'Encryption, anonymity and markets', in Thomas, D and Loader, B (eds), *Cybercrime: Law Enforcement, Security and Surveillance in the Information Age*, Routledge, 2000, at 137.

[132] CoE Report 1990, above, n 66, at 86 et seq.

[133] *Governor of Brixton Prison and another, ex parte Levin* [1996] 4 All ER 350.

held that the nature of the communication process meant that the foreign jurisdiction where the attacked machine was located was engaged. However, the Internet operates on a store-and-forward basis, so what would the courts hold in a cyberspace environment? At a policy level, Paul Boateng, then Home Office minister, has suggested the following approach:

> Jurisdiction over a database should not now depend only on where it happens to be physically stored. Where the owners of the system have set it up to be accessible from another jurisdiction, it should be regarded as present in that jurisdiction for law enforcement purposes.[134]

- *Data access*: the circumstances leading to access will vary. Access to the data in the foreign jurisdiction may be achieved because the data is an openly available resource, such as a public website. If access is subject to control mechanisms, the suspect may exercise legitimate control over access, through passwords for example, of which the agency has knowledge, either with cooperation from the suspect or arising from forensic analysis. However, while a suspect may have information enabling access, the access may still be unauthorized; for example, the suspect may have obtained unlawful access and control a 'botnet' where data is stored. Finally, the agency may 'hack' access to the data, circumventing or breaking the access control mechanisms. In the first and second situations, a breach of law in the foreign jurisdiction is unlikely to arise, as the access is likely to be considered authorized. In the latter two situations, an unlawful act may be committed in the course of gaining access, under both domestic[135] and foreign law, which may impact on the investigative process and the evidential product.
- *Data obtaining*: having accessed the foreign data, the agency will generally obtain a copy of the data. How will such copying be characterized in terms of police powers? Additionally, the agency may decide to delete or modify the data itself, or the means by which the data is accessed, in order to prevent its further use and abuse. Again, are such activities legitimate in terms of the powers of the agency under domestic law[136] and does their exercise constitute an offence in the foreign jurisdiction, even potentially an act of war?

5.65 As well as being under the control of a suspect, foreign data may be under the joint control of a third party, such as a communication service provider (CSP) or financial institution, such as messages stored in a web-based email account. An investigator will often therefore have a choice between direct obtaining and approaching the third party for access. The formal procedure for obtaining data from the third party in the latter scenario is discussed later in this chapter. Were the investigator to directly obtain, there is the additional issue of potential liability for infringing the rights of, or causing harm to, the foreign third party.

5.66 These issues will first be examined under UK law and then international developments and comparative jurisdictions will be considered.

---

[134] Comment made in March 1999. Quoted in Sussmann, M, 'The critical challenges from international high-tech and computer-related crime at the millennium', 9 *Duke J of Comp & Int'l L* 451 (1999), at 453 fn 5.
[135] eg CMA, s 1.
[136] eg ibid, s 3.

English law

In the first scenario, the access is carried out in the course of the exercise of statutory powers **5.67** to enter and search premises.[137] In a networked environment, however, what is the geographical scope of such warrants? Under the Police and Criminal Evidence Act 1984, a constable may require 'any information which is stored in any electronic form and is accessible from the premises to be produced in a form in which it can be taken away ...'.[138] On the face of it, this provision would appear to enable law enforcement officers to obtain information held on remote systems under a single search warrant, since information in electronic form will be accessible from a networked computer on the searched premises.[139] In terms of the other three scenarios, no provisions of English law would appear to provide express powers to carry out such acts, although they would seem ordinary within a standard investigative process.

Accessing remote data became problematic for UK law enforcement agencies during the **5.68** early 1990s, as a consequence of the Computer Misuse Act 1990. Certain electronic bulletin boards, containing illegal material such as virus code, began placing messages at the point of access to the site stating that 'law enforcement officials are not permitted to enter the system'. While the Act contained a saving provision in respect of 'powers of inspection, search or seizure', such warnings were considered to be potentially effective in restricting the police from simply monitoring the use made of such bulletin boards without technically committing an offence.[140] As a consequence, the Computer Misuse Act was amended in 1994 to prevent law enforcement agencies committing an offence of 'unauthorized access'.[141] The amendment was limited to the issue of 'access', so it would not legitimize the use of 'hacking' and related techniques by law enforcement agencies to circumvent data security measures utilized on remote systems.

In 2015, the saving provision was further amended in three important ways. First, the saving **5.69** provision was extended to apply all the offences, rather than only to the s 1(1) offence. This greatly expands the ability of law enforcement agencies (LEAs) to engage in more disruptive forms of proactive intervention against targets, subject to appropriate authorization.[142] Second, the 'bulletin board' amendment was also extended to all the offences in respect of consent to 'access' any program or data. While 'access' is not a necessary feature of all integrity offences, such as Distributed Denial of Service attacks,[143] it will generally be a component. Third, the saving provision is now applicable not just to powers granted to inspect, search, and seize, but also to 'any other enactment by virtue of which the conduct in question is authorised or required'.[144] This would include, for example, authorized interferences with property.[145] Taken together, these amendments were clearly designed to remove

---

[137] See further paras 4.274–4.279.

[138] s 19(4), as amended by the Criminal Justice and Police Act 2001, Sch 2(2), para 13(2)(a). See also s 20, which extends this provision to powers of seizure conferred under other enactments, such as the CMA, s 14.

[139] For a discussion about how such data can be obtained, see Sealey, P, 'Remote forensics', 1 *Digital Investigation* 261 (2004).

[140] See Home Affairs Committee, *Computer Pornography*, Report No 126, HMSO, February 1994, at xii, paras 31–2.

[141] The Criminal Justice and Public Order Act 1994, s 162, amending s 10 of the CMA.

[142] eg under RIPA, Pt II, as 'directed surveillance' or ISA, s 7.

[143] See paras 3.294 et seq.

[144] Inserted by the Serious Crime Act 2015, s 44(2)(b) and (c).

[145] eg Police Act 1997, Pt III or ISA, s 5.

any legal uncertainties concerning the conduct of LEAs to interfere with the integrity of computers, their programs or data, whether domestically or internationally.[146] However, while conduct in breach of foreign laws can be authorized to be carried out by the Secret Intelligence Service or Government Communication Headquarters (GCHQ),[147] the police cannot be granted such powers. In the light of the July 2005 terrorist attacks, the police called for new powers 'to attack identified websites', which would have significant cross-border implications;[148] although no such powers have been granted. However, while this provides protection in a domestic context, LEAs can still be in breach of computer-integrity offences in other jurisdictions.

5.70   In terms of police powers, a distinction can be made between the exercise of specific coercive powers, such as powers of search or surveillance, and general investigative activities. As with any public body, all police actions must have appropriate *vires*, otherwise they may be subject to control by the courts by way of judicial review and found unlawful.[149] Any subsequent criminal proceedings consequent on an unlawful act may be stayed for abuse of process; although the court will only exercise its discretion in exceptional circumstances.[150] In the scenarios outlined previously, there would need to be either an express power or the acts 'may fairly be regarded as incidental to, or consequential upon'[151] an authorized police activity, ie examination of seized material, questioning of suspect and general investigative activities.

5.71   However, in all cases, the exercise of police powers is subject to the jurisdictional limitation placed on the police under the Police Act 1996: 'A member of a police force shall have all the powers and privileges of a constable throughout England and Wales and the adjacent United Kingdom waters.'[152] For other law enforcement agencies, similar jurisdictional limitations may be expressly provided for or implied.[153]

5.72   As a consequence of the jurisdictional limitation, investigators are obliged to give mind to the legality of any extra-territorial activity, since evidence obtained unlawfully from a foreign state may be excluded by a court, either as an abuse of process[154] or through the exercise of statutory discretion.[155] However, prior to such a decision, the court would first need to

---

[146] The legality of GCHQ hacking was to be raised before the Investigatory Powers Tribunal in May 2015, in proceedings brought by Privacy International, but the amendments came into effect on 3 May 2015. See Bowcott, O, 'Intelligence officers given immunity from hacking laws, tribunal told', *The Guardian*, 15 May 2015, available at <http://www.theguardian.com/uk-news/2015/may/15/intelligence-officers-have-immunity-from-hacking-laws-tribunal-told>.

[147] ISA, s 7 'Authorisation of acts outside the British Islands'.

[148] See Association of Chief Police Officers (ACPO), 'Chief Police Officers recommend changes to counter the terrorist threat', Press Release (55/05), 21 July 2005.

[149] See eg *R v Robin Edward Hounsham and others* [2005] EWCA Crim 1366.

[150] See Lord Bingham in *Attorney-General's Reference (No 2 of 2001)* (HL (E)) [2004] WLR 1, at 13H.

[151] *A-G v Great Eastern Railway Co* (1880) 5 App Cas 473.

[152] Police Act 1997 (PA), s 30(1) 'Jurisdiction of constables'. In addition, PA, s 93, authorization to interfere with property is limited to property in the 'relevant area', which is limited to various territorial limits (ibid, s 93(6)).

[153] eg in respect of the National Crime Agency, see Crime and Courts Act 2013, s 10, Sch 5, Pt 4, para 12.

[154] See *R v Loosely (Attorney General's Reference No 3 of 2000)* [2001] UKHL 53; [2001] 4 All ER 897.

[155] Police and Criminal Evidence Act 1984, s 78(1):

> In any proceedings the court may refuse to allow evidence on which the prosecution proposes to rely to be given if it appears to the court that, having regard to all the circumstances in which the evidence was obtained, the admission of the evidence would have such an adverse effect on the fairness of the proceedings that the court ought not to admit it.

determine whether to characterize police access as a territorial or extra-territorial exercise of power; then whether the activity is unlawful, under domestic or foreign law, either through breach of specific provisions, such as unauthorized access, or based on general principles of breach of national sovereignty and the comity of nations implied into the operation of such principles. Were the remote data to be accessed through the voluntary actions of the suspect, then such challenges are less likely to arise.

International developments

In an attempt to minimize the inevitable conflicts of law arising from 'direct penetration', **5.73** efforts have been made at an intergovernmental level to address extra-territorial searches under public international law. In a Council of Europe report from 1989, consideration was given to the possibility of legalizing such activities in certain circumstances and under certain conditions, giving the following examples:

- that it would be used only for the taking of measures destined to preserve the status quo, that is, so that the data cannot be tampered with;
- that the data would not be used unless the involved state gives its consent;
- that the nature or seriousness of the offence justifies the penetration;
- that there is a strong presumption that the time needed for resorting to a traditional procedure of letters rogatory would compromise the search for truth;
- that the investigating authorities inform the authorities of the other state.[156]

However, it felt that the time was not yet ripe for such a proposal to be pursued. In a subsequent Council of Europe recommendation, it was noted that search powers could extend to other connected computers, but only within the jurisdiction.[157] Extending that power to computers located in other jurisdictions should only occur where 'immediate action is required' and only on a legal basis that avoids 'possible violations of state sovereignty and international law'.[158] However, it was also accepted that there was an urgent need for further international agreement on the issue.

The first significant movement in the area was within the G8 forum. At a meeting of Justice **5.74** and Interior ministers in Moscow in October 1999, a document entitled 'Principles on Transborder Access to Stored Computer Data' was adopted.[159] As well as calling upon states to enable the rapid preservation of data and expedited mutual legal assistance procedures, there was also agreement that access could be achieved without authorization from another state for the purpose of:

(a) accessing publicly available (open source) data, regardless of where the data is located geographically;

---

[156] CoE Report 1990, above, n 66, at 88.

[157] Council of Europe Recommendation No R (95) 13, concerning problems of procedural law connected with information technology, 11 September 1995, and Explanatory Memorandum (1996), available at <https://books.google.co.uk/books?id=pC5d2wAud10C&printsec=frontcover&source=gbs_ge_summary_r&cad=0#v=onepage&q&f=false>, Principle 3.

[158] ibid, Principle 17.

[159] Principles on Transborder Access to Stored Computer Data, adopted in Moscow, 20 October 1999, available at <http://www.usdoj.gov/ag/events/g82004/99TransborderAccessPrinciples.pdf>.

(b) accessing, searching, copying, or seizing data stored in a computer system located in another State, if acting in accordance with the lawful and voluntary consent of a person who has the lawful authority to disclose to it that data.[160]

5.75 Within the Council of Europe, the negotiators on the Cybercrime Convention agreed two sets of provisions that addressed the obtaining of access to data stored in another jurisdiction, without requiring authorization of the state in which the data resides. First, a person in the territory of the Member State may be subject to a 'production order' that extends to data that is in that person's 'possession or control', which could clearly include data held in another jurisdiction.[161] Alternatively, a service provider 'offering its service in the territory' may be required to disclose 'subscriber information'[162] relating to such services in the provider's 'possession or control',[163] which could obviously mean that an order may be served where both provider and data reside in a foreign jurisdiction. In both scenarios, the person subject to the request is usually a third party who is considered to have relevant data to the investigation, but is not a suspect. While the procedure is coercive, it is not intrusive in the same manner that search and seizure procedures are; the former comprising requests for the disclosure of data, backed by legal sanction, the latter involving the obtaining of access to data for the purpose of seizure.

5.76 'Possession and control' reflects the terminology used under English criminal procedure.[164] 'Possession' would seem a narrower concept than 'control', even though it may extend beyond physical possession to constructive possession under certain legal systems.[165] The concept of having 'control' over data can be viewed from different perspectives, including managerial, technical, or legal; the latter encompassing rights in respect of the data, 'whether legislative, executive, administrative, judicial, contractual or consensual'.[166]

5.77 Whether a third party or service providers can be said to have 'possession or control' over data has itself become a contentious issue as a consequence of the Snowden revelations since June 2013. In particular, service providers with US parents have been at pains to make clear that data they hold in facilities outside of the US on behalf of non-US customers does not necessarily come within the concept of 'possession and control'. Rackspace, for example, has stated that it takes the view that it has neither possession nor control over its customer stored data, since customers have the technical capability 'to lock Rackspace out, control of passwords used to access their data, and the security of data stored on those servers to the exclusion of others', as well as having contractual responsibility for the protection of any data stored with Rackspace.[167] In deciding whether a US parent company can be compelled

---

[160] ibid, para 6.
[161] Convention on Cybercrime, Art 18(1)(a).
[162] Defined at Art 18(3), it is any data relating to a subscriber to the service other than 'traffic data or content data'. See also paras 4.157 et seq.
[163] Convention on Cybercrime, Art 18(1)(b).
[164] See Criminal Procedure Rules, Pt 6, 'Investigation orders and warrants', which refers to 'possession, custody or power' (para 6.7) and to 'possession or control' (para 6.15).
[165] Explanatory Report to the Convention on Cybercrime, above, n 65, para 173.
[166] ibid, para 38.
[167] Statement issued by Alan Schoenbaum, General Counsel of Rackspace, 9 June 2013, available at <https://community.rackspace.com/general/f/34/p/791/1347>. See also 'Thoughts on Foreign Data Storage and the Patriot Act', Verizon Policy Blog, 27 January 2014, available at <http://publicpolicy.verizon.com/blog/entry/thoughts-on-foreign-data-storage-and-the-patriot-act>.

to require a foreign subsidiary to disclose customer data to US authorities, a court would likely focus on the nature of the relationship between the parent and its subsidiary.[168]

This issue is at the heart of on-going proceedings in the US, between the US Government **5.78** and Microsoft. The case arose from a search and seizure warrant issued against Microsoft in December 2013 in respect of an @msn.com account. Microsoft determined that the email account content resided on its servers based in Dublin, Ireland.[169] As a consequence, it challenged the validity of the warrant, arguing that the search and seizure was extra-territorial and therefore the US courts could not authorize such conduct. The motion to quash was denied by the New York Magistrate,[170] and this decision was subsequently upheld by the US District Court in July 2014.[171] In order to facilitate a prompt appeal, Microsoft subsequently agreed to be found in contempt for failing to comply with the order of the court,[172] and the appeal was heard in September 2015. The appeal generated numerous amicus briefs, from technology companies, trade associations, and advocacy groups,[173] as well as a draft Congressional bill.[174]

There are a large number of issues being argued in this case, which can be grouped into **5.79** three categories: (a) the extra-territorial reach of US law; (b) mechanisms for international cooperation; and (c) the impact of European data protection law. It is beyond the scope of this book to examine each issue in detail, but each is relevant in the context of this chapter.

On the reach of US law, the central argument concerns the nature of the request being **5.80** made by the warrant. The issue concerns interpretations of the Electronic Communications Privacy Act and, specifically, the Stored Communications Act.[175] Does the 'warrant' compel Microsoft to disclose 'information in its possession, custody or control regardless of the location of that information',[176] which is akin to an administrative subpoena and requires no judicial finding; or is it a search and seizure, which requires a judicial finding of probable cause, for which Microsoft is being compelled to act as an agent of the requesting LEA? If the answer to this question is the former, then a next issue to be determined is whether such compelled disclosure only extends to Microsoft's business records or includes the private records of its customers; which is the same point raised by Rackspace and Verizon, as noted above.[177] As part of its response, the Government quotes from Microsoft's terms of service,

---

[168] eg, *United States v Vetco, Inc*, 691 F2d 1281 (9th Cir 1981), where the court required the US entity to produce data held by a subsidiary outside of the US.

[169] Certain account information, such as the customer's address book was held in the US and was duly handed over to the authorities.

[170] *In the matter of a warrant to search a certain e-mail account controlled and maintained by Microsoft Corporation*, 15 F Supp 3d 466, 472 (SDNY 2014) ('Magistrate's Decision').

[171] Decision of District Judge, Hon. Loretta A. Preska, 31 July 2014.

[172] Order of District Judge, Hon. Loretta A. Preska, 8 September 2014.

[173] See Smith, B, 'Business, Media and Civil Society Speak Up in Key Privacy Case', *Digital Constitution Blog*, 15 December 2014, available at <http://digitalconstitution.com/2014/12/business-media-civil-society-speak-key-privacy-case/>.

[174] The Law Enforcement Access to Data Stored Abroad Act of 2015, introduced into the Senate by Mr Hatch et al. See <http://www.hatch.senate.gov/public/_cache/files/e7759b0c-672a-49dd-a2cb-b0955421f6f0/LEADS%20Act%20section-by-section,%20February%2012,%202015.pdf>.

[175] ie 18 USC s 2703, 'Required disclosure of customer communications or records'.

[176] Magistrate's Decision, 15 F Supp 3d 466, at 472, citing *Marc Rich & Co, AG v United States*, 707 F2d 663 (2d Cir 1983), which states that the 'test for production of documents is control, not location' (at 667).

[177] See para 5.77. Also *United States v Warshak*, 631 F3d 266 (6th Cir 2010), at 288, that the 'government may not compel a commercial ISP to turn over the contents of a subscriber's emails without first obtaining a warrant based on probable cause'.

which it argues contains provisions indicating sufficiency of 'control' to enable it to comply with the warrant.[178]

5.81 Whichever interpretation is upheld, a second line of argument advanced by Microsoft is that there are bilateral mutual legal assistance procedures in place between the US and Ireland,[179] which is the most appropriate way to access remote data, rather than asserting extra-territorial reach, breaching principles of international law, and undermining the position of US businesses abroad.[180] The Government argues that mutual legal assistance (MLA) is only one of a variety of means of obtaining evidence located in a foreign territory, so LEAs must be free to choose whichever means is most efficacious.[181] They also note that the nature of such 'cloud' services means the location of data can move rapidly between jurisdictions, rendering use of MLA procedures more uncertain.[182]

5.82 The data protection angle is essentially analogous to our earlier discussion about domestic LEAs breaking the laws of foreign jurisdictions. Microsoft argues that by disclosing personal data under the warrant it would be in potential breach of its obligations under Irish data protection law. In response, the Government notes that US law recognizes that genuine conflicts of law can arise, which may require 'a careful balancing of the interest involved',[183] but that the interests of US criminal law enforcement generally outweigh the foreign prohibition.[184]

5.83 If Microsoft prevails, then it will likely result in the US Government calling for amendments to domestic law, as well as taking steps to improve MLA procedures. If the Government's position is upheld, then it will raise difficult questions for US service providers when trying to convince non-US customers that their data is protected from the long arm reach of US law enforcement.

5.84 Article 32 of the Convention addresses a second situation where law enforcement can obtain direct access to remotely held data. The two circumstances where such access may be obtained are virtually identical to those contained in the G8 document. Article 32 can be seen as constituting the most radical component of the whole Convention, representing an apparent erosion of the traditional concept of sovereignty, and has therefore also been its most controversial. From a state perspective, it has been deemed unacceptable by countries such as Russia, which has led to calls for either its removal or the development of an alternative international instrument within a different forum, specifically the United Nations (UN). While from a civil society perspective, concerns have been expressed that it enables national regimes protecting individual rights to be circumvented. For the Council of Europe itself, debates over its interpretation and future scope have provided the most significant workload to date for the Cybercrime Convention Committee (T-CY).

---

[178] Brief for the United States of America, 9 March 2015, at 42 ('US Brief').

[179] Treaty on Mutual Legal Assistance in Criminal Matters between the United Kingdom of Great Britain and Northern Ireland and the Republic of the Philippines, Cm 8398, which entered into force on 11 August 2009.

[180] Microsoft's Appellant Brief, 8 December 2014.

[181] US Brief, above, n 178, at 49 et seq.

[182] ibid, at 51–2.

[183] *United States v First National City Bank*, 396 F2d 897 (2d Cir 1968), at 901.

[184] US Brief, above, n 178, at 16.

As already noted, Art 32 specifies two distinct circumstances where one party may access **5.85** stored data in another state, without the latter's prior authorization.[185] The former is generally considered less controversial that the latter:

a. access publicly available (open source) stored computer data, regardless of where the data is located geographically; or
b. access or receive, through a computer system in its territory, stored computer data located in another Party, if the Party obtains the lawful and voluntary consent of the person who has the lawful authority to disclose the data to the Party through that computer system.

The former circumstance would presumably be applicable where information was con- **5.86** tained on a public website, and was first proposed by the G8 countries in 1997.[186]

The latter would extend, for example, to a person's email stored in another country by a ser- **5.87** vice provider, such as Hotmail. While the Convention provision could be viewed as eroding traditional sovereign rights, it also represents an extra-territorial extension of domestic procedural jurisdiction, which may strengthen sovereignty in a transnational cyberspace environment. Article 32 details two circumstances all parties to the Convention could accept, but does not preclude other situations being authorized under national law.

Within the European Union, further harmonization of rules governing transborder access **5.88** has been advanced by the Commission, first under a Framework Decision on a 'European Evidence Warrant' (EEW)[187] and, more recently, under the 'European Investigation Order'. Under both instruments, Member States must enable the execution of an EEW or EIO 'without further formality'.

Other jurisdictions may take a more permissive approach to extra-territorially obtained **5.89** evidence than the UK. In 2000, as part of an investigation into the activities of two Russian hackers, Vasiliy Gorshkov and Alexey Ivanov, the Federal Bureau of Investigation (FBI) in the United States accessed computers in Russia via the Internet, using surreptitiously obtained passwords to download data from computers operated by the accused already under arrest in the US.[188] At an evidentiary hearing, Gorshkov first sought to have the evidence suppressed on the grounds that it was obtained in violation of the Fourth Amendment.[189] The court held that the Fourth Amendment was not applicable to 'non-resident alien's property outside the territory of the United States'.[190] In addition, were the

---

[185] However, a party may decide to give notification to the state where the data resides. See T-CY, Guidance Note No 3, *Transborder access to data (Article 32)*, 3 December 2014, para 3.3.

[186] G8, Principles and Action Plan to Combat High-tech Crimes, Principle VII.

[187] Council Framework Decision 2008/978/JHA of 18 December 2008 on the European evidence warrant for the purpose of obtaining objects, documents and data for use in proceedings in criminal matters, OJ L 350, 30 December 2008

[188] *United States v Gorshkov*, 2001 WL 1024026 (WD Wash 2001).

[189] The Fourth Amendment states:

The right of the people to be secure in their persons, houses, papers, and effects, against unreasonable searches and seizures, shall not be violated, and no Warrants shall issue, but upon probable cause, supported by Oath or affirmation, and particularly describing the place to be searched, and the persons or things to be seized.

[190] *Gorshkov*, 2001 WL 1024026 (WD Wash 2001), at *3.

Fourth Amendment to be applicable, the court considered the actions to be reasonable in all the circumstances, therefore meeting the requirements of the Fourth Amendment.[191]

5.90 Of critical relevance to our discussion in this section, the court in *Gorshkov* also held that the FBI's act of copying data was not a 'seizure' under the Fourth Amendment 'because it did not interfere with the Defendant's or anyone else's possessory interest in the data'.[192] While this may be true at a technical level, ie a copied document does not interfere with the source document,[193] one has to question whether it is appropriate as a matter of legal principle to rely on such a distinction. Indeed, the US courts have subsequently held that a 'seizure occurs when the Government interfere in some meaningful way with the individual's possession of property',[194] which has been reflected in the Federal Rules on Criminal Procedure, where 'on-site copying' is seen as equating to a 'seizure'.[195]

5.91 The issue has been addressed previously in a Council of Europe Recommendation on criminal procedure.[196] The Recommendation states: 'The legal remedies that are provided for in general against search and seizure should be equally applicable in case of search in computer systems and in case of seizure of data therein.'[197] This suggests equality of treatment between physical and virtual seizures, which is not the position adopted by the court in *Gorshkov*. Indeed, a further principle reiterates the need for equality: 'Where automatically processed data is functionally equivalent to a traditional document, provisions in the criminal procedural law relating to search and seizure of documents should apply equally to it.'[198] The Explanatory Report to the Recommendation notes that the different purposes of 'seizure' are 'to safeguard evidence, or to safeguard the object in order to possibly confiscate it or give it back to its lawful owner when it has been illegally acquired'.[199] While the first purpose is clearly present in all investigations, whatever the environment, the other purposes may only sometimes be necessary, for example where the defendant has child pornographic images. To achieve confiscation in an electronic environment, law enforcement officers have two choices; physical seizure of the equipment on which the data resides or render the data technically beyond use, either through deletion or making inaccessible, such as the use of encryption. However, the Report notes that in many situations the ability to copy data, rather than seize in the traditional sense, confers a benefit to the person subject to the procedure.[200] Clearly, any such benefits would be lost were the courts then to treat the procedure as something other than seizure, with the associated legal protections.[201]

---

[191] Gorshkov was eventually given a three-year jail sentence. See Department of Justice, 'Russian computer hacker sentenced to three years in prison', Press Release, 4 October 2002, available at <http://www.justice.gov/archive/criminal/cybercrime/press-releases/2002/gorshkovSent.htm>.

[192] *Gorshkov*, 2001 WL 1024026 (WD Wash 2001), at *3.

[193] This is true in terms of the document's content, but not in respect of the meta-data concerning the document's attributes or properties, which may record the fact that the original document was accessed at the time and date of copying.

[194] *United States v Ganias*, 755 F3d 125 (2d Cir 2014), at 133, 137.

[195] Federal Rules on Criminal Procedure, Title VIII, Rule 41(e)(2)(B).

[196] Recommendation No R (95) 13, above, n 157.

[197] ibid, Principle 2.

[198] ibid, Principle 4.

[199] Explanatory Memorandum, above, n 157, para 54.

[200] ibid, para 57.

[201] See also the Australian decision, *Australian Securities and Investments Commission v Rich and Another* [2005] NSWSC 62, which noted that the 'process of copying to storage devices brought to the premises, information stored in electronic form, involved the seizure of electronic things'.

In other international instruments, we see divergent approaches to the issue. The G8 **5.92** principles expressly distinguish between acts of copying and seizing data,[202] while the Commonwealth 'Model Computer and Computer-related Crimes Bill' incorporates an expansive definition of 'seizure', which puts the matter beyond doubt:

> ... 'seize' includes:
> (a) make and retain a copy of computer data, including by using onsite equipment; and
> (b) render inaccessible, or remove, computer data in the accessed computer system; and
> (c) take a printout of output of computer data.[203]

A second argument raised by the defence in *Gorshkov* was that the actions of the FBI agents **5.93** were in breach of Russian law. On this, the court held that Russian law was not applicable and even if it were, the agents had complied sufficiently.[204] However, in retaliation for this breach of sovereignty, the Russian authorities charged the FBI agent responsible for the intrusion with hacking, not with any anticipation of success, but as a 'matter of principle'.[205]

Under Australian law, the issue of liability raised in *Gorshkov* would not seem to arise, since **5.94** specific statutory protection from *any* liability is granted to certain law enforcement agencies 'for any computer-related act done outside Australia',[206] although this would presumably not prevent a challenge being raised against the use in court of any evidence so obtained.

In New Zealand, specific procedures have been adopted for a 'remote access search', which **5.95** is 'a search of a thing such as an Internet data storage facility that does not have a physical address that a person can enter and search'.[207] Such a search can be authorized under a warrant and when executing the warrant the person can 'use reasonable measures to gain access to the thing to be searched'.[208] On completion of the search, the investigating officer must send an electronic message to the email address of the location searched giving notice about who and when the search was carried out.[209]

Moving evidence: Mutual legal assistance

Evidence residing abroad may be obtained by LEAs through a range of mechanisms. **5.96** Broadly speaking, these mechanisms can be distinguished into formal legal mechanisms for the provision of assistance; informal voluntary cooperation between the requesting LEA and a relevant foreign person (eg LEA or service provider); or direct engagement with the material (eg open source). This section considers the first of these—mutual legal assistance between national law enforcement agencies and prosecuting authorities—although a cybercrime investigation will often comprise a mix of all three approaches. In *Levin*, for

---

[202] G8 Principles, above n 186.

[203] Commonwealth Model Law on Computer and Computer Related Crime, LMM(02)17, October 2002, Art 11.

[204] *Gorshkov*, 2001 WL 1024026 (WD Wash 2001), at *4 fn 4.

[205] Seitz, N, 'Transborder search: A new perspective in law enforcement?', 7(1) *Yale Journal of Law and Technology* 23 (2004–5), at 32. See also Brenner, S and Koops, B-J, 'Approaches to cybercrime jurisdiction', 4 *Journal of High Technology Law* 1 (2004).

[206] Criminal Code Act 1995, No 12 (Cth), para 476.5 'Liability for certain acts'. The relevant agencies are the Australian Secret Intelligence Service and the Defence Signals Directorate.

[207] Search and Surveillance Act 2012, s 3(1).

[208] ibid, s 111(a).

[209] ibid, s 132.

example, assistance was required not only from the St Petersburg police, but also the local telephone company. Obtaining assistance in a timely and efficient manner will often be critical to the success of a cybercrime investigation. Historically, however, MLA procedures have been notoriously slow and bureaucratic, 'on a timescale of months, rather than days';[210] therefore most mutual assistance occurs through informal cooperation and liaison between authorities.[211]

5.97 As with other areas of criminal procedure, different rules and procedures exist, or are being established, for the movement of evidence between the UK and other EU Member States compared with the procedures governing the movement of such evidence between the UK and non-EU states. Among European Union Member States, mutual legal assistance is primarily governed by the European Convention on Mutual Assistance in Criminal Matters (1959), which has subsequently been supplemented on a number of occasions, most recently by the 2000 Convention.[212] Parts of the 2000 Convention have been incorporated into English law through the Crime (International Co-operation) Act 2003, which repeals and replaces parts of the Criminal Justice (International Co-operation) Act 1990. In addition the Eurojust initiative is designed to facilitate the exchange of information between authorities and cross-border cooperation in the investigation and prosecution of serious and organized crime.[213]

5.98 While the 1959 and 2000 Conventions still remain in force, they will be replaced from May 2017 with a new EU procedure, the European Investigation Order. This will represent the latest stage of an evolution within the EU from traditional MLA processes to embracing the 'principle of mutual recognition'. While mutual recognition has been at the heart of the European project for many years,[214] it was only in 1999 that the Council accepted it as the 'cornerstone of judicial co-operation in both civil and criminal matters within the Union'.[215] It was not until the Lisbon Treaty that the principle was enshrined in the Treaty on the Functioning of the European Union (TFEU).[216] This shift from MLA to 'mutual recognition' is a fundamental one in terms of the nature of cooperation between two states. Under the former, assistance is based on an exercise of discretion by the recipient state and the request being assessed as valid under its law, a process that can take considerable time. By contrast, under mutual recognition, a request is deemed legally valid by default; on the

---

[210] United Nations Office of Drug and Crime (UNODC), *Comprehensive Study on Cybercrime* (draft), February 2013, at 206, available at <https://www.unodc.org/documents/organized-crime/UNODC_CCPCJ_EG.4_2013/CYBERCRIME_STUDY_210213.pdf> which also reports a median response time of 150 days.

[211] See Crown Prosecution Service Guidance, 'Evidence and Information from Abroad: Informal Enquiries and Letters of Request' ('CPS Guidance').

[212] EU Convention on Mutual Assistance in Criminal Matters, OJ C 197/1, 12 July 2000 ('MLA Convention'). See also Explanatory Report to the MLA Convention, above, n 116. Between Commonwealth countries, MLA is governed by the 'Scheme Relating to Mutual Assistance in Criminal Matters' (the 'Harare Scheme'). With the US, the UK signed a bilateral 'Treaty on Mutual Legal Assistance in Criminal Matters' in 1994 (TS 014/1997, Cm 3546).

[213] See para 5.199 for a description of Eurojust.

[214] See generally Janssens, C, *The Principle of Mutual Recognition in EU Law*, Oxford University Press, 2013.

[215] Tampere European Council (15–16 October 1999), Presidency Conclusions, 'Towards a Union of Freedom, Security and Justice', para 33, available at <http://www.europarl.europa.eu/summits/tam_en.htm>.

[216] OJ C 83/47, 30 March 2010, Art 82(1).

basis that the issuing authority followed recognized procedures, thereby enabling immediate and direct execution of the request.

This evolution is reflected in a series of EU instruments. In 2003, a measure was adopted on **5.99** the 'freezing' of evidence.[217] However, obtaining the transfer of the evidence required a second process, which undermined its efficiency. To address this issue, an European Evidence Warrant (EEW) procedure was adopted.[218] The EEW was limited, however, to 'evidence which exists and is readily available', while evidence that requires further investigative activities to be carried out in the executing state, such as real-time interception and covert surveillance, as well as access to data retained by CSPs, was to be addressed in a second instrument 'in due time'.[219]

Due to the limitations of the EEW, a new measure was adopted based on a single instrument, **5.100** the European Investigation Order Directive (EIO).[220] It covers nearly all forms of investigative procedure[221] and will be applicable in twenty-six of the twenty-eight Member States.[222] Reflecting its mandatory nature, the grounds for non-recognition or non-execution are limited, including source protection, national security interests, or the fundamental rights of an individual.[223] Refusal on the grounds that the conduct is not an offence in the executing state is also permissible, although not where the offence is listed in Annex D, which includes 'computer-related crime', and it would be punishable by a tariff of at least three years.[224] In addition, the executing state may choose an alternative investigation measure if it 'would achieve the same result by less intrusive means'.[225] In terms of handling the EIO, a principle of non-discrimination is imposed, requiring that the measure be 'carried out with the same celerity and priority as for a similar domestic case', as well as a default position of thirty days from receipt.[226] As with other mutual recognition measures in the criminal law field, especially the EAW, the EIO has been generated opposition, especially from those concerned that individual rights may be excessively encroached upon and are not adequately safeguarded.[227]

---

[217] Council Framework Decision 2003/577/JHA on the execution in the European Union of orders freezing property or evidence, OJ L 196/45, 2 August 2003.

[218] Council Framework Decision 2008/978/JHA on the European evidence warrant for the purpose of obtaining objects, documents and data for use in proceedings in criminal matters, OJ L 350/72, 30 December 2008.

[219] See Council of the European Union, Justice and Home Affairs Council Meeting, Press Release No 9409/06 (Presse 144), 1–2 June 2006, available at <http://www.consilium.europa.eu/uedocs/cms_data/docs/pressdata/en/jha/89875.pdf>.

[220] EIO, above, n 123.

[221] ibid, Art 3.

[222] Denmark and Ireland are not included, although the latter can opt in at some point in the future; while the UK opted in.

[223] EIO, above, n 123, Art 11. In addition, where the EIO involves interception, an executing state may refuse where the measure would not have been authorized for a similar domestic case (ibid, Art 30(5)). Although these exceptions are optional, where the ground for refusal involves an incompatibility with fundamental rights, refusal is effectively mandatory. See *NS v Secretary of State for the Home Department* [2012] 2 CMLR 9.

[224] EIO, above, n 123, Art 11(1)(g).

[225] ibid, Art 10(3).

[226] ibid, Art 12.

[227] eg Fair Trials International, 'Response to the adopted European Investigation Order Directive', Position Paper, March 2014, available at <http://www.fairtrials.org/wp-content/uploads/EIO-Position-Paper1.pdf>

5.101   The Extradition Act 2003 details mechanisms for the mutual provision of evidence, either obtaining evidence from abroad for use in the UK or assisting overseas authorities to obtain evidence from the UK. In the former situation, a judge, on the application of a prosecuting authority (eg the CPS) or a person charged in the proceedings (ie the defendant), may issue requests for evidence from abroad.[228] Such a request, historically known as a 'letter rogatory' or *'commission rogatoire'*, will only be made where it appears that an offence has been committed and that proceedings have been instituted or an investigation is underway.[229] The request may be sent to a court in the relevant jurisdiction, to an authority designated in the jurisdiction for receipt of such requests or, in cases of urgency, the International Criminal Police Organisation (INTERPOL).[230] The evidence, once received, should then only be used for the purpose specified in the request, known as the 'specialty principle':

> Evidence obtained by virtue of a letter of request shall not without the consent of such an authority . . . be used for any purpose other than that specified in the letter: and when any document or other article obtained pursuant to a letter of request is no longer required for that purpose (or for any other purpose for which such consent has been obtained), it shall be returned to such an authority unless that authority indicates that the document or article need not be returned.[231]

5.102   Requests for UK-based evidence by overseas authorities must be sent to the Secretary of State at the Home Office, referred to as the 'territorial authority'.[232] The Secretary of State may then nominate a court to receive the requested evidence. As well as achieving the disclosure of particular evidence, the MLA procedure also provides for the obtaining of evidence. The Secretary of State may direct that a warrant be applied for from the courts in order that a search can be undertaken and evidence seized. Law enforcement agencies may also obtain a warrant to intercept communications, as discussed above. However, such coercive powers may only be exercised where the conduct constitutes an appropriate offence in both the requesting country and under the laws of England and Wales, the so-called 'double criminality' principle, as also required in extradition proceedings.[233]

5.103   In terms of informal mechanisms for obtaining evidence from abroad, as the CPS notes, such assistance is 'dependent in many cases on their own domestic laws, how good the relations are generally between the country and the UK and, frankly, the attitude and opinions of the people on the ground to whom the request is made'![234] While informal requests are the norm, often in the course of preparing a formal request, they are less frequent in cybercrime cases, where the evidence required often involves either the seizure of equipment (eg a server) or disclosure of information by a foreign communication service provider, both of which often require the use of coercive powers, only available through the formal mechanisms referred to above. However, in this scenario, an alternative informal approach may also exist where the perpetrator's activities constitute an offence under foreign law, as

---

[228]   Crime (International Co-operation) Act 2003, Chapter 2, ss 7–12.

[229]   ibid, s 7(1).

[230]   ibid, s 8.

[231]   ibid, s 3(7). This principle is also generally present in extradition treaties, requiring the requesting state only to prosecute the accused for the crimes detailed in the extradition request: see Extradition Act 2003, s 95.

[232]   Crime (International Co-operation) Act 2003, ss 13 and 28(9). In practice, this is the UK Central Authority for Mutual Legal Assistance (UKCA) located in the Home Office.

[233]   See ibid, ss 16–18.

[234]   See CPS Guidance, above, n 211.

well as the UK. As such, the foreign authorities can choose to investigate without formal request even though they have no real intention to pursue a domestic prosecution. Such an approach can be viewed as a version of the 'double criminality' principle, where the act is in actuality an offence in both jurisdictions rather than theoretically.[235]

The operation of mutual legal assistance procedures has inevitably become considerably **5.104** more complex in a cyberspace environment, where the location of relevant resources may involve a variety of jurisdictions in respect of access to a single forensic source. In October 2004, for example, a US-based managed hosting company, Rackspace, received a subpoena, pursuant to an MLA Treaty, requesting delivery up of certain log file information[236] pertaining to an independent media organization, Indymedia.[237] The originating request came from a public prosecutor in Italy. To comply with the request for the information, Rackspace shut down the hosting server in London and delivered up drives to the FBI from that server. The purported reason for providing the physical drives, rather than merely the information requested, was described in the following terms:

> Rackspace employees searched for the specific information requested in the subpoena but were unable to locate this information prior to the strict delivery deadline imposed by the FBI. In order to comply with the mandated deadline, Rackspace delivered copied drives to the FBI. Shortly thereafter, Rackspace succeeded in isolating and extracting the relevant files responsive to the subpoena and immediately asked that the drives be returned by the FBI. The FBI returned the drives, and it was our understanding that at no time had they been reviewed by the FBI. The relevant files were then delivered to the FBI.[238]

The case raises two particular issues of interest. First, execution of a legitimate bilateral **5.105** MLA request required implementation in a third country, the UK, with no involvement from domestic law enforcement[239] or seeming consideration of the legality of such action under English law. This renders the process open to legal challenge, as well as exposing Rackspace to potential liability. Second, the nature of the timescales involved in compliance with the order meant that the intermediary, Rackspace, felt the need to exceed the terms of the request. It can be seen as illustrating an inevitable tension between the need for speed, with the corresponding initiatives to reduce the procedural lag, and the ability of a requested party to appropriately respond. While data preservation is a relatively straightforward process, accessing the requested data may be considerably more problematic.[240]

Improving MLA has risen up the political agendas in both the UK and US over recent years **5.106** as the need for forensic material from the major US social media providers (eg Facebook,

---

[235] Such an approach has been adopted in the US, according to a statement made by Michael Sussman, Senior Counsel, US Department of Justice, Criminal Division, Computer Crime and Intellectual Property Section at an Academy of European Law conference in Trier, Germany, 20 February 2003.

[236] Data concerning use of the resource.

[237] See generally Electronic Frontier Foundation, 'Indymedia server takedown', August 2005, available at <https://www.eff.org/cases/indymedia-server-takedown>.

[238] According to an email from Rackspace to CNet, quoted in 'Details on FBI's secret call for Indymedia Logs', *CNet*, 2 August 2005, available at <http://www.cnet.com/news/details-on-fbis-secret-call-for-indymedia-logs/>.

[239] In response to parliamentary questions from MPs, Richard Allan and Jeremy Corbyn (20 October 2004, Col 725W), John McDonnell MP (27 October 2004, Col 1278W), and Lynne Jones (11 November 2004, Col 895W), to Home Office minister Caroline Flint, who replied: 'I can confirm that no UK law enforcement agencies were involved in the matter.'

[240] See further paras 4.224–4.255.

Twitter, Yahoo!, and Google) has become more prevalent,[241] and alternative more direct routes have become more problematic, especially following the Snowden revelations. In September 2014, the UK Government appointed Sir Nigel Sheinwald as special envoy on intelligence and law enforcement data sharing specifically to improve access to data, including MLA.[242] In the US, the tech industry has been lobbying Congress complaining of 'insufficient staffing and investment by the US' and supporting the Department of Justice's appropriations request to fund reform of the MLA process.[243]

5.107   Although there are no special conditions governing the admissibility of computer-derived material under English rules of evidence, prosecutors will often be challenged to prove the reliability of any such evidence presented. Auditable procedures will need to be adhered to, often supported by independent expert witnesses, to show the probative value of any evidence generated.[244] Where such evidence has been generated abroad, compliance with such procedures, and evidence of such compliance, is much more complex and vulnerable to defence claims of errors, technical malfunction, prejudicial interference, or fabrication, especially where the evidence was obtained through informal means, and is therefore more likely to be subject to an application to exclude.[245]

Moving people: Extradition

5.108   Clearly when a UK-based computer system is 'hacked', the perpetrator may be located anywhere in the world. Therefore, if a prosecution is to be mounted, the accused has to be brought to the UK. The formal procedure under which persons are transferred between states for prosecution is known as 'extradition'. Either bilateral or multilateral treaties or agreements between states generally govern extradition.[246] The first case of an extradition to the UK for a computer misuse was that of Joseph Popp in 1991 from the United States.[247] The case involved the distribution of an 'AIDS' diskette that contained a Trojan Horse virus and a demand for payment. Although successfully extradited, at trial, the judge dismissed the prosecution on eleven counts of blackmail on the grounds that he was unfit to plead due to mental illness. In the absence of such a treaty, the state where the perpetrator resides is not required under any rule of public international law to surrender the person. In such situations, informal mechanisms may be used to bring the perpetrator to justice. In the case of *Levin*, for example, the accused was enticed to leave Russia, with which the US did not

---

[241]   eg a 60% increase in foreign evidence requests and a 1000% increase in requests for computer records over the last decade. See US DOJ Fiscal Year (FY) 2015 Budget Request, 'Mutual legal assistance treaty process reform + $24.1 million in total funding', available at <http://www.justice.gov/sites/default/files/jmd/legacy/2014/07/13/mut-legal-assist.pdf>.

[242]   See Cabinet Office, 'Sir Nigel Sheinwald appointed Special Envoy on intelligence and law enforcement data sharing', Press Release, 19 September 2014, available at <https://www.gov.uk/government/news/sir-nigel-sheinwald-appointed-special-envoy-on-intelligence-and-law-enforcement-data-sharing>.

[243]   See letters dated 31 March 2014, 3 November 2014, and 23 April 2015 from the Application Developers Alliance, Business Software Alliance, Computer and Communications Industry Association, and others.

[244]   See generally ACPO, 'Good Practice Guide for Computer Based Evidence', Appendix IV, available at <http://www.cps.gov.uk/legal/assets/uploads/files/ACPO_guidelines_computer_evidence[1].pdf>.

[245]   See further paras 6.82–6.85.

[246]   eg Council Decision 2009/820/CFSP on the conclusion on behalf of the European Union of the Agreement on extradition between the European Union and the United States of America and the Agreement on mutual legal assistance between the European Union and the United States of America, OJ L 291/40, 23 October 2009.

[247]   See Wilding, E, 'Popp goes the weasel', *Virus Bulletin* 2, January 1992, available at <https://www.virusbtn.com/pdf/magazine/1992/199201.pdf>.

have an extradition treaty, to travel to the UK. As soon as he landed in a country with which the US did have an extradition arrangement, ie the UK, he was arrested.[248] Similarly, in *Gorshkov*, the suspects were lured from Russia to Seattle in the United States.[249]

In an action for extradition, the applicant is generally required to show that the actions of **5.109** the accused constitute a criminal offence exceeding a minimum level of seriousness in both jurisdictions, ie the country from which the accused is to be extradited and the country to which the extradition will be made. This is referred to as the 'double criminality' principle. In *Levin*, the defendant was accused of committing wire and bank fraud in the United States. No direct equivalent offences exist in English law, and therefore Levin was charged with sixty-six related offences, including ss 2 and 3 of the Computer Misuse Act. At that time, the s 1 unauthorized access offence only attracted a maximum penalty of six months, which meant that it was not an extraditable offence,[250] although this was reformed when the Act was amended in 2006.[251] Conversely, in the cyber-espionage case, *Haephrati*, the defendants were charged with some nine offences under Israeli law, including infringement of privacy,[252] which has no equivalent under English law. However, the extradition hearing charge was conspiracy to defraud, which was considered broad enough to cover the defendants' activities.

Under the Extradition Act 1989, an extradition offence had to be punishable by a minimum **5.110** twelve-month imprisonment in both states.[253] The Cybercrime Convention also provides that the offences it details should be extraditable provided that they are punishable under the laws of both parties 'by deprivation of liberty for a maximum period of at least one year, or by a more severe penalty'.[254] It also provides that the Convention itself may be the legal basis for extradition in the absence of a treaty between the relevant states.[255] The 1989 Act was repealed and replaced by the Extradition Act 2003, under which 'double criminality' is no longer required for offences listed in Schedule 2 (as specified in the European Arrest Warrant Scheme) in relation to 'Category 1' territories, which are part of the European Arrest Warrant Scheme.[256]

Extradition is a complex and often lengthy process, involving, at least in common law juris- **5.111** dictions, both judicial and executive decision-taking. In *Levin*, for example, the defendant was arrested in March 1995 and yet the judicial process was not completed until June 1997. One of the most notorious examples of the extradition process was that involving Gary McKinnon. In June 2005, extradition proceedings were commenced against McKinnon,

---

[248] See also *Yarimaka v Governor of HM Prison Brixton; Zezev v Government of the United States of America* [2002] EWHC 589 (Admin).

[249] *Gorshkov*, 2001 WL 1024026 (WD Wash 2001), at *1.

[250] CMA, s 1(3).

[251] See 'Revision of the Computer Misuse Act', Report of an Inquiry by the All Party Parliamentary Internet Group (June 2004), paras 95 et seq.

[252] Protection of Privacy Law 5741-1981, s 5.

[253] Extradition Act 1989, s 2(1). See also *R v Bow Street Magistrates' Court, ex parte Allison* [1998] 3 WLR 1156, where the court held that ss 2 and 3 of the CMA were extradition crimes (confirmed by the House of Lords, at 625G).

[254] Convention on Cybercrime, Art 24(1).

[255] ibid, Art 24(4).

[256] Designated by the Secretary of State under s 1(1), which could include non-EU states. As of October 2005, Category 1 territories are the 24 EU Member States: Extradition Act 2003 (Designation of Part 1 Territories) Order 2003 (SI No 3333), as amended, s 2.

who was accused of hacking into US military and NASA computers during 2001 and 2002, causing more than $700,000 of damage, as well as disrupting critical military systems at a naval weapons station.[257] In May 2006, a judge at Bow Street Magistrates' Court held that the extradition could proceed, subject to the decision of the Home Secretary. The judge stated that he was satisfied with assurances given by the US Government that McKinnon would not face terrorism charges, and felt that extradition would not incompatible with his Convention rights.[258] The Secretary of State subsequently ordered McKinnon's extradition in July 2006. McKinnon appealed, but the High Court and the House of Lords dismissed the various grounds that were advanced.[259] Having been diagnosed with Asperger's Syndrome, he then appealed to the European Court of Human Rights and the Home Secretary on the grounds that his rights under Arts 3 and 8 would be infringed. The former rejected his application for interim measures,[260] while the latter reaffirmed her order for McKinnon's extradition.[261] The decision of the Home Secretary resulted in judicial review proceedings, which were again unsuccessful.[262] His extradition was ordered again, which generated further judicial review proceedings that were then adjourned given a change of government. During this period, campaigners on behalf of McKinnon were so successful at maintaining the profile of the story that his case was even raised in discussions between the US President and the UK Prime Minister.[263] Finally, in October 2012, the Home Secretary, Theresa May, decided not to extradite McKinnon stating that 'McKinnon's extradition would give rise to such a high risk of him ending his life that a decision to extradite would be incompatible with Mr McKinnon's human rights'.[264] The whole episode finally came to an end in December 2012, when the CPS and Metropolitan Police decided not to proceed with a domestic prosecution, since the 'prospects of a conviction … which reflects the full extent of his alleged criminality are not high'.[265] This was largely due to the unwillingness of the US authorities to make available the necessary material and witnesses relating to the case.

5.112   Having taken ten years, the McKinnon case can either be viewed as an exceptional case or as an example of the inherent difficulties arising in extradition proceedings. As an exception, McKinnon was a vulnerable individual who engendered strong feelings and support, as well as managing to engage the attention of politicians. As a case study, it illustrates a couple of key issues. First, the extradition of nationals is inevitably more fraught than that of foreigners passing through the jurisdiction. Indeed, the UK is one of the few countries that are prepared to extradite their own nationals. Given this position, the Convention requires a Member State to establish jurisdiction over its own nationals and to prosecute them where,

---

[257] See *United States v Gary McKinnon*, Indictment, November 2002, available at <http://news.findlaw.com/hdocs/docs/cyberlaw/usmck1102vaind.pdf>.

[258] 'Judge greenlights extradition of "Pentagon hacker"', *The Register*, 10 May 2006, available at <http://www.theregister.co.uk/2006/05/10/pentagon_hacker_packs_bags/>.

[259] *McKinnon v Government of the United States of America & others* [2007] EWHC 762 (Admin) and [2008] UKHL 59 respectively.

[260] European Court of Human Rights, Press Release No 601, 'European Court of Human Rights refuses request for interim measures by Gary McKinnon', 28 August 2008.

[261] Letter from the Treasury Solicitor on behalf of the Secretary of State, 13 October 2008.

[262] *R (on the application of McKinnon) v Secretary of State for Home Affairs* [2009] EWHC 2021 (Admin).

[263] 'Cameron and Obama discuss computer hacker Gary McKinnon', *BBC*, 20 July 2010, <http://www.bbc.co.uk/news/uk-10704452>.

[264] Theresa May statement, above, n 93.

[265] 'Joint CPS/MPS statement on the case of Gary McKinnon', *CPS News Brief Blog*, 14 December 2002, available at <http://blog.cps.gov.uk/2012/12/gary-mckinnon.html>.

as a matter of national law, such persons may not be extradited to a requesting state where the crime was committed.[266] However, as the McKinnon case shows, an ability to prosecute may be fatally undermined by evidential problems.

Finally on this issue, it must be noted that the McKinnon case contributed to existing **5.113** public concern about the UK extradition process, which resulted in the Government deciding to amend the law on extradition. First, the role of the executive has been diminished, leaving the High Court to consider appeals 'on human rights grounds'.[267] Second, a 'forum bar' has been implemented, under which the courts have the ability to bar an extradition, if it is 'would not be in interests of justice'.[268] In making such a decision, a judge must first decide that 'a substantial measure' of the defendant's conduct was carried out in the UK; then regard must be had to various 'specified matters', which map closely the Eurojust 2003 Guidelines, discussed earlier.[269]

A second issue from *McKinnon* was not the need to meet the minimum threshold of 'double **5.114** criminality', as noted in *Levin* above, but rather the differential regarding the maximum penalties applicable to such criminality. Under UK law, the maximum tariff would likely have been five years for a s 3 offence under the Computer Misuse Act 1990 (as in force at the time). In the US, the indictment listed seven counts of computer fraud and related activity, each of which carried a maximum sentence of ten years.[270] These sentences could run consecutively, depending on the decision of the federal judge, giving a possible total of seventy years. The reality was that such an outcome was extremely unlikely.[271] However, in terms of generating support, such differential sentencing regimes provided fuel for claims of unfairness in the extradition process.

In order to simplify the extradition process within the EU, the concept of the 'European **5.115** Arrest Warrant' has been established.[272] The Council Decision abolished the formal extradition procedure in favour of a simplified process in which a warrant issued by a Member State court will be granted mutual recognition by other Member States and will result in the arrest and surrender of the requested person. The surrender may be conditional upon the acts detailed in the warrant being an offence in the executing state.[273] However, certain offences, including 'computer related crime',[274] which are punishable in the issuing Member State by a custodial sentence of a maximum of at least three years (eg Computer Misuse Act 1990, ss 2 and 3) will be subject to automatic execution of the warrant, ie

---

[266] Convention on Cybercrime, Arts 22(3) and 24(6).

[267] Extradition Act 2003, s 108(7).

[268] ibid, ss 19B (category 1 territories) and 83A (category 2 territories).

[269] See paras 5.37–5.40.

[270] The indictment is available at <news.findlaw.com/hdocs/docs/cyberlaw/usmck1102vaind.pdf>.

[271] Indeed, McKinnon was offered a plea bargain of 4 years by the US authorities, the latter part of which could have been served in the UK, which he refused. See Green, DA, 'Why did it take ten years to block the extradition of Gary McKinnon?', *New Statesman*, 16 October 2012, available at <http://www.newstatesman.com/politics/2012/10/gary-mckinnon>.

[272] Council Framework Decision 2002/584/JHA on the European arrest warrant and the surrender procedures between Member States, OJ L 190/1, 18 July 2002, as amended by Council Framework Decision 2009/299/JHA enhancing the procedural rights of persons and fostering the application of the principle of mutual recognition to decisions rendered in the absence of the person concerned at the trial, OJ L 81/24, 27 March 2009.

[273] ibid, Art 2(4).

[274] Extradition Act 2003, Sch 2, at para 11.

surrender, without consideration of the dual criminality requirement. Extradition under such circumstances will also be available even though some element of the conduct occurred in the UK.[275]

5.116 Part I of the Extradition Act 2003 implements the EAW, providing for a maximum ten-day period from the date of the judicial order for completion of an extradition to a Category 1 territory, ie a Member State of the EU, unless an appeal has been lodged.[276] Part II specifies that extradition to a non-EAW country, referred to as a 'Category 2' territory, should take place within 28 days from the date of the Secretary of State's order,[277] although the 'double criminality' principle continues to be applicable.[278]

5.117 These provisions amend extradition procedures with the US, which are reflected in a new extradition treaty between the UK and the US.[279] This Treaty has given rise to controversy regarding the different evidential standards that potentially exist when persons are sent to the US, where prima facie evidence is required, ie evidence sufficient to justify conviction unless challenged or contradicted by evidence adduced by the defence, compared with obtaining suspects from the US, where evidence 'as would provide a reasonable basis to believe that the person sought committed the offence', or 'probable cause', must be shown.[280] The reality of these distinctions was considered insignificant in a review of the UK's extradition procedures in 2011,[281] and the Government subsequently rejected calls for reform.[282]

5.118 As with the obtaining of evidence, while there are formal procedures governing extradition, there are also informal elements involved prior to, or alternate to, extradition. In a situation of cross-border hacking, for example, the perpetrator will often have committed offences in more than one country. As such, a decision may need to be made by the national authority where the perpetrator is located (eg the CPS), whether to commence a domestic prosecution or comply with a request for extradition. Where extradition is available, a process of negotiation should take place between the relevant states about the most appropriate forum to prosecute.

D. Harmonization Initiatives

5.119 Computer and cybercrime have an obvious international dimension, and governments have recognized the need to ensure that legal protection is harmonized among nations. Attempts have been made within numerous regional and international organizations and

---

[275] See *Office of the King's Prosecutor, Brussels v Cando Armas* [2005] UKHL 67.

[276] Extradition Act 2003, s 35.

[277] ibid, s 117.

[278] ibid, s 137(2)(b).

[279] United States No 1 (2003), Extradition Treaty between the Government of the United Kingdom of Great Britain and Northern Ireland and the Government of the United States, Washington, March 2003, Cm 5821, ratified by the President on 6 December 2006, entered into force 26 April 2007.

[280] ibid, Art 8(3)(c). See 'Enron trio lose extradition fight', *BBC News*, 21 February 2006, available at <http://news.bbc.co.uk/2/hi/business/4735292.stm>.

[281] Baker, S, Perry, D, and Doobay, A, *A Review of the United Kingdom's Extradition Arrangements* (September 2011), Pt 8, available at <https://www.gov.uk/government/uploads/system/uploads/attachment_data/file/117673/extradition-review.pdf>.

[282] Theresa May statement, above, n 93.

fora, including the G8, the Association of Southeast Asian Nations (ASEAN) states,[283] and the United Nations,[284] to achieve a harmonized approach to legislating against computer crime and thereby try to prevent the appearance of 'computer crime havens'. The first major attempt was under the auspices of the Organisation for Economic Co-operation and Development (OECD). It published a report in 1986, which listed five categories of offence that it believed should constitute a common approach to computer crime.[285] However, the most significant institutions in the field have been the Council of Europe and the European Union.

As well as explicit initiatives at harmonization, informal harmonization can also be seen **5.120** between legal systems that have historical connections, based on common legal traditions that generally reflect a colonial past and on-going influence. The UK's Computer Misuse Act 1990, for example, is manifest in the legislation adopted in Singapore,[286] Malaysia,[287] Brunei,[288] and Sri Lanka.[289]

As reflected in this book, harmonization initiatives have tended to address both substantive **5.121** offences and criminal procedure, the former adopting a narrow focus, in terms of categories of offence, the latter having potential generic applicability to all forms of crime. In terms of substantive offences, national legal traditions have generally proved a greater barrier to harmonization than in the field of criminal procedure. Inevitably, national criminal codes exhibit a variety of means of conceiving an activity that are not present when considering the process of investigation. A fraudulent act, for example, may be criminalized from the perspective of the perpetrator (eg dishonest intent), the victim (eg deception), or the manner by which it is carried out (eg wire fraud). Such divergence tends to be less pronounced in offences of more recent origin, such as money laundering, which gives them a distinct advantage over more traditional offences, especially in a transnational context where issues of mutual legal assistance and extradition are involved.[290] Greater harmonization of laws also helps reduce the likelihood of jurisdictional conflicts, discussed already in this chapter. In terms of criminal procedure, national differences tend to be more principle-based, reflecting cultural concerns about privacy and the proper limits of police powers.

Council of Europe

The Council of Europe was founded in 1949 to defend human rights, parliamentary dem- **5.122** ocracy and the rule of law, in part through harmonization agreements on legal matters.[291] Its most significant legal achievement to date is the Convention for the Protection of Human

---

[283] See the e-ASEAN Framework Agreement, 22–25 November 2000, Singapore, available at <http://www.eppo.go.th/inter/asean/asean-sec/infs4_afw.htm>.

[284] See *United Nations Manual on the Prevention and Control of Computer-related Crime*, Sales No E95IV5. Published in the *International Review of Criminal Policy*, Nos 43 and 44, 1996, available at <http://www.unodc.org/pdf/Manual_ComputerRelatedCrime.PDF>.

[285] 'Computer-Related Criminality: Analysis of Legal Policy in the OECD Area', Report DSTI-ICCP 84.22, 18 April 1986.

[286] Computer Misuse Act 1993.

[287] Computer Crimes Act 1997.

[288] Computer Misuse Order 2000.

[289] Computer Crimes Act 2006.

[290] Interview with Terry Palfrey, CPS, 2 February 2006.

[291] Statute of the Council of Europe, CETS 001, opened for signature 5 May 1949, entered into force 3 August 1949, Art 1(b).

Rights and Fundamental Freedoms, adopted in 1950 and enforced through the European Court of Human Rights in Strasbourg.[292] It currently comprises forty-seven countries within Europe,[293] although observer status has been granted to four non-European countries: the United States, Canada, Japan, and Mexico.[294] Over the years, it has published an extensive number of reports in the field of criminal law, as well as adopting recommendations and treaties, addressing law reform on both substantive and procedural issues.

5.123 In 1985, a select committee of experts, the European Committee on Crime Problems, was established under the auspices of the Council of Europe to consider the legal issues raised by computer crime. The final report was published in September 1989,[295] addressing substantive, procedural, and international aspects. As part of the Committee's work, it produced guidelines for national legislatures on a 'Minimum list of offences necessary for a uniform criminal policy on legislation concerning computer-related crime'.[296] The list of offences included: computer fraud; computer forgery; damage to computer data or computer programs; computer sabotage; unauthorized access; unauthorized interception; unauthorized reproduction of a computer program; and unauthorized reproduction of a topography. These eight offences were seen by all Member States to be the critical areas of computer misuse that required provisions in criminal law. In addition, the Report put forward an 'optional list' of four offences that failed to achieve consensus among Members, but was thought to be worthy of consideration.[297] The Report was published with a Council of Ministers Recommendation urging governments to take account of the Report when reviewing and initiating legislation in this field: Recommendation No R (89) 9, 13 September 1999.

5.124 Following the 1989 Recommendation, the Council of Europe shifted its attention to the issue of prosecution of computer crime and the particular problems faced by law enforcement agencies, as recommended by the Committee.[298] A second committee of experts commenced work in October 1992. In September 1995, the Council of Ministers adopted a Recommendation addressing issues of search and seizure, the admissibility of evidence, and international mutual assistance: Recommendation No R (95) 13 concerning problems of procedural law connected with information technology.[299]

5.125 Despite these various initiatives, Council of Europe Recommendations are not binding legal instruments on Member States and inevitably, therefore, such harmonizing measures had limited effect. However, the growth of the Internet as a transnational environment for the commission of crime has refocused the attention of policy makers on the need for harmonized criminal laws in the area. As a consequence, in April 1997, the Council of Europe embarked on the adoption of a Convention in the area, which Member States would have an obligation to implement.

---

[292] European Convention on Human Rights, 4 November 1950, entered into force 3 November 1953, 213 UNTS 222 (ECHR), as amended by Protocol No 11 (ETS No 155).

[293] See Council of Europe website, <http://www.coe.int>.

[294] As provided for under Council of Europe Statutory Resolution (93)26 on observer status, adopted 14 May 1993.

[295] CoE Report 1990, above, n 66..

[296] ibid, Appendix I.

[297] ie alteration of computer data or computer programs; computer espionage; unauthorized use of a computer; and unauthorized use of a protected computer program.

[298] CoE Report 1990, above, n 66, at 83.

[299] See also Recommendation 95 (13) and the Explanatory Memorandum, above, n 157.

Convention on cybercrime

In November 2001, the Council of Ministers adopted the 'Convention on Cybercrime', which **5.126** was opened for signature in Budapest on 23 November 2001, and has since been signed by forty-five of the forty-seven members of the Council of Europe.[300] However, of particular significance to the status of the Convention, four non-members were involved in the drafting process, the United States, Japan, South Africa, and Canada, and became signatories.[301] The Convention also contains a mechanism whereby other non-members can be invited to accede to the Convention, with the unanimous consent of the Committee of Ministers.[302] To date, four states have acceded to the Convention: Australia, Dominican Republic, Mauritius, Sri Lanka, and Panama.[303] Once five states ratified the Convention, through implementation into national law, it entered into force,[304] which occurred on 1 July 2004.

The Convention addresses issues of substantive and procedural criminal law, which Member **5.127** States are obliged to take measures to implement in national law, as well as issues of international cooperation.

In terms of offences, Section 1 distinguishes four categories of offence: **5.128**

- 'Offences against the confidentiality, integrity and availability of computer data and systems': ie illegal access, illegal interception, data interference, systems interference and misuse of devices (Arts 2–6).[305]
- 'Computer-related offences': ie forgery and fraud (Arts 7–8).
- 'Content-related offences': ie child pornography (Art 9).
- 'Offences related to and infringements of copyright and related rights' (Art 10).

Relevant aspects of these provisions have been examined in detail in Chapter 3. In addition, the Convention addresses related liability issues in relation to attempts and aiding or abetting (Art 11) and corporate liability (Art 12).

Section 2 of the Convention addresses procedural provisions that Member States are obliged **5.129** to implement in national law. These include measures to enable the 'expedited preservation of stored computer data' (Art 16); 'expedited preservation and partial disclosure of traffic data' (Art 17);[306] the production and search and seizure of computer data (Arts 18–19); the 'real-time collection of traffic data' (Art 20); and the interception of content data (Art 21). The majority of these measures contains specific rules applicable to 'service providers', which are recognized as a key forensic tool and source:

---

[300] Convention on Cybercrime and Explanatory Report to the Convention, above, n 65. Number of signatories as at 2 February 2016. See Appendix II in this volume.

[301] All except South Africa have observer status in the Council of Europe. For the US, the Convention entered into force on 1 January 2007.

[302] Convention on Cybercrime, Art 37.

[303] As at 2 February 2016.

[304] Convention on Cybercrime, Art 36(3). Three of the ratifications had to be Council of Europe Members. As at 26 November 2015, all but 8 Member States had ratified the Convention.

[305] Devices, including passwords, being produced or used with the intent to commit one of the offences within the category.

[306] ' "Traffic data" means any computer data relating to a communication by means of a computer system, generated by a computer system that formed a part in the chain of communication, indicating the communication's origin, destination, route, time, date, size, duration, or type of underlying service' (Art 1(d)). See further paras 4.182–4.194.

(i) any public or private entity that provides to users of its service the ability to communicate by means of a computer system, and

(ii) any other entity that processes or stores computer data on behalf of such communication service or users of such service.[307]

This is recognized as encompassing 'a broad category of persons', not only those that provide communication services, but also those that simply process data on behalf of users of communication services, such as hosting and caching services.[308] These services are distinguished from a 'mere provider of content' who does not also 'offer communication or related data processing services'.[309] The boundary lines between these different entities can have important implications for the exercise of law enforcement powers, yet the line is far from clear in our age of convergence. Indeed, in 2014, the UK Government amended the RIPA to make it clear that the applicable term, 'telecommunication services', included 'providers whose services are internet-based (such as web-based email) as well as those providing infrastructure for connection to the internet';[310] partly in response to challenges from providers as to the applicability of the original provisions to their services.

5.130 Section 3 addresses the issue of jurisdiction (Art 22). Relevant aspects of these provisions have been examined in detail in Chapter 4 and previous sections of this chapter.

5.131 In terms of international cooperation, the Convention addresses issues of extradition (Art 24), mutual legal assistance between national law enforcement agencies (Arts 25–34) and the establishment of a 24/7 network of points of contact to support such assistance (Art 35). The concept of promoting mutual assistance through information exchange dates back to the establishment of INTERPOL;[311] although a contact network for cybercrime is based on the experience of one established among the G8 states in 1997, which was intended to facilitate cooperation through informal channels of communications, to supplement the formal mutual legal assistance procedures.[312] The network already has over fifty participant countries.[313]

5.132 When becoming a signatory or depositing an instrument of ratification, a state may make various 'declarations' that it intends to meet its obligations through the requirement of additional elements, the possibility of which is provided for under the terms of specific articles.[314] Lithuania, for example, has chosen to criminalize illegal access only by infringing security measures, as permitted for under Art 2.[315] States may also make 'reservations', but

---

[307] Convention on Cybercrime, Art 1(c).

[308] Explanatory Report to the Convention on Cybercrime, above, n 65, para 26.

[309] ibid, para 27.

[310] Home Office, 'Data Retention and Investigatory Powers Bill—Human Rights Memorandum', Bills (14–15) 024, para 5. Section 5 of the Data Retention and Investigatory Powers Act 2014, inserted a new subsection (8A) in s 2.

[311] See Art 2(1) of the Constitution of the International Criminal Police Organization-Interpol, available at <http://www.interpol.int/About-INTERPOL/Legal-materials/The-Constitution>. INTERPOL has developed a secure police network, 'I-24/7', which covers some 190 countries. See INTERPOL, 'Data exchange', available at <http://www.interpol.int/INTERPOL-expertise/Data-exchange>.

[312] Explanatory Report to the Convention on Cybercrime, above, n 65, para 298.

[313] Comment from Kevin McNulty, Home Office in UN, 'Criminalization of computer wrongdoing prerequisite for combating cybercrime', Press Release (SOC/CP/332), 22 April 2005.

[314] Convention on Cybercrime, Art 40.

[315] Declaration contained in the instrument of ratification deposited on 18 March 2004. For a complete list of declarations, see <http://conventions.coe.int/Treaty/Commun/ListeDeclarations.asp?NT=185&CM=8&DF=&CL=ENG&VL=1>.

only where the option exists in respect of an article.[316] Denmark, for example, has stated that in relation to child pornography, national law does not criminalize images 'appearing to be a minor engaged in sexually explicit conduct', as permitted under Art 9(4).[317] Such declarations and reservations obviously represent a limitation to the harmonization objective, but are also a standard feature of such international treaties.

As well as the on-going remit of the European Committee on Crime Problems (CDPC) to keep under review all areas of criminal law, the Convention also contains a specific mechanism for periodic consultation between the parties, concerning implementation issues, legal, policy, and technological developments, and possible amendment of the Convention, a mechanism which is provided for under Art 44. The first such multilateral consultation meeting of the T-CY was held in March 2006, and it holds an annual Plenary meeting.[318]   **5.133**

The remit of the T-CY, as stated at Art 46(1), is to consider the effective use and implementation of the Convention; exchange information about policy, legal and technological developments, and consider supplements or amendments to the Convention. To date, the activities and outputs from the T-CY represent a significant body of materials relating to the Convention. The T-CY has published guidance notes on eight topics, six of which have been formally adopted by the Committee.[319] It has organized regular public events, engaged in information gathering exercises, and carried out assessment reports of Member State implementation. The T-CY can also make recommendations for the adoption of Protocols to the Convention and is considering such a possibility with respect to the articles on mutual assistance and international cooperation.   **5.134**

The comprehensive nature of the Convention, as well as the geographical spread of its signatories, means it is likely to remain the most significant international legal instrument in the field for the foreseeable future. Other intergovernmental organizations have also endorsed it, such as the leaders of the Asia-Pacific Economic Cooperation (APEC) states, in 2002, and the Organization of American States (OAS) in 2004, which recommended that members implement the principles of the Convention and even consider accession.[320] In 2005, the international police organization, INTERPOL, adopted a resolution describing the Convention as 'providing a minimal international legal and procedural standard' and recommending that its 190 member countries consider joining it.[321] The success of the Cybercrime Convention as a spur to harmonization can be measured not only on the basis of the number of signatories, including non-European countries, but also as the source of other harmonization initiatives, such as the Commonwealth 'Model Computer and Computer-related Crimes Bill' (October 2002), addressing the needs of some fifty-three developed and developing nations.   **5.135**

---

[316] Convention on Cybercrime, Art 42.

[317] Reservation contained in the instrument of ratification deposited on 21 June 2005.

[318] See generally Council of Europe, 'Action against cybercrime', available at <http://www.coe.int/t/dghl/cooperation/economiccrime/cybercrime/T-CY/Default_TCY_en.asp>.

[319] ibid. The content of these notes are examined elsewhere in the book, as appropriate, but primarily in Chapters 3 and 4.

[320] OAS Conclusions and Recommendations of the Fifth Conference of Ministers of Justice and Attorney General, Washington DC, 28–30 April 2004, IV Cyber-crime at 8, available from <http://www.oas.org/juridico/english/remjaV_final_report.pdf>. See also the OAS Portal on Cyber-Crime, <http://www.oas.org/juridico/english/cyber.htm>.

[321] Resolution from the Sixth International Conference on Cyber Crime, Egypt, April 2005.

5.136 Much criticism has been directed at the Cybercrime Convention over the years, on a range of grounds and from different quarters. First, the lack of transparency in the actual drafting process has been a source of frustration and anger, with the process seen as being totally dominated by the interests of law enforcement, rather than incorporating a multiple stakeholder dialogue.[322] Second, criticism has come from human rights groups[323] and other bodies with responsibilities to protect individual rights[324] for alleged incursions on those rights and the absence of sufficient protections incorporated in the Convention, other than the general statements contained in Art 15, which were incorporated relatively late into the drafting process. Third, service providers have complained about the resource burdens placed upon them as a consequence of their obligations to assist law enforcement agencies. Fourth, the Convention has been criticized for failing to address key areas of cybercrime, such as identity theft.[325] Fifth, certain states, most notably Russia and China, the former being a member of the Council of Europe, have expressed serious reservations about the Convention, particularly concerning Art 32 on transborder access.[326] One consequence of these criticisms has been calls for a treaty to be drafted under the auspices of the United Nations.[327]

Additional protocol

5.137 After the adoption of the Convention in 2001, an additional protocol to the Convention was agreed by Member States, 'concerning the criminalisation of acts of a racist and xenophobic nature committed through computer systems', in January 2003.[328] Such issues were considered during the drafting of the main instrument, but consensus could not be reached, therefore the approach of drafting a separate instrument was agreed.[329] As at April 2015, thirty-six Member States had signed the Protocol, as well as two non-Member States, Canada and South Africa. The Protocol entered into force in March 2006, with the fifth ratification.[330]

5.138 The Protocol requires the establishment of a range of substantive offences concerning 'racist or xenophobic material', defined in the following terms:

---

[322] See eg American Civil Liberties Union, 'Seven Reasons the US should reject the International Cybercrime Treaty', 18 December 2003, Reason No 7, 'The treaty was drafted in a closed and secretive manner', available at <https://www.aclu.org/seven-reasons-us-should-reject-international-cybercrime-treaty>.

[323] ibid, Reason No 1, 'The treaty lacks privacy and civil liberties protections'.

[324] Working Party, Opinion 4/2001 on the Council of Europe's Draft Convention on Cyber-crime (WP 41), 22 March 2001, Art 29, available at <http://ec.europa.eu/justice/data-protection/article-29/documentation/opinion-recommendation/files/2001/wp41_en.pdf>.

[325] Gercke, M, '10 years Convention on Cybercrime: Achievements and failures of the Council of Europe's instrument in the fight against Internet-related crimes', 12(5) *Computer Law Review International* 142 (2013).

[326] Ordinance of the Russian President, 'On signing the Convention on Cyber Crime', 15 November 2005. Note that the G8 'transborder access' principles adopted in October 1999 (see para 5.73 above) occurred during the last months of Boris Yeltsin's presidency of Russia.

[327] See Yong, P, 'New China criminal legislations in the progress of harmonization of criminal legislation againstcybercrime',December2011,availableat<https://rm.coe.int/CoERMPublicCommonSearchServices/DisplayDCTMContent?documentId=09000016803042f0>.

[328] Additional Protocol to the Convention on Cybercrime, concerning the criminalisation of acts of a racist and xenophobic nature committed through computer systems, ETS No 189, 28 January 2003 ('Additional Protocol').

[329] Explanatory Report to the Additional Protocol, para 4. Available at <https://rm.coe.int/CoERMPublicCommonSearchServices/DisplayDCTMContent?documentId=09000016800d37ae>.

[330] Additional Protocol, above, n 328, Art 10(1). As of 1 September 2006, there are seven ratifications.

any written material, any image or any other representation of ideas or theories, which advocates, promotes or incites hatred, discrimination or violence, against any individual or group of individuals, based on race, colour, descent or national or ethnic origin, as well as religion if used as a pretext for any of these factors.[331]

The offences include the dissemination of such material (Art 3); threats and insults motivated by racism or xenophobia (Arts 4 and 5); and the denial of genocide and crimes against humanity (Art 6).

The dissemination of such material, whether through active distribution or passive 'making available', is only an offence when made 'to the public', thereby protecting an individual's private communications and correspondence, as provided for under Art 8 of the ECHR.[332] The boundary between private and public communications will depend primarily on the subjective intent of the sender, although it would be for the tribunal of fact to determine in the circumstances of a case.[333] **5.139**

Owing to the complexities of legislating against such material, Member States have considerable autonomy not to adopt such measures, or parts of a measure, where, for example, issues of freedom of expression under Art 10 of the ECHR conflict.[334] Member States are obliged to extend the procedural elements of the Convention to the Protocol offences.[335] **5.140**

In terms of existing English law, the Public Order Act 1986 criminalizes acts intending to stir up racial and religious hatred, which includes threatening and insulting words, as well as displays.[336] These provisions would therefore seem generally to cover the offences detailed in Arts 3–5. Indeed, the offence in relation to religious hatred goes beyond that required under the Protocol, which is only concerned with religion to the extent that it is used as an alibi or substitute for the racism.[337] The Art 6 offence has no equivalence under English law; although prosecutions of ISPs under such laws in France and Germany were *causes célèbres* in terms of Internet regulation.[338] The Terrorism Act 2006 criminalizes the glorification of the commission of terrorist acts,[339] which clearly has similarities with the 'approval' of crimes against humanity. The UK Government has not yet signed the Protocol; the previous Government having stated that it will 'not ratify the protocol as it does not allow us to maintain our criminal threshold for this sort of offence'.[340] **5.141**

G8 initiatives

First established in 1975, the G8 comprises the leading industrialized nations.[341] While lacking the institutional structure of other intergovernmental bodies, its membership ensures that it has a significant influence on setting international policy agendas, such as **5.142**

---

[331] ibid, Art 2(1).
[332] Explanatory Report to the Additional Protocol, above, n 329, para 29.
[333] ibid, paras 30–1.
[334] Additional Protocol, above, n 328, Art 3(3).
[335] ibid, Art 8.
[336] Public Order Act 1986 (POA), ss 18–23 and s 29B–F respectively.
[337] Explanatory Report to the Additional Protocol, above, n 329, para 21.
[338] See generally para 2.241.
[339] TA 2006, s 1(3).
[340] Response by Vernon Coaker, then Parliamentary Under-Secretary of State (Home Office), HC Deb, 29 January 2008, c209W.
[341] ie the United States, France, Germany, Russia, the United Kingdom, Japan, Canada, and Italy.

debt relief for the least developed nations. In respect of computer and cybercrime, the G8 governments have adopted a number of declarations following the adoption of a set of ten principles and an Action Plan 'to combat High-tech Crime' in December 1997.[342]

5.143　The first principle lies at the heart of harmonization initiatives in the criminal field and that is to prevent the emergence of safe havens, where crimes could be carried out with potential impunity. In terms of substantive offences, only offences in respect of the confidentiality, integrity, and availability of data and systems are called for.[343] Most of the subsequent principles concern law enforcement capacity and cooperation. The potentially most controversial principle is the ninth: 'To the extent practicable, information and telecommunications systems should be designed to help prevent and detect network abuse, and should also facilitate the tracing of criminals and the collection of evidence.' While the first part could be interpreted simply as a call for better security measures, the second part could be seen as a call to alter the current manner in which the Internet and cyberspace operates to reduce the potential for anonymous activities, especially when considered in the light of point 7 of the Action Plan: 'Work jointly with industry to ensure that new technologies facilitate our effort to combat high-tech crime by preserving and collecting critical evidence.' This implies law enforcement involvement in the development of new technologies and the standards upon which they operate, which may be seen as meddling with existing open, dynamic, and private sector processes, embodied by entities such as the Internet Engineering Task Force.

5.144　At subsequent meetings, 'high-tech' crime has been a constant theme in G8 statements and recommendations, particularly at meetings of Justice and Interior Ministers. The G8 states have addressed a range of issues that relate directly or indirectly to the subject matter of this book and have resulted in various initiatives.

5.145　In 1999, the G8 adopted a set of principles 'on transborder access to stored data'. Following the events of 11 September 2001, the G8 Justice and Interior Ministers adopted a 'Recommendation on Transnational Crime', which addressed all three categories of cybercrime,[344] and in which all G8 members stated their intention to become parties to the Cybercrime Convention—which effectively means Russia, since the others are already signatories. In addition, they also put forward 'Recommendations for Tracing Networked Communications Across National Borders in Terrorist and Criminal Investigations', which called for governments to consider a range of measures including data retention on the grounds of 'public safety'.[345] At the Gleneagles meeting in 2005, tackling intellectual property rights (IPR) privacy and counterfeiting was addressed, with calls for steps to be taken to '[e]nhance detection and deterrence of the distribution and sale of counterfeit goods through the internet and combat online theft'.[346]

---

[342] Meeting of G8 Justice and Interior Ministers, Washington DC, 10 December 1997, available at <http://www.library.utoronto.ca/g7/adhoc/justice97.htm>.

[343] ibid, Principle IV.

[344] Available at <http://www.npa.go.jp/sosikihanzai/kokusaisousa/kokusai1/transg8rece.htm>. See in particular, Pt IV, Section D, 'Hi-Tech and Computer-Related Crimes'.

[345] Available at <http://www.coe.int/t/dg1/legalcooperation/economiccrime/cybercrime/Documents/Points%20of%20Contact/24%208%20Recommendations%20for%20Tracing%20Networked%20Communications%20Acros_en.pdf>.

[346] See G8 Declaration, 'Reducing IPR piracy and counterfeiting through more effective enforcement', July 2005, available at <https://www.eff.org/files/filenode/EFF_PK_v_USTR/foia-ustr-acta-response1-doc46.pdf>.

United Nations

The United Nations comprises a multitude of agencies, a number of which have an interest **5.146** in discrete issues addressed in this book. The International Telecommunications Union, for example, has promoted global standards in relation to lawful intercept capabilities for law enforcement access.[347] As a truly global intergovernmental institution, the perspective of UN agencies inevitably tends to encompass to a greater extent the needs of developing countries than the organizations discussed above.

One particular area of concern has been to assist developing countries to establish the cap- **5.147** acity and expertise to be able to deal effectively with computer crime issues. To support such initiatives, the UN published a first 'Manual on the prevention and control of computer-related crime' in 1994.[348]

In the area of child protection, the United Nations Children's Fund (UNICEF), with the **5.148** support of the Office of the High Commissioner for Human Rights, has taken a particular interest in child pornography, under its Convention on the Rights of the Child.[349] In 2000, an 'Optional Protocol to the Convention on the Rights of the Child on the sale of children, child prostitution and child pornography' was adopted, entering into force in January 2002,[350] which the UK ratified in 2009.[351] It defines 'child pornography' in the following terms: '… means any representation, by whatever means, of a child engaged in real or simulated explicit sexual activities or any representation of the sexual parts of a child for primarily sexual purposes'.[352] This formulation would seem broad enough to cover virtual images created without directly involving a child. The Protocol calls upon States to criminalize the '[p]roducing, distributing, disseminating, importing, exporting, offering, selling or possessing' of such material.[353]

Computer crime and cybercrime issues have been the subject of a number resolutions from **5.149** the United Nations General Assembly. The first in 1990, where the General Assembly endorsed the recommendations of the Eighth United Nations Congress on the Prevention of Crime and the Treatment of Offenders, which included a resolution on computer-related crimes.[354] In 2001, a second General Assembly resolution was adopted, 'Combating the criminal misuse of information technologies'.[355] The resolution made a series of general recommendations to Member States concerning the need to eliminate safe havens and to improve cooperation between national law enforcement agencies.

Computer-related crime was one of the topics considered during a workshop at the Eleventh **5.150** United Nations Congress on Crime Prevention and Criminal Justice, held in Bangkok in April 2005. At the meeting, it was reported that the UN is in the process of negotiating

---

[347] eg ITU Resolution 1115, Doc C97/135-E, 27 June 1997.
[348] United Nations, *International Review of Criminal Policy*, Nos 43 and 44, Sales No E.94.IV.5, 1994, available at <http://www.unodc.org/pdf/Manual_ComputerRelatedCrime.PDF>.
[349] Adopted by UN General Assembly Resolution 44/25, 20 November 1989.
[350] Adopted by UN General Assembly Resolution 54/263, 25 May 2000, available at <http://www.ohchr.org/EN/ProfessionalInterest/Pages/OPSCCRC.aspx>.
[351] Miscellaneous Series No 9 (2008), Cm 7490.
[352] ibid, Art 2(3).
[353] ibid, Art 3(1)(c).
[354] UN General Assembly Resolution 45/121, 14 December 1990.
[355] UN General Assembly Resolution 55/63, 22 January 2001.

a UN Convention of Cybercrime, both to build on the achievements of the Council of Europe's work, as well as address some of the criticisms it has faced 'regarding the effective protection of human rights, the protection of customer privacy and the high cost of cooperating with law enforcement investigators.'[356]

5.151   Over recent years, the two leading UN agencies in the area have been the United Nations Office on Drugs and Crime (UNODC), which has taken the lead on discussions about a potential Convention, and the International Telecommunication Union (ITU), which has focused on the cyber-security aspects of cybercrime. The UNODC has viewed cybercrime as a component of its work on transnational organized crime. Its work has primarily been concerned with capacity building,[357] international cooperation, awareness raising, and data collection.[358] It also established an 'Open-ended intergovernmental expert group' to examine the topic in 2011.[359] Despite discussions, no substantive progress has been made with regard to the drafting and adoption of an UN Convention on Cybercrime. The ITU's cyber-security work has included guidelines for industry on child online protection.[360]

Commonwealth

5.152   The Commonwealth 'Model Computer and Computer-related Crimes Bill' was recommended for use by Law Ministers in November 2002.[361] The instrument was drafted in reaction to the Council of Europe Cybercrime Convention, and closely follows its structure and content. However, the membership of the Commonwealth, comprising some fifty-three developed and developing nations, particularly African states, extends well beyond Europe and therefore represents an important harmonization initiative in the area.

5.153   Despite its title, the scope of the instrument in terms of substantive offences is primarily directed to computer-integrity offences, similar to the EU Framework Decision,[362] the exception being the issue of child pornography. The procedural law provisions encompass all forms of criminal investigation involving ICTs, which also interact with existing Commonwealth mutual legal assistance instruments, specifically the 'Harare scheme'.[363]

5.154   As discussed previously, the Model Law adopts a distinct phraseology, 'without lawful excuse or justification', for determining the criminality of the acts of access, interference, and interception. The offence of interference with data and systems differs from the other international instruments, but is similar to UK and US law, by including recklessness as a basis for liability, thereby potentially covering accidental damage caused by a hacker.

---

[356] Congress Discussion Guide, A/CONF.203/PM.1, 11 February 2005, para 190. See also Macan-Markar, M, 'Developing countries not immune from Cybercrime—UN', Inter Press Service, 25 April 2005, available at <http://www.ipsnews.net/2005/04/technology-developing-countries-not-immune-from-cyber-crime-un/>.

[357] eg UNODC, *Comprehensive Study on Cybercrime*, above, n 210.

[358] eg UNODC Cybercrime Repository, <https://www.unodc.org/cld/index-cybrepo.jspx>.

[359] See generally the Report of the Secretary-General on 'Promotion of activities relating to combating cybercrime, including technical assistance and capacity-building', E/CN.15/2013/24, 5 March 2013.

[360] See generally 'ITU Cybersecurity activities', available at <http://www.itu.int/en/action/cybersecurity/Pages/default.aspx>.

[361] Communiqué of the Law Ministers' meeting, Kingstown, St Vincent and the Grenadines, 18–21 November 2002, para 17.

[362] Commonwealth Model Law, above, n 203, Art 2.

[363] Scheme relating to Mutual Legal Assistance in Criminal Matters within the Commonwealth, as amended by Law Ministers in April 1990, November 2002, and October 2005.

Recklessness is also a basis for liability in respect of illegal devices, however, which would seem an inappropriate over-criminalization, although it would seem to be further qualified by the need for intention in respect of use.[364]

Most recently, the Secretariat has established and led the Commonwealth Cybercrime **5.155** Initiative (CCI), which brings together a consortium of Commonwealth organizations, other international organizations, law enforcement agencies, partner states, and private sector members to offer a range of capacity building assistance, from the establishment of legal frameworks to the technical expertise required of investigators and prosecutors.[365]

Other regional initiatives

There has been a range of regional initiatives on cybercrime, which share the objective of **5.156** harmonizing national rules in order to avoid data havens and to improve international cooperation in the investigation and prosecution of cybercrime. In December 2010, the League of Arab States adopted a 'Convention on Combating Information Technology Offences'.[366] In August 2011, the Council of Ministers of the Economic Community of West African States (ECOWAS) adopted a 'Directive on Fighting Cybercrime within ECOWAS'.[367] In November 2012, the Ministers responsible for Telecommunications, Postal, and ICT in the Southern African Development Community (SADC) endorsed a Model Law on Computer Crime and Cybercrime.[368] In June 2014, the African Union adopted a 'Convention on Cyber Security and Personal Data Protection'.[369] Each of these measures addresses both substantive and procedural law issues and substantially overlaps with the others. Differences designed to reflect the particular cultural traditions and needs of the member states tend to be relatively minor, although drafting differences have the potential to generate new areas of legal uncertainty and potential disharmony.

Computer and cybercrime issues may not figure high on the reform agenda of develop- **5.157** ing nations, but coupled with broader ICT law reform initiatives, to facilitate electronic commerce, such as the African Union Convention, and similar initiatives taking place in important regional trading partners, such issues are receiving increasing attention.

European Union

The UK's membership of the European Union means that policies, initiatives, and meas- **5.158** ures originating from the European institutions, related directly or indirectly to the subject matter of this book, are important to our understanding of domestic criminal law and policy. As greater European integration has been sought and achieved, so the areas of overlap

---

[364] Commonwealth Model Law, above, n 203, Art 9(1).

[365] CCI Operating Framework, available at Annex B to the Report of the Commonwealth Working Group of Experts on Cybercrime, LLM(14)14, available at <http://thecommonwealth.org/sites/default/files/news-items/documents/Report_of_the_Commonwealth_Working_Group_of_Experts_on_Cybercrime_May_2014.pdf>.

[366] Done at Cairo, the Arab Republic of Egypt, 12 December 2012.

[367] C/DIR 1/08/11.

[368] Similar model law initiatives, jointly funded by the International Telecommunications Union and the European Commission, have been developed in the Caribbean (HIPCAR) and the Pacific Island countries (ICB4PAC).

[369] EX.CL/846(XXV). Adopted by the Twenty-third Ordinary Session of the Assembly of the Union, Malabo, 27 June 2014. The African Union comprises 54 African states, with only Morocco not being a member.

have extended, encompassing substantive offences, penalties, procedural mechanisms, and inter-Member State institutional arrangements. This section reviews each of these areas in turn. First, however, the question of EU competence in matters of criminal policy must be briefly considered.[370]

Matters of competence

5.159　Most aspects of criminal law and procedure were originally outside the competence of the Community institutions under the Treaty establishing the European Community (EC Treaty), generally referred to as the 'first pillar'.[371] Instead, such issues lay within the sphere of competence of the Member States, under the 'third pillar', Title VI of the Treaty on European Union (TEU), in the context of providing EU citizens with 'a high level of safety within an area of freedom, security and justice'.[372] In some cases, however, complementary measures were adopted under both pillars, which has created its own problems.[373]

5.160　With the coming into force of the Lisbon Treaty in 2009, the EU institutions were granted two key competences in the field of criminal law, as detailed in TFEU:

Article 83(1)—The Council and Parliament can adopt directives establishing minimum rules on defining criminal offences and applicable sanctions for 'serious crime with a cross-border dimension', which specifically includes computer crimes.

Article 83(2)—Where approximation of criminal laws is essential to ensure effective implementation of a EU policy already subject to harmonizing measures.[374]

For our purposes, the primary implications of these new competences have been as follows: (a) a need to change the legal basis for earlier measures, which has itself given rise to an opportunity to reconsider, recast, and extend the rules; (b) other proposed measures have become unblocked as the process shifted from one requiring unanimity among the Member State governments to the 'ordinary legislative procedure';[375] and (c) the nature of the obligations placed upon Member States in terms of requiring them to amend domestic criminal law.

5.161　As well as fundamentally altering EU competence in the field of criminal law, the changes to the legal framework resulting from the Lisbon Treaty have also had very particular implications for the UK, resulting from two opt-out procedures the framework included as part of the Lisbon settlement. For pre-Lisbon EU measures concerning policing and criminal law, the UK was able to 'block' opt-out of all 130 measures, which it did in July 2013, and then opt back in to some 35 of the measures.[376] For post-Lisbon measures, the UK can decide on a case-by-case basis, within three months of a proposal being presented, whether

---

[370] For a more comprehensive treatment, see Summers, S et al, *The Emergence of EU Criminal Law: Cyber crime and the regulation of the Information Society*, Hart Publishing, 2014.

[371] See Case 203/80 *Casati* [1981] ECR 2595 and Case C-226/97 *Lemmens* [1998] ECR I-3711.

[372] TEU, Art 29.

[373] See generally White, S, 'Harmonisation of criminal law under the first pillar', 31 *European Law Review* 81 (2006).

[374] See Communication from the Commission, 'Towards an EU Criminal Policy: Ensuring the effective implementation of EU policies through criminal law', COM(2011) 573 final, 20 September 2011.

[375] TFEU, Arts 289(1) and 294, ie co-decision making between the Council and Parliament and no Member State vetoes in Council.

[376] TEU, Protocol 36, Title VII, Art 10(4) and (5), OJ C 326/322, 26 October 2012. See also HM Government, *Decision pursuant to Article 10 of Protocol 36 to The Treaty on the Functioning of the European Union*, Cm 8671, July 2013.

to opt in to the adoption and application of the measure. Once it has opted in, it cannot later decide to opt out.[377] While these opt-out/opt-in procedures distinguish the UK from the vast majority of the other Member States, to date they have not had much impact in the areas of substantive and procedural law of concern in this book, since there is considerable commonality of interests in tackling cybercrime.

From an organizational perspective, competence for criminal matters generally falls **5.162** to be considered by the European Council's 'Justice and Home Affairs' ministers,[378] the European Parliament's Committee on Civil Liberties, Justice and Home Affairs,[379] and the 'Justice' Directorate-General of the European Commission.[380] Reflecting the position in the UK, the Commission places issues of cybercrime within the topic of organized crime.

It must also be borne in mind that over the past ten years, the Community has adopted a **5.163** broad range of measures addressed at various aspects of the Internet, especially electronic commerce activities, many of which have an indirect impact on computer and cybercrime. Legal instruments in fields such as copyright,[381] 'electronic identification and trust services',[382] export control,[383] and data protection, contain regulatory measures designed to strengthen the rights of persons and enhance security and trust in cyberspace. In addition, the Commission has funded research activities on a range of topics related to cybercrime, addressing issues of substantive and procedural law, as well as technical issues.[384] These matters have generally fallen under the competence of the Directorate-Generals of the European Commission for Internal Market and Communications Networks, Content and Technology, but are generally beyond the scope of this book.

Substantive offences

In May 1997, the Justice and Home Affairs Council requested that the Commission fund **5.164** a study on computer crime, which was presented to the Council in April 1998.[385] On the basis of this study, the Commission adopted a Communication on network security and computer crime that included proposals for legislative measures in the area addressing both substantive and procedural issues.[386] While recognizing the work being carried out by the Council of Europe, including the adoption of a common position during the negotiations

---

[377] TFEU, Protocol 21, OJ C 326/295, 26 October 2012.

[378] <http://www.consilium.europa.eu/en/council-eu/configurations/jha/>.

[379] <http://www.europarl.europa.eu/committees/libe_home_en.htm>.

[380] <http://ec.europa.eu/justice_home/index_en.htm>.

[381] Directive 2001/29/EC on the harmonisation of certain aspects of copyright and related rights in the information society, OJ L 167/10, 22 June 2001.

[382] Regulation 910/2014 on electronic identification and trust services for electronic transactions in the internal market and repealing Directive 1999/93/EC, OJ L 257/73, 28 August 2014.

[383] Council Regulation (EC) No 428/2009 setting up a Community regime for the control of exports, transfer, brokering and transit of dual-use items, OJ L 134/1, 29 May 2009.

[384] eg Cyber Tools On-Line Search for Evidence (CTOSE), available at <http://cordis.europa.eu/project/rcn/60288_en.html>.

[385] European Commission, 'Legal Aspects of Computer-Related Crime in the Information Society' ('COMCRIME Study'), 1 January 1998, available at <http://www.oas.org/juridico/english/COMCRIME%20Study.pdf>.

[386] Communication from the European Commission to the Council and the European Parliament, 'Creating a Safer Information Society by Improving the Security of Information Infrastructures and Combating Computer-related Crime', COM(2000) 890 final ('2000 Communication'), s 7.1.

on the Convention,[387] the perceived advantages for the Commission of legislative activity at an EU level are the ability to 'go further' than the approximation achieved by the Convention, as well as adopt a binding instrument within a shorter period of time, with the added force of EU enforcement mechanisms.[388] The Commission was also keen to establish a forum for all interested stakeholders to share knowledge and experience, as well as raise public awareness of the risks.[389]

5.165 The EU has adopted a range of legislative measures covering activities within the three categories of offences discussed in Chapter 3: computer-related, content-related, and computer-integrity. The following briefly reviews these measures, focusing in particular on financial fraud, child protection issues, and the protection of information systems. It should also be noted that each issue originates within a different aspect of EU policy.

5.166 *Fraud.* Computer-related fraud falls squarely in with other measures addressing organized crime, money laundering, and proceeds from crime. In May 2001, the Council adopted a Framework Decision on fraud,[390] which includes a provision expressly addressing computer-related fraud, as one form of behaviour involved in such fraud:

> Each Member State shall take the necessary measures to ensure that the following conduct is a criminal offence when committed intentionally:
>
> performing or causing a transfer of money or monetary value and thereby causing an unauthorised loss of property for another person, with the intention of procuring an unauthorised economic benefit for the person committing the offence or for a third party, by:
>
> — without right introducing, altering, deleting or suppressing computer data, in particular identification data, or
>
> — without right interfering with the functioning of a computer programme or system.[391]

The wording is similar to the Convention provision, although it had not then been finalized, and therefore the provision was based on Council of Europe Recommendation No R (89) 9.[392]

The provision distinguishes input and output frauds that focus on the manipulation of accounting data itself, from changes made to the applications data, in the form of software or programs that process accounting data.

5.167 Member States were obliged to transpose the provisions of the Decision by 2 June 2003,[393] although no Member States had notified the Commission of their relevant measures by that date,[394] an indication both of the procedural weakness of so-called 'third

---

[387] Common Position of 27 May 1999 adopted by the Council on the basis of Art 34 of the Treaty on European Union, on negotiations relating to the Draft Convention on Cyber Crime held in the Council of Europe, OJ L 142/1, 5 June 1999 .

[388] ibid, at 17. This last assertion was in contradiction with the adoption of framework decisions, for which no EU enforcement mechanism existed.

[389] A provisional website was established, but has since disappeared.

[390] Fraud Decision, above, n 62.

[391] ibid, Art 3, 'Offences related to computers'.

[392] Recommendation No. R (89) 9 of the Committee of Ministers to Member States on Computer-related Crime, at 37–8, available <https://wcd.coe.int/com.instranet.InstraServlet?command=com.instranet.CmdBlobGet&InstranetImage=610660&SecMode=1&DocId=702280&Usage=2>.

[393] Fraud Decision, above, n 62, Art 14.

[394] Report from the Commission based on Art 14 of the Council Framework Decision of 28 May 2001 combating fraud and counterfeiting of non-case means of payment {SEC(2004) 532}, COM/2004/0346 final, s 1.1.2 ('First Art 14 Report').

pillar' instruments,[395] as well as their perception by Member States. By April 2004, the Commission was able to report that seven Member States had indicated compliance with the Art 3 provision, either because their existing law was broadly conceived (eg Spain and Germany) or national provisions had been appropriately amended (eg France, Finland, and Ireland).[396] In its Second Report, the Commission was able to report that an additional eleven Member States had indicated compliance with the provision. Of these, Portugal, Sweden, and Slovakia had addressed such acts through computer crime provisions, rather than general fraud law.[397]

Interestingly, the UK was one of those indicating compliance, despite the recognized **5.168** problems with frauds involving the deception of a machine, which has subsequently been addressed in the Fraud Act 2006. The only express amendment made under English law to transpose the terms of the Decision into national law was in respect of the Forgery and Counterfeiting Act 1981.[398] The Act criminalizes the use of any instrument in a forgery or fraud, but only criminalizes possession of a specific list of instruments.[399] This list required amendment to include all of those instruments referred to in the Decision, such as debit cards.

Child protection. As noted in Chapter 3, the Internet is seen as raising a wide range of issues **5.169** for child safety and protection, which can be broadly distinguished into concerns about the content available to children over the Internet, and concerns about the use of the Internet to abuse children, specifically child pornography. Both aspects have been the subject of initiatives at a EU level and were highlighted in a 1996 Commission Communication 'on illegal and harmful content on the Internet',[400] which was endorsed by the Parliament and Council.[401]

A Council Framework Decision specifically addressing the issue of child pornography on **5.170** the Internet was adopted in 2000.[402] This first instrument required Member States to take measures to encourage and enable Internet users to report suspected child pornographic images, through hotlines such as that operated by the Internet Watch Foundation,[403] as well as promoting the effective investigation and prosecution of perpetrators, at both a national level and through greater Member State cooperation.[404] The need for law enforcement to work with industry is recognized; while Member States are called upon to consider measures that would place 'Internet providers under a duty' to assist law enforcement,

---

[395] ie enforcement proceedings could not be taken by the European Commission.

[396] First Art 14 Report, above, n 394 s 2.2.3.

[397] Second report from the Commission based on Art 14 of the Council Framework Decision of 28 May 2001 combating fraud and counterfeiting of non-case means of payment {SEC(2006) 188}, COM/2006/ 65 final, s 2.3.

[398] The amendment was made under the Crime (International Co-operation) Act 2003, s 88.

[399] Forgery and Counterfeiting Act 1981 (FCA), at 5(5).

[400] COM(1996) 487, Brussels, 16 October 1996.

[401] Parliamentary Resolution ... on intermodality and intermodal freight transport in the European Union, OJ C 150/38, 19 May 1997 and Council Resolution on a Model Agreement for setting up a Joint Investigation Team, OJ C 70/1, 6 March 1997.

[402] Council Decision 2000/375/JHA to combat child pornography on the Internet, OJ L 138/1, 9 June 2000.

[403] ibid, Art 1(1).

[404] ibid, Art 2.

through the establishment of notice and take-down procedures, the retention of traffic data, and related actions.[405]

5.171 Child pornography has been the subject of further, more prescriptive measures, harmonizing Member State substantive law.[406] Child pornography is conceived broadly to include 'realistic images of a child', which differentiates the position in Europe from that in the US.[407] However, Member States are given the option of excluding the production and possession of 'realistic images' from criminal liability where it is solely for the person's private use and it involves no risk of dissemination,[408] where presumably the harm is considered to be *de minimis*. The Directive requires Member States to criminalize acts of sexual abuse, the sexual exploitation of children, child pornography and solicitation of children for sexual purposes (ie 'grooming').[409]

5.172 In respect of child pornography, five types of conduct may comprise the offence: (a) production; (b) 'distribution, dissemination and transmission'; (c) 'offering, supplying and making available'; (d) 'acquisition or possession'; and (e) 'knowingly obtaining access'.[410] By grouping acquisition with possession, the Decision potentially avoids a blur between the acts of production and possession that exists under English law due to the process of downloading being equated to the offence of 'making'. In terms of sanction, the offences should attract terms from between one and three years. In a previous measure, maximum prison terms of up to ten years were mandated in certain 'aggravating circumstances', such as where the activity takes place in the context of a criminal organization.[411]

5.173 As well as criminalizing conduct, the Directive also contains a range of measures designed to protect children. Those convicted should be prevented from 'exercising at least professional activities involving direct and regular contact with children'.[412] Professionals working with children should be able to report suspicions without breaching their confidentiality obligations.[413] Victims should also be given all necessary 'assistance, support and protection', including in the course of the investigation and any subsequent criminal proceedings.[414]

5.174 In terms of prevention, the Directive requires Member States to take a range of measures, including the removal of material and the blocking of websites. In terms of the former, a removal scheme is mandated for material hosted in the jurisdiction, while efforts should also be taken against foreign material.[415] With regard to the more controversial issue of blocking, Member States *may* take measures, and only if subject to 'transparent procedures and adequate safeguards'.[416] Both measures take place in the UK, through the work of the

---

[405] ibid, Art 3.

[406] Directive 2011/92/EU on combating the sexual abuse and sexual exploitation of children and child pornography, and replacing Council Framework Decision 2004/68/JHA, OJ L 335/1, 17 December 2011.

[407] ibid, Art 1(c)(iv). See para 3.168.

[408] Directive 2011/92/EU, above, n 406, Art 5(8).

[409] ibid, Arts 3–6.

[410] ibid, Art 5(2)–(6).

[411] Council Framework Decision 2004/68/JHA on combating the sexual exploitation of children and child pornography, OJ L 13/44, 20 January 2004, Art 5(2).

[412] ibid, Art 10.

[413] ibid, Art 16.

[414] ibid, Arts 18–20.

[415] ibid, Art 25(1).

[416] ibid, Art 25(2). See European Parliament, 'Child pornography: MEPs doubt effectiveness of blocking web access', Press Release, 15 November 2010. See also Demeyer, K, Lievens, E, and Dumortier, J, 'Blocking

Internet Watch Foundation (IWF), an industry-funded body operating largely without a specific regulatory framework, although subjecting itself to a range of accountability measures designed to ensure transparency and provide safeguards.[417]

Attacks against information systems. In the area of computer-integrity offences, a first meas- **5.175**
ure was adopted in 2005: Council Framework Decision 2005/222/JHA of 24 February on attacks against information systems.[418] This was repealed and replaced by a Directive in 2013.[419] Member States had an obligation to transpose it into national law by 4 September 2015.[420] While UK law was largely already compliant with the terms of the Framework Decision 2005, amendments were made to the Computer Misuse Act 1990,[421] Likewise, with the Integrity Directive, the UK choose to opt-in to the measure[422] and has again amended the 1990 Act.[423]

The Integrity Directive criminalizes five distinct acts: illegal access, illegal system inter- **5.176**
ference, illegal data interference, illegal interception, and tools used for committing offences.[424] The generic issues concerning such integrity offences and the specific provisions are examined in detail in Chapter 3; however, certain features of the Integrity Directive are worthy of further consideration.

In contrast to the UK, a distinction is made between a system and the data it processes, both **5.177**
of which are covered by the s 3 offence under the Computer Misuse Act 1990. While such a distinction is not inherently problematic for UK law, the issue of defining 'systems' and 'data' does raise broader concerns in respect of their use within the Integrity Directive's concept of 'without right': 'means conduct referred to in this Directive, including access, interference, or interception, which is not authorised by the owner or by another right holder of the system or of part of it, or not permitted under national law'.[425]

Such a broad formulation raises questions about where the boundary exists between the system and the data, whether in the form of programs or other forms of software component, which reside on the system. To the extent that the concept grants rights of control to those attached to the system, rather than the data, difficult decisions may have to be made by a court as to which camp a component falls.

Under the Integrity Directive, an offence would also be committed where such access or **5.178**
interference is not 'permitted under national law', whether such access is authorized or not. This seems a problematic formulation. In what circumstances is it appropriate to impose criminal liability for access or interference in the absence of any form of authorization control exercised by the system owner? While it may be perfectly appropriate to grant criminal

---

and Removing Illegal Child Sexual Content: Analysis from a Technical and Legal Perspective', 4 *Policy & Internet* 1 (2012).

[417] The IWF established a national notice and take-down system in December 2006, while an international version was launched in January 2013. Blocking or filtering access to URLs was commenced in 2004. See further para 2.277 and IWF website, at <http://www.iwf.org.uk>.
[418] Framework Decision 2005, above, n 68.
[419] Integrity Directive, above, n 64.
[420] ibid, Art 16.
[421] Explanatory Note to the Police and Justice Act 2006, para 297.
[422] Official Report, House of Commons, Cols 1051–8. See further para 4.161.
[423] Explanatory Note to the Serious Crimes Act 2015, para 128.
[424] Integrity Directive, above, n 64, Arts 3–7
[425] ibid, Art 1(d).

law protection for certain types of system, such as critical infrastructure, or data, such as official secrets or personal data, these are subject to separate treatment and should not need the protection of computer-integrity offences.

5.179 Under the Computer Misuse Act 1990 (CMA), commission of the s 1 offence involves the *actus reus* to 'cause a computer to perform any function'. As with the Convention, the Framework Decision permitted Member States to require a second *actus reus* of 'infringing a security measure'.[426] One reason advanced for such a provision was to ensure that those that owned the systems and the data implemented some form of protection, in order to benefit from the protection of criminal law. Only seven of the twenty Member States to which the Framework Decision was applicable chose to adopt this option.[427] Under the Integrity Directive, the option has now become part of the harmonized offence;[428] meaning that 'infringing a security measure' should be a threshold fact to be determined by a court. The European Parliament introduced this amendment, although no reasoning is given.[429] When amending UK law, the Government did not address this through its amendments to the Computer Misuse Act 1990, which potentially renders it non-complaint.

5.180 Article 4 requires Member States to criminalize interference with an intention to cause 'serious hindering or interruption'. The word 'serious' is not defined, so it is left to Member States to determine any criteria. Such a threshold is not present in the s 3 offence of unauthorized acts, where the prosecution is not required to show any intention in respect of the 'seriousness' of the damage, although it would generally be relevant at sentencing.[430] However, in 2015, the Government decided to introduce a new offence into the 1990 Act of 'unauthorised acts causing, or creating a risk of, serious damage'.[431] In setting a threshold, EU law takes the same approach as the Cybercrime Convention[432] and a similar approach to the US Computer Fraud and Abuse Act, which details a range of threshold outcomes that must be present when damage is caused, from an aggregate monetary loss of \$5,000 to some threat to public safety.[433] In contrast to UK and US law, however, recklessness does not constitute a basis for liability. The provision also ends with a qualification from the obligation to legislate 'for cases which are not minor', which is also present in the other offences. While a *de minimis* threshold has a certain appeal for the other offences and is designed to exclude 'cases that would *in abstracto* be covered by the basic definition, but are considered not to harm the protected legal interest',[434] it makes little sense where there is a second threshold of 'seriousness', since the concept of an intentionally serious interference that is minor seems nonsense, even if the distinction being made is one between the interference the perpetrator intends to carry out and that which was actually achieved.

---

[426] Convention on Cybercrime, Art 2.

[427] Report from the Commission to the Council, based on Article 12 of the Framework Decision, COM(2008) final, 14 July 2008, at 4. Those countries were Austria, Finland, Germany, Hungary, Italy, Latvia, and Lithuania.

[428] Integrity Directive, above, n 64, Art 3.

[429] Position of the European Parliament adopted at first reading on 4 July 2013, P7_TC1-COD(2010)0273. See also Chapter 3, n. 584.

[430] However, 'serious' interference is the standard required for it to comprise an act of terrorism (Terrorism Act 2000, s 1(2)(e)). See paras 3.295–3.296.

[431] CMA, s 3ZA. See further para 3.304.

[432] Article 4(2) refers to 'serious harm' as an option for data interference, while for system interference (Art 5), 'serious hindering' is the mandated threshold.

[433] 18 USC s 1030(a)(5)(B).

[434] Commission proposal for the Integrity Directive, COM(2010) 517 final, 30 September 2010, at 7.

The most significant innovation of the Framework Decision and the Integrity Directive **5.181**
over that of the Convention is in respect of the harmonization of penalties. The Convention
simply requires Member States to implement 'effective, proportional and dissuasive criminal sanctions'.[435] The Integrity Directive imposes a sliding scale of minimum tariffs:

- Two years in respect of all the offences;[436]
- A tariff of at least three years for data or system interference 'where a significant num-
  ber of information systems have been affected through the use of a tool, referred to in
  Article 7';[437]
- The highest tariff of at least five years, where they are committed in context of organized
  crime, cause 'serious damage' or target a 'critical infrastructure information system'.[438]

In the UK, certain forms of 'serious damage' were already be covered by the Terrorism Act **5.182**
2000, which classifies as terrorist acts actions 'designed seriously to interfere with or seriously disrupt an electronic system'.[439] In the UK, the 2015 amendments to the 1990 Act
raised the maximum tariff to life imprisonment where serious damage is caused to 'human
welfare' or national security through an unauthorized act in relation to a computer.[440] The
tariff for the Computer Misuse Act s 1 basic offence of 'unauthorised access' was raised from
six months to two years in 2006.

Under the Integrity Directive, provisions address the liability of legal persons, identical to **5.183**
those contained in the EU measures on fraud and child pornography.[441] These provisions
are designed, in part, to address organized crime as a common thread behind all such
activities. The liability of legal persons, such as corporations, under criminal law must be
distinguished into, first, those situations where the legal person is held directly liable for the
commission of an offence, either as the principal or jointly with a natural person; and second, situations where liability attaches on the basis that the legal person is liable for the acts
and omissions of its employees, generally referred to as 'vicarious liability'.

The Integrity Directive addresses both categories of liability. A legal person may be held **5.184**
liable, under criminal or civil law, where the illegal access or interference was for the benefit of any person who had a 'leading position within the legal person', ie where the person
has the power to represent the legal person, or the authority to take decisions on behalf of
the legal person or exercise control.[442] It is interesting to note that the use of the concept of
authorization in this context is much closer to the UK use of the term under the Computer
Misuse Act than it is in relation to the offences themselves, where authorization is linked
to ownership and right holder, rather than control. Liability may also arise where a 'lack
of supervision or control' by the legal person has made possible the commission of the
offences, which would seem implicit in the concept of vicarious liability.[443]

---

[435] Convention on Cybercrime, Art 13.
[436] Integrity Directive, above, n 64, Art 9(2).
[437] ibid, Art 9(3).
[438] ibid, Art 9(4).
[439] Terrorism Act 2000, s 1(2)(e).
[440] CMA, s 3ZA(7).
[441] Integrity Directive, above, n 64, Arts 10 and 11.
[442] ibid, Art 10(1).
[443] ibid, Art 10(2).

5.185   *Other initiatives.* The other area of substantive criminal law in the computer crime field where EU measures have been pursued are in respect of content-related crimes. There have been proposals on criminal measures for use in the enforcement of intellectual property rights, which were designed to complement an instrument on enforcement through civil proceedings.[444] The Commission justified the need for EU-scale harmonization of criminal law in this field on a number of grounds, including the proper functioning of the Internal Market; the threat posed by such activities to consumers and national economies; as well as the increasing involvement of organized crime.[445] The proposal generated significant controversy and was eventually withdrawn in 2010.[446]

5.186   As part of its broader policy initiative in the area of illegal and harmful content, referred to above in respect of child abuse images, a Commission Communication in 2000 suggested the need for action in the area of racism and xenophobia,[447] similar to the Council of Europe's Additional Protocol. A proposal was published in 2002 and adopted in 2008.[448] In contrast to the Protocol, it does not distinguish activities that occur over the Internet, based on the principle that 'what is illegal offline remains illegal online', otherwise referred to as technology neutrality.

5.187   In July 2013, the UK Government decided to exercise its opt-out in respect of the 2008 Decision.[449] Strangely, however, as part of its mitigation for this decision it states that the UK is a signatory to the Additional Protocol, which it is clearly not![450] Another stated concern with the measure is the possibility that by being party to it, the UK would then be subject to Court of Justice rulings on the 2008 Decision, which could result in the need to establish new offences, such as 'Holocaust denial'.[451]

5.188   Post-Lisbon, the EU has become an important source of harmonization for substantive criminal law. The qualitative nature of EU measures can be distinguished from other regional and international harmonization instruments in two key areas. First, the extent to which Member States are given options to legislate are minimized, thereby reducing the scope for variation and enhancing harmonization. Second, the ability to mandate minimum penalties further advances the depth of harmonization between Member States. For the UK, however, the position is less clear due to its ability to opt out and opt in to measures, which generates its own disruption to harmonization.

Procedural matters

5.189   In the area of procedural law, while the Commission has noted that '[m]ore than in any other transnational crime, the speed, mobility and flexibility of computer crime challenge

---

[444] Proposal for a European Parliament and Council Directive on criminal measures aimed at ensuring the enforcement of intellectual property rights, COM(2005)276 final, 12 July 2005. See further para 3.125.

[445] Proposal for Directive on criminal measures, above, n 444, at 2.

[446] OJ C 252/7, 18 September 2010.

[447] 2000 Communication, above, n 386, at 17.

[448] Council Framework Decision 2008/913/JHA of 28 November 2008 on combating certain forms and expressions of racism and xenophobia by means of criminal law, OJ L 328/55, 6 December 2008 ('2008 Decision').

[449] HM Government, *Decision pursuant to Article 10 of Protocol 36 to The Treaty on the Functioning of the European Union*, Cm 8671, July 2013, paras 192–204.

[450] ibid, para 198.

[451] See HM Government, 'Response to the House of Lords EU Committee Inquiry on the UK's 2014 opt-out decision', 6 January 2014, at 8–9.

the existing rules of criminal procedural law',[452] any measure is clearly potentially applicable against all types of crime, including drugs, organized crime, and terrorism. In addition to those measures discussed earlier in this chapter, the EAW, EEW, and EIO, the Community has adopted or proposed other measures addressing police and judicial cooperation which are designed to enhance law enforcement agency cooperation and therefore more effective enforcement throughout the Union.

With regard to obtaining data 'in transmission', an early procedural initiative was a Council **5.190** resolution aimed at coordinating Member State requirements for lawful intercept capability, adopted in 1995.[453] The Resolution recognized that telecommunications liberalization and the development of the Internet had challenged traditional interception rules. It detailed a list of requirements considered necessary by the law enforcement community, including access to communications data, so called 'call associated data'.[454] The initiative does not, however, address concerns that diverse reactions to the changing environment by Member States may lead to distortions of the Single Market.

In terms of lawful intercept, substantial harmonization has taken place within European **5.191** industry at the standards level, under the auspices of the European Telecommunications Standardisation Institute.[455] In addition, legal initiatives have addressed cross-border cooperation, under the EU Convention on Mutual Assistance provisions,[456] as well as rules protecting an individual's communications privacy.[457] However, since the 1995 Resolution, no harmonization measure of a more binding nature has been adopted at Community level addressing the nature of the obligations placed by the state on communication service providers. As a consequence, we have indeed seen Member States adopt divergent approaches on a range of issues, from 'intercept capability' to the treatment of costs,[458] which undermines the concept of a Single Market for the European communications market.

To improve access to data 'at rest' in the course of an investigation, the Commission pub- **5.192** lished a proposal for a Council Framework Decision 'on the exchange of information under the principle of availability'.[459] The measure was designed to complement and supplement existing and future MLA procedures, such as the EEW, by making certain types of information available to a police force or other agency from another Member State ('requesting authority') when that information is already available to an 'equivalent'[460] competent authority in the source Member State ('source authority'). Under the proposal, a source authority would not have had an obligation to 'collect or store' information for the sole

---

[452] 2000 Communication, above, n 386, at 18.
[453] Council Resolution of 17 January 1995 on the lawful interception of telecommunications, OJ C 329/1, 4 November 1996.
[454] ibid, Annex.
[455] eg the ETSI standards for 'lawful intercept', available at <http://www.etsi.org/technologies-clusters/technologies/security/lawful-interception>.
[456] See paras 5.54–5.57.
[457] Directive 2002/58/EC of the European Parliament and of the Council concerning the processing of personal data and the protection of privacy in the electronic communications sector, OJ L 201/37, 31 July 2002, Art 5.
[458] See paras 4.152–4.156.
[459] Proposal for a Council Framework Decision on the exchange of information under the principle of availability, COM(2005) 490 final, 12 October 2005 ('Availability Proposal').
[460] ibid, Art 3(c).

purpose of supplying to a requesting authority,[461] but it would be required to provide access to designated types of information that are already available. Such access would either be through direct online access, 'without intervention of another authority or party',[462] or upon individual request. The proposal was highly controversial and was subsequently withdrawn with the coming into force of the Lisbon Treaty.[463]

5.193 The EIO enters into force on 22 May 2017 and will replace the European conventions on mutual assistance, of 1959 and 2000, as well as the 2003 Decision on the freezing of evidence and the EEW.[464] As with the EU's substantive law measures, the position of the UK with respect to these various procedural instruments is complicated both by the UK's opt-out and opt-in capabilities, as well as more prosaic political positioning around the issue of the UK's continued membership of the EU. The EAW, for example, was one of the measures that the UK Government decided it would opt back into, following the wholesale opt-out in July 2013. This was achieved, in the face of some opposition, prior to the 1 December 2014 deadline.[465] With regard to the EIO, the UK Government decided to opt-in in July 2010.

5.194 To address the obvious concerns about the potential abuse of such broad access rights for law enforcement agencies, the EU adopted a measure 'on the protection of personal data processed in the framework of police and judicial cooperation in criminal matters'.[466] This is also currently undergoing reform, with a proposal for a Directive.[467]

5.195 Other procedural measures have been in reaction to initiatives taken within other fora, such as the G8. In 2001, for example, the Council recommended that Member States that had not yet joined the G8 network of twenty-four-hour contact points should do so.[468]

5.196 Procedural law measures are considered likely to engage issues of human rights and the fundamental freedoms guaranteed by Community law. In *Bickel*, for example, the Court of Justice noted that although criminal procedure was generally a matter for Member States, such provisions must operate within Community law and, therefore, 'may not discriminate against persons to whom Community law gives the right to equal treatment or restrict the fundamental freedoms guaranteed by Community law'.[469]

---

[461] ibid, Art 2(2). While not under an obligation, the source authority can choose to cooperate with the requesting authority and obtain requested information using its domestic powers. See Home Office consultation, 'Acquisition and disclosure of communications data' (June 2006), para 7.14.

[462] Availability Proposal, above, n 459, Art 3(f).

[463] Commission Communication, 'Consequences of the entry into force of the Treaty of Lisbon for ongoing interinstitutional decision-making procedures', COM(2009) 665 final, 2 December 2009, Annex 2.

[464] EIO, above, n 123, Art 34.

[465] See Commission Decision 2014/858/EU, OJ L 345/6, 1 December 2014, and The Criminal Justice and Data Protection (Protocol No 36) Regulations 2014, SI No 3141.

[466] Council Framework Decision 2008/977/JHA of 27 November 2008 on the protection of personal data processed in the framework of police and judicial cooperation in criminal matters, OJ L 350/60, 30 December 2008.

[467] Proposal for a Directive on the protection of individuals with regard to the processing of personal data by competent authorities for the purposes of prevention, investigation, detection or prosecution of criminal offences or the execution of criminal penalties, and the free movement of such data, COM(2012) 10 final, 25 January 2012.

[468] Council Recommendation of 25 June 2001 on contact points maintaining a 24-hour service for combating high-tech crime, OJ C 187/5, 3 July 2001.

[469] Case C-274/96 *Bickel and Franz* [1998] ECR I-7637, para 17. See also Case C-186/87 *Cowan* [1989] ECR 195, para 19.

Institutional developments

Complementing the procedural initiatives, various developments have taken place designed **5.197**
to improve the institutional arrangements between the Member States. Such activities
combine two distinct approaches: the establishment of new mechanisms for joint working
between national authorities and the establishment of European institutions designed to
supplement the activities at a Member State level. The latter is obviously a unique feature of
European Union law that goes beyond traditional intergovernmental instruments.

In terms of improving Member State cooperation against cross-border crime, the 2000 **5.198**
Convention on Mutual Assistance provides for the establishment of 'Joint Investigation
Teams' (JITs),[470] comprising law enforcement officials from two or more jurisdictions.
However, due to the delay in the Convention entering into force through Member
State ratifications, JITs were initially also governed by a framework decision.[471] Under
English law, the concept of an 'international joint investigation team' is defined in the
following terms:

any investigation team formed in accordance with—
(a) any framework decision on joint investigation teams adopted under Article 87 of the
    Treaty on the Functioning of the European Union;
(b) the Convention on Mutual Assistance in Criminal Matters between the Member States
    of the European Union, and the Protocol to that Convention, established in accordance
    with that Article of that Treaty; or
(c) any international agreement to which the United Kingdom is a party and which is speci-
    fied for the purposes of this section in an order made by the Secretary of State.[472]

Such JITs may be established where the investigation involves 'difficult or demanding
investigations' or the nature of the case requires 'coordinated, concerted action',[473] which
clearly may be applicable to computer and cybercrime investigations. Under such arrangements,[474] a law enforcement agent will be seconded to an authority in another Member
State and may be present when an investigative measure is carried out and carry out certain
investigative tasks.[475] These procedures can be seen as complementing developments in UK
law, introduced under the Criminal Justice Act 2003, which has enabled civilian experts to
be granted powers of search and seizure.[476]

In terms of institutional responses at an EU level, there have been two key institutional **5.199**
initiatives: Europol and Eurojust:

---

[470] MLA Convention, Art 13.
[471] Council Framework Decision 2002/465/JHA 'on joint investigation teams'; OJ L 162/1, 20 June
2002. Art 5 states that the decision ceases to have effect when the 2000 Convention has entered into force
in all Member States.
[472] Crime and Courts Act 2013, Sch 4, para 5. See also Police Act 1996, s 88(7). In terms of (c), see also
the International Joint Investigation Teams (International Agreement) Order 2004 (SI No 1127), which
specifies the Schengen Agreement.
[473] MLA Convention, Art 13(1).
[474] See Council Recommendation of 8 May 2003 on a model agreement for setting up a joint investigation
team (JIT), OJ C 121/1, 23 May 2003.
[475] MLA Convention, Art 13(4) and (5) respectively. Note that the police authority will be liable for any
wrongful acts of such a seconded person to the same extent that it would for the unlawful conduct of its
constables: Police Act 1996, s 88(6).
[476] CJA, s 2. See further para 6.109.

- *Europol* was originally established in 1995 by a Convention under the TEU, but has since become an entity of the European Union.[477] A further change is currently being discussed, which would re-establish Europol under a Regulation.[478] Europol's objective is to improve cooperation between the competent authorities in the Member States 'in preventing and combating organized crime, terrorism and other serious forms of serious crime affecting two or more Member States'.[479] Computer crime is explicitly recognized as one category of serious crime against property that Europol could be asked to address.[480] In 2012, the Commission called for the establishment of a European Cybercrime Centre (EC³) as part of Europol.[481] EC³ was launched in January 2013 and become fully operational in 2015.
- *Eurojust* was established in 2002 to improve judicial cooperation between Member States in relation to the investigation and prosecution of serious crimes, particularly when carried out as part of a criminal organization.[482] As with Europol, computer crime is listed as a type of crime over which Eurojust has competence to act.[483]

5.200 As noted in the 2000 Communication, Community policy in the area of computer crime and security must be as concerned with proactive prevention measures as it is with 'ensuring that the law enforcement authorities have the appropriate means to act'.[484] As a consequence, the Commission adopted a further Communication on 'Network and Information Security'[485] in 2001, which proposed a number of measures, including strengthening national Computer Emergency Response Teams (CERTs), as well as consideration of the need to organize a European warning and information system.

5.201 In 2002, the Council called upon the Commission to consider the establishment of a 'cybersecurity task force' to enhance the individual and collective response of Member States to network and information security problems.[486] In response, the Commission proposed the establishment of the 'European Network and Information Security Agency' (ENISA), on the grounds that the technical and organizational complexity of the response to security issues required under various European measures, specifically in relation to communications regulation and data protection issues, could constitute an obstacle to the Internal Market. As a consequence, a regulation was adopted, establishing ENISA.[487] The UK subsequently challenged the legal basis for the regulation, claiming that Art 95 of the Treaty of the European

---

[477] Convention based on TEU, Art K.3 on the establishment of a European Police Office; OJ C 316/2, 27 November 1995 and Council Decision 2009/371/JHA establishing the European Police Office (Europol), OJ L 121/37, 15 May 2009.

[478] Commission proposal for a Regulation on the European Union Agency for Law Enforcement Cooperation and Training (Europol) and repealing Decisions 2009/371/JHA and 2005/681/JHA, COM(2013) 173 final, 27 March 2013.

[479] ibid, Art 3.

[480] ibid, Annex.

[481] Commission Communication, 'Tackling Crime in our Digital Age: Establishing a European Cybercrime Centre', COM(2012) 140 final, 28 March 2012.

[482] Council Decision (2002/187/JHA) of 28 February 2002 setting up Eurojust with a view to reinforcing the fight against serious crime, OJ L 63/1, 6 March 2002 ('Eurojust Decision'). See generally Europol website, at <https://www.europol.europa.eu/>. The Decision was amended by Council Decision 2009/426/JHA, OJ L 138/14, 4 June 2009.

[483] Eurojust Decision, above, n 482, Art 4(1)(b), first indent.

[484] 2000 Communication, above, n 386, at iv.

[485] COM(2001) 298 final, 6 June 2001.

[486] Council Resolution of 28 January on a common approach and specific actions in the area of network and information security, OJ C 43/2, 16 February 2002.

[487] Regulation (EC) No 460/2004 establishing the European Network and Information Security Agency, OJ L 77/1, 13 March 2004. See also ENISA website, at <https://www.enisa.europa.eu/>.

Communities was designed to harmonize national laws, not establish advisory agencies. However, the European Court of Justice rejected this submission, finding that ENISA was a 'measure for approximation'.[488] ENISA has since been placed under a revised regulation.[489]

Finally, it should be noted that all the substantive, procedural, and institutional meas-   **5.202**
ures discussed above are directed at improving law enforcement throughout the Union. However, concerns have been expressed that as a consequence the security elements of the policy agenda for 'freedom, security and justice' have received a disproportionate share of attention and support than the other elements.[490] There was a proposal for a framework decision harmonizing procedural rights under criminal proceedings,[491] although it was withdrawn following entry into force of the Lisbon Treaty. At an institutional level, the Council of Bars and Law Societies of Europe (CCBE) have promoted the concept of establishing a European Criminal Law Ombudsman,[492] although this has yet to be taken up by the Commission or Council.

E. Concluding Remarks

A very high proportion of cybercrime will involve an international element, compared with   **5.203**
more traditional crimes. The international dimension may arise in respect of whether an offence has been committed or not, or it may form an element of the forensic process, the obtaining of evidence. In terms of substantive rules, the concern of policy makers and legis-lators about cybercrime has been reflected in moves to extend the reach of relevant offences beyond traditional jurisdictional principles. In terms of criminal procedures, the concern has been to improve the speed and efficiency of international cooperation in order to better reflect the fast-moving environment in which cybercrime operates. Such enhanced cooper-ation may have improved the obtaining of evidence in a transnational context; however, significant issues continue to exist in respect of the usage of such evidence in the course of a prosecution, especially ensuring appropriate accountability in the exercise of such powers, as well as the location of any subsequent criminal proceedings.

As cybercrime has become an element of the 'war on terrorism', harmonization and cooper-   **5.204**
ation have gathered pace and re-engaged the attention of legislators. Such initiatives can be seen as extensions of state authority in the face of the erosion of state control, different faces of national sovereignty. Despite the early aterritorial assertions for cyberspace, cybercrime activities take place and have effects in and between territories. As such, governments may be prepared to trade a loss of some degree of de jure state control, in terms of criminal procedure, reflecting their loss of de facto control, in return for extended jurisdictional reach, enhancing state authority. The deal may not be viewed as good, but simply the best available!

---

[488] Case C-217/04, *United Kingdom v European Parliament and Council* [2006] ECR I-03771, at 8.

[489] Regulation (EC) No 526/2013 concerning the European Union Agency for Network and Information Security (ENISA) and repealing Regulation (EC) No 460/2004, OJ L 165/41, 18 June 2013.

[490] See eg Douglas-Scott, S, 'The rule of law in the European Union—Putting security into the area of freedom, security and justice', 29 *European Law Review* 210 (2004).

[491] Commission proposal for a Council Framework Decision on certain procedural rights in criminal proceedings throughout the European Union, COM(2004) 328 final, 28 April 2004.

[492] CCBE, 'Proposal for the establishment of a European Criminal Law Ombudsman', December 2004, available at <http://www.ccbe.eu/fileadmin/user_upload/NTCdocument/criminal_law_ombudsm1_1183714563.pdf>.

6

EVIDENTIAL ISSUES: PRESENTING DATA

A. Introduction

Having carried out the investigations and obtained what appears to be sufficient evidence, **6.01** the next stage in the criminal justice process is the prosecution of the computer criminal, a process of presenting evidence to a court or tribunal of fact. Evidential rules tend to be very specific to each jurisdiction, but as with many areas of law, a broad distinction can be made between civil and common law systems. In civil law systems, criminal proceedings are generally based upon a judge(s) acting as an investigator, gathering and evaluating the evidence. By contrast, common law criminal proceedings are generally adversarial, with evidence being presented and challenged by the prosecutor and the defendant's legal advisers before a jury and judge.

Prosecuting counsel will present evidence with the objective of showing to the requisite **6.02** criminal standard, of 'beyond reasonable doubt', that the defendant is guilty of committing all, or some, of the offences for which he has been charged. On the other hand, defence counsel will be concerned, unless a guilty plea is submitted, to tender evidence that either challenges or contradicts the version of events indicated by the prosecution or offers an alternative version, with the objective of raising sufficient doubt in the minds of the court for the defendant to be acquitted. The process is governed by a complex set of rules and procedures designed, primarily, to safeguard the rights of the defendant. Computer and network-derived evidence, whether obtained from the victim, accused, third parties, or generated by the investigators themselves, may present a range of issues that need to be addressed, whether by the prosecution, defence, or court.

This chapter examines the legal framework governing the use of computer- and network- **6.03** derived evidence in criminal proceedings before the English courts, in the first instance either a Magistrates' Court or Crown Court, from pre-trial to the hearing. Pre-trial issues revolve first around the need for each side to disclose relevant material to the other side. Once disclosure has occurred, each side may apply to the court for certain evidence to be excluded from consideration on various grounds, raising questions of admissibility. The value or weight given to the evidence that is considered by the court will be the next potential point for argument, raising questions of probative value. The critical role of expert witnesses and the manner in which computer- and network-derived evidence is presented in court will complete our examination of evidential issues.

6.04   While the focus of attention remains with the prosecution of cybercrimes, the discussion is obviously applicable to any offence where computer- and network-derived evidence is involved. However, it is not within the scope of this book to provide a comprehensive treatment of all aspects of criminal evidence.[1] In addition, because of the degree of specificity in national evidential rules, reference to comparative jurisdictions will be more limited than in other parts of the book.

6.05   The nature of the evidence being presented to court will be determined by a range of factors already considered in the book. First, the nature of the offences with which the perpetrator has been charged, as examined in Chapter 3, will dictate what issues will have to be proved in a court of law. In a case of phishing, for example, if the defendant were charged with fraud, then evidence would have to be adduced that the person intended to make a representation causing loss to another;[2] while if, instead, the defendant was charged with money laundering offences, then evidence is required to show that the person knowingly acquired, used, or possessed 'criminal property'.[3]

6.06   The choice of charge will also have resource implications that, as for all areas of public administration, may be a determinant factor. The prosecutions arising from the software piracy case Operation Blossom,[4] for example, generated some £18.4 million in defence costs,[5] which was seen by some as resulting from the choice of charge made against the defendants and the resultant volume of material that required review.[6] Third, the availability of evidence obtained through the forensic process, examined in Chapter 4, will often dictate the charges laid against the perpetrator. Seized data may be encrypted, for example, such that the prosecution has to proceed merely on the basis of the evidence that is accessible and legible. Fourth, the conduct may involve international elements in jurisdictions with whom no suitable procedure exists for obtaining evidence, as considered in Chapter 5, which can render evidence gathering effectively impossible.

6.07   Concerns about the evidential value of computer- and network-derived evidence extend to civil proceedings as much as criminal. Evidential issues have been central to many of the debates about the legality of electronic commerce. Such debates have tended to focus on three key issues, the validity, enforceability, and admissibility of electronic methods of doing business. In some jurisdictions, electronic evidence was, and still is, unacceptable

---

[1] For a general treatment, see Roberts, P and Zuckerman, A, *Criminal Evidence*, 2nd edn, Oxford University Press, 2010; and May, R et al, *May on Criminal Evidence*, 6th edn, Sweet & Maxwell, 2015.

[2] Fraud Act 2006, s 2.

[3] Proceeds of Crime Act 2002, s 329.

[4] See para 3.107.

[5] Dyer, C, 'Lawyers charged £28m in legal aid for two cases', *The Guardian*, 31 May 2006, available at <http://www.theguardian.com/politics/2006/may/13/ukcrime.immigrationpolicy>.

[6] Interview with Peter Sommer, 21 June 2006.

before the courts. In others, the position was, and remains, unclear, creating legal uncertainty that in itself is seen as an obstacle to the growth of electronic commerce. In response, international, regional, and national initiatives have been adopted to try and address the issue. The United Nations Commission on International Trade Law (UNCITRAL) Model Law on Electronic Commerce (1996),[7] for example, addresses the admissibility and evidential weight of data messages:

(1) In any legal proceedings, nothing in the application of the rules of evidence shall apply so as to deny the admissibility of a data message in evidence:
  (a) on the sole ground that it is a data message; or,
  (b) if it is the best evidence that the person adducing it could reasonably be expected to obtain, on the grounds that it is not in its original form.

(2) Information in the form of a data message shall be given due evidential weight. In assessing the evidential weight of a data message, regard shall be had to the reliability of the manner in which the data message was generated, stored or communicated, to the reliability of the manner in which the integrity of the information was maintained, to the manner in which its originator was identified, and to any other relevant factor.[8]

The Commonwealth Secretariat has also issued a 'Model Law on Electronic Evidence'.[9]   **6.08**
While such initiatives have primarily focused on the use of computer-derived evidence in a commercial context, the law reforms have sometimes extended to the criminal field as well.[10] As with our discussion on digital investigations, where relevant, brief reference will also be made to the comparative rules of evidence in civil proceedings.

B. Pre-trial Disclosure

A fundamental element of an individual's right to a fair trial under Art 6 of the European   **6.09**
Convention on Human Rights (ECHR) is the principle of 'equality of arms', such that the defendant is put, as far as possible, in the same position as the state prosecutor in respect of access to legal advice and the evidence upon which he is to be tried.[11] To meet this obligation requires that the prosecution disclose to the defendant the evidence that they have and intend to use in the course of the prosecution. While disclosure is a critical component in the fairness of the trial process, it is also considered to be 'one of the most abused', resulting in substantial inefficiencies in the operation of the criminal justice system and obstructing justice.[12] The difficulty of handling computer-derived material is one area where the disclosure process can struggle to function properly.

---

[7] 36 ILM 197 (1997) ('UNCITRAL 1996'), available at <http://www.uncitral.org/uncitral/en/uncitral_texts/electronic_commerce/1996Model.html>.

[8] ibid, Art 9.

[9] Commonwealth Secretariat, 'Draft Model Law on Electronic Evidence', in Commonwealth Secretariat, *2002 Meeting of Commonwealth Law Ministers and Senior Officials: Kingstown, St Vincent and the Grenadines, 18–21 November 2002*, Commonwealth Secretariat, 2003, available at <http://dx.doi.org/10.14217/9781848598188-11-en>.

[10] UNCITRAL 1996, Art 1 states that it applies to data used in the context of commercial activities, but the Commission notes that a state may want to extend the applicability to any kind of data. The Commonwealth Model explicitly includes criminal proceedings (Art 2).

[11] See *Jespers v Belgium* (1981) 27 DR 61 and *X v FRG* (1984) 8 EHRR 225.

[12] Court of Appeal, 'Disclosure: A Protocol for the control and management of unused material in the Crown Court', 2006, para 1. See also Ormerod, D, 'Improving the disclosure regime', 7 *E & P* 102 (2003) and Redmayne, M, 'Disclosure and its discontents', *Criminal Law Review* 441 [2004].

6.10 Under English law, the process of disclosure is governed primarily by the Criminal Procedure and Investigations Act 1996 (CPIA). This Act details the nature of the duty upon the investigator and prosecution to retain and disclose material obtained or generated in the course of an investigation to the defence and vice versa. While disclosure is an element of criminal proceedings, and is therefore a topic for this chapter, disclosure issues first arise in the course of an investigation, as an element of criminal procedure, as discussed in Chapter 4.[13] The principle of fairness that lies at the heart of the prosecutor's disclosure obligation extends backwards to the investigative stage, placing a duty upon an investigator to pursue all reasonable lines of inquiry, whether supporting the case against the suspect or otherwise.[14] So, for example, if a suspect claims that a seized computer was used by more than one person, the claim must be investigated, both in terms of interviewing the other persons and the analysis carried out of the data found on the hard disk. In terms of handling and disclosing computer- and network-derived evidence, there are no specific statutory provisions, although some guidance has been developed to assist prosecutors.

6.11 The prosecutor's duty continues throughout the course of the proceedings,[15] and extends both to evidence that the prosecution intends to use in the furtherance of its case, as well as 'unused'[16] material that might undermine its case or assist the case of the accused, generally referred to as the 'undermine or assist' test.[17] The duty to obtain, retain, and disclose unused material is governed by a code of practice issued by the Secretary of State,[18] applicable to police officers;[19] Guidelines issued by the Attorney-General,[20] applicable to both the police and the Crown Prosecution Service (CPS); and a CPS Disclosure Manual.[21]

6.12 In terms of criminal proceedings, material obtained in the course of an investigation can be divided into four broad categories:

- non-sensitive evidence that is to be adduced by the prosecution as part of its case, which is disclosable;
- non-sensitive unused material in the possession of the prosecution or a third party, which is disclosable since it may undermine or assist the defendant;[22]

---

[13] Indeed, rules of discovery are sometimes not considered rules of evidence in the strict sense.

[14] Criminal Procedure and Investigations Act 1996 (CPIA), s 23(1)(a). See also Crown Prosecution Office (CPS), Disclosure Manual, para 3.5, available at <http://www.cps.gov.uk/legal/d_to_g/disclosure_manual/> ('CPS Disclosure Manual'); and Chapter 4.

[15] CPIA, s 7A 'Continuing duty to disclose'.

[16] Unused in the sense that it does not form part of the prosecution's case.

[17] CPIA, s 3(1)(a).

[18] ibid, s 23. Brought into force by the Criminal Procedure and Investigations Act 1996 (Code of Practice) Order 2015 (SI No 861). For latest version of the 'Code', see Criminal Procedure and Investigations Act Code of Practice, 16 February 2015, available at <https://www.gov.uk/government/publications/criminal-procedure-and-investigations-act-code-of-practice> ('CPIA Code').

[19] As well as any other person charged with the duty of conducting an investigation (CPIA, s 26). The Code distinguishes between the 'investigator' involved in the conduct of the investigation and who must retain relevant material, from the 'disclosure officer', the person responsible for examining the material and meeting the disclosure obligations towards the prosecutor and accused (ibid, s 2.1).

[20] Attorney-General's Guidelines on Disclosure, 3 December 2013, available at <https://www.gov.uk/government/publications/attorney-generals-guidelines-on-disclosure-2013>.

[21] CPS Disclosure Manual, above, n 14.

[22] The Court of Appeal, above, n 12, has criticized prosecutors for failing to apply the 'undermine and assist' test, thereby increasing the volume of material in this category.

- sensitive unused material in the possession of the prosecution or a third party, which is not disclosable if it is the subject of an application for a public interest immunity (PII) certificate;[23]
- material in the possession of the prosecution or a third party that is considered irrelevant to the prosecution.[24]

In the course of criminal proceedings, a prosecutor is required to provide copies of, or the **6.13** ability to inspect, material of any kind that has come into the prosecutor's possession or has been inspected by him in relation to the case,[25] referred to as the 'golden rule of full disclosure'.[26] However, this duty is subject to three exceptions:

- that the material meets the 'undermine and assist' test, such that '[n]eutral material or material damaging to the defendant' does not need to be disclosed;[27]
- that the material is considered sensitive, requiring protection from disclosure through the court grant of PII;
- that the material is the product of an interception.

In respect of determining the applicability of the first exception, while the test is an objective one, ie that 'which might reasonably be considered', it is for the prosecutor to make the initial judgement. However, the defence can challenge what the prosecutor has disclosed and apply to the court for an order requiring such disclosure.[28]

Sensitive material is that which the prosecution considers should not be disclosed to the **6.14** defence, because it would constitute 'a real risk of serious prejudice to an important public interest'.[29] As noted by the European Court of Justice:

> The entitlement to disclosure of relevant evidence is not an absolute right. In any criminal proceedings there may be conflicting interests . . . which must be weighed against the rights of the accused. In some cases it may be necessary to withhold certain evidence from the defence so as to preserve the fundamental rights of another individual or to safeguard an important public interest.[30]

The types of public interest engaged include matters of national security; information that could undermine an investigative process, such as the identity of an informant or surveillance location; or material that may facilitate the commission of other offences or hinder their prevention and detection, such as child pornography images.[31] Such protections may extend to the persons based in foreign jurisdictions, operating on behalf of foreign investigators,[32] as well as other state interests.[33] Such matters are obviously similar to those

---

[23] Material falling into this category will generally be treated in one of three ways: (a) if considered to meet the 'undermine or assist' test, it will need to be reclassified as non-sensitive, eg through redaction of the sensitive parts; (b) be the subject of a PII application; or (c) if considered not to meet the test, be reclassified as irrelevant to the case.

[24] As determined by the prosecutor.

[25] CPIA, s 3(2) and (3).

[26] *H and C* [2004] UKHL 3, para 36 *per* Lord Bingham.

[27] ibid, para 35.

[28] CPIA, s 8.

[29] CPIA Code, above, n 18, para 6.15.

[30] *Edwards and Lewis v United Kingdom* (2005) 40 EHRR 24, para 53. However, for criticism of such a balancing approach, see Ashworth, A and Redmayne, M, *The Criminal Process*, 4th edn, Oxford University Press, 2010, at 248.

[31] CPIA Code, above, n 18. See also the CPS Disclosure Manual, above, n 14, para 8.4.

[32] *Alibhai and others* [2004] EWCA Crim 681, para 86.

[33] CPS Disclosure Manual, above, n 14, para 35.86.

justifying state interference in an individual's right to privacy through covert investigative techniques.[34]

6.15 An unusual issue relating to the duty to disclosure arose in *Crown Prosecution Service v LR*,[35] involving child sexual abuse images. Part of the defendant's case was that some images were of adults, not children. In order to receive legal advice, it was necessary to examine the material. The CPS was concerned about the conditions under which such access was granted to the defendant, proposing that they use a glass-walled room with a policeman standing outside. This was rejected as a breach of the defendant's right to confidential discussions with his lawyer. In the absence of any alternative arrangement, the court then ordered disclosure of a copy of the images. The CPS refused, however, on the grounds that making such as copy would constitute an offence and, second, that the safe handling and retention of the images could not be assured. The CPS stated that they were not trying to deprive the defendant of his disclosure rights, but the problem concerned the method of disclosure. The CPS appealed the judge's order to disclose and indicated that the defendant would be acquitted if the appeal failed. The Court of Appeal showed little sympathy for the CPS's argument, and the appeal was dismissed, with the court stressing the importance of respecting a defendant's right to a fair trial.

6.16 Where sensitive material is involved, the prosecution must apply for a court order not to disclose certain materials in the public interest.[36] Clearly, such non-disclosure could have serious implications for the fairness of a trial; therefore the judiciary are required to act as the guarantors of such fairness by considering the proportionality of each such request and keeping the question under constant review.[37] Ultimately, if such sensitive material satisfies the 'undermine or assist' test, but the prosecution refuses to allow its disclosure, then the prosecution may have to be halted.

6.17 A failure by the prosecutor to disclose aspects of his case prior to the trial may result in the evidence being held inadmissible. A failure to comply with the duty of disclosure in respect of unused material, because it is lost or destroyed (which is quite conceivable when dealing with computer-derived evidence, for example data held in volatile RAM dependent on batteries), may result in the proceedings being stayed for abuse of process.[38] A failure by the defence to disclose may result in the judge or jury drawing an inference from such behaviour.[39]

6.18 The primary obligation to disclose copies contrasts with the position in civil proceedings, as a matter of law, where disclosure comprises simple notification that a document exists, or existed, which then generally gives rise to a right to inspect, and then a right to request a copy, on condition that the requesting party pays reasonable copying costs.[40] In practice,

---

[34] See generally Chapter 4.

[35] [2010] EWCA Crim 924.

[36] CPIA, s 3(6). See also Criminal Procedure Rules (as in force on 6 October 2014) (CPR), Pt 22.3, available at <http://www.legislation.gov.uk/uksi/2014/1610/pdfs/uksi_20141610_en.pdf>.

[37] Lord Bingham, in *H and C* [2004] UKHL 3, para 36.

[38] *R (on the application of Ebrahim) v Feltham Magistrates Court* [2001] 2 Cr App R 23. See generally Martin, S, 'Lost and destroyed evidence: The search for a principled approached to abuse of process', 9 *E & P* 158 (2005).

[39] CPIA, s 11. See *Tibbs* [2000] 2 Cr App R 309.

[40] CPR, Pt 31 'Disclosure and Inspection of Documents', rr 31.2, 31.3, and 31.15, respectively.

however, both systems operate similarly on the basis of the provision of lists, referred to as 'disclosure schedules' in criminal proceedings, which detail the availability of the unused material.[41] Two schedules are prepared by the disclosure officer, one detailing the non-sensitive material, the other the sensitive material; only the former is disclosed to the defence.

The disclosure obligation has certain implications for digital investigations. First, the vol- **6.19** ume of material involved will often be very substantial. Seized data storage media, such as hard drives and CDs, may contain the equivalent of many thousands of pieces of paper. It is estimated, for example, that an average hard disk can store over 200 gigabytes of data, which if printed would produce a stack of A4 paper 10m pages long;[42] which means producing hard copies of all the material will generally be unfeasible. Only a small proportion of this material may be actually used by the prosecution, but it must all be detailed in the 'disclosure schedule' and be made available to the defence for examination. Indeed, it is also sometimes the case that the volumes involved mean that not all of the material has been examined by the investigators. In such situations, the disclosure officer may simply have to state the reasons why the material has not been examined and the fact that it is not known whether such material meets the 'undermine or assist' test.[43]

In most cases, the defence will be provided with copies of the material, whether in hard copy **6.20** or electronic form; however, in certain circumstances, that may not always be appropriate because the provision of copies would be impracticable or undesirable, and the defence may instead be given an opportunity to inspect the material,[44] such as being given an opportunity to interrogate a database.

A 'disclosure schedule' for data storage media will generally need to include the following **6.21** information:

- Each item containing stored data should be identified, which may include hard disks, memory sticks, and CDs/DVDs.
- A description of what steps have been taken, by whom, to examine and analyse the information held on the storage media, on a chronological basis (eg a log detailing times and duration of access).
- A listing of the information held on the media, either compiled by the investigator (eg through the use of tools such as Encase), based on keyword searches[45] or 'sampling',[46] or present on the media itself (eg a directory structure).

Second, evidence will often be generated in the course of an investigation by expert exam- **6.22** iners, as well as that obtained by the investigation. Evidence generated by the investigative process will also need to be disclosed, but will often require the defence to retain its own experts. The availability of suitable experts is often a problem in this environment, because of the lack of professional standards in the area of computing.

---

[41] CPIA Code, above, n 18, paras 6.2 et seq.
[42] ACPO, 'Good Practice Guide for Computer Based Evidence' ('ACPO Guide'), para 7.4.2: see Appendix 4 of this volume.
[43] ibid, para 7.4.7.
[44] CPIA, ss 3(3)(b), 4(b).
[45] CPS Disclosure Manual, above, n 14, Annex H 'The use of keyword searches and digital evidence recovery officers'.
[46] See Attorney-General's Guidance, above, n 20, at A44, which notes that sampling may need to be carried out more than once.

6.23 As well as seized material, there may be substantial evidence held by a victim or another third party, to whom access may need to be obtained, but which they may be unwilling or inefficient about providing. While difficulties obtaining third-party evidence may impact on the fairness of a trial, the demand for such information may also interfere with the rights of the third party, such as the privacy or confidentiality of information. In *Alibhai*,[47] for example, the defendants appealed against a conspiracy to deal dishonestly in counterfeit Microsoft products on the basis of inadequate disclosure. The complaint related to material in possession of Microsoft, the FBI, and an informant, not material held by the prosecution authorities. The court rejected the appeal, stating that it must be shown that the prosecution must suspect that such evidence was likely to undermine or assist and, even if it did, the prosecutor also has a 'margin of consideration' in respect of how such situations are handled.[48]

6.24 One coercive mechanism for obtaining access to information that a third party is unwilling to provide is for the prosecution to ask the court to issue a 'witness summons', under the Criminal Procedure (Attendance of Witnesses) Act 1965.[49] This could require the third party to produce a specified 'document or thing', such as data storage media, provided it was 'likely to be material evidence',[50] and could state such production be carried out prior to trial for the purpose of enabling inspection by the prosecution.[51] It would not be available, however, where the third party is based outside the jurisdiction.

Intercept evidence

6.25 One category of evidence that is not required to be disclosed is that obtained through the interception of a person's communications, 'intercept product':

> Material must not be disclosed under this section to the extent that it is material the disclosure of which is prohibited by section 17 of the Regulation of Investigatory Powers Act 2000.[52]

The rationale behind this rule is that certain investigative methods of law enforcement agencies need to be protected from disclosure, since such knowledge may undermine the ability of law enforcement to use such techniques. To protect the source of intercept evidence, the product of the intercept is consequentially excluded from being admitted into court.[53] Intercept product can therefore only be used to assist in the process of an investigation, rather than form part of the prosecution case. Indeed, it has been stated in the Criminal Appeal Court, by Latham LJ, that s 17 is not 'concerned with questions of admissibility', rather it is a prohibition on disclosure,[54] a statement which, with respect, seems hard to accept 'given the very sweeping language in which section 17(1) is expressed'![55]

---

[47] *Alibhai and others* [2004] EWCA Crim 681.
[48] ibid, paras 62 et seq.
[49] Alternatively, the Magistrates' Courts Act 1980, s 97.
[50] Criminal Procedure (Attendance of Witnesses) Act 1965 (CPAW), s 2.
[51] ibid, s 2A.
[52] CPIA, s 3(7).
[53] Regulation of Investigatory Powers Act 2000 (RIPA), s 17. See further paras 6.69–6.79.
[54] *Scotting* [2004] EWCA Crim 197 at 14.
[55] Stated by Lord Bingham in *Attorney-General's Reference (No 5 of 2002) sub nom R v W* [2004] UKHL 40, at 20.

In addition, law enforcement agencies have a general duty to destroy any intercept prod-   **6.26**
uct as soon as it is no longer necessary for any statutory purpose.[56] However, it may be
retained for certain 'authorised purposes', including where 'it is necessary to ensure that a
person conducting a criminal prosecution has the information he needs to determine what
is required of him by his duty to secure the fairness of the prosecution'.[57] In such a situation,
it may subsequently be disclosed to the prosecutor, referred to as a 'Preston briefing',[58] for
a determination to be made. In addition, 'where the exceptional circumstances of the case
make the disclosure essential in the interests of justice', a trial judge may order that the intercept product be disclosed to himself, but not to the defence.[59]

The investigating officer is therefore placed in a potentially difficult situation, having both   **6.27**
to gather the evidence that will form the basis of any proceedings, as well as carry out
'the essential function' of making decisions about whether information intercepted could
impact on the fairness of the prospective proceedings. While the inadmissibility of intercept evidence from court will generally work to the advantage of a defendant, it may obviously be disadvantageous where exculpatory material is present.[60] These complexities would
not be necessary were intercept evidence made generally admissible.

International material

A cybercrime will often involve international components and, therefore, foreign-sourced   **6.28**
evidence may comprise a key element of the prosecution's case and will be subject to disclosure obligations. Obviously much material may be derived from systems and networks
based in foreign jurisdictions, such as a Facebook account. Prosecution requests for unused
material from abroad may arise in two situations. First, where the investigator is discharging his duty to pursue all reasonable lines of inquiry. Second, when the investigator or prosecutor suspects that material held by a third party would be disclosable, because it meets the
'undermine and assist' test, were it to be in the possession of the prosecution.[61]

The requirement of disclosure in respect of unused material may present particular prob-   **6.29**
lems, arising from the different legal traditions that exist; misunderstandings about the
request as implying incompetence or impropriety on behalf of the foreign entity;[62] or it may
interfere with a separate on-going investigation in that foreign jurisdiction.[63]

As considered in Chapter 5, such material will generally be obtained through mutual   **6.30**
assistance procedures or using a 'letter of request', requested by either the prosecution or
defence, or more informal and direct techniques between investigators. Issues may obviously arise concerning the means by which a foreign third party has obtained the material
being requested in the first place, such as the use of covert surveillance techniques. If there

---

[56] RIPA, at s 15(3).
[57] ibid, at s 15(4)(d). See *Gibbs* [2004] EWCA Crim 3431.
[58] CPS Disclosure Manual, above, n 14, para 27.19. The term relates to the House of Lords' decision in
Preston [1994] 2 AC 130, 164B.
[59] RIPA, at s 18(7)(b), (8). See also Attorney-General's Guidance for Prosecutors, 'Section 18 RIPA
Prosecutors Intercept Guidelines England and Wales', 29 November 2012.
[60] See Mirfield, P, 'Regulation of Investigatory Powers Act 2000 (2): Evidential Aspects', *Criminal Law
Review* 91 [2005].
[61] CPS Disclosure Manual, above, n 18, para 35.3.
[62] ibid, para 35.5.
[63] Interview with Peter Sommer, 21 June 2006.

are prima facie grounds for the prosecution to suspect that the material had been obtained unlawfully, further investigations may need to be carried out.[64] However, in such circumstances it may be virtually impossible for the defence to adequately check the veracity of what is presented by the prosecution or, conversely, what was available but not produced.[65]

C. Abuse of Process

6.31 Under English law, the courts have an inherent jurisdiction to control their own proceedings to prevent an injustice occurring.[66] By 'staying' criminal proceedings, the court effectively brings those proceedings to an end, without the need to consider fully the evidence being adduced by either side. Although staying a trial for abuse of process overlaps with issues of fairness, addressed in part through the exclusionary evidential rules examined below, particularly s 78 of the Police and Criminal Evidence Act 1984 (PACE), the English courts have viewed the doctrine as having wider import, as expressed by Lord Griffiths in *ex parte Bennett*:[67]

> In the present case there is no suggestion that the appellant cannot have a fair trial . . . If the court is to have the power to interfere with the prosecution . . . it must be because the judiciary accept the responsibility for the maintenance of the rule of law that embraces a willingness to oversee executive action and to refuse to countenance behaviour that threatens either basic human rights or the rule of law . . . The courts, of course, have no power to apply direct discipline to the police or the prosecuting authorities, but they can refuse to allow them to take advantage of abuse of power by regarding their behaviour as an abuse of process and thus preventing a prosecution.[68]

6.32 While our concern with abuse of process lies with this indirect supervision of the investigative process, as examined in Chapter 4, the doctrine may also be applicable to the actual trial process, arising for example where pre-trial publicity is considered to undermine the possibility of finding an unbiased jury.

6.33 In a computer-integrity case, *Bevan*,[69] the defendant hacker, known as 'Kuji', was accused of conspiring to obtain unauthorized access to systems and committing unauthorized modifications to data belonging to the United States Air Force and the Lockheed Space and Missile Company. He was eventually acquitted when the Crown offered no evidence, after having been asked by the judge to consider its position and make submissions as to 'abuse of process' in relation to its conduct of the case.

6.34 While an abuse claim could emerge from the exercise of both coercive and covert investigative techniques, it is the latter where case law has tended to focus. In *Grant*,[70] for example, the use of a covert listening device in a police exercise yard to record conversations between the accused and his solicitor was held to be an abuse, rendering the conviction unsafe. As

---

[64] *Hardy* [2003] 1 Cr App R 30, para 53.
[65] Loof, R, 'Obtaining, adducing and contesting evidence from abroad: A defence perspective on cross-border evidence', *Criminal Law Review* 40 [2011].
[66] See Roberts and Zuckerman, above, n 1, at 69 et seq.
[67] *R v Horseferry Road Magistrates' Court, ex parte Bennett* [1994] 1 AC 42.
[68] ibid, at 62.
[69] Woolwich Crown Court, 21 November 1997.
[70] [2005] EWCA Crim 1089.

already discussed, the use of covert techniques is more prevalent in a cyberspace environment, where the identity and location of suspects are more difficult to establish, victims are less likely or willing to report crime, or the investigation concerns the commission of consensual offences, such as intellectual property crimes and child abuse images.[71]

Among covert techniques, there is obviously a broad range of activities that may be undertaken by a law enforcement agent, varying with respect to extent of participation in the commission of the criminal conduct, the degree of intrusion, and/or level of deception carried out against a suspect. A specific class of covert technique that has raised abuse of process issues is the involvement of state agencies through the provision of opportunities for, or the encouragement or incitement of, the commission of crimes. Two examples considered in Chapter 4 were the operation of honeypots, in the form of hacking targets or decoy illegal content providers, and the participation in peer-to-peer (P2P) file-sharing communities.[72] The use of such online deception techniques may be subject to claims of entrapment, leading to an order to stay proceedings for abuse of process.   **6.35**

A finding of entrapment may either prevent legal proceedings from being pursued or fatally undermine the success of a prosecution. As a legal concept, entrapment is concerned with the involvement of public law enforcement authorities and their agents in the inducement or commission of a crime. As such, the use of deception techniques by strictly non-public entities should not give rise to a claim of entrapment.[73]   **6.36**

In common law jurisdictions, a claim of entrapment has been characterized as having differing legal remedies. In practical terms, such differences will generally have the same outcome, the failure to prosecute successfully. However, such characterization will impact on the manner in which the claim is treated within the proceedings and may consequentially impact on the handling of cross-border computer crime investigations.   **6.37**

In the US, entrapment is characterized in the federal courts as a substantive defence, which if upheld would mean that the crime was not considered to have been committed.[74] As such, it is an issue to be decided by a jury rather than the judiciary. In Canada, entrapment gives rise to a stay of proceedings, with the court effectively preventing the proceedings commencing.[75] In Australia, the issue has been treated as an evidential issue, the courts exercising their discretion to exclude evidence obtained through entrapment.[76] Under English law, the issue of how to characterize entrapment was examined in detail by the House of Lords in *Looseley (Attorney-General's Reference No 3 of 2000)*.[77]   **6.38**

The court confirmed earlier case law that entrapment did not constitute a substantive defence under English law.[78] The exclusion of entrapment-based evidence on the grounds that it would have an adverse effect on the fairness of the proceedings, under s 78 of the   **6.39**

---

[71] See Lord Hoffman's comments in *Looseley (Attorney-General's Reference No 3 of 2000)* [2001] UKHL 53, at 66.

[72] See paras 4.104–4.120.

[73] However, see further Hofmeyr, K, 'The problem of private entrapment', *Criminal Law Review* 319 [2006].

[74] *Sherman v United States*, 356 US 369 (1957).

[75] *R v Mack* (1988) 44 CCC (3d) 513.

[76] *Ridgeway v The Queen* (1995) 184 CLR 19.

[77] [2001] UKHL 53; [2001] 4 All ER 897.

[78] *Sang* [1980] AC 402.

PACE, was also rejected as the appropriate remedy. The court held that the inherent jurisdiction of a court to stay proceedings to protect the integrity of the judicial system[79] was the most appropriate remedy under English law.[80] In reaching its decision, the court also examined those factors that may be considered relevant to a decision to stay proceedings in a situation of entrapment, and it is these factors that bear directly on the use of deception techniques in the investigation of computer and cybercrime.

6.40 The House of Lords dismissed the predisposition of a defendant to commit such a crime as a determinative factor, effectively rejecting the US Supreme Court's approach. In the context of a honeypot, for example, the fact that a person can be shown to have had the necessary intent to hack into a system will not excuse unacceptable activities by the law enforcement agencies.[81] Therefore, the perspective of the court's inquiry into the circumstances of the entrapment will be in respect of the conduct of the relevant law enforcement agency. The court examined a range of relevant factors that were appropriate for consideration.

6.41 First, whether the activities of the agency were 'no more than might have been expected from others in the circumstances',[82] which may include 'some degree of deception [and] importunity'.[83] This should be an 'unexceptional opportunity' for the suspect to offend.[84] In the case under consideration, 'the undercover officer presented himself to Looseley as an ideal customer for a drugs deal, but ... he did not go beyond that portrayal and ... presented himself exactly as someone in the drugs world would expect to see a heroin addict.' This included an initial call by the officer asking 'can you sort us out a couple of bags', to which the accused affirmatively replied, a trip to the accused's flat and a drive to procure the heroin. Two further drug purchases ensued under similar circumstances. However, the degree of persistence in making contact with a suspect could render the process abusive, depending on the frequency and the pressure applied, for example, bombarding a suspect with emails that eventually led to an agreement to deal.

6.42 Second, the degree of intrusiveness: 'It should not be used in a random fashion, and used for wholesale "virtue-testing", without good reason.'[85] In illustrating what constitutes random virtue testing, Lord Hoffmann cites the example given by the Canadian High Court in *Mack*[86] of the wallet full of money left in plain sight in a park by an officer seeking to improve his performance statistics and without any basis for suspicion as to anyone in the park. This scenario constitutes an abuse of state power preying on the weakness of human nature for an improper purpose and is to be contrasted with authorized exercises conducted pursuant to an investigation and under direction of a supervisor.[87] The nature of the offence,

---

[79] In *Looseley*, it is also described as 'an abuse of process' (para 18 *per* Lord Nicholls) and an 'abuse of executive power' (para 40 *per* Lord Hoffmann).

[80] Although it was recognized that a stay of proceedings may arise procedurally through a claim made under Police and Criminal Evidence Act 1984 (PACE), s 78.

[81] *Looseley*, para 22 *per* Lord Nicholls and para 68 *per* Lord Hoffmann.

[82] ibid, para 23 *per* Lord Nicholls; see also ibid, para 55 *per* Lord Hoffmann and para 102 *per* Lord Hutton.

[83] *Ridgeway v The Queen* (1995) 184 CLR 19, at 92 per McHugh J, quoted with approval in *Looseley*, para 23 *per* Lord Nicholls.

[84] *Looseley*, para 23 *per* Lord Nicholls.

[85] ibid, para 24 *per* Lord Nicholls.

[86] [1988] 2 SCR 903.

[87] *Looseley*, paras 58–60 *per* Lord Hoffman.

the manner in which the crime is committed, the difficulty of detection or the unwillingness of the victims to report, may make entrapment a necessary tool of investigation.[88]

Third, the agency's actions must be carried out in good faith and there must be reasonable **6.43** grounds for suspicion, either in respect of a particular person or place.[89] However, where the activity is carried out on the basis of a place or location, such as an online bulletin board or 'Hangout', it may be that the proportionate policing response is that of a surveillance operation, rather than proactive entrapment.[90] Suspicion of a particular person may obviously be based on his past criminal activities, which does make the defendant's predisposition potentially relevant. However, it would be wrong for an investigator's action to transform the nature of a person's wrongdoing, as occurred in *Moon*,[91] where the prosecution conceded that the defendant was only a drug user, who had been converted into a supplier through the persistent efforts of the undercover police officer. By analogy, inciting a hobbyist hacker to trade confidential data, or a possessor of child abuse images to supply such material, could similarly be considered abusive.

The alternative scenario posited in *Mack* of the handbag left in a bus station where incidents **6.44** of theft have been reported is cited as an illustrative example of how reasonable suspicion may exist without the need for it to be focused on a particular individual.[92] Another example cited in *Looseley* of how this factor may apply in a decoy situation where no one person is the object of reasonable suspicion is *Williams v DPP*.[93] In this case police, investigating thefts from vehicles in Essex, left an unattended van containing cartons of cigarettes visible and with the back door open. The arrest of the accused was found not to constitute an abuse of power. Rather, it was 'an authorised investigation into actual crime and the fact that the defendants may not have been previously suspected or even thought of offending was their hard luck'.[94]

To ensure good faith, the investigative activity should be subject to appropriate supervi- **6.45** sion. This should generally arise through compliance with the Regulation of Investigatory Powers Act 2000 (RIPA) Codes; although, as with the exclusionary rules examined below, 'minor infractions to the provisions of RIPA' may not require the determination of a stay of proceedings.[95]

Fourth, the nature of the agency involvement in the crime, particularly in respect of any **6.46** inducements that may be held out. The agency may provide the opportunity for the accused to commit the crime, but not cause its commission.[96] This is noted to be 'a most important factor' but not necessarily decisive.[97] Where the line is drawn, however, is not to be determined by 'mechanical application of a distinction between "active" and "passive" conduct

---

[88] ibid, para 26 *per* Lord Nicholls and para 66 *per* Lord Hoffmann.
[89] ibid, para 27 *per* Lord Nicholls and para 65 *per* Lord Hoffmann.
[90] See Ormerod, D, 'Entrapment: Restating Principles and Reviewing Recent Developments', Paper delivered at CPS Conference, *Prosecuting Organised Crime*, 24 March 2006, para 4.16.
[91] [2004] EWCA Crim 2872.
[92] *Looseley*, para 65 *per* Lord Hoffmann.
[93] [1994] 98 Cr App R 209, cited by *Looseley*, para 65 *per* Lord Hoffmann.
[94] *Looseley*, para 65 *per* Lord Hoffmann.
[95] *Paulssen* [2003] EWCA 3109, para 29. See also *Brett* [2005] EWCA Crim 983, where the court stated that an abuse may arise where the codes have been 'flouted or ignored'.
[96] *Looseley*, para 50 *per* Lord Hoffmann.
[97] ibid.

on the part of the undercover policeman or informer.'[98] Thus, it would be 'absurd' in some instances for the officer to wait for an offer silently, such as in a test purchase.[99] Notably, in doing what the ordinary purchaser will do may require him to exercise a certain degree of persistence to overcome wariness or in another circumstance to show enthusiasm for the enterprise. Thus, 'a good deal of active behaviour in the course of an authorised operation may therefore be acceptable without crossing the boundary ...'[100]

6.47 Each of these factors needs to be considered in terms of their applicability to the operation of an online investigation. According to the court, deception per se does not indicate entrapment, as some level of deception may be an inevitable by-product of an effective investigation. While the honeypot is generally made available to the world at large, via a public network such as the Internet, the nature of the technique means that the 'visitor' is confronted with security measures which have to be breached in order to gain entry to the honeypot. Such steps would seem to go well beyond any concept of 'virtue-testing'. The repeated breach of security points or delving many folder levels down in a secure area is well beyond 'casual attempts to rattle the door' that someone not inclined to hack a system might do.[101] In the past, organizations have invited the public to attack their network either as a marketing stunt or for other reasons, but the opposite should be the basis upon which a 'real' honeypot would operate. Moreover, given the ability to document extensive attempts on defence and other targeted computer systems[102] it would appear that a honeypot investigation could be objectively justified as being in good faith and based on reasonable suspicion related to the site (or others by that same entity).

6.48 Further, as noted in the introduction, the nature of the technology renders network-based crime extremely difficult to investigate, which makes the use of honeypots a necessary tool. There is also a clear unwillingness to report such crime by victims, particularly among commercial organizations keen to avoid any adverse publicity. Thus, this factor would also weigh in favour of their use.

6.49 One additional aspect considered by the Law Lords in *Looseley* was whether the ECHR, and specifically the 'right of fair trial' provided for under Art 6(1), modified the treatment of entrapment under English law. The use of *'agents provocateurs'* has been considered previously by the European Court of Human Rights in *Teixeira de Castro v Portugal*.[103] In finding that the applicant has been deprived of his 'right of fair trial', the absence of previous suspicion in respect of the applicant and the lack of supervision over the investigation were relevant factors in the court's finding. Clearly, honeypots and P2P infiltration are not generally designed with a specific person in mind; rather, they are concerned with suspicious activities towards a particular place, ie a network which is accessible from other networks or a file-sharing community. In terms of supervision, there should be a commonality

---

[98] ibid, at 69.
[99] ibid.
[100] ibid.
[101] Schwartz, M, 'To Trap a Thief', *Computerworld*, 2 April 2001, available at <http://www.computerworld.com/article/2591588/lan-wan/to-trap-a-thief.html>.
[102] eg Verton, D, 'Cyberattacks against Pentagon on the rise', *Computerworld*, 14 December 2000, available at <http://www.computerworld.com/article/2589482/technology-law-regulation/cyberattacks-against-pentagon-on-the-rise.html> reporting that 'malicious hackers and other criminals' had penetrated the Pentagon network security over 14,000 times in the first seven months of 2000.
[103] (1998) 4 BHRC 533.

of interests in that an appropriately supervised operation, as well as addressing concerns regarding the rights of the perpetrator, will generate evidence with sufficient probative value, discussed further below.

D. Admissibility

While much time, resource, and effort may have been expended in the course of a digital investigation, as discussed in Chapter 4, the product of such forensic activity may not be permitted to be adduced as evidence in any subsequent criminal proceedings. Admissibility is concerned with the ability to submit evidence into court for consideration by the judge and/or jury. In civil law systems, the investigating judge generally determines the issue; while in common law systems, complex admissibility rules have historically existed to govern the issue, based in statute and case law. Our interest in questions of admissibility concern the extent to which the forensic product derived from computers and networks may be excluded from the court. Indeed, challenges to the admissibility of such evidence are a key defence strategy in cybercrime prosecutions.[104] The more vulnerable computer- and network-derived evidence is to exclusion, the more problematic will be the prosecution of computer and cybercrimes.

6.50

For our purposes, evidential exclusions can be broadly divided into two categories: the first focuses on the material itself, the second on the circumstances surrounding the obtaining of the material for use as evidence. In the first, the unreliability of the material is the primary policy concern, either because the person was not witness to the facts, as in hearsay, or because the reliability of the source from which it is derived is considered vulnerable, as computers were treated in the early years. In the second, the policy concerns are the activities of the investigators in obtaining the material. This can be further subdivided into 'protective exclusions', where the objective is to protect the investigative process, which is the case with the current inadmissibility of intercept product, data obtained 'in transmission', and 'fairness exclusions', where the rights of the defendant have been, or could be, infringed were the material to be admitted.

6.51

These exclusions may occur through statutory prohibition, through judicial determination, or a combination of both. As a statutory prohibition, the RIPA expressly prohibits intercept product from being admitted into court. Such material is considered to be for intelligence, not evidential purposes: protecting the investigative process from examination. A court has the right to exercise discretion not to admit evidence based on a concern to ensure the fairness of any criminal proceedings and, to a lesser extent, to regulate the conduct of law enforcement agencies. In the latter scenario, evidence may be excluded because it involved the commission of an offence by the investigator, or a breach of a procedural obligation designed to protect the rights of the suspect.[105] Evidential exclusion may operate as an alternative to a judicial stay for abuse of process.

6.52

---

[104] Smith, R, Grabosky, P, and Urbas, G, *Cyber Criminals on Trial*, Cambridge University Press, 2004, at 62.
[105] See Kerr, O, 'Lifting the "fog" of Internet surveillance: How a suppression remedy would change computer crime law', 54 *Hastings Law Journal* 805 (2003).

6.53 As well as fair trial concerns arising from breaches of procedural rules governing the investigative process, such as the codes made under PACE[106] or the codes under the RIPA,[107] the concept of a fair trial is also enshrined in human rights instruments, specifically the ECHR, Art 6, to which the UK courts must give consideration.[108] Similar 'due process' concerns are present in all developed legal systems.[109] In addition, a trial may be considered unfair where the investigative process involved a breach of other human rights, such as the right to privacy, under ECHR, Art 8.

6.54 Law enforcement agencies must therefore give mind to such exclusionary rules in the course of a digital investigation, since their application may be triggered by the choice and manner in which the investigation is carried out. The following briefly reviews four historical grounds for excluding digital evidence, the first two of which have largely or wholly disappeared.

Real and hearsay evidence

6.55 The historic basis for the presentation of evidence in court is through the use of witnesses, persons capable of giving testimony about what they witnessed and being subjected to cross-examination by the opposing counsel. As such, documentary evidence has historically been treated somewhat cautiously due to the perceived difficulties of challenging such evidence. A fundamental distinction has existed in English law between the concepts of 'real' and 'hearsay' evidence. Real evidence is direct from the witness, while hearsay may be described as 'second-hand' evidence, the truth of which cannot be directly testified to in court. Many documentary records are submitted into court as hearsay evidence, either replacing a witness who is unable to provide oral testimony or because the person recording the information did not directly witness the recorded event.

6.56 Whether computer-derived evidence is real or hearsay in a particular instance will depend on the nature of the information being fed into, or produced by, the computer system. Where computers are operating in a mechanistic way, as automatic recording systems or simply as calculating tools, the evidence they produce is real.[110] This point was addressed by the House of Lords in *Levin*,[111] which involved the defendant hacking into a funds transfer system operated by the US company Citibank. The defendant objected to the admission of computer printouts detailing the subsequent unauthorized transfers on the grounds that they were hearsay. In rejecting this claim, Lord Hoffman stated:

> The printouts are tendered to prove the transfers of funds which they record. They do not assert that such transfers took place. They record the transfers themselves, created by the interaction between whoever purported to request the transfers and the computer program in Parsippany.[112]

---

[106] eg Code B: 'Code of practice for searches of premises by police officers and the seizure of property found by police officers on persons or premises' (in force since 27 October 2013).

[107] See generally Chapter 4.

[108] Human Rights Act 1998, s 6.

[109] eg in the US, the Fifth and Fourteenth Amendments to the Constitution.

[110] eg *The Statute of Liberty* [1968] 2 All ER 195, involving a printout from a fully automated radar tracking system; and *Castle v Cross* [1984] Crim LR 682, involving the printout of a breath-testing machine. In *Sophocleous v Ringer* [1988] RTR 52, the courts held that where a computer was used as a tool to facilitate analysis, then the hearsay conditions did not apply.

[111] [1997] AC 741.

[112] ibid, at 746. See also *R v Pettigrew* [1980] 71 Cr App R 39; and *Minors* [1989] 1 WLR 441.

An appropriate formulation for making the distinction between real and hearsay computer-derived evidence would seem to be that accepted by the court in *Coventry Justices ex parte Bullard*,[113] where it was suggested that it was necessary to distinguish 'between computer print-outs containing information implanted by a human and print-outs containing records produced without human intervention'.[114] In *Skinner*,[115] the court rejected a defence claim that electronically copying an image from one computer to another rendered them hearsay. To attempt to remove any uncertainty, the Criminal Justice Act 2003 defines a hearsay statement of fact or opinion to include only those statements 'made by a person', not by machine.[116]

Owing to its perceived unreliability, the law has historically excluded hearsay evidence from **6.57** court. However, as documentary evidence has become the norm in most cases, legal reform has removed many of the barriers to the admissibility of hearsay evidence.[117] The Criminal Justice Act 2003, Part 11, Chapter 2, further enhanced the admissibility of hearsay evidence in criminal proceedings by codifying existing rules (eg by the agreement of the parties to the proceedings)[118] and removing the common law rule against the admissibility of hearsay evidence. Categories of documents considered admissible include 'business' documents,[119] although there is special exclusionary discretion where the statement may be considered unreliable due to:

(a) its contents, (b) the source of the information, (c) the way in which or the circumstances in which the information was supplied or received, or (d) the way in which or circumstances in which the document concerned was created or received.[120]

This would seem potentially arguable against documents supplied by a victim's computer system that has been subject to an unauthorized act by the defendant, since the unauthorized act could be the circumstance that renders the evidence unreliable. A similar argument was made in *Levin* in respect of PACE, s 69, but was rejected.[121]

The Criminal Justice Act 2003 provides that a hearsay statement includes those that appear **6.58** to the court to have been made by a person to cause 'a machine to operate on the basis that the matter is as stated'.[122] However, where a representation is made by a machine, but depends on the accuracy of the information supplied to it by a person, then such a representation is not admissible unless the accuracy of the information can be proved (although the machine is presumed to be properly set or calibrated),[123] which reflects both the previous common law position[124] as well as the old computer adage: 'garbage in, garbage out'. The Act also provides that authenticated copies of a document containing the statement may be

---

[113] (1992) 95 Cr App R 175.
[114] ibid, at 178.
[115] [2005] EWCA Crim 1439.
[116] Criminal Justice Act 2003 (CJA), s 115(2).
[117] For civil proceedings, see the Civil Evidence Act 1995.
[118] CJA, s 114(1)(c).
[119] ibid, s 117, ie 'created or received by a person in the course of a trade, business, profession or other occupation, or as the holder of a paid or unpaid office' (2)(a).
[120] ibid, s 117(7).
[121] [1997] QB 65, 77.
[122] CJA, s 115(3)(b).
[123] ibid, s 129.
[124] *Wood* (1983) 76 Cr App R 23.

used, although clearly files stored over time, under different applications, may differ from the original.[125]

6.59 Despite this liberalization in respect of the admissibility of hearsay, the courts also retain a general discretion to exclude such evidence, where:

> the court is satisfied that the case for excluding the statement, taking account of the danger that to admit it would result in undue waste of time, substantially outweighs the case for admitting it, taking account of the value of the evidence.[126]

Given the volume of material potentially generated from digital media in a computer crime investigation, both content and meta-data, this discretion to exclude may prove valuable to the courts.

Computer-derived

6.60 Until 2000, English law had special rules governing the admissibility of evidence derived from computers in criminal proceedings. Such rules reflected a widely held view that computers 'are not infallible ... occasionally malfunction ... often have "bugs"' and therefore 'must be regarded as imperfect devices'.[127] However, the rules presented an increasing obstacle to the prosecution of computer-based crime and led to their eventual repeal. Despite the reform, other common law jurisdictions continue to impose special conditions on the admissibility of computer-derived evidence, such as Botswana,[128] even though the Commonwealth Secretariat has drafted a 'Model Law on Electronic Evidence' designed to facilitate and harmonize reform on the issue.[129] In addition, many of the issues raised in relation to this 'old' admissibility requirement continue to be relevant in respect of questions concerning the exclusion of hearsay evidence and the probative value of computer-derived evidence, especially in relation to issues of data integrity.

6.61 Under the Police and Criminal Evidence Act 1984, all computer evidence, both real and hearsay,[130] had to comply with s 69:

> (1) In any proceedings, a statement in a document produced by a computer shall not be admissible as evidence of any fact stated therein unless it is shown—
> > (a) that there are no reasonable grounds for believing that the statement is inaccurate because of improper use of the computer;
> > (b) that at all material times the computer was operating properly, or if not, that any respect in which it was not operating properly or was out of operation was not such as to affect the production of the document or the accuracy of its contents.

To satisfy a court that the s 69(1) conditions had been met, it was necessary to obtain either a signed statement or oral testimony from a person who occupies 'a responsible position' in relation to the operation of the computer system.[131] Therefore, the evidential burden fell on the party relying on the computer evidence, generally the prosecution.

---

[125] Tapper, C, 'Electronic evidence and the Criminal Justice Act 2003', 10(7) *Computer and Telecommunications Law Review* 164 (2004).

[126] CJA, s 126(1).

[127] *Minors* [1989] 1 WLR 441, 443D–E per Steyn, J.

[128] Electronic Records (Evidence) Act 2014.

[129] Draft Model Law, above, n 9.

[130] *Shephard* [1993] AC 380.

[131] Police and Criminal Evidence Act 1984, Sch 3, Pt II, paras 8 and 9. See *R v Shephard* [1993] 1 All ER 225.

The broad nature of the language used in s 69(1) presented obvious opportunities for a party **6.62** to challenge computer-derived evidence. The conditions were therefore the subject of significant consideration by the courts, requiring the court to hold a trial within a trial (*voir dire*).

In a networked environment, one issue that arose is the extent to which s 69(1) was to **6.63** be complied with in respect of each and every machine involved in the processing of the evidential information. In *Cochrane*,[132] the court upheld an appeal concerning a prosecution for theft of monies from a building society's cash machines because the Crown were unable to adduce evidence about the operation of the company's mainframe computer that had authorized the withdrawal, as well as the cash machine itself. However, identifying all the potential computers would obviously be problematic in an open networked environment such as the Internet, where data can pass through numerous intermediary machines. In *Waddon*,[133] the court held that the computers involved in the transmission of an image across the Internet were not involved in its 'production' when printed from the investigator's computer and therefore did not require certification under s 69. Network-derived evidence does, however, raise the possibility of challenge both in respect of the provenance of any data and the nature of any intermediate processing that may have occurred. In a cloud-computing environment, for example, a user may utilize a Software-as-a-Service application that may reside on a third-party Platform-as-a-Service, which depends on an Infrastructure-as-a-Service operated by another provider. Such complex ecosystems may present possibilities for evidential challenge against cloud-derived evidence.[134]

In terms of the system 'operating properly', two broad categories of argument would be **6.64** pursued by defence counsel. First, the system had faults, errors or other malfunctions that impacted on the reliability of the data produced from the system. Second, that the criminal conduct itself had generated such faults, errors or malfunctions in the computer system and/or its data content.

With respect to the first argument, the House of Lords was asked to consider the issue in **6.65** *DPP v McKeown and Jones*.[135] Here an intoximeter used to analyse the amount of alcohol in a person's breath was found to have an inaccurate clock. In the Divisional Court, the defendants successfully argued that the clock's inaccuracy rendered the statement detailing the level of alcohol present in the defendant inadmissible on the grounds that s 69(1)(b) could not be complied with. This was subsequently overturned in the House of Lords, with Lord Hoffmann stating:

> A malfunction is relevant if it affects the way in which the computer processes, stores or retrieves the information used to generate the statement tendered in evidence. Other malfunctions do not matter.[136]

Expert testimony would still be required, however, as to the source and impact of any discernable malfunction within a computer on its various data processing functions.

---

[132] [1993] Crim LR 48.
[133] [2000] All ER (D) 502.
[134] See Taylor, M et al, 'Digital evidence in cloud computing systems', 26(3) *Computer Law and Security*, 304 (2010). See also Millard, C, *Cloud Computing Law*, Oxford University Press, 2013.
[135] [1997] 1 WLR 295.
[136] *McKeown and Jones* [1997] 1 WLR 295, at 302.

6.66   As an example of the second argument, in *Levin*,[137] defence counsel challenged certain evidence presented by Citibank on the grounds that since the accused had improperly used the computer system operated by Citibank, the requirements of s 69(1)(a) could not be satisfied. The court rejected this argument noting that 'unauthorised use of the computer is not of itself a ground for believing that the statements recorded by it were inaccurate'.[138] Clearly, were there more extensive evidence of deliberate or unintended modification to data held on the system, the value of such computer-derived evidence could be open to challenge on such grounds. To prevent this argument being deployed against the admissibility of computer-derived evidence, the Commonwealth 'Model Computer and Computer-related Crimes Bill' includes the following provision:

> In proceedings for an offence against a law of [enacting country], the fact that:
> (a) it is alleged that an offence of interfering with a computer system has been committed; and
> (b) evidence has been generated from that computer system; does not of itself prevent that evidence from being admitted.[139]

6.67   Section 69(1)(b) also required that a computer must have been 'operating properly' at the 'material time'. In *Connolly v Lancashire County Council*,[140] audit records were submitted with respect to the correct operation of a computerized weighbridge. However, the records related to an examination of the weighbridge system carried out nearly three months prior to the date of the alleged offence. The records were not accepted by the courts as evidence that the system was operating properly at the 'material time'. A party may therefore need to be able to show that any system from which evidence is derived was functioning appropriately at the time the evidence was generated, for example through audit records.

6.68   Despite the generally favourable attitude of the courts to the admission of computer-derived evidence, considerable disquiet had been voiced against the s 69 conditions. In response, the Law Commission proposed reform of the rules to re-introduce the pre-1984 maxim *omnia praesumuntur rite esse acta*, a common law presumption that things have been done properly.[141] It justified this change of position on five grounds, although the fifth was subsequently resolved by the House of Lords decision in *McKeown*:

- That the majority of inaccuracies were due to errors in data entry and were obvious (the 'garbage in, garbage out' adage again).
- Developments in the complexity of ICTs rendered compliance with s 69 increasingly impracticable.

---

[137] *Governor of Brixton Prison and another, ex parte Levin* [1996] 4 All ER 350.
[138] ibid, at 359c. It is interesting to note that the judge refers to the recording of statements, whereas s 69(1) is only concerned with the production of statements.
[139] Draft Model Law, above, n 9, Art 20.
[140] (1994) RTR 79.
[141] See Law Commission, 'Evidence in Criminal Proceedings: Hearsay and Related Topics', Consultation Paper No 138, HMSO, 1995; and Law Com No 245, 'Evidence in Criminal Proceedings: Hearsay and Related Topics', HMSO, 1997, Pt XIII and Recommendation 50.

- A relying party may not be in a position to comply with the conditions, since they are simply a recipient of the computer-derived document, which may have been produced by a computer located in another jurisdiction.
- The conditions were only applicable to tendered evidence, not to processes external to the trial, such as the forensic analysis carried out by an expert.[142]

The presumption effectively shifts the burden of proof with respect to the reliability of com- **6.69** puter evidence from the party submitting the evidence to the party against whom the evidence is being adduced, therefore considerably reducing the likelihood of a challenge being raised. A similar reform was adopted with respect to the admissibility of computer evidence in civil proceedings by the Civil Evidence Act 1995, repealing the special provisions for computer evidence under s 5 of the Civil Evidence Act 1968. The repeal of s 69 came into force in April 2000.[143]

Network-derived: Intercept evidence

As discussed previously, one category of evidence that is considered, as a class, to be inad- **6.70** missible is data obtained 'in transmission' through interception: network-derived evidence. Section 17(1) of the RIPA provides that:

(1) Subject to section 18, no evidence shall be adduced, question asked, assertion or disclosure made or other thing done in, for the purposes of or in connection with any legal proceedings or Inquiries Act proceedings which (in any manner)—
   (a) discloses, in circumstances from which its origin in anything falling within subsection (2) may be inferred, any of the contents of an intercepted communication or any related communications data; or
   (b) tends (apart from any such disclosure) to suggest that anything falling within subsection (2) has or may have occurred or be going to occur.
(2) The following fall within this subsection—
   (a) conduct by a person falling within subsection (3) that was or would be an offence under section 1(1) or (2) of this Act or under section 1 of the Interception of Communications Act 1985;
   (b) a breach by the Secretary of State of his duty under section 1(4) of this Act;
   (c) the issue of an interception warrant or of a warrant under the Interception of Communications Act 1985;
   (d) the making of an application by any person for an interception warrant, or for a warrant under that Act;
   (e) the imposition of any requirement on any person to provide assistance with giving effect to an interception warrant.[144]

The purpose of the exclusion is to protect from disclosure, forensic inquiry, and defence counsel matters related to the operation of the warrant regime under s 5 of the RIPA, and the activities of the intelligence and law enforcement agencies. The provision is applicable in both criminal and civil proceedings.

---

[142] Law Com No 245, paras 13.6–13.11.
[143] Youth Justice and Criminal Evidence Act 1999, s 60.
[144] The exceptions under s 18 include disclosure.

6.71 By contrast, interception evidence *would* be admissible when it does not reveal anything about the activities of UK law enforcement agencies. So, for example, where a communication service provider engages in interception in the course of enforcing provisions of the Communications Act 2003, as provided for under the RIPA, s 3(3), the intercept product would be admissible.[145] Likewise, as stated by Lord Bingham:

> . . . there was no rule of law or practice which rendered inadmissible in criminal proceedings the product of any unofficial or private eavesdropping activity.[146]

Such evidence would also be admissible if it comes from an interception carried out in another country, even though it reveals information about the activities of foreign law enforcement agencies.[147]

6.72 Section 17 replicated the position adopted under the previous regime, the Interception of Communications Act 1985 (IOCA) at s 9, which had consumed considerable judicial attention, including three visits to the House of Lords.[148] However, questions of interpretation have continued to come before the courts, which is perhaps to be expected given the increasing use of intercept evidence in the fight against organized crime and the obvious opportunity the provision gives a defence counsel to have incriminating evidence excluded from the court.

6.73 In *Attorney-General's Reference (No 5 of 2002) sub nom R v W*,[149] the House of Lords was asked to consider the scope of the s 17 exclusion, specifically whether it prevented a court from investigating whether an interception had taken place on a private or public telecommunication system. The original case concerned the suspected disclosure of confidential and sensitive information by certain police officers to unauthorized persons, including journalists. The prosecution served evidence that the interception had taken place on a 'private telecommunication system', while defence asserted that it has occurred on a 'public telecommunication system'. When the trial judged ruled that the defence were unable, by virtue of s 17, to make such an assertion, defence asked for the prosecution's evidence to be excluded on the grounds of not being fair, under the Police and Criminal Evidence Act 1984, s 78, to which the judge agreed. As a consequence, the prosecution's case failed.

6.74 On appeal by the Attorney-General, the Court of Appeal overturned the decision of the trial judge,[150] but recognizing the complexities of the issues referred it on to the House of Lords. The Lords noted that under the 1985 regime, the exclusion under s 9 had not prevented the courts from considering the public or private nature of the telecommunication system, a then particularly critical distinction as the 1985 Act only addressed interception when carried out over a public system.[151] Lord Bingham then went on to state:

---

[145] eg Communications Act, s 125. Similar provisions were contained in the Interception of Communications Act 1985, s 1(3)(a), and were considered in *Morgans v DPP* [2001] 1 AC 315.

[146] In *Attorney-General's Reference (No 5 of 2002) sub nom R v W* (2005) 1 AC 167, at 174H. See also *Avocet Hardware plc v Morrison*, EAT, 17 February 2003 (re: incorrect exclusion of private intercept evidence); also *Senat* (1968) 52 Cr App R 282.

[147] See *R v P and others* [2001] 2 All ER 58.

[148] ie *Preston* [1994] 2 AC 130; *Morgans v DPP* [2001] 1 AC 315; *Sargent* [2003] 1 AC 347.

[149] [2004] UKHL 40; [2005] 1 AC 167.

[150] [2003] EWCA Crim 1632, [2003] 1 WLR 2902.

[151] See eg *Ahmed (Iftikhar)* [1995] Crim LR 246; *Effik* [1994] 3 All ER 458, HL(E); *Allen and Bunting* [2001] Crim LR 739.

Save where necessary to preserve the security of warranted interception, there is no reason why it should have been sought to exclude the product of any lawful interception where relevant evidence in any case whether civil or criminal.[152]

Therefore, while s 17 potentially excludes evidence of an intercept carried out on either a public or private telecommunication system, where the intercept was lawful, by virtue of s 1(5) (ie under s 3, s 4, or s 1(5)(c)), the evidence would be admissible.[153] As a consequence, the courts must be able to inquire as to the lawfulness of the intercept in those circumstances, which would include establishing whether the interception has been carried out on a public or private system and, if private, whether it was carried out by, or on behalf of, the person 'with a right to control' the system.[154]

Such a strident purposive approach should minimize the number of situations where intercept evidence is subject to exclusion, although it can also be argued that precise drafting is particularly critical in the field of criminal procedure.[155] However, the issue continues to be live, as a result of the Government's 'war on terrorism' and consequential new legal powers and problems, such as the detention of suspects under Part 4 of the Anti-terrorism, Crime and Security Act 2001, where part of the evidence comprised inadmissible intercepts.[156] Over the years, there have been calls from a number of parliamentary committees for a reform of the current rules, to bring the UK into line with nearly all other jurisdictions that allow the admission of intercept evidence.[157] In the US, for example, intercept evidence is only excluded where it is obtained unlawfully.[158]   **6.75**

The Prime Minister commissioned a review of the current position in July 2003, to examine whether the use of intercept evidence would secure more convictions of those engaged in organized crime and terrorism. The then Home Secretary, Charles Clarke, announced the Government's conclusions in January 2005.[159] The review did not make a recommendation about whether the current system should change, focusing instead on the perceived benefits and risks. It reported that a change would improve convictions of some serious criminals, but not terrorists,[160] which seems a surprising assertion given that their criminal conduct is likely to be of a similar nature.   **6.76**

The Government concluded, therefore, that there were insufficient benefits to bring in changes at the current time. It also felt that the main risks could not currently be mitigated 'partly because of the difficulty of assessing the impact of major changes expected in   **6.77**

---

[152] [2005] 1 AC 167, at 179E.

[153] ibid, at 182G, interpreting s 18(4), an approach which is supported in the Explanatory Notes to the Regulation of Investigatory Powers Act, para 142.

[154] Which excludes the intercept conduct from criminal liability, see Regulation of Investigatory Powers Act 2000 (RIPA), s 1(6).

[155] See eg Rees, T and Ormerod, D, 'Evidence: Regulation of Investigatory Powers Act 2000, s. 17(1) – interception of telephone conversation', *Criminal Law Review* 222 [2005].

[156] *A and others v Secretary of State for the Home Department* [2005] 3 All ER 169.

[157] See eg Privy Counsellor Review Committee, *Anti-terrorism, Crime and Security Act 2001: Review Report*, HC 100, HMSO, December 2003 ('the Newton Committee'), paras 208–15; and the Joint Parliamentary Committee on Human Rights, 18th Report, July 2004, paras 54–6.

[158] 18 USC s 2515 'Prohibition of use as evidence of intercepted wire or oral communications'.

[159] Commons Hansard, vol 430, No 28, 26 January 2005, Col 19WS.

[160] ibid, accordingly it is claimed that it 'would not have made a critical difference in supporting criminal prosecution of those detained under ATCSA (Part 4) powers' (ie those represented in *A and others v Secretary of State for the Home Department* [2005] 3 All ER 169).

communications technologies over the next few years',[161] but which appears an open-ended unsupported position based on a conception that technological developments are going to plateau or stabilize sufficiently at some point in the future!

6.78 The issue did not go away, however, and a bill permitting the use of intercept evidence in criminal proceedings in respect of serious crime and terrorism was introduced into the Lords in October 2005.[162] The Home Secretary again considered a change to the existing position, as opposition from the law enforcement community diminished, as indicated in evidence given to the Home Affairs Committee by Andy Hayman, on behalf of ACPO:

> I have personally moved my position. I originally started off by being fairly unsupportive of the notion of using the material, mainly on the basis that it was starting to disclose methodology to the other side. I think that is now well and truly worn-out because I think most people are aware of that . . . The next point which I had reservations about was the true logistics about transcribing the material, where you could go into reams of material. Again, that is a fairly moot point now, given that you can be very selective about the things you are going to transcribe if you are very precise on your investigation and focused. I think I am moving, as I know ACPO is, to a conclusion that in a selected number of cases, not just for terrorism but also for serious crime, it would be useful. I think also it does make us look a little bit foolish that everywhere else in the world is using it to good effect.[163]

However, the Home Secretary reiterated that two problems for Government remained to be solved. First, the concern that disclosures about intelligence activities may prejudice the interests of the intelligence services; as noted by Baroness Ramsey of Cartvale in a Lords debate arguing against a change in the current position:

> This is not a matter of principle, it is a question of practicality and the effect of such a move on the efficiency and productivity of the services and agencies engaged in interception.[164]

A second problem is the issue of disclosure and the potential volume of material involved.[165]

6.79 The review did put forward a proposal for a 'preferred legal model' for the use of intercept evidence, were reform to be accepted, which would result in the possible issuance of three different kinds of intercept warrant: 'intelligence only, non-evidential and evidential'.[166] The first two would continue to be issued by the Secretary of State, while the last would be authorized by a judge. A partial change, as proposed by the review, would likely present another layer of complexity for the courts to struggle with.

6.80 Another review of the issue was carried out by the Privy Council in 2007, chaired by Sir John Chilcot.[167] The report supported the principle that intercept evidence should be admissible in court, subject to various qualifications. The Government accepted the recommendations

---

[161] Commons Hansard, above, n 159.

[162] Interception of Communications (Admissibility of Evidence) Bill, 10 October 2005. Introduced into the Lords by Lord Lloyd of Berwick. See Lords Hansard, 18 November 2005, Cols 1301 et seq. The Bill was reintroduced into the Lords in the 2012–14 session, but again to no effect.

[163] Home Affairs Select Committee, *Fourth Report: Terrorism Detention Powers*, HC 910-1, 3 July 2006, para 113 ('Home Affairs Report').

[164] Lords Hansard, 18 November 2005, Col 1306.

[165] ibid. See also Home Affairs Report, above n 163, para 115.

[166] Commons Hansard, vol 430, No 28, 26 January 2005, Col 19WS.

[167] *Privy Council Review of Intercept as Evidence*, Report, Cm 7324, 30 January 2008, available at <https://www.gov.uk/government/uploads/system/uploads/attachment_data/file/228513/7324.pdf>.

of the Privy Council and commissioned further work on its implementation. However, by 2009, the Government had concluded that, although the operational requirements could be achieved, in terms of safeguarding the work of the law enforcement and intelligence agencies, the model would not be 'legally viable, in terms of ensuring continued fairness at trial'.[168] The matter was therefore moved to the file called 'needs further work'.

At some point, therefore, the Government may have to concede that the complexities cre- **6.81** ated by the admissibility provisions outweigh any possible benefits, and that such evidence should simply be subject to an application for public interest immunity,[169] on a case-by-case basis, rather than as a class. It is widely expected that the current rules will not survive for much longer, since '[o]utside the Government there is universal support for the use of intercept evidence in court'.[170]

Section 78

While the previous grounds for exclusion have direct relevance to computer- and network- **6.82** derived evidence, there is also a general power given to courts to exclude evidence on grounds of fairness. At s 78(1) of the Police and Criminal Evidence Act 1978, it states:

> In any proceedings the court may refuse to allow evidence on which the prosecution proposes to rely to be given if it appears to the court that, having regard to all the circumstances, including the circumstances in which the evidence was obtained, the admission of the evidence would have such an adverse effect on the fairness of the proceedings that the court ought not to admit it.

This statutory provision extends the court's power to exclude beyond that already existing under common law.[171] The wording of the provision makes it clear that considerations of fairness extend back to the manner in which the evidence was obtained, not just the trial itself. A determination to exclude under s 78 is not to be seen as an exercise of discretion in the same manner that occurs when a court orders a stay for abuse of process, engaging in a balancing exercise of the various interests present, since where a court holds that admission of a piece of evidence *would have* an adverse effect of the fairness of the proceedings, it is duty bound to exclude it.[172]

The application of this provision has been significantly enhanced with the coming into **6.83** force of the Human Rights Act 1998 and the subsequent incorporation of the European Convention on Human Rights. Not only have courts been obliged to consider its application as a matter of course, defence counsel have more frequently made claims for evidence to be excluded on such grounds, particularly breach of a person's right to privacy under

---

[168] Home Office Report, *Intercept as Evidence*, Cm 7760, December 2009.

[169] Civil Procedure and Investigations Act 1996, s 3(6). See also the CPR, r 22.3.

[170] Home Affairs Report, above, n 163, para 116. In September 2006, the Attorney-General, Lord Goldsmith, also came out publicly in favour of changing the current rules: see Dyer, C, 'Courts set to admit wiretap evidence', *The Guardian*, 21 September 2006, available at <http://www.theguardian.com/politics/2006/sep/21/ukcrime.immigrationpolicy>. See also the *Intercept evidence: Lifting the ban*, Justice Report, October 2006, which carried out a comparative review of other common law jurisdictions and concluded that the 'current ban is archaic, unnecessary and counter-productive'.

[171] *Sang* [1980] AC 402.

[172] *Chalkley* [1998] QB 848, at 874. However, Ashworth and Redmayne, above, n 30, at 322, suggest that other statements concerning s 78 in *Chalkley* should be disregarded.

Art 8.[173] However, despite the large amount of case law on s 78, few clearly discernable principles governing its application have been seen to have emerged.[174]

6.84 Since the investigative activities of public law enforcement agencies have been placed under a consolidated framework, under the RIPA, there have been numerous challenges on the basis that evidence was gathered either without authorization, or the form of authorization was incorrect, for example the surveillance should have been viewed as an act of interception.[175] To date, however, such applications appear to have been largely unsuccessful.[176] It is perhaps inevitable that this would generate substantial scope for legal argument during the first years of a new regime, and it is likely that such issues will be raised less frequently over time.

6.85 Where a procedural code is applicable to the actions of an investigator, the code will be admissible as evidence in criminal proceedings for consideration by a court.[177] The more technical the breach, the less likely are the courts to exclude the evidence;[178] conversely, where the rule breach causes a 'significant and substantial'[179] disadvantage to the defendant the evidence will be excluded.[180] The sole consideration when deciding to exclude under s 78 is one of fairness; therefore, a court should not exclude simply to punish the investigating agency for its failure to comply with a code provision,[181] since it already has jurisdiction to order a stay for abuse of process. Some uncertainty continues to exist in respect of the treatment of evidence obtained in another jurisdiction, under circumstances that differ from those procedural rules applicable under English law.[182]

E. Probative Value or Evidential Weight

6.86 As noted in the discussion on admissibility, defence applications to have evidence excluded will generally target either the reliability of the evidence itself or the process under which such evidence was obtained. Where such applications are rejected and the evidence admitted, the defence have a second opportunity to challenge the reliability of evidence during trial by casting doubt on the probative value or weight that should be given by the judge and/or jury to such evidence in proving all the elements of the offence. The defence objective is to raise sufficient doubt to undermine the standard of proof required of the prosecution, that of 'beyond reasonable doubt'.

6.87 With the removal of the s 69 obstacle to the admissibility of computer-derived evidence, the question generally becomes one of probative value: what weight or value should be given to

---

[173] eg *Khan v United Kingdom* (2001) 31 EHRR 45.
[174] See Ashworth and Redmayne, above, n 30, at 320 et seq.
[175] eg *R v E* [2004] EWCA Crim 1243, [2004] 2 Cr App R 484.
[176] As of September 2006, no reported cases under RIPA have excluded evidence under PACE, s 78.
[177] PACE, s 67(11) and RIPA, s 72(3). They are also admissible in civil proceedings.
[178] *Blackwell* [1995] 2 Cr App R 625, at 641.
[179] *Quinn* [1990] Crim LR 581.
[180] Ashworth and Redmayne, above, n 30, at 320–1.
[181] *Delaney* (1989) 88 Cr App R 338, at 341. See also Ormerod, D and Perry, D (eds), *Blackstone's Criminal Practice 2016*, Oxford University Press, para F.2.24.
[182] See Gane, C and Mackarel, M, 'The admissibility of evidence obtained from abroad into criminal proceedings: The interpretation of mutual legal assistance treaties and use of evidence irregularly obtained' 4(2) *European Journal of Crime, Criminal Law and Criminal Justice* 98 (1996), at 116.

such evidence? Statute provides little or no guidance on this issue. The Police and Criminal Evidence Act did contain the following provision in respect of computer-derived evidence, although it has been repealed along with s 69:

> In estimating the weight, if any, to be attached to a statement regard shall be had to . . . in particular—
>
> (a) to the question whether or not the information . . . was supplied to the relevant computer . . . contemporaneously with the occurrence or existence of the facts . . .; and
>
> (b) to the question whether or not the person concerned with the supply of information . . . had any incentive to conceal or misrepresent the facts.[183]

While the courts are no longer instructed to consider these particular issues, such matters can obviously still be relevant on the facts of a specific case.

In the absence of statutory guidance, a court may be referred to other sources of guidance **6.88** that may be considered relevant to either the conditions in which the evidence was held by the forensic source or the manner in which it was obtained by the party adducing such evidence, generally the investigating agency.

Advice has been developed by standards-making and industry bodies that address good **6.89** practice and procedure in respect of the maintenance of digital evidence and its handling in the course of an investigation. At a national level, for example, the British Standards Institution issued a 'Code of Practice for Legal Admissibility and Evidential Weight of Information Stored Electronically'[184] in 1999, which subsequently formed the basis of an international standard: ISO 15489 'Information and documentation—Records management'.[185] Another ISO standard was adopted in 2012, 'Guidelines for identification, collection, acquisition, and preservation of digital evidence',[186] which is designed to ensure that the forensic process is carried out in a sufficiently robust manner to enable the product to be used as evidence. These standards assist users of information systems to meet their organizational, regulatory and legal needs, although compliance with the recommended procedures may obviously support an assertion of probative value in the course of criminal proceedings. The Information Assurance Advisory Council has published guidance, 'Digital Evidence, Digital Investigations and E-Disclosure',[187] which addresses the need for organizations to have a 'forensic readiness plan' to enable them to respond appropriately and effectively to future requirements to produce reliable electronic evidence.

In terms of law enforcement, as noted in Chapter 4, national agencies have issued good **6.90** practice guidance about handling computer-derived evidence, which disseminates the lessons garnered by experienced computer crime investigators.[188] While designed to support

---

[183] PACE, Sch 3, Part II: Provisions Supplementary to s 69, at 11.

[184] Standard No DISC PD 0008:1999, 15 July 1999, withdrawn 23 December 2003.

[185] 15 September 2009, available at <http://www.iso.org/iso/catalogue_detail?csnumber=31908>.

[186] ISO/IEC 27037:2012, 15 October 2015, available at <http://www.iso.org/iso/catalogue_detail?csnumber=4438>.

[187] First published in September 2005, the 4th edn was published in November 2013, available from <http://www.iaac.org.uk/media/1347/iaac-forensic-4th-edition.pdf>.

[188] eg in the UK, the ACPO Good Practice Guide for Digital Evidence, 5th edn, March 2012, available as <http://library.college.police.uk/docs/acpo/digital-evidence-2012.pdf>; in the US, the Department of Justice manual, *Searching and seizing computers and obtaining electronic evidence in criminal investigations*, Office of Legal Education Executive Office for United States Attorneys, 2009, available at <http://

investigators, such guidance also inevitably provides potential grounds upon which defence counsel, or their expert witness, may challenge the probative value of computer-derived evidence, where such guidance has not been followed. It has been noted in relation to the ACPO guide, for example, that failure to comply with Principle 3, which requires that all relevant processes be auditable and capable of being replicated, is a common ground for challenging prosecution evidence.[189]

6.91 In general the features that computer-derived evidence must exhibit can be drawn from the field of data security, since the features that an organization needs to protect its data are comparable to the features that evidence should display: authenticity, integrity, and accountability.[190]

Authenticity

6.92 Authenticity is concerned with the origin of the material and can be further subdivided into two tests. The first is the need to establish a link between the material being adduced as evidence and the accused. Such evidence depends on investigators being able to adequately address the 'identity problem' considered in Chapter 4. This may create a forensic challenge for a number of reasons, obviously more so in a networked environment, whether open, such as the Internet, or closed, such as a corporate network.

6.93 The location of the source computer may mean that multiple users had potential access to the machine at the relevant time, which can make it difficult to show 'beyond reasonable doubt' that the accused was the person with 'his fingers on the keyboard'. In *Vatsal Patel*,[191] the accused was a contract programmer at Dun and Bradstreet who was alleged to have installed 'wrecking programs' on the organization's network to delete completed development work, in order to extend the period of his lucrative contract. He was acquitted, however, because the prosecution was unable to prove that it was Patel who had initiated the programs, partly due to the physical position of the relevant terminal behind a concrete pillar!

6.94 In a networked environment, where the illegal content or the act is only evidenced from remote sources, authenticity will mean establishing an adequate evidential link between the material and the virtual identity used, and then between that and the defendant. As much as machines may have multiple users, online identities may be shared, compromised, or 'spoofed', where someone deliberately inserts incorrect identification details into a message.

6.95 Even when it is beyond dispute that the source computer belongs to the suspect, a second course of challenge is for the accused to deny that he was aware that such illegal or incriminating material was present on his machine: the so-called 'Trojan horse' defence and its variants. As noted in Chapter 2, widespread ignorance about the manner in which

---

www.justice.gov/sites/default/files/criminal-ccips/legacy/2015/01/14/ssmanual2009.pdf>; while the EU and Council of Europe have published an 'Electronic evidence guide' (Version 1, March 2013), available at <http://www.coe.int/en/web/cybercrime/trainings>.

[189] Interview with Peter Sommer, 21 June 2006.

[190] See also Turner, P, 'Digital provenance—interpretation, verification and corroboration', 2 *Digital Investigation* 45 (2005), who proposes an expanded list of attributes for 'good provenance': unique, unambiguous, concise, repeatable, and comprehensible.

[191] Aylesbury Crown Court, 2 July 1993. Reported in 5(1) *Computers and Law* (1993), available at <http://www.computerevidence.co.uk/Cases/Patel/Articles/Patel.htm>.

computers and the Internet work, coupled with the technical reality that data can be placed surreptitiously on a remote machine (eg 'spyware'), means that such claims can be a fruitful basis for disputing prosecution evidence.

In *Mould*,[192] for example, the accused maintained that the indecent images found on his **6.96** machine had got there accidentally and unknowingly. To counter this claim, the prosecution was required to adduce evidence that showed that Mould had an interest in paedophile material and had previously accessed newsgroups, chat rooms, and websites concerned with such material. In *Schofields*,[193] the prosecution was unable to offer evidence against the defence expert's report that a 'Trojan horse' virus found on the machine of the accused could have placed the indecent images on the hard drive without his knowledge.[194] In *Caffrey*,[195] the jury acquitted the defendant of a s 3(1) offence under the Computer Misuse Act 1990 even though the prosecution expert witness stated that no evidence of the presence of a 'Trojan horse' virus could be found. The defendant argued that it was impossible to test every file on the computer and that the virus could be designed to self-destruct leaving no trace, which seems to have sown sufficient doubt in the minds of the jurors.

To assist the process of linking the material with the accused, Barrett describes a 'scene- **6.97** of-habitation' analysis process, which involves examining 'innocent' as well as 'criminal' information contained in the seized media.[196] By examining the suspect's normal usage of a range of applications, such as email, patterns may be discerned that can reinforce an assertion of authorship. In *Takenaka (UK) Ltd v Frankl*,[197] evidence linking the defendant to the sending of certain defamatory emails included emails send to the defendant's wife, using a different account but sent in proximity; communications that recognized the presence of the computer in the defendant's hotel room; and email extracts saved in a Word document.[198] Such an approach does raise potential legal concerns, however, where material is deemed outside the scope of the original search warrant, or it involves collateral intrusion on an individual's privacy, whether the suspect's or a third party's.

A second authenticity test is to link the material to the relevant computer or system, the **6.98** 'computer source' test. This is partly an extension of the person/material test, since people operate in a networked environment through computers, whether using a PC, tablet, or a smartphone. However, it also arises from the manner in which some environments operate. For example, what is displayed on a computer screen when a 'webpage' is downloaded over the Internet may potentially comprise a mosaic of material drawn from different computers based in different jurisdictions, the image being assembled only at the moment it is requested.[199] Such mechanisms have apparently been used for the distribution of child abuse images. As well as raising problematic forensic issues in terms of identifying the source of such material, it may offer a potential defence against a charge for supply.

---

[192] [2001] 2 Cr App R (S) 8.
[193] Reported in The Times Online, 18 April 2003.
[194] This also arose in *Julian Green*, Exeter Crown Court, July 2003.
[195] Southwark Crown Court, 17 October 2003.
[196] Barrett, N, *Traces of Guilt*, Bantam Press, 2004, at 214 et seq.
[197] [2001] EWCA Civ 348.
[198] ibid, para 22; although in this case the standard of proof is civil rather than criminal.
[199] eg in a web environment, image files (<IMG SRC ...>) are often stored separately from text files (<A HREF ...>).

Integrity

6.99 In terms of integrity, the concern is to be able to show that the material is accurate and complete. This essentially reflects the 'operating properly' test that was previously an admissibility test under s 69. While the burden of proof has been shifted, the party adducing computer-derived evidence may still need to ensure that they have the necessary evidence, whether oral or documented, to be able to refute any serious challenge raised as to the integrity of evidence derived from a computer or network. For a complex system, this may require an array of witnesses with familiarity of the different components and services comprising, or connected to, the system.

Accountability

6.100 Accountability is concerned with the circumstances under which evidence is obtained and subsequently handled. Computer and network-derived evidence is notoriously vulnerable to alteration, which extends from the manner of obtaining it, the acquisition process discussed in Chapter 4, to the handling of such evidence by investigators, prosecutors, and expert witnesses at all stages until trial, the 'chain of custody test'.[200] This could be relevant, for example, where a digital copy of an original item of evidence was being relied upon in court.[201]

6.101 A simple example of the vulnerability of digital evidence to alteration is a document created using Microsoft Word. As well as the document, the application generates meta-data about the document, for example detailing the time and date the document was created, modified, and accessed.[202] However, an investigator, when accessing such a document, may inadvertently alter the document in some way and therefore alter such meta-data.[203] Alterations made to a file once it is in the possession of an investigator obviously create a strong basis upon which to raise a challenge to the probative value of evidence. Law enforcement agencies therefore need to follow procedures designed to minimize such accountability threats and ensure the provenance of any adduced evidence, including disk 'imaging'[204] techniques and screen shots.[205]

F. Expert Witnesses

6.102 The complexities of obtaining and presenting computer-derived evidence to a court will mean that in many cases experts will be required to assist the court. The expert may be required to explain to the judge and jury in court the evidence being adduced, since much computer- and network-derived evidence is unintelligible to the normal person.[206] The

---

[200] Sommer, P, 'Digital footprints: Assessing computer evidence', *Criminal Law Review*, Special Edition (December 1998).

[201] *Kajala v Noble* (1982) 75 Cr App R 149.

[202] To view these details, on the menu go to File, Properties, Statistics.

[203] eg if you go to the menu, Tools, Word Count, recounting the words in a document constitutes a recorded modification.

[204] Where a complete copy of the computer's permanent memory is preserved. Also referred to as 'bit stream imaging methodology', see Kenneally, E and Brown, C, 'Risk sensitive digital evidence collection', 2 *Digital Investigation* 101 (2005).

[205] eg using Lotus ScreenCam.

[206] See Barrett, N, *Traces of Guilt*, Bantam Press, 2004, at 69–70, who describes expert witnesses as having three principal tasks: to describe the computer and its operation of relevance to the case; to assist counsel's understanding; and to appear in court and address any questions put.

person will generally be primarily concerned with the properties of the ICTs from which the evidence is derived, rather than the content of the retrieved material. An expert essentially acts as an interpreter, addressing those matters 'likely to be outside the experience of and knowledge of a judge or jury'.[207] As such, the role of an expert is not simply to present facts, but also to offer opinions and interpretations on matters on which he has expertise.[208] Indeed, the ability to state opinions distinguishes an expert from the general rule applicable to witnesses that they should only give evidence of facts they have perceived,[209] although it must be clear to the court on what facts any expert opinions are based.[210]

In the adversarial common law system, both the prosecution and defence teams may need **6.103** to make use of the services of 'expert witnesses', although they are both under a duty to be 'objective and unbiased'.[211] By contrast, in civil law systems, such as France and Germany, an official expert will be nominated by the court that has a different status from a witness.[212] The benefits of one system over the other have been a much debated topic over the years.[213]

The nature of the criminal process, and indeed in civil proceedings, means the prosecution **6.104** expert will often be engaged at an earlier stage in the proceedings than the defence expert. A prosecution expert may carry out a range of tasks, from assisting law enforcement in the investigation and collection of evidence at the scene of the crime, to analysing the seized material and presenting it in court. The defence expert will be looking for any flaws in the evidence itself; the procedure under which it was collected, analysed, and presented; possible arguments that may be used by defence counsel; or, indeed, confirming to the instructing solicitor that the evidence does not support the defendant's contentions, which may facilitate a guilty plea.[214]

One problem with experts in the fields of computer and communications technologies is **6.105** the huge range of systems and applications that may be involved and therefore the range of skills being required of an expert. An expert in Unix systems, for example, may not be able to assess IP-based transmission protocols and networks. The technology is also developing so rapidly that an expert's knowledge, if he is no longer actively working in an area, may become outdated relatively rapidly. Therefore, a complex case may require the use of a series of experts.[215] However, there is also a general absence of formalized professionalism within the field of computing, which means that it may be difficult for lawyers to assess whether the skills of an expert are appropriate and sufficient for the tasks being asked of him, let alone whether he has the necessary communication skills to present effectively in a court of law.[216] Expertise will generally comprise a mix of qualifications and experience.

---

[207] Lord Mansfield in *Folkes v Chadd* (1782) 3 Doug KB 157.
[208] As a consequence, such evidence is sometimes referred to as 'opinion evidence'. See CPR, Pt 33 'Expert Evidence'.
[209] *Blackstone's Criminal Practice 2016*, above, n 181, at F10.
[210] *Golizadeh* [1995] Crim LR 232, where it was held that there is no requirement to actually produce the computer print-out that contained the facts on which the expert's opinion was derived.
[211] CPR, r 33.2(1)(a).
[212] However, variations exist in both systems. See generally Spencer, J, 'Evidence', in Delmas-Marty, M and Spencer, JR (eds), *European Criminal Procedures*, Cambridge University Press, 2005, at 632 et seq.
[213] For a review of the issues, see Roberts and Zuckerman, above, n 1, at 300 et seq.
[214] Interview with Peter Sommer, 21 June 2006.
[215] Kelman, A and Sizer, R, *The Computer in Court*, Ashgate, 1982.
[216] In March 2008, Terence 'Jim' Bates was convicted on four counts of making false statements in evidence in respect to his qualifications as a computer expert. See the related case, *Bates v Chief Constable of the Avon & Somerset Police* [2009] EWHC 942 (Admin).

6.106 As discussed previously, there are attempts to promote and enhance the professional status of computer forensic experts. In the UK, there was an attempt to establish an organization, the Council for the Registration of Forensic Practitioners, which eventually folded through lack of funding.[217] The Society of Expert Witnesses[218] provides a database of witnesses, but only offers five names in the field of information technology. This is not a market sector suffering from oversupply! In the US, there is a High Technology Criminal Investigators Association (HTCIA)[219] and internationally, there is the International Association of Computer Investigative Specialists (IACIS).[220]

6.107 The problem of resource has already been mentioned in respect of law enforcement, prosecution, and judicial experience in the area, but as the numbers quoted illustrate, the problem extends to all aspects of the legal process. Levels of financial remuneration obviously also have an impact on the supply of experts. Prosecution experts will be funded from limited police budgets, while defence experts will often have to negotiate with the Legal Aid Agency,[221] responsible for legal aid, with rates for both falling well below market rates.[222]

6.108 The shortage of qualified and experienced experts is further exacerbated when apparent mistakes occur, which attract the glare of publicity. In 2003, for example, Brian Stevens, a police officer involved in the Soham murder case, was arrested on accusations of possessing child abuse images on his computer. At trial, however, the CPS offered no evidence and admitted that the prosecution expert, Brian Underhill, had made critical errors in assessing the relevant evidence.[223] After such cases, experts tend to become more difficult to find and those that do are more cautious in their assessments, which may reduce the number of successful prosecutions.

6.109 In terms of the law, the use of experts is subject to certain procedural rules, which must be followed. For example, for an expert to accompany the police in the execution of a search warrant, the presence of the expert should be detailed in the warrant issued by the court.[224] During the execution of a search, the duty of experts is to assist law enforcement, although an appropriately 'authorised' person has the same search-and-seizure powers as the accompanying police officers, which is designed to facilitate the use of skilled civilians in searches involving computers, provided they are exercised in the company and under the supervision of a constable.[225]

---

[217] See Home Department Written Question, from Chris Grayling to the Home Secretary, available at <http://www.theyworkforyou.com/wrans/?id=2009-05-11d.273039.h>.

[218] See <http://www.sew.org.uk>.

[219] See <http://www.htcia.org/>.

[220] See <http://www.iacis.com>.

[221] See <https://www.gov.uk/government/organisations/legal-aid-agency>.

[222] See the Society of Expert Witnesses, 'Expert Fees under Attack', available at <https://www.sew.org.uk/ed/001_MoJCP1809/index.cfm>.

[223] See Vasagar, J and Hall, S, 'Soham policeman cleared of child porn charges after computer evidence blunder', *The Guardian*, 21 August 2003, available at <http://www.theguardian.com/uk/2003/aug/21/childprotection.children>.

[224] PACE, s 16(2): 'a warrant may authorise persons to accompany any constable'. See *Lord Advocate's Reference No 1 of 2002* (2002) SLT 1017, in which the accused, who was investigated for being part of the 'Wonderland Club' that traded in child pornography, successfully argued in the first instance that evidence obtained by a civilian employee was inadmissible on the grounds that his actions rendered the search irregular. This was overturned on appeal.

[225] PACE, s 16(2A) and (2B).

With rights come responsibilities, however, and legal controls governing the activities of **6.110** public law enforcement agencies will also be applicable to expert witnesses, such as the Police and Criminal Evidence Act Codes of Practice.[226] As such, a failure to comply may result in a court exercising its discretion to exclude evidence unfairly obtained.[227]

During the course of proceedings, the experts will submit reports detailing various tech- **6.111** nical issues relating to the computer or network-derived evidence. Expert reports are subject to pre-trial requirements to disclose,[228] which would extend to unused material that meets the 'undermine or assist' test, such as data analysis that casts doubt on the identity of the perpetrator.[229] Under the Criminal Justice Act 2003, the accused is required to give notification of the names of any experts he has instructed, although this provision is still not yet in force.[230] The Bill initially proposed that the defence would be required to disclose unused expert reports, although this was amended after claims that such a process would have a 'chilling effect' on the use of experts by the defence.[231] However, there are still concerns that the prosecution could effectively raise an inference in the mind of a jury based on the absence of a defence expert report, despite evidence that experts were consulted.

The admissibility of expert testimony as hearsay evidence is governed by common law rules, **6.112** rather than statute, having been preserved despite the recent liberalization of the hearsay rule.[232] When considering whether to admit expert testimony, the court has generally asked two questions:

> [W]hether study and experience will give a witness's opinion an authority which the opinion of one not so qualified will lack;[233] and, if the first is held, Is the witness appropriately skilled, knowledgeable and competent to offer such an opinion?[234]

In other evidential fields, controversy about the admissibility of expert testimony has arisen **6.113** where the expertise is considered 'novel and untried', ie where the science underpinning the expertise is not well established.[235] In the US, the Supreme Court has laid down a number of factors that a court, acting as 'gatekeeper', should give mind to when considering the relevance and reliability of expert testimony, such as whether the technique can be, or has been, tested; whether the technique has been peer-reviewed and published; any knowledge about reported error rates relating to the use of the technique, and finally, its 'general acceptance' within the relevant community.[236] While such questions about evidence in respect of the manner in which ICTs operate are unlikely to be raised, a challenge could arise where the

---

[226] PACE, s 67(9): 'Persons other than police officers who are charged with the duty of investigating offences or charging offenders shall in the discharge of that duty have regard to any relevant provision of a code.'

[227] *Halawa v FACT* [1995] 1 Cr App Rep 21; [1995] Crim LR 409.

[228] CPR, Pt 24 'Disclosure of Expert Evidence'.

[229] CPS Disclosure Manual, above, n 14, Chapter 23, 'Disclosure of unused forensic science material' and Annex K 'Guidance Booklet for Experts'.

[230] CJA, s 35, inserting s 6D into the CPIA.

[231] Ashworth and Redmayne, above, n 30, at 245.

[232] CJA, s 118(1)8. See further paras 6.54–6.58 above.

[233] *Robb* (1991) 93 Cr App R 161, 165 *per* Bingham LJ.

[234] ibid.

[235] eg *Gilfoyle* [2001] 2 Cr App R 57. See also O'Brian Jr, W, 'Court scrutiny of expert evidence: Recent decisions highlight the tensions', 7 *E & P* 172 (2003), at 181.

[236] *Daubert v Merrell Dow Pharmaceuticals, Inc*, 509 US 579, at 593–4, 113 S Ct 2786 (1993).

expert utilizes novel forensic techniques, such as self-authored software tools, to analyse and present conclusions about data under investigation.

6.114 There are two important statutory provisions governing the admissibility of expert testimony. First, an 'expert report' is granted statutory admissibility, which enables the court and jury to have copies of the report while the expert is being cross-examined.[237] Second, where more than one person is involved in the preparation of components of the report, such as a team of 'forensic computer analysts' or 'digital evidence recovery officers'[238] working on the contents of a hard disk, then one expert is permitted to express opinions or make inferences based on such material.[239] There are currently no provisions under the Criminal Procedure Rules governing the actual presentation of expert evidence in court; although the court retains the right to remove the status of 'expert' from a witness during the course of a trial and 'limit his evidence to factual matters'.[240]

6.115 The role of the expert in determining certain matters is restricted, and should not supplant what is more properly an issue for the jury to decide. For example, a cyber-forensic expert may be able to indicate that relevant evidence was written by the same person, based on common traits in the forensic data, but will not be in a position to give his opinion as to whom that person is, since this may be based on other evidence adduced by the prosecution.[241] In *Land*,[242] the court held that in determining whether a indecent image was that of a child, it was a question to be determined by the jury, rather than being the subject of a determination by an expert. Likewise, determinations of obscenity are questions for a jury to decide, not for expert determination.[243]

6.116 The prosecution expert will usually draft a technical report, which will then be disclosed to the defence and reviewed by their expert, who will draft a response report. Generally, although there will be areas of disagreement and challenge between the two reports, the experts will also be encouraged to identify those issues upon which there is agreement and these points will form the contents of a single report for submission to the court and consideration by the jury. This may include, for example, an agreed glossary of terms to describe various elements and operations of systems and networks. The degree of cooperation that occurs between experts will depend on a range of factors, including judicial direction and the strategy being pursued by counsel. The experts will then be called upon to give evidence during the course of the trial in respect of the outstanding contentious issues.

6.117 In some cases, questions raised during a trial may relate not only to the facts being tendered, but the expertise of the expert themselves.[244] As with any witness in court, an expert witness has immunity from suit in respect of any evidence he has given to the court of law.[245]

---

[237] Criminal Justice Act 1988, s 30. The leave of the court is required where the expert will not give oral evidence.

[238] CPS Disclosure Manual, above, n 14, Annex H, para 3.

[239] Criminal Justice Act 2003, s 127.

[240] *G* [2004] 2 Cr App R 38, para 33.

[241] See *Doheny* [1997] 1 Cr App R 369, at 374, which concerned DNA material.

[242] (1998) 1 CAR 301.

[243] *Stamford* [1972] 2 QB 391.

[244] *G* [2004] 2 Cr App R 38, concerning a prosecution witness in a serious fraud case.

[245] See *X (Minors) v Bedfordshire County Council* [1995] 2 AC 633.

G. Court Presentation

Approaches to the presentation of computer-derived evidence will generally vary depend-   **6.118**
ing on whether magistrates or a judge alone are being addressed, or judge and jury in the
Crown Court. In the latter case, while it is the role of the jury to decide matters of fact, such
as indecency or intention, the judge will generally play a critical role in terms of deciding
on the admissibility of evidence; directing that a weak case be dismissed; summing up the
facts, and the giving of any direction to the jury on relevant issues to have in mind when
engaged in its deliberations.[246] While an expert witness is expected to direct his forensic
explanations to the jury, the judge will also question the testimony presented.[247] The ability of an expert witness to clearly explain the technical issues involved, from the basics to
the minutiae, the interpretations, and the areas of dispute, can therefore be critical to the
outcome of a trial.

As such, the presentation of computer-derived evidence in court will not only depend on   **6.119**
the use of expert witnesses, but may also require the presence of appropriate technology in
the court room, such as PCs, to enable the judge and jury to fully appreciate and handle
the material being considered. In terms of appreciation, the use of graphical presentations
can enhance understanding of the environment within which certain events took place. In
terms of handling the volumes of material involved, in a complex fraud trial for example,
digital media significantly improve the ability and speed of accessing relevant material. At a
general policy level, the use of ICTs is also a central component of the Government's strategy to modernize the criminal justice system, although the use of technology within the
court system is a topic beyond the scope of this book.[248]

At trial, both prosecution and defence will need to explain to the judge and jury the nature   **6.120**
of the events that took place in respect of the activities of the suspect, with or without the
help of expert witnesses. As discussed above, cybercrimes may present a particular challenge in terms of presenting the operation of diverse and complex forms of technological
interaction, from email to Internet relay chat (IRC) and P2P file exchanges, in an easily accessible manner. One mechanism for addressing such issues is through the use of
computer-based interactive demonstrators to illustrate particular online environments,
such as chat rooms. From a defence perspective, the use of such tools may present issues in
terms of the impression that these demonstrators may establish in the minds of the jury.[249]
A person's chosen chat room name, for example, may be considered weird or unusual, but
reflects an aspect of cyber-culture of which a jury will need to be made aware, rather than
leaving them to make inappropriate assumptions about that person.[250]

---

[246] See Crown Court Bench Book, Judicial Studies Board (now called the Judicial College), available at
<https://www.judiciary.gov.uk>.

[247] See eg Barrett, N, *Traces of Guilt*, Bantam Press, 2004, at 318–25.

[248] See generally the Criminal justice system efficiency programme, at <www.justice.gov.uk/about/
criminal-justice-system-efficiency-programme>.

[249] Interview with Peter Sommer, 21 June 2006.

[250] For a discussion of virtual identities, see Turkle, S, *Life on the Screen: Identity in the Age of the Internet*,
Simon & Schuster, 1997.

6.121 In a New Zealand computer-integrity case, *Garrett*,[251] for example, one of the issues for the court to decide was whether to permit the prosecution to run a demonstration of how a program, known as 'Back Orifice',[252] operated, the functions it was capable of performing and the log files and associated evidence that it generated. Defence counsel objected on the grounds that it may be mistakenly viewed by the jury as establishing the fact of the infection and the consequences that flowed, which was in dispute. The court allowed the evidence to be admitted, on the grounds that it was necessary because the jury could not be expected to carry out their own examination; it was not attempting to be a reconstruction of events, and on the basis that the jury be given adequate warning as to the nature and purpose of the demonstration.

H. Concluding Remarks

6.122 Computer and network-derived evidence is prevalent in the vast majority of legal proceedings today, whether civil or criminal. Computers are an integral element of our daily activities, and they automatically generate records of such activities, whether operating within the home or across a global network.

6.123 Such evidence was initially viewed with considerable distrust by legislators, the legal profession and public alike, often borne primarily out of ignorance. In some jurisdictions, the formal evidential rules have required amendment to facilitate the use of such evidence, while in others, a change in attitude from the judiciary was required.

6.124 There remains considerable scope to challenge computer- and network-derived evidence, whether primary or secondary, based in part on the forensic processes discussed in Chapter 4. For law enforcement agencies it has required appropriate training and resources to ensure that such evidence can form the basis of a successful prosecution. From a defence perspective, there are concerns that the scarcity of resources in this complex area can impact on the quality of representation that defendants receive.

---

[251] [2001] DCR 912 (Judge Harvey).
[252] See further 'Back Orifice', Wikipedia, available at <https://en.wikipedia.org/wiki/Back_Orifice>.

7

COMPUTER CRIMES
AND DIGITAL INVESTIGATIONS

A. In Review

Over the course of the preceding six chapters, we have considered a vast array of issues **7.01** generated by our examination of computer crimes and digital investigations. The structure has followed the classic course of criminal law: first identifying the criminal conduct; then the investigative gathering of forensic material; and finally its presentation before a court of law in criminal proceedings. In terms of subject matter, however, while the overriding topic is computer and cybercrimes, the book, as implied by the title, could also be viewed as two separate books: computer crimes and digital investigations.

As noted throughout the text, many of the issues of digital investigations considered in **7.02** Chapter 4, the first half of Chapter 5 and Chapter 6, are just as applicable and relevant to other forms of criminal conduct as those computer crimes considered in Chapter 3. Criminal investigations increasingly rely on forensic material generated by a suspect's communications activities or residing on computers; globalization means jurisdictional issues are more prevalent; and the treatment of computer- and network-derived evidence, while no longer viewed with widespread suspicion, requires expertise to guide us.

The notion of computer crime adopted in this book is itself open to challenge. A structure **7.03** was imposed on the criminal activities, distinguishing between crimes where the computer was the tool, the content illegal, or the computer the target. This schema does not describe the real world, but provided a framework within which we could analyse such criminality. Of our three categories, however, computer-related and content-related crimes are not widely considered to be 'proper' computer crimes since the computer is simply another means of committing a traditional form of crime. Computers may already be, or are likely soon to become, the dominant instrument of such criminality, as is the case for the appropriation and misuse of information, fraud, intellectual property, and child abuse images, but the conduct itself predates our current technological environment.

To what extent, therefore, is it any longer relevant to talk about computer crime as a discrete **7.04** area of study? This question returns us to an earlier debate about wine and bottles: what is novel about computer crime? This book accepts that only computer integrity offences can really be considered to present unique forms of criminality. While analogies can be drawn with traditional legal concepts, such as trespass, damage, and obstruction, none has proved sufficiently robust to address the range of conduct being carried out in an ICT environment, hence the need for *sui generis* statutory offences. Such discrete legislative initiatives also serve to focus attention on such activities, enhancing their status in the minds of the general public. The legal treatment of conduct aimed at compromising the integrity, confidentiality, and availability of computers and networks, and the data they process, clearly requires examination.

7.05   Novelty is not only about new forms of activity, however, but also traditional activities placed in a radically new context. Computers and the Internet present such a context and, as such, all three categories of computer crime would seem to demand the attention of legal practitioners and deserve academic study.

B. Changing Landscape and Shifting Priorities

7.06   It is trite to refer to the pace and scale of change that is occurring in the field of information and communication technologies, but it is necessary nonetheless. Rapid change is occurring at all levels, from the devices being connected to networks by end-users, to the services, and capacities of the networks themselves. Policy makers and legislators are required to consider such developments when trying to tackle harmful behaviours and appropriately capture the criminal conduct. Law enforcement agencies have to address such developments when investigating those engaged in such conduct. Prosecutors, judges, and juries are confronted with this evolving environment when asked to act or decide on matters in relation to such criminality.

7.07   The inescapable reality of this changing landscape places an inevitable limit on the achievements of all the different participants in the criminal process. New activities will emerge that fall outside the existing code, while terms and terminology will no longer accurately describe the environment to which they apply. The problems that ICTs have generated for our legal system are by no means unique to the area of criminal law. Abiding by regulatory principles such as 'technology neutrality' can go some way to mitigating obsolescence, but can struggle in the face of criminal imagination and innovation. The rigid application of the principle would seem just as capable of leading to the drafting of inappropriate rules, where technological developments are treated as not making a difference, when they clearly do. In other areas of activity, particularly those where regulatory authorities have a remit to intervene, a wait-and-see attitude is often viewed as the preferable approach to handling a fast moving technical and market environment. However, such an approach seems less appropriate and acceptable where substantial harms result and criminality is involved, and it is not an option likely to appeal to politicians and the general public.

7.08   Digital investigators require the necessary technical skills, resource, and investigative powers. However, the data problems cannot all be addressed in a comprehensive manner. The volume and diverse sources of potential forensic material, as well as their examination, are always likely to be subject to time and resource constraint, even though some costs can be placed upon or shared with those that generate and hold such data, such as communication service providers. It is also likely that tools will be increasingly utilized by criminals to place forensic material permanently beyond the reach of investigators.[1] This may mean fewer 'smoking guns' and more prosecutions where the proverbial body is never found. It effectively shifts the focus to circumstantial evidence, from primary content. Such a development may demand a rethink of criminal policy.

While technological and market developments may undermine the task of law enforcement, they also offer a mechanism for crime control, to reduce the occurrence and impact of computer crime. Virus software can reduce the incidence of malware entering systems; automated software upgrades patch exposed vulnerabilities; and effective backup routines can enable swift data recovery in the event of loss or damage. The implementation of such techniques represents a growing cost to organizations, but such costs are minor compared to the risks associated with being a victim of computer crime or, indeed, of any other form of data vulnerability. **7.09**

Although not a criminology text, we must acknowledge that vastly differing reasons motivate computer criminals, although it appears that 'intellectual joy-riding' is increasingly taking a back seat in the face of industrialized computer crime. As the ex-hacker, Bevan, has noted, 'recreational hacking is the same, but the volume of people on the net means far more are involved in genuinely nefarious activities'.[2] If accurate, this shift is significant, since much historic and some current debate around computer crime has been fixated with the non-malevolent motivations of groups of perpetrators, reflected in cases from Gold and Schifreen in the mid-1980s to the UFO seeker Gary McKinnon. **7.10**

A key theme that has dominated our deliberations has been the shifting priorities of policy makers, legislators, and law enforcement when addressing computer crime. Over time, the profile and place of computer crime on the public agenda rises and falls. In the media, computer crime continues to be viewed as synonymous with computer integrity offences; while the Internet is portrayed as both the scene and source of every conceivable form of illegality. **7.11**

There are numerous studies and statistics that have and can be quoted to illustrate the changing nature of computer crime, the scale, the perpetrators, and the cost. The reliability of some of this work may be challenged, but its overall influence on policy makers is undoubted. We can see examples of evidence-based and precautionary anecdote-based policy making. Denial-of-service attacks are an example of the former, where the emergence of a new form of criminal activity exposed a lacuna in existing law. The Government's decision to criminalize the possession of extreme pornography would seem to be an example of the latter. Even where evidence of threats emerge, novel in either form, scale, or context, legislative initiatives may result, less from a lack of law, more as a political response to the need to be seen doing something, identity theft being an example. **7.12**

Three dominant concerns at the forefront of UK criminal policy are organized crime, terrorism, and child protection issues. In each, computer crime plays an important, but secondary, role. As such, computer crime has become subsumed into a broader crime control strategy. **7.13**

---

[1] Goodman, MD, 'Why the police don't care about computer crime', 10 *Harvard Journal of Law and Technology* 465 (1997).

[2] Quoted in Bowcott, O, 'Pentagon's pursuit of "scapegoat" hacker hides real threat from the web', *The Guardian*, 11 June 2005, available at <http://www.theguardian.com/technology/2005/jun/11/hacking.internetcrime>.

7.14 While the fight against child abuse images is both high profile and politically uncontroversial, tackling other forms of content-related crime generates greater controversy and tends to get mixed up in the minds of legislators and the general public with broader concerns about harmful content made available over the Internet. The Government has adopted, or is considering, a number of measures criminalizing content, but experience to date suggests that legislating in the area does not necessarily translate into significant enforcement activity.

7.15 There is some evidence to suggest that advantage may be being taken of the consensus present around the issue of child abuse images to promote broader content-control strategies, such as filtering, thereby circumventing some of the controversies inherent in the subject matter itself. Policy makers make liberal reference to child abuse investigations in support of granting law enforcement powers that are applicable across all types of computer crime. Such practices are also adopted in the private sector, with rights-holders keen to associate the enforcement activity surrounding the illegal use of their products and services with the broader fight against organized crime and terrorism.

7.16 In an Internet context, shifting priorities at a national level have then to be reconciled with shifting priorities at an international level, in fora such as the United Nations. Differing national concerns can result in inaction, despite agreement about the criminal nature of particular forms of conduct. In the area of child abuse images, for example, the US and Russia are major sources of such material,[3] but both have been considered weak on enforcement in the past, for very different reasons. In the US, First Amendment concerns would seem to constrain action, while Russia is keen to deny the existence of such activities on its soil. As a consequence, evidence suggests that criminals exploit this situation, regularly shifting their material between these jurisdictions, sometimes on a daily basis.

C. Laws, Code, and Rules

7.17 This book has broadly examined four different categories of rule relating to cybercrime. First, criminal code addressing crimes that may, or may not, be committed using computers and networks, ie computer-related and content-related crimes. Second, technology-specific criminal code adopted expressly to grant protection to activities carried out using computers and networks, ie the computer integrity offences. Third, criminal procedure governing the investigative activities of public law enforcement agencies carried out in a digital environment; and fourth, evidential rules governing the use of data obtained through the investigative process in the prosecution of the perpetrator of the criminal act.

7.18 Each set of rules has been examined primarily from an English law perspective, with comparative examples and international instruments considered where relevant and of value. The adequacy and appropriateness of each set of rules has been evaluated against various criteria, as a coherent, workable set of rules, proportionate in terms of meeting their objectives, adopting a widely accepted position that the use of criminal law should be kept to a minimum. Criminalization of an activity is only justified if it is both necessary and practical.[4]

---

[3] See Internet Watch Foundation (IWF) Annual & Charity Report 2013, at 14, available at <https://www.iwf.org.uk/assets/media/annual-reports/annual_report_2013.pdf.pdf>.

[4] Law Commission, *Legislating the Criminal Code: Misuse of Trade Secrets*, Consultation Paper No 150, The Stationery Office, 1997, para 3.43.

The nature of criminal law, and English criminal law in particular, means that criminal **7.19** activities do not often fall into the neat categories of offence that have been designed for them. The variety of applicable offences represents, in part, a choice to be made by prosecutors, based on a range of factors such as the availability of evidence. It was noted that the change in policing priorities to tackle terrorism and organized crime has also resulted in a shift from focusing on individual criminal behaviours towards capturing the dynamics of groups through social network analysis. Both these factors have an impact on how computer crimes are treated.

Computing and network professionals live in a world of codes, protocols, and standards, a **7.20** rule-based environment that has been aptly labelled by Lessig as 'West-coast code', having a similar nature and function to some extent as 'East-coast code', the laws emanating from the US Congress, in terms of regulating cyberspace.[5] However, technology professionals are often to be heard bemoaning the problems that exist 'at the edge of the network', outside the environment designed and controlled by the professionals, inhabited by people or machines that the people (poorly) control. If it wasn't for the problems 'at the edge of the network', so the story goes, the network would have the reliability, security, and all those other good things that 'West-coast code' has the potential to offer us.

While this may not be an entirely fair portrayal, it does raise the question whether simi- **7.21** lar problems can be said to exist at the edge of the criminal code? Are the problems of the criminal code in a cyberspace environment simply a consequence of the manner in which such code is created, ie the legislative process, and the environment in which it operates, ie human relations; or is it, to a certain extent, a limitation of the code itself?

The one thing you can generally say about 'either/or' propositions is that the truth probably **7.22** lies somewhere along the continuum between the two! Not wishing to appear relativist, but for many complex issues facing modern society there are no right answers, simply compromises based on some form of consensus. For the questions posed above, this means that both the manner and the environment lie at the root of many of the problems discussed in this book, from anecdotal law making to a rapidly evolving technological environment behind which the law will inevitably lag. However, it may also be argued that some of the problems of the criminal code are not a result of the failure of the code, but are inherent limitations of 'East-coast code', for example the criminal code. Limitations that have to be recognized, worked around, but ultimately accepted and lived with.

Three distinct but closely interrelated elements lie 'at the edge of the criminal code', and **7.23** have caused problems throughout the book: language, circumstance, and discretion. The code is largely written down, but our language cannot always capture the complexities of the world around us. Such language limitations are not always a failure of imagination, either on behalf of the legislature or judiciary, but are also spaces that words cannot adequately fill. Just as steganography exploits the redundant data in digitized information, so criminals sometimes operate in the regions between our carefully drafted criminal codes. During the course of our deliberations, we have had to consider a range of boundary issues, where the legal terminology and that which it attempts to capture are blurred in an ICT environment, such as computer/data, supply/possession, and content/communications data.

---

[5] See Lessig, L, *Code and Other Laws of Cyberspace*, Basic Books, 2000.

7.24 The need to consider all the circumstances and facts in a criminal case can be seen as analogous to the individuality that lies at the heart of the human condition, requiring us to look at each case and make decisions appropriate to that circumstance. Decisions have to be made not only about the guilt or otherwise of a suspect, but often about a mass of other matters that form part, or are a consequence, of the criminal act. For the whole criminal process to work fairly and efficiently, taking account of both language spaces and circumstances, discretion has to be exercised. Discretion should not be arbitrary, and should be appropriately constrained by widely accepted principles, practices, and procedures within and outside the criminal code, but discretion it remains.

7.25 Similarities may perhaps be seen to exist with the problems faced by those who, over recent decades, have attempted to create legal expert systems, using ICTs to build systems that capture the legal decision-making process.[6] While such initiatives have been valuable, they have not generally led to widespread adoption within legal education or practice. This has been due, in large part, to the problems developers have experienced in appropriately capturing all but the most straightforward of legal processes. Indeed, it could be said that legal expert systems represent the inherent differences and difficulties when reconciling law with computer code.

D. Regulating and Policing Cyberspace

7.26 Issues of cybercrime can be seen as lying at the heart of the future of cyberspace and the Internet. Debates within fora, such as the World Summit on the Information Society (WSIS),[7] have focused on issues of governance, specifically control of the domain name system, which underpins the successful operation of the Internet. At the Tunis meeting in 2005, it was agreed that the Secretary-General of the United Nations would convene a 'multi-stakeholder policy dialogue called the Internet Governance Forum (IGF)'.[8] However, national and international approaches to tackling cybercrime go to the heart of how the Internet is used in future decades. The libertarian origins of cyberspace still have a real impact on governmental moves to regulate the Internet, haunted by the ever-present but diffuse threat hanging over them that regulation will somehow strangle the golden goose.

7.27 What many of the themes examined in this book raise are questions of how to balance between potentially conflicting objectives, rights, and interests. Both policy and law represent the outcomes of such balancing exercises, revisited and recast over time to reflect the changing landscape and shifting priorities. Computer crime and digital investigations present different aspects of this on-going balancing process.

7.28 In terms of substantive law, the criminal code must, as a minimum, achieve a balance between being comprehensive enough to capture the activities considered worthy of criminalization, and over-extending the reach of criminal law to activities for which it is not appropriate. For criminal procedure, a fundamental balance has to be found between the

---

[6] See eg Susskind, R, *Expert Systems in Law*, Oxford University Press, 1989.
[7] See generally <http://www.itu.int/wsis/>.
[8] See <http://www.intgovforum.org/>.

rights of the suspect, in terms of privacy and fair trial, as well as other individuals collaterally involved in, or impacted by, an investigation, and the needs of law enforcement to investigate and prosecute offenders.

Balancing the privacy needs of users against the safety and security of the wider public is one **7.29** of the key on-going debates within the area. *Where* the line is drawn between the two objectives is not primarily a legal issue, especially in a system that lacks clear constitutional protections. In terms of *how* that line is drawn, however, issues of law and regulation, conceived in a broad sense, are an essential part of the solution. In that regard, Reitinger proposes four models.[9] Under the 'market' model, the market is left to its own devices, such that ICT products and services will have the security features we need, when we are prepared to pay for them. The 'incentive' model is the 'market' model with governmental intervention to provide incentives that encourage a favourable outcome in terms of public policy objectives. The 'regulatory' model involves government imposing an outcome, but allows the market to choose between different technological solutions. Finally, under the 'mandatory' model, government ignores the market and imposes a solution. Issues may move between models over time, as political priorities shift in the ways discussed above. Large-scale data retention is an example of such movement, from 'incentive' to 'mandatory' (and is currently being reconsidered again).

While self-regulatory initiatives generally focus on the providers of goods and service **7.30** over the Internet, the suppliers of ICT equipment, whether soft, firm, or hard, and communication service providers, attention must also focus on educating and empowering end-users to take measures against computer crimes. Media literacy initiatives can better equip end-users to be aware of the risks encountered when communicating over the Internet, as well as steps that can be taken to mitigate or prevent becoming a victim of computer crime.[10]

Cyberspace clearly cannot be viewed simply in terms of public and private spaces, any more **7.31** than the nation state can preserve traditional sovereign control. In the real world, the police have a role in active policing of public spaces, and we are seeing the emergence of analogous practices in cyberspace, such as the Virtual Global Taskforce. However, the blurring of the boundary between private and public space, and between the jurisdictions of nation states, raises important issues in terms of criminality, international law, and the proper exercise of state power.

Effective policing involves a variety of strategies; cybercrime policing is particularly dependent on the intermediaries through whom we obtain access to the Internet: communication **7.32** service providers. While it is entirely appropriate that policing computer and cybercrime involves a mix of public and private law enforcement activities, concerns arise about the transparency and proper limits or controls placed over the private sector and cooperative practices.

---

[9] See Reitinger, PR, 'Encryption, anonymity and markets', in Thomas, D and Loader, B (eds), *Cybercrime: Law Enforcement, Security and Surveillance in the Information Age*, Routledge, 2000, at 139.

[10] eg Ofcom's Media Literacy site includes a page devoted to guidance concerning Internet security and safety: see <htttp://www.ofcom.org.uk/advice/media_literacy/>.

E. Where Next?

7.33 With the assurance that a student text book will be periodically updated and reissued, getting things rights, whether legal or otherwise, becomes more of a damage limitation exercise: if not now, next time! The fate of this book is more uncertain and therefore gaps and mistakes may go on to haunt the author. One type of mistake that can be made concerns predictions for the future, the 'where next?' of computer crime. In successive editions, past predictions can be a source of interest and further discussion; for the single edition, they can undermine faith in the preceding analysis and form amusing references in the work product of others.

7.34 When the author began his career, computer law issues were considered relatively exotic and distinct. Some twenty years later, many of the issues that concerned us then have become mainstream legal issues, at least for practitioners, if not for law students. Much the same is true of many of the issues examined in this book. For CSPs, for example, law enforcement issues are simply one aspect of a range of regulatory compliance obligations to which they must give adequate consideration. Computer crimes and digital investigations have become typical, if not yet ordinary.

7.35 In terms of criminal law, controlling content over the Internet seems likely to dominate the attention of policy makers and politicians for the foreseeable future. Successful models of enforcement, such as that achieved in the field of child abuse images, are likely to be seized upon by governments and imposed across an ever-wider range of issues, resulting in an increasingly mediated access to the Internet. Innovative ways of attacking, exploiting, and interfering with computer and communication technologies are likely to regularly emerge, challenging investigators and prosecutors alike. However, such integrity threats can be expected to attract policy makers only to the extent that they are carried out against, or on a scale, which is perceived to threaten a nation's critical infrastructure.

7.36 A common concern voiced by digital investigators is that the 'technology has outstripped the legislation'.[11] While we must accept this as an inevitable feature of the landscape, what are the possible consequences? At one extreme, there is the possibility that technology may reach a state, as mentioned above, where our use of ICTs no longer provides a valuable source of forensic material for investigators. Data criminals will be able to operate using identities and from locations that are effectively hidden, processing information protected by unbreakable codes. To address this scenario, already part reality, governments may be tempted to give law enforcement agencies further wide-ranging powers to intrude and disrupt such online criminalities. This may include revisiting *ex ante* demands that suppliers of networks and devices design their equipment in a manner supportive of such policing methods.

7.37 Computer crimes and digital investigations will comprise a substantial part of criminal policy, law, and practice over the coming years, as information becomes the cornerstone of the global economy. To examine such developments and the evolving legal framework may require a third edition!

---

[11] Quoted in Warren, P, 'Lifting the veil on Internet voices', *The Guardian*, 27 July 2006, available at <http://www.theguardian.com/technology/2006/jul/27/guardianweeklytechnologysection>.

Appendices

APPENDIX 1

Computer Misuse Act 1990 (c. 18)

An Act to make provision for securing computer material against unauthorised access or modification; and for connected purposes.

[29th June 1990]

Be it enacted by the Queen's most Excellent Majesty, by and with the advice and consent of the Lords Spiritual and Temporal, and Commons, in this present Parliament assembled, and by the authority of the same, as follows:—

Computer misuse offences

1.—(1) A person is guilty of an offence if—
   (a) he causes a computer to perform any function with intent to secure access to any program or data held in any computer[, or to enable any such access to be secured];
   (b) the access he intends to secure[, or to enable to be secured] is unauthorised; and
   (c) he knows at the time when he causes the computer to perform the function that that is the case.

(2) The intent a person has to have to commit an offence under this section need not be directed at—
   (a) any particular program or data;
   (b) a program or data of any particular kind; or
   (c) a program or data held in any particular computer.

[(3) A person guilty of an offence under this section shall be liable—
   (a) on summary conviction in England and Wales, to imprisonment for a term not exceeding 12 months or to a fine not exceeding the statutory maximum or to both;
   (b) on summary conviction in Scotland, to imprisonment for a term not exceeding 12 months or to a fine not exceeding the statutory maximum or to both;
   (c) on conviction on indictment, to imprisonment for a term not exceeding two years or to a fine or to both.]

Unauthorised access to computer material.

Notes

Words in brackets inserted by Police and Justice Act 2006, s. 35. The maximum penalty was originally 6 months imprisonment, which was raised to 12 months by Serious Crime Act 2015, Sch. 4, para. 7(a).

2.—(1) A person is guilty of an offence under this section if he commits an offence under section 1 above ('the unauthorised access offence') with intent—
   (a) to commit an offence to which this section applies; or
   (b) to facilitate the commission of such an offence (whether by himself or by any other person); and the offence he intends to commit or facilitate is referred to below in this section as the further offence.

(2) This section applies to offences—
   (a) for which the sentence is fixed by law; or
   (b) for which a person of twenty-one years of age or over (not previously convicted) may be sentenced to imprisonment for a term of five years (or, in England and Wales, might be so sentenced but for the restrictions imposed by section 33 of the Magistrates' Courts Act 1980).

(3) It is immaterial for the purposes of this section whether the further offence is to be committed on the same occasion as the unauthorised access offence or on any future occasion.

(4) A person may be guilty of an offence under this section even though the facts are such that the commission of the further offence is impossible.

[(5) A person guilty of an offence under this section shall be liable—
   (a) on summary conviction in England and Wales, to imprisonment for a term not exceeding 12 months or to a fine not exceeding the statutory maximum or to both;

Unauthorised access with intent to commit or facilitate commission of further offences.

(b) on summary conviction in Scotland, to imprisonment for a term not exceeding 12 months or to a fine not exceeding the statutory maximum or to both;

(c) on conviction on indictment, to imprisonment for a term not exceeding five years or to a fine or to both.]

Notes

Words in brackets inserted by Police and Justice Act 2006, s. 52, Sch. 14, para. 17. The maximum prison term on summary conviction was raised from 6 to 12 months by Serious Crime Act 2015, Sch. 4, para. 7(b).

Unauthorised acts with intent to impair operation of computer, etc.

[**3.**— (1) A person is guilty of an offence if—

(a) he does any unauthorised act in relation to a computer;

(b) at the time when he does the act he knows that it is unauthorised; and

(c) either subsection (2) or subsection (3) below applies.

(2) This subsection applies if the person intends by doing the act—

(a) to impair the operation of any computer;

(b) to prevent or hinder access to any program or data held in any computer;

(c) to impair the operation of any such program or the reliability of any such data; or

(d) to enable any of the things mentioned in paragraphs (a) to (c) above to be done.

(3) This subsection applies if the person is reckless as to whether the act will do any of the things mentioned in paragraphs (a) to (d) of subsection (2) above.

(4) The intention referred to in subsection (2) above, or the recklessness referred to in subsection (3) above, need not relate to—

(a) any particular computer;

(b) any particular program or data; or

(c) a program or data of any particular kind.

(5) In this section—

(a) a reference to doing an act includes a reference to causing an act to be done;

(b) 'act' includes a series of acts;

(c) a reference to impairing, preventing or hindering something includes a reference to doing so temporarily.

(6) A person guilty of an offence under this section shall be liable—

(a) on summary conviction in England and Wales, to imprisonment for a term not exceeding 12 months or to a fine not exceeding the statutory maximum or to both;

(b) on summary conviction in Scotland, to imprisonment for a term not exceeding 12 months or to a fine not exceeding the statutory maximum or to both;

(c) on conviction on indictment, to imprisonment for a term not exceeding ten years or to a fine or to both.]

Notes

Words in brackets substituted by Police and Justice Act 2006, s. 36. The maximum penalty was originally 5 years imprisonment. The maximum prison term on summary conviction was raised from 6 to 12 months by Serious Crime Act 2015, Sch. 4, para. 7(c).

[**3ZA**—(1) A person is guilty of an offence if—

Unauthorised acts causing, or creating risk of, serious damage

(a) the person does any unauthorised act in relation to a computer;

(b) at the time of doing the act the person knows that it is unauthorised;

(c) the act causes, or creates a significant risk of, serious damage of a material kind; and

(d) the person intends by doing the act to cause serious damage of a material kind or is reckless as to whether such damage is caused.

(2) Damage is of a 'material kind' for the purposes of this section if it is—

(a) damage to human welfare in any country;

(b) damage to the environment in any country;

(c) damage to the economy of any country; or

(d) damage to the national security of any country.

(3) For the purposes of subsection (2)(a) an act causes damage to human welfare only if it causes—

(a) loss to human life;

(b) human illness or injury;

(c) disruption of a supply of money, food, water, energy or fuel;

(d) disruption of a system of communication;

(e) disruption of facilities for transport; or

(f) disruption of services relating to health.

(4) It is immaterial for the purposes of subsection (2) whether or not an act causing damage—

    (a) does so directly;

    (b) is the only or main cause of the damage.

(5) In this section—

    (a) a reference to doing an act includes a reference to causing an act to be done;

    (b) 'act' includes a series of acts;

    (c) a reference to a country includes a reference to a territory, and to—

        (i) any place in, or part or region of, a country or territory;

        (ii) the territorial sea adjacent to a country or territory.

(6) A person guilty of an offence under this section is (unless subsection (7) applies) liable, on conviction on indictment, to imprisonment for a term not exceeding 14 years, or to a fine, or to both.

(7) Where an offence under this section is committed as a result of an act causing or creating a significant risk of—

    (a) serious damage to human welfare of the kind mentioned in subsection (3)(a) or (3)(b), or

    (b) serious damage to national security, a person guilty of the offence is liable, on conviction on indictment, to imprisonment for life, or to a fine, or to both.]

Notes

Words in brackets inserted by Serious Crime Act 2015, s. 41(2). To implement article 9(4) of Directive 2013/40/EU 'on attacks against information systems'.

[**3A.**— (1) A person is guilty of an offence if he makes, adapts, supplies or offers to supply any article—

    (a) intending it to be used to commit, or to assist in the commission of, an offence under section 1, 3 or 3ZA.

    (b) A person is guilty of an offence if he supplies or offers to supply any article believing that it is likely to be used to commit, or to assist in the commission of, an offence under section 1, 3 or 3ZA.

(2) A person is guilty of an offence if he obtains any article with a view to its being supplied for use to commit, or to assist in the commission of, an offence under section 1, 3 or 3ZA.

(3) A person is guilty of an offence if he obtains any article—

    (a) intending to use it to commit, or to assist in the commission of, an offence under section 1, 3 or 3ZA, or

    (b) with a view to its being supplied for use to commit, or to assist in the commission of, an offence under section 1, 3 or 3ZA.

(4) In this section 'article' includes any program or data held in electronic form.

(5) A person guilty of an offence under this section shall be liable—

    (a) on summary conviction in England and Wales, to imprisonment for a term not exceeding 12 months or to a fine not exceeding the statutory maximum or to both;

    (b) on summary conviction in Scotland, to imprisonment for a term not exceeding 12 months or to a fine not exceeding the statutory maximum or to both;

    (c) on conviction on indictment, to imprisonment for a term not exceeding two years or to a fine or to both.]

Making, supplying or obtaining articles for use in offence under section 1, 3 or 3ZA

Notes

Words in brackets inserted by Police and Justice Act 2006, s. 37. Further minor amendments were made by Serious Crime Act 2015, s. 41(3), 42 and Sch. 4, paras. 8. The maximum prison term on summary conviction was raised from 6 to 12 months by Serious Crime Act 2015, Sch. 4, para. 7(d).

Jurisdiction

Territorial scope of [offences under this Act].

4.—(1) Except as provided below in this section, it is immaterial for the purposes of any offence under section 1, 3 or 3ZA above—

(a) whether any act or other event proof of which is required for conviction of the offence occurred in the home country concerned; or

(b) whether the accused was in the home country concerned at the time of any such act or event.

(2) Subject to subsection (3) below, in the case of such an offence at least one significant link with domestic jurisdiction must exist in the circumstances of the case for the offence to be committed.

(3) There is no need for any such link to exist for the commission of an offence under section 1 above to be established in proof of an allegation to that effect in proceedings for an offence under section 2 above.

(4) Subject to section 8 below, where—

(a) any such link does in fact exist in the case of an offence under section 1 above; and

(b) commission of that offence is alleged in proceedings for an offence under section 2 above;

section 2 above shall apply as if anything the accused intended to do or facilitate in any place outside the home country concerned which would be an offence to which section 2 applies if it took place in the home country concerned were the offence in question.

[(4A) It is immaterial for the purposes of an offence under section 3A whether the accused was in the home country concerned at the time of any act or other event proof of which is required for conviction of the offence if there is a significant link with domestic jurisdiction in relation to the offence.]

(5) This section is without prejudice to any jurisdiction exercisable by a court in Scotland apart from this section.

(6) References in this Act to the home country concerned are references—

(a) in the application of this Act to England and Wales, to England and Wales;

(b) in the application of this Act to Scotland, to Scotland; and

(c) in the application of this Act to Northern Ireland, to Northern Ireland.

Notes

Words in brackets in heading to section 4 inserted by Police and Justice Act 2006, s. 52, Sch. 14, para. 18 and further amended by Serious Crime Act 2015, Sch. 4, para. 9. Section 4A inserted by the Serious Crime Bill 2014, s. 43(3).

Significant links with domestic jurisdiction.

5.—(1) The following provisions of this section apply for the interpretation of section 4 above.

[(1A) In relation to an offence under section 1, 3, 3ZA or 3A, where the accused was in a country outside the United Kingdom at the time of the act constituting the offence there is a significant link with domestic jurisdiction if—

(a) the accused was a United Kingdom national at that time; and

(b) the act constituted an offence under the law of the country in which it occurred.

(1B) In subsection (1A)—

'country' includes territory;

'United Kingdom national' means an individual who is—

(a) a British citizen, a British overseas territories citizen, a British National (Overseas) or a British Overseas citizen;

(b) a person who under the British Nationality Act 1981 is a British subject; or

(c) a British protected person within the meaning of that Act.]

(2) In relation to an offence under section 1, either of the following is a significant link with domestic jurisdiction—

(a) that the accused was in the home country concerned at the time when he did the act which caused the computer to perform the function; or

[(b) that any computer containing any program or data to which the accused by doing that act secured or intended to secure unauthorised access, or enabled or intended to enable unauthorised access to be secured, was in the home country concerned at that time.]

(3) In relation to an offence under section 3, either of the following is a significant link with domestic jurisdiction—

(a) that the accused was in the home country concerned at the time when [he did the unauthorised act (or caused it to be done)]; or [(b) that the unauthorised act was done in relation to a computer in the home country concerned.]

[(3A) In relation to an offence under section 3ZA, any of the following is also a significant link with domestic jurisdiction—

(a) that the accused was in the home country concerned at the time when he did the unauthorised act (or caused it to be done);

(b) that the unauthorised act was done in relation to a computer in the home country concerned;

(c) that the unauthorised act caused, or created a significant risk of, serious damage of a material kind (within the meaning of that section) in the home country concerned.]

Notes

Subsections 1A, 1B and 3A inserted by Serious Crime Act 2015, s. 43(4) and 43(5). Other words in brackets inserted by Police and Justice Act 2006, s. 52, Sch. 14, para. 19(2) and (3).

6.—(1) On a charge of conspiracy to commit an [offence under this Act] the following questions are immaterial to the accused's guilt—

(a) the question where any person became a party to the conspiracy; and

(b) the question whether any act, omission or other event occurred in the home country concerned.

(2) On a charge of attempting to commit an offence under this Act above the following questions are immaterial to the accused's guilt—

(a) the question where the attempt was made; and

(b) the question whether it had an effect in the home country concerned.

[(3)]

(4) This section does not extend to Scotland.

Territorial scope of inchoate offences related to [offences under this Act].

Notes

Words in brackets in section heading inserted by Police and Justice Act 2006, s. 52, Sch. 14, para. 20(a) and further amended by Serious Crime Act 2015, Sch. 4, para. 10(2). Words in brackets inserted by Police and Justice Act 2006, s. 52, Sch. 14, para. 20(b). Subsection (3) repealed under Serious Crime Act 2007, s. 92, Sch. 14, para. 1. Insertions of 'Act' in body made by Serious Crime Act 2015, Sch. 4, paras. 10(3) and (4).

7.—

[(1)–(2) …]

(3) The following subsections shall be inserted after section 1(1) of the [1981 c. 47.] Criminal Attempts Act 1981—

'(1A) Subject to section 8 of the Computer Misuse Act 1990 (relevance of external law), if this sub-section applies to an act, what the person doing it had in view shall be treated as an offence to which this section applies.

(1B) Subsection (1A) above applies to an act if—

(a) it is done in England and Wales; and

(b) it would fall within subsection (1) above as more than merely preparatory to the commission of an offence under section 3 of the Computer Misuse Act 1990 but for the fact that the offence, if completed, would not be an offence triable in England and Wales.'

[(4)]

Territorial scope of inchoate offences related to offences under external law corresponding to offences under [sections 1 to 3].

Notes

Subsections (1) and (2) repealed by the Criminal Justice (Terrorism and Conspiracy) Act 1998, Sch. 2, Pt II, para. 1. Words in section heading inserted by Police and Justice Act 2006, s. 52, Sch. 14, para. 21. Subsection (4) repealed under the Serious Crime Act 2007, s. 92, Sch. 14, para. 1.

8.—(1) A person is guilty of an offence triable by virtue of section 4(4) above only if what he intended to do or facilitate would involve the commission of an offence under the law in force where the whole or any part of it was intended to take place.

[(2) …]

(3) A person is guilty of an offence triable by virtue of section 1(1A) of the Criminal Attempts Act 1981 […] only if what he had in view would involve the commission of an offence under the law in force where the whole or any part of it was intended to take place.

Relevance of external law.

(4) Conduct punishable under the law in force in any place is an offence under that law for the purposes of this section, however it is described in that law.

(5) Subject to subsection (7) below, a condition specified in subsections (1) [or] (3) above shall be taken to be satisfied unless not later than rules of court may provide the defence serve on the prosecution a notice—

    (a) stating that, on the facts as alleged with respect to the relevant conduct, the condition is not in their opinion satisfied;

    (b) showing their grounds for that opinion; and

    (c) requiring the prosecution to show that it is satisfied.

(6) In subsection (5) above 'the relevant conduct' means—

    (a) where the condition in subsection (1) above is in question, what the accused intended to do or facilitate;

    [(b) …]

    (c) where the condition in subsection (3) above is in question, what the accused had in view.

(7) The court, if it thinks fit, may permit the defence to require the prosecution to show that the condition is satisfied without the prior service of a notice under subsection (5) above.

(8) If by virtue of subsection (7) above a court of solemn jurisdiction in Scotland permits the defence to require the prosecution to show that the condition is satisfied, it shall be competent for the prosecution for that purpose to examine any witness or to put in evidence any production not included in the lists lodged by it.

(9) In the Crown Court the question whether the condition is satisfied shall be decided by the judge alone.

(10) In the High Court of Justiciary and in the sheriff court the question whether the condition is satisfied shall be decided by the judge or, as the case may be, the sheriff alone.

Notes

Subsections (2) and (6)(b) repealed by the Criminal Justice (Terrorism and Conspiracy) Act 1998, Sch. 2, Pt II, para. 1. Subsection (5) amended by Criminal Justice (Terrorism and Conspiracy) Act 1998, Sch. 1, Pt II, para. 6(1)(b). Subsection (3) amended by the Serious Crime Act 2007, Sch. 14, para. 1.

British
citizenship
immaterial.

9.—(1) [Except as provided by section 5(1A), in] any proceedings brought in England and Wales in respect of any offence to which this section applies it is immaterial to guilt whether or not the accused was a British citizen at the time of any act, omission or other event proof of which is required for conviction of the offence.

(2) This section applies to the following offences—

    (a) any [offence under the Act];

    [(b) …]

    (c) any attempt to commit an offence under this Act above; and

    [(d) …]

Notes

Words in subsection (1) inserted by Serious Crime Act 2015, Sch. 4, para. 11(2). Subsection (2)(b) repealed by the Criminal Justice (Terrorism and Conspiracy) Act 1998, Sch. 2, Pt II, para. 1. Subsection (2)(d) repealed by the Serious Crime Act 2007, Sch. 14, para. 1. Words substituted in subsections (2)(a) and (c) inserted by Police and Justice Act 2006 and Serious Crime Act 2015.

Miscellaneous and general

Savings

10. Sections 1 to 3A have effect without prejudice to the operation—

    (a) in England and Wales of any enactment relating to powers of inspection, search or seizure or of any other enactment by virtue of which the conduct in question is authorised or required; and

    (b) in Scotland of any enactment or rule of law relating to powers of examination, search or seizure or of any other enactment by virtue of which the conduct in question is authorised or required.

[and nothing designed to indicate a withholding of consent to access to any program or data from persons as enforcement officers shall have effect to make access unauthorised for the purposes of any of those sections.

In this section –

'enactment' means any enactment, whenever passed or made, contained in—
(a) an Act of Parliament;
(b) an Act of the Scottish Parliament;
(c) a Measure or Act of the National Assembly for Wales;
(d) an instrument made under any such Act or Measure;
(e) any other subordinate legislation (within the meaning of the Interpretation Act 1978);
'enforcement officer' means a constable or other person charged with the duty of investigating offences; and withholding consent from a person 'as' an enforcement officer of any description includes the operation, by the person entitled to control access, of rules whereby enforcement officers of that description are, as such, disqualified from membership of a class of persons who are authorised to have access.]

Notes

Words in brackets inserted by the Criminal Justice and Public Order Act 1994, s. 162(1). Wording underlined inserted by the Serious Crime Act 2015, s. 44.

11.—[(1)–(7) …]

Proceedings for offences under section 1.

Notes

Section repealed by Police and Justice Act 2006, s. 52, Sch. 14, para. 23.

12.—[(1)–(4) …]

Notes

Section repealed by Police and Justice Act 2006, s. 52, Sch. 14, para. 24.

Conviction of an offence under section 1 in proceedings for an offence under section 2 or 3.

13.—(1) A sheriff shall have jurisdiction in respect of an offence under section 1 or 2 above if—

Proceedings in Scotland.

(a) the accused was in the sheriffdom at the time when he did the act which caused the computer to perform the function; or
[(b) any computer containing any program or data to which the accused by doing that act secured or intended to secure unauthorised access, or enabled or intended to enable unauthorised access to be secured, was in the sheriffdom at that time.]
(2) A sheriff shall have jurisdiction in respect of an offence under section 3 above if—
(a) the accused was in the sheriffdom at the time when [he did the unauthorised act (or caused it to be done)]; or
(b) [the unauthorised act was done in relation to a computer in the sheriffdom].
[(2A) A sheriff shall have jurisdiction in respect of an offence under section 3ZA above if—
(a) the accused was in the sheriffdom at the time when he did the unauthorised act (or caused it to be done), or
(b) the computer in relation to which the unauthorised act was done was in the sheriffdom at the time.
[(2B) A sheriff shall have jurisdiction in respect of an offence under section 3A above if—
(a) the accused was in the sheriffdom at the time when
(i) he made, adapted, supplied or offered to supply the article intending it to be used as mentioned in subsection (1) of that section,
(ii) he supplied or offered to supply the article believing that it would be used as mentioned in subsection (2) of that section, or
(iii) he obtained the article intending to use it, or with a view to its being supplied for use, as mentioned in subsection (3) of that section; or

(b) the offence related to the commission of an offence under section 1, 3 or 3ZA above (in the way described in subsections (1) to (3) of section 3A above) and any computer as mentioned in subsection (1)(b), (2)(b) or (2A)(b) of this section was in the sheriffdom at the time the accused carried out the act constituting the offence under section 3A above.]

[(3)–(7) …]

(8) In proceedings in which a person is charged with an offence under section 2 or 3 above and is found not guilty or is acquitted of that charge, he may be found guilty of an offence under section 1 above if on the facts shown he could have been found guilty of that offence in proceedings for that offence […].

(9) Subsection (8) above shall apply whether or not an offence under section 1 above has been libelled in the complaint or indictment.

(10) A person found guilty of an offence under section 1 above by virtue of subsection (8) above shall be liable, in respect of that offence, only to the penalties set out in section 1.

[(10A) Where an offence under section 1, 3 or 3A above is committed outside Scotland, the person committing the offence may be prosecuted, tried and punished for the offence—

(a) in any sheriff court district in Scotland in which the person is apprehended or is in custody, or

(b) in such sheriff court district as the Lord Advocate may direct,

as if the offence had been committed in that district; and the offence is, for all purposes incidental to or consequential on the trial or punishment, deemed to have been committed in that district.]

(11) This section extends to Scotland only.

Notes

Words in brackets in subsections (1) and (2) inserted, and subsections (3)–(7) and words in (8) repealed, by Police and Justice Act 2006, s. 52, Sch. 14. Subsections 2A, 2B and 10A inserted by the Serious Crime Act 2014, s. 43(6) and (7).

Search warrants for offences under section 1.

[14 …]

Notes

Section repealed by Police and Justice Act 2006, s. 52, Sch. 14, para. 26.

Extradition where Schedule 1 to the Extradition Act 1989 applies.

[15 …]

Notes

Section repealed by Extradition Act 2003, s. 220, Sch. 4.

Application to Northern Ireland.

16.—(1) The following provisions of this section have effect for applying this Act in relation to Northern Ireland with the modifications there mentioned.

[(1A) In section 1(3)(a)—

(a) the reference to England and Wales shall be read as a reference to Northern Ireland; and

(b) the reference to 12 months shall be read as a reference to six months.]

(2) In section 2(2)(b)—

(a) the reference to England and Wales shall be read as a reference to Northern Ireland; and

(b) the reference to section 33 of the Magistrates' Courts Act 1980 shall be read as a reference to Article 46(4) of the Magistrates' Courts (Northern Ireland) Order 1981.

[(2A) In section 2(5)(a)—

(a) the reference to England and Wales shall be read as a reference to Northern Ireland; and

(b) the reference to 12 months shall be read as a reference to six months.]

[(3) …]

[(3A) In section 3(6)(a)—

(a) the reference to England and Wales shall be read as a reference to Northern Ireland; and

(b) the reference to 12 months shall be read as a reference to six months.]

[(3B) In section 3A(4)(a)—

(a) the reference to England and Wales shall be read as a

reference to Northern Ireland; and

(b) the reference to 12 months shall be read as a reference to six months.]

(4) [Subsection (7) below shall apply in substitution for subsection (3) of section 7];.

[(5)–(6) …]

(7) The following paragraphs shall be inserted after Article 3(1) of that Order—

'(1A) Subject to section 8 of the Computer Misuse Act 1990 (relevance of external law), if this paragraph applies to an act, what the person doing it had in view shall be treated as an offence to which this Article applies.

(1B) Paragraph (1A) above applies to an act if—

(a) it is done in Northern Ireland; and

(b) it would fall within paragraph (1) as more than merely preparatory to the commission of an offence under section 3 of the Computer Misuse Act 1990 but for the fact that the offence, if completed, would not be an offence triable in Northern Ireland.'

(8) In section 8—

[(a) …]

(b) the reference in subsection (3) to section 1(1A) of the Criminal Attempts Act 1981 shall be read as a reference to Article 3(1A) of that Order.

(9) The references in sections 9(1) and 10 to England and Wales shall be read as references to Northern Ireland.

[(9A) In section 10 the definition of 'enactment' shall be read as including a reference to an enactment, whenever passed or made, contained in Northern Ireland legislation or in an instrument made under such legislation.]

[(10)–(12) …]

Notes

Subsections (5), (6) and (8)(a) repealed and subsection (4) amended by the Criminal Justice (Terrorism and Conspiracy) Act 1998. Subsections (1A), (2A), (3A) and (3B) inserted, and subsections (3), (10)–(12) repealed, by Police and Justice Act 2006. Subsection (4) amended by the Serious Crime Act 2007. Subsection 9A inserted by the Serious Crime Act 2015, s. 44(3).

[16A. — (1) Where a county court judge is satisfied by information on oath given by a constable that there are reasonable grounds for believing—

(a) that an offence under section 1 above has been or is about to be committed in any premises, and

(b) that evidence that such an offence has been or is about to be committed is in those premises,

he may issue a warrant authorising a constable to enter and search the premises, using such reasonable force as is necessary.

(2) The power conferred by subsection (1) above does not extend to authorising a search for material of the kinds mentioned in Article 11(2) of the Police and Criminal Evidence (Northern Ireland) Order 1989 (privileged, excluded and special procedure material).

(3) A warrant under this section—

(a) may authorise persons to accompany any constable executing the warrant; and

(b) remains in force for twenty-eight days from the date of its issue.

(4) In exercising a warrant issued under this section a constable may seize an article if he reasonably believes that it is evidence that an offence under section 1 above has been or is about to be committed.

(5) In this section 'premises' includes land, buildings, movable structures, vehicles, vessels, aircraft and hovercraft.

(6) This section extends only to Northern Ireland.]

Northern Ireland: search warrants for offences under section 1

Notes

Section inserted by Police and Justice Act 2006, s. 52, Sch. 14, para. 28.

17.—(1) The following provisions of this section apply for the interpretation of this Act.

(2) A person secures access to any program or data held in a computer if by causing a computer to perform any function he—

(a) alters or erases the program or data;

(b) copies or moves it to any storage medium other than that in which it is held or to a different location in the storage medium in which it is held;

Interpretation.

(c) uses it; or

(d) has it output from the computer in which it is held (whether by having it displayed or in any other manner);

and references to access to a program or data (and to an intent to secure such access [or to enable such access to be secured]) shall be read accordingly.

(3) For the purposes of subsection (2)(c) above a person uses a program if the function he causes the computer to perform—

(a) causes the program to be executed; or

(b) is itself a function of the program.

(4) For the purposes of subsection (2)(d) above—

(a) a program is output if the instructions of which it consists are output; and

(b) the form in which any such instructions or any other data is output (and in particular whether or not it represents a form in which, in the case of instructions, they are capable of being executed or, in the case of data, it is capable of being processed by a computer) is immaterial.

(5) Access of any kind by any person to any program or data held in a computer is unauthorised if—

(a) he is not himself entitled to control access of the kind in question to the program or data; and

(b) he does not have consent to access by him of the kind in question to the program or data from any person who is so entitled.

[but this subsection is subject to section 10.]

(6) References to any program or data held in a computer include references to any program or data held in any removable storage medium which is for the time being in the computer; and a computer is to be regarded as containing any program or data held in any such medium.

[(7) …]

(8) [An act done in relation to a computer is unauthorised if the person doing the act (or causing it to be done)—

(a) is not himself a person who has responsibility for the computer and is entitled to determine whether the act may be done; and

(b) does not have consent to the act from any such person.

In this subsection 'act' includes a series of acts.]

(9) References to the home country concerned shall be read in accordance with section 4(6) above.

(10) References to a program include references to part of a program.

Notes

Words in brackets in subsection (5) inserted by the Criminal Justice and Public Order Act 1994, s. 162(2). Other amendments and repeals were made by the Police and Justice Act 2006, s. 52, Sch. 14, para. 29.

Citation, commencement etc.

18.—(1) This Act may be cited as the Computer Misuse Act 1990.

(2) This Act shall come into force at the end of the period of two months beginning with the day on which it is passed.

(3) An offence is not committed under this Act unless every act or other event proof of which is required for conviction of the offence takes place after this Act comes into force.

Council of Europe Convention on Cybercrime
Budapest, 23 November 2001 and Additional Protocol (2003)

Preamble

The Member States of the Council of Europe and the other States signatory hereto,

Considering that the aim of the Council of Europe is to achieve a greater unity between its members;

Recognising the value of fostering co-operation with the other States parties to this Convention;

Convinced of the need to pursue, as a matter of priority, a common criminal policy aimed at the protection of society against cybercrime, *inter alia*, by adopting appropriate legislation and fostering international co-operation;

Conscious of the profound changes brought about by the digitalisation, convergence and continuing globalisation of computer networks;

Concerned by the risk that computer networks and electronic information may also be used for committing criminal offences and that evidence relating to such offences may be stored and transferred by these networks;

Recognising the need for co-operation between States and private industry in combating cybercrime and the need to protect legitimate interests in the use and development of information technologies;

Believing that an effective fight against cybercrime requires increased, rapid and well-functioning international co-operation in criminal matters;

Convinced that the present Convention is necessary to deter action directed against the confidentiality, integrity and availability of computer systems, networks and computer data as well as the misuse of such systems, networks and data by providing for the criminalisation of such conduct, as described in this Convention, and the adoption of powers sufficient for effectively combating such criminal offences, by facilitating their detection, investigation and prosecution at both the domestic and international levels and by providing arrangements for fast and reliable international co-operation;

Mindful of the need to ensure a proper balance between the interests of law enforcement and respect for fundamental human rights as enshrined in the 1950 Council of Europe Convention for the Protection of Human Rights and Fundamental Freedoms, the 1966 United Nations International Covenant on Civil and Political Rights and other applicable international human rights treaties, which reaffirm the right of everyone to hold opinions without interference, as well as the right to freedom of expression, including the freedom to seek, receive, and impart information and ideas of all kinds, regardless of frontiers, and the rights concerning the respect for privacy;

Mindful also of the right to the protection of personal data, as conferred, for example, by the 1981 Council of Europe Convention for the Protection of Individuals with regard to Automatic Processing of Personal Data;

Considering the 1989 United Nations Convention on the Rights of the Child and the 1999 International Labour Organization Worst Forms of Child Labour Convention;

Taking into account the existing Council of Europe conventions on co-operation in the penal field, as well as similar treaties which exist between Council of Europe Member States and other States, and stressing that the present Convention is intended to supplement those conventions in order to make criminal investigations and proceedings concerning criminal offences related to computer systems and data more effective and to enable the collection of evidence in electronic form of a criminal offence;

Welcoming recent developments which further advance international understanding and co-operation in combating cybercrime, including action taken by the United Nations, the OECD, the European Union and the G8;

Recalling Committee of Ministers Recommendations No. R (85) 10 concerning the practical application of the European Convention on Mutual Assistance in Criminal Matters in respect of letters rogatory for the interception of telecommunications, No. R (88) 2 on piracy in the field of copyright and neighbouring rights, No. R (87) 15 regulating the use of personal data in the police sector, No. R (95) 4 on the protection of personal data in the area of telecommunication services, with particular reference to telephone services, as well as No. R (89) 9 on computer-related crime providing guidelines for national legislatures concerning the definition of certain computer crimes and No. R (95) 13 concerning problems of criminal procedural law connected with information technology;

Having regard to Resolution No. 1 adopted by the European Ministers of Justice at their 21st Conference (Prague, 10 and 11 June 1997), which recommended that the Committee of Ministers support the work on cybercrime carried out by the European Committee on Crime Problems (CDPC) in order to bring domestic criminal law provisions closer to each other and enable the use of effective means of investigation into such offences, as well as to Resolution No. 3 adopted at the 23rd Conference of the European Ministers of Justice (London, 8 and 9 June 2000), which encouraged the negotiating parties to pursue their efforts with a view to finding appropriate solutions to enable the largest possible number of States to become parties to the Convention and acknowledged the need for a swift and efficient system of international co-operation, which duly takes into account the specific requirements of the fight against cybercrime;

Having also regard to the Action Plan adopted by the Heads of State and Government of the Council of Europe on the occasion of their Second Summit (Strasbourg, 10 and 11 October 1997), to seek common responses to the development of the new information technologies based on the standards and values of the Council of Europe;

Have agreed as follows:

CHAPTER I – USE OF TERMS

Article 1 – Definitions

For the purposes of this Convention:

(a) 'computer system' means any device or a group of interconnected or related devices, one or more of which, pursuant to a program, performs automatic processing of data;

(b) 'computer data' means any representation of facts, information or concepts in a form suitable for processing in a computer system, including a program suitable to cause a computer system to perform a function;

(c) 'service provider' means:
   (i) any public or private entity that provides to users of its service the ability to communicate by means of a computer system, and
   (ii) any other entity that processes or stores computer data on behalf of such communication service or users of such service.

(d) 'traffic data' means any computer data relating to a communication by means of a computer system, generated by a computer system that formed a part in the chain of communication, indicating the communication's origin, destination, route, time, date, size, duration, or type of underlying service.

CHAPTER II – MEASURES TO BE TAKEN AT THE NATIONAL LEVEL

SECTION 1 – SUBSTANTIVE CRIMINAL LAW

Title 1 – Offences against the confidentiality, integrity and availability of computer data and systems

Article 2 – Illegal access

Each Party shall adopt such legislative and other measures as may be necessary to establish as criminal offences under its domestic law, when committed intentionally, the access to the whole or any part of a computer system without right. A Party may require that the offence be committed by infringing security measures, with the intent of obtaining computer data or other dishonest intent, or in relation to a computer system that is connected to another computer system.

Article 3 – Illegal interception

Each Party shall adopt such legislative and other measures as may be necessary to establish as criminal offences under its domestic law, when committed intentionally, the interception without right, made by technical means, of non-public transmissions of computer data to, from or within a computer system, including electromagnetic emissions from a computer system carrying such computer data. A Party may require that the offence be committed with dishonest intent, or in relation to a computer system that is connected to another computer system.

Article 4 – Data interference

1. Each Party shall adopt such legislative and other measures as may be necessary to establish as criminal offences under its domestic law, when committed intentionally, the damaging, deletion, deterioration, alteration or suppression of computer data without right.
2. A Party may reserve the right to require that the conduct described in paragraph 1 result in serious harm.

Article 5 – System interference

Each Party shall adopt such legislative and other measures as may be necessary to establish as criminal offences under its domestic law, when committed intentionally, the serious hindering without right of the functioning of a computer system by inputting, transmitting, damaging, deleting, deteriorating, altering or suppressing computer data.

Article 6 – Misuse of devices

1. Each Party shall adopt such legislative and other measures as may be necessary to establish as criminal offences under its domestic law, when committed intentionally and without right:
   (a) the production, sale, procurement for use, import, distribution or otherwise making available of:
      (i) a device, including a computer program, designed or adapted primarily for the purpose of committing any of the offences established in accordance with Articles 2 through 5;
      (ii) a computer password, access code, or similar data by which the whole or any part of a computer system is capable of being accessed, with intent that it be used for the purpose of committing any of the offences established in Articles 2 through 5; and
   (b) the possession of an item referred to in paragraphs a.i or ii above, with intent that it be used for the purpose of committing any of the offences established in Articles 2 through 5. A Party may require by law that a number of such items be possessed before criminal liability attaches.
2. This article shall not be interpreted as imposing criminal liability where the production, sale, procurement for use, import, distribution or otherwise making available or possession referred to in paragraph 1 of this article is not for the purpose of committing an offence established in accordance with Articles 2 through 5 of this Convention, such as for the authorised testing or protection of a computer system.
3. Each Party may reserve the right not to apply paragraph 1 of this article, provided that the reservation does not concern the sale, distribution or otherwise making available of the items referred to in paragraph 1 a.ii of this article.

Title 2 – Computer-related offences
Article 7 – Computer-related forgery

Each Party shall adopt such legislative and other measures as may be necessary to establish as criminal offences under its domestic law, when committed intentionally and without right, the input, alteration, deletion, or suppression of computer data, resulting in inauthentic data with the intent that it be considered or acted upon for legal purposes as if it were authentic, regardless whether or not the data is directly readable and intelligible. A Party may require an intent to defraud, or similar dishonest intent, before criminal liability attaches.

Article 8 – Computer-related fraud

Each Party shall adopt such legislative and other measures as may be necessary to establish as criminal offences under its domestic law, when committed intentionally and without right, the causing of a loss of property to another person by:

(a) any input, alteration, deletion or suppression of computer data,

(b) any interference with the functioning of a computer system, with fraudulent or dishonest intent of procuring, without right, an economic benefit for oneself or for another person.

Title 3 – Content-related offences
Article 9 – Offences related to child pornography

1. Each Party shall adopt such legislative and other measures as may be necessary to establish as criminal offences under its domestic law, when committed intentionally and without right, the following conduct:
    (a) producing child pornography for the purpose of its distribution through a computer system;
    (b) offering or making available child pornography through a computer system;
    (c) distributing or transmitting child pornography through a computer system;
    (d) procuring child pornography through a computer system for oneself or for another person;
    (e) possessing child pornography in a computer system or on a computer-data storage medium.
2. For the purpose of paragraph 1 above, the term 'child pornography' shall include pornographic material that visually depicts:
    (a) a minor engaged in sexually explicit conduct;
    (b) a person appearing to be a minor engaged in sexually explicit conduct;
    (c) realistic images representing a minor engaged in sexually explicit conduct.
3. For the purpose of paragraph 2 above, the term 'minor' shall include all persons under 18 years of age. A Party may, however, require a lower age-limit, which shall be not less than 16 years.
4. Each Party may reserve the right not to apply, in whole or in part, paragraphs 1, sub-paragraphs d. and e, and 2, sub-paragraphs b. and c.

Title 4 – Offences related to infringements of copyright and related rights
Article 10 – Offences related to infringements of copyright and related rights

1. Each Party shall adopt such legislative and other measures as may be necessary to establish as criminal offences under its domestic law the infringement of copyright, as defined under the law of that Party, pursuant to the obligations it has undertaken under the Paris Act of 24 July 1971 revising the Bern Convention for the Protection of Literary and Artistic Works, the Agreement on Trade-Related Aspects of Intellectual Property Rights and the WIPO Copyright Treaty, with the exception of any moral rights conferred by such conventions, where such acts are committed wilfully, on a commercial scale and by means of a computer system.
2. Each Party shall adopt such legislative and other measures as may be necessary to establish as criminal offences under its domestic law the infringement of related rights, as defined under the law of that Party, pursuant to the obligations it has undertaken under the International Convention for the Protection of Performers, Producers of Phonograms and Broadcasting Organisations (Rome Convention), the Agreement on Trade-Related Aspects of Intellectual Property Rights and the WIPO Performances and Phonograms Treaty, with the exception of any moral rights conferred by such conventions, where such acts are committed wilfully, on a commercial scale and by means of a computer system.
3. A Party may reserve the right not to impose criminal liability under paragraphs 1 and 2 of this article in limited circumstances, provided that other effective remedies are available and that such reservation does not derogate from the Party's international obligations set forth in the international instruments referred to in paragraphs 1 and 2 of this article.

Title 5 – Ancillary liability and sanctions
Article 11 – Attempt and aiding or abetting

1. Each Party shall adopt such legislative and other measures as may be necessary to establish as criminal offences under its domestic law, when committed intentionally, aiding or abetting the

commission of any of the offences established in accordance with Articles 2 through 10 of the present Convention with intent that such offence be committed.

2. Each Party shall adopt such legislative and other measures as may be necessary to establish as criminal offences under its domestic law, when committed intentionally, an attempt to commit any of the offences established in accordance with Articles 3 through 5, 7, 8, and 9.1.a and c. of this Convention.

3. Each Party may reserve the right not to apply, in whole or in part, paragraph 2 of this article.

Article 12 – Corporate liability

1. Each Party shall adopt such legislative and other measures as may be necessary to ensure that legal persons can be held liable for a criminal offence established in accordance with this Convention, committed for their benefit by any natural person, acting either individually or as part of an organ of the legal person, who has a leading position within it, based on:
   (a) a power of representation of the legal person;
   (b) an authority to take decisions on behalf of the legal person;
   (c) an authority to exercise control within the legal person.

2. In addition to the cases already provided for in paragraph 1 of this article, each Party shall take the measures necessary to ensure that a legal person can be held liable where the lack of supervision or control by a natural person referred to in paragraph 1 has made possible the commission of a criminal offence established in accordance with this Convention for the benefit of that legal person by a natural person acting under its authority.

3. Subject to the legal principles of the Party, the liability of a legal person may be criminal, civil or administrative.

4. Such liability shall be without prejudice to the criminal liability of the natural persons who have committed the offence.

Article 13 – Sanctions and measures

1. Each Party shall adopt such legislative and other measures as may be necessary to ensure that the criminal offences established in accordance with Articles 2 through 11 are punishable by effective, proportionate and dissuasive sanctions, which include deprivation of liberty.

2. Each Party shall ensure that legal persons held liable in accordance with Article 12 shall be subject to effective, proportionate and dissuasive criminal or non-criminal sanctions or measures, including monetary sanctions.

SECTION 2 – PROCEDURAL LAW

Title 1 – Common provisions

Article 14 – Scope of procedural provisions

1. Each Party shall adopt such legislative and other measures as may be necessary to establish the powers and procedures provided for in this section for the purpose of specific criminal investigations or proceedings.

2. Except as specifically provided otherwise in Article 21, each Party shall apply the powers and procedures referred to in paragraph 1 of this article to:
   (a) the criminal offences established in accordance with Articles 2 through 11 of this Convention;
   (b) other criminal offences committed by means of a computer system; and
   (c) the collection of evidence in electronic form of a criminal offence.

3. (a) Each Party may reserve the right to apply the measures referred to in Article 20 only to offences or categories of offences specified in the reservation, provided that the range of such offences or categories of offences is not more restricted than the range of offences to which it applies the measures referred to in Article 21. Each Party shall consider restricting such a reservation to enable the broadest application of the measure referred to in Article 20.
   (b) Where a Party, due to limitations in its legislation in force at the time of the adoption of the present Convention, is not able to apply the measures referred to in Articles 20 and 21 to communications being transmitted within a computer system of a service provider, which system: (i) is being operated for the benefit of a closed group of users, and (ii) does not employ public communications networks and is not connected with another computer system, whether public or

private, that Party may reserve the right not to apply these measures to such communications. Each Party shall consider restricting such a reservation to enable the broadest application of the measures referred to in Articles 20 and 21.

Article 15 – Conditions and safeguards

1. Each Party shall ensure that the establishment, implementation and application of the powers and procedures provided for in this Section are subject to conditions and safeguards provided for under its domestic law, which shall provide for the adequate protection of human rights and liberties, including rights arising pursuant to obligations it has undertaken under the 1950 Council of Europe Convention for the Protection of Human Rights and Fundamental Freedoms, the 1966 United Nations International Covenant on Civil and Political Rights, and other applicable international human rights instruments, and which shall incorporate the principle of proportionality.
2. Such conditions and safeguards shall, as appropriate in view of the nature of the procedure or power concerned, *inter alia*, include judicial or other independent supervision, grounds justifying application, and limitation of the scope and the duration of such power or procedure.
3. To the extent that it is consistent with the public interest, in particular the sound administration of justice, each Party shall consider the impact of the powers and procedures in this section upon the rights, responsibilities and legitimate interests of third parties.

Title 2 – Expedited preservation of stored computer data
Article 16 – Expedited preservation of stored computer data

1. Each Party shall adopt such legislative and other measures as may be necessary to enable its competent authorities to order or similarly obtain the expeditious preservation of specified computer data, including traffic data, that has been stored by means of a computer system, in particular where there are grounds to believe that the computer data is particularly vulnerable to loss or modification.
2. Where a Party gives effect to paragraph 1 above by means of an order to a person to preserve specified stored computer data in the person's possession or control, the Party shall adopt such legislative and other measures as may be necessary to oblige that person to preserve and maintain the integrity of that computer data for a period of time as long as necessary, up to a maximum of ninety days, to enable the competent authorities to seek its disclosure. A Party may provide for such an order to be subsequently renewed.
3. Each Party shall adopt such legislative and other measures as may be necessary to oblige the custodian or other person who is to preserve the computer data to keep confidential the undertaking of such procedures for the period of time provided for by its domestic law.
4. The powers and procedures referred to in this article shall be subject to Articles 14 and 15.

Article 17 – Expedited preservation and partial disclosure of traffic data

1. Each Party shall adopt, in respect of traffic data that is to be preserved under Article 16, such legislative and other measures as may be necessary to:
   (a) ensure that such expeditious preservation of traffic data is available regardless of whether one or more service providers were involved in the transmission of that communication; and
   (b) ensure the expeditious disclosure to the Party's competent authority, or a person designated by that authority, of a sufficient amount of traffic data to enable the Party to identify the service providers and the path through which the communication was transmitted.
2. The powers and procedures referred to in this article shall be subject to Articles 14 and 15.

Title 3 – Production order
Article 18 – Production order

1. Each Party shall adopt such legislative and other measures as may be necessary to empower its competent authorities to order:
   (a) a person in its territory to submit specified computer data in that person's possession or control, which is stored in a computer system or a computer-data storage medium; and

(b) a service provider offering its services in the territory of the Party to submit subscriber information relating to such services in that service provider's possession or control.

2. The powers and procedures referred to in this article shall be subject to Articles 14 and 15.

3. For the purpose of this article, the term 'subscriber information' means any information contained in the form of computer data or any other form that is held by a service provider, relating to subscribers of its services other than traffic or content data and by which can be established:

(a) the type of communication service used, the technical provisions taken thereto and the period of service;

(b) the subscriber's identity, postal or geographic address, telephone and other access number, billing and payment information, available on the basis of the service agreement or arrangement;

(c) any other information on the site of the installation of communication equipment, available on the basis of the service agreement or arrangement.

Title 4 – Search and seizure of stored computer data

Article 19 – Search and seizure of stored computer data

1. Each Party shall adopt such legislative and other measures as may be necessary to empower its competent authorities to search or similarly access:

(a) a computer system or part of it and computer data stored therein; and

(b) a computer-data storage medium in which computer data may be stored in its territory.

2. Each Party shall adopt such legislative and other measures as may be necessary to ensure that where its authorities search or similarly access a specific computer system or part of it, pursuant to paragraph 1.a, and have grounds to believe that the data sought is stored in another computer system or part of it in its territory, and such data is lawfully accessible from or available to the initial system, the authorities shall be able to expeditiously extend the search or similar accessing to the other system.

3. Each Party shall adopt such legislative and other measures as may be necessary to empower its competent authorities to seize or similarly secure computer data accessed according to paragraphs 1 or 2. These measures shall include the power to:

(a) seize or similarly secure a computer system or part of it or a computer-data storage medium;

(b) make and retain a copy of those computer data;

(c) maintain the integrity of the relevant stored computer data;

(d) render inaccessible or remove those computer data in the accessed computer system.

4. Each Party shall adopt such legislative and other measures as may be necessary to empower its competent authorities to order any person who has knowledge about the functioning of the computer system or measures applied to protect the computer data therein to provide, as is reasonable, the necessary information, to enable the undertaking of the measures referred to in paragraphs 1 and 2.

5. The powers and procedures referred to in this article shall be subject to Articles 14 and 15.

Title 5 – Real-time collection of computer data

Article 20 – Real-time collection of traffic data

1. Each Party shall adopt such legislative and other measures as may be necessary to empower its competent authorities to:

(a) collect or record through the application of technical means on the territory of that Party, and

(b) compel a service provider, within its existing technical capability:

(i) to collect or record through the application of technical means on the territory of that Party; or

(ii) to co-operate and assist the competent authorities in the collection or recording of, traffic data, in real-time, associated with specified communications in its territory transmitted by means of a computer system.

2. Where a Party, due to the established principles of its domestic legal system, cannot adopt the measures referred to in paragraph 1.a, it may instead adopt legislative and other measures as may be necessary to ensure the real-time collection or recording of traffic data associated with specified communications transmitted in its territory, through the application of technical means on that territory.

3. Each Party shall adopt such legislative and other measures as may be necessary to oblige a service provider to keep confidential the fact of the execution of any power provided for in this article and any information relating to it.

4. The powers and procedures referred to in this article shall be subject to Articles 14 and 15.

Article 21 – Interception of content data

1. Each Party shall adopt such legislative and other measures as may be necessary, in relation to a range of serious offences to be determined by domestic law, to empower its competent authorities to:
   (a) collect or record through the application of technical means on the territory of that Party, and
   (b) compel a service provider, within its existing technical capability:
      (i) to collect or record through the application of technical means on the territory of that Party, or
      (ii) to co-operate and assist the competent authorities in the collection or recording of, content data, in real-time, of specified communications in its territory transmitted by means of a computer system.

2. Where a Party, due to the established principles of its domestic legal system, cannot adopt the measures referred to in paragraph 1.a, it may instead adopt legislative and other measures as may be necessary to ensure the real-time collection or recording of content data on specified communications in its territory through the application of technical means on that territory.

3. Each Party shall adopt such legislative and other measures as may be necessary to oblige a service provider to keep confidential the fact of the execution of any power provided for in this article and any information relating to it.

4. The powers and procedures referred to in this article shall be subject to Articles 14 and 15.

Section 3 – Jurisdiction

Article 22 – Jurisdiction

1. Each Party shall adopt such legislative and other measures as may be necessary to establish jurisdiction over any offence established in accordance with Articles 2 through 11 of this Convention, when the offence is committed:
   (a) in its territory; or
   (b) on board a ship flying the flag of that Party; or
   (c) on board an aircraft registered under the laws of that Party; or
   (d) by one of its nationals, if the offence is punishable under criminal law where it was committed or if the offence is committed outside the territorial jurisdiction of any State.

2. Each Party may reserve the right not to apply or to apply only in specific cases or conditions the jurisdiction rules laid down in paragraphs 1.b through 1.d of this article or any part thereof.

3. Each Party shall adopt such measures as may be necessary to establish jurisdiction over the offences referred to in Article 24, paragraph 1, of this Convention, in cases where an alleged offender is present in its territory and it does not extradite him or her to another Party, solely on the basis of his or her nationality, after a request for extradition.

4. This Convention does not exclude any criminal jurisdiction exercised by a Party in accordance with its domestic law.

5. When more than one Party claims jurisdiction over an alleged offence established in accordance with this Convention, the Parties involved shall, where appropriate, consult with a view to determining the most appropriate jurisdiction for prosecution.

Chapter III – International co-operation

Section 1 – General principles

Title 1 – General principles relating to international co-operation

Article 23 – General principles relating to international co-operation

The Parties shall co-operate with each other, in accordance with the provisions of this chapter, and through the application of relevant international instruments on international co-operation in criminal matters, arrangements agreed on the basis of uniform or reciprocal legislation, and domestic laws, to the widest extent possible for the purposes of investigations or proceedings concerning criminal offences related to computer systems and data, or for the collection of evidence in electronic form of a criminal offence.

Title 2 – Principles relating to extradition

Article 24 – Extradition

1. (a) This article applies to extradition between Parties for the criminal offences established in accordance with Articles 2 through 11 of this Convention, provided that they are punishable under the laws of both Parties concerned by deprivation of liberty for a maximum period of at least one year, or by a more severe penalty.
    (b) Where a different minimum penalty is to be applied under an arrangement agreed on the basis of uniform or reciprocal legislation or an extradition treaty, including the European Convention on Extradition (ETS No. 24), applicable between two or more parties, the minimum penalty provided for under such arrangement or treaty shall apply.
2. The criminal offences described in paragraph 1 of this article shall be deemed to be included as extraditable offences in any extradition treaty existing between or among the Parties. The Parties undertake to include such offences as extraditable offences in any extradition treaty to be concluded between or among them.
3. If a Party that makes extradition conditional on the existence of a treaty receives a request for extradition from another Party with which it does not have an extradition treaty, it may consider this Convention as the legal basis for extradition with respect to any criminal offence referred to in paragraph 1 of this article.
4. Parties that do not make extradition conditional on the existence of a treaty shall recognise the criminal offences referred to in paragraph 1 of this article as extraditable offences between themselves.
5. Extradition shall be subject to the conditions provided for by the law of the requested Party or by applicable extradition treaties, including the grounds on which the requested Party may refuse extradition.
6. If extradition for a criminal offence referred to in paragraph 1 of this article is refused solely on the basis of the nationality of the person sought, or because the requested Party deems that it has jurisdiction over the offence, the requested Party shall submit the case at the request of the requesting Party to its competent authorities for the purpose of prosecution and shall report the final outcome to the requesting Party in due course. Those authorities shall take their decision and conduct their investigations and proceedings in the same manner as for any other offence of a comparable nature under the law of that Party.
7. (a) Each Party shall, at the time of signature or when depositing its instrument of ratification, acceptance, approval or accession, communicate to the Secretary General of the Council of Europe the name and address of each authority responsible for making or receiving requests for extradition or provisional arrest in the absence of a treaty.
    (b) The Secretary General of the Council of Europe shall set up and keep updated a register of authorities so designated by the Parties. Each Party shall ensure that the details held on the register are correct at all times.

Title 3 – General principles relating to mutual assistance

Article 25 – General principles relating to mutual assistance

1. The Parties shall afford one another mutual assistance to the widest extent possible for the purpose of investigations or proceedings concerning criminal offences related to computer systems and data, or for the collection of evidence in electronic form of a criminal offence.
2. Each Party shall also adopt such legislative and other measures as may be necessary to carry out the obligations set forth in Articles 27 through 35.
3. Each Party may, in urgent circumstances, make requests for mutual assistance or communications related thereto by expedited means of communication, including fax or email, to the extent that such means provide appropriate levels of security and authentication (including the use of encryption, where necessary), with formal confirmation to follow, where required by the requested Party. The requested Party shall accept and respond to the request by any such expedited means of communication.

4. Except as otherwise specifically provided in articles in this chapter, mutual assistance shall be subject to the conditions provided for by the law of the requested Party or by applicable mutual assistance treaties, including the grounds on which the requested Party may refuse co-operation. The requested Party shall not exercise the right to refuse mutual assistance in relation to the offences referred to in Articles 2 through 11 solely on the ground that the request concerns an offence which it considers a fiscal offence.

5. Where, in accordance with the provisions of this chapter, the requested Party is permitted to make mutual assistance conditional upon the existence of dual criminality, that condition shall be deemed fulfilled, irrespective of whether its laws place the offence within the same category of offence or denominate the offence by the same terminology as the requesting Party, if the conduct underlying the offence for which assistance is sought is a criminal offence under its laws.

Article 26 – Spontaneous information

1. A Party may, within the limits of its domestic law and without prior request, forward to another Party information obtained within the framework of its own investigations when it considers that the disclosure of such information might assist the receiving Party in initiating or carrying out investigations or proceedings concerning criminal offences established in accordance with this Convention or might lead to a request for co-operation by that Party under this chapter.

2. Prior to providing such information, the providing Party may request that it be kept confidential or only used subject to conditions. If the receiving Party cannot comply with such request, it shall notify the providing Party, which shall then determine whether the information should nevertheless be provided. If the receiving Party accepts the information subject to the conditions, it shall be bound by them.

Title 4 – Procedures pertaining to mutual assistance request in the absence of applicable international agreements

Article 27 – Procedures pertaining to mutual assistance requests in the absence of applicable international agreements

1. Where there is no mutual assistance treaty or arrangement on the basis of uniform or reciprocal legislation in force between the requesting and requested Parties, the provisions of paragraphs 2 through 9 of this article shall apply. The provisions of this article shall not apply where such treaty, arrangement or legislation exists, unless the Parties concerned agree to apply any or all of the remainder of this article in lieu thereof.

2. (a) Each Party shall designate a central authority or authorities responsible for sending and answering requests for mutual assistance, the execution of such requests or their transmission to the authorities competent for their execution.

(b) The central authorities shall communicate directly with each other;

(c) Each Party shall, at the time of signature or when depositing its instrument of ratification, acceptance, approval or accession, communicate to the Secretary General of the Council of Europe the names and addresses of the authorities designated in pursuance of this paragraph;

(d) The Secretary General of the Council of Europe shall set up and keep updated a register of central authorities designated by the Parties. Each Party shall ensure that the details held on the register are correct at all times.

3. Mutual assistance requests under this article shall be executed in accordance with the procedures specified by the requesting Party, except where incompatible with the law of the requested Party.

4. The requested Party may, in addition to the grounds for refusal established in Article 25, paragraph 4, refuse assistance if:

(a) the request concerns an offence which the requested Party considers a political offence or an offence connected with a political offence, or

(b) it considers that execution of the request is likely to prejudice its sovereignty, security, *ordre public* or other essential interests.

5. The requested Party may postpone action on a request if such action would prejudice criminal investigations or proceedings conducted by its authorities.

6. Before refusing or postponing assistance, the requested Party shall, where appropriate after having consulted with the requesting Party, consider whether the request may be granted partially or subject to such conditions as it deems necessary.

7. The requested Party shall promptly inform the requesting Party of the outcome of the execution of a request for assistance. Reasons shall be given for any refusal or postponement of the request. The requested Party shall also inform the requesting Party of any reasons that render impossible the execution of the request or are likely to delay it significantly.

8. The requesting Party may request that the requested Party keep confidential the fact of any request made under this chapter as well as its subject, except to the extent necessary for its execution. If the requested Party cannot comply with the request for confidentiality, it shall promptly inform the requesting Party, which shall then determine whether the request should nevertheless be executed.

9. (a) In the event of urgency, requests for mutual assistance or communications related thereto may be sent directly by judicial authorities of the requesting Party to such authorities of the requested Party. In any such cases, a copy shall be sent at the same time to the central authority of the requested Party through the central authority of the requesting Party.

   (b) Any request or communication under this paragraph may be made through the International Criminal Police Organisation (Interpol).

   (c) Where a request is made pursuant to sub-paragraph a. of this article and the authority is not competent to deal with the request, it shall refer the request to the competent national authority and inform directly the requesting Party that it has done so.

   (d) Requests or communications made under this paragraph that do not involve coercive action may be directly transmitted by the competent authorities of the requesting Party to the competent authorities of the requested Party.

   (e) Each Party may, at the time of signature or when depositing its instrument of ratification, acceptance, approval or accession, inform the Secretary General of the Council of Europe that, for reasons of efficiency, requests made under this paragraph are to be addressed to its central authority.

Article 28 – Confidentiality and limitation on use

1. When there is no mutual assistance treaty or arrangement on the basis of uniform or reciprocal legislation in force between the requesting and the requested Parties, the provisions of this article shall apply. The provisions of this article shall not apply where such treaty, arrangement or legislation exists, unless the Parties concerned agree to apply any or all of the remainder of this article in lieu thereof.

2. The requested Party may make the supply of information or material in response to a request dependent on the condition that it is:

   (a) kept confidential where the request for mutual legal assistance could not be complied with in the absence of such condition, or

   (b) not used for investigations or proceedings other than those stated in the request.

3. If the requesting Party cannot comply with a condition referred to in paragraph 2, it shall promptly inform the other Party, which shall then determine whether the information should nevertheless be provided. When the requesting Party accepts the condition, it shall be bound by it.

4. Any Party that supplies information or material subject to a condition referred to in paragraph 2 may require the other Party to explain, in relation to that condition, the use made of such information or material.

SECTION 2 – SPECIFIC PROVISIONS

Title 1 – Mutual assistance regarding provisional measures

Article 29 – Expedited preservation of stored computer data

1. A Party may request another Party to order or otherwise obtain the expeditious preservation of data stored by means of a computer system, located within the territory of that other Party and in respect of which the requesting Party intends to submit a request for mutual assistance for the search or similar access, seizure or similar securing, or disclosure of the data.

2. A request for preservation made under paragraph 1 shall specify:

   (a) the authority seeking the preservation;

(b) the offence that is the subject of a criminal investigation or proceedings and a brief summary of the related facts;

(c) the stored computer data to be preserved and its relationship to the offence;

(d) any available information identifying the custodian of the stored computer data or the location of the computer system;

(e) the necessity of the preservation; and

(f) that the Party intends to submit a request for mutual assistance for the search or similar access, seizure or similar securing, or disclosure of the stored computer data.

3. Upon receiving the request from another Party, the requested Party shall take all appropriate measures to preserve expeditiously the specified data in accordance with its domestic law. For the purposes of responding to a request, dual criminality shall not be required as a condition to providing such preservation.

4. A Party that requires dual criminality as a condition for responding to a request for mutual assistance for the search or similar access, seizure or similar securing, or disclosure of stored data may, in respect of offences other than those established in accordance with Articles 2 through 11 of this Convention, reserve the right to refuse the request for preservation under this article in cases where it has reasons to believe that at the time of disclosure the condition of dual criminality cannot be fulfilled.

5. In addition, a request for preservation may only be refused if:

(a) the request concerns an offence which the requested Party considers a political offence or an offence connected with a political offence, or

(b) the requested Party considers that execution of the request is likely to prejudice its sovereignty, security, *ordre public* or other essential interests.

6. Where the requested Party believes that preservation will not ensure the future availability of the data or will threaten the confidentiality of or otherwise prejudice the requesting Party's investigation, it shall promptly so inform the requesting Party, which shall then determine whether the request should nevertheless be executed.

7. Any preservation effected in response to the request referred to in paragraph 1 shall be for a period not less than sixty days, in order to enable the requesting Party to submit a request for the search or similar access, seizure or similar securing, or disclosure of the data. Following the receipt of such a request, the data shall continue to be preserved pending a decision on that request.

Article 30 – Expedited disclosure of preserved traffic data

1. Where, in the course of the execution of a request made pursuant to Article 29 to preserve traffic data concerning a specific communication, the requested Party discovers that a service provider in another State was involved in the transmission of the communication, the requested Party shall expeditiously disclose to the requesting Party a sufficient amount of traffic data to identify that service provider and the path through which the communication was transmitted.

2. Disclosure of traffic data under paragraph 1 may only be withheld if:

(a) the request concerns an offence which the requested Party considers a political offence or an offence connected with a political offence; or

(b) the requested Party considers that execution of the request is likely to prejudice its sovereignty, security, *ordre public* or other essential interests.

Title 2 – Mutual assistance regarding investigative powers

Article 31 – Mutual assistance regarding accessing of stored computer data

1. A Party may request another Party to search or similarly access, seize or similarly secure, and disclose data stored by means of a computer system located within the territory of the requested Party, including data that has been preserved pursuant to Article 29.

2. The requested Party shall respond to the request through the application of international instruments, arrangements and laws referred to in Article 23, and in accordance with other relevant provisions of this chapter.

3. The request shall be responded to on an expedited basis where:

(a) there are grounds to believe that relevant data is particularly vulnerable to loss or modification; or

(b) the instruments, arrangements and laws referred to in paragraph 2 otherwise provide for expedited co-operation.

Article 32 – Trans-border access to stored computer data with
consent or where publicly available

A Party may, without the authorisation of another Party:

(a) access publicly available (open source) stored computer data, regardless of where the data is located geographically; or

(b) access or receive, through a computer system in its territory, stored computer data located in another Party, if the Party obtains the lawful and voluntary consent of the person who has the lawful authority to disclose the data to the Party through that computer system.

Article 33 – Mutual assistance regarding the real-time collection of traffic data

1. The Parties shall provide mutual assistance to each other in the real-time collection of traffic data associated with specified communications in their territory transmitted by means of a computer system. Subject to the provisions of paragraph 2, this assistance shall be governed by the conditions and procedures provided for under domestic law.

2. Each Party shall provide such assistance at least with respect to criminal offences for which real-time collection of traffic data would be available in a similar domestic case.

Article 34 – Mutual assistance regarding the interception of content data

The Parties shall provide mutual assistance to each other in the real-time collection or recording of content data of specified communications transmitted by means of a computer system to the extent permitted under their applicable treaties and domestic laws.

Title 3 – 24/7 Network

Article 35 – 24/7 Network

1. Each Party shall designate a point of contact available on a twenty-four hour, seven-day-a-week basis, in order to ensure the provision of immediate assistance for the purpose of investigations or proceedings concerning criminal offences related to computer systems and data, or for the collection of evidence in electronic form of a criminal offence. Such assistance shall include facilitating, or, if permitted by its domestic law and practice, directly carrying out the following measures:

(a) the provision of technical advice;

(b) the preservation of data pursuant to Articles 29 and 30;

(c) the collection of evidence, the provision of legal information, and locating of suspects.

2. (a) A Party's point of contact shall have the capacity to carry out communications with the point of contact of another Party on an expedited basis.

(b) If the point of contact designated by a Party is not part of that Party's authority or authorities responsible for international mutual assistance or extradition, the point of contact shall ensure that it is able to co-ordinate with such authority or authorities on an expedited basis.

3. Each Party shall ensure that trained and equipped personnel are available, in order to facilitate the operation of the network.

CHAPTER IV – FINAL PROVISIONS

Article 36 – Signature and entry into force

1. This Convention shall be open for signature by the member States of the Council of Europe and by non-member States which have participated in its elaboration.

2. This Convention is subject to ratification, acceptance or approval. Instruments of ratification, acceptance or approval shall be deposited with the Secretary General of the Council of Europe.

3. This Convention shall enter into force on the first day of the month following the expiration of a period of three months after the date on which five States, including at least three member States of the Council of Europe, have expressed their consent to be bound by the Convention in accordance with the provisions of paragraphs 1 and 2.

4. In respect of any signatory State which subsequently expresses its consent to be bound by it, the Convention shall enter into force on the first day of the month following the expiration of a period of three months after the date of the expression of its consent to be bound by the Convention in accordance with the provisions of paragraphs 1 and 2.

Article 37 – Accession to the Convention

1. After the entry into force of this Convention, the Committee of Ministers of the Council of Europe, after consulting with and obtaining the unanimous consent of the Contracting States to the Convention, may invite any State which is not a member of the Council and which has not participated in its elaboration to accede to this Convention. The decision shall be taken by the majority provided for in Article 20.d. of the Statute of the Council of Europe and by the unanimous vote of the representatives of the Contracting States entitled to sit on the Committee of Ministers.

2. In respect of any State acceding to the Convention under paragraph 1 above, the Convention shall enter into force on the first day of the month following the expiration of a period of three months after the date of deposit of the instrument of accession with the Secretary General of the Council of Europe.

Article 38 – Territorial application

1. Any State may, at the time of signature or when depositing its instrument of ratification, acceptance, approval or accession, specify the territory or territories to which this Convention shall apply.

2. Any State may, at any later date, by a declaration addressed to the Secretary General of the Council of Europe, extend the application of this Convention to any other territory specified in the declaration. In respect of such territory the Convention shall enter into force on the first day of the month following the expiration of a period of three months after the date of receipt of the declaration by the Secretary General.

3. Any declaration made under the two preceding paragraphs may, in respect of any territory specified in such declaration, be withdrawn by a notification addressed to the Secretary General of the Council of Europe. The withdrawal shall become effective on the first day of the month following the expiration of a period of three months after the date of receipt of such notification by the Secretary General.

Article 39 – Effects of the Convention

1. The purpose of the present Convention is to supplement applicable multilateral or bilateral treaties or arrangements as between the Parties, including the provisions of:

   • the European Convention on Extradition, opened for signature in Paris, on 13 December 1957 (ETS No. 24);

   • the European Convention on Mutual Assistance in Criminal Matters, opened for signature in Strasbourg, on 20 April 1959 (ETS No. 30);

   • the Additional Protocol to the European Convention on Mutual Assistance in Criminal Matters, opened for signature in Strasbourg, on 17 March 1978 (ETS No. 99).

2. If two or more Parties have already concluded an agreement or treaty on the matters dealt with in this Convention or have otherwise established their relations on such matters, or should they in future do so, they shall also be entitled to apply that agreement or treaty or to regulate those relations accordingly. However, where Parties establish their relations in respect of the matters dealt with in the present Convention other than as regulated therein, they shall do so in a manner that is not inconsistent with the Convention's objectives and principles.

3. Nothing in this Convention shall affect other rights, restrictions, obligations and responsibilities of a Party.

Article 40 – Declarations

By a written notification addressed to the Secretary General of the Council of Europe, any State may, at the time of signature or when depositing its instrument of ratification, acceptance, approval or accession, declare that it avails itself of the possibility of requiring additional elements as provided for under Articles 2, 3, 6 paragraph 1.b, 7, 9 paragraph 3, and 27, paragraph 9.e.

Article 41 – Federal clause

1. A federal State may reserve the right to assume obligations under Chapter II of this Convention consistent with its fundamental principles governing the relationship between its central government and constituent States or other similar territorial entities provided that it is still able to co-operate under Chapter III.

2. When making a reservation under paragraph 1, a federal State may not apply the terms of such reservation to exclude or substantially diminish its obligations to provide for measures set forth in Chapter II. Overall, it shall provide for a broad and effective law enforcement capability with respect to those measures.

3. With regard to the provisions of this Convention, the application of which comes under the jurisdiction of constituent States or other similar territorial entities, that are not obliged by the constitutional system of the federation to take legislative measures, the federal government shall inform the competent authorities of such States of the said provisions with its favourable opinion, encouraging them to take appropriate action to give them effect.

Article 42 – Reservations

By a written notification addressed to the Secretary General of the Council of Europe, any State may, at the time of signature or when depositing its instrument of ratification, acceptance, approval or accession, declare that it avails itself of the reservation(s) provided for in Article 4, paragraph 2, Article 6, paragraph 3, Article 9, paragraph 4, Article 10, paragraph 3, Article 11, paragraph 3, Article 14, paragraph 3, Article 22, paragraph 2, Article 29, paragraph 4, and Article 41, paragraph 1. No other reservation may be made.

Article 43 – Status and withdrawal of reservations

1. A Party that has made a reservation in accordance with Article 42 may wholly or partially withdraw it by means of a notification addressed to the Secretary General of the Council of Europe. Such withdrawal shall take effect on the date of receipt of such notification by the Secretary General. If the notification states that the withdrawal of a reservation is to take effect on a date specified therein, and such date is later than the date on which the notification is received by the Secretary General, the withdrawal shall take effect on such a later date.

2. A Party that has made a reservation as referred to in Article 42 shall withdraw such reservation, in whole or in part, as soon as circumstances so permit.

3. The Secretary General of the Council of Europe may periodically enquire with Parties that have made one or more reservations as referred to in Article 42 as to the prospects for withdrawing such reservation(s).

Article 44 – Amendments

1. Amendments to this Convention may be proposed by any Party, and shall be communicated by the Secretary General of the Council of Europe to the Member States of the Council of Europe, to the non-member States which have participated in the elaboration of this Convention as well as to any State which has acceded to, or has been invited to accede to, this Convention in accordance with the provisions of Article 37.

2. Any amendment proposed by a Party shall be communicated to the European Committee on Crime Problems (CDPC), which shall submit to the Committee of Ministers its opinion on that proposed amendment.

3. The Committee of Ministers shall consider the proposed amendment and the opinion submitted by the CDPC and, following consultation with the non-member States Parties to this Convention, may adopt the amendment.

4. The text of any amendment adopted by the Committee of Ministers in accordance with paragraph 3 of this article shall be forwarded to the Parties for acceptance.

5. Any amendment adopted in accordance with paragraph 3 of this article shall come into force on the thirtieth day after all Parties have informed the Secretary General of their acceptance thereof.

Article 45 – Settlement of disputes

1. The European Committee on Crime Problems (CDPC) shall be kept informed regarding the interpretation and application of this Convention.

2. In case of a dispute between Parties as to the interpretation or application of this Convention, they shall seek a settlement of the dispute through negotiation or any other peaceful means of their choice, including submission of the dispute to the CDPC, to an arbitral tribunal whose decisions

shall be binding upon the Parties, or to the International Court of Justice, as agreed upon by the Parties concerned.

Article 46 – Consultations of the Parties

1. The Parties shall, as appropriate, consult periodically with a view to facilitating:
    (a) the effective use and implementation of this Convention, including the identification of any problems thereof, as well as the effects of any declaration or reservation made under this Convention;
    (b) the exchange of information on significant legal, policy or technological developments pertaining to cybercrime and the collection of evidence in electronic form;
    (c) consideration of possible supplementation or amendment of the Convention.
2. The European Committee on Crime Problems (CDPC) shall be kept periodically informed regarding the result of consultations referred to in paragraph 1.
3. The CDPC shall, as appropriate, facilitate the consultations referred to in paragraph 1 and take the measures necessary to assist the Parties in their efforts to supplement or amend the Convention. At the latest three years after the present Convention enters into force, the European Committee on Crime Problems (CDPC) shall, in co-operation with the Parties, conduct a review of all of the Convention's provisions and, if necessary, recommend any appropriate amendments.
4. Except where assumed by the Council of Europe, expenses incurred in carrying out the provisions of paragraph 1 shall be borne by the Parties in the manner to be determined by them.
5. The Parties shall be assisted by the Secretariat of the Council of Europe in carrying out their functions pursuant to this article.

Article 47 – Denunciation

1. Any Party may, at any time, denounce this Convention by means of a notification addressed to the Secretary General of the Council of Europe.
2. Such denunciation shall become effective on the first day of the month following the expiration of a period of three months after the date of receipt of the notification by the Secretary General.

Article 48 – Notification

The Secretary General of the Council of Europe shall notify the Member States of the Council of Europe, the non-member States which have participated in the elaboration of this Convention as well as any State which has acceded to, or has been invited to accede to, this Convention of:
(a) any signature;
(b) the deposit of any instrument of ratification, acceptance, approval or accession;
(c) any date of entry into force of this Convention in accordance with Articles 36 and 37;
(d) any declaration made under Article 40 or reservation made in accordance with Article 42;
(e) any other act, notification or communication relating to this Convention.

In witness whereof the undersigned, being duly authorised thereto, have signed this Convention.

Done at Budapest, this 23rd day of November 2001, in English and in French, both texts being equally authentic, in a single copy which shall be deposited in the archives of the Council of Europe. The Secretary General of the Council of Europe shall transmit certified copies to each Member State of the Council of Europe, to the non-member States which have participated in the elaboration of this Convention, and to any State invited to accede to it.

ADDITIONAL PROTOCOL TO THE CONVENTION ON CYBERCRIME, CONCERNING THE CRIMINALISATION OF ACTS OF A RACIST AND XENOPHOBIC NATURE COMMITTED THROUGH COMPUTER SYSTEMS

Strasbourg, 28.01.2003

The Member States of the Council of Europe and the other States Parties to the Convention on Cybercrime, opened for signature in Budapest on 23 November 2001, signatory hereto;

Considering that the aim of the Council of Europe is to achieve a greater unity between its members;

Recalling that all human beings are born free and equal in dignity and rights;

Stressing the need to secure a full and effective implementation of all human rights without any discrimination or distinction, as enshrined in European and other international instruments;

Convinced that acts of a racist and xenophobic nature constitute a violation of human rights and a threat to the rule of law and democratic stability;

Considering that national and international law need to provide adequate legal responses to propaganda of a racist and xenophobic nature committed through computer systems;

Aware of the fact that propaganda to such acts is often subject to criminalisation in national legislation;

Having regard to the Convention on Cybercrime, which provides for modern and flexible means of international co-operation and convinced of the need to harmonise substantive law provisions concerning the fight against racist and xenophobic propaganda;

Aware that computer systems offer an unprecedented means of facilitating freedom of expression and communication around the globe;

Recognising that freedom of expression constitutes one of the essential foundations of a democratic society, and is one of the basic conditions for its progress and for the development of every human being;

Concerned, however, by the risk of misuse or abuse of such computer systems to disseminate racist and xenophobic propaganda;

Mindful of the need to ensure a proper balance between freedom of expression and an effective fight against acts of a racist and xenophobic nature;

Recognising that this Protocol is not intended to affect established principles relating to freedom of expression in national legal systems;

Taking into account the relevant international legal instruments in this field, and in particular the Convention for the Protection of Human Rights and Fundamental Freedoms and its Protocol No. 12 concerning the general prohibition of discrimination, the existing Council of Europe conventions on co-operation in the penal field, in particular the Convention on Cybercrime, the United Nations International Convention on the Elimination of All Forms of Racial Discrimination of 21 December 1965, the European Union Joint Action of 15 July 1996 adopted by the Council on the basis of Article K.3 of the Treaty on European Union, concerning action to combat racism and xenophobia;

Welcoming the recent developments which further advance international understanding and co-operation in combating cybercrime and racism and xenophobia;

Having regard to the Action Plan adopted by the Heads of State and Government of the Council of Europe on the occasion of their Second Summit (Strasbourg, 10-11 October 1997) to seek common responses to the developments of the new technologies based on the standards and values of the Council of Europe;

Have agreed as follows:

CHAPTER I – COMMON PROVISIONS
Article 1 – Purpose

The purpose of this Protocol is to supplement, as between the Parties to the Protocol, the provisions of the Convention on Cybercrime, opened for signature in Budapest on 23 November 2001 (hereinafter referred to as 'the Convention'), as regards the criminalisation of acts of a racist and xenophobic nature committed through computer systems.

Article 2 – Definition

1. For the purposes of this Protocol:

'racist and xenophobic material' means any written material, any image or any other representation of ideas or theories, which advocates, promotes or incites hatred, discrimination or violence, against any individual or group of individuals, based on race, colour, descent or national or ethnic origin, as well as religion if used as a pretext for any of these factors.

2. The terms and expressions used in this Protocol shall be interpreted in the same manner as they are interpreted under the Convention.

Chapter II – Measures to be taken at national level

Article 3 – Dissemination of racist and xenophobic material through computer systems

1. Each Party shall adopt such legislative and other measures as may be necessary to establish as criminal offences under its domestic law, when committed intentionally and without right, the following conduct: distributing, or otherwise making available, racist and xenophobic material to the public through a computer system.

2. A Party may reserve the right not to attach criminal liability to conduct as defined by paragraph 1 of this article, where the material, as defined in Article 2, paragraph 1, advocates, promotes or incites discrimination that is not associated with hatred or violence, provided that other effective remedies are available.

3. Notwithstanding paragraph 2 of this article, a Party may reserve the right not to apply paragraph 1 to those cases of discrimination for which, due to established principles in its national legal system concerning freedom of expression, it cannot provide for effective remedies as referred to in the said paragraph 2.

Article 4 – Racist and xenophobic motivated threat

1. Each Party shall adopt such legislative and other measures as may be necessary to establish as criminal offences under its domestic law, when committed intentionally and without right, the following conduct: threatening, through a computer system, with the commission of a serious criminal offence as defined under its domestic law, (i) persons for the reason that they belong to a group, distinguished by race, colour, descent or national or ethnic origin, as well as religion, if used as a pretext for any of these factors, or (ii) a group of persons which is distinguished by any of these characteristics.

Article 5 – Racist and xenophobic motivated insult

1. Each Party shall adopt such legislative and other measures as may be necessary to establish as criminal offences under its domestic law, when committed intentionally and without right, the following conduct:

   insulting publicly, through a computer system, (i) persons for the reason that they belong to a group distinguished by race, colour, descent or national or ethnic origin, as well as religion, if used as a pretext for any of these factors; or (ii) a group of persons which is distinguished by any of these characteristics.

2. A Party may either:
   (a) require that the offence referred to in paragraph 1 of this article has the effect that the person or group of persons referred to in paragraph 1 is exposed to hatred, contempt or ridicule; or
   (b) reserve the right not to apply, in whole or in part, paragraph 1 of this article.

Article 6 – Denial, gross minimisation, approval or justification of genocide or crimes against humanity

1. Each Party shall adopt such legislative measures as may be necessary to establish the following conduct as criminal offences under its domestic law, when committed intentionally and without right: distributing or otherwise making available, through a computer system to the public, material which denies, grossly minimises, approves or justifies acts constituting genocide or crimes against humanity, as defined by international law and recognised as such by final and binding decisions of the International Military Tribunal, established by the London Agreement of 8 August 1945, or of any other international court established by relevant international instruments and whose jurisdiction is recognised by that Party.

2. A Party may either
   (a) require that the denial or the gross minimisation referred to in paragraph 1 of this article is committed with the intent to incite hatred, discrimination or violence against any individual or group of individuals, based on race, colour, descent or national or ethnic origin, as well as religion if used as a pretext for any of these factors, or otherwise
   (b) reserve the right not to apply, in whole or in part, paragraph 1 of this article.

Article 7 – Aiding and abetting

Each Party shall adopt such legislative and other measures as may be necessary to establish as criminal offences under its domestic law, when committed intentionally and without right, aiding or abetting the commission of any of the offences established in accordance with this Protocol, with intent that such offence be committed.

CHAPTER III – RELATIONS BETWEEN THE CONVENTION AND THIS PROTOCOL

Article 8 – Relations between the Convention and this Protocol

1. Articles 1, 12, 13, 22, 41, 44, 45 and 46 of the Convention shall apply, *mutatis mutandis*, to this Protocol.

2. The Parties shall extend the scope of application of the measures defined in Articles 14 to 21 and Articles 23 to 35 of the Convention, to Articles 2 to 7 of this Protocol.

CHAPTER IV – FINAL PROVISIONS

Article 9 – Expression of consent to be bound

1. This Protocol shall be open for signature by the States which have signed the Convention, which may express their consent to be bound by either:

    (a) signature without reservation as to ratification, acceptance or approval; or
    (b) subject to ratification, acceptance or approval, followed by ratification, acceptance or approval.

2. A State may not sign this Protocol without reservation as to ratification, acceptance or approval, or deposit an instrument of ratification, acceptance or approval, unless it has already deposited or simultaneously deposits an instrument of ratification, acceptance or approval of the Convention.

3. The instruments of ratification, acceptance or approval shall be deposited with the Secretary General of the Council of Europe.

Article 10 – Entry into force

1. This Protocol shall enter into force on the first day of the month following the expiration of a period of three months after the date on which five States have expressed their consent to be bound by the Protocol, in accordance with the provisions of Article 9.

2. In respect of any State which subsequently expresses its consent to be bound by it, the Protocol shall enter into force on the first day of the month following the expiration of a period of three months after the date of its signature without reservation as to ratification, acceptance or approval or deposit of its instrument of ratification, acceptance or approval.

Article 11 – Accession

1. After the entry into force of this Protocol, any State which has acceded to the Convention may also accede to the Protocol.

2. Accession shall be effected by the deposit with the Secretary General of the Council of Europe of an instrument of accession which shall take effect on the first day of the month following the expiration of a period of three months after the date of its deposit.

Article 12 – Reservations and declarations

1. Reservations and declarations made by a Party to a provision of the Convention shall be applicable also to this Protocol, unless that Party declares otherwise at the time of signature or when depositing its instrument of ratification, acceptance, approval or accession.

2. By a written notification addressed to the Secretary General of the Council of Europe, any Party may, at the time of signature or when depositing its instrument of ratification, acceptance, approval or accession, declare that it avails itself of the reservation(s) provided for in Articles 3, 5 and 6 of this Protocol. At the same time, a Party may avail itself, with respect to the provisions of this Protocol, of the reservation(s) provided for in Article 22, paragraph 2, and Article 41, paragraph 1, of the

Convention, irrespective of the implementation made by that Party under the Convention. No other reservations may be made.

3. By a written notification addressed to the Secretary General of the Council of Europe, any State may, at the time of signature or when depositing its instrument of ratification, acceptance, approval or accession, declare that it avails itself of the possibility of requiring additional elements as provided for in Article 5, paragraph 2.a, and Article 6, paragraph 2.a, of this Protocol.

Article 13 – Status and withdrawal of reservations

1. A Party that has made a reservation in accordance with Article 12 above shall withdraw such reservation, in whole or in part, as soon as circumstances so permit. Such withdrawal shall take effect on the date of receipt of a notification addressed to the Secretary General of the Council of Europe. If the notification states that the withdrawal of a reservation is to take effect on a date specified therein, and such date is later than the date on which the notification is received by the Secretary General, the withdrawal shall take effect on such a later date.

2. The Secretary General of the Council of Europe may periodically enquire with Parties that have made one or more reservations in accordance with Article 12 as to the prospects for withdrawing such reservation(s).

Article 14 – Territorial application

1. Any Party may at the time of signature or when depositing its instrument of ratification, acceptance, approval or accession, specify the territory or territories to which this Protocol shall apply.

2. Any Party may, at any later date, by a declaration addressed to the Secretary General of the Council of Europe, extend the application of this Protocol to any other territory specified in the declaration. In respect of such territory, the Protocol shall enter into force on the first day of the month following the expiration of a period of three months after the date of receipt of the declaration by the Secretary General.

3. Any declaration made under the two preceding paragraphs may, in respect of any territory specified in such declaration, be withdrawn by a notification addressed to the Secretary General of the Council of Europe. The withdrawal shall become effective on the first day of the month following the expiration of a period of three months after the date of receipt of such notification by the Secretary General.

Article 15 – Denunciation

1. Any Party may, at any time, denounce this Protocol by means of a notification addressed to the Secretary General of the Council of Europe.

2. Such denunciation shall become effective on the first day of the month following the expiration of a period of three months after the date of receipt of the notification by the Secretary General.

Article 16 – Notification

The Secretary General of the Council of Europe shall notify the Member States of the Council of Europe, the non-member States which have participated in the elaboration of this Protocol as well as any State which has acceded to, or has been invited to accede to, this Protocol of:
(a) any signature;
(b) the deposit of any instrument of ratification, acceptance, approval or accession;
(c) any date of entry into force of this Protocol in accordance with its Articles 9, 10 and 11;
(d) any other act, notification or communication relating to this Protocol.

In witness whereof the undersigned, being duly authorised thereto, have signed this Protocol.

Done at Strasbourg, this 28th day of January 2003, in English and in French, both texts being equally authentic, in a single copy which shall be deposited in the archives of the Council of Europe. The Secretary General of the Council of Europe shall transmit certified copies to each member State of the Council of Europe, to the non-member States which have participated in the elaboration of this Protocol, and to any State invited to accede to it.

APPENDIX 3

Directive 2013/40/EU of the European Parliament and of the Council of 12 August 2013 on Attacks Against Information Systems and Replacing Council Framework Decision 2005/222/JHA

THE EUROPEAN PARLIAMENT AND THE COUNCIL OF THE EUROPEAN UNION,[1]

Having regard to the Treaty on the Functioning of the European Union, and in particular Article 83(1) thereof,

Having regard to the proposal from the European Commission,

After transmission of the draft legislative act to the national parliaments,

Having regard to the opinion of the European Economic and Social Committee,[2]

Acting in accordance with the ordinary legislative procedure,[3]

Whereas:

(1) The objectives of this Directive are to approximate the criminal law of the Member States in the area of attacks against information systems by establishing minimum rules concerning the definition of criminal offences and the relevant sanctions and to improve cooperation between competent authorities, including the police and other specialised law enforcement services of the Member States, as well as the competent specialised Union agencies and bodies, such as Eurojust, Europol and its European Cyber Crime Centre, and the European Network and Information Security Agency (ENISA).

(2) Information systems are a key element of political, social and economic interaction in the Union. Society is highly and increasingly dependent on such systems. The smooth operation and security of those systems in the Union is vital for the development of the internal market and of a competitive and innovative economy. Ensuring an appropriate level of protection of information systems should form part of an effective comprehensive framework of prevention measures accompanying criminal law responses to cybercrime.

(3) Attacks against information systems, and, in particular, attacks linked to organised crime, are a growing menace in the Union and globally, and there is increasing concern about the potential for terrorist or political ly motivated attacks against information systems which form part of the critical infrastructure of Member States and of the Union. This constitutes a threat to the achievement of a safer information society and of an area of freedom, security, and justice, and therefore requires a response at Union level and improved cooperation and coordination at international level.

(4) There are a number of critical infrastructures in the Union, the disruption or destruction of which would have a significant cross-border impact. It has become apparent from the need to increase the critical infrastructure protection capability in the Union that the measures against cyber attacks should be complemented by stringent criminal penalties reflecting the gravity of such attacks. Critical infrastructure could be understood to be an asset, system or part thereof located in Member States, which is essential for the maintenance of vital societal functions, health, safety, security, economic or social well-being of people, such as power plants, transport networks or government networks, and the disruption or destruction of which would have a significant impact in a Member State as a result of the failure to maintain those functions.

---

[1] http://eur-lex.europa.eu, © European Union, 1998–2015
[2] OJ C 218, 23.7.2011, p. 130
[3] Position of the European Parliament of 4 July 2013 (not yet published in the Official Journal) and decision of the Council of 22 July 2013.

(5) There is evidence of a tendency towards increasingly dangerous and recurrent large-scale attacks conducted against information systems which can often be critical to Member States or to particular functions in the public or private sector. This tendency is accompanied by the development of increasingly sophisticated methods, such as the creation and use of so-called 'botnets', which involves several stages of a criminal act, where each stage alone could pose a serious risk to public interests. This Directive aims, inter alia, to introduce criminal penalties for the creation of botnets, namely, the act of establishing remote control over a significant number of computers by infecting them with malicious software through targeted cyber attacks. Once created, the infected network of computers that constitute the botnet can be activated without the computer users' knowledge in order to launch a large-scale cyber attack, which usually has the capacity to cause serious damage, as referred to in this Directive. Member States may determine what constitutes serious damage according to their national law and practice, such as disrupting system services of significant public importance, or causing major financial cost or loss of personal data or sensitive information.

(6) Large-scale cyber attacks can cause substantial economic damage both through the interruption of information systems and communication and through the loss or alteration of commercially important confidential information or other data. Particular attention should be paid to raising the awareness of innovative small and medium-sized enterprises to threats relating to such attacks and their vulnerability to such attacks, due to their increased dependence on the proper functioning and availability of information systems and often limited resources for information security.

(7) Common definitions in this area are important in order to ensure a consistent approach in the Member States to the application of this Directive.

(8) There is a need to achieve a common approach to the constituent elements of criminal offences by introducing common offences of illegal access to an information system, illegal system interference, illegal data interference, and illegal interception.

(9) Interception includes, but is not necessarily limited to, the listening to, monitoring or surveillance of the content of communications and the procuring of the content of data either directly, through access and use of the information systems, or indirectly through the use of electronic eavesdropping or tapping devices by technical means.

(10) Member States should provide for penalties in respect of attacks against information systems. Those penalties should be effective, proportionate and dissuasive and should include imprisonment and/or fines.

(11) This Directive provides for criminal penalties at least for cases which are not minor. Member States may determine what constitutes a minor case according to their national law and practice. A case may be considered minor, for example, where the damage caused by the offence and/or the risk to public or private interests, such as to the integrity of a computer system or to computer data, or to the integrity, rights or other interests of a person, is insignificant or is of such a nature that the imposition of a criminal penalty within the legal threshold or the imposition of criminal liability is not necessary.

(12) The identification and reporting of threats and risks posed by cyber attacks and the related vulnerability of information systems is a pertinent element of effective prevention of, and response to, cyber attacks and to improving the security of information systems. Providing incentives to report security gaps could add to that effect. Member States should endeavour to provide possibilities for the legal detection and reporting of security gaps.

(13) It is appropriate to provide for more severe penalties where an attack against an information system is committed by a criminal organisation, as defined in Council Framework Decision 2008/841/JHA of 24 October 2008 on the fight against organised crime,[4] where a cyber attack is conducted on a large scale, thus affecting a significant number of information systems, including where it is intended to create a botnet, or where a cyber attack causes serious damage, including where it is carried out through a botnet. It is also appropriate to provide for more severe penalties where an attack is conducted against a critical infrastructure of the Member States or of the Union.

(14) Setting up effective measures against identity theft and other identity-related offences constitutes another important element of an integrated approach against cybercrime. Any need for Union action against this type of criminal behaviour could also be considered in the context of evaluating the need for a comprehensive horizontal Union instrument.

---

[4] OJ L 300, 11.11.2008, p. 42

(15) The Council Conclusions of 27 to 28 November 2008 indicated that a new strategy should be developed with the Member States and the Commission, taking into account the content of the 2001 Council of Europe Convention on Cybercrime. That Convention is the legal framework of reference for combating cybercrime, including attacks against information systems. This Directive builds on that Convention. Completing the process of ratification of that Convention by all Member States as soon as possible should be considered to be a priority.

(16) Given the different ways in which attacks can be conducted, and given the rapid developments in hardware and software, this Directive refers to tools that can be used in order to commit the offences laid down in this Directive. Such tools could include malicious software, including those able to create botnets, used to commit cyber attacks. Even where such a tool is suitable or particularly suitable for carrying out one of the offences laid down in this Directive, it is possible that it was produced for a legitimate purpose Motivated by the need to avoid criminalisation where such tools are produced and put on the market for legitimate purposes, such as to test the reliability of information technology products or the security of information systems, apart from the general intent requirement, a direct intent requirement that those tools be used to commit one or more of the offences laid down in this Directive must be also fulfilled.

(17) This Directive does not impose criminal liability where the objective criteria of the offences laid down in this Directive are met but the acts are committed without criminal intent, for instance where a person does not know that access was unauthorised or in the case of mandated testing or protection of information systems, such as where a person is assigned by a company or vendor to test the strength of its security system. In the context of this Directive, contractual obligations or agreements to restrict access to information systems by way of a user policy or terms of service, as well as labour disputes as regards the access to and use of information systems of an employer for private purposes, should not incur criminal liability where the access under such circumstances would be deemed unauthorised and thus would constitute the sole basis for criminal proceedings.
This Directive is without prejudice to the right of access to information as laid down in national and Union law, while at the same time it may not serve as a justification for unlawful or arbitrary access to information.

(18) Cyber attacks could be facilitated by various circumstances, such as where the offender has access to security systems inherent in the affected information systems within the scope of his or her employment. In the context of national law, such circumstances should be taken into account in the course of criminal proceedings as appropriate.

(19) Member States should provide for aggravating circumstances in their national law in accordance with the applicable rules established by their legal systems on aggravating circumstances. They should ensure that those aggravating circumstances are available for judges to consider when sentencing offenders. It remains within the discretion of the judge to assess those circumstances together with the other facts of the particular case.

(20) This Directive does not govern conditions for exercising jurisdiction over any of the offences referred to herein, such as a report by the victim in the place where the offence was committed, a denunciation from the State of the place where the offence was committed, or the non-prosecution of the offender in the place where the offence was committed.

(21) In the context of this Directive, States and public bodies remain fully bound to guarantee respect for human rights and fundamental freedoms, in accordance with existing international obligations.

(22) This Directive strengthens the importance of networks, such as the G8 or the Council of Europe's network of points of contact available on a 24 hour, seven-day-a- week basis. Those points of contact should be able to deliver effective assistance thus, for example, facilitating the exchange of relevant information available and the provision of technical advice or legal information for the purpose of investigations or proceedings concerning criminal offences relating to information systems and associated data involving the requesting Member State. In order to ensure the smooth operation of the networks, each contact point should have the capacity to communicate with the point of contact of another Member State on an expedited basis with the support, inter alia, of trained and equipped personnel. Given the speed with which large-scale cyber attacks can be carried out, Member States should be able to respond promptly to urgent requests from this network of contact points. In such cases, it may be expedient that the request for information be accompanied by telephone contact in order to ensure that the request is processed swiftly by the requested Member State and that feedback is provided within eight hours.

(23) Cooperation between public authorities on the one hand, and the private sector and civil society on the other, is of great importance in preventing and combating attacks against information systems. It is necessary to foster and improve cooperation between service providers, producers, law enforcement bodies and judicial authorities, while fully respecting the rule of law. Such cooperation could include support by service providers in helping to preserve potential evidence, in providing elements helping to identify offenders and, as a last resort, in shutting down, completely or partially, in accordance with national law and practice, information systems or functions that have been compromised or used for illegal purposes. Member States should also consider setting up cooperation and partnership networks with service providers and producers for the exchange of information in relation to the offences within the scope of this Directive.

(24) There is a need to collect comparable data on the offences laid down in this Directive. Relevant data should be made available to the competent specialised Union agencies and bodies, such as Europol and ENISA, in line with their tasks and information needs, in order to gain a more complete picture of the problem of cybercrime and network and information security at Union level and thereby to contribute to formulating a more effective response. Member States should submit information on the modus operandi of the offenders to Europol and its European Cybercrime Centre for the purpose of conducting threat assessments and strategic analyses of cybercrime in accordance with Council Decision 2009/371/JHA of 6 April 2009 establishing the European Police Office (Europol).[5] Providing information can facilitate a better understanding of present and future threats and thus contribute to more appropriate and targeted decision-making on combating and preventing attacks against information systems.

(25) The Commission should submit a report on the application of this Directive and make necessary legislative proposals which could lead to broadening its scope, taking into account developments in the field of cybercrime. Such developments could include technological developments, for example those enabling more effective enforcement in the area of attacks against information systems or facilitating prevention or minimising the impact of such attacks. For that purpose, the Commission should take into account the available analyses and reports produced by relevant actors and, in particular, Europol and ENISA.

(26) In order to fight cybercrime effectively, it is necessary to increase the resilience of information systems by taking appropriate measures to protect them more effectively against cyber attacks. Member States should take the necessary measures to protect their critical infrastructure from cyber attacks, as part of which they should consider the protection of their information systems and associated data. Ensuring an adequate level of protection and security of information systems by legal persons, for example in connection with the provision of publicly available electronic communications services in accordance with existing Union legislation on privacy and electronic communication and data protection, forms an essential part of a comprehensive approach to effectively counteracting cybercrime. Appropriate levels of protection should be provided against reasonably identifiable threats and vulnerabilities in accordance with the state of the art for specific sectors and the specific data processing situations. The cost and burden of such protection should be proportionate to the likely damage a cyber attack would cause to those affected. Member States are encouraged to provide for relevant measures incurring liabilities in the context of their national law in cases where a legal person has clearly not provided an appropriate level of protection against cyber attacks.

(27) Significant gaps and differences in Member States' laws and criminal procedures in the area of attacks against information systems may hamper the fight against organised crime and terrorism, and may complicate effective police and judicial cooperation in this area. The transnational and borderless nature of modern information systems means that attacks against such systems have a cross-border dimension, thus underlining the urgent need for further action to approximate criminal law in this area. In addition, the coordination of prosecution of cases of attacks against information systems should be facilitated by the adequate implementation and application of Council Framework Decision 2009/948/JHA of 30 November 2009 on prevention and settlement of conflict of jurisdiction in criminal proceedings.[6] Member States, in cooperation with the Union, should also seek to improve international cooperation relating to the security of

---

[5] OJ L 121, 15.5.2009, p. 37
[6] OJ L 328, 15.12.2009, p. 42

information systems, computer networks and computer data. Proper consideration of the security of data transfer and storage should be given in any international agreement involving data exchange.

(28) Improved cooperation between the competent law enforcement bodies and judicial authorities across the Union is essential in an effective fight against cybercrime. In this context, stepping up the efforts to provide adequate training to the relevant authorities in order to raise the understanding of cybercrime and its impact, and to foster cooperation and the exchange of best practices, for example via the competent specialised Union agencies and bodies, should be encouraged. Such training should, inter alia, aim at raising awareness about the different national legal systems, the possible legal and technical challenges of criminal investigations, and the distribution of competences between the relevant national authorities.

(29) This Directive respects human rights and fundamental freedoms and observes the principles recognised in particular by the Charter of Fundamental Rights of the European Union and the European Convention for the Protection of Human Rights and Fundamental Freedoms, including the protection of personal data, the right to privacy, freedom of expression and information, the right to a fair trial, the presumption of innocence and the rights of the defence, as well as the principles of legality and proportionality of criminal offences and penalties. In particular, this Directive seeks to ensure full respect for those rights and principles and must be implemented accordingly.

(30) The protection of personal data is a fundamental right in accordance with Article 16(1) TFEU and Article 8 of the Charter on Fundamental Rights of the European Union. Therefore, any processing of personal data in the context of the implementation of this Directive should fully comply with the relevant Union law on data protection.

(31) In accordance with Article 3 of the Protocol on the position of the United Kingdom and Ireland in respect of the Area of Freedom, Security and Justice, annexed to the Treaty on European Union and to the Treaty on the Functioning of the European Union, those Member States have notified their wish to take part in the adoption and application of this Directive.

(32) In accordance with Articles 1 and 2 of the Protocol on the position of Denmark annexed to the Treaty on European Union and to the Treaty on the Functioning of the European Union, Denmark is not taking part in the adoption of this Directive and is not bound by it or subject to its application.

(33) Since the objectives of this Directive, namely to subject attacks against information systems in all Member States to effective, proportionate and dissuasive criminal penalties and to improve and encourage cooperation between judicial and other competent authorities, cannot be sufficiently achieved by the Member States, and can therefore, by reason of their scale or effects, be better achieved at Union level, the Union may adopt measures in accordance with the principle of subsidiarity as set out in Article 5 of the Treaty on European Union. In accordance with the principle of proportionality, as set out in that Article, this Directive does not go beyond what is necessary in order to achieve those objectives.

(34) This Directive aims to amend and expand the provisions of Council Framework Decision 2005/222/JHA of 24 February 2005 on attacks against information systems.[7] Since the amendments to be made are of substantial number and nature, Framework Decision 2005/222/JHA should, in the interests of clarity, be replaced in its entirety in relation to Member States participating in the adoption of this Directive,

HAVE ADOPTED THIS DIRECTIVE:

Article 1

Subject Matter

This Directive establishes minimum rules concerning the definition of criminal offences and sanctions in the area of attacks against information systems. It also aims to facilitate the prevention of such offences and to improve cooperation between judicial and other competent authorities.

---

[7] OJ L 69, 16.3.2005, p. 67

Article 2
Definitions

For the purposes of this Directive, the following definitions shall apply:

(a) 'information system' means a device or group of inter- connected or related devices, one or more of which, pursuant to a programme, automatically processes computer data, as well as computer data stored, processed, retrieved or transmitted by that device or group of devices for the purposes of its or their operation, use, protection and maintenance;

(b) 'computer data' means a representation of facts, information or concepts in a form suitable for processing in an information system, including a programme suitable for causing an information system to perform a function;

(c) 'legal person' means an entity having the status of legal person under the applicable law, but does not include States or public bodies acting in the exercise of State authority, or public international organisations;

(d) 'without right' means conduct referred to in this Directive, including access, interference, or interception, which is not authorised by the owner or by another right holder of the system or of part of it, or not permitted under national law.

Article 3
Illegal access to information systems

Member States shall take the necessary measures to ensure that, when committed intentionally, the access without right, to the whole or to any part of an information system, is punishable as a criminal offence where committed by infringing a security measure, at least for cases which are not minor.

Article 4
Illegal system interference

Member States shall take the necessary measures to ensure that seriously hindering or interrupting the functioning of an information system by inputting computer data, by transmitting, damaging, deleting, deteriorating, altering or suppressing such data, or by rendering such data inaccessible, intentionally and without right, is punishable as a criminal offence, at least for cases which are not minor.

Article 5
Illegal data interference

Member States shall take the necessary measures to ensure that deleting, damaging, deteriorating, altering or suppressing computer data on an information system, or rendering such data inaccessible, intentionally and without right, is punishable as a criminal offence, at least for cases which are not minor.

Article 6
Illegal interception

Member States shall take the necessary measures to ensure that intercepting, by technical means, non-public transmissions of computer data to, from or within an information system, including electromagnetic emissions from an information system carrying such computer data, intentionally and without right, is punishable as a criminal offence, at least for cases which are not minor.

Article 7
Tools used for committing offences

Member States shall take the necessary measures to ensure that the intentional production, sale, procurement for use, import, distribution or otherwise making available, of one of the following tools, without right and with the intention that it be used to commit any of the offences referred to in Articles 3 to 6, is punishable as a criminal offence, at least for cases which are not minor:

(a) a computer programme, designed or adapted primarily for the purpose of committing any of the offences referred to in Articles 3 to 6;

(b) a computer password, access code, or similar data by which the whole or any part of an information system is capable of being accessed.

Article 8

Incitement, aiding and abetting and attempt

1. Member States shall ensure that the incitement, or aiding and abetting, to commit an offence referred to in Articles 3 to 7 is punishable as a criminal offence.
2. Member States shall ensure that the attempt to commit an offence referred to in Articles 4 and 5 is punishable as a criminal offence.

Article 9

Penalties

1. Member States shall take the necessary measures to ensure that the offences referred to in Articles 3 to 8 are punishable by effective, proportionate and dissuasive criminal penalties.
2. Member States shall take the necessary measures to ensure that the offences referred to in Articles 3 to 7 are punishable by a maximum term of imprisonment of at least two years, at least for cases which are not minor.
3. Member States shall take the necessary measures to ensure that the offences referred to in Articles 4 and 5, when committed intentionally, are punishable by a maximum term of imprisonment of at least three years where a significant number of information systems have been affected through the use of a tool, referred to in Article 7, designed or adapted primarily for that purpose.
4. Member States shall take the necessary measures to ensure that offences referred to in Articles 4 and 5 are punishable by a maximum term of imprisonment of at least five years where:
   (a) they are committed within the framework of a criminal organisation, as defined in Framework Decision 2008/841/JHA, irrespective of the penalty provided for therein;
   (b) they cause serious damage; or
   (c) they are committed against a critical infrastructure information system.
5. Member States shall take the necessary measures to ensure that when the offences referred to in Articles 4 and 5 are committed by misusing the personal data of another person, with the aim of gaining the trust of a third party, thereby causing prejudice to the rightful identity owner, this may, in accordance with national law, be regarded as aggravating circumstances, unless those circumstances are already covered by another offence, punishable under national law.

Article 10

Liability of legal persons

1. Member States shall take the necessary measures to ensure that legal persons can be held liable for offences referred to in Articles 3 to 8, committed for their benefit by any person, acting either individually or as part of a body of the legal person, and having a leading position within the legal person, based on one of the following:
   (a) a power of representation of the legal person;
   (b) an authority to take decisions on behalf of the legal person;
   (c) an authority to exercise control within the legal person.
2. Member States shall take the necessary measures to ensure that legal persons can be held liable where the lack of supervision or control by a person referred to in paragraph 1 has allowed the commission, by a person under its authority, of any of the offences referred to in Articles 3 to 8 for the benefit of that legal person.
3. The liability of legal persons under paragraphs 1 and 2 shall not exclude criminal proceedings against natural persons who are perpetrators or inciters of, or accessories to, any of the offences referred to in Articles 3 to 8.

Article 11

Sanctions against legal persons

1. Member States shall take the necessary measures to ensure that a legal person held liable pursuant to Article 10(1) is punishable by effective, proportionate and dissuasive sanctions, which shall include criminal or non-criminal fines and which may include other sanctions, such as:
   (a) exclusion from entitlement to public benefits or aid;
   (b) temporary or permanent disqualification from the practice of commercial activities;
   (c) placing under judicial supervision;

455

(d) judicial winding-up;

(e) temporary or permanent closure of establishments which have been used for committing the offence.

2. Member States shall take the necessary measures to ensure that a legal person held liable pursuant to Article 10(2) is punishable by effective, proportionate and dissuasive sanctions or other measures.

Article 12
Jurisdiction

1. Member States shall establish their jurisdiction with regard to the offences referred to in Articles 3 to 8 where the offence has been committed:

   (a) in whole or in part within their territory; or

   (b) by one of their nationals, at least in cases where the act is an offence where it was committed.

2. When establishing jurisdiction in accordance with point (a) of paragraph 1, a Member State shall ensure that it has jurisdiction where:

   (a) the offender commits the offence when physically present on its territory, whether or not the offence is against an information system on its territory; or

   (b) the offence is against an information system on its territory, whether or not the offender commits the offence when physically present on its territory.

3. A Member State shall inform the Commission where it decides to establish jurisdiction over an offence referred to in Articles 3 to 8 committed outside its territory, including where:

   (a) the offender has his or her habitual residence in its territory;

   or

   (b) the offence is committed for the benefit of a legal person established in its territory.

Article 13
Exchange of information

1. For the purpose of exchanging information relating to the offences referred to in Articles 3 to 8, Member States shall ensure that they have an operational national point of contact and that they make use of the existing network of operational points of contact available 24 hours a day and seven days a week. Member States shall also ensure that they have procedures in place so that for urgent requests for assistance, the competent authority can indicate, within eight hours of receipt, at least whether the request will be answered, and the form and estimated time of such an answer.

2. Member States shall inform the Commission of their appointed point of contact referred to in paragraph 1. The Commission shall forward that information to the other Member States and competent specialised Union agencies and bodies.

3. Member States shall take the necessary measures to ensure that appropriate reporting channels are made available in order to facilitate the reporting of the offences referred to in Article 3 to 6 to the competent national authorities without undue delay.

Article 14
Monitoring and statistics

1. Member States shall ensure that a system is in place for the recording, production and provision of statistical data on the offences referred to in Articles 3 to 7.

2. The statistical data referred to in paragraph 1 shall, as a minimum, cover existing data on the number of offences referred to in Articles 3 to 7 registered by the Member States, and the number of persons prosecuted for and convicted of the offences referred to in Articles 3 to 7.

3. Member States shall transmit the data collected pursuant to this Article to the Commission. The Commission shall ensure that a consolidated review of the statistical reports is published and submitted to the competent specialised Union agencies and bodies.

Article 15

Replacement of Framework Decision 2005/222/JHA

Framework Decision 2005/222/JHA is hereby replaced in relation to Member States participating in the adoption of this Directive, without prejudice to the obligations of the Member States relating to the time limit for transposition of the Framework Decision into national law.

In relation to Member States participating in the adoption of this Directive, references to the Framework Decision 2005/222/JHA shall be construed as references to this Directive.

Article 16

Transposition

1. Member States shall bring into force the laws, regulations and administrative provisions necessary to comply with this Directive by 4 September 2015.
2. Member States shall transmit to the Commission the text of the measures transposing into their national law the obligations imposed on them under this Directive.
3. When Member States adopt those measures, they shall contain a reference to this Directive or shall be accompanied by such a reference on the occasion of their official publication. The methods of making such a reference shall be laid down by the Member States.

Article 17

Reporting

The Commission shall, by 4 September 2017, submit a report to the European Parliament and the Council, assessing the extent to which the Member States have taken the necessary measures in order to comply with this Directive, accompanied, if necessary, by legislative proposals. The Commission shall also take into account the technical and legal developments in the field of cybercrime, particularly with regard to the scope of this Directive.

Article 18

Entry into force

This Directive shall enter into force on the twentieth day following that of its publication in the Official Journal of the European Union.

Article 19

Addressees

This Directive is addressed to the Member States in accordance with the Treaties.

Done at Brussels, 12 August 2013.

For the European Parliament	*For the Council*
The President	*The President*
M. SCHULZ	L. LINKEVIČIUS

APPENDIX 4

Association of Chief Police Officers Good Practice Guide
for Digital Evidence

INTRODUCTION TO THE GUIDE FOR DIGITAL EVIDENCE

It gives me great pleasure to introduce the 5th version of the ACPO Good Practice Guide for Digital Evidence. Much effort has been put in to ensure that the right information is available to practitioners and managers in the fight against cyber crime. I would like to thank all those who contributed to its creation for their efforts in drawing together their expert knowledge in tackling the criminal misuse of current and emerging technologies. The review board drew together people from academia, private and the public sector and has been an excellent example of collaborative working.

Since taking the UK policing lead for e-Crime in April 2008, I have overseen the creation of the Police Central e-Crime Unit. The team has grown from strength to strength through partnership working leading to the formation of a centre of excellence for cyber crime and the successful prosecution of cyber criminals. It is only through bringing together the expertise in policing across the UK, the capability and best practice within industry, support of Government and the Criminal Justice System that we will combat those responsible for cyber crime.

I am pleased that there has been recognition of a need to co-ordinate the UK response to cyber security issues through the establishment of the Office of Cyber Security and the Cyber Security Operations Centre. This approach will combine the various industries, law enforcement and agencies' hard work to corral them into a single effort to gather intelligence, enforcement capability and create the right framework of policy and doctrine to better enable us all to tackle the major issues identified.

This guide has changed from version 4, where it centred on computer based evidence; the new revision reflects digital based evidence and attempts to encompass the diversity of the digital world. As such this guide would not only assist law enforcement but the wider family that assists in investigating cyber security incidents. I commend all to read and make use of the knowledge and learning contained in this guide to provide us with the right tools to carry out our role.

Janet Williams QPM

Deputy Assistant Commissioner

Metropolitan Police Service

ACPO lead for the e-Crime Portfolio

FOREWORD

It seems that whenever a review of ACPO guidance is carried out we are in the middle of technological changes that have vast impact on the work that is done within digital forensic units. It is a testament to the authors of the original four guiding principles for digital forensics that they still hold today, and one of the key early decisions of the review board was to keep those four principles, with only a slight change of wording to principle four.

We work in an area of constant change. There is a continuing need to re-evaluate and revise our capacities to perform our duties. There is a need to recover and analyse digital data that can now be found within the many devices that are within day to day use, and can supply vital evidence in all our investigations.

Hence a second key early decision was to change the title of the document to ACPO Good Practice Guide for Digital Evidence. This would hopefully encompass all aspects of digital evidence and remove the difficulty about trying to draw the line to what is or isn't a computer and thus falling within the remit of this guide.

459

It is important that people who work within the arena of digital forensics do not just concentrate on the technology, as essential as that is, but that the processes we use are fit for the purpose, and that skills and capacities within units reflect the demands that are made on them. A prime example of this is the use of the word 'triage'. It has been a subject of much discussion within the forensic community. It should be noted that it does not mean a single triage tool rather it is a complete process where certain tools will play a part but are not the whole solution.

This guide is not intended to be an A–Z of digital forensics, or a specific "how to do" instruction manual. It should paint an overall picture and provides an underlying structure to what is required within Digital Forensic Units (DFUs). Therefore, the guide has been produced as a high-level document without the specific guidance included in previous versions, as this guidance is now available elsewhere. Where relevant, links to other guidance documents will be given.

In this document Digital Forensic Unit is used to cover any type of group that is actively involved in the processing of digital evidence.

1. SECTION 1—APPLICATION OF GUIDE

1.1 When reading and applying the principles of this guide, any reference made to the police service also includes the Scottish Crime and Drugs Enforcement Agency (SCDEA) and the Police Service for Northern Ireland (PSNI) unless otherwise indicated.

1.2 This guide is primarily written for the guidance of UK law enforcement personnel who may deal with digital evidence. This will include:
- Persons who are involved in the securing, seizing and transporting of equipment from search scenes with a view to recovering digital evidence, as well as in the identification of the digital information needed to investigate crime;
- Investigators who plan and manage the identification, presentation and storage of digital evidence, and the use of that evidence;
- Persons who recover and reproduce seized digital evidence and are trained to carry out the function and have relevant training to give evidence in court of their actions. **Persons who have not received appropriate training and are unable to comply with the principles should not carry out this category of activity;**
- Persons who are involved in the selection and management of persons who may be required to assist in the recovery, identification and interpretation of digital evidence.

1.3 Since the previous version of the guide was published, the Forensic Science Regulator has published new draft Codes of Conduct and Practice covering forensic science throughout the UK. All practitioners working in the field of digital forensics must abide by these codes.

2. SECTION 2—THE PRINCIPLES OF DIGITAL EVIDENCE

2.1 Principles

2.1.1 **Principle 1:** No action taken by law enforcement agencies, persons employed within those agencies or their agents should change data which may subsequently be relied upon in court.

2.1.2 **Principle 2:** In circumstances where a person finds it necessary to access original data, that person must be competent to do so and be able to give evidence explaining the relevance and the implications of their actions.

2.1.3 **Principle 3:** An audit trail or other record of all processes applied to digital evidence should be created and preserved. An independent third party should be able to examine those processes and achieve the same result.

2.1.4 **Principle 4:** The person in charge of the investigation has overall responsibility for ensuring that the law and these principles are adhered to.

2.2 Explanation of the Principles

2.2.1 All digital evidence is subject to the same rules and laws that apply to documentary evidence.

2.2.2 The doctrine of documentary evidence may be explained thus: the onus is on the prosecution to show to the court that the evidence produced is no more and no less now than when it was first taken into the possession of law enforcement.

2.2.3 Operating systems and other programs frequently alter, add and delete the contents of electronic storage. This may happen automatically without the user necessarily being aware that the data has been changed.

2.2.4 In order to comply with the principles of digital evidence, wherever practicable, proportionate and relevant an image should be made of the device. This will ensure that the original data is preserved, enabling an independent third party to re-examine it and achieve the same result, as required by principle 3.

2.2.5 This may be a physical / logical block image of the entire device, or a logical file image containing partial or selective data (which may be captured as a result of a triage process). Investigators should use their professional judgement to endeavour to capture all relevant evidence if this approach is adopted.

2.2.6 In cases dealing with data which is not stored locally but is stored at a remote, possibly inaccessible location it may not be possible to obtain an image. It may become necessary for the original data to be directly accessed to recover the data. With this in mind, it is essential that a person who is competent to retrieve the data and then able to give evidence to a court of law makes any such access. Due consideration must also be given to applicable legislation if data is retrieved which resides in another jurisdiction.

2.2.7 It is essential to display objectivity in a court of law, as well as the continuity and integrity of evidence. It is also necessary to demonstrate how evidence has been recovered, showing each process through which the evidence was obtained. Evidence should be preserved to such an extent that a third party is able to repeat the same process and arrive at the same result as that presented to a court.

2.2.8 It should be noted that the application of the principles does not preclude a proportionate approach to the examination of digital evidence. Those making decisions about the conduct of a digital investigation must often make judgements about the focus and scope of an investigation, taking into account available intelligence and investigative resources. This will often include a risk assessment based on technical and non-technical factors, for example the potential evidence which may be held by a particular type of device or the previous offending history of the suspect. Where this is done it should be transparent, decisions should be justifiable and the rationale recorded.

2.2.9 Application of the four principles will also be informed by:

- The Forensic Science Regulator's forthcoming Codes of Practice and Conduct;
- The guidance around digital forensic process improvements developed by the National Policing Improvement Agency's Forensic 21 programme and those engaged in the collection, examination or reporting of digital evidence should also refer to that guidance.

3. Section 3—Plan

3.1 This also refers to the:

- The NPIA Forensic21 HTCU Computer Examination Process, 2011
- The SCDEA HTCU Guidance.

3.2 The proliferation of digital devices and the advances in digital communications mean that digital evidence is now present or potentially present in almost every crime.

3.3 Digital evidence can be found in a number of different locations:

- Locally on an end-user device—typically a user's computer, mobile/smart phone, satellite navigation system, USB thumb drive, or digital camera;
- On a remote resource that is public—for example websites used for social networking, discussion forums, and newsgroups;

- On a remote resource that is private—an internet Service Provider's logs of users' activity, a mobile phone company's records of customers' billing, a user's webmail account, and increasingly common, a user's remote file storage;
- In transit—for example mobile phone text messages, or voice calls, emails, or internet chat.

3.4 It would be quite common for evidence of a crime to be in more than one of the locations mentioned above. However it might be much easier to obtain the evidence from one location rather than another; careful consideration should be given to the resources required to obtain the evidence.

3.5 For example, if evidence is required of contact between two mobile phone numbers, the best method would be to obtain call data from the Communication Service Providers via the force SPOC, rather than to request a forensic examination of the mobile phones. The call data is likely to be more comprehensive than call logs from a mobile phone and the times and dates can be relied upon, which is not necessarily the case with logs from a mobile phone.

3.6 In addition, investigators seeking to capture 'in transit' evidence must be aware of the implications under the Regulation of Investigatory Powers Act (RIPA) and the need to seek appropriate authorities for doing so. Further information is available from force SPOCs.

3.7 With the above in mind, it is important that investigators develop appropriate strategies to identify the existence of digital evidence and to secure and interpret that evidence throughout their investigation.

3.8 Due consideration should always be given by the investigators of the benefits to the overall investigation of conducting any digital forensic work. Proportionality should be assessed when a digital forensic strategy is being considered to ensure that limited resources for digital forensic investigation are directed appropriately.

4. Section 4—Capture

4.1 This also refers to:

- Retrieval of Video Evidence and Production of Working Copies from Digital CCTV Systems v2.0;
- Network forensics and volatile data collection—Appendix A;
- Crimes involving websites, forums and blogs—Appendix B.

4.2 Physical Crime Scenes

4.2.1 There are many different types of digital media and end-user devices, which may be encountered during a search of a crime scene, all of which have the potential to hold data which may be of value to the investigation. In order to preserve the data and achieve best evidence, these items must be handled and seized appropriately, and should be treated with as much care as any other item that is to be forensically examined. This section is intended to assist individuals to ensure their actions in relation to seizure are correct.

4.3 Proportionality Issues Relating to Seizure

4.3.1 Proportionality issues relating to seizure are:

- Before seizing an item, consider whether the item is likely to hold evidence. For example, is this a family computer or a computer belonging to a suspect?
- Ensure that details of where the item was found are recorded, which could assist in prioritising items for examination at a later stage;
- Consider when the offence was committed; when seizing CCTV, give consideration to narrowing down what is seized, by camera and/or time period. Check whether another system may be better placed to record the evidence;
- Differentiate between mobile phones found on a suspect (likely to be in current use) and phones found in a drawer (may not be in current use), as different levels of examination may be possible for these;
- Also consider that evidence may be stored online, or on an internet service provider's systems, and end-user devices may only be needed to obtain the details necessary to request this

evidence from the service provider. If so, it is best to seize items in current usage, i.e. computers connected to the internet.

4.3.2 Digital devices and media should not be seized just because they are there. The person in charge of the search must have reasonable grounds to remove property and there must be justifiable reasons for doing so. The search provisions of PACE Legislation Codes of Practice equally apply to digital devices and media in England, Wales and Northern Ireland. In Scotland, officers should ensure they are acting within the terms of the search warrant.

4.3.3 Due regard should also be given to the application of the European Convention of Human Rights.

4.4 Before Attending a Scene to Capture Digital Evidence

4.4.1 Persons responsible for the seizure of digital devices, or for on-scene capture of data, should ensure:
- They have the necessary equipment. (Refer to the First Responder's Guide for a detailed breakdown);
- They have considered potential sources of evidence and know what is likely to be relevant, where possible.

4.4.3 Where an investigation is likely to involve the examination of user-created digital images, consideration should be given to the question of seizing of cameras and other devices capable of taking digital photographs. For example, in cases where a suspect is believed to have taken indecent photographs of children, seizure of devices capable of taking digital photos could be useful not only for the data they store, but also to link these devices to previously identified indecent photographs by the examination of digital metadata (EXIF data).

4.4.3 Where necessary, specialist advice from a force's Digital Forensic Unit should be sought in advance. If given sufficient information about the investigation, DFUs will be able to advise on which items are most likely to provide the evidence sought.

4.5 When Attending A Scene

4.5.1 To comply with principle 3, records must be kept of all actions taken in relation to digital evidence, which could include photographs/diagrams of equipment locations, details of any information provided by persons present, and records of any actions taken at the scene.

4.5.2 Refer to the First Responder's Guide for detailed guidance on seizure for individual items. However, persons attending a scene should be especially aware that **systems which are powered on (running) need to be handled with care**, as there is the potential to make unwanted changes to the evidence if these are not dealt with correctly. Such systems should only be accessed by appropriately trained personnel. In addition, volatile data of evidential value may be lost.

4.6 Capturing Online Evidence

4.6.1 In some investigations the capture of digital evidence may be from an online rather than a physical location. Detailed guidance on securing this evidence can be found in 'Crimes involving websites, forums and blogs' and 'Network forensics and volatile data'.

4.6.2 Online evidence can roughly be split into that which is publicly available (e.g. forum postings, where the forum does not require a login to view) and that which is private (e.g. Facebook account information). There may be scope to obtain both (e.g. by capturing the text of a forum posting and then requesting the account details of the user who made the posting from the forum owner). Investigators should be aware of the potential issues when capturing publicly available data, Including the 'footprints' which are left when accessing a site, which can alert a website owner to law enforcement interest.

4.6.3 Records should be kept of all actions taken when capturing online evidence in order to comply with principle 3.

5. Section 5—Analyse

5.1 This also refers to:
- The NPIA Forensics21 HTCU Computer Examination Process, 2011;
- Forensic Science Regulator's Codes of Practice and Conduct;
- Digital Imaging Procedure v2.1.

5.2 Devices seized as part of a search will typically be submitted to the force Digital Forensic Unit in accordance with force policy. Due to the volume and complexity of data stored on digital devices, it is not possible or desirable to extract all data held on a device for review by investigators. Instead, a forensic strategy needs to be formulated to enable the examination to be focused on the relevant data.

5.3 The National Policing Improvement Agency is currently formulating suggested processes for digital examinations involving computer and phone devices. Readers should refer to these processes for more specific detail of best practice digital examination processes. Other types of digital examinations should follow the same principles, briefly summarised below.

5.4 The investigator needs to properly consider the nature and purpose of the digital examination. The investigator must be clear on what priorities are placed on the examination as it may well be that key information needs to be found in order to preserve evidence that may exist elsewhere. This is particularly the case where it relates to the existence of additional evidence, offenders and victims.

5.5 When submitting evidence to Digital Forensic Units, investigators must supply specific requirements. It is not practically possible to examine every item of digital data and clear tasking is needed to ensure that the digital forensic practitioner has the best chance of finding any evidence which is relevant to the investigation.

5.6 For more complex or lengthy investigations, an initial triage/review of the digital evidence (whether or not this is done using a specific triage tool) will give investigators and practitioners a better understanding of the nature of the digital evidence held. The forensic strategy should be regularly reviewed to take account of any changes in the direction of the investigation, which may occur as a result of digital forensic examination (for example, finding emails identifying a co-conspirator) or investigations elsewhere (a witness identifying another person as being of interest to the investigation). For this reason it is vital that the investigator and the digital forensic practitioner communicate regularly regarding the progress of the investigation.

5.7 If initial examination results in a large amount of data to be reviewed, consideration must be given to who is best placed to review that data. Often this will be the investigator, due to their greater knowledge of the case. Dependent on the source, this data may include:
- Internet history records;
- E-mails;
- Instant Messaging Logs;
- Media files (images and videos);
- Text documents;
- Spreadsheets;
- CCTV;
- Text Messages.

5.8 Collaboration with the Digital Forensic Unit will ensure that the significance of any reviewed data is not misunderstood. For example, when reviewing keyword hits which exist in deleted files, the significance of a hit's location may need explanation from a digital forensic practitioner.

5.9 For mobile phone examinations, different levels of examination may be appropriate depending on the intelligence relating to the device and the requirements of the investigation. For example, a phone which has been found in a drawer may be examined only to retrieve the necessary information to request billing details and to establish whether it is owned by the suspect (level 1). A phone which is known to be in regular use by a suspect in a high profile investigation may be subject to a much more in-depth examination involving the retrieval of deleted data and potentially the physical removal and examination of memory chips (level 4). These examination levels are outlined in the NPIA mobile phone SOPs.

5.10 INTERPRETATION OF DIGITAL DATA

5.10.1 As with other forensic evidence, interpretation is often required to ensure the evidential weight of recovered digital evidence is clear. Practitioners who undertake the interpretation of digital data must be competent to do so and have had sufficient training to undertake the task assigned to them.

5.10.2 As an example, the presence of indecent images of children on a computer would not in itself be sufficient evidence of possession, as the possessor must be aware of the existence of the images. A digital forensic practitioner may interpret the presence of other digital evidence (such as a list of recently opened files, recent search terms, the name and location of folders/files containing the material, or whether or not the computer is password protected) to establish the likelihood of the user being aware of the existence of these images.

5.10.3 Establishing the provenance of digital evidence is another key task of the forensic practitioner, who must use their knowledge and skills to identify not just that the evidence exists but also how it came to be there. This is common to all forensic disciplines; for example, the presence of a defendant's fingerprint on a bottle at the crime scene may not have any bearing on whether the defendant committed the crime if the bottle may have been carried there by someone else. It is the responsibility of the practitioner to carry out analysis to identify provenance where necessary, to mitigate the risk of their findings being misinterpreted.

5.10.4 Often the role of the digital forensic practitioner will be to make investigators and prosecutors aware of the limitations of the digital evidence as well as its strengths.

5.10.5 It must also be borne in mind that the development of digital technology is dynamic and the practitioners may well face significant challenges to their knowledge. It is not possible to be an expert in all aspects of digital forensic examination, but a practitioner should be aware of the limits of their knowledge and where further research or additional specialist knowledge is required.

6. SECTION 6—PRESENT

6.1 This also refers to:
- NPIA Forensics21 process maps;
- CPS disclosure manual, annex K.

6.2 Communication of the results of a digital forensic examination may be through a number of means:
- Verbally to an investigator/officer throughout a case;
- By a statement or report on conclusion of the case;
- In court if witness evidence is required.

6.3 In all cases a digital forensic practitioner must be aware of their duty of impartiality and that they must communicate both the extent and the limitations of the digital forensic evidence. This is especially important as, due to the nature of digital forensic evidence, it is not always immediately understandable by the layman.

6.4 Verbal Feedback

6.4.1 This should be given regularly throughout the progress of an examination. In this way it will enable the investigator to pursue relevant lines of enquiry as these become evident, and will ensure that the practitioner is up-to-date with any information required to better target their investigation.

6.4.2 It is important that this communication be recorded for potential disclosure at a later date. Good practice would be for a verbal conversation to be followed up via email, or to be recorded in contemporaneous notes.

6.5 Statements or Reports

6.5.1 The statement or report is the ultimate product of the examination. It should outline the examination process and the significant data recovered. Whilst an initial report may be relatively brief, the practitioner should be in a position to produce a full technical report should one later be required.

6.5.2 The report should be written to be understandable to the reader; this may include the use of a glossary, diagrams/screenshots to illustrate points, the use of examples and avoidance of technical jargon.

6.5.3 When particular items are reproduced in a report, care should be taken to ensure that the representation is accurate. For example, pictures should not be reproduced at a larger size without this being made clear in the report. If a report is produced digitally, items should be reproduced where possible in their original file formats, to ensure that those viewing will see the item as close as possible to its original appearance. If this is not appropriate (for example, if a file needs to be converted to a more common format for reviewing) then the fact that it has been converted must be stated in the report. Where it is not possible to reproduce the item as it would have originally been viewed, for example, when a webpage is retrieved some time after the original page was accessed, this must also be clearly stated in the report.

6.5.4 The report should make clear the strength of any conclusions reached and always identify where an opinion is being given, to distinguish this from fact. Where opinion evidence is provided, the practitioner must state the facts on which this is based, and how he or she came to this conclusion.

6.6 Witness Evidence

6.6.1 A practitioner may need to testify about not only the conduct of the examination, but also the validity of the procedure and their experience and qualifications to conduct the examination.

6.6.2 Expert witness training should be considered for digital forensic practitioners so they are familiar with the process of giving evidence and aware of their responsibilities as witnesses. A digital forensic practitioner will not always be giving expert evidence and should clearly understand the distinction between expert evidence and evidence of fact.

6.6.3 When giving evidence, practitioners must make clear when they are expressing facts and when they are giving opinions, as above. Practitioners, when giving expert evidence, must take care to do so only where it relates to their own area of expertise and remember that their duty when giving evidence (whether it be in report form or as a witness) is to the court, regardless of which party has instructed them.

6.7 Contemporaneous Notes

6.7.1 It is worth repeating at this point that full records should be made of all actions taken. These must be disclosed to the defence who may subsequently cause a further examination to be conducted. A significant part of such an examination will be to validate the actions and results of the original examination. Such records are also part of the unused material for the case under investigation.

7. SECTION 7—GENERAL

7.1 Training and Education

7.1.1 Also refers to:
  • ACPO Good Practice and Advice Guide for Managers of e-Crime Investigations ('Managers' Guide').

7.1.2 The general principle of training in digital investigation significantly differs from usual police training. Owing to the rapidly changing environment of technology, there is a requirement for the continuous but essential retention and updating of skills.

7.1.3 Readers should refer to the section concerning training in the Good Practice and Advice Guide for Managers of e-Crime Investigations.

7.1.4 It is also the personal responsibility of any person working within the area of digital forensics to maintain their knowledge of the subject areas they are involved in. Formal training is just one route, but there is also a vast amount of open-source information available for self development and awareness. (Practitioners should be mindful that the veracity of open-source information cannot always be established, and should critically evaluate any information sourced in this way.) Professional development can also be progressed by attending conferences and technical workshops, conducting independent research, participating in online specialist forums or by discussions with subject matter experts in other forces or agencies.

7.1.5 Police personnel should also be aware of POLKA (Police On-Line Knowledge Area), an information sharing resource where there are digital forensic communities that discuss numerous topics and a library of some relevant documentation.

7.2 Welfare in the Workplace

7.2.1 Also refers to:

- ACPO Good Practice and Advice Guide for Managers of e-Crime Investigations.

7.2.2 There are a number of aspects concerning the welfare of staff working within the digital forensic area and the risks associated with that type of work:

- The psychological effect of viewing disturbing material including indecent images of children (IIOC);
- Electrical safety;
- Ergonomics, including working with Display Screen Equipment (DSE);
- Biohazards.

7.2.3 Both staff and managers should be aware of the potential impacts of these and take steps to minimise their effect. For further details, refer to the Managers' Guide.

7.3 Digital Forensic Contractors

7.3.1 Also refers to:

- ACPO Good Practice and Advice Guide for Managers of e-Crime Investigations;
- Forensic Regulator's Codes of Practice and Conduct.

7.3.2 Where the services of commercial forensic service providers are required by law enforcement, it is important to select external consulting witnesses/forensic practitioners carefully. Any external practitioner should be familiar with, and agree to comply with, the principles of digital evidence referred to in this guide.

7.3.3 Selection of external providers, particularly in the more unusual or highly technical areas, can be a problem for the investigator. Digital forensic units may be able to offer more advice on the criteria for selection.

7.3.4 Readers should refer to the ACPO Managers' Guide for further suggestions on the practical aspects of selecting an external forensic service provider (including such aspects as security clearance and physical security requirements or procurement issues). They should also ensure that any forensic service provider engaged on law enforcement work is able to work in accordance with the Forensic Regulator's Codes of Practice and Conduct which requires ISO accreditation (ISO 17025 and ISO 17020). The Regulator will expect compliance for all digital forensic services by 2014, but procurement frameworks and contracts should be looking at compliance for external service providers in advance of this date.

7.3.5 When engaging the services of digital forensic contractors, processes and policies for the retention of case-related data should be considered, both on an ongoing basis and following the termination of the contract. Contractors and those engaging them must comply with the terms of the Data Protection Act, and with any local policies of the engaging organisation.

7.4 Disclosure

7.4.1 Also refers to:

- Attorney General's Guidelines on Disclosure (revised April 2005);
- CPS Disclosure Manual.

7.4.2 The particular issues relating to disclosure of digital evidence are typically those of volume. A digital investigation may involve the examination of a vast amount of data and it is not always straightforward for investigators and prosecutors to discharge their disclosure obligations in respect of this. For example, the average hard disk is now larger than 200 gigabytes and this, if printed out on A4 paper, would be 10,000,000 pages long. In addition, the nature of digital evidence means it is not always possible to create a static representation which preserves the nature of the original evidence (e.g. of a database) and in some cases data can only be disclosed electronically, such as CCTV.

7.4.3 The Criminal Procedure and Investigations Act 1996 (CPIA) came into force on 1 April 1997[1] The Act, together with its Code of Practice, introduced a statutory framework for the recording, retention, revelation and disclosure of unused material obtained during criminal investigations commenced on or after that date.

7.4.4 Additional guidance for investigators and prosecutors to assist them in complying with their statutory duties is set out in the Attorney General's Guidelines on Disclosure (revised April 2005). ACPO and the CPS have also agreed detailed joint operational instructions for handling unused material, currently set out in the Disclosure Manual.

7.4.5 What follows should be regarded as a very brief summary of some of the relevant guidance in the Disclosure Manual. It is not intended as a replacement for the detailed guidance provided in the Manual itself.

7.4.6 Even in relatively straightforward cases, investigators may obtain, and even generate, substantial quantities of material. Some of this material may in due course be used as evidence: for example, physical exhibits recovered from the scene of the crime or linked locations, CCTV material, forensic evidence, statements obtained from witnesses and tape recordings of defendants interviewed under caution before charge. The remaining material is the 'unused material', and it is this material which is the subject of the procedure for disclosure created under the CPIA.

7.4.7 Generally material must be examined in detail by the disclosure officer or the deputy but, exceptionally, the extent and manner of inspecting, viewing or listening will depend on the nature of the material and its form. For example, it might be reasonable to examine digital material by using software search tools. If such material is not examined in detail, it must nonetheless be described on the disclosure schedules accurately and as clearly as possible. The extent and manner of its examination must also be described together with justification[2] for such action.

7.4.8 The CPIA Code of Practice also provides guidance concerning the duty to pursue all reasonable lines of enquiry, in relation to computer material.[3] Examination of material held on a computer may require expert assistance and, in some cases, Digital Evidence Recovery Officers (DEROs) may be commissioned to help extract evidence and assist with unused material. DEROs may be police officers, police staff or external service providers. The use of DEROs and related matters is discussed in detail in Annex H of the Disclosure Manual.

7.4.9 It is important that the material is inspected and described on the unused material schedule, in accordance with the above guidance, as it is the schedules (non-sensitive and sensitive) which are, in due course, revealed to the prosecutor, in order that the latter can comply with the duty under section 3 CPIA to provide primary disclosure to the accused (or initial disclosure, where the criminal investigation in question has commenced on or after 4 April 2005).

7.4.10 Whether the material is disclosed under section 3 of the CPIA, following service of a statement, or after an application for specific disclosure under section 8 of the Act, disclosure may be in the form of providing a copy or copies of the material in question to the defence. It may also be by permitting the defence (or a suitable expert, instructed by the defence) access to the actual material. Guidance concerning this is set out in the Disclosure Manual, 30.8–30.13.

7.4.11 It is important to note that where the computer material consists of sensitive images falling within section 1(1)(a) of the Protection of Children Act 1978, the guidance set out in the Memorandum of Understanding Between CPS and ACPO concerning Section 46 Sexual Offences Act 2003 (signed on 4th October 2004) should be followed.

---

[1] It has recently been amended in key respects following the implementation of some of the provisions of Part V of the Criminal Justice Act 2003, as of 4 April 2005.

[2] Paragraph 27, Attorney General's Guidelines on Disclosure (2005)

[3] CPIA Code of Practice, paragraph 3.5

7.4.12 In Scotland, the question of disclosure is fundamentally different from that in England and Wales and is one specifically for the Procurator Fiscal. The question of disclosure was judicially considered in the case of McLeod Petitioner, 1988, SLT233. There is no obligation upon the Crown to produce every document in their possession that has any connection with the case. It is the duty of the Procurator Fiscal to disclose anything that is relevant to establish the guilt or innocence of the accused. The court will not lightly interfere with the view of the Procurator Fiscal.

7.5 Legislation

7.5.1 Also refers to:

- Legislation.gov.uk;
- ACPO Good Practice and Advice Guide for Managers of e-Crime Investigations.

7.5.2 A wide variety of legislation may apply in examinations of digital evidence. Some of the most relevant is detailed below.

i. *Computer Misuse Act 1990 (UK-wide)*

(http://www.legislation.gov.uk/ukpga/1990/18/introduction)

S1 Unauthorised Access To Computer Material

- It is an offence to cause a computer to perform any function with intent to gain unauthorised access to any program or data held in any computer. It will be necessary to prove the access secured is unauthorised and the suspect knows this is the case. This is commonly referred to as 'hacking'.
- The Police and Justice Bill 2006 amended the maximum penalty for Section 1 offences. The offence is now triable either way, i.e. in the Magistrates Court or the Crown Court. The maximum custodial sentence has been increased from six months to two years.

S2 Unauthorised Access with Intent to Commit Other Offence

- An offence is committed as per S1 but the S1 offence is committed with the intention of committing an offence or facilitating the commission of an offence. The offence to be committed must carry a sentence fixed by law or carry a sentence of imprisonment of 5 years or more. Even if it is not possible to prove the intent to commit the further offence, the S1 offence is still committed. Max penalty: 5 years imprisonment.

S3 Unauthorised Acts with Intent to Impair Operation

- An offence is committed if any person does an unauthorised act with the intention of impairing the operation of any computer. This 'impairment' may be such that access to data is prevented or hindered or that the operation or reliability of any program is affected. This offence carries a maximum penalty of ten years imprisonment. This offence is used instead of the Criminal Damage Act 1971, since it is not possible to criminally damage something that is not tangible. The Police and Justice Bill 2006 amended the original Section 3 Computer Misuse Act offence, unauthorised modification, and increased the maximum penalty to ten years imprisonment.

S3A Making, Supplying or Obtaining Article for Use in S1 or S3 offences

- The Police and Justice Bill 2006 created a new S3A offence of making, supplying (including offers to supply) or obtaining articles for use in S1 or S3 computer misuse offences. The maximum penalty for this offence is two years imprisonment.

S10 Saving For Certain Law Enforcement Powers

- This section explains that S1 of the Act has effect without prejudice to the operation in England, Wales or Scotland of any enactment relating to powers of inspection, search and seizure.

S17 Interpretation

- This section assists by explaining the meaning of some of the words and phrases used within the Act.

ii. *The Police & Criminal Evidence Act 1984*

(http://www.legislation.gov.uk/ukpga/1984/60/contents)

- This legislation does not apply in Scotland unless officers from England, Wales and Northern Ireland are using their cross-border policing powers and procedures.

- Schedule 1 details the procedure by which special procedure material and excluded material can be obtained.
- A circuit judge can order that such material be produced to a constable for him to take away or that such material be made available for the constable to access within seven days of the order. For information held on a computer, an order can be made that the material is produced in a visible and legible form in which it can be taken away. Or, an order can be made giving a constable access to the material in a visible and legible form within seven days of the order.

S8 Search Warrant

- A justice of the peace can issue a search warrant, if it is believed an indictable offence has been committed and evidence of that offence is on the premises. This warrant may, as per S16 of PACE, also authorise persons who can accompany the officers conducting the search for example a computer expert.

S19 General Power of Seizure

- This details the power by which an officer can seize items and the circumstances in which they can be seized.

S20 Extension of Powers of Seizure to Computerised Information

- This section details the power for requiring information held on a computer to be produced in a form in which it can be taken away and in which it is visible and legible.

S21 Access and Copying

- This section details the power in relation to having items seized accessed and copied to other relevant parties.

S22 Retention

- This details the circumstances in which seized property can be retained.

S78 Exclusion of Unfair Evidence

- The court can exclude evidence where, with regard to all the circumstances, it would have an adverse effect on the fairness of the proceedings.

iii. Criminal Justice & Police Act 2001 (England, Wales & NI)

(http://www.legislation.gov.uk/ukpga/2001/16/contents)

S50 (re search and seizure—bulk items)

- Describes the power by which an item can be seized, if it is believed it may be something or it may contain an item or items for which there is a lawful authorisation to search.

S50 (1)

- Where a person is lawfully on premises carrying out a search and it is not practicable to determine at the time if an item found is something that he is entitled to seize, or if the contents of an item are things that he is entitled to seize, the item can be taken away for this to be determined. There must be reasonable grounds for believing the item may be something for which there was authorisation to search.

S50 (2)

- Where a person is lawfully on premises and an item for which there is a power to seize is found, but it is contained within an item for which there would ordinarily be no power to seize and it is not practicable to separate them at the time, both items can be seized.

7.5.3 Factors to be considered prior to removing such property:
    - How long would it take to determine what the item is or to separate the items?
    - How many people would it take to do this within a reasonable time period?
    - Would the action required cause damage to property? If the items were separated, would it prejudice the use of the item that is then seized?
    - Once seized, the items must be separated or identified as soon as practicable. Any item found, which was seized with no power to do so, must be returned as soon as reasonably practicable.

Items of legal privilege, excluded material and special procedure material, should also be returned as soon as practicable, if there is no power to retain them.

7.5.4 It should be noted that the use of this act gives additional rights (such as the right to be present during examination) to the owner of the property.

7.5.5 Equivalent powers in Scotland are granted under:

- Civic Government Scotland Act 1982;
- Criminal Procedure Scotland Act 1995;
- Common Law.

7.5.6 Sexual Offences Act 2003 (http://www.legislation.gov.uk/ukpga/2003/42/contents) 46 Criminal proceedings, investigations etc. E+W+N.I.

(1) After section 1A of the Protection of Children Act 1978 (c. 37) insert—

'1B Exception for criminal proceedings, investigations etc.

(1) In proceedings for an offence under section 1(1)(a) of making an indecent photograph or pseudo-photograph of a child, the defendant is not guilty of the offence if he proves that—

    (a) it was necessary for him to make the photograph or pseudo-photograph for the purposes of the prevention, detection or investigation of crime, or for the purposes of criminal proceedings, in any part of the world,

    (b) at the time of the offence charged he was a member of the Security Service, and it was necessary for him to make the photograph or pseudo-photograph for the exercise of any of the functions of the Service, or

    (c) at the time of the offence charged he was a member of GCHQ, and it was necessary for him to make the photograph or pseudo-photograph for the exercise of any of the functions of GCHQ.

(2) In this section "GCHQ" has the same meaning as in the Intelligence Services Act 1994.'

7.5.7 Coroners and Justice Act 2009 (Came into force on 06 April 2010) (http://www.legislation.gov.uk/ukpga/2009/25/contents)

7.5.8 CPS guidance regarding prohibited images of children can be found at:

https://www.cps.gov.uk/legal/p_to_r/prohibited_images_of_children/

Sections 62–68 deal with 'possession of prohibited images of children'.

7.5.9 The offence targets certain non-photographic images of children, possession of which is not covered by previously existing legislation.

7.5.10 A prohibited image is pornographic and concentrates on genitals or shows a sex act and is grossly offensive, disgusting, or otherwise of an obscene character.

7.5.11 An image is of a child if impression conveyed is that of a child or the predominant impression is that of a child despite some physical characteristics shown are not those of a child.

7.5.12 If the image is in a series then the context of the series can be used to determine if the individual image is prohibited or not.

7.5.13 Classified films are excluded (unless an individual is in possession of a still or clip that has been extracted solely or principally for the purpose of sexual arousal).

7.5.14 There is a defence of having a legitimate reason for possession, or having not seen the image and not knowing, nor having cause to suspect, it was a prohibited image.

7.5.15 The maximum penalty is 3 years' imprisonment.

7.6 Other Legislation

7.6.1 For additional guidance or information in relation to legislation not listed, investigators may wish to consult the Police National Legal Database (PNLD) or the UK Legislation website (which replaces the Office of Public Sector Information (OPSI) and Statute Law databases), available online at http://www.legislation.gov.uk.

Glossary of Terms/Abbreviations Used in this Guide

ACPO: Association of Chief Police Officers

DFU: Digital Forensic Unit

NPIA: National Police Improvement Agency

IIOC: Indecent Images Of Children

SPOC: Single Point Of Contact

RIPA: Regulation Of Investigatory Powers Act

RIPSA: Regulation Of Investigatory Powers (Scotland) Act

DPA: Data Protection Act

CCTV: Closed Circuit Television

IP Address: Internet Protocol Address—numerical address assigned to device in a computer network that uses the Internet protocol for communications.

PACE: Police & Criminal Evidence Act 1984

SIM: A subscriber identity module or subscriber identification module (SIM) on a removable SIM card securely stores the service-subscriber key (IMSI) used to identify a subscriber on mobile telephony devices (such as mobile phones and computers).

PUK: PIN Unlock Key (PUK)

CSP/ISP: Communications Service Provider/Internet Service Provider

References

- ACPO Good Practice and Advice Guide for Managers of e-Crime Investigations ('Managers' Guide'),
  http://www.acpo.police.uk/documents/crime/2011/20110301%20CBA%20ACPO%20managers_guide_v10.1.4%20for%20ecrime%20investigations_2011.pdf
- Attorney General's Guidelines on Disclosure (revised April 2005)
  http://www.cps.gov.uk/legal/a_to_c/attorney_generals_guidelines_on_disclosure/
- Crimes involving websites, forums and blogs
- CPS disclosure manual
  http://www.cps.gov.uk/legal/d_to_g/disclosure_manual/
- Digital Imaging Procedure v2.1
  http://tna.europarchive.org/20100413151426/http://scienceandresearch.homeoffice.gov.uk/hosdb/publications/cctv-publications/DIP_2.1_16-Apr-08_v2.3_(Web)47aa.html?view=Standard&pubID=555512
- First Responder's Guide
- Forensic Science Regulator's Codes of Practice and Conduct
  http://www.homeoffice.gov.uk/publications/agencies-public-bodies/fsr/codes-conductpractice?view=Standard&pubID=868070
- Network forensics and volatile data collection
- NPIA Forensics21 HTCU Computer Examination Process, 2011
- NPIA mobile phone SOPs
- Retrieval of Video Evidence and Production of Working Copies from Digital CCTV Systems v2.0
  http://tna.europarchive.org/20100413151426/http://scienceandresearch.homeoffice.gov.uk/hosdb/publications/cctv-publications/66   08_Retrieval_of_Video_Ev13c4f.html?view=Standard&pubID=585513
- SCDEA guidance

Acknowledgements

Review Board members

Paul Birch (Serious Fraud Office)

Lisa Burrell (Police Central e-Crime Unit)

Rick Conway (Surrey Police)

Steve Edwards (Police Central e-Crime Unit)

Dennis Edgar-Neville (Canterbury University/British Computer Society)

Danny Faith (NTAC/F3)

Steve Guest (IACIS)

Dan Haagman (7-Safe)

Sonny Hanspal (NPIA)

Keith McDevitt (SCDEA)

Jelle Niemantsverdriet (VerizonBusiness)

Bev Nutter (MPS-DEFS)

Harry Parsonage (Nottingham Police)

Peter Salter (PSNI)

Lindy Shepherd (Cranfield University)

Paul Slater (PWC)

Rob Watson (7-Safe)

Alastair Wilson (SCDEA)

Mark Wilson (MPS-DOI)

Paul Wright (VerizonBusiness)

Other acknowledgments

Esther George (CPS)

Jane Stevenson (Workplace Wellbeing)

Eddie Fisher (MPS-DEFS)

Appendix A

Network Forensics

Home and corporate network environments

Networks of computers are becoming more common in the domestic environment and are well established in corporate settings. In the home, they are usually based around the broadband Internet connection, which often also offers functionality to set up a small internal (and often wireless) network within the household. In corporate environments, more advanced network setups can be found, for which no generic description can be given.

The use of wireless networks in both the corporate and home environment is also increasing at a considerable rate. To the forensic investigator, this presents a number of challenges and an increased number of potential artefacts to consider. Owing to the potential complexity of 'technical' crime scenes, specialist advice should be sought when planning the digital evidence aspect of the forensic strategy.

Wireless devices

A whole range of wired and wireless devices may be encountered:

- Network devices which connect individual systems or provide network functionality: Switches, hubs, routers, firewalls (or devices which combine all three).
- Devices to connect individual computers to the network, such as network cards (which can also be embedded within the computer)
- Devices to set up a wireless network: Wireless Access Points.
- Printers and digital cameras.
- Bluetooth (small range wireless) devices—PDAs, mobile phones, dongles.
- Hard drives which can be connected to the network.

Wireless networks cannot be controlled in the same way as a traditionally cabled solution and are potentially accessible by anyone within radio range. The implications of this should be carefully considered when planning a search or developing the wider investigative strategy. A device, such as a computer or a hard drive, may not be located on the premises where the search and seizure is conducted.

Home networks and data

If devices are networked, it may not be immediately obvious where the computer files and data, which are being sought, are kept. Data could be on any one of them. Networks, both wired and wireless, also enable the users of the computers to share resources; such as printers, scanners and connections to the Internet. It may well be the case that if one of the computers is connected to the Internet, some or all of the others are also.

With the widespread use of broadband type Internet subscriptions such as ADSL and cable, the Internet connection is nowadays likely to be of an 'always on' type connection. This implies that even if no-one is apparently working on a computer or using the Internet, there may be data passing to and from computers or between the network and the Internet. If a wired network is present, there will usually be a small box (called a 'hub' or a 'switch') also present, connecting the computers together. Hubs, switches and routers look very much the same as one another. The network cables are usually connected at the rear.

The network may also be connected to another device (called a Cable Modem or a ADSL Modem) providing access to the Internet. Sometimes, the hub/switch/router mentioned before are combined with these modems in one device.

One wire from a modem will usually be connected to the telephone or television cable system and another wire will be connected either to one of the computers present or directly to the network hub, or the modem itself may be incorporated within the hub in a modem/router.

Operation planning in networked environments

When planning an operation involving a network, consider carefully the possibility of remote access, i.e. person(s) accessing a network with or without permissions from outside the target premises. Investigators should consider the possibility of nefarious activity being carried out through the insecure network of an innocent party. The implications of such a scenario are that search warrants could be obtained on the basis of a resolved Internet Protocol address, which actually relates to an innocent party. The implications are potentially unlawful searches, legal action taken against the relevant investigative agency and a waste of resources.

Consider also the possibility of a computer's access to remote online storage, which may physically reside in a foreign jurisdiction. This can include web-based services for email, photo or document storage or other applications offered via the Internet. There will be legal issues in relation to accessing any such material. Legal advice should be sought prior to any access or retrieval and often the provider of the particular service will have to be contacted to ensure that material is preserved while the relevant mutual legal assistance requests are being arranged.

Network detection

Network detecting and monitoring is a specialist area and should not be considered without expert advice. Recommendations for dealing with networks and wireless implementations involve the following steps:

- Identify and check network devices to see how much network or Internet activity is taking place. Consider using a wireless network detector to determine whether wireless is in operation and to locate wireless devices. Consideration should also be given to mobile Internet devices such as 3G or GPRS dongles or phones, which operate using the mobile phone network;
- As you do so, consider photographing the layout of the network and the location of the machines connected to it, so as to allow a possible future reconstruction;
- Once satisfied that no data will be lost as a result, you may isolate the network from the Internet. This is best done by identifying the connection to the telephone system or wireless communications point and unplugging it from the telephone point. Keep modems and routers running, as they may need to

be interrogated to find out what is connected to them. Owing to their nature, it is particularly difficult to ascertain what is connected to a wireless network;

- Trace each wire from the network devices to discover the computer to which it is connected. This
may not be possible in premises where cables may be buried in conduits or walls (advice in this case
should be sought from the local IT administrator, if available, as to the set up of the system). Make a
note of each connection. Note which computer is connected to which number 'port' on the network
device (hub / switch / router or multi function device). Label each connection in such a way that the
system can be rebuilt exactly as it stands, should there be any future questions as to the layout. It is
highly recommended that pictures be taken of the setup;
- Consider making a connection to the access point/router in order to establish the external IP address.
Most modern networks use Network Address Translation (NAT) which means that they communicate with an internal IP address and never get assigned and external IP one. In a wireless environment, remember that no cables are used between a PC and other devices. However, there will still
be some physical cabling to each device (which could include a network cable to the wired network,
power cables etc.), the configuration of which should be recorded. Please also note that Cable / ADSL
modems can have wireless capabilities built in.
- Once satisfied that the evidential impact is acceptable, you may remove each connection in turn from
the network device once it has been identified. This will isolate each computer in turn from the network. The same can be done with cabling into wireless devices;
- Seize and bag all network hardware, modems, original boxes and CDs / floppy disks etc. (provided
they are easily removable);
- Subsequently treat each device as you would a stand-alone device;
- Remember that the data which is sought may be on any one of the computers on the network. Officers
should make a decision based on the reasonable assumption that relevant data may be stored on a
device before seizing that device;
- Bear in mind the possibility that the network may be a wireless network as well as a wired one,
i.e. certain computers may be connected to the network via conventional network cabling. Others
may be connected to that same network via the mains system, and others may be connected via a
wireless link;
- Also, bear in mind that any mobile phones and PDAs may be wireless or Bluetooth enabled and connected to a domestic network.

Concerns with remote wireless storage often focus around the inability to locate the device. In this
instance, it would be impossible to prove that an offence had been committed. Artefacts on seized computers might provide evidence that a remote storage device has been used, however the analysis of such
artefacts will take time and this cannot often be done during the onsite seizure.

Corporate network environments

When dealing with computer systems in a corporate environment, the forensic investigator faces a
number of differing challenges. If the system administrator is not part of the investigation then seek
their assistance. The most significant is likely to be the inability to shut down server(s) due to company
operational constraints. In such cases, it is common practice that a network enabled 'forensic software'
agent is installed, which will give the ability to image data across the network 'on-the-fly', or to a network share or a locally connected removable storage medium such as a USB hard drive.

Other devices could be encountered which may assist the investigation. For example, routers and firewalls can give an insight into network configuration through Access Control Lists (ACLs) or security
rule sets. This may be achieved by viewing the configuration screens as an administrator of the device.
This will require the user names and passwords obtained at the time of seizure or from the suspect during interview.

By accessing the devices, data may be added, violating Principle 1 but, if the logging mechanism is
researched prior to investigation, the forensic footprints added during investigation may be taken into
consideration and therefore Principle 2 can be complied with.

In the case of large company networks, consider gaining the advice and assistance of the network
administrator/ support team (assuming that they are not suspects).

Volatile Data Collection

In certain circumstances, it may be necessary or advisable for computer forensic investigators to gather evidence from a computer whilst its running or in a 'live' state. This technique has become a common practice as, even though some changes to the original evidence will be made, this method often allows access to evidence which would have been unavailable if the power is removed from a system. In order to capture volatile data on a device the device WILL have to be accessed. Therefore changes WILL be caused by the examiner.

Special consideration should be given to Principle 2 of the guidelines, as conducting live-forensics implies access to the original evidence. Any person doing this needs to be competent and fully aware of the impact their actions have and should be prepared to explain their reasons for taking this route.

Live forensics approach

By profiling the footprint of trusted forensic tools used to gather volatile data, the digital forensic examiner can understand the impact of using such tools and can explain any artefacts left by the tools.

In order to ensure that a consistent approach is used and the chance of errors is minimized, it is recommended to use a scripted approach using a number of basic and trusted tools. Regardless of the tools used, it is advisable to start with capturing the contents of RAM, the volatile memory.

If other tools are used before the contents of the RAM are stored, it is very likely that running the forensic tools will overwrite parts of the RAM.

Other examples of information, which might be available in the dump of the RAM contents, can be retrieved using different tools:

- listings of running processes;
- logged on and registered users;
- network information including listening, open and closing network ports;
- ARP (address resolution protocol) cache;
- Registry information.

The tools used to capture this volatile information are generally run from removable media like a USB stick, DVD or CD-ROM or a floppy disk. A USB stick is generally most convenient, as the output of the tools can be written back to the stick. Writing tool output to the original drive should be avoided whenever possible, as this changes the contents of the hard drive and can destroy potential evidence. Again, principle 2 does allow the investigator to do this, but a conscious decision will have to be made and the process written down.

When inserting USB devices the examiner must ensure that they know the details of the serial numbers of the devices they are connecting so that they can be eliminated when analysing the date captured.

When in doubt as to whether or not to use live forensics, consult with the digital forensic examiner for advice. And, it should be noted that in live forensics it is not always possible to know upfront which approach will yield the best results. Whichever method is chosen, remember to take meticulous notes—as dictated by principle 3.

Summary of steps

A summary of the steps to be taken is shown below. Documentation of all actions, together with reasoning, should also apply when following such steps:

- Perform a risk assessment of the situation—Is it evidentially required and safe to perform volatile data capture?
- If so, install volatile data capture device to a removable data carrier (such as a USB stick)—preferably, this has already been done prior to starting the operation;
- Plug the data carrier into the machine and start the data collection script;
- Once complete, stop the device (particularly important for USB devices, which if removed before proper shutdown can lose information);
- Remove the device;
- Verify the data output on a separate forensic investigation machine (not the suspect system);
- Immediately follow with standard power-off procedure.

The capture and analysis of volatile data no doubt presents the investigator with technical challenges. However, as cases become more complex and connectivity between devices and public networks proliferate, with an increase in more advanced malware, which cannot always be retrieved using more traditional disk forensics, the above recommendations will need to be considered.

It is vitally important that only someone with the relevant training and is competent to do so should take any of these actions.

Appendix B

Crimes Involving Websites, Forums, and Blogs

Where a crime involves evidence displayed on a website the most convenient method of recovering the evidence may be by engaging the assistance of suitably trained staff to visit the website and take copies of the evidential content. In order to do this the officer taking report of the matter needs to obtain the address of the website, for example, http://www.acpo.police.uk, or if it is a specific page within the site.

http://www.acpo.police.uk/about_pages/structure.html.

When carrying out any evidence recovery it is essential that an audit trail of all activity carried out by the investigator is recorded in a log. The recommended method for copying a website is to visit the site and record the relevant pages using video capture software so there is a visible representation of how they look when visited at the time. If video capture software is not available then the pages can be saved as screenshots. It is also advisable to follow this by capturing the web pages themselves either by using website copying software or saving the individual pages. Copying the pages themselves, as well as obtaining a visual record, means that the code from the web pages is also secured should that become relevant later.

This work should be conducted from a computer which has been specifically set up to be non-attributable on the Internet. Failure to use an appropriate system may lead to the compromise of other police operations. Anyone visiting a website generally exposes a certain amount of information to the website, for example it is common on police systems to have a web browser which is branded with the forces name. This branding is exposed to a website being visited and so may be recorded in logs on the site along with other information amongst which, will include the pages visited.

If it appears likely that the evidence on the website might be lost by a delay in carrying out the above procedures then the person reporting may be asked to make a copy of the evidence by whatever means they are capable of (either printing, screenshot or saving pages), alternatively this could be done by the person receiving the report. Before taking these steps every effort should be made to secure the services of a competent person to carry out this work as failing to capture the information correctly could have a detrimental impact on the investigation.

Where there is difficulty in capturing the evidence by visiting the site it might be possible to make an official request to the owner of the site by whatever legal procedures are required within the jurisdiction. The CSP/ISP SPOC or Digital Forensic Unit can usually advise on the appropriate procedures.

By making a request to the service provider hosting the site it may be possible to recover evidence of who has created the web page or posting. It is not unusual for details of the user such as name, address, phone number, banking details, email address, and alternative email address to be recorded by a host.

If there is a requirement to identify who has committed some activity on a website, for example where a fraud has been committed by purchasing goods from a website or by posting a message on a website, the likelihood is that the suspect may be traceable from logs on the site. When any user accesses the Internet they are allocated a unique address known as an IP address and their Internet Service Provider (ISP) keeps logs of the times and dates and the identity of the user allocated any IP address.

When a user visits a site and conducts some activity, for example logs on, posts a message, or makes a purchase, it is likely that the user's IP address has been logged by the website. It is often possible to obtain copies of logs from websites if there is a requirement to see who has been active on a website by making a request via the force CSP/ISP SPOC.

If the evidence is no longer available to be retrieved by any of the above means, and where the use of resources can be justified by the seriousness of the case, it may be possible to recover evidence of the site contents from an end user device that has been used to view the site by conducting a forensic examination of the device.

Where investigators wish to carry out open source intelligence research on the Internet they should be trained to do so and conduct the research from a computer which cannot be attributed to the investigator's agency.

Covert Interaction on the Internet

In circumstances where investigators wish to communicate covertly with an online suspect they MUST use the services of a Nationally Accredited and Registered (CII). CIIs have received specialist training which addresses the technical and legal issues relating to undercover operations on the Internet.

Crimes Involving Email Communication

There are generally two methods of sending and receiving email, one by using a web browser and accessing email online for example at the Hotmail, Windows Live, Yahoo or Google websites. In these circumstances the mail is stored on the webmail server and is read through the user's browser. The other method is to access email using a program such as Outlook or Windows Mail to download mail to the user's computer. The program is used to view and store the emails locally.

Where the evidence in a case involves an email sent from a person who the police want to trace the key evidence is usually found in what is known as the email's 'Full Internet Header'. Each email sent over the Internet contains this header which is normally not visible to the user. It contains details of the route taken across the Internet by the email and includes the IP address of the sender. Even where an email has been sent with a fictitious email address which has been registered with false details, it is often possible to identify the sender from the Full Internet Header.

In order to obtain the Full Internet Header the person taking the incident report needs to ascertain which of the two methods the recipient uses to access their email. Where it is web based identify the webmail host (i.e. Hotmail, Yahoo etc.) or if by a program on the computer ascertain what program and version number of the program. The version number can usually be found in the program's Help on the menu bar under an item called 'About'.

Each webmail provider and email program treat the Full Internet Header differently and if the officer or user does not know how to display the header the details of the webmail provider or program need to be passed to a specialist in the Digital Forensic Unit or CSP/ISP SPOC who will be able to provide advice. Once the header has been exposed the relevant email should be printed together with the header, and may also be saved electronically. Depending upon the seriousness of the case and the volume of email evidence, advice may be sought from the digital forensics unit on the most appropriate method of securing and retaining the email evidence.

Once the full header has been obtained the force CSP/ISP SPOC will be able to use this to conduct enquiries to attempt to identify the sender from the originating IP address.

Where an email address of a suspect is known but there is no email available from which a full header can be obtained, it may be possible to identify the user of the email address and their location. Depending upon the email service provider various details of the user may be recorded together with the first registration IP address and a varying period of IP address login history. These details may be obtained by making an appropriate CSP/ISP SPOC request for the email address. In conducting such enquiries it needs to be recognised that it is a trivial exercise to send an email with a false email address in the 'From:' field of an email.

On some occasions the investigating agency might access a user's email account with written authority from the user in order to secure evidence. Where this is the case, if third party material is exposed as a consequence of viewing the user's emails, advice should be sought as to whether a Directed Surveillance Authority should be in place in addition to the user's authority. Even if the password and log in details are available. For example as a result of the Forensic examination authority and formal authority is required to access the email account.

Where justified by the investigation, consideration may be given to accessing messages on an email provider's server by obtaining the appropriate RIPA authority.

Crimes Involving Internet Chat

Users can employ a number of different devices to engage in chat on the Internet. There are three main ways to chat—using a website's chat facility, for example Facebook, using an instant messenger program like Windows Live Messenger, or much less commonly, using Internet Relay Chat (IRC).

Where an incident is reported which involves the use of chat the person taking the report needs to ascertain what method of chat was being used, i.e. what is the name of the website hosting the chat and its full Internet address, or what program is being used. The key evidence to be secured is

- any information which may identify the suspect party, and
- the content of any chat.

If the chat is web-based the details of the website, any chat room name and the user name of the suspect should be obtained together with the times and dates of any chat activity. If the chat facility is part of a social networking site the user will most likely have a unique ID number as well as a user name. This is usually visible in the web browser's address bar when viewing a user's profile or when the mouse pointer is moved over the user name. The force CSP/ISP SPOC or Digital Forensic Unit can provide help in finding this ID number. If the chat is by instant messenger program then the user name of the suspect should be obtained together with the associated email address which is usually available from the contact list of the person reporting. Generally a user's contact list can be accessed from any computer connected to the Internet so if it is considered that the user's computer might be retained for a forensic examination then it should not itself be used to access the contact list.

There is usually an option for a user to save chat logs but more often than not the default setting is for logs not to be saved. If the user has saved chat logs that contain evidence, the logs should be saved to removable media for production as evidence, if no removable media is available they should be printed out. Users are able to engage in chat from many types of device in addition to computers. Where the circumstances of the case warrant it, an end-user device could be submitted for forensic examination in order to recover evidence of the suspect's contact details and chat content. Where a suspect's user details are obtained it may be possible to identify the suspect by making the appropriate CSP/ISP SPOC requests. In the event that the chat has been conducted using IRC the following details should be obtained—the IRC program used, the name of the IRC server, the channel and any usernames. Further advice should then be sought from the Digital Forensic Unit.

Communications in the course of a transmission

Digital evidence in transit may be any form of communication using the Internet or a telecommunications network such as email, chat, voice calls, text messages, and voice-mail. Where such evidence is sought advice should be obtained from the force Covert Authorities Bureau.

Appendix C

Crime Scenes

There are many different types of digital media and end-user devices, which may be encountered during a search of a crime scene, all of which have the potential to hold data which may be of value to the investigation. In order to preserve the data and achieve best evidence, these items must be handled and seized appropriately, and should be treated with as much care as any other item that is to be forensically examined. This section is intended to assist individuals to ensure their actions in relation to seizure are correct.

The following guidance deals with the majority of scenarios that may be encountered. The general principles, if adhered to, will ensure the best chance of evidence being recovered in an uncontaminated and, therefore, acceptable manner.

Items found during a search will normally fall into the broad categories of computer-based media items, CCTV systems and mobile devices. These are considered separately below.

Proportionality

Before seizing an item, consider whether the item is likely to hold evidence (eg, is this a family computer or a computer belonging to a suspect?) Ensure that details of where the item was found are recorded. Consider when the offence was committed; when seizing CCTV, give consideration to narrowing down what is seized, by camera and/or time period. Check whether another system may be better placed to record the evidence.

Differentiate between mobile phones found on a suspect and phones found in a drawer, as different levels of examination may be possible for these. Also consider that evidence may be stored online, or on an internet service provider's systems, and end-user devices may only be needed to obtain the details necessary to request this evidence from the service provider. If so, it is best to seize items in current usage, i.e. computers connected to the internet.

Digital devices and media should not be seized just because it is there. The person in charge of the search must have reasonable grounds to remove property and there must be justifiable reasons for doing so. The search provisions of PACE Legislation Codes of Practice equally apply to digital devices and media in England, Wales and Northern Ireland. In Scotland, officers should ensure they are acting within the terms of the search warrant.

Due regard should also be taken concerning any possible contravention of the European Convention of Human Rights.

What to take to a scene

The following is a suggested list of equipment that might be of value during planned searches. This basic tool-kit should be considered for use in the proper dismantling of digital systems as well as for their packaging and removal:

- Property register;
- Exhibit labels (tie-on and adhesive);
- Labels and tape to mark and identify component parts of the system, including leads and sockets;
- Tools such as screw drivers (flathead and crosshead), small pliers, and wire cutters for removal of cable ties;
- A range of packaging and evidential bags fit for the purpose of securing and sealing heavy items
- such as computers and smaller items such as PDAs and mobile phone handsets;
- Cable ties for securing cables;
- Flat pack assembly boxes—consider using original packaging if available;
- Coloured marker pens to code and identify removed items;
- Camera and/or video to photograph scene in situ and any on-screen displays;
- Torch;
- Forensically sterile storage material.

In addition, the following items may be useful when attending scenes to retrieve CCTV:

- Laptop with USB and network connectivity. A selection of proprietary replay software could be installed, to enable the downloaded data to be checked;
- External CD/DVD writer;
- USB hard drives.

Records to be kept

To comply with principle 3, records must be kept of all actions taken in relation to digital evidence, for example:
- Sketch map/photographs of scene and digital equipment;
- Record location and contact details;
- If a business, record opening hours;
- Details of all persons present where digital equipment is located;
- Details of digital items - make, model, serial number;
- Details of connected peripherals;
- Remarks/comments/information offered by user(s) of equipment;
- Actions taken at scene showing exact time;

• Notes/photographs showing state of system when found.

Computer based devices and media

This includes desktop or laptop PCs and Apple Macintosh systems, digital cameras, memory cards, USB sticks, external hard drives and games consoles, amongst other items. Mobile devices which have wireless connectivity/ communications capability (such as tablet computers and satellite navigation systems) fall under the heading of 'mobile devices'.

Systems which are powered on (running) need to be handled with care, as there is the potential to make unwanted changes to the evidence if these are not dealt with correctly. Such systems should only be accessed by appropriately trained officers In addition, volatile data of evidential value may be lost. Be aware of the potential to lose other valuable data, particularly when dealing with business systems, which could give rise to a claim for damages. In these cases expert advice should be sought before seizing a business system which is powered on.

Desktop and laptop computers/games consoles

The scene should be fully documented by written notes and/or a photographic record. If a device is powered on, it needs to be handled carefully to preserve any volatile data and to avoid unwanted changes to the stored data.

Consider removing the device from any network, as devices can be remotely accessed, causing alteration to the data—but balance this against the possibility of losing data of evidential value, such as the list of currently open connections. If unsure, seek expert advice.

Seizure steps:

1. Secure and take control of the area containing the equipment;
2. Move people away from any computers and power supplies and do not allow any interaction with digital devices by suspect;
3. Photograph or video the scene and all the components including the leads in situ. If no camera is available, draw a sketch plan of the system and label the ports and cables so that system/s may be reconstructed at a later date;
4. Allow any printers to finish printing.

If switched off:

5. Do not, in any circumstance, switch the computer on;
6. Make sure that the computer is switched off, by moving the mouse – some screen savers may give the appearance that the computer is switched off, but hard drive and monitor activity lights may indicate that the machine is switched on;
7. Be aware that some laptop computers may power on by opening the lid. Remove the battery from the laptop. Seize any power supply cables for future use.

If switched on:

8. Record what is on the screen by photographing it and by making a written note of the content of the screen;
9. Do not touch the keyboard or click the mouse. If the screen is blank or a screen saver is present, the investigator should be asked to decide if they wish to restore the screen. If so, a short movement of the mouse should restore the screen or reveal that the screen saver is password protected. If the screen restores, photograph or video it and note its content. If password protection is shown, continue as below, without any further touching of the mouse. Record the time and activity of the use of the mouse in these circumstances. (For games consoles, or tablet computers, the equivalent would be moving the controller joystick or touching the touchscreen);
10. If the system may contain valuable evidence in its current state (for example, if it is currently displaying a relevant document or an instant message conversation), seizing officers should seek expert advice from their local digital forensic unit as this may be lost if the power is lost. This is especially important if the suspect is a technically knowledgeable user who may be using encryption, as there may be no way to retrieve evidence stored in encrypted volumes once the power is lost;

11. Consider advice from the owner/user of the computer but make sure this information is treated with caution;
12. Remove the main power source battery from laptop computers. However, prior to doing so, consider if the machine is in standby mode. In such circumstances, battery removal could result in avoidable data loss. This is normally evident by a small LED (light) lit on the casing. In this case, officers should seek advice from their local digital forensic unit;
13. Unplug the power and other devices from sockets on the computer itself (i.e. not the wall socket). When removing the power supply cable, always remove the end connected to the computer, and not that attached to the socket. This will avoid any data being written to the hard drive if an uninterruptible power supply is fitted. If the equipment was switched on, do not close down any programs or shut down the computer, as this will cause changes to the stored data and may trigger wiping software to run, if this is installed;
14. Ensure that all items have signed and completed exhibit labels attached to them. Failure to do so may create difficulties with continuity and cause the equipment to be rejected by the digital forensic unit;
15. Search the area for diaries, notebooks or pieces of paper with passwords on them, often attached or close to the computer;
16. Ask the user about the setup of the system, including any passwords, if circumstances dictate. If these are given, record them accurately;
17. Allow the equipment to cool down before removal;
18. Track any cables that can be seen as they made lead you to other devices in other rooms.

Mobile devices

This includes mobile phones, smartphones, and other devices which may have wireless connectivity/communications capability such as tablet computers, personal digital assistants (PDAs), personal media players and satellite navigation systems.

1. Secure and take control of the area containing the equipment. Do not allow others to interact with the equipment;
2. Photograph the device in situ, or note where it was found, and record the status of the device and any on-screen information;
3. If the device is switched on, power it off. It is important to isolate the device from receiving signals from a network to avoid changes being made to the data it contains. For example, it is possible to wipe certain devices remotely and powering the device off will prevent this. However, in exceptional circumstances the decision may be made to keep the device on. Timely access to the handset data is critical the decision may be made to leave the device switched on. Consideration may be given to place the handset in a Faraday environment to further prevent signal reception. In such circumstances advice should be sought from the DFU.
4. Seize cables, chargers, packaging, manuals, phone bills etc. as these may assist the enquiry and minimise the delays in any examination;
5. Packaging materials and associated paperwork may be a good source of PIN/PUK details;
6. Be aware that some mobile phone handsets may have automatic housekeeping functions, which clear data after a number of days. For example, some Symbian phones start clearing call/event logs after 30 days, or any other user defined period. Submit items for examination as soon as possible.

Handling and transporting digital evidence

Digital Devices

Handle with care. If placing in a car, place upright where it will not receive serious physical shocks. Keep away from magnetic sources (loudspeakers, heated seats & windows and police radios).

Hard disks

As for all digital devices protect from magnetic fields. Place in anti-static bags, tough paper bags or tamper evident cardboard packaging or wrap in paper and place in aerated plastic bags.

Removable storage

Floppy disks, memory sticks, memory cards, CDs/DVDs) Protect from magnetic fields. Do not fold or bend. Do not place labels directly onto floppy disks or CDs/DVDs. Package in tamper-force approved packaging to avoid interaction with the device whilst it is sealed.

Other items

Protect from magnetic fields. Package correctly and seal in plastic bags. Do not allow items to get wet.

Other Considerations

1. If fingerprints or DNA evidence are likely to be required, always consult with the investigator;
2. Using aluminium powder on electronic devices can be dangerous and result in the loss of evidence.

Before any examination using this substance, consider all options carefully. The equipment should be stored at normal room temperature, without being subject to any extremes of humidity and free from magnetic influence such as radio receivers. Dust, smoke, sand, water and oil are also harmful to electronic equipment. Some devices are capable of storing internal data (such as the time and date set on the system) by use of batteries. If the battery is allowed to become flat, internal data will be lost. It is not possible to determine the life expectancy of any one battery. However, this is an important consideration when storing a device for long periods before forensic examination and should be addressed in local policy.

Appendix D

Developing a Digital Investigation Strategy

The investigation of crimes and incidents in which digital evidence is involved, particularly the Internet, presents some unique challenges to the investigator. The explosion of the availability and use of technology, the growth of virtual storage, development of 'Cloud Services' (online services) and the convergence of mobile and traditional computer technology has resulted in most investigations having a digital element of some description.

Investigators need to have a greater understanding of the use of digital evidence if interviews of witnesses and suspects are to be effective. This is particularly the case in serious or complex investigations where a failure to identify and secure volatile digital data could have a significant impact on the conduct of the investigation.

It is important that investigators develop appropriate strategies to identify the existence of digital evidence and to secure and interpret that evidence. Irrespective of the size or complexity the investigator should consider five primary stages.

• Data Capture and search and seizure at crime scenes;
• Data Examination;
• Data Interpretation;
• Data Reporting;
• Interview of Witness and Suspects.

Investigators should seek the advice of their force Telecoms/ISP SPOC, Network Investigators and Digital Forensic Units at the earliest opportunity to formulate a written digital forensic strategy.

Due consideration should always be given by the investigators of the benefits to the overall investigation of conducting any digital forensic work.

Data Capture Strategy

The investigator should develop a Data Capture Strategy to identify and secure all relevant digital evidence. Other than a requirement to react to immediate events the investigator should be able to plan this strategy in advance.

Where a crime or incident is reported, early consideration should be given to the potential to glean evidence from the Internet or end user devices which have a digital memory capacity and from which evidence / intelligence may be retrieved.

Social Network Sites

Priority—Establish the use of Social Networking, Online Communities, Online Storage and other Cloud Services by witnesses and suspects. Whilst this may be revealed by the examination of seized devices it may be gleaned more quickly if asked during interview.

Many current investigations involve Social Networking Sites. It is imperative that early consideration is made around securing Social Networking Profiles that fall within the investigation. The best evidence is available from the service provider however they are often located outside of the UK and may or may not secure the content on the appropriate request via the force CSP/ISP SPOC. As such the investigator should always secure a copy of what is seen by them as this may be the only opportunity to secure this evidence before it changes.

Open Source Research

The internet is a huge repository of information much of it of value to the investigator. Research by properly **trained** staff, preferably with access to a stand alone computer, will enable the investigator to get the best from the vast amount of information that is now held online. In addition to this the force CSP/ISP SPOCs will be able to give advice on the type of data that can potentially be obtained from ISP's, web mail and web based providers.

Care should be taken when undertaking Internet research from any computer linked to the Police National Network (pnn) as a digital footprint will be left and may reveal the law enforcement interest. This will not be obvious to the general internet user but will most certainly be clear to the hosts or providers of the service and those who are particularly technically aware and monitoring IP addresses.

Registration details are often asked for and whilst in some instances they will inevitably be fictitious, on many occasions they will include the following;

- IP log on;
- Name and Address;
- Landline and Mobile phone Numbers;
- Banking data;
- Emails used;
- Username and passwords;
- Linked accounts.

Whilst law enforcement are used to working with RIPA, RIPSA and the DPA to obtain information this legislation only applies within the UK. Many services are based outside of the UK based organisations.

It is essential that the CSP/ISP SPOC is engaged at the earliest opportunity to these enquiries with the objective of preserving known time critical data.

National Technical Assistance Centre (NTAC)

If encrypted files are located or suspected it is important that the suspect is asked for them, failure to do so may result in an offence under sec 49 of RIPA. Encryption is difficult to break and assistance can be sought via the Digital Forensic Unit from the National Technical Assistance Centre (NTAC) in London.

The National Technical Assistance Centre (NTAC) provides technical support only to public authorities, particularly law enforcement agencies and the intelligence services. It includes a facility for the complex processing of lawfully obtained protected electronic information.

NTAC is the leading national authority for all matters relating to the processing of protected information into an intelligible format and the disclosure of key material.

All public authorities should consult with NTAC at the earliest opportunity when considering exercising the powers in Part III of the Regulation of Investigatory Powers Act (RIPA).

A public authority cannot serve any notice under Section 49 of RIPA or, when the authority considers it necessary, seek to obtain appropriate permission, without the prior written approval of NTAC.

Investigating Crimes where Digital Evidence may be present

The proliferation of digital devices and the advances in digital communications mean that digital evidence is now present or potentially present in almost every crime.

Digital evidence can be found in a number of different locations,

- Locally on an end-user device—typically a users computer, mobile/smart phone, satellite navigation system, USB thumb drive, or digital camera;
- On a remote resource that is public—for example websites used for social networking, discussion forums, and newsgroups;
- On a remote resource that is private—an Internet Service Provider's logs of users' activity, a mobile phone company's records of customers' billing, a user's webmail account, and increasingly common,
- a user's remote file storage;
- In transit—for example mobile phone text messages, or voice calls, emails, or Internet chat.

Investigating Different Types of Crime and Identifying Sources of Evidence

It would be quite common for evidence of a crime to be in more than one of the locations mentioned above. However it might be much easier to obtain the evidence from one location rather than another; careful consideration should be given to the resources required to obtain the evidence.

For example, if evidence is required of contact between two mobile phone numbers, the best method would be to obtain call data from the Communication Service Providers via the force SPOC, rather than to request a forensic examination of the mobile phones. The call data is likely to be more comprehensive than call logs from a mobile phone and the times and dates can be relied upon, which is not necessarily the case with logs from a mobile phone.

Covert Forensic Computing

Some investigations may require consideration of gathering digital intelligence in a covert manner. It is evidently not appropriate to discuss covert tactics within this document however opportunities exist to capture digital data online and physically from devices in a covert manner where the appropriate authorities are in place.

Data Examination Strategy

Devices seized as part of a search will be forwarded to the force Digital Forensic Unit in accordance with force policy.

The investigator needs to properly consider the nature and purpose of the digital examination.

The investigator must tailor the needs of the digital examination not only based on the investigation requirements but the ability of the Digital Forensic Unit to deliver it. The better the briefing the better the advice will be.

The Investigator must be clear on what priorities are placed on the examination as it may well be, as previously stated, that key information needs to be found in order to preserve evidence that may exist elsewhere. This is particularly the case where it relates to the existence of additional evidence, offenders and victims. A preview of content may be appropriate albeit the limitations of this approach will require to be properly understood.

Priorities may also be set on the type of data to be extracted and viewed by persons other than the Digital Forensics Unit as this may reduce the burden on the unit and increase the likelihood of the delivery of the data. This will of course depend on the nature of the examination. But could include:

- Internet History;
- Emails;
- Evidence of webmail;
- Instant Messaging Logs;
- Media Files (images & videos);
- Social Networks;
- Forums & Chat Rooms;
- Cloud Services / Virtual Storage;

- File Sharing programs;
- Usernames / Passwords;
- Encrypted Files;
- Word Documents;
- Spreadsheets.

The discussion between the investigator and digital forensic unit should result in an agreed digital extraction/ examination plan to achieve an agreed outcome. The plan may need to be reviewed as the evidential picture and priorities change.

Data Interpretation Strategy

Staff tasked by the investigator to undertake the digital data extraction / examination must be competent to do so and have had sufficient training to undertake the task assigned to them. It must be borne in mind that the development of digital technology is dynamic and the examiners may well face significant challenges to their knowledge.

It is the role of the Digital Evidence Examiner to provide the investigator with a report/statement accounting for the examination of the devices as part of the investigation. The report should account in full for the parameters set for the examination, data extracted and data examined. There should also be provision to provide an interpretation of technical aspects of the examination relevant to the provision of evidence in the case.

The investigator should have a full discussion with the examiner ahead of the production of any reports to ensure all the relevant evidence is contained in the report and that the processes used adhered to the ACPO Principles governing handling digital based evidence. These principles are explained in the section headed 'The Principles of Digital Evidence' in this guide.

Data Reporting

The report is the ultimate product of the examination. It should outline the examination process and the significant data recovered. Whilst an initial report may be relatively brief, the examiner should be in a position to produce a full technical report should one later be required.

Examination notes must be preserved for disclosure or testimony purposes and, if required, the preparation of a full technical report. In Scotland, they will be preserved as productions to be used as evidence in court.

An examiner may need to testify about not only the conduct of the examination, but also the validity of the procedure and their experience and qualifications to conduct the examination.

The role of the examiner is to secure from any seized material true copy of any data that they may contain Forensic hardware should be subject to initial and periodic testing. It is worth repeating at this point that full records should be made of all actions taken. These can be made available to the defence who may subsequently cause a further examination to be conducted. A significant part of such an examination will be to validate the actions and results of the original examination. Such records are also part of the unused material for the case under investigation.

It is important to remember that legislation continues to change to keep up with technological and societal change. It is important, therefore, to consider the legal requirements and restrictions when examining digital evidence. Recent case law and precedents set at higher courts are important considerations when preparing an evidence package for an investigator This applies, in particular, to the use of the Internet and files downloaded from the Internet; or material accessible from foreign jurisdictions i.e. online data stores.

Interview of Witnesses and Suspects

The interview of witnesses/suspects is a crucial opportunity to identify key information about the nature and use of digital data relative to the investigation in hand. As such those involved must be properly briefed and competent to undertake the interview having the necessary understanding of the areas to explore.

Consideration should be given to consulting with a trained Interview Advisor with a view to the compilation of an appropriate interview strategy.

Bear in mind that the digital examination of devices seized will take time and may not necessarily reveal vital information that the witness / suspect may be aware of. Typically this may include:

- Web Mail Addresses / Username & Passwords / shared or sole use;
- Social Network Profiles / Username & Passwords / shared or sole use;
- Use of Forums & Chat Rooms / Username & Passwords;
- Use of Cloud Services / Username & Passwords / shared or sole use;
- Use of Virtual Storage / Username & Passwords / shared or sole use;
- Use of Role Play Gaming Sites / Username & Passwords / shared or sole use;
- Use of Auction sites / Username & Passwords / shared or sole use;
- Use of Online Banking;
- List of User Names;
- Use of Encryption / Encryption Keys;
- User Names of contacts;
- Use of the devices;
- Websites Visited;
- Internet Service Provider.

This list is not exhaustive.

WORKBOOK FOR THE CREATION OF
ACPO GUIDANCE/PRACTICE ADVICE

This workbook, with all sections completed, must be included in the final document as an Appendix and submitted, through the Head of the Business Area, to the Programme Support Office for quality assurance prior to submission to Cabinet for approval as ACPO Doctrine.

ACPO equality impact assessment template (diversity audit) as agreed with the CRE

1. Identify all aims of the guidance/advice

1.1 Identify the aims and projected outcomes of the guidance/advice:
1.2 Which individuals and organisations are likely to have an interest in or likely to be affected by the proposal?

2. Consider the evidence

2.1 What relevant quantitative data has been considered?	
Age	
Disability	
Gender	
Race Religion / Belief	
Sexual Orientation	

2.2 What relevant qualitative information has been considered?

Age	
Disability	
Gender	
Race	
Religion / Belief	
Sexual Orientation	

2.3 What gaps in data/information were identified?

Age	
Disability	
Gender	
Race	
Religion / Belief	
Sexual Orientation	

2.4 What consideration has been given to commissioning research?

Age	
Disability	
Gender	
Race	
Religion / Belief	
Sexual Orientation	

3. Assess likely impact

3.1 From the analysis of data and information has any potential for differential/adverse impact been identified?

Age	

Disability	
Gender	
Race	
Religion / Belief	
Sexual Orientation	

3.2 If yes explain any intentional impact:

Age	
Disability	
Gender	
Race	
Religion / Belief	
Sexual Orientation	

3.3 If yes explain what impact was discovered which you feel is justifiable in order to achieve the overall proposal aims. Please provide examples:

Age	
Disability	
Gender	
Race	
Religion / Belief	
Sexual Orientation	

3.4 Are there any other factors that might help to explain differential/adverse impact?

Age	
Disability	
Gender	
Race	

Religion / Belief	
Sexual Orientation	

4. Consider alternatives

4.1 Summarise what changes have been made to the proposal to remove or reduce the potential for differential/adverse impact:
4.2 Summarise changes to the proposal to remove or reduce the potential for differential/adverse impact that were considered but not implemented and explain why this was the case:
4.3 If potential for differential/adverse impact remains explain why implementation is justifiable in order to meet the wider proposal aims:

5. Consult Formally

5.1 Has the proposal been subject to consultation? If no, please state why not. If yes, state which individuals and organisations were consulted and what form the consultation took:	
Age	
Disability	
Gender	
Race	
Religion / Belief	
Sexual Orientation	
5.2 What was the outcome of the consultation?	
Age	
Disability	
Gender	

Race	
Religion / Belief	
Sexual Orientation	

5.3 Has the proposal been reviewed and/or amended in light of the outcomes of consultation?

5.4 Have the results of the consultation been fed back to the consultees?

6. Decide whether to adopt the proposal

6.1 Provide a statement outlining the findings of the impact assessment process. If the proposal has been identified as having a possibility to adversely impact upon diverse communities, the statement should include justification for the implementation:

7. Make Monitoring Arrangements

7.1 What consideration has been given to piloting the proposal?

7.2 What monitoring will be implemented at a national level by the proposal owning agency and/or other national agency?

7.3 Is this proposal intended to be implemented by local agencies that have a statutory duty to impact assess policies? If so, what monitoring requirements are you placing on that agency?

8. Publish Assessment Results

8.1 What form will the publication of the impact assessment take?

BIBLIOGRAPHY

BOOKS

Akdeniz, Y, *Internet Child Pornography and the Law: National and International Responses*, Ashgate: 2008.

Arkin, S (ed), *Prevention and Prosecution of Computer and High Technology Crime*, Matthew Bender, 1990.

Arlidge, A and Parry, J, *Arlidge and Parry on Fraud*, Sweet & Maxwell, 2005.

Ashworth, A, and Horder, J. *Principles of Criminal Law*, 7th edn, Oxford University Press, 2009.

Ashworth, A and Redmayne, M, *The Criminal Process*, 4th edn, Oxford University Press, 2010.

Ashworth, A, Macdonald, A, and Emmerson, B, *Human Rights and Criminal Justice*, 3rd edn, Sweet & Maxwell, 2012.

Bantekas, I and Nash, S, *International Criminal Law*, Routledge Cavendish, 2003. Barrett, N:
  (a) *Digital Crime: Policing the Cybernation*, Kogan Page, 1997.
  (b) *Traces of Guilt*, Corgi, 2009.

Bently, L and Sherman, B, *Intellectual Property Law*, 4th edn, Oxford, 2014.

Bequai, A, *Technocrimes*, Lexington Books, 1987.

Blackstone's Criminal Practice, Oxford University Press, 2016.

Boister, N, *An Introduction to Transnational Criminal Law*, Oxford University Press: 2012.

Boni, WC, and Kovacich, GL, *I-Way Robbery: Crime on the Internet*, Butterworth, 1999.

Brenner, S, *Cyberthreats and the Decline of the Nation-State*, Routledge: 2014.

Casey, E, *Digital Evidence and Computer Crime*, 3rd edn, Academic Press, 2011.

Cassese, A, et al, *International Criminal Law*, 3rd edn, Oxford University Press, 2013.

Clifford, R, *Cybercrime: The Investigation, Prosecution and Defence of a Computer-related Crime*, 3rd edn, Carolina Academic Press, 2011.

Clough, J., *Principles of Cybercrime*, Cambridge University Press: 2010.

Coppel, P (ed), *Information Rights: Law and Practice*, 4th ed, Hart Publishing, 2014.

Cornwall, H, *Data Theft*, Mandarin, 1990.

Coupland, D, *Microserfs*, Flamingo, 1995.

Delmas-Marty, M and Spencer, JR (eds), *European Criminal Procedures*, Cambridge University Press, 2002.

Duff, R and Green, S (eds), *Defining Crimes*, Oxford University Press, 2005.

Endicott, T., *Vagueness in Law*, Oxford University Press, 2000.

Farr, R, *The Electronic Criminals*, Fontana, 1977.

Furnell, S, *Cybercrime: Vandalizing the Information Society*, Pearson, 2002.

Gibson, W, *Neuromancer*, HarperCollins, 1984.

Gillespie, A, *Child Pornography: Law and Policy*, Routledge-Cavendish, 2011.

Glenny, M, *DarkMarket: Cyberthieves, CyberCops, and You,* The Bodley Head, 2011

Gurry on Breach of Confidence, 2nd ed., OUP, 2012.

Grabosky, P, Smith, RG, and Dempsey, G, *Electronic Theft: Unlawful Acquisition in Cyberspace*, Cambridge University Press, 2001.

Grady, MF and Parisi, F, *The Law and Economics of Cybersecurity*, Cambridge, 2006.

Grewlich, K, *Governance in Cyberspace*, Kluwer Law International, 1999.

Hafner, K and Markoff, J, *Cyberpunk: Outlaws and Hackers on the Computer Frontier*, Simon and Schuster, New York, 1991.

Harfield, C and Harfield, K, *Covert Investigations: A Practical Guide for Investigators*, 3rd Edn, Oxford University Press, 2012.

Hirst, M, *Jurisdiction and the Ambit of the Criminal Law*, Oxford University Press, 2003.

Hollinger, RC (ed), *Crime, Deviance and the Computer*, Dartmouth, 1997.

The Honeynet Project, *Know Your Enemy: Learning about Security Threats*, 2nd edn, Addison-Wesley Professional, 2004.

Janssens, C., *The Principle of Mutual Recognition in EU Law*, OUP, 2013.

Jewkes, Y (ed), *Dotcons: Crime, Deviance and Identity on the Internet*, Willan, 2003.

Jewkes, Y, and Yar, M, *Handbook of Internet Crime*, Willan, 2009.

Jordan, T and Taylor, PA, *Hactivism and Cyberwars: Rebels with a Cause*, Routledge, 2004.

Keefe, P, *Chatter: Dispatches from the Secret World of Global Eavesdropping*, Random House, 2005.

Kelman, A and Sizer, R, *The Computer in Court*, Ashgate, 1982.

Koops, B-J and Brenner, S (eds), *Cybercrime Jurisdiction: A Global Survey*, TMC Asser Press, 2006.

Latham, E, *Bombs and Bandwidth: The Emerging Relationship Between Information Technology and Security*, New Press, 2003.

Lessig, L, *Code and Other Laws of Cyberspace*, Basic Books, New York, 2000.

Levy, S, *Hackers*, Penguin, 1984.

Lilley, P, *Hacked, Attacked & Abused*, Kogan Page, 2002.

Littman, J, *The Watchman: The twisted life and crimes of serial hacker Kevin Poulson*, Little, Brown & Co, 1997.

Mason, S., (ed), *Electronic Evidence*, 3rd ed., LexisNexis, 2012.

Marsden, C., *Internet Co-Regulation*, Cambridge University Press, 2011.

McKay, S., *Covert Policing: Law and Practice*, 2nd edn, OUP, 2015.

McKnight, G, *Computer Crime*, Michael Joseph, 1973.

Millard, C., *Cloud Computing Law*, OUP, 2013.

Millwood Hargrave, A and Livingstone, S, *Harm and Offence in Media Content*, Intellect 2006.

Mitnick, K and Simon, WL, *Art of Intrusion: The Real Stories Behind the Exploits of Hackers, Intruders and Deceivers*, Hungry Minds, 2005.

Naughton, J, *A Brief History of the Future*, Phoenix, 2000.

Naylor, R, *Wages of Crime: Black Markets, Illegal Finance, and the Underworld Economy*, Cornell University Press, 2004.

Newman, G and Clarke, R, *Superhighway Robbery: Preventing e-Commerce Crime*, Willan Publishing, 2003.

Ormerod, D, and Laird, K, *Smith & Hogan Criminal Law*, 14th edn, Oxford University Press, 2015.

Packer, H, *The Limits of the Criminal Sanction*, Stanford University Press, 1969.

Parker, D,
    (a) *Crime by Computer*, Charles Scribner's Sons, 1976.
    (b) *Fighting Computer Crime: A New Framework for Protecting Information*, Wiley, New York, 1998.

Powles, S, Waine, L, and May, R and, *Criminal Evidence*, 6th edn, Sweet & Maxwell, 2015.

Price, M and Verhulst, S, *Self-Regulation and the Internet*, Kluwer Law International, 2005.

Raymond, E, *The New Hacker's Dictionary* 3rd edn, MIT Press, 1996.

Reed, C,
    (a) *Internet Law: Text and Materials*, 2nd edn, Cambridge University Press, 2004.
    (b) *Making Laws for Cyberspace*, Oxford University Press, 2012

Richardson, M, *Cyber Crime: Law and Practice*, Wildy, Simmonds and Hill Publishing, 2014.

Roberts, P and Zuckerman, A, *Criminal Evidence*, 2nd edn, Oxford University Press, 2010.

Schmitt, M, (ed) *Tallinn Manual on the International Law Applicable to Cyber Warfare*, Cambridge University Press, 2013

Schneier, B, *Secrets and Lies: Digital Security in a Networked World*, Wiley, 2000.

Shapiro, C and Varian, H, *Information Rules: A Strategic Guide to the Network Economy*, HBS Press, 1998.

Shotton, M, *Computer Addiction?: A Study of Computer Dependency*, Taylor & Francis, 1989.

Sieber, U, *The International Handbook on Computer Crime*, Wiley, 1986.

Simester, AP, Spencer, JR, Sullivan, GR and Virgo GJ, *Criminal Law: Theory and Doctrine* 5th edn, Hart, 2013.

Smith, ATH, *Property Offences*, Sweet & Maxwell, 1994.

Smith, R, Grabosky, P, and Urbas, G, *Cyber Criminals on Trial*, Cambridge University Press, 2004.

Sofaer, A and Goodman, S, *The Transnational Dimension of Cyber Crime and Terrorism*, Hoover Institution, 2001.

Spitzner, L, *Honeypots: Tracking Hackers*, Addison-Wesley, 2002.

Sterling, B, *The Hacker Crackdown: Law and Disorder on the Electronic Frontier*, Penguin Books, 1994.

Stoll, C, *Cuckoo's Egg*, Pocket Books, 1998.

Summers, S., et al., *The Emergence of EU Criminal Law: Cyber crime and the regulation of the Information Society*, Hart Publishing, 2014.

Tapper, C, *Computer Law*, 4th edn, Longman, 1989.

Tapper, C, *Cross & Tapper on Evidence*, 12th edn, Oxford University Press, 2010.

Taylor, M and Quayle, E, *Child Pornography: An Internet Crime*, Brunner-Routledge, 2003.

Taylor, P, *Hackers: Crime and the Digital Sublime*, Routledge, 1999.

Thomas, D and Loader, B (eds), *Cybercrime: Law Enforcement, Security and Surveillance in the Information Age*, Routledge, 2000.

Turkle, S, *Life on the Screen: Identity in the Age of the Internet*, Simon & Schuster, 1997.

Wacks, R, *Personal Information, Privacy and the Law*, Clarendon Press, 1989.

Walden, I, *Telecommunications Law and Regulation*, Oxford University Press, 2012.

Wall, DS,
    (a) (ed) *Crime and the Internet: Cybercrimes and Cyberfears*, Routledge, 2001.
    (b) (ed) *Cyberspace Crime*, Dartmouth, 2003.
    (c) *Cybercrime: The Transformation of Crime in the Information Age*, Polity, 2007.

Wall, DS, and Williams, M, (ed) *Policing Cybercrime: Networked and Social Media Technologies and the Challenges for Policing*, Routledge, 2014

Warren, P and Streeter, M, *Cyber Alert: How the World is Under Attack from a New Form of Crime*, Vision Publishing, 2005.

Wasik, M, *Crime and the Computer*, Clarendon Press, 1991.

Westby, JC, *International Guide to Combating Cybercrime*, American Bar Association, Chicago, 2003.

Whiteside, T, *Computer Capers*, Sidgwick and Jackson, 1979.

Wilding, E, *Computer Evidence*, Sweet & Maxwell, 1997.

Williams, V, *Surveillance and Intelligence Law Handbook*, Oxford University Press, 2006.

ARTICLES

Akdeniz, Y, 'The regulation of pornography and child pornography on the Internet' 1997 (1) *The Journal of Information Law and Technology*, available at: <http://www2.warwick.ac.uk/fac/soc/law/elj/jilt/1997_1/akdeniz1/>.

Anderson, R, Needham, R, and Shamir, A, 'The steganographic file system', pp 73–82, in Ausmith, D (ed), *Information Hiding*, Springer-Verlag, 1998.

Anderson, R. and others, 'Measuring the Cost of Cybercrime', pp. 265-300, in *The Economics of Information Security and Privacy*, Pt. IV, 2013

Andrews S, 'Who Holds the Key?—A comparative study of US and European encryption policies', 2000 (2) *The Journal of Information, Law and Technology* <http://elj.warwick.ac.uk/jilt/00-/andrews.html>.

Armstrong, HL and Forde, PJ, 'Internet anonymity practices in computer crime', *Information Management & Computer Security*, vol 11, No 5, 2003.

Ashworth, A, and Blake, M, 'The presumption of innocence in English criminal law' [1996] Crim LR 306.

Bacigalupo, E, 'The use of technical means in interception and surveillance of private communications', pp 131–42, in Militello, V and Huber, B, (eds) *Towards a European Criminal Law Against Organised Crime*, Edition Iuscrim, 2001.

Baldwin, R and Hawkins, K, 'Discretionary justice: Davis reconsidered' [1984] *Public Law* 570.

Barlow, JP, 'Crime and puzzlement: In advance of the law on the electronic frontier', pp 1–24, *Whole Earth Review*, 68, Fall 1990.

Baron, R, 'A critique of the international cybercrime treaty', pp 263–278, *CommLaw Conspectus* 10 (2002).

Barton, P and Nissanka, V, 'Cyber-crime—criminal offence or civil wrong?' pp 401–5, *Computer Law and Security Report*, vol 19, No 5, 2003.

Bazelon, D, Choi, Y, and Conaty, J, 'Computer Crimes', 43 *American Criminal Law Review* 259, 2006.

Bell, E, 'The Prosecution of Computer Crime', pp 308–25, *Journal of Financial Crime*, vol 9, No 4, 2002.

Bennett, D., "The challenges facing computer forensic investigations in obtaining information from mobile devices for use in criminal investigations", 20 August 2011, available at <www.forensicfocus.com>.

Birnhack, MD, and Elkin-Koren, N, 'The invisible handshake: The reemergence of the state in the digital environment', 8 *Va JL & Tech* 6, 2003.

BloomBecker, JJB, 'Computer crime and abuse', pp 34–41, *The EDP Auditor Journal*, II, 1990.

Boehm, F. and M. Cole, "Data Retention after the judgement of the Court of Justice of the European Union", available at

Bowden, C, 'The US surveillance programmes and their impact on EU citizens' fundamental rights', Report for the European Parliament, 2013

Brenner, S,
(a) 'Is there such a thing as "virtual crime"', 4 *California Criminal Law Review* 1, 2001.
(b) 'In defense of cyberterrorism', 2 *The University of Illinois Journal Of Law, Technology & Policy* 1, 2002 (with Marc D Goodman).
(c) 'Organised cybercrime? How cyberspace may affect the structure of criminal relationships', *North Carolina Journal of Law and Technology*, vol 4, No 1, Fall 2002.
(d) 'Transnational evidence-gathering and local prosecution of international cybercrime', 20 *The John Marshall Journal of Computer and Information Law* 347, 2002 (with Joseph Schwerha IV).
(e) 'Toward a criminal law for cyberspace: Distributed security', 10 *BU J Sci & Tech L* 2, 6–11, 2004.
(f) 'Distributed security: Moving away from reactive law enforcement', *International Journal of Communications Law and Policy*, Special Issue Cybercrime, Spring 2005.
(g) 'Defining cybercrime: A review of state and federal law', pp 13–95, in Clifford, R, *Cybercrime: The Investigation, Prosecution and Defence of a computer-related crime*, 2nd edn, Carolina Academic Press, 2006.
(h) 'Law, Dissonance, and Remote Computer Searches', *North Carolina Journal of Law & Technology,* 14(1) (2012), 43.

Brenner, S and Goodman, M, 'Cybercrime: The need to harmonize national penal and procedural laws', International Society for the Reform of Criminal Law 16th Annual Conference Technology and Its Effects on Criminal Responsibility, Security and Criminal Justice, 2002.

Brenner, S and Koops, B-J, 'Approaches to cybercrime jurisdiction', 4 *Journal of High Technology Law* 1, 2004.

Broucek, V and Turner, P, 'Intrusion detection: Issues and challenges in evidence acquisition', pp 149–64, *International Review of Law Computers & Technology*, vol 18, No 2, 2004.

Burden, K and Palmer, C, 'Cyber crime—A new breed of criminal?', pp 222–7, *Computer Law and Security Report*, vol 19, No 3, 2003.

Calabresi, G, and Douglas Melamud, A, "Property Rules, Liability Rules and Inalienability: One View of the Cathedral" [1971], 85 *Harvard law Review*. 1089.

Campbell, D., "GCHQ and me: My life unmasking British eavesdroppers', 3 August 2015, available at www.firstlook.org/theintercept/.

Cangemi, D, 'Procedural law provisions of the Council of Europe Convention on Cybercrime', pp 165–71, *International Review of Law Computers & Technology*, vol 18, No 2, 2004.

Chandler, JA,
(a) 'The changing definition and image of hackers in popular discourse', pp 229–51, *International Journal of the Sociology of Law*, vol 24, No 2, 1996.
(b) 'Security in cyberspace: Combating distributed denial of service attacks', 1 *University of Ottawa Law and Technology Journal* 231, 2003–04.

Charney, S, 'Combating cybercrime: A public-private strategy in the digital environment', paper written for the Eleventh United Nations Congress on Crime Prevention and Criminal Justice, 18–23 April 2005, Bangkok, Thailand.

Christie, AL, 'Should the law of theft extend to information?', pp 349–60, *The Journal of Criminal Law*, vol 69, No 4, 2005.

Clayton, R, 'Anonymity and traceability in cyberspace', University of Cambridge, Computer Laboratory, Technical Report, UCAM-CL-TR-653, November 2005. Available at <http://www.cl.cam.ac.uk/techreports/UCAM-CL-TR-653.html>.

Conte, A, 'Crime and terror: New Zealand's criminal law reform since 9/11', pp 635–64, *New Zealand Universities Law Review*, vol 21, No 4, 2005.

Cormack, A, 'Logfiles', JANET Guidance Note GD/NOTE/008, June 2004, available at <http://www.ja.net/services/publications/technical-guides/logfiles.pdf>. Cross, JT,
(a) 'Trade secrets, confidential information, and the criminal law', 36 *McGill Law Journal*, 524, 1991.
(b) 'Protecting confidential information under the criminal law of theft and fraud', 11 *Oxford Journal of Legal Studies* 264, 1991.

Davies, CR, 'Protection of intellectual property—A myth?, pp 398–410, *The Journal of Criminal Law*, vol 68, pt 5, October 2004.

Davies, L, 'Packets and bits: Forensic investigation on the Internet—Paper trails and coolie crumbs', *The Litigator* 35, 1997.

Davis, RH, 'Social network analysis: An aid in conspiracy investigations', *FBI Law Enforcement Bulletin* pp 11–19, 1981.

Decroos, M, 'Criminal jurisdiction over transnational speech offenses', pp 365–400, *European Journal of Crime, Criminal Law and Criminal Justice*, vol 13, No 2005.

de Hert, P. and M. Kopcheva, 'International mutual legal assistance in criminal law made redundant: A comment on the Belgium Yahoo! case' (2011) *Computer Law and Security Review*, 27.

Demeyer, K., Lievens, E. and Dumortier, J. (2012), "Blocking and Removing Illegal Child Sexual Content: Analysis from a Technical and Legal Perspective". *Policy & Internet*, 4: 1–23.

Denning, D, 'Cyberterrorism: The logic bomb versus the truck bomb', *Global Dialogue*, Autumn, pp 29–37, 2000.

Denning, D and Baugh, W, 'Hiding crimes in cyberspace', pp 105–31, in Thomas, D and Loader, B (eds), *Cybercrime: Law Enforcement, Security and Surveillance in the Information Age*, Routledge, 2000.

Douglas-Scott, 'The rule of law in the European Union—Putting security into the area of freedom, security and justice', pp 219–42, 29 *European Law Review*, 2004.

Duff, RA, 'Subjectivism, objectivism and criminal attempts', pp 19–44, in *Harm and Culpability* (Simester, AP and Smith, ATH, eds), Clarendon Press, 1996.

Ellison, L and Akdeniz, Y, 'Cyber-stalking: The regulation of harassment on the Internet', in Walker, C (ed), *Crime, Criminal Justice and the Internet* (special edition, *Criminal Law Review*), Sweet & Maxwell, London, 1998.

Endeshaw, A, 'Theft of information revisited' *Journal of Business Law*, 187, 1997.

Esposito, LC, 'Regulating the Internet: The new battle against child pornography', *Case Western Reserve Journal of International Law*, 1998, vol 30, No 2/3, 541.

Feiler, L., "The Legality of the Data Retention Directive in Light of the Fundamental Rights to Privacy and Data Protection", *European Journal of Law and Technology*, Vol. 1,Issue 3, 2010.

Flanagan, A, 'The law and computer crime: Reading the script of reform', pp 98–117, *International Journal of Law and Information Technology*, vol 13, No 1, 2005.

Fletcher, M, 'Extending "indirect effect" to the third pillar: the significance of *Pupino*?', pp 863–77, 30 *European Law Review*, December 2005.

Forest Wolfe, D, 'The Government's right to read: Maintaining state access to digital data in the age of impenetrable encryption', *Emory Law Journal* 711, 2000.

Fournier, R., and others, "Comparing pedophile activity in different P2P systems", *Social Sciences* 2014, 3, 314–325.

Freedman, CD,
   (a) 'Criminal misappropriation of confidential commercial information and cyberspace: Comments on the issues', pp 147–62, 13 *International Review of Law, Computers and Technology*, 1999.
   (b) *"The New Law of Criminal Organizations in Canada"* (2007) 85(2) Canadian Bar Review 171

Froomkin, M, 'It came from Planet Clipper: The battle over cryptographic key "escrow"', *U Chi L Forum* 15, 1996.

Gane, C, and Mackarel, M, 'The admissibility of evidence obtained from abroad into criminal proceedings: The interpretation of mutual legal assistance treaties and use of evidence irregularly obtained' (1996) 4 Eur J Crime, Crim L & Crim Just 98, 116

Garrie, D, Armstrong, M, and Harris, D, 'Voice over Internet Protocol and the Wiretap Act: Is your conversation protected?' p 97, *Seattle University Law Review*, vol 29, 2005.

Gillespie, AA,
   (a) 'Children, chatrooms and the law', [2001] *Criminal Law Review*, 435.
   (b) 'The Sexual Offences Act 2003: (3) Tinkering with 'child pornography', [2004] *Criminal Law Review*, 361.
   (c) 'Child pornography: Balancing substantive and evidential law to safeguard children effectively from abuse', pp 29–49, *International Journal of Evidence & Proof*, vol 9, No 1, 2005.
   (d) 'Restricting access to the internet by sex offenders' *Int J Law Info Tech* (2011) 19 (3): 165-186.

Goldstone, D, and Shave, B, 'International dimensions of crimes in cyberspace', 22 *Fordham International Law Journal* 1924, 1999.

Goodman, MD, 'Why the police don't care about computer crime', 10 *Harvard Journal of Law and Technology* 465, 1997.

Grabosky, P, 'Virtual criminality: Old wine in new bottles', 10 *Social & Leg Studies* 243, 2001.

Grabosky, PN and Smith, R, 'Digital crime in the twenty-first century', pp 8–26, *Journal of Information Ethics*, Spring 2001.

Grover, D, 'Dual encryption and plausible deniability', pp 37–40, *Computer Law and Security Report*, vol 20, No 1, 2004.

Haggerty, Karran, Lamb and Taylor, 'A framework for the forensic investigation of unstructured email relationship data', *International Journal of Digital Crime and Forensics*, 3(3), 1-18, 2011.

Haines, J and Johnstone, P, 'Global cybercrime: New toys for the money launderers', pp 317–25, *Journal of Money Laundering Control*, vol 2, No 4.

Hammond, RG, 'Theft of Information', pp 252–64, *Law Quarterly Review*, vol 100, April 1984.

Hatcher, M, McDannell, J, and Ostfeld, S, 'Computer crimes', 36 *American Criminal Law Review*, 397.

Hirst, M, 'Cyberobscenity and the ambit of English criminal law', *Computers and Law*, vol 13, No 2, 2002.

Hoey, A, 'Techno-cops: Information technology and law enforcement', pp 69–90, *International Journal of Law and Information Technology*, vol 6, No 2, 1996.

Hofmeyr, K, 'The problem of private entrapment' [2006] Crim LR 319.

Hollinger, RC,

(a) 'Hackers: Computer heroes or electronic highwayman?', pp 6–17, *Computers and Society*, 21, 1991.

(b) 'Crime by computer: Correlates of software piracy and unauthorized account access', pp 2–12, *Security Journal*, 4, 1993.

Hosein, I, 'The sources of laws: Policy dynamics in a digital and terrorized world', pp 187–99, *The Information Society*, vol 20, No 3, 2004.

Hosein, I and Pascuual, A, 'Understanding traffic data and deconstructing technology-neutral regulations', March 2002, available at <http://www.it46.se/docs/papers/unece-latest-escuderoa-hoseini.pdf>.

International Journal of Communications Law and Policy, Special Issue on Cybercrime, Issue 9, Part II, Autumn 2004.

Jarvie, N, 'Control of cybercrime—Is an end to our privacy on the Internet a price worth paying?' *Computer and Telecommunications Law Review*, Part 1: 76–81 (9(3)), Part 2: 110–15 (9(4)), 2003.

Jordan, T and Taylor, P, 'A sociology of hackers', pp 757–80, *Sociological Review,* November 1998.

Kabay, M, 'Studies and surveys of computer crime', 2001, available from <http://www.securitystats.com/reports/Studies_and_Surveys_of_Computer_Crime.pdf>.

Karnow, C, 'Launch of warning: Aggressive defense of computer systems', pp 87–102, *Yale Journal of Law and Technology*, Fall 2004–05.

Katyal, NK,

(a) 'Criminal law in cyberspace', 149 *University of Pennsylvania Law Review* 1003, 2001.

(b) 'The dark side of private ordering', pp 193–217 in Grady, MF and Parisi, F, *The Law and Economics of Cybersecurity*, Cambridge, 2006.

Kelman, A, 'The regulation of virus research and the prosecution for unlawful research?' Commentary, *The Journal of Information, Law and Technology*, 1997(3), <https://www2.warwick.ac.uk/fac/soc/law/elj/jilt/1997_3/kelman1/>.

Kenneally, E, 'The Internet is the computer: The role of forensics in bridging the digital and physical divide', pp 41–4, *Digital Investigation* 2, 2005.

Kenneally, E and Brown, C, 'Risk sensitive digital evidence collection', *Digital Investigation* (2005) 2, 101–19.

Kent, G, 'Sharing Investigation-specific Data With Law Enforcement - An International Approach', (2014), <http://papers.ssrn.com/sol3/papers.cfm?abstract_id=2472413>.

Kerr, I and Gilbert, D, 'The role of ISPs in the investigation of cybercrime', pp 163–72, Chapter 20 in *Information Ethics in the Electronic Age* (Mendina, T and Britz, J eds), McFarland Press, 2004.

Kerr, O,

(a) 'Cybercrime's scope: interpreting "access" and "authorization" in computer misuse statutes', *New York University Law Review* 1596, 2003.

(b) 'Lifting the "fog" of Internet surveillance: How a suppression remedy would change computer crime law', 54 *Hastings Law Journal* 805, 2003.

(c) 'Digital evidence and the new criminal procedure', *Columbia Law Review*, January 2005.

(d) 'Fourth Amendment Seizures of Computer Data', *Yale Law Journal,* 119 (2010), 700.

Koops, BJ,

(a) 'Commanding decryption and the privilege against self-incrimination', pp 431–445, in *New Trends in Criminal Investigation: Volume 2*, (eds Breur, Kommer, Nijboer and Reijntjes), Intersentia, 2000.

(b) 'Should ICT regulation be technology-neutral?', pp 77–108, in Koops, B-J et al (eds), *Starting Points for ICT Regulation*, TMC Asser Press, 2006.

Kosta, E, "The Way to Luxemburg: National Court Decisions on the Compatibility of the Data Retention Directive with the Rights to Privacy and Data Protection", (2013) 10:3 *SCRIPTed* 339

Kshetri, N, 'The simple economics of cybercrimes', pp 33–9, *IEEE Security and Privacy*, vol 4, Issue 1, January/February 2006; available at <http://papers.ssrn.com/sol3/papers.cfm?abstract_id=881421>.

Lanham, D, 'Larsonneur revisited' [1976] Crim LR 276.

Levi, M, 'The organisation of serious crimes', pp 878–913, *The Oxford Handbook of Criminology*, 3rd edn, Oxford University Press, 2002.

Lewis, BC, 'Prevention of computer crime amidst international anarchy', 41 *American Criminal Law Review* 1353, 2004.

Lewis, O, 'Information security & electronic eavesdropping—a perspective', pp 165–8, *Computer Law and Security Report*, vol 7, No 4, 1991.

Lipson, HF, *Tracking and tracing cyber-attacks: technical challenges and global policy issues*, CERT Coordination Center, Special Report CMU/SEI-2002-SR-009, November 2002 at 10, <http://resources.sei.cmu.edu/library/asset-view.cfm?assetid=5831>.

Loof, R, 'Obtaining, adducing and contesting evidence from abroad: A defence perspective on cross-border evidence' (2011) Crim L.R. 1, pp. 40–57

Macan-Markar, M, 'Developing countries not immune from cybercrime—UN', Inter Press Service, posted 25 April 2005, available at <http://www.ipsnews.net/africa/internaasp?idnews=28430>.

Mann D and Sutton, M, 'NETCRIME: More change in the organization of thieving', pp 201–29, 38 *British Journal of Criminology*, 1998.

Martin, G., "The case of the hacked refrigerator – Could 'The Internet of Things' connect everything?", 5 February 2014, available at <http://alumni.berkeley.edu/california-magazine/just-in/2014-03-05/case-hacked-refrigerator-could-internet-things-connect>

McAfee, *Virtual Criminology Report: North American Study into Organised Crime and the Internet*, July 2005, available at <http://www.softmart.com/mcafee/docs/McAfee%20 NA%20Virtual% 20Criminology%20Report.pdf>.

McGee, S., R. Sabett and A. Shah, "Adequate attribution: A framework for developing a national policy for private sector use of active defense", 8 J. Bus. & Tech. L. 1 (2013)

Mirfield, P, 'Regulation of Investigatory Powers Act 2000 (2): Evidential aspects' [2005] Crim LR 91.

Moitra, SD,
    (a) 'Analysis and modelling of cybercrime: prospects and potential', *Max Planck Institute for Foreign and International Criminal Law*, available at: <https://www.mpicc.de/shared/data/pdf/fa-moitra03.pdf>.
    (b) 'Developing policies for cybercrime: Some empirical issues', pp 435–64, *European Journal of Crime, Criminal Law and Criminal Justice*, vol 13, No 3, 2005.

Nikkel, B, 'Domain name forensics: A systematic approach to investigating an internet presence', *Digital Investigation* 1, 247–55, 2004.

Noam, E, 'Beyond liberalization II: The impending doom of common carriage', pp 435–52, *Telecommunications Policy*, vol 18, No 6, 1994.

Nykodym, N, Taylor, R, and Vilela, J, 'Criminal profiling and insider cyber crime', pp 408–14, *Computer Law and Security Report*, vol 21, No 5, 2005.

O'Brian Jr, W, 'Court scrutiny of expert evidence: Recent decisions highlight the tensions' 7 *E & P* 172, 2003.

O'Brien, M, 'Clear and present danger? Law and the regulation of the Internet', pp 151–64, *Information & Communications Technology Law*, vol 14, No 2, 2005.

O' Floinn and Ormerod, D,:
    (a) 'Social networking sites, RIPA and criminal investigations', *Crim. L. R.* 2011, 10, 766-789
    (b) 'Social Networking Material as Criminal Evidence', *Criminal Law Review*, 7 (2012), 486.

Olivenbaum, JM, '<CTRL><ALT><DEL>: Rethinking federal computer crime legislation', 27 *Seton Hall Law Review* 574, 1997.

Ormerod, D,
  (a) 'Case Comment', [2000] Crim LR, May, 385–388.
  (b) 'Improving the disclosure regime', pp 102–129, *International Journal of Evidence and Proof*, vol 7, no 2, 2003.
  (c) 'Telephone intercepts and their admissibility', [2004] Crim LR 15.
  (d) 'Entrapment: Restating principles and reviewing recent developments', paper delivered at CPS Conference, *Prosecuting Organised Crime*, 24 March 2006.
Paganini, P., 'Sinkholes: Legal and Technical Issues in the Fight against Botnets' (28 May 2014), available at <http://resources.infosecinstitute.com/sinkholes-legal-technical-issues-fight-botnets/>
Palfrey, T,
  (a) 'Case Comments', [2000] Crim L.R, May, 385–388.
  (b) 'Surveillance as a response to crime in cyberspace', pp 173–93, *Information and CommunicationsTechnology Law*, vol 9, No 3, 2000.
  (c) 'Is fraud dishonest? Parallel proceedings and the role of dishonesty', pp 518–40, *The Journal of Criminal Law*, vol 64, pt 5, 2000.
  (d) 'Cybercrimes and the fight against Hi-Tech criminality', paper delivered at a seminar organised by the European Institute of Public Administration, in Bucharest, 21–22 February 2005.
Philippsohn, S, 'Trends in cybercrime: An overview of current financial crimes on the Internet', 20 *Computers & Security*, pp 53–69, 2001.
Podgor, ES, 'International computer fraud: A paradigm for limiting national jurisdiction', 35 *UC Davis Law Review*, 267.
Poullet, Y, 'The fight against crime and/or the protection of privacy: A thorny debate!', pp 251–73, *International Review of Law Computers & Technology*, vol 18, No 2, 2004.
Quinn, K, 'Computer evidence in criminal proceedings: Farewell to the ill-fated s 69 of the Police and Criminal Evidence Act 1984', pp 174–187, *International Journal of Evidence and Proof*, vol 5, No 3, 2001.
Rauhofer, J, and Mac Sithigh, D, "The Data Retention Directive Never Existed", (2014) 11:1 SCRIPTed 118.
Redmayne, M, 'Disclosure and its discontents' [2004] Crim LR 441.
Reid, AS and Ryder, N, 'The case of Richard Tomlinson: The spy who emailed me', pp 61–78, *Information and Communications Technology Law*, vol 9, No 1, 2000.
Reidenberg, J,
  (a) 'Lex Informatica: The formulation of information policy rules through technology', 76 *Texas Law Review*, 553, 1998.
  (b) 'States and Internet enforcement', 1 *University of Ottawa Law and Technology Journal*, 1, 18, 2004.
Reitinger, PR,
  (a) 'Compelled production of plaintext and keys', 171, *University of Chicago Legal Forum*, 1996.
  (b) 'Encryption, anonymity and markets', in Thomas, D and Loader, B (eds), *Cybercrime: Law Enforcement, Security and Surveillance in the Information Age*, Routledge, 2000.
Rowbottom, J, 'Obscenity laws and the Internet: Targeting the supply and demand', pp 97–109, [2006] *Criminal Law Review*.
Rowland, D, 'Data retention and the war against terrorism—A considered and proportionate response?', (3) *Journal of Information, Law and Technology (JILT)* 2004, available at <http://www2.warwick.ac.uk/fac/soc/law/elj/jilt/2004_3/rowland/>.
Ryan, PS, 'War, peace or stalemate: Wargames, wardialing, wardriving and the emerging market for hacker ethics', *Virginia Journal of Law & Technology*, vol 9, No 7, Summer 2004.
Salgado, R, 'Legal issues', pp 225–52, in *Know your Enemy*, Addison-Wesley, 2004.
Samuelson, P, 'Legally speaking: Can hackers be sued for damages caused by computer viruses?, pp 666–9, *Communications of the ACM*, 32, 1989.
Sealey, P, 'Remote forensics', pp 261–65, *Digital Investigation* 1, 2004.

Seitz, N, 'Transborder search: A new perspective in law enforcement?', pp 23–50, *Yale Journal of Law and Technology*, Fall 2004–05.

Shytov, A, 'Indecency on the Internet and international law', pp 260–80, *International Journal of Law and Information Technology*, vol 13, No 2, 2005.

Sinrod, E and Reilly, W, 'Cyber-crimes: A practical approach to the application of Federal computer crime laws', pp 177–229, *Santa Clara Computer and High Technology Law Journal*, vol 16, May 2000.

Smith, G, 'An Electronic Pearl Harbor? Not likely', *Issues on Science and Technology*, 15, pp 68–73, Fall 1998.

Soghoian, C., 'Caught in the Cloud: Privacy, Encryption and Government Back Doors in the Web 2.0 Era', *Journal on Telecommunications and High Technology Law*, 8(2) (2010), 359.

Sommer, P,

(a) 'Digital footprints: Assessing computer evidence', *Criminal Law Review*, Special Edition, December 1998.

(b) 'Evidence in Internet paedophilia cases', pp 176–84, *Computer and Telecommunications Law Review*, vol 8, No 7, 2002.

(c) 'Evidence from cyberspace: Downloads, logs and captures', pp 33–42, *Computer and Telecommunications Law Review*, vol 8, No 2, 2002.

(d) 'Intrusion detection systems as evidence', pp 67–76, *Computer and Telecommunications Law Review*, vol 8, No 3, 2002.

(e) 'Computer misuse prosecutions', pp 25–6, *Computers and Law*, vol 16, No 5, December/January 2006.

Spence, M and Endicott, T, 'Vagueness in the scope of copyright', pp 657–80, *Law Quarterly Review*, vol 121, No 4, 2005.

Spencer, JR, 'Codifying criminal procedure' [2006] Crim LR 279.

Steele, D, 'Eavesdropping on electromagnetic radiation emanating from video display units' (1989–90) 32 *Criminal Law Quarterly*, 253.

Sussmann, M, 'The critical challenges from international high-tech and computer-related crime at the millennium', 9 *Duke J of Comp & Int'l L* 451.

Tapper, CB, 'Criminality and copyright', pp 266–79, in Vaver, D, and Bently, L (eds), *Intellectual Property in the New Millennium*, Cambridge University Press, 2004.

Taylor, M, Holland, G, and Quayle, E, 'Typology of paedophile picture collections', 74 *Police Journal* 97, 2001.

Taylor, MJ, Haggerty, D, Gresty and Hegarty, R, "Digital evidence in cloud computing systems", pp. 304-308, *Computer Law and Security Review*, 26(3), 2010

Thomas, D, 'Criminality on the electronic frontier', pp 17–35, in Thomas, D and Loader, B (eds), *Cybercrime: Law Enforcement, Security and Surveillance in the Information Age*, Routledge, 2000.

Turner, P, 'Digital provenance—interpretation, verification and corroboration', pp 45–9, *Digital Investigation* 2, 2005.

Urbas, G, 'Cybercrime, Jurisdiction and Extradition: The Extended Reach of Cross-Border Law Enforcement', *Journal of Internet Law*, 16(1) (2012), 7.

Vegh, S, 'Hackivists or cyberterrorists? The changing media discourse on hacking' 7(10) *First Monday*, at <http://firstmonday.org/issues/issue7_10/vegh/index.html>.

Walden, I,

(a) 'Computer crime', pp 295–29, Chapter 8 in *Computer Law*, 7th edition, Reed (ed), Oxford University Press, 2011.

(b) 'Crime and Security in Cyberspace', pp 51–68, in *Cambridge Review of International Affairs*, vol 18, No 1, April 2005.

(c) 'Harmonising computer crime laws in Europe', pp 321–36 in *European Journal of Crime, Criminal Law and Criminal Justice*, vol 12, No 4, 2004.

(d) 'Addressing the data problem', pp 18–31, *Information Security Technical Report*, vol 8, No 2, 2003.

(e) 'Honeypots: A sticky legal landscape' (with Anne Flanagan), pp 317–70, in *Rutgers Computer and Technology Law Journal*, vol 29, No 2, 2003.

Walden, I., and M. Wasik, 'The Internet: Access Denied Controlled!', pp. 377–387, [2011] *Crim. L.R.*, Issue 5.

Walker, C, 'Email interception and RIPA: the Court of Appeal rules on the "right to control" defence', pp 22–4, *Communications Law*, vol 11, No 1, 2006.

Wall, DS,
  (a) 'Policing and the regulation of the Internet', pp 79–91, in Walker, C (ed), *Crime, Criminal Justice and the Internet* (special edition, *Criminal Law Review*), Sweet & Maxwell, London, 1998.
  (b) 'Cybercrimes: New wine, no bottles?', in Davies, P, Francis, P, and Jupp, V (eds), *Invisible Crimes: Their Victims and their Regulation*, Macmillan, 1999.
  (c) 'Policing the Internet: Maintaining order and law on the cyberbeat', Chapter 7, pp 154–75, in Walker, C and Wall, D (eds), *The Internet, Law and Society*, Longman, 2000.
  (d) 'The Internet as a conduit for criminals', pp 77–98, in *The Criminal Justice System and the Internet*, Pattavina, A (ed), Thousand Oaks, 2005.

Wallace, RP, Lusthaus, A, and King, JH, 'Computer crimes', 42 *American Criminal Law Review* 223, 2005.

Warren, P, 'Smash and grab, the hi-tech way', *The Guardian*, 19 January 2006.

Wasik, M, 'Hacking, viruses and fraud', Chapter 12, pp 272–93, in Walker, C and Wall, D (eds), *The Internet, Law and Society*, Longman, 2000.

Wegener, H, 'Guidelines for national criminal codes on cybercrime', available at <http://www.itis-ev.de/infosecur>, 31 July, 2003.

White, M, 'Far right extremists on the Internet', pp 234–50, in Thomas, D and Loader, B (eds), *Cybercrime: Law Enforcement, Security and Surveillance in the Information Age*, Routledge, 2000.

White, S, 'Harmonisation of criminal law under the first pillar', pp 81–92, 31 *European Law Review*, February 2006.

Wible, B, 'A site where hackers are welcome: Using hack-in contests to shape preferences and deter computer crime', pp 1577–624, *Yale Law Journal*, vol 112, No 6, 2003.

Williams, K, 'Controlling Internet child pornography and protecting the child', pp 3–24, *Information & Communications Technology Law*, vol 12, No 1, 2003.

Williams, P, 'Organised crime and cybercrime: synergies, trends and responses', 2001, available from <http://www.crime-research.org>.

Wilson, W, 'The structure of criminal defences' [2005] Crim LR 108.

Wong Yang, D and Hoffstadt, B, 'Countering the cyber-crime threat' 43 *American Criminal Law Review* 201, 2006.

Yong, P., 'New China Criminal Legislations in the Progress of Harmonization of Criminal Legislation against Cybercrime', December 2011, available at <https://rm.coe.int/CoERMPublicCommonSearchServices/DisplayDCTMContent?documentId=09000016803042f0>.

Zhengchuan Xu, Qing Hu, and Chenghong Zhang: "Why computer talents become computer hackers", *Communications of the ACM*, April 2013, vol. 56, no. 4.

REPORTS, OFFICIAL DOCUMENTS

All Party Parliamentary Internet Group:
  Report on 'Communications Data', January 2003.
  Report on 'Revision of the Computer Misuse Act', June 2004.

Association of Chief Police Officers, 'Good Practice Guide for Computer Based Evidence' (3rd edn).

Association Internationale pour la Protection de la Propriété Intellectuelle (AIPPI) Summary Report, 'Criminal law sanctions with regard to the infringement of intellectual property rights' (Question 169), 2002. Available from <http://www.aippi.org>.

Attorney-General:
  Guidance on Disclosure, April 2005.
  Section 18 RIPA Prosecutors Intercept Guidelines England and Wales.

'guidelines for prosecutors on the use of the common law offence of conspiracy to defraud', available at <https://www.gov.uk/use-of-the-common-law-offence-of-conspiracy-to-defraud--6>

Cabinet Office, Performance and Innovation Unit Report, *Encryption and Law Enforcement*, May 1999.

Computer Security Institute and Federal Bureau of Investigation ('CSI/FBI Survey'), *Computer Crime and Security Survey*, annually since 1995, available from <http://www.goci.com>.

Council of Europe:

'Extraterritorial criminal jurisdiction', 1990.

Cybercrime Convention Committee paper, *Strengthening co-operation between law enforcement and the private sector—Examples of how the private sector has blocked child pornographic sites*, T-CY (2006) 04, 20 February 2006.

T-CY Guidance Note # 2, 'Provisions of the Budapest Convention covering botnets', T-CY (2013) 6E Rev

Electronic evidence guide (Ver. 1, March 2013)

T-CY Guidance Note # 5, 'DDOS attacks', T-CY (2013) 10E Rev

T-CY, Guidance Note # 3, *Transborder access to data (Article 32)*, 3 December 2014

Crown Prosecution Service

Code for Crown Prosecutors (2013)

Guidelines for prosecutors on assessing the public interest in cases involving the media, September 2012

Department of Trade and Industry:

Dealing with Computer Misuse, HMSO, 1992.

Consultation Document, *Building Confidence in Electronic Commerce* (URN 99/642), March 1999.

European Commission:.

Commission Communication to the Council and the European Parliament on 'Critical Infrastructure Protection in the fight against terrorism', COM(2004) 702 final, Brussels, 20 October 2004.

Commission Communication to the European Parliament and the Council on 'the implications of the Court's judgment of 13 September 2005' (Case C 176/03 *Commission v Council*), COM(2005) 583 final, Brussels, 23 November 2005.

Green Paper on a European Programme for Critical Infrastructure Protection, COM(2005) 576 final, 17112005.

Commission Communication, 'Consequences of the entry into force of the Treaty of Lisbon for ongoing interinstitutional decision-making procedures' COM(2009) 665 final, 2.12.2009.

Commission Communication, 'Towards an EU Criminal Policy: Ensuring the effective implementation of EU policies through criminal law', COM(2011) 573 final, 20.9.2011

Commission Communication, 'Tackling Crime in our Digital Age: Establishing a European Cybercrime Centre', COM(2012) 140 final, 28.3.2012

Commission Staff Working Document, *E-commerce Action Plan*, 2012-2015, Brussels, 23.4.2013

Europol:

Computer-related crime within the EU: Old crimes new tools; new crimes new tools (2002).

HM Government

A Strong Britain in an Age of Uncertainty: The National Security Strategy (Cm 7953), October 2010

Decision pursuant to Article 10 of Protocol 36 to The Treaty on the Functioning of the European Union, Cm 8671, July 2013

Serious and Organised Crime Strategy (Cm 8715), October 2013

Response to the House of Lords EU Committee Inquiry on the UK's 2014 opt-out decision (6 January 2014)

Home Affairs Committee Report No 126: 'Computer Pornography', HMSO, February 1994.

Home Office:

Consultation Paper, *Interception of Communications in the United Kingdom*, Cm 4368, June 1999.

Consultation Paper, *Accessing Communications Data: Respecting Privacy and Protection the Public from Crime*, 11 March 2003.

Discussion Paper, *Counter-Terrorism Powers: Reconciling Security and Liberty in an Open Society*, Cm 6147, February 2004.

Online Report 62/04, *The future of netcrime now: Part 1— threats and challenges*.

Online Report 63/04, *The future of netcrime now: Part 2— responses*.

Criminal Statistics: England and Wales 2003, Cm 6361, 2004.

Requests for Mutual Legal Assistance in Criminal Matters: Guidelines for Authorities Outside the United Kingdom (12th edn), March 2015

Consultation Paper, 'The initial transposition of Directive 2006/24/EC on the retention of data generated or processed in connection with the provision of publicly available electronic communications services or of public communications networks and amending Directive 2002/58/EC', March 2007.

Investigation of Protected Electronic Information, 2007.

Intercept as Evidence, December 2009, Cm 7760

Surveillance Camera Code of Practice, June 2013

Circular, *Serious Crime Act 2015*, March 2015.

Counting Rules for Recorded Crime, available at https://www.gov.uk/government/publications/counting-rules-for-recorded-crime.

Cyber crime: A review of the evidence, Research Report 75, October 2013. Available at https://www.gov.uk/government/publications/cyber-crime-a-review-of-the-evidence

Covert Human Intelligence Sources: Code of Practice, December 2014

Covert Surveillance and Property Interference, December 2014.

Acquisition and Disclosure of Communications Data, March 2015.

Interception of Communications Code of Practice, January 2016.

Equipment Interference Code of Practice, January 2016.

Consultation Paper, *On the possession of extreme pornographic material*, August 2005.

Online Report 09/06, *Fraud and technology crimes: Findings for the 2003/04 British Crime Survey, the 2004 Offending, Crime and Justice Survey and administrative sources*.

Consultation Paper, *Investigation of Protected Electronic Information*, June 2006.

Consultation Paper, *New Powers Against Organised and Financial Crime*, Cm 6875, HMSO, July 2006.

Consultation on the possession of extreme pornographic material: Summary of responses and next steps, August 2006.

Independent Reviewer of Terrorism Legislation, *A Question of Trust*, June 2015.

Information Assurance Advisory Council, *Digital Evidence, Digital Investigations and E-Disclosure*, 4th edition, November 2013.

Information Commissioner, *What Price Privacy? The unlawful trade in confidential personal information*, 10 May 2006.

Intellectual Property Office,

Report: *Penalty Fair? Study of criminal sanctions for copyright infringement available under the CDPA 1988*, 2015

A consultation on changes to the penalties for offences under sections 107(2A) and 198(1A) of the Copyright Designs and Patents Act (Penalties for Online Copyright Infringement, 18 July 2015

Intelligence and Security Committee report, *Privacy and Security: A modern and transparent legal framework*, HC 1075, March 2015

Interception of Communications Commissioner:

Report for 2002 (September 2003).

Report for 2003 (July 2004).

Law Commission:
> Working Paper No 31, *The Mental Element in Crime*, HMSO, 1970.
> Report No 55, *Report on Forgery and Counterfeit Currency*, HMSO, 1973.
> Report No 91, *Report on the Territorial and Extraterritorial Extent of the Criminal Law*, Cm 75, HMSO, 1978.
> Working Paper No 110, *Computer Misuse*, HMSO, 1988.
> Report No 177, *A Criminal Code for England and Wales*, HMSO, 1989.
> Report No 180, *Jurisdiction over Offences of Fraud and Dishonesty with a Foreign Element*, Cm 318, HMSO, 1989.
> Report No 186, *Computer Misuse*, Cm 819, HMSO, 1989.
> Report No 243, *Offences of Dishonesty: Money Transfers*, HMSO, 1996.
> Consultation Paper No 150, *Legislating the Criminal Code: Misuse of Trade Secrets*, HMSO, 1997.
> Consultation Paper No 155, *Legislating the Criminal Code: Fraud and Deception*, HMSO, 1999.
> Report No 276, *Fraud*, Cm 5569, HMSO, 2002.
> Report No 300, *Inchoate Liability for Assisting and Encouraging Crime*, Cm 6878, HMSO, July 2006.
> *Tenth Programme of Law Reform*, 2008.

National Criminal Intelligence Service report, 'Project Trawler: Crime on the Information Highways' (1999), available at <http://www.cyber-rights.org>.

National Infrastructure Security Co-ordination Centre:
> Briefing 08/2005, *Targeted Trojan Email Attacks*, 16 June 2005.
> Briefing 11a/2005, *Botnets—The threat to the Critical National Infrastructure*.

OECD, 'Computer-Related Criminality: Analysis of Legal Policy in the OECD Area', Report DSTI-ICCP 8422 of 18 April 1986.

Office of Communications (Ofcom) (and formerly Oftel):
> *Guidelines for the Interconnection of Public Electronic Communication Networks*, May 2003.
> Research Document, 'Online protection: A survey of consumer, industry and regulatory mechanisms and systems', 21 June 2006.

Office of the President, *The National Strategy to Secure Cyberspace* 39 (Feb 2003), at <http://www.whitehouse.gov/pcipb/cyberspace_strategy.pdf>.

Oxford Internet Institute survey report, *The Internet in Britain*, May 2005: available from <http://www.oii.ox.ac.uk/>.

Privy Council Review of Intercept as Evidence, 30 January 2008, Cm 7324.

RAND Technical Report, Handbook of Legal Procedures of Computer and Network Misuse in EU Countries, 2006; available from <http://www.rand.org>.

Royal United Services Institute, Independent Surveillance Review, *A Democratic Licence to Operate*, July 2015

Sentencing Guidelines Council (formerly the Sentencing Panel):
'The Panel's Advice to the Court of Appeal on Offences Involving Child Pornography', August 2002.
'Sexual Offences Act 2003: Consultation Guideline', June 2006.

Serious and Organised Crime Agency, The United Kingdom Threat Assessment of Serious Organised Crime: 2006/7, 31 July 2006.

United Nations:
> *United Nations Manual on the Prevention and Control of Computer-related Crime*, United Nations publication, Sales No E95IV5. Published in the *International Review of Criminal Policy*, Nos 43 and 44, 1996: available at <http://www.uncjin.org/Documents/EighthCongress.html#congress>. 'Measures to Combat Computer-related Crime', Workshop 6: Background Paper (A/CONF203/14), presented at the Eleventh United Nations Congress on Crime Prevention and Criminal Justice, Bangkok, April 2005.

United Nations Office on Drugs and Crime, *Comprehensive Study on Cybercrime*, draft, (February 2013)

US Department of Defense, Annual Report to Congress, *The Military Power of the People's Republic of China*, 20 July 2005.

US Department of Justice Report, *Searching and Seizing Computers and Obtaining Electronic Evidence in Criminal Investigations*, July 2002 (available at <http://www.usdoj.gov/criminal/cybercrime>).

United States Sentencing Commission, *Guidelines Manual* (2014), available at <http://www.ussc.gov/guidelines-manual/2014/2014-ussc-guidelines-manual>.

World Federation of Scientists, Permanent Monitoring Panel on Information Security, *Towards a Universal Order of Cyberspace: Managing Threats from Cybercrime to Cyberwar*, August 2003.

INDEX